Equine Husbandry & Equestrian Sports

Major General (Dr) B. S. Panwar
AVSM, SM (RETD.)

Colonel (Dr) K. N. Yadav

ibdc publishers
PUBLISHING GREEN

Published by

Khushnuma Complex Basement
7, Meerabai Marg (Behind Jawahar Bhawan),
Lucknow 226 001 U.P. (INDIA)
Tel. : 91-522-2209542, 2209543, 2209544, 2209545
Fax : 0522-4045308
E-Mail : ibdco@airtelmail.in

First Edition 2010

ISBN 978-81-8189-477-9

Composed & Designed at :

Panacea Computers
3rd Floor, Agarwal Sabha Bhawan, Subhash Mohal
Sadar Cantt. Lucknow-226 002
Phone : 0522-2483312, 9335927082, 9335927082
E-mail : prasgupt@rediffmail.com

Cover Designed at :

Dot-n-Line
9/5, Rana Pratap Marg, Opp. Botanical Garden, Lucknow
Phone : 9415349259

Printed at:

Salasar Imaging Systems
C-7/5, Lawrence Road Industrial Area
Delhi - 110 035
Tel. : 011-27185653, 9810064311

Preface

Equine management is a multi disciplinary concept and in-depth knowledge is required to achieve optimal results in terms of health, production and work energy output. No doubt, sufficient theoretical knowledge and practical training can only help in scientific management of equine stock. Accordingly, with a view to generate increased awareness and scientific know-how in the field of equine husbandry to the students of veterinary profession in various Agricultural/Veterinary Universities, academicians engaged in teaching animal management to undergraduate courses, there is a felt need of having a standard textbook which deals with the fundamental concepts of equine management in the Indian context. Concepts to be meaningful are to be related to environment and foreign textbooks often are of limited help to the teachers, the teachers and the taught with regard to India's equine production, its resources and specific requirement. The authors of this textbook, who have vast experience in all aspects of modern scientific equine husbandry practices, have strived hard to bring this textbook which deals with the basics of equine management in totality.

The book is in consonance with the syllabi requirement of undergraduate students of Veterinary Colleges in India. It will make an extremely interesting reading not only to students but to all equine lovers and those actively engaged in the field of equestrian sports. In addition to covering all important concepts of equine husbandry, the book includes chapters on Feeds and Feeding, Reproduction and Breeding as well as on Maintenance of Helath and Disease Control.

The Chapters on Doping in equines, FEI Rules to conduct the Equestrian Sports ,Welfare of horses, Equine Dentistry will be of immense value to the readers. The hallmark of the book is its chapter 30 dealing with Equine management in Nuclear, Biological and Chemical Disaster.

While compiling the text of this book, the authors have consulted various text/referecne books, journals and other pulished/unpublished technical literature including material on web world pertaining to the subject matter and the same wherever quoted/reproduced in the text is hereby duly acknowledged.

ABOUT THE AUTHORS

Maj. Gen. (Dr) B. S. Panwar, AVSM, SM (Retd)

Maj Gen (Dr) B. S. Panwar, AVSM,SM (Retd), former "Head of Service, RVC", was born on September 5, 1945. He obtained his BVSc & AH and MVSc degrees from G B Pant University of Agri.and Technology, Pantnagar. He was commissioned in Army(RVC) on January 1, 1969. While in service, he continued his academic persuit and obtained PhD (Vety. Medicine) from JNKVV Jabalpur. His professionalism of highest order was recognized at all levels and earned him laurels by award of prestigious fellowships of National Institute of Communicable Diseases (FISCD) and National Academy of Veterinary Sciences (FNAVSC). He has been the Panel Veterinarian with the Fedration Equistrian Internationale (FEI), Vice President, Equestrian Fedration of India (EFI), and Vice President, Defence Service Officers Institute. During his long tenure lasting almost 37 years, in Army, he had a very wide a exposure having served at almost all important positions of RVC. His key areas of professional interest include Epidemiology and control of communicable disease, modernization in disease diagnostic techniques and Therapeutic approach, Geographical surveillance of diseases in Army animals, Equine Reproduction, Cryo preservation of equine Semen and Embryo Transfer Technology, Specialized Breeding and Training of Sports horses as well as of Army Dogs, Technical updation of Veterinarians and Para Veterinary personnel and improving the man management practices in RVC. He has been directly related with Defence Research and Development Organization (DRDO) projects related to Veterinary Science in Armed Forces. In recognition of his distinguished service of exceptional order and devotion to duty, General B. S. Panwar was confirred with, Army Commander's Commendation Card, Chief of the Army Staff Commendation Card, Sena Medal AVSM (Ati Vsihisht Seva Medal) is a medal awarded for distinguished service of an exceptional order in the Indian Army and finally Ati Vishisht Seva Medal SM (Sena Medal) in a medal awarded for exceptional devotion to duty or corerage as have special significance in the service by His Excellency, the President of India.

He can be contacted at; bspanwar@rediffmail.com or B.R. House, A1-26, Defence Enclave, Meerut-250 001.

Col. K. N. Yadav

Col K. N. Yadav was commissioned on 29 Now 1982 in Remount Veterinary Crops (RVC) of Indian Army. He obtained his BVSc & AH with Honours Certificate from JNKVV Jabalpur and Post Graduated (MVSc) in Animal Breeding from HAU, HISSAR. He did his National Diploma in Equine Husbandary Medicine and Surgery from RVC Centre and College with distinction and also awarded Membership of National Academy of Veterinary Sciences for his distinguished service to the profession. Col Yadav has attended and qualified All Arms Equitation and Management Course of 11 month duration and Dog Training Course with army officers of other nations at RVC Centre and College.

The author has wide experience on equines and related fields for over 25 years. In Army , he had been Instructor for Equine Breeding and Genetics for officers at RVC Centre and College, Breeding Officer in Equine Breeding Stud and Commanded hospitals at Himalayan region, as well as North Eastern region and peace station. Under Defence Research and Development Organization (DRDO) the author was on deputation at Field Research Lab now known, Defence Institute for High Altitude Research(DIHAR) Leh, Ladakh(J & K) as Deputy Director where he handled various research projects on Equines, Bovines, Double Hump Camel, Poultry as well as Rural Development and Forestry. Before serving in Army Col. K. N. Yadav started his career as Cattle Development Officer at BAIF, Urulikanchan, served as Veterinary Officer at a Dairy Development Corporation for Short Duration and Asstt. Prof (Astt. Dairy Cattle Breeder) at college of Veterinary Sci. and A.H. Jabalpur for two years.

He was co-opted in Leh, ladakh region to carry out the Embryo Transfer trials in Yak, for the first time in India. Col. Yadav commaneded the Remount and Veterinary Squadron (NCC) at Madras Veterinary College and was responsible for shaping few meritorious horse riders who achieved laurel at national level in equestrian sports. Equine and Bovine fertility improvement programme with modern managemental approach is his special area of interest and had achieved success with repute. Presently, he is serving as Senior Veterinary Officer at a Mill Farm with a mandate to render professional expertisation.

He has published various research papers/technical articles and had been Asstt. Editor of Journal of Remount and Veterinary Crops. He can be contacted at Knyadavyadav@yahoo.co.in or Yadav Bhavan, Sihora (Sagar) - 470 120, Madhya Pradesh

Contents

CHAPTER		PAGE
1.	Introduction	1
2.	The Horse Through Ages	9
3.	The Points of the Horse and Dentition	29
4.	Care of Teeth and Dentistry	37
5.	Systems of Breeding	43
6.	Selection Procedure	53
7.	Reproductive Cycle	73
8.	Specialized Management of Breeding Stock	93
9.	Artificial Insemination and Frozen Semen Technique	133
10.	Embryo Transfer Technology	163
11.	Common Reproductive Disorders	175
12.	Description of the Horse	197
13.	Examination for Soundness	219
14.	Stabling	239
15.	Grooming and Stable Management	247
16.	Care of Feet and Shoeing	279
17.	Principles of Equine Feeding	305
18.	Types of Feed and Fodder	317
19.	Feeding Standards and Nutritional Requirments	329
20.	Practical Feeding of Various Classes	355

21.	Storage of Feed	375
22.	Saddlery	383
23.	Transportation	409
24.	Antimicrobial Therapy	415
25.	Important Diseases and their Prevention	423
	EQUESTRIAN SPORTS	
26.	Historical Background	509
27.	Dressage	519
28.	Drug Abuse and Dope Testing	549
29.	Welfare Requirement of Horses in Equestrian Sports	567
30.	Conservation of Indigenous Equine Species	585
31.	Equine Management in Nuclear, Biological and Chemical Disaster	601
Index		637

Chapter 1

Introduction

The **Horse** *Equus caballus* is derived from the Anglo Saxon word Hors which means swiftness. It is logical to suppose that this genus was able to survive the vicissitude of time and animal attack due to its speed. Probably the horse is the last animal which was domesticated by mankind and the earliest trace of horse hitched to a chariot goes back about 2000 B.C. The mounted horses were given place in Olympic Games in 648 B.C.

There are vast territories in the plains of northern and north-western regions, in the hills and foothills,arid and semi-arid regions and many other parts of the country where horses, ponies, mules and donkeys are the most valuable pack animals for transportation of men and material. In spite of the road development and introduction of mechanical transport in most parts of the country, the economics of haulage of goods and transportation of men and material over short distances are still in favour of draught animals.

Army, paramilitary forces and the police make use of horses for mobility, patrolling, riot control duties and the like. Horses are also widely used for races, polo, equestrian sports, hunting and various other purposes. Although, owing to development of modern methods of communication and transport, requirement of horses for transportation has declined world over, yet our country has still retained their usefulness as pack and riding animals.

Mules have their use both in military establishments and civilian occupations for haulage of goods. These animals have the greatest use as pack animals in different mountaineous regions. They get preference over hill ponies because of their greater strength, sturdiness and sure-footedness.

The donkey is an important animal in the economy of landless labourers, small and marginal farmers and other poorer sections of the society, both in rural and urban areas. The crisis in the conventional energy sector and looming shortage of petroleum products would demand that sufficient attention is bestowed on the sound animal husbandry practices for the upkeep and further development of horses, ponies, donkeys, and mules, for their efficient and economic utility.

Systemic horse breeding in India dates back to 1779 when British Army created the stud Department for breeding horses in India with a view to meet their requirement of horses for army. Seven studs were set up in different parts of the country which played a vital role to make locally-bred animals available to army and also improved the quality of indigenous equines. Further, keeping in view the ever increasing requirement of horses and mules in army and with an aim to rehabilitate the Indian soldiers who left Army after world war I, four breeding areas were set up at Shahpur, Chenab, Montgomery and Pindi for breeding horses and mules. However, after world war II and subsequent mechanization, the requirement of horses and mules in army was reduced significantly. As a result, breeding areas located in southern part were gradually closed whereas those in western part formed part of Pakistan after partition in 1947.

In the post-Independent India, Meerut breeding area was opened with its headquarters at Babugarh in 1948, and breeding operations were started in various centres in UP, Punjab and Rajasthan to meet the requirement of army animals and to improve the quality of local equines. Subsequently, for Punjab and Rajasthan, seperate breeding area was opened with its headquarters at Jalandhar Cantonment. However, the number of horses and mules available from these resourses were not able to meet the requirement of army, as such. Equine breeding studs were established by Army at Babugarh in 1957 and at Hisar in 1965. Over a period of time, these breeding studs developed role models in the country and met the requirements of army in totality leading to gradual closing of breeding areas earstwhile functioning under the aegies of army. Meanwhile, many privately owned studs were opened in various parts of the country for breeding thoroughbred horses primarily for racing in the turf clubs. Simaltaneously, some state governments opened studs for provision of quality stallion services to farmers so as to conserve the local breeds and to improve the quality of equines used for haulage of men and materials.

The equine production is closely associated with the functional requirement of each country viz Thoroughbreds for racing, Warm blood horses for equestrian sports, Half breds and indigenous breeds for saddle horses, pack ponies and mules for haulage of goods etc. Presently, the equine breeding activity in India is going on through various state's owned horse breeding centres and private stud farms. However, for want of realistic equine breeding policy,the quality of indigenous breeds of horses could not be significantly improved for want of good germ plasm and adoption of indiscriminate breeding activities.

It is worth mentioning that in the field of equine breeding, army has done a commendable work by improving the quality of horses and mules to meet its own requirements and also successfully upgraded the horse flesh for equestrian sports which has proved their mettle not only within country but also internationally through organized and systematic breeding activities. Army equine breeding studs are producing not only thorough0breds but also halfbreds and quarter breds of various blood line to maintain the quality animals in army and also the life line of equestrian sports in the country.

Similarly, owing to lack of sound breeding policies and planned upgradation of indigenous breeds of horses being used for haulage of goods, such animals underwent indiscriminate breeding and very few good specimens are left behind which are sturdy, relatively disease resistant and are most suited to the agro-climatic conditions prevailing in the country

Population Trend of Equines in the Country

Population trend in respect of horses/ponies, donkeys and mules as recorded by periodic animal census in India from 1951 to 2000 is given below:

	Population Trend of Equines (in 000s)		
Year	*Horses and Ponies*	*Donkeys*	*Mules*
1951	1514	1249	61
1956	1484	1057	39
1961	1327	1096	53
1966	1148	1054	75
1972	942	994	75
1977	916	917	89
1982	900	1024	131
1987	784	960	169
1992	826	970	197
2000	990	-	-

The broad conclusion that can be drawn from the census data with reasonable degree of accuracy is that beginning from 1951, there has been a continuous decline in the population of equines in the country. Further, over the years, there is a gradual decrease in the population of horses and ponies where as increasing trend in population of mules is evident. The changing trends of population amongst equines depict the requirement of animals for haulage of goods and even amongst horses and ponies, horse population might be decreasing more in proportion to pony population. *However, due to some serious efforts in past, 1992 and 2000 figures in above table show that the downward trends has been arrested.*

Indigenous Horses :-

India has five reconized breeds of indigenous horses which are named as per the geographical area in which they are widely available and used as saddle or pack animals. The details are as under :

Kathiawari - These horses have their breeding tract in Gujarat. These are well known for pace and speed.

Marwari - These horses closely resemble those of Kathiawari breed. They are mainly found in several districts of Rajasthan. These are riding horses, tough and sturdy with easy pace.

Bhutia **-** Horses of this breed are slow moving type and are mainly found in hilly sub-mountainous tracts of Himalayan ranges. These horses can walk long distances in hills and are sure-footed.

Spiti **-** From the Himalayan area of India and almost similar to Bhutia in type and conformation but slightly smaller in overall size. Its height is about 1.22 meter, hardy with plenty of stamina, well muscled with a short, thick neck, straight shoulders, short back and strong limbs and feet.

Manipuri :-Horses of this breed are being bred over centuries in erstwhile Manipur State. They possess good speed for use in plains and the sure-footedness required for work in the hills. Manipuri horses are reputed for their intelligence and are widely used for polo, racing and as pack animals.

Over the years, these native breeds are being either bred indiscriminately within themselves or cross bred with various other breeds. Each breed has got its own conformation, temperament and typical movement. In the chosen breed, long stride, carrying head and neck high, a well-laid-out shoulder and not too short a back are important while selecting the performance

The difficulties in carrying out improvement in native horses and ponies is lack of pedigree or performance records for proper selection of breeding stock. Presently, the selection is primarily based on phenotypical characters such as temperament, typical movements, general conformation, long stride, a well laid out shoulder, carriage of head and neck etc Besides the Indian Breeds of horses, some other breeds such as Baluchi, Hirzai, Unmol and Connemara are also being bred and maintained by some farmers and local breeders in our country and these are also being indiscriminately bred with local equines.

The need of the hour is to create a strong gene pool, containing genes for performance as the modern competititon horse and pony by infusing superior germ plasm using Arab and thoroughbred blood lines. In this regard, the Peruvian Paso horse, which is one of the oldest and purest breeds in the world, is a good case study. This breed originated from a small horse in east Russia and is now known for its highly individual four beat lateral gait which is inbred and inherent as a result of 450 years of selective breeding. Similarly, the Trakehner breed of horses is one of the oldest in Europe with a history reaching back over 400 years. This breed also originated from a small horse by cross breeding with thoroughbreds and is now well known for its verstality and stamina.

Further, the Shetland breed of horse, was earliar considered just suitable rides for tiny tots or harness ponies. But now they are genuine performance ponies. The sire 'Jack' of Londonderry stable contributed greatly for improvement of this breed in that of 490 foals entered in stud book at that time 248 were of Jack and 160 were from his eight grandsons.

It is also pertinent to know that, the Mongolian horse which descended from Tarpan, has been developed through regular selection over 1000 years. In modern days Mongolian mares are cross bred with Don and Trotter stallions imported from Russia. Also these are cross bred with Budenny and Through-bred stallions as part of programme to evolve a 3-breed new horse that can hold its own against the best performance.

At present there are 200 breeds of horses in the world. Horses have entered into human heart through their common sense, and excellence in both work and sports. India also possesses some valuable stock of indigenous breeds which are capable of further development and propagation. Most of the Indian breeds are well-adopted for the specialized type of work they are required to perform, however, the need of the hour is to ensure that this noble animal is conserved and further developed. Experience of many foreign countries does show that with careful selection of pure breeds and through cross breeding,many countries have succeeded in raising equines of distinction and this story of success can be repeated in India too. Accordingly, we have to define our goals and suitably formulate policies to streamline the equine breeding so as to improve our indigenous stock and also evolve ideal horse flesh for competitive performance.

Donkeys:

It is the most simple and unselfish member of equine family. It is a very hardy animal which can work incessantly on poor forage. It is mainly used as a pack animal and is sure-footed. The Nubian ass is the parent of present days donkeys. Donkeys were domesticated at about 4000 B.C. in both Mesopotamia and Eqypt.

There are two types of donkeys - small grey and large white which are commonly seen in India. The small size donkey seen throughout the country is dark grey with Zebra strippings on limbs, neck and quarters. The large white is seen mostly in the Kathiawar region of Gujarat state. It is light grey to white in colour. Large white asses (Khol) are endangered dwindling species the strength of which is gradually falling down and presently these animals are confined in a sanctuary.

Mule - Among equines, mules are hybrid, born out of cross between a donkey stallion and horse mare. They inherit the size, speed, strength and appearance from the dam whereas disposition, hardiness, patience, endurance, longevity, toughness and sure-footedness comes from the sire. The opposite cross between she-ass and stallion pony, "Hinny" is not very common. Both males and females are sterile. The height of mules in use varies from 1.25 to 1.45 metres. Mules like ponies, have the greatest use as pack animals in plane as well as mountainous terrains for transportation of men and materials. They get preference over hill ponies because of their greater strength, sturdiness and sure-footedness. In the planes, mule drawn carriages are used for transport of goods in moderately big numbers, over short distances in towns and cities with good roads.

Equestrian Awareness

With a view to impart equestrian training to young boys and girls at school and college level which helps the nation to spot young talents in equestrian sports for national/international competitions, and with the increasing equestrian awareness, there are greater demands for horses for sporting purposes, so as to keep the equestrian sports alive and develop it to an extent where our riders can compete in international arena.

Futuristic Approach

The country has no dearth of natural resources with regard to availability of equine stock though not of a very superior quality. The tremendous utility potential of equines in the nation is enough to prove the necessity of preservation of indigenous breeds and organized programmes at states and national level. The achievements till date are certainly not up to the mark and much efforts to be done in this regard as discussed elsewhere in this textbook.

Further, there is a definite need for giving special consideration to equines for their utilization to the best possible advantage of the owners under the prevailing conditions and the anticipated change of circumstances in coming decades. Such an effort will provide the long overdue fillip to equine developmental activities and restore the pride, the country once possessed in having a few of world's best equine breeds.

It is amply clear that our country has tremendous potential for equine utility and given the right impetus and thought, can create wonders in improving the socio-economic status of the weaker and poorer sections of the society. The main emphasis needs to be laid to strengthen the organized and systematic breeding activities, improve management as well as related equine husbandry practices and to undertake selective breeding and upgradation programmes. These measures alongwith rational preventive and therapeutic approaches to existing and emerging equine diseases in progressive manner, will certainly bring constructive improvements in equine resources of our country.

Chapter 2

The Horse Through Ages

The horse is descended from a small primitive four toed animal that inhabited the river banks during the early Eocene epoch. About 50 million years ago this "dawn horse" not larger than fox, was approximately 25 cm in height and bearing little resemblance to the modern horse. It was named Eohippus (Eo is the Greek word for "dawn" and hippus is the Greek word for "horse"). From Eohippus to the thoroughbred, dramatic changes occurred in size and shape. There were also remarkable evolutionary changes in the teeth and chewing methods, the size of the skull and brain, and the length of the neck and legs and also the four toes were reduced to a single sturdy hoof. The major source of knowledge as far as the evolution of the horse is concern, is based on the very rich fossil deposits of western North America.

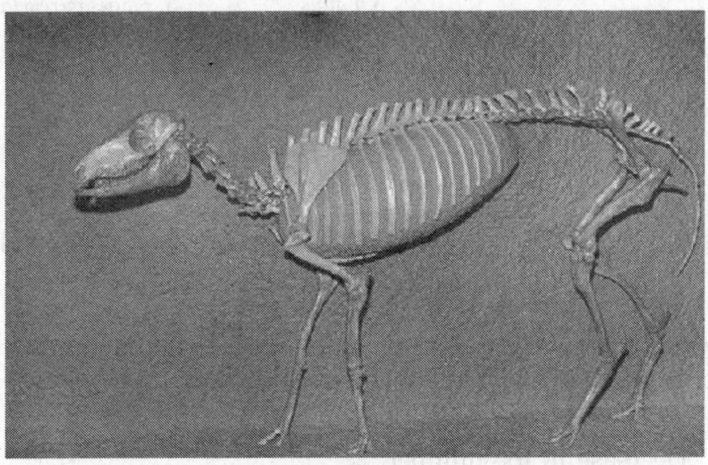

Fig 2.1 EOHIPPOS

Scientifically, horse is ***Perrissodactyla Quadripad.*** As per the latest Taxonomical Classification(2000) all equines are placed as under:

Order — Perrissodactyla
Family — Equidae
Genus — Equus
Subgenus — **Equus:** e g., Horses
Subgenus — **Asinus:** e.g., Ass, Onager, Kiang
Subgenus — **Hippotigris:** e.g., Zebra

The equine family tree can be depicted as under:

The Equine Family

Horse		**Ass**	**Zebra**
Equus caballus (64) * * *All the horses domesticated* @ *The only wild horse* available in the world (True wild horse)	*Equus przewalski* (66) @	**1.** *Equus hemionus* (Mongolian/ Asiatic wild Ass) (56)	Three species exist in Africa **1.** *Equus zebra* (Cape Colony zebra or Mountain zebra) (32)
		2. *Equus kyang* (Tibetan wild Ass) (54)	**2.** *Equus Gvevyi*- (Somaliland zebra) (46)
		3. *Equus onager*(persian wild Ass) (56)	3. *Equus burchelli*- (Common zebra of East Africa) (44)
		4. *Equus asinus* - African wild Ass. (It is the ancestor of donkeys) (62)	

(Figures in parenthesis indicate the Chromosome numbers)

VARIOUS EVOLUTIONARY STAGES

The equine evolution is classical example of gradual adaptation to changing environment . The most distinct changes were-

- Increase in size
- Decrease in toe number
- Switching over from Browsing to Grazing

Like the family as a whole, the genus Equus evolved in North America and spread from there into the whole world somewhere 47-50 million years ago. Horse is the last species to be domesticated by mankind about 6000 years ago somewhere in the region now known as Modern Russia and the Ukraine.

Eohippus - was a common ancestor of all horse families which was 25 cm high, 50 million years ago.

Mesohippus - Its height was 60 cm and it was three toed animal.

Merychippus - Its height was approx 100 cm and by then, out of three toes, the central toe started increasing in size.

Pliohippus - Its height was 1.25 mtr and by then, it developed into single toe.

Equus - Its height and size was variable and there was further increase in size of hoof. It is by now two million years old.

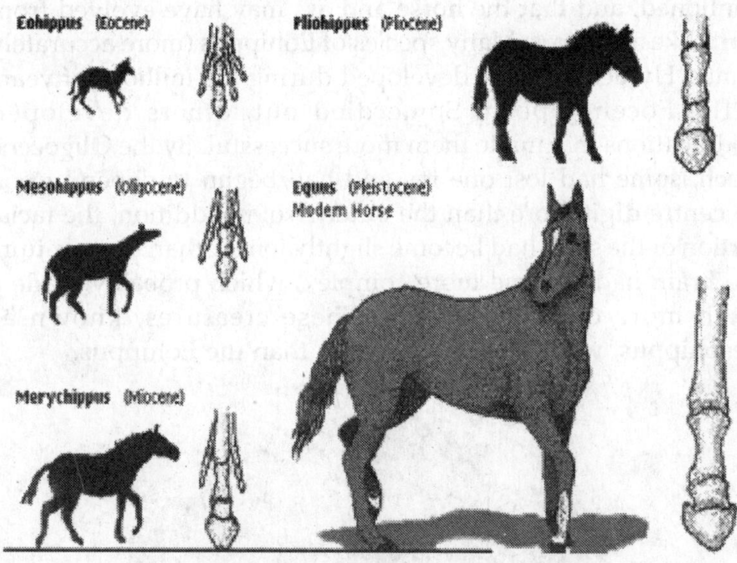

Fig. 2.2 : EVOLUTION

Today, probably eight distinct species of the genus Equus appear in the family equidae. Some of these species are known to interbreed and produce fertile offsprings, an example being the Mongolian wild horse crossed with the domestic horse. The distinction between a breed and a species is not always clear-cut. Usually, groups of animals that cannot interbreed are classified as distinct species. While the various breed crosses are quite fertile, equine species, lack hybrid fertility stems owing to differences in chromosome number. Usually, three divergent types of animals are considered to be within the equine family: the horse, the ass, and the zebra. These have chromosome differences among members of each of these types.

It is difficult to determine whether all of the present-day species evolved from a common ancestor or whether some represent stages of recent equine evolution. The fact that all present species hybridize, even though most are infertile, indicates that they are not too distant from a common ancestor. However, it is believed that the zebra is the most primitive of the three types mentioned, and that the horse and ass may have evolved from zebra-like ancestors. Many species of Eohippus (more accurately termed Hyracotherium) developed during the millions of years of the Eocene epoch. Some died out, others developed modifications that made them more successful. By the Oligocene epoch, some had lost one toe and had begun to depend upon the centre digit more than the outer two; in addition, the facial portion of the skull had become slightly longer than the cranium. The brain had become more complex, which probably made a much more cunning animal. These creatures, known as Mesohippus, were 15 to 20 cm taller than the Eohippus.

Fig 2.3 : EQUUS PRZEWALSKI

Some species that developed from Mesohippus were better adapted to open grazing than to a forest habitat. Accordingly, their dependence upon the middle toe increased. Grazing rather than browsing created a problem, with teeth wearing away from the abrasive action of sand in the grass. To overcome this, more successful grazers developed teeth with longer crowns and enamel ridges with cement between which was much like the horse teeth of today. The skull length also increased to facilitate grazing. Ultimately, the most successful equine species of this epoch turned out to be Merychippus.

By the middle of the Pliocene epoch, some one toed species of equines, had evolved. Throughout the years, generation after generation, it increased in size and Pliohippus eventually resembled some zebras of today.

Equus was the typical equine of the Pleistocene epoch. No one knows how many species of this genus have evolved and died out in the thousands of years since then. The ancestors of the contemporary equine moved across the land of the Bering Strait and into Europe and Asia. They eventually migrated as far as the southern tip of Africa.

It is also believed that during ice ages the Equus have migrated over land bridges to Europe, Africa and Asia. The disappearance of these land bridges as the ice receded some 10,000 years ago prevented horse population making reverse journey.

Three types of equines that are of special interest today developed in the old world. In the southern and eastern parts of Africa, the zebra species evolved. The various ass or "half ass" species developed in northern Africa and Asia Minor, while the horse species developed in Mongolia and Russia. Several species of wild horses are known to have existed, all of which have become extinct except *Equus przewalski* and *Equus caballus.*

There is much evidence that *Equus caballus* developed along two lines, often referred to as heavy horses and light horses. The light horse had a short face, a narrow snout, with slender legs and body. The heavy horse had a long, narrow skull with a prominent face and massive bones of the body and legs. Another difference is the enamel patterns of the teeth of the two.

Modern members of the equine family have been divided into seven species. The two species of horse, as mentioned, are *Equus caballus* and *Equus przewalski*. There are probably two species of the ass type. *Equus kiang* has still not been determined by karyotype to be a separate species, and there is doubt about the separate species status of *Equus onager* and *Equus hemionus* because of their identical chromosome number. Further, little doubt also exists regarding three species of zebras: *Equus zebra, Equus grevyi, and Equus burchelli.*

Other than chromosome number,measurement or count of various bones of the body is also used in differentiating species. A study has revealed much variation in vertebrae number among the equine species.

Table 2.1. Varying Numbers of Vertebrae in the Equine Species.

Animal		*Thoracic Vertebrae*				*Lumbar Vertebrae*			
		17	18	18 ½	19	5	5 ½	6	7
Domestic horse	(55)	4	50	1	-	6	1	48	-
Shetland Pony	(7)	-	7	-	-	-	-	7	
Arabian	(7)	4	3	-	-	I	-	6	
Przewalski's	(32)	-	23	-	9	16	-	16	
Ass	(11)	1	10	-	-	9	-	2	
Mille	(6)	2	4	-	-	1	-	5	
Hemione	(9)	-	8	-	1	9	-	-	
Zebra	(49)	7	41	-	1	5	-	44	
Grevyi zebra	(14)	-	14	-	-	1	-	12	1

(The number in parentheses represent the number of specimens examined by the workers).

Ancient Horse Types

The various horse breeds of today seem to have developed from few ancient types of about 10,000 years ago. It is believed that the 'Tarpan', cold blooded European horse, the 'hot-blooded' oriental horse and *Equus przewalski*, have made valuable contribution to the heritage of the modern horse.

Tarpan: It was small and buckskin coloured. These horses either developed from ancient pony types or superseded this type and heavily contributed to its development. It was known as wild horse of Europe.

The Cold-blooded European horse: It was an ancient inhabitant of European forests and its pure strains created the 'Great Horse' of medieval times, which in turn were used to develop draft breeds as well as some light horses. These large horses had relatively longer upper arm and leg with much shorter lower leg and forearm. This gave rise to a deeper chest and thicker body than the lighter horses of same wither height. The ancient horses had large rounded hooves, suggestive of soft forest or meadow habitat.

The Hot-blooded Oriental horse: It was believed to be small, probably between 1.32 to 1.37 m, and might have been similar to Tarpan with thin hair and a delicate bone structure. This ancient horse had a dished face with a small muzzle. This horse may have had great speed.

Equus przewalski : This ancient horse links closely to the ass and zebra. The height ranges 1.22 to 1.42 m, colour yellowish dun with mealy muzzle and dark mane and tail, a dorsal stripe down the back and zebra markings on the legs. It is considered true wild horse, being a different species from the domesticated horse. However, the hybrid of *Equus przewalski* and *Equus caballus* are fertile. This breed is considered as foundation stock for all domesticated horses. The Russian explorer Col. Przewalski in 1881 discovered this species in north west part of Mongolia. This horse is very wild and timid towards human. It has massive head with small ears, big jaw and very big teeth. Neck is short and shoulder is straight. Hindquarters are very strong. Legs have fine bones and cannon bones are short.

Development of Breeds

Ancient horse breeding and selection for a prolonged period brought about development of three basic light horse breeds i.e. Arabian, Barb and Turk. Evidence suggests that the domestication of the heavy horse and inbreeding with light horse was used mostly for pulling chariots rather than for riding. Selective breeding for larger horses was probably quite effective in early Persia, as evidenced by horse racing and polo playing at that time. Large war horses on the other hand, were probably produced by crosses with the heavy horse or the cold-bloods.

In 1680 B.C., light type horses spread with infiltrators, along the northern coast of Africa and Egypt. As a result of environmental and breeding selection, a new type of horse developed which was later known as 'Barb'. It was docile, tough horse and able to exist on poor feed. It had a relatively long head with a low set tail. Most of these interbred with Arabian horses and the product was called North African horse. Throughout the history of horse domestication, various groups of people have bred the Arabian horse. The Bedouins of the Arabian desert have called theirs, the Elite Arab or the original Arab. In some areas, the heavy horse developed into specific breeds without much crossing with the light horse and vice versa.

It is also believed that even before Persians began horse breeding, some of the Asian wild horses had migrated into western and northern Europe. However, because of severe environment, they evolved over hundreds of generations, into somewhat smaller horses now referred to as Celtic ponies. Exmoor breed of today, greatly resembles Celtic pony. These animals served as foundation stock for most of the pony breeds. Some of the ponies were later bred with heavy horses, producing still other breeds.

Ancestry of the Breeds and Modem Breed of Horses

A few horses found throughout the world, can be classified as foundation breeds because of their ancient origin and important contributions to the development of more recent breeds. Besides recognized breeds of horses, many specific types of horses have developed because of various environmental factors and the need of man. Important breeds of horses are listed as under:

Arabian	Barb	Turkmene	Tarpan
British Ponies	Ardennes	Konic	Holstein
Andalusian	Percheron	Lipizzaner	Kladruber
Shire	Criollo	Cleveland Bay	Thoroughbred
Hackney	Suffolk	Trakenhner	

The Indian breeds of horses include:-

Kathiawari	Marwari	Manipuri
Bhutia	Spiti	

In addition, modern breeds of horses include :-

The Albino	The Appaloosa	The Bashkir Curly
The Belgian	The Buckskin	The Chickasaw
The Clydesdale	The Fjord	The Friesian
The Galiceno	The Gotland	The Hackney pony
The Haflinger	The Hanoverian	The Knabstrup
The Morgan	The Nonius	The Orlov Trotter
The Paint	The Palonllno	The Peruvian paso
The Pinto	The Pony of America	
The quarter horse	The American saddle horse	
Spanish barb	Spotted horse	
Standard bred	The Tennessee walking horse	

Arabian: The **Arabs** did not get horse in beginning of **Christian era**. Camel ride used to be the mode of transport for them. **Prophet Mohammed** (PBUH) in seventh century AD realized the decisive importance of good cavalry for war. Presently, Arabian horses of quite diversified 'types can be found throughout the world. The people of many countries, outside Arabia, have bred their own distinct type of Arabian horse for years. Such Arabian horses have been bred extensively in England, Egypt, Poland, the United States, Spain, Germany and also elsewhere.

Arab horse breeding is best example in *animal breeding history* envisaging the principle of selection coupled with inbreeding, careful rearing and tough endurance test. This concept of breeding is often practiced according to strain fads. Today's strains are quite different from the strains developed by the Bedouins of the desert. They are more like nationalities, developed within the past 100 years.

The Arabian horse is characterized by its distinctive head. The bulging forehead and concave face gives a dished appearance. The eyes are large and set low in the head. A slight bulge at the back of the head and a light muzzle give the head a wedge-shaped appearance. The neck is arched, large and rounded. The back is short, straight, and rather level at the hip, reflecting the long, somewhat horizontally set pelvic bones. The short back usually reflects a missing thoracic vertebra rather than a missing lumbar vertebra.

The Arabian horse has contrived to the development of warm-blooded breed of horse and has even been crossed with the ancient Barb and Turk horses to give our modern Barb and Turkmene breeds. In this respect, the Arabian could be considered to be the original source of the hot-blood or, as the Arabian enthusiasts would put it, the only pure breed.

The modern Arabian breed is the product of the horse breeders of the Arabian desert during the last 1000 years. The blood of these horses was exported from time to time, principally to countries that exerted some political influence over the desert breeders. The Arabian breed in Persia has, therefore, been more or less continually infused with blood from the Arabian desert horse.

Barb: Coming out of Persia, in addition to early Arabian and Turkmene horses, was another horse called the Numidian. These horses were known to have been in Egypt in 1600 BC. The breed was later modified by the desert environment and the needs of the people as it moved across North Africa during the following centuries. This horse became known as the Barb from the Barbary states, now Ethopia, Somalia and other parts of North Africa. These horses reportedly reached Spain by 1000 B.C.

The native country of the Barb is northern Africa. The Libyan barb contains a strong mixture of Arabian blood, various local strains and other mixtures as well. A relatively pure strain of the Barb is found in Algeria. Several types among these strains indicate infusion of some outside blood even in the Algerian barb. This outside blood is mostly Arabian.

The Barb has contributed to the development of other important breeds. Offsprings of the famous Godolphin barb (1689) were used as the original stock for development of the English thoroughbred. The Barb stallion, 'Guzman', founded the Spanish breed, 'Guzmanes'. The horses brought to America by the spanish explorers were strong in barb blood. These horses had an influence on the development of the wild horses of North America and even some of the modern, South American breeds.

Turkmene: The Turkmene horses were well known in 1000 B.C. as race horses. They probably originated from the same Syrian stock from which the early Arabian breed was developed, King Darius of Persia reportedly had 30,000 horsemen mounted on Turkmene horses. At about 500 B.C., the game of polo originated in Persia and was played on these horses. The breed spread into Europe and Asia, where it contributed to the development of others, such as the thoroughbred - principally by Byerly Turk - and several Russian breeds, the Karabiar, the Jornad, and the Achal-Teke.

The modern Turkmene breed is found in Russia. These horses are of exceptional stamina and endurance, as well as are extremely fast. They have a long neck with a medium-sized head carried high, fairly prominent withers, long back, pronounced croup, and a sloping hip.

The Turkmene, Barb, and Arabian breeders of today, claim the early Persian horses as the ancentry of their breeds.

Thoroughbred: During the 16th century, the English were avid horse breeders and the sport of horse racing developed. At this time, the English ponies were being crossed with the Arabian and Barb horses. This crossing increased the size and speed of the English horses and brought out a new type. Perhaps some Andalusian blood was introduced to give even more height to the horse.

Two hundred years of intensive breeding of thoroughbreds has concentrated the hot-blood and developed thoroughbred horse to a very prepotent breed. Thoroughbred breeding is the best example of targeted selection for the particular trait which is speed. The thoroughbreds are the ***Lord of Race track;*** they are the **fastest**. The thoroughbred English has been developed over the years by selective breeding of the following categories:-

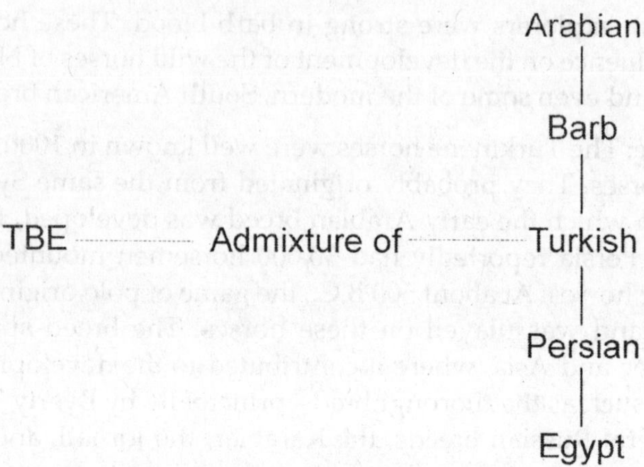

Thoroughbred crosses have been used to refine many other breeds. The Cleveland bay, although developed from cold-blooded horses, is now classified by some authorities as a warm-blooded breed due to extensive crossing with the thoroughbred. The quarter horse and other North American breeds have been developed and improved by infusing much thoroughbred blood. Since the turn-of-the century, thoroughbred sires have gained popularity in many countries by the number of stakes winners they have sired.

Breeds of Indian Horses

The Marwari

The **Marwari** or **Malani** is an ancient breed of horse from the Marwar region in the state of Rajasthan, India. The Marwari was a warrior mount for the Rathore rulers of Marwar, including the war horse of Maharana Pratap Chetak. Selective breeding of these horses may have begun in the early 12th century.

An elegant medium height, strong horse with track record of bravery and loyalty in the battle fields of medieval period. Now famous for traveling long distances, have strong feet and hoof, has his home in the area called "Malani" which is part of Barmer district of Marwari in the villages namely Nagar, Gudha, Jasol, Sindhari, Bakhasar and some areas of Sanchor Tehsil. These areas are said to be the nucleus of the breed "Marwari Horse".

The nearby Pali and Jalore districts have some famous breeders of Marwari breed. The others who are fond of Marwari Horse have taken it to the districts of Udaipur, Jaipur, Ajmer and even to Gujarat and Kathiawar and to other states. The horse stock, of the breed is maintained for breeding, travel, marriage ceremonies and personal interest. A good number of Marwari Horses can be seen in fairs of Pushkar, Tilwara and Naguar.

Fig 2.4 : Marwari Horse

The bardic literature of Rajasthan speaks very high of Marwari Horses, of their heroic exploits, leaping up to Haudus of elephant crossing over the high barrier walls of cities and forts. Few of the famous horses are **"Chetak"** of Maharana of Pabuji, and Veer Durga Dasji's horse "Arbud."

It is difficult to exactly trace the origin of true Marwari horse with precision but undoubtedly it has connections with "Arab" and may have mixed with Turkmenian breed, the horses of Alexander's army which were of this breed. However by selective breeding for the need of the warriors of the middle ages was evolved a breed which can survive well in difficult arid terrain. The growing demand of horses was in battle field of Indigenous breed which could withstand intense heat and cold, could cover long distances with speed, and has hard strong hoof and feet, gave impetus to development of Marwari breed.

Characteristics of Marwari Horses:

Head: The head is refined, relatively long and wide between eyes, with a medium muzzle and a shallow firm mouth.

Face: Long flat, broad with light forehead.

Ears: The medium-sized ears are curved inward at the tips and often touching the length varying from 9 to 15 cm located 90 degree axis and can rotate 180 degrees.

Eyes: Large eyes, set widely and reflect intelligence and a placid disposition.

Nose : Spacious, slightly Roman, the nostrils are full and sensitive.

Jaws: Well developed jaws imply great strength.

Neck: The head joins the neck at about 45 degree angle, proportionate with good musculature, the neck blends into sloping shoulders. It is clean at the throat.

Shoulders: Long, set at an angle of about 45 degree, well muscular, the slopes of shoulder blends into the withers.

Withers: Medium high, well defined and slightly higher than croup (about 1 to 2 cm high)

Chest: Broad, deep chested, wide round girth the muscling on the inside of the forearm gives the appearance of inverted "V."

Back: The short saddle back is powerful. The barrel or girth is deep with well sprung ribs. The underline or belly is longer than the back and does not cut high into the flank.

Rear Quarters: They are broad deep and heavy, well muscular, the croup is long slope gently from hip to the tail set. The hip muscle extends down into stifle.

Stifle: The stifle is deep; when viewed from rear extends out below the hip and above the gaskin. When viewed from the rear the stifle is the widest part of the animal.

Gaskin: It is wide and shows related thickness both inside and outside when seen from rear.

Hock: The hock is broad, clean, strong low set and free of excess tissue. The muscling lies well into the hock joint. There is no play in the hock joint except directly forward.

Fig 2.5 : Marwari Horse

Cannon: The cannon bones are short with hock and knee joints low to the ground. The cannon bones both front and rear show a perpendicular position and appear quite broad when viewed from side. The tendon, back and below the knees and hocks appear sharply separated from the bone and from each other.

Pastern and Hoof: The ankle is well formed and strong to withstand shock and strain, the medium length pastern denote strength. They have a slightly forward slope about 45 degrees, viewed from either the front or rear. The legs cannons and pastern are straight. The hoof is oblong. Its size balances with the overall size of the individual animal, it has overall same slope as the pastern. The sole and the wall are very strong.

Average Height: Stallion 155 cm (145 to 169) cm, Mares 153 cm (142 to 163) cm

Average shank measurement - 20.5 cm in Stallions and 20.0 cm in Mares.

Colours: A wide variety of colours is observed in Marwari breed horses. The most prevalent body colours are dark brown, bay, chestnut, dun, gray, flea-bitten gray, skewbald, piebald:

The Kathiawari: The Kathiawari has fhe same history as that of Marwari but having been bred in the Kathiawar region of Gujarat , it acquires the name of Kathiawari. Breeding line and environmental differences have distinctively given certain separate features to the Kathiawari from it's cousin the Marwari. Such as ears, eyes, nose and in it's built up structure

Although the Kathiawari and Marwari are separate breeds, yet virtually identical, both having descended from the indigenous Indian country breeds crossed with Arab stock. They tend to be generally bad tempered but extremely tough with lots of stamina, and they thrive on little food. Varying in height from 142 to 152 cm. They are very light and narrow, with weak necks and quarters, low set tail and sickle hocks. Any colour is found including piebald and skewbalds. The ears curve inwards with the tips almost touching at the points, thus indicating the Arab influence.

The Manipuri: Bred in the hill state of Assam and the Himalayas, the Manipuri is a descendant of both the Mongolian wild horse and the Arab. It has been claimed as the original polo pony, as a result of the British tea planters using it to play the local polo game in 1850. (The game was reputed to have been introduced to the State of Manipur in the seventh century). Physique of this horse is typical like that of pony but is very quick and maneuverable. A sturdy pony, height varying 112 to 132 cm, tough, surefooted and can be of any colour. It is deep through the girth, with a good shoulder, short back and well developed quarters. The legs are short with plenty of bone and the feet are hard.

Fig. 2.6 : Manipuri

The Bhutia: A thick-set pony from the Himalayan mountain area of India. The Bhutia is principally used as a pack pony on the mountain passes. It is sure-footed, extremely hardy and intelligent, with plenty of stamina and the ability to live frugally. Usually grey in colour, it is strong and sturdy with muscular quarters and good bone. It stands 132 to 137 cm in height.

The Spiti. The name Spiti has been taken from the famous *Spiti river* of Indian state of Himachal Pradesh. From the Himalayan area of India, the Spiti is bred principally by the Kanyat tribesmen. very similar to Bhutia in type and conformation. Although smaller, Its height is only about 122 cm, but it is hardy and with plenty of stamina. Well muscled with a short, thick neck, straight shoulders, short back and strong limbs and feet, the Spiti, like the Bhutia, tend to be temperamental. Both the Spiti and the Bhutia are closely related, and very similar to the 'Tibetan Nanfan' about whom very little is known. They are mostly used for transportation in the mountains.

Fig 2.7 Spiti

The Zanskari:

Zanskari horses are bred in the high altitude i.e. Zanskar region of Ladakh in eastern Jammu and Kashmir State of India. Physique of this horse is very similar to the Spiti pony but are more adaptable for higher altitudes where they are used as work horses

HYBRIDS: These are the crosses between various subgenus and many times progenies are found superior to the parents due to exploitation of genetic interaction called Hybrid vigour.

(i) Mule: ***Cross of Donkey Stallion*** X ***Horse Mare***

The largest hybridization in Asia is carried out in India amongst the organized stud farms and in some rural areas which is very successful for utility.

(ii) Hinny: Reciprocal cross of Mule.

Cross of Horse Stallion X ***Donkey Mare***

(Does not have much utility.)

(iii) Zeony: ***Cross of Shetland Pony Mare*** X ***Zebra Stallion***

(iv) Zebroid: ***Cross of Horse Stallion*** **X** ***Zebra Mare***

The hybrids have better heat tolerance for tropical climate and are fairly disease resistant.

Cloned Mule : First Equid to be Successfully Cloned

The first clone ever produced was a tadpole in 1952, using embryonic cells. Cloning made headlines in 1997 when Scottish scientists created "Dolly", a Finn Dorset sheep. Dolly's creation was significant in that she was the first mammal cloned from the cell of an adult animal. Since then, researchers have cloned a number of large and small animals including sheep, goats, cows, mice, pigs, cats, rabbits, and a gaur.

Fig. 2.8 : First & Second Cloned Mule

Working together with the University of Idaho, and Utah State University, Dr. Vanderwall headed up a team of scientists and geneticists to attempt what, to date, had never been done successfully. On May 29, 2003, the University of Idaho announced the successful cloning and resulting birth of ***Idaho Gem***. Born on ***May 4th, 2003***, Idaho Gem is the result of the cloning of a 45 day embryo which was the product of breeding Taz' sire and dam. On June 9th and July 27th 2003, second ("Utah Pioneer") and third cloned mules were born to join Idaho Gem and increased the success of this ground-breaking research project. Researchers believe that their success can have a major impact on the preservation of endangered species such as Przewalskis horse

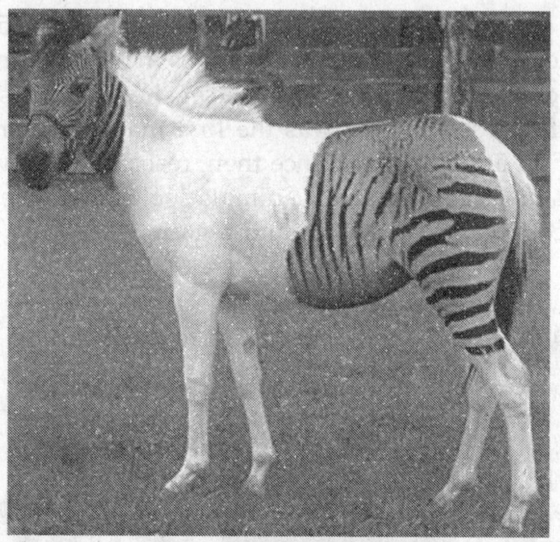

Fig.2.9 : Equine Hybrid Born to a Horse Dather and a Zebra Mother During 2006 at Schloss Holte, Germany.

Fig. 2.10 : Indian Donkey

Fig 2.11 : Wild Ass

Chapter **3**

The Points of the Horse and Dentition

The "points" of the horse are the terms used to indicate the several regions alluded to.

Commencing at the top of the head, the part immediately between and behind the ears is called the "poll"; the "forehead" is from the poll down to the level of the eyes. From the level of the eyes downwards to the nostrils is the "face," and the lower part, including nostrils, mouth and chin, is generally termed as "muzzle". By taking hold of the inner side of the nostril, one is able to see some distance up it, to note that it rapidly gets very narrow, and to see on the floor of it, rather towards the inner side, a small hole, which looks as if it had been made with a punch. This opening is the end of a small canal which starts from the inner side of the lower eyelid and allows the tears to flow without running over the face.

If a finger is passed into the nostril at its upper angle, it enters a blind pouch or cul-de-sac, which is known as the "false nostril".

Starting again from the poll: the top of the neck from which the mane springs is called the "crest" and passing the hand down, the raised portion is called the "withers". The withers rise slightly from the end of the neck and slope away down to the back; they are situated immediately over the top of the shoulder-blade. Behind the withers lies the "back"; behind the back, are the "loins", "croup" and "dock." The "back" runs as far from behind the shoulder-blade as a hunting saddle reaches, the "Loins" from there to the top of the quarter, and the "croup" from thence on to the root of the tail or "dock.". Coming back to the head, the space between the branches of the jaw is called the "jowl" and just behind it is the "throat." Running down the lower part of each side of the neck, from the angle of the jaw to just in front of the shoulder, is a well-marked shallow groove in which the large blood vessels of the head and neck lie. On the left side, the "gullet" (oesophagus) also lies in this groove, and its position may be accurately noted whenever the animal swallows a mouthful of food. Beneath these grooves and in the center line, the "windpipe" (trachea) is found and may be traced from the throat to the base of the neck where it enters the chest, the rings of cartilage of which it is composed, being easily felt beneath the skin.

At the lower part of the neck where it joins the body is the "breast," in the centre of which may be felt the point of the breast-bone (sternum). This bone runs backwards between the forelegs and terminates in a broad piece of cartilage with a slightly upward curve which is seen just behind the point of the elbow; this is the "girth-place."

The ribs, eighteen pairs in number,springing from the backbone above and attached to the breast-bone (sternum) below, form a cage for the organs of the chest and belly which extends from between the front of the shoulders to the loins. They may be felt from behind the shoulder backwards, and the space between the last rib and the hind-quarter is termed as "flank." The regions occupied by the "chest" and "belly" respectively may be estimated by drawing a line, curved forward in its length, from the loins above to the girth-place below. The "forehead" includes head, neck and fore-limbs. The "quarters" are the whole of the parts from flank to tail.

Turning one's attention now to the foreleg, the "shoulder-blade" slopes downwards and forwards to the "point of the shoulder" where, with the "arm-bone," or humerus, it forms the shoulder-joint; this latter being continued backwards and downwards to the "elbow-joint". The whole of this region from the top of the shoulder-blade down to the elbow and including the large mass of muscles behind the bones constitutes the "shoulder". The "forearm" reaches from the elbow to the knee, the bones being covered with muscles, except on the inside, where they lie close under the skin. The bone forming the "point of the elbow" may be felt projecting prominently at the back of the elbow-joint. On the inner side of the arm may be noted a horny prominence, the "chestnut" or "castor".

From below the knee to the next joint, the bone running down the front of the leg is termed the "cannon", "shank" or "shin," and the tendons from the bend of the knee down the back of the same area, are familiar to all as the "back-tendons". This brings us to the "fetlock" joint, and below this the "pastern" slopes downwards and forwards to the *hoof.* Behind the fetlock, in a tuft of hair, is a small mass of horn. This is known as the "ergot," and is largest in common bred horses. The region round the top of the hoof is called the "coronet" and usually there is a slight bulging forward of the skin at this point.

Commencing now at the top of the hind-quarter, we find, about a good hand's breadth behind the last rib, a body prominence just beneath the skin, the "point of the hip"; the projection of the quarter just below the root of the tail or "dock" is the "point of the quarter" or "buttock" and about midway between the point of the hip and buttock, lying deeply in the muscles, is the "hip-joint". The hip-bone runs from the hip-joint to the "stifle" which is the large joint found behind the lower part of the flank; from here the "thigh" runs backwards and downwards to the "hock-joint" and the prominent bunch of muscles found over the outside of the lower part of the thigh is often called the "gaskin" or "second thigh". The "hamstring" is the thick, strong tendon running from the muscles at the back of the thigh to the "point of the hock". Below the hock the same terms are used as in the foreleg. The "chestnut" in the hind leg is situated on the inner and lower part of the hock, and is smaller than the corresponding one in front.

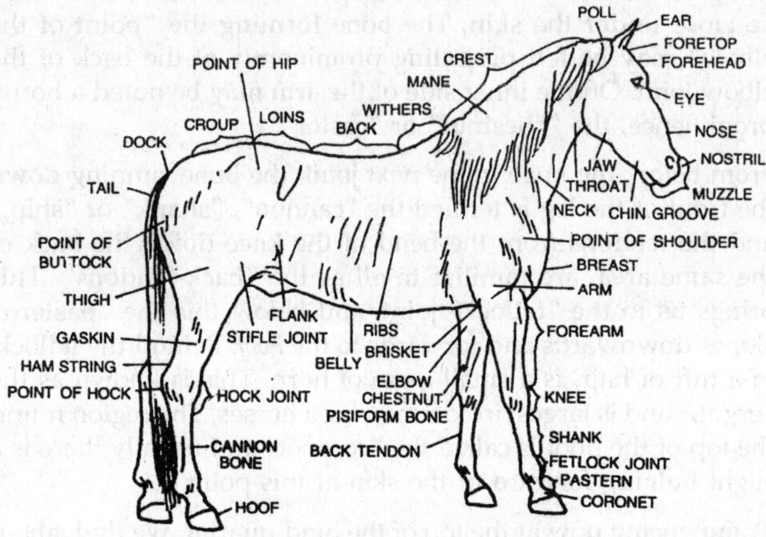

Fig. 3.1 : Points of the Horse.

Dentition

The horse's teeth, unlike those of man or the dog, do not grow to a certain length and remain so. On the contrary, they continue to grow and be worn away until old age. As horses get older, definite changes are observed in shape and appearance of their teeth, and it is owing to these that they form such a good guide to the animal's age.

The age of the horse may be told with practical accuracy by the appearances of the incisor teeth. There are two complete sets of these, i.e. the original temporary milk or foal teeth, subsequently replaced by permanent or horse teeth.

The differences between temporary and permanent teeth are as follows:

- The temporary teeth are small and white, have a distinct neck, and a short fang, which practically disappears as the teeth get older, from the pressure of the growing permanent teeth beneath, until its remnant is pushed out of the jaw.

- The permanent teeth are larger, stronger, and browner in colour, have no marked neck and a long, stout fang.

The Parts of a Tooth : The surface which bites on the food or its fellow in the opposite jaw is the table or wearing surface. The mark is the blackened depression which is seen on the table. It is lined by a distinct, narrow, pearly-white ring of enamel. This latter is easily seen and felt, as it stands up a little above the level of the rest of the surface. In a new tooth, the mark is very broad and deep, but with age and wear, it becomes shallower and smaller, till finally it disappears altogether. The blackening of the mark is due to discolouration from the food during mastication, and is not present in the new tooth.

The crown of the tooth is that part which is above the gum, and the point where the gum and tooth meet is the neck.

The fang is the part within the jaw. It is hollow and its cavity (fanghole) contains the blood-vessels and nerves which nourish and sensitize the tooth. As the tooth grows up, the fang-hole becomes filled in with tooth substance of a lighter colour than the remainder, and when the wear reaches this level, it appears on the table of the tooth as a small white spot in the centre, or in front of the mark, if that has not already disappeared.

Number of teeth: There are six incisors, at first milk teeth (temporary), and later on replaced by permanent teeth, in each jaw. The two in the centre of the jaw are called "centrals," the next tooth on either side is known as a "lateral" and the outermost on each side of the jaw is the "corner" tooth.

In the male, a tush appears behind the corner tooth on both side of each jaw when the horse is reaching maturity. This is a permanent tooth only.

The molar teeth are six on each side of jaws. The 1st, 2nd, and 3rd are first temporary and then permanent, but the 4th, 5th and 6th only appear as permanent teeth. Practically, they may be left out of consideration for our purpose.

- At birth, the foal has two central temporary incisors teeth in each jaw. At about two months, the lateral temporary teeth are out, and at six to eight months the corner temporary incisors are out through the gum.

- At one year, the whole of the temporary incisors are in wear, the corner tooth being little worn and looking "shelly" i.e., the inner side of the tooth not yet grown up level with the front.
- At two years to two years and three months, there may be some sign of the centrals giving place to the permanent teeth which are to succeed them. The gum may be red and swollen and the teeth loose.
- Care should be taken against mistaking a two-year-old for a six-year old mouth. This has frequently been done, but will not occur if one is familiar with the difference between the temporary and permanent teeth in appearance.
- At two years and six months, the central permanent incisors appear and at three years they are in full wear.
- At three and a half years, the permanent lateral incisors are also visible.
- At four years and six months, the corner permanent teeth are cut and at five years are in wear, but not fully.
- Between four and five years the tush is cut, at first it has a sharp point and edges, but these gradually become rounded with age.
- At six years, the corner teeth are in full wear over their whole surface, the marks are broad, but those of the central teeth are smaller, and show more wear than those of the laterals and the laterals more than the corners. The wearing surfaces of the teeth are broad ones, the centrals showing perhaps a tendency to become triangular.
- With the mouth closed (see Plate III) and looked at from the side the teeth are upright and meet each other squarely, the upper corner tooth projecting slightly beyond that of the lower jaw, at the posterior corner.
- From six years onwards, the changes are as follows:

The marks get smaller, rounded, and may disappear from the central teeth at about ten years. In some teeth, however they persist for much longer periods, the variation being due to the depth of the mark and the thickness of its enamel lining, and also the manner in which the upper and lower incisors make contact with each other. In an "undershot" mouth, the "marks" may persist for a long time.

The fang-hole makes its appearance on the wearing surface of the central teeth at about eight years, as a transverse line, in front of the mark. With increasing age it becomes a "spot" rather than a line, and as the mark disappears, it occupies the center of the table.

The shape of the wearing surface becomes changed from the broad oval to triangular, the back of the tooth forming the apex of the triangle.

The teeth become longer and project forwards with age, instead of meeting each other in the perpendicular or nearly so.

At and after seven years, there is a distinct notch on the upper corner incisors, where it overlaps its fellow in the lower jaw (plate IV). It is frequently broken off and sometimes removed by unscrupulous persons.

At ten years "Galvayne's mark," a depression on the outer side of the upper corner incisor appears; it reaches half-way down the tooth at fifteen, to the bottom at twenty, is half grown out at twenty-five, and disappears at thirty (plate IV).

All changes appearing in the tables of the central teeth are seen in the laterals the following year and in the corners a year later.

The changes are given here for precise dates, but variations are considerable and can be learned by practice only.

All the points already mentioned should be taken into consideration when determining the age of an animal, and too much reliance should not be placed on a single tooth without taking into consideration the whole mouth.

In case of doubt, the following points (apart from the teeth) are often present in old horses: sunken eyes, a sunken cavity above the eye, grey hairs in coat, and sunken anus.

Bishoping: It is attempting to make an old mouth look younger, as follows: The teeth are filed short and level, a false "mark" is gouged out of the center of the table and blackened with caustic.

The trick may be detected by: (1) closing the mouth, when the teeth will not meet naturally; (2) by observing the absence of the enamel rim to the false mark and errors of its shape due to slips of the gouge; (3) occasionally the traces of the rasp or file used to shorten the teeth are in evidence.

When ageing a horse, one should always look at the same time for signs of crib-biting, in which case the front teeth will be unusually worn, sometimes down to the gums.

Chapter **4**

Care of Teeth and Dentistry

Dental Care is one of the neglected aspect in equine husbandry but gaining importance in the *modern managemental system* especially with performance horses. It is necessary part of the grooming and health care programme. Poor mastication causing colic and sometimes poor performance of otherwise known to be good performer may be due to painful dental problems. Sometimes horse may not show noticeable signs at all because some horses simply adapt to their discomfort.

Indications of Dental Problem:

(i) Horse takes long time to eat and excessive salivation .

(ii) Takes only grain or the hay or have preference for one over the other.

(iii) Evidence of Dysphagia, Halitosis, or quidding (half masticated material thrown out of mouth.

(iv) While eating tilting head one side or preferring to drink warm water rather than cold.

(v) While riding tossing of head or over reacting to bit, tail wringing, pulling against bit, bit chewing, tongue rolling, fighting the bit, or resisting bridling.

(vi) Swelling of Jaw, traces of nasal discharge.

(vii) Passing of undigested whole grains in feces.

(viii)Loss of body condition.

(ix) Poor performance, such as lugging on the bridle, failing to turn or stop, even bucking.

Routine Checkup Method:

Oral exams should be an essential part of an annual physical examination by a veterinarian. Every dental exam provides the opportunity to perform routine preventative dental maintenance. Periodical checkup every six months for young horses till five years of age and annually thereafter is necessary by opening the mouth with or without the help of Mouth guage and pulling tongue one side; all molars and incisors of both side should be examined critically with the help of flash light.

Method of Teeth Labeling:

For proper recording of dental problem, teeth labeling as per Nomenclature of dentistry is required. Other than usual anatomical system of nomenclature in which function is denoted by first letter (I - Incisors; C - Canines; P - Premolars; and M - Molars) the latest modified Triadan system of labeling is more logical and easy for this purpose. Infact, this system is an additional help for identification of individual horse and accelerates the recording process.

The horse's teeth are divided into four ***Dental Quadrants (arcade)*** each having specific number as under:

Upper Right quadrant – 1

Upper Left quadrant – 2

Lower left quadrant – 3

Lower Right quadrant – 4

The horses have 11 teeth on each side of the dental quadrants. The numbering begins from first central incisor of that quadrant (tooth-1) and ends at last Molar (tooth-11)

The first digit indicates the dental quadrant (arcade) of jaw and last two digits indicate the specific tooth.

For example, "301" is first central incisor of left dental quadrants of lower jaw and "311" is last molar of same side of jaw.

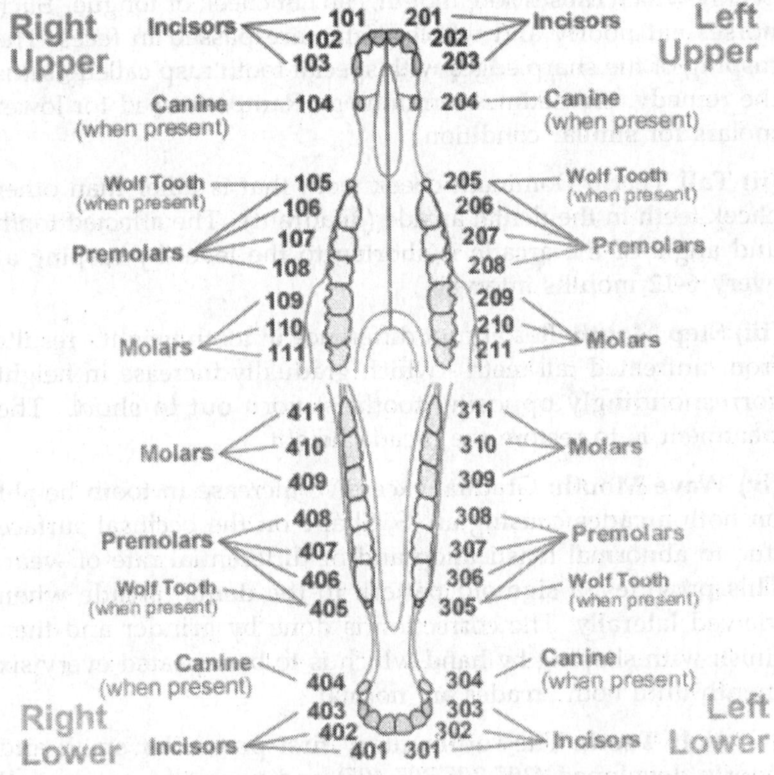

Fig 4.1 : The Triadan system dental nomenclature in equine.

104, 204,304 and 404	—	Canines of respective quadrants.
105,205,305, and 405	—	First Pre-molar or wolf teeth of right and left Upper, left and right Lower jaws respectively.

Common Dental Problems and Remedies:

(i) Hooks: It is most commonly encountered dental problem. The sharp edges develop on the outside edge of upper molars and the inside edge of lower molars, due to uneven wear and tear. Therefore, the chewing surface of molars do not meet evenly which causes sore mouth, can cut cheek or tongue. Such horses eat poorly and whole grains are passed in feces. The rasping of the sharp edges with special tooth rasp called *float* is the remedy. Sometimes terminology Ramps is used for lower molars for similar condition.

(ii) Tall Teeth: Dominant cheek teeth that is taller than other cheek teeth in the dental arcade (quadrant). The affected tooth and angle of the arcade is shorten to the level by rasping at every 6-12 months interval.

(iii) Step Mouth: It is abrupt difference in tooth height - results from untreated tall teeth - which gradually increase in height correspondingly opposing tooth is worn out to short. The treatment is to restore the arcade height.

(iv) Wave Mouth: Gradual excessive increase in tooth height on both arcades causing an 'S' Shape on the occlusal surface due to abnormal mastication and or differential rate of wear. This provides, a sigmoid pattern to the dental arcade when viewed laterally. The correction is done by grinder and then finish with shaping by hand which is to be repeated every six month until both arcades are normal.

(v) Wolf Teeth: The rudimentary first pre-molar small and poorly developed *(205,205,305,405)* and normally upper wolf teeth *(105, 205)* only erupt.

Wolf teeth are rarely found and generally absent in mare. The bit hitting wolf teeth is very painful to horse. A horse with sore wolf teeth may carry its head to one side to escape pressure from bit (over-check bit). The horses with wolf teeth creates training problem. It is advisable to remove wolf teeth in performance horses. Burgess wolf teeth extractor is used for extraction. The cylinder end is placed over the tooth and rotated in both direction applying pressure. After setting the handle in gum, extractor is moved back and forth but never in lateral movements. After removing tooth, gum (gingiva) is allowed to heal.

(vi) Too Long Canine Teeth: In older horses the canine also known as tushes, may grow too long and strike the opposite gum, causing sores. The reduction of length of canine tooth will facilitate bit insertion and prevents tongue injury. By tooth nipper canine is clipped to half length and the rough surface is filed with float.

(vii) Impacted tooth: Deciduous teeth those fail to fall out, preventing underlying permanent teeth from erupting. The caps interfere with chewing in young horse and hence should be pulled off by dental forceps and elevator.

(viii) Dental Caries: The dental caries or decay is destruction of dental cementum, enamel and dentin secondary to fermentation of carbohydrates producing acidic pH causing destruction of tooth material. Eighty percent of horses after 15 years of age suffer from this problem. This is also known as Infundibular necrosis. The routine dental maintenance and flushing by Metronidazole prevents the condition.

(ix) Periodontitis: This is inflammation of gingival with progression to formation of gingival pockets which leads to resorption of alveolar bone, loss of gingival attachment destruction of periodontal ligament and subsequently loosening of teeth. It is most common dental disease of horses. Animal shows symptoms of dysmasesis, quidding, dropping of grain, head tilt and salivation. Treatment includes correction of any malocclusion and routine dental maintenance flushing out of the trapped food and packing the packets with metronidazole, till the restoration of gingiva and grind the opposing tooth with rotary burr and shortened by 2-3 mm.

(x) Smooth Mouth: This is the condition of old aged horse that develops as teeth are lost or worn down to the gingival surface. Severely limited occlusal surface effects the grinding efficiency and thus mastication.

(xi) Bit Seat: It is the procedure in which the rostral edges of second pre-molar teeth (106,206,306 and 406) are rounded off to allow an area for a bit and associated soft tissues to rest against the teeth.

known as tushes they grow too long and strike the opposite gum causing sores. The reduction of length of canine tooth will facilitate bit insertion and prevents tongue injury. The tooth of upper canine is clipped to half length and the rough surface is filed with float.

(vii) Impacted tooth: Deciduous teeth those fail to fall out, preventing unerupting permanent teeth from emerging. The caps interfere with chewing in young horse and hence should be pulled out by dental forceps and elevator.

(viii) Dental Caries: The dental caries or decay is destruction of dental cementum, enamel and dentin secondary to fermentation of carbohydrates producing acidic pH causing destruction of tooth material. Eighty percent of horses after 15 years of age suffer from this problem. This is also known as infundibular necrosis. The routine dental maintenance and flushing by Metronidazole prevents the condition.

(ix) Periodontitis: This is inflammation of gingiva with progression to formation of gingival pockets which leads to resorption of alveolar bone, loss of gingival attachment, destruction of periodontal ligament and subsequently loosening of teeth. It is most common dental disease of horses. Animal shows symptoms of dysmastesis, quidding, dropping of grain, head tilt and salivation. Treatment includes correction of any malocclusion and routine dental maintenance, flushing out of the trapped food and packing the pockets with metronidazole, till the restoration of gingiva and grind the opposing teeth with rotary burr and shortened by 2-3 mm.

(x) Smooth Mouth: This is the condition of old aged horse that developed as teeth are lost or worn down to the gingival surface. Severely limited occlusal surface affects the grinding efficiency and thus mastication.

(xi) Bit Seat: It is the procedure in which the rostral edges of second pre-molar teeth (106,206,306 and 406) are rounded off to allow an area for a bit and associated soft tissues to rest against the teeth.

Chapter **5**

Systems of Breeding

There are only two general categories or systems of breeding for the pure bred horse breeder: (1) Continuous outbreeding, which involves stallions that are unrelated to the mares of the herd, or (2) some form of inbreeding.

Those who are successfully producing non-registered horses also seem to have two categories of breeding systems (I) grading up and (2) crossbreeding.

Grading Up : Grading up is the use of good purebred stallions of the same breed generation after generation or crossbreeding to bring together certain combinations which are desirable for the type of horses that are being bred.

The grading up of horses is generally a sound practice because one can substitute genes for outstanding performance for the genes in the foundation stock. With six generations of grading up, practically all of the genes of the outstanding purebred are substituted for the genes with which the programme was started. It must be emphasized that to make this method successful, one must use stallions of outstanding merit in each generation. Too frequently, breeders breed non-descript mares to stallions of low merit in order to avoid a high stallion fee. It is not necessary to breed to a stallion of exceptional merit initially, but using a stallion of low merit at any time should be avoided.

Many of the coat colour are used by breeders as a technique of grading up with much success. The type of breeding is probably the only realistic answer for breeders of Appaloosas, Palominos, *Pintos,* and other breeds. It is difficult to make progress in selection when a large number of traits are being selected.

Therefore, the colour breeder can take advantage of the years of breeding and selection in another breed (if a breed can be found of the type desired). Within six generations, a breeder can incorporate over 98 per cent of the genes of that breed into his own stock, and at the same time, maintain the desired colour.

Two hundred years ago, some Arabian horse breeders were using a system of grading up in Poland. It was extremely difficult to obtain purebred horses from the desert during those times, but a few good Arabian stallions were imported.

This situation was ideal for the breeding technique of grading up. A number of farms were canying on breeding programmes for hundreds of years and with a view to upgrade their stock, the valuable mares were crossed with the imported Arabian stallions. The continued breeding of horses with a grading up system brings the horses involved one step closer to purity with each generation. As illustrated in Table 7.1, impure genes are halved with each generation, and with the thirteenth generation, the breeding herd is absolutely pure.

There is no attempt made here to debate the desirability of' 'almost pure" horses versus the absolutely pure. From a practical point of view, 200 years of grading up produced a horse indistinguishable from a purebred. However, no breed has been "pure" forever and proper selection within each new generation can produce increased effectiveness of the system. If the original mares have a few genes that might be especially desirable, these genes can be selectively maintained throughout years of breeding so that eventually one can attain an almost pure strain of horse along with some unique characteristics. On the other hand, if the purebred characteristics are all that is desired, selection over the years can eliminate every visible characteristics of the original mares.

Table 5.1 : Percentage of the Genes of the Purebred by Generations of use of Purebred Stallions in a Grading-up Programme

Generation	*Per cent of purebred Genes*
1	50.00
2	75.00
3	87.50
4	93.75
5	96.88
6	98.49
7	99.25
8	99.63
9	99.82
10	99.91
11	99.96
12	99.98
13	99.99

The key to successful grading up is the use of a purebred stallion in each generation. The crossing to two half-bred horses is not grading up and it is almost impossible to visualize what can happen in 12 or 13 generations. This period is more than a life time for most and some horse breeding programme have maintained such a continuous breeding upgradation.

Crossbreeding and Hybrid Vigour: The other non purebred system of breeding available for both horse and mule breeders, is crossbreeding which is used by horse breeders to make genetic combinations to further the purpose for which the horses or mules are being produced. The crossing of existing breeds has been used to put certain colours or colour patterns into a breed. Crossbreeding has also been used to give hybrid vigour, as the Arabian horses have been used to produce horses with great endurance and stamina.

The greatest use of crossbreeding was in the production of work stock in which the horse stallion was bred to jennies to produce hinnies or the jack was bred to horse mares to produce mules. The majority of the crosses were jack to horse mares to produce mules. Large draught type mares of various breeds of horses are bred to mammoth jacks to produce draught mules for specific purposes, whereas smaller and more active mares, are bred to jacks to produce farm mules and mules used for general purpose.

The mule is remarkably vigorous as a work animal and has many desirable characteristics viz sturdiness, greater strength than ponies and sure footedness. As mules are hybrids, born out of cross between a donkey stallion and horse mare, they inherit size, speed, strength and appearance from the dam whereas disposition, hardiness, patience, endurance, longevity, toughness and surefootedness comes from the sire. The opposite cross between she ass and stallion pony hinny is not very common. Mules, both males and females are sterile. The height of mules usually varies from 125 to 145 cm.

Inbreeding: The subject of inbreeding brings many things to mind. Some will consider it an aspect to avoid in a breeding programme, others will view it as a mysterious technique understood by only the greatest of breeders. The actual definition of inbreeding is the breeding of animals more closely related than the average of the breed, or population.

Inbreeding in excess can be bad. Inbreeding without ruthless selection will be deleterious. On the other hand, without inbreeding, it is impossible to develop homozygosity, which brings predictability to a breeding programme.

Before embarking on any type of inbreeding programme, one should consider those factors that will determine its success. The three basic factors that determine the success or failure of inbreeding programmes are: (1) the merit of the breeder's horse foundation material, (2) the effectiveness of the selection programme, and (3) the rate of inbreeding. The merit of the horse foundation material reflects how well the horses perform, how free they are from inherited lethals and defects, and how fertile the brood mares in the herd are. If the herd is relatively free of inherited defects of all kinds, highly fertile and performing at a high level, then a breeder can expect success using his own stallions in a breeding programme. A master at selection and one who is ruthless enough to keep only those horses having outstanding merit for breeding, will probably do well with inbreeding. The flaw is that people who work with horses are often swayed in their judgement by a horse who has a particularly good personality even though it may be extremely weak in other respects. Although, disposition and temperament should not be slighted, all of the attributes needed by a horse must be considered rather than only one or two. If one inbreeds rapidly (sire to daughter, son to dam, or full brother to sister) over a period of time, the genes tend to occur in the homozygous condition at a rapid rate.

The exact amount of inbreeding can never be accurately determined because there is never enough information about the breeding of all ancestors. Many breeds of horses carry a much higher amount of inbreeding than suspected.

Desirable and undesirable gene combinations will be produced in the homozygous state. Unfortunately, some undesirable recessive genes when in the homozygous condition, can mask the expression of a large number of desirable genes, and result in considerable numbers of undesirable horses. With a slower rate of inbreeding, selection can be more effective, and the less desirable material can be culled gradually without a large financial loss. Also, one can avoid the extreme of fixation that eliminates the opportunity to select.

Studies with most animals have shown that mild inbreeding with rigid selection, generally results in initial improvement, but with inbreeding at 25 to 50 percent (62.5 to 75 percent homozygosity), some loss in vigour usually occurs.

Line breeding: The principal method of increasing homozygosity in horse breeding is the practice of line breeding, which is thoughtfully approached by breeders who want to preserve certain desirable characteristics found in a particular animal. Generally, this is a stallion with an outstanding performance record or he may have been a halter champion. Less frequently, the object of a line breeding programme is a mare.

Line breeding is an attempt to get as much blood of a particular stallion or mare into the animals of the herd as possible, while at the same time keeping inbreeding as low as possible. The theory of inbreeding is excellent, but if one decides that a particular horse is outstanding and concentrates the blood of that horse in his herd, the merit of such a programme is no better than the judgement as to whether the horse is truly outstanding. However, if a breeder, through selection based on performance, decides on line breeding the programme is sound because the animals selected for line breeding have proven that they transmit outstanding performance.

Many years ago the Bedouins on the Arabian desert were practicing line breeding. Although, they did not use that term but their practices had the same effect as modern line breeding to certain stallions. The Arabs line bred to famous mares, and as a result developed, what has since been called strains. They were interested only in the bottom line of a pedigree and a stallion was important because of his dam. They developed very well-known strains such as Seglawi, Abeyan, and Jilfan.

Breeders have recognized the importance of line breeding because they can observe the prepotency that results in future generations. Breeding a champion to another completely unrelated champion may produce a winner, but he will seldom be a breeding horse. He will lack prepotency. His offspring will miss the mark that he made in almost every instance.

Inbreeding tends to accentuate faults as well as outstanding traits, but not to the same extent in all horses. Some offsprings will inherit most of the best traits, and few of the faults. Intelligent selection along the way improves the line. Often breeders will line breed to members of a particular family, not confining their aim to one individual. This approach provides several sources of the specific genetic material desired in a variety of combinations. As a result, the offsprings tend to have more variety at first, and then by selection, more vigorous line bred stock can be developed.

Outcrossing: As mentioned earlier, outcrossing tends to

increase heterosis although it is not as pronounced as that produced by crossbreeding. Outcrossing is the breeding of two unrelated lines within a breed. The amount of inbreeding decreases, so it is the opposite of line breeding.

Charles Leicester, in his book Bloodstock Breeding, gives valuable information on the merits of outcrossing versus line breeding. He classified as outbred, those horses that have no name appearing twice in the first four generations of their pedigrees. In addition, he classified inbred horses into four categories (1) those inbred at the fourth generation, (2) those inbred with the same name occuring at the third and at the fourth generation of their pedigree (3) those inbred at the third generation, and (4) those more closely inbred.

With this classification, Leicester investigated the percentages of these types within the general thoroughbred population and among various types of winners. The general population contained 56.8 per cent outbreds. Yet each of the five categories of winners analyzed had a lower percentage of outbreds. His survey shows that although winners are more highly inbred than the general population, the parents of winners were more highly inbred than the winners. This study exemplifies the relationship between prepotency and heterosis, as explained earlier. The breeder is always faced with the paradox of breeding for the best trait through outcrossing and at the same time breeding for the best breeding. Outcrossing does help in producing winners, but the chances of these winners becoming great breeders are diminished.

Important Considerations in Equine Breeding Programme

Breeders cannot change Mendelian genetics, nor the number of genes involved in traits, nor their linkage relationships. They cannot change the physiological interactions of gene products, but they can hope through selective mating to realize gene combinations that consistently result in high quality stock.

Ann T. Bowling

Before starting the actual breeding programme in a stud, stallion having particular strong trait or traits that need strengthening in the herd, should be identified. At the same time, it must be ensured that additional weakness is not brought into the herd. Accordingly, the stallion selected to strengthen the weakness in the herd, must not have undesirable traits. If a stallion with one undesirable trait is used for correction of another undesirable trait already existing in the herd, it may result in spread of two undesirable traits instead of only one. Hence, it would be better to use a stallion with no undesirable traits, even though he is not outstanding in the trait that needs correction in a specific herd.

It is essential to be completely objective and ruthless with a view to have an effective breeding programme which has no place for sympathy towards an animal or for personal whims and fancies. Every attempt should be made to see that the environment is the same for all of the animals. A particularly appealing foal, if given special care and training, may develop into a desirable animal, however, it must be remembered that many foals, who might be less appealing in early life, may have the genetic potential to develop into desirable animals if given special care and training. Environmentally produced differences in horses are not inherited and will not be transmitted. In fact, it is often wise to select animals who were developed under the type of environment in which they are expected to perform for example, if stock horses are being developed for carrying in rough, rugged terrain, selection under such conditions is more desirable than under conditions that are not severe. Animals who have inherited weaknesses will tend to break down under the rugged environment. As a consequence, they will not be ideal animal for breeding. Further, such animals might never show their inherited weaknesses under a less-rugged environment.

The ideal environment for horse breeding programme should aim at availability of plenty of forage of good quality, on an area that compels the horses to take considerable exercise over fairly rough land in order to obtain the forage. Where the land area is highly productive and level, the animals may have to be forced to exercise a great deal. Since forced exercise will ensure that the animals do not become fatty and will give greater strength to their feet and legs to enable them to carry any excess weight they may acquire. Regular exercise, even if it is quite strenuous, will not harm an animal who is genetically sound. However, it may bring out inherited weakness possessed by some horses. An environment that will be useful in distinguishing the animals which are genetically most capable, for the purpose they are to fulfill, should be ensured. For example, animals who are being bred for endurance in travelling should be made to travel long distances every day to determine whether they can do so without developing unsoundnesses. This practice is useful as a selection tool in deciding whether to keep the horse for breeding or not. Similarly, horses that are bred for jumping ability should be made to jump as soon as the horse is mature enough and soundly conditioned to undertake required levels of jumping so that those lacking the ability to do so or those who go unsound from jumping, can be culled from the breeding programme before they leave any offspring. Horses who are bred for high speed at short distance should be forced to run at their highest possible speed, to detect those animals who lack the ability, and also those who become unsound from the strain of fast speed. However, a horse must be properly conditioned before high speed is forced. In addition, it is always best to know the capabilities of a horse before it is selected for breeding as much variation exists amongst the horses and one should keep only those that meet the needs of the type of horse being bred.

References

Ann T. Bowling (1995) CMK Record, SI/3: page 5/6 Fall, 1995.

area is highly productive and levels, the animals may have to be urged to exercise a great deal, since forced exercise will ensure that the animals do not become fatty and will give greater strength to their feet and legs to enable them to carry any excess weight they may acquire. Regular exercise, even if it is quite strenuous, will not harm an animal which is genetically sound. However, it may bring out inherited weaknesses possessed by some horses. An environment that will be useful in distinguishing the animals which are genetically most capable for the roles they are to fulfill should be ensured. For example, animals which are being bred for endurance in travelling should be made to travel long distances every day to determine whether they can do so without developing unsoundnesses. This practice is useful as a selection tool in deciding whether to keep the horse for breeding or not. Similarly, horses that are bred for jumping ability should be made to jump as soon as the horse is mature enough and soundly conditioned to undertake required levels of jumping so that those lacking the ability to do so or those who go unsound from jumping, can be culled from the breeding programme before they leave any offspring. Horses who are bred for high speed at short distance should be forced to run at their highest possible speed, to detect those animals who lack the ability and also those who become unsound from the strain of fast speed. However, a horse must be properly conditioned before high speed is forced. In addition, it is always best to know the capabilities of a horse before it is selected for breeding as much variation exists amongst the horses and one should keep only those that meet the needs or the type of horse being bred.

References

Ann T. Bowling (1996), CMK Report(s) 3, page 76 Fall 1995.

Chapter 6

Selection Procedure

Selection may be defined as the differential reproduction of what is desired. It is a process in which certain individuals in a population are given an opportunity to produce offsprings, while others are devoid of this opportunity. This is an important tool in the hands of a breeder for changing of gene frequency to develop a type for a particular purpose. The characteristics of a specific type that the breeder is trying to develop can be vital as more than one trait is desired in an ideal horse e.g. size, specific muscling type, temperament and correct conformation.

In actual animal breeding practice, selection is a decision making procedure and the choice is generally based on records available. Accordingly, the frequency of selection also depends upon the accuracy of records and number of records available with us.

Types of Selection

Selection is mainly of two types :

1. **Natural selection:** In the natural selection, the particular environment in which the population lives is the main operative factor in nature. It is not man made and is generally based on the principle of survival of the fittest.

Factors Affecting Natural Selection.

- Difference in mortility of the individuals in a population i.e. it may be in early life or after sexual maturity has been attained.
- Difference in the sexual maturity as such, which in turn affects the reproduction potential.

- Intensity of sexual activity - Individuals indulging in more sexual activity are likely to produce more offsprings.

2. **Artificial selection:** It is the selection made by the breeder. In this, the efforts are directed to increase the frequency of desirable genes or combination of genes in a population by locating and saving the superior parents and their subsequent breeding.

Methods of Selection

Tandem selection. In this method, selection is practiced for only one trait at a time, till the goal set for this trait is achieved. Thereafter, selection is directed for another trait till the progress of this trait is achieved and so on. This system of selection is the simplest one and is most useful for colour breeding. The establishment of a particular colour breed is compatible with the gaining of one desirable trait at a time. In this case, colour has top priority. Further, coat colour that involves more than one gene, can be obtained step by step. Once the desired colour has been established in the herd, the breeder can go on to another trait as size, height and so on. However, this system of selection may prove to be unsatisfactory if a large number of traits are required to be improved in a herd.

Minimum Culling Level Selection: In this method, a few characters are considered at a time. Even for each trait, a minimum standard is set and every animal must meet the standard of each of the character, otherwise it is rejected from breeding population. This system is particularly useful in stallion selection from a very high quality herd. This method does not provide comparative advantages and if an animal is exceptionally good in one character but little inferior in another character, it will still be rejected. As such, the breeder is unable to utilize the outstanding performance in two or three traits at the expense of inferiority in one trait. The effectiveness of this method depends upon the standards kept for each of the characters. This method is extremely useful for all or none trait, such as defects and reduced fertility in horses where mare either does or does not have a foal. Similarly, traits that show continous variations such as speed, body size, could be selected by setting minimum standards, below which all horses are culled. However, if very high standards are kept, the number of animals selected to become parents will be very small, resulting in gradual extinction of population. On the other hand, if low standards are kept, then adequate number of animals are not culled to achieve the goal. Further, in this system, no provision exists for priority rating of traits. This is considered a handicap to the system because some characteristics are harder to come than others and ought to be rated higher on the priority list. For example, hypothetical data of four potential stallions is given in following table and those not reaching the minimum in anyone trait are to be culled:

Table 6.1

Trait	*minimum*	*Stallions*			
		1	2	3	4
Height (m)	1.60	1.58	1.60	1.62	1.63
Weight (kg)	450	450	425	500	500
Disposition	7	10	8	10	7
Conformation	8	9	10	7	8

Analysis of above data reveals that stallion 1 falls short in height, stallion 2 in weight, stallion 3 in conformation and stallion 4 would be the only one qualifying for breeding programme, though he is not as good in several points as some of the other stallions which will be culled in the true spirit of the selection system.

The Index System or Total Score Method or Score Card Method: The most effective method of mass selection is the Index System. This method removes disadvantages of previous two methods, in that a certain value is assigned for each character depending upon the heritability or economic value of that character. This method involves the developing of an index or point system for each trait considered important in the selection process. Those traits with a higher priority can be assigned a higher total of points, thus balancing the more important traits carefully against those deserving less consideration. However, the more traits used in selection, the less progress can be made in anyone year. Selection for four traits is half as efficient as for one. Similarly, selection for as many as 16 traits, will reduce selection efficiency by half again. Therefore, if breeder is concerned about a dozen or more traits, it is going to take him about four times longer to reach his goal than a breeder selecting for only one trait. Grading should be consistant from year to year. The exact method of grading with all the variables of each trait identified in terms of how they affect the total value of that trait, should be described in the beginning. Further, an important consideration in assigning a certain value to a trait is its heritability i.e. a ratio of how much a trait. is produced by the environment in relation to genetic factors. For example, weight is strongly influenced by environmental factors, such as amount of food available and weather. But even under ideal conditions, each horse has a certain genetic potential for weight at a particular age. The heritability of body weight is reported to be approximately 25 per cent. Similarly, coat colour has higher heritability and the shape of head and body conformation are also quite highly heritable. Therefore, traits which are less heritable should be awarded less value in proportion to their importance while establishing an index.

Example of Index Method

In equine breeding, the breeder allots points for various traits to the breeding animals, keeping in view their relative importance in selection process. The higher priority is given to those traits which have got more importance and lower priority to those traits which deserve less importance. The animals scoring maximum, are selected and those scoring minimum are rejected.

Table 6.2: Grading Chart of the Type for Index Selection System

Trait Total	*Possible value*	*Fillies*									
		1	*2*	*3*	*4*	*5*	*6*	*7*	*8*	*9*	*10*
Height	100	80	100	75	80	100	0	100	50	100	100
Weight	30	25	30	25	30	30	10	30	15	30	30
Tail set	200	100	50	175	100	150	200	100	100	0	200
Head	200	100	50	200	100	150	200	0	100	150	200
Straightness Of legs	250	250	250	200	200	750	200	250	125	250	0
Disposition	155	100	50	140	100	0	150	130	75	150	150
Action	200	100	25	200	100	50	200	150	100	200	200
General conformation	100	50	25	90	70	80	50	50	50	50	100
Value of pedigree	80	10	60	80	80	80	80	50	40	80	80
Speed	75	50	40	50	50	75	25	25	40	75	60
Colour	10	10	5	8	5	10	5	10	5	10	10
Gene Quality	100	50	45	90	60	50	80	50	50	75	80
Total	1500	925	680	1333	975	1025	1200	945	750	1070	1210

In the above example, ten fIllies are graded for selection. If a breeder is selecting only 20 per cent for replacement, then the two highest scoring fillies will be selected. However, each breeder is likely to have his own list of traits and each will vary as to the possible value of each trait. This choice of trait is based on the perception of each breeder, keeping in View the importance of each trait relative to others.

Basis of Selection or Aids for Selection

In breeding, mostly the selection is made on the basis of records of the individual and its relatives. The kind of relatives an individual may have, may be described as under :

Collateral Relatives –

Sons		Sire [	G Dam
			G Sire
Progeny-	The Individual -	Ancestors	
			G Sire
Daughters		Dam [	G Dam

The Selection aids fall into four general categories :

(a) Appearance (b) Pedigree (c) Performance records (d) Production records

Appearance:- In equine breeding, the horse's selection is done by phenotypic examination of horse. The experienced horse-man can see defects in conformation and abnormalities of the eyes, feet, legs and also respiratory abnormalities e.g. heaves and roaring. The animals having above mentioned abnormalities should be discarded. Similarly, many lamenesses have a genetic predisposition e.g. a hock with faulty conformation is more likely to develop a spavin than one of the sound conformation. Accordingly, all animals which harbour inheritable genetic abnormalities, should be excluded from the breeding programme e.g. long sloppy pastern, calf knees, bowed legs, knocked knees, toe in, toe out, curb, cow hocks etc. If a horse has 'toes in' at the front feet, it will have a tendency to swing the front feet in circle, a motion called paddling. If 'toes out', it will tend to throw the front feet inwards in a circle motion known as winging. A horse may also tend to strike the supporting leg with the striding foot, a motion causing interference. Similarly, some horses tend to overstride with the hind feet and catch the heel of the front foot with the toe of the hind foot, which is known as forging. Horses with short straight pasterns, tend to walk in a stilted way and will be uncomfortable for riding. Such horses are more likely to stumble than a horse with normal pastern.

All these undesirable patterns of movement are to be avoided in a stallion because these reflect defects in conformation which are under genetic control. Further, with a view to see that various actions of animal are smooth and whether stumbling occurs or not, it is good to watch the horse while moving. Horse should also be viewed from the front, from behind and from the side as they move in the walk and the trot paces. It is also wise to move a horse vigorously during examination so that defects in respiration e.g. broken wind or heaves and roaring etc will be exhibited,

Selection on the Basis of Pedigree Information or record

A pedigree is simply a record of ancestory and accurate pedigree information is essential to a breeder for selection programme. In equine practice, certain internationally recognised records are available.

Thoroughbred Record Sire Book: It gives pedigree record as well as pedigree cross reference index. This pedigree index is helpful for planning inbreeding and outcrossing. Minimum four generations should be considered to avoid inbreeding but eight generations are ideal for superiority of performance. A breeder must keep a check on the amount of inbreeding in each horse, whether for performance or for the production of breeding stock. The only sure check is pedigree. How much each pedigree contributes to an individual, is explained as follows:

1st generation	50%
2nd	25%
3rd	12.5 %
4th	6.25%
5th	3.12%
6th	1.56%
7th	0.78%
8th generation	0.39%

9th	0.19%
	0.095%
10th -	0.047%
11th	0.023%
12th	0.011%
13th	0.005%
14th	

To specify the influence of ancestors, each" generation must be considered 100 per cent. Accordingly, the influence of tall male grand stallion sire will be 25 per cent but the influence must be expressed through the son of the grand stallion. Frequently, it is believed that the son is a 50 percent replica of the father but in reality, the son receives one allele of each gene from his sire. Only those stallion that are completely homogenous will transmit the same quality each time.

Performance Record:- Selection based on performance of an individual progeny is called progeny testing. Accurate record of individual animal, if incorporated correctly in the pedigree, then the performance record is good indication of what the genetic constitution of the animal is and how it should transmit. Pedigree without performance records are usually of little value in terms of indicating the genetic value of an animal. Moreover, a pedigree without performance records does reflect the inbreeding that was involved in the production of the individual. Further, pedigree containing records of performance should be evaluated, keeping in mind several considerations which are as follows:

(a) Pedigree is man made and can be considered important only if the breeders, who kept the pedigree records, were honest and accurate.

(b) Records of low performance in a pedigree are as important as records of outstanding performance. A foal with one outstanding great grand sire and one great grand sire with very low performance is likely to exhibit inheritance for low and for high performance. Similarly, the name of an outstanding animal in the pedigree of a horse should not be over estimated and performance of all the others in the pedigree should be considered.

(c) A pedigree with performance records must show records on all the animals, as a missing record is assumed to be absent to make the horse book better than the real record.

(d) Performance of the stallion and mare is much more important than performance of animals more apart in a pedigree. Unless an outstanding ancestor appears several times in the pedigree, it can be given only minor consideration especially when it is five or six generations apart from the animal being evaluated.

Performance records most commonly recorded are, racing speed, money earned or contests won, records of winning at halter and in some cases, colour development and changes throughout life. In addition, records should be kept on disposition, cow sense, jumping ability and all other heritable characters. These records become increasingly valuable as they accumulate generation after generation. Performance records are important as the basis of improvement through selection when heritability of the trait is high (0.5 or more). These traits include speed with estimated heritability at 0.45 and wither height, at 0.63. Similarly, traits that are intennediate in heritability (20 to 30 percent), will respond to selection. However, traits which are lowly heritable (5 to 15 percent), generally do not respond greatly to selection.

Performance has been indexed as a means of comparing all horses on the basis of one figure. The average earning index is often used in race horses and a horse under consideration is compared with the average of his breed. Similarly, draught horse index has been composed of four major categories namely, (1) pulling power in relation to body weight, (2) score for soundness of feet and legs, (3) foreleg breadth, (4) chest breadth. However, considerable research work is further required to be undertaken for developing and standardization of various other indices of performance records.

Production Records

Production record is of immense aid to the horse breeders to make good improvement in breeds. These records are most comprehensive summary of stallions' records. In the annual thoroughbred record sire book, every sire of a winner is listed as the year passes. Each winner is identified by name, age and with pertinent information about his winning offsprings. In addition, complete production record of stallions and their ranking for the various categories i.e. highest class of race won by each winner, the claiming price, average distance run, number of starts, times won, placed or showed, total amount won by all offsprings. Similarly, records of top ranking sires are made for the following categories - (i) average earning per start, (ii) average earning per trainer (iii) percent of winners (iv) number of winners and (v) number of races won. Broodmares' sires are also ranked in the same way. Another important production record may be the record of top sires alongwith the prices at their yearling sale. The availability of such records is a tremendous asset to breeders to plan their breeding programme.

Selection Intensity

The rate of genetic progress is affected by the intensity of selection. The factor for intensity of selection is not quite proportional to the fraction culled. The intensity factor increases at an increasing rate as the fraction selected declines. These factors are a relative measure of how much the selected group will exceed the average of the population from which selected animals are taken. For the intensity factors to apply, selection must be made entirely on predicted genetic value.

A chart showing the selection intensity factors is as follows :

Selection percentage	*Selection intensity factor*
100	0.00
90	0.20
85	0.27 No Culling
75	0.42 Usual level of selection of mares
70	0.50

60	0.64	
50	0.80	
40	0.97	Range for selecting Dams of stallion.
30	1.16	
10	1.40	
5	1.75	
4	2.067	Possible range for selecting stallions.
3	2.27	
2	2.42	
1	2.67	

The heritability of a trait determines how accurately the genetic value of a sire or dam can be assessed. The accuracy (percentage) is equal to the square root of the heritability which is expressed as h^2. For example, if heritability of racing ability is 0.50 or 50 per cent, then accuracy in determining the best sire and dam from racing records will be square root of 0.50 i.e. 71 per cent.

The heritability estimates of certain traits in horses are as follows:

	Average heritability	
Fertility		
	5% (only 5% *success, if done on the basis of selection, since it is primarily due to environment and various other factors.)*	
Gestation		
	Spanish Mares	34%
	Arabian Mares	49%
	Speed in thoroughbred	35%
Trotting characteristics		
	Speed	37%
	Pace length	50%

Galloping		
	Pace length	56%
	Style	55%
Jumping		
	Winner over obstacles	18%
	Style	71%
Body measurements		
	Height at withers	81%
	Girth	20%
	Cannon bone circumference	20%
	Body Length	39%
	Body weight	27%
Pulling		
	Pulling power	26%
	Pulling power per unit	14%
Body weight		
	Walking speed	41%

Negative Genetic Association - There are certain traits, that have a negative genetic association as they are known to be somewhat antagonistic to each other. For example, if selection is undertaken for a straight or upright shoulder on one hand and a long smooth stride on the other hand, these characteristics do not go together, instead selection for the sloping shoulder should have positively contributed to a longer stride. Accordingly, this consideration must be kept in mind while planning selection programme, otherwise selection for one such trait will automatically cause a decline in other corresponding traits and vice versa. This phenomenon is also referred to as teeter-totter of selection.

Selection Criteria to Improve Fertility: Low fertility of brood mare is a serious problem in stud farm. The trait is lowly heritable therefore selection is ineffective and hence attention to environmental factors such as time of mating, nutrition, management and disease control is indicated. The mare is having longer oestrus period average 5-7 days and the ovulation as a rule occur 1-2 days before the end of oestrus. The time of covering in relation to the time of ovulation is very important because of limited life of both spermatozoa and ovum in female genital tract. The aging of gametes in reproductive tract will effect fertility and the sperm should wait for ova rather than ova waiting for sperm. The chromosomal aberration and fetal absorption is more in older parents.

Mares with more incidence of twin ovulations in oestrus cycle should be preferred less. Wind suckers and those mares with abnormal reproductive anatomy should not be selected for breeding as they are more prone to abortions. Non heritable pathological and functional disorders responsible for low fertility or sterility should be treated by paying proper attention to each mare.

Selection criteria for Racing Ability: Ability to win race for which money is at stake has the high genetic transmissibility and in horse industry the covering fees of the particular stallion is based on his race performance as well as earning index. The stamina for racing ability is also breed specific. The thoroughbreds who are the fastest racer has got better ability to stay on race track for longer time than the quarter horse. Moderate to high heritability of trait indicates that the selection of horse based on their racing performance will bring the genetic improvements in the next generation and therefore progeny produced out of good racer will have the genetic potential to excel provided favourable environment and training is given.

Selection Criteria for Behaviour and Temperament: The horses possess personalities and temperament like human beings. Horse intelligence is associated with their mentality and reasoning power. It is experienced that the donkey possesses more reasoning power than horse. The genetics does play in determining the equine behaviour. The two negative traits that seem to passed through equine family lines with some frequency are fearfulness and reactivity. Thoroughbred and Arabians are generally considered more flighty and reactive than quarter horses and warmbloods. Yet certain blood lines in Arabs and the thoroughbreds produce horses that are totally calm and docile.

Certain horses has tendency to buck when ridden despite proper training which is undesirable behaviour. The analysis of breeding data has shown that heritability of behaviour is moderate to high in certain breeds therefore mare/stallions showing undesirable behavioral characteristics should be culled to become future parents.

Selection on Basis of Type and Conformation for Saddle and Draught Horses

Type -

It is referred to the physical form and features that fits individual for a particular function. To know, what is the most desirable form and structure, one must become familiar with the parts of the horse and the unique characteristics for specific purpose based on that one must be able to evaluate and compare body conformation.

What is a Good Horse?

Front view	Ideal quality	Faults
Head	Well proportionate to rest of body, appearance, full fore head with great width between the eyes. Broad jaw and strongly muscled. Ear medium size, well carried and attractive.	Plain headed, Weak jaw, Parrot mouth, Roman nose and Pig mouth etc.
Faminity or Masculanity	Stallion should give a masculine expression. Mare should give an overfall famine expression.	
Chest capacity	Deep and wide	Narrow chest

Set of front legs	Straight, true and squarely set forelegs.	
Rear view	Wide and muscular over the croup and through the quarter.	Lacking width and length over the croup and muscularity through rear quarter.
Set of hind legs	Straigth, true and squarely set hind legs.	Crooked hind legs.
Soundness	Sound and free from blemishes.	Unsound, blemished.
Action		
At walk	Easy, prompt, balanced, long step with each foot carried forward in a straight line. Feet lifted off ground.	Short step with feet not lifeted off ground.
At trot	Rapid, straight, elastic trots with joints well flexed.	Winging, forging and Interfering.
At canter	Slow collected canter which is readily extended on either lead.	Fast and extended canter.
Side view		
Style and beauty	High carriage of head, active ears, Alert disposition and beauty of Conformation.	
Faults to be seen at overall side view are		Poor withers, back too long, lacking middle and long croup.
Balance and Symmetry	All parts well developed and nicely blend together.	Lacking balance and symmetry.
Neck	Fairly long neck, carried high and clean cut.	Short thick and ewe neck.
Shoulder	Sloping shoulders (about 45° angle.	Straight shoulder.
Top line	Short strong back and loin, with a long nicely turned and heavily muscled Croup and a well high set tail. Withers clearly defined and of the same height as the high point of croup.	Sway back and steep croup.
Coupling	Short coupling as denoted by the last rib being close to the hip.	Long coupling.

Middle	Ample middle due to long and well sprung ribs.	Lacking middle.
Rear flank	Well laid down in the rear flank.	High cut rear flank and Wasp waisted.
Arms, fore arms and gaskin	Well muscled.	Lacking muscles.
Legs, feet and pastern	Straight, true and squarely set Pastern should be sloppy (45o), Hooves large, dense and wide at heels.	Crooked legs, straight pastern, small hooves, and contracted heels.
Body type	Showing plenty of breed type i.e. size, colour, shape of body, head and action true to the breed respresented.	Lacking breed type.

Selection on the Basis of Type and Conformation for Saddle and Draught Horses

Saddle_ Race and Light Horse

- Height at the withers and over the croup should be atleast equal to the length of body. This a desirable quality of galloper horse.
- Depth of body at withers should be considerably less than half the height.
- Gaskin should be broad and neck should be long.
- Forelegs should be lighter.
- Horse should not be thick between the upper ends of shoulder blades.
- Withers should be high and should run far back.
- Hind legs should be long.
- Hocks should possess the ability of being fully straightened out as well as bent.
- The loins behind the cantle should be flat on account of presence of largely developed muscles.

Draught Horse / Heavy Cart Horse :

- Legs should be short. Consequently, the animal will be longer in the body than height at withers or at croup. It will be deeper from withers to brisket than from brisket to ground.

- Muscles, bones, tendons and ligaments should be as thick and strong as possible.
- The shoulders should be sloppy in cart horses which work on rough ground, and somewhat upright in those horses which work on smooth roads.
- Height over the croup should be low than the height at withers;

Polo Pony:

- Hardiness and speed with sufficient staying and weight carrying power are two chief requirements of polo pony. So it should be lighter in front, should carry its head and neck well and have sloppy shoulders, strong hocks and its hind legs well under it. The fact is, it should be "goose romped".
- The animal should have a great ability of suddenly stopping, turning round and galloping off in opposite direction and all this work is to be done chiefly by hind quarters.
- The temperament of animal should be fearless and must be intelligent enough to judge the placement of polo ball.

HERITABLE GENETIC DEFECTS OF EQUINES:

By definition, the genetic defects are the pathologic condition of proven genetic origin. There are certain diseases which are reported to be inherited in equines. Some commonly occurring genetic defects are :-

Scrotal Hernia: Commonly observed in mule foal. It is due to incomplete dominant gene.

Umbilical Hernia: Simple recessive character which can be eliminated by selection.

Cryptorchidism: May be unilateral or bilateral which is suspected to have genetic pre-disposition.

Genetic infertility: This may be due to chromosomal abnormality which can be detected by Karyotyping of the individual. The abnormality may result into developmental defects, abortions, or infertility. If abnormality involves sex chromosomes in mare this will result into infertility with small aplastic ovaries in apparently healthy animal. In stallion the condition like *XXY (Kleinfelter Syndrome*) causes infertility.

Hyperkalemic Periodic Paralysis (HPP): It is a dominant heritable defect and can be eliminated by proper selection. The affected horse shows intermittent muscular tremors followed by weakness and collapse or sudden death. Common in quarter horses breed.

Anterior Segment Dysgenesis (ASD): Genetic eye defect most common in chocolate colour horses and in Rocky Mountain Horses. In USA has shown that ASD is caused by single gene having codominant inheritance. In future a genetic DNA marker will be able to detect the defect more precisely.

Congenital Aniridia: Characterised by the absence of iris with secondary cataract in Belgium breed. The trait is dominant in inheritance.

Combined Immune Deficiency Syndrome (CID): This condition is mostly observed In Arabian foals .

Overo Lethal White Syndrome : The homozygous dominant autosomal gene results to non viable embryo and in recessive form, animal shows albinism which may be coupled with congenital defects of intestinal tract especially colonic atresia and hence most of the time do not survive

Counselling for Genetic Disease of Horses:

Dead or deformed foals produced by purebred parents represent an economic and emotional loss to the horse breeder. In order to avoid producing such defective foals in the future, the breeder may seek guidance in determining whether their origin is environmental or genetic. Only a few, genetic diseases of horses have been rigorously defined. As per the latest policy of American Veterinary Medical Association(AVMA) and American Association of Equine Practitioners; genetic diseases which are corrected surgically should be accompanied by sterilization to prevent perpetuation of the genetic flaw. For successful genetic selection against any disease in equine population, the prerequisite is presence of measurable genetic variation of that defects amongst individuals.

Chapter 7

Reproductive Cycle

In reproductive terminology the equines are classified as
" Seasonally Polyoestrous ,Monotoccous,Spontaneous Ovulator."

Equines have several unique aspects of reproductive endocrinology and pregnancy. Unlike other large animal species e.g., Cattle, selection practiced in horse is only related to their ability to walk or run. The established practice is to breed them as early in the year as possible since their age is counted from 1st January, irrespective of the month in which they might have been born.

Sexual Behaviour

Stallions as well as mares show seasonal variations to a great extent in their sexual behaviour. The breeding season of a stallion is not clearly demarcated and it is possible to collect semen throughout the year, although significant seasonal variations have been reported in reaction time, number of mounts per ejaculate, volume of gel free semen, total number of spermatozoa per ejaculate, sperm agglutination and motility in fresh as well as diluted semen. In addition, greater seasonal effects have been reported on semen plasma as compared to spermatozoa. Further, spermatozoa and other semen characteristics in second ejaculate are more affected by season as compared to first ejaculate. Mares depict greater seasonal variations in their reproduction cycle as compared to other domestic animals. The majority of mare population are seasonally polyoestrous, although, some mares can produce foals at any time of the year as true polyoestrous. Behavioural oestrus often unaccompanied by ovulation is noticed in some mares during a restricted breeding season and conception rates in mares bred during such period is low. Based on the breeding season, mares can be classified into three categories :

(a) Defined breeding season

(b) Transitory breeding season

(c) Year round breeding

In **defined breeding season**, mares menifest several oestrous cycles during a restricted breeding season which coincide with largest length of days of the year. This type of breeding peculiarity is seen in wild breed of horses. In **transitory breeding** season, oestrous cycle is depicted throughout year but ovulation accompanied oestrus is menifested during breeding season only. **Year round breeding** is characterized by mares manifesting oestrous cycle accompanied by ovulation throughout the year.

Mares exhibit seasonally polyoestrous characterstics and the breeding and nonbreeding seasons occur during summer and winter months respectively. The cyclic reproductive behaviour during breeding season is mediated by the stimulatory and inhibitory actions of oestradiol and progesterone. Photoperiod is considered to be most important environmental signal which entrains the pitituary gonadal axis. The exposure of mare to additional hours of sunlight during winter months is known to induce oestrus and may advance the onset of breeding season.

Stallion's Reproductive Parameters

Sexual Maturity

Attaining correct sexual maturity and use of stallion for natural or artificial breeding is guided largely by the managerial considerations. The testes of the stallion are either already present in the scrotum at the time of birth or may descend at one to three weeks of age. Postnatal growth of testes, however, starts during 11th month. Further, left testis grows faster than right testis which is accompanied by gradual outward development of seminiferous tubules around the right testis.

Semen Production

The reproductive parameters and characteristics of semen with average values are given below :

Table: Reproductive Parameters and Characteristics Values (Average)

Sexual maturity	Postnatal growth of testes	1 year
	Sperms appear in testes	1 year
	Sperms appear in ejaculate	13 months
	Sexual maturity	2 years
Testicular and Epididymal morphology	Testicular weight (gm)	150-170 gm
	Epididymal weight (gm)	20-30 gm
	Volume of tubules/testes	55-70%
	Length of tubules/testes	2300-2600 m
	Weight (without tunica albuginea)	14-20 gm
Spernatogenesis and sperm transport in male tract.	Life span of primary spermatocytes	19 days
	Life span of secondary spennatocytes	0.7 days
	Life span of spermatids with round nuclei	8.7 days
	Life span of spermatids with elongated nuclei	10 days
	Interval of labelled sperm to enter epididymis	35 days
	Interval for labelled sperm to appear in ejaculate	40 days
	Tiltle of transport of sperm in excurrent ducts	8-11 days

The ejaculate of stallion is consisted of six to nine jets which results from the contraction of urethra. The volume of each succeeding jet in the ejaculate becomes approximately half of the initial jet. Further, first three jets contain 2/3 or more of the spermatozoa and the basic constituents. The gelatinous material which forms gel of semen is secreted by seminal vesicles and the volume may vary from stallion to stallion. Generally, it is 1/3 of ejaculate and does not have any significant effect on sperm motility or its fertilizing ability.

The biochemical characterstics of various semen fractions are given below :

Semen Fraction	*Origin*	*Physical Characterstics*	*Biochemical Characterstics*
Presperm	Urethral glands	Watery	High NaCl content, no ergothioniene, Citric acid or glyceryl phosphoryl Choline (GPC).
Sperm-rich	Epididymal and Ampullary glands	Milky	High sperm concentration, non viscous, rich in ergothioneine and GPC, Little NaCl and citric acid.
Post sperm	Seminal vesicle	Highly viscous	Low sperm concentration. High content of citric acid, low ergothioneine and GPC.
Penile drip	Tail end sample	Watery	No spermatozoa, lacks any secretory products of epididymis, ampulla and Seminal vesicles (eg GPC, citric acid).

Semen characteristics are influenced by the degree of sexual stimulation, age, testicular size, frequency of ejaculation and method of semen collection. As explained earlier, seasonal variation also influences the physical and biochemical characteristics of semen as well as blood hormone levels. Accordingly, the libido of stallion and sperm output is related with natural breeding season of mares. The pattern of seminal and sexual behaviour is related to plasma testosterone levels of stallion which is also influenced by season. Although, 500 x 10^6 motile spermatozoa per insemination are considered enough for fertilization, yet the minimal number of spermatozoa necessary for maximal conception rate has not yet been clearly established.

Ejaculation

Semen is ejaculated wider high pressure directly into the uterus. During the process of ejaculation the urethral diverticulum of the penis is in close apposition to the external cervical orifice of the mare. The process of emission is related with the number of jets per ejaculate which varies with an average of eight. Initial jet occurs in a stream with distinct spatter and contains 80 per cent of ejaculated spermatozoa whereas the latter jets are associated with low pressure and low concentration of sperm cells and ergothioneine. The terminal jets contain no mucous fraction.

Mare's Reproductive Parameters

The unique characterstics of reproductive and ovulation cycles of mare are summarized below:

	Reporductive Parameters	Value Range and (Average)
Oestrous Cycle	Duration of oestrus	2-11 days (5)
	Length of oestrous cycle - Normal	16-24 days (22)
	Short	10-16 days
	Long	29 days
	Number of oestrous cycles/year	3-16 days
	Length of dioestrus	15 days
	Time from onset of oestrus to ovulation	4.3 - 10 day
	Time from end of oestrus to ovulation	1-2 days
Ovulation	Size of preovulatory follicles (cm)	3-6 (4.5)
	Frequency of twin ovulations without oestrus	3-30%
	Incidence of ovulations without oestrus	50%
Corpus Luteum	Corpus luteum palpable after ovulation	1-18 days
	During non pregnancy	2-3 months
	State of pregnancy when corpus luteum regresses	5-7 months
Pregnancy	Stage when ovulation and new corpora lutea formed in gestation under influences of Pregnant Mare Serum Gonadotrophin (PMSG)	40-60 days
	Interval from foaling to foal heat	5-18 days

Reproductive Parameters Specific to Mares

Development of Ovary	During foetal life. Cortical tissue entirely surrounds the medullary portion. During neonatal life cortical tissue becomes confined to one area and is nearly surrounded by medullary tissue.
Site of ovulation on ovarian surface	Follicles can only ovulate through the surface of the ovary adjacent to cortical tissue ("ovulation fossa").
Accessory ovulation during luteal phase of oestrous cycle and pattern of follicular growth.	Ovulation unaccompanied by oestrous occurs. A small group of follicles develops during late dioestrous, some of which enlarge differentially to ovulate during subsequent oestrous. Remaining follicles may ovulate during early luteal phase and others regress without ovulation.
Gonadotrophins associated with ovulation.	Prolonged rise of Leutinizing hormone(LH) surge during oestrous which continues after ovulation.
Life span of corpus luteum during non pregnancy	Spontaneous prolongation of CL life span is common; corpora lutea that fails to regress at normal time persist for two months.
Follicle Stimulating Hormone(FSH) content of pituitary.	High
Ovarian response to FSH	Low
Egg transport in oviduct	Mare's oviduct can discriminate between fertilized and Unfertilized egg. Non fertilized eggs may be retained in oviducts during pregnancy and Non pregnancy up to seven months.
Presence of placental hormone secreted (PMSG)	PMSG formed in large quantities by endometrial cups during early pregnancy
Secondary Corpora lutea	Remain functional until mid pregnancy.

OESTROUS CYCLES

Signs of Oestrus

The characteristic signs of oestrus in mares include, large and swollen vulva with loose labial folds. The vulva becomes scarlet or orange coloured, wet, glossy and covered with a film of transparent mucus. Highly vascular mucosa of vagina with tendency to accumulate thin watery mucus. Cervix dilates during oestrus to the extent of permiting passage of two to four fingers as compared to insertion of only one finger during dioestrus. Mares assume a stance characterstic of urination. Tail is raised, urine is expelled in small amounts and the clitoris is exposed by prolonged rhythmic contraction(winking). The duration of oestrus varied. It is prolonged in old mares as well as in mares under-fed, during the beginning of breeding season and in twin ovulation.

Behavioral Changes in Horse Mare

During diestrus, the mare is totally disinterested in stallion and will kick, bite and chase him. While teasing testing, she will not stand quite when approach by teasing pony but 1 or 2 days before estrus it becomes more passive and will not object to the presence of teaser or stallion. During oestrus, she is receptive to stallion and allows to bite and chew on neck and flanks.

Behavioral changes in donkey mare

Donkey mare is shy in expressing its oestrus behaviour.It holds her head low and makes typical chewing motion of its jaws and also flaxes the pelvis. Signs consistent with behavioural oestrus include:

1. Mouth clapping (i.e., frequent vertical opening and closing of the mouth accompanied by stretching and lowering of the head and holding the ears back);
2. Winking (rhythmic eversion of the clitoris from ventral labiae);
3. Raising the tail;
4. Urination;
5. Posturing (i.e., abducted rear legs, arched tail, tipped pel-

vis, and lowered perineal area); and, of course,

6. Standing to be mounted.

Interestingly, it is noted that mouth clapping began almost one day earlier, and lasted almost one day later, than expression of other positive signs of oestrus.

Follicular Growth and Ovulation

In mare, the pattern of follicular development is less well defined. A small group of follicles develop during late dioestrus and one of them enlarges differentially, matures, and ovulates during the ensuing oestrus. The remaining follicles may continue to develop and one or more may ovulate during the early luteal phase. The other follicles regress without ovulating. This pattern of follicular growth causes a high incidence of multiple ovulations at the ovulation fossa, equally in the right and left ovaries. The frequency of twin ovulations may range from 30 per cent depending on the breed and season of year. It is rare in pony breeds and during the spring season, the incidence of twin pregnancy varies from 1 per cent to 5 per cent. However, twin live births occur only in a few cases as one member of the twins usually dies before birth. Pre-ovulatory follicles increase in size from 3 to 6 cm between days 6 and 1 before ovulation, but just before ovulation, they measure 3 to 6 cm in diameter. Rarely can ovulation occur from follicles less than 2 cm in diameter. A few ovulatory follicles may develop to 10 cm in diameter, persist up to two months and then regress, affecting the normal length of oestrus. Some follicles soften and then become turgid again before ovulation whereas others remain turgid throughout. Palpation of the ovary just before and after ovulation occasionally may provoke pain. In half of oestrus periods, two or more follicles other than the one about to ovulate are over 25 mm in diameter and are palpable.

Half of these regress before ovulation and the rest regress after ovulation. Ovulation, occuring during the luteal phase of the oestrous cycle is not accompanied by oestrus and may cause confusion during routine rectal examinations of mares. These ovulations do not affect plasma progestogen concentration or any other characteristic of the oestrous cycle. It is not known whether dioestrus ovulations are fertile.

Keeping in view the lengthy oestrus in mares, mating is required to be synchronized with ovulation in order to ensure fertilization. The time of ovulation can be detected by repeated rectal palpations. Prior to ovulation, one of the ovaries enlarges and the developing follicles occupy most of the ovarian stroma. The injection of 2,000 iu of Human Chorionic Gonadotrophin (hCG) hastens the time of ovulation and shortens the duration of oestrus. Repeated injection of hCG does not appear to cause refractoriness.

Corpus Luteum

Most ovulations occur on days 3,4 or 5 of oestrus, 24 to 48 hours prior to the end of behavioural oestrus (ie. the time of ovulation is more closely related to the end than to the onset of oestrus). Follicular size and the day of ovulation are consistent in mares from one cycle to another. Ovulation takes place after the first meiotic division. The fertility of mating gradually rises to a peak about two days before the end of oestrus and then falls sharply on the last day. The ruptured folicles can be palpated up to 24 hrs after ovulation as a soft fluctuant area. The developing corpus luteum, however, cannot be detected by rectal examination 48 hours after ovulation because it develops within the ovarian stroma. The corpus luteum reaches only one half to three fourths the size of the follicle at the time of ovulation. The maximal size is attained at 14 days, when luteal cells enlarge and have a peripheral vacuolation. Spontaneous prolongation of the corpus luteum, accompanied by follicular activity and without any signs of oestrus for periods of two to three months, is common. Corpora lutea that fail to regress at the normal time, persist for about two months and are characterized by having a white connective tissue core. Most of the granulosa cells that undergo luteinization 24 hours after ovulation become secretory.

Endocrine Control of Oestrous Cycles

Gonadotropin Releasing Hormone (GnRH) secreted by the hypothalamus of the brain, GnRH has a controlling influence over other reproductive hormones. Early in the year stimulation of the pineal gland by light - either natural or artificial - causes a reduction of melatonin secretion, which in turn allows GnRH to be secreted by the hypothalamus, thereby stimulating the production of other hormones (FSH, LH). The exact connection between decreased melatonin production and increased GnRH levels is not understood. In anestrus mares GnRH is released in a pulsatile manner with long period between secretions, resulting in undetectable blood levels of the hormone. In estrus mares secretion is continuous with additional pulses ranging from every 2 hours in diestrus mares, to twice hourly during estrus.

In normally cycling mares, two surges of follicle stimulating hormone (FSH) occur at approximately 20 and 11 days prior to ovulation. Both FSH and leutinizing hormone (LH) concentrations surge around the time of ovulation. The late oestrus/early dioestrus surge of FSH appears to initiate development of up to 20 follicles. The mid dioestrus surge may be important for the subsequent development of follicles destined to ovulate 10 to 13 days later.

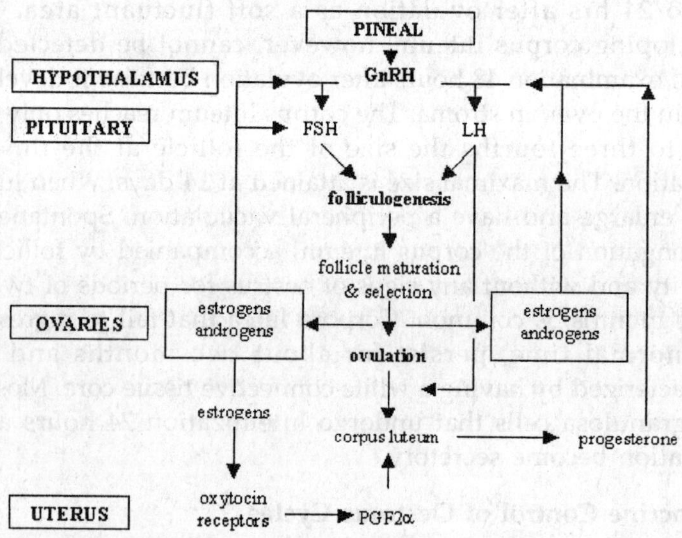

Fig. 7.1 : ***Hormones Active During the Estrous Cycle of the Mare***

FSH and LH : The ovary of the mare is less sensitive to FSH than that of the cow, ewe and goat. The administration of HCG shortens oestrus and hastens ovulation. Injection of HCG is frequently used in an attempt to decrease the number of inseminations or matings/cycle and to synchronize ovulation time, more accurately with mating. The regulation of LH secretion involves two mechanisms (1) a central nervous system pituitary component which is independent of ovarian influences, (2) an ovarian (steroidal) component that modifies the primary LH rhythm during the breeding season. Level of LH increase by the onset of oestrus, reaching a maximum at one to two days after ovulation. This rise in LH may stimulate maturation of the follicle throughout oestrus

An inverse relationship between progesterone and LH levels occurs, suggesting a negative feedback, but there is no such relationship between FSH and progesterone concentrations. LH levels show a prolonged rise during oestrus that continues after ovulation. A significant decrease from peak levels is not observed until the third day after ovulation. From this time onwards, levels continue to decline toward dioestrus values. The pattern of plasma LH in the mare differs from other species of domestic animals showing persistence of high concentrations of LH which results from a long half life of the endogenous LH. This in turn may be responsible for the relatively large number of second ovulation detected in many oestrous cycles. It seems that LH may be sensitive to progesterone feedback control, in that levels do not start to rise until after the corpus luteum has regressed completely. On the other hand, high circulating progesterone levels apparently do not constitute an effective negative feedback control mechanism once LH release has begun. In the mare, the uterus exerts its luteolytic effect on the corpus luteum primarily through a systemic utero-ovarian pathway mediated with secretion of prostagladin.

Estrogens: There are several forms of estrogen occurring in the mare. In the non-pregnant mare estradiol is the most active; in the pregnant mare there are several, but the most important to note is estrone sulphate. Estradiol in the estrus mare is secreted by the follicle and serves several purposes. Its presence is associated with the behavioural displays common to estrus. Estradiol also causes the relaxation of the cervix during estrus. Estrogen presence has a *negative* impact on FSH, *but a positive* impact on LH; It is thought that there is a link between sufficient estradiol levels and early pregnancy maintenance, perhaps as a result of an effect of estradiol on uterine condition; In the pregnant mare estrone sulphate is secreted by the feto-placental unit (FPU). Levels rise gradually until about day 70 post-conception ovulation, when they rise dramatically and remain elevated until about day 210, when they start to slowly drop again until shortly before foaling. The presence of estrone sulphate in the mare's blood from about day 70 of pregnancy onwards can be used as a reliable indicator of fetal viability as its levels drop rapidly following fetal failure.

Progesterone:

- Progesterone is the hormone that, among other things, in non-pregnant mares prevents the display of estrus. It is also, in part, responsible for increasing uterine and cervical tone in the diestrus mare.
- Progesterone is secreted by the Corpus Luteum (CL) that is formed in the evacuated follicles left behind after the mare has ovulated.
- Luteal Progesterone has a positive impact on FSH and a negative impact on LH.

In the absence of ovulation, with or without follicular growth, there are prolonged periods of low progesterone levels. The daily intramuscular injection of 100 mg or more of progesterone during the midcycle prevents oestrus and ovulation, but a dose of 50 mg per day inhibits only oestrus. The interval between termination of treatment and oestrus appears to depend upon dosage to counteract habitual abortion in the mare. It is usual to administer 250 to 500 mg every 10 to 30 days.

- **Prostaglandin**
  - Pulsatile secretion of Prostaglandin F2á (PGF_2a) by the lining of the uterus commences if pregnancy is not detected at about day 14 post-ovulation.
  - The presence of PGF2á causes the "lycing" of the CL and an almost immediate drop in circulating levels of progesterone, which permits the mare to start displaying estrus.
  - This pulsatile secretion actually continues for several more days.
  - PGF2á also causes contraction of smooth muscles - which includes the uterus.

- **Inhibin**
  - Inhibin is a follicular hormone that in addition to estrogen quietens the positive impact that progesterone has on FSH follicular maturation and selection.

A Brief Sequential Overview of the Regular Estrous Cycle

- **Key Features:**
  - The entire estrous cycle from ovulation to ovulation takes approximately 21 days;
  - Ovulation of a follicle occurs, releasing the ova for potential fertilization;
  - The cavity left behind on the ovary by the evacuated follicle fills rapidly with blood and in some cases forms a **Corpus Hemorrhagicum** prior to creation of luteal tissue to become a **Corpus Luteum** (CL) as a result of the presence of LH;
  - By about 5 days after ovulation, the CL is fully functional and secreting progesterone. This is also known as the luteal phase;
  - FSH action, early in diestrus, may produce a mid-cycle follicle that will sometimes ovulate, but more usually regresses;
  - Around day 13 post-ovulation, the endometrium of

the uterus secretes **PGF2á** which causes the destruction ("lycing") of the CL, which will then permit onset of estrus behaviour;

- FSH activity in late diestrus cause the selection of a dominant follicle (or possibly two) which, under the influence of increasing estrogen levels in early estrus, will develop to reach ovulatory status approximately 21 days after the previous ovulation.
- The mare will display receptive behaviour (estrus) towards the stallion for 5-7 days and will ovulate in the last 24-48 hours of that display period.

Induction of Oestrus and Ovulation :

Saline Infusion: The technique of intrauterine saline infusion has been used routinely to induce oestrus in anoestrus mares. Anoestrus mares are affected only near the beginning and end of the breeding season when anovulatory heats are induced. Dioestrus mares infused between 5th and 9th day return to heat four days earlier than expected and induced oestrus is accompanied by ovulation. Mares in prolonged dioestrus may show ovulatory heats within three to nine days of infusion. Repeated infusions are clinically harmless but post infusion bacteriologic swabs from the uterus are positive.

Photostimulatory Method: The major external factor causing the mare to start cycling regularly, is the amount of daylight to which she is exposed. This can be artificially extended very simply by using a light source of sufficient power and duration to suggest to the mare that spring is closer than it actually is. It is believed however, from observation of other species that the animal must go through some period of "short days" prior to entering the photostimulatory period, although exact duration of short days is unknown. The first plan consists of extending the natural daylight by two to two and one-half hours of artificial lighting immediately following sunset. The time that the artificial light is turned on should be adjusted each week so that it keeps pace with the sunset. The second plan is to subject the mares to a 1 hour pulse of artificial light nine and one half to ten and one half hours after the onset of darkness. Either of these plans can be achieved by the use of a timer on the light, or manual management. At least 60 to 80 days of phototropic stimulation are needed prior to the onset of normal cycling. Therefore, if breeding is desired in February, the lighting programme should be commenced no later than December 1st.

The use of exogenous hormones to stimulate the mare to ovulate earlier in the year is also practiced. This is most commonly used in the form of the synthetic analogue altrenogest or to use a better known commercial name: "Regumate". Regumate is administered orally. There are injectable forms of progesterone which are cheaper, but the oral form may be preferable in view of the repeated dosing requirement. It is believed that progestogens hasten the first ovulation, but only in mares which are on the verge of, or have just started, cycling. It should therefore be used in conjunction with, not instead of, one of the lighting regimes noted above. Treatment is carried out daily for 15 days, at regular dosage rates, after the mare has been subjected to photostimulation for the requisite period.

Synchronization of Oestrus.

It allows mares to be inseminated at predetermined times without the need to detect oestrus or palpate the ovaries. The ovarian activity in mare is effectively influenced by induction of luteolysis with prostaglandin F2a (PGF2a) or its analogue as well as induction of ovulation during the follicular phase by an injection of hCG.

***Progesterone and Estradiol Combination*:** The use of the combined steroids progesterone and estradiol (or "P & E") is the accepted method for maximum control. This is normally presented as a course of 10 daily injections, with a dose of prostaglandin F2á being given at the same time as the 10th dose. Estrus will usually commence in 4 days time, and by day 18 of treatment, 90% of mares will have a 35 mm follicle present that will respond to hCG administration by ovulating within 36-42 hours. This results in 75-80% of mares ovulating in the evening of day 19 or early morning of day 20 of treatment. The daily dosage for a 1,000-1,500 lb horse is 150mg of progesterone and 10 mg of estradiol 17â. The dosage levels should be proportionately increased for horses of a larger size.

Fertilization and Implantation: After ovulation, fertilization is the union of a viable ovum and spermatozoa which usually occurs in the oviduct. The gelatinous mass enclosing the ovum gets detached from the egg within two days and the fertilized ova are transported in the uterus. Non-fertilized ova may be retained in the oviduct of pregnant/non-pregnant mares for a prolonged period up to 7 months followed by degeneration and fragmentation. This phenomenon is more common in heavy breeds and more often in early pregnancies. Although, the blastocyte in mare is quite close to the uterine epithelieum, yet it takes about 2 months for implantation to begin. At this stage, blastoyte is about 5 cm in diameter. It acquires an albumin coat during third week of fertilization which is preceded by a group of columnar cells and the trophoblastic disc in the trophoblastic wall of chorion. trophoblastic is concerned with ingestion of uterine milk and to help the attachment. By about 10th week, the villi from the chorion penetrate into mucosal fold of the uterine wall and by 14th week, implantation is completed.

Gestation: Gestation may be descried as the period which extends from fertilization of the ovum to the expulsion of a fully developed and viable foal. In mare, duration of oestrus is longer with some uncertainty of ovulation time, as such the exact parturition time cannot be predicted and wide variations are observed in the gestation period which can be attributed to delayed implantation. Accordingly, the length of gestation in equines ranges from 335 days in mares to 365 days in ass. Similarly, gestation period in case of hybrids, ranges from 345 days in mares to 355 days in ass. Further, it is believed that the length of gestation is controlled by the hereditary influence and the genotype of the dam and foetus. In addition, endocrine mechanism, size of foetus, foetal metabolism and seasonal variation are also considered to influence the gestation period.

Placenta and Placentation: Placenta is an intimate apposition or the fusion of foetal organs to the maternal tissues for physiological exchange. The placental membranes can be differentiated into the (i) amnion (ii) allantois (iii) serosa. The amnion surrounds the foetus whereas the serosa is outer most membranes in contact with endothelium and the inner layer of allantois is fused to amnion and outer layer to the serosa forming chorio-allantois. The allantois is continuous with bladder via uterus which is located in the umbilical cord. The chorio-allantois brings the foetal blood vessels in close contact with umbilical arteries and veins which are located in the connective tissue between the allantois and chorion. The placenta of the mare is classified as diffuse, micro cotyledonary and epitheliochorial type. The outer surface of the chorion is closely studded with tufts of branching villi that enter into corresponding invaginations in the endometrium to form small globular structures known as microcotyledons, which are a distinctive feature of the mature equine placenta and are fully formed by the fifth month of gestation. The primary folds of trophoblast become elaborately subdivided as gestation proceeds. These changes are reflected in the structure of the maternal crypts, which receive the foetal villi. Within each microcotyledon, chorionic and uterine epithelia are in intimate contact and a microvillous junction is formed at the foetal maternal boundary.

Placental Barrier: The following mechanisms control the passage of gases, nutrients, ions or hormones across the placental barrier (1) those related to diffusion across the placental tissues i.e. permeability, diffusion distances, total surface area and concentration gradients between maternal and foetal blood vessels; (2) speed of supply and removal on either side of the placenta, the presence or absence of specialized exchange areas, the direction of blood flow in these areas and the existence of shunts or unequal flows; and (3) specialized mechanisms that assist the passage of substances and, in the case of oxygen, differences in haemoglobin oxygen affinity and oxygen capacity between foetus and mother.

The primary corpus luteum that develops at the site of the fertile ovulation regresses about day 160 of gestation and is replaced by secondary corpora lutea. The primary and secondary corpora lutea and the placenta contribute to the total progesterone pool during pregnancy. The luteal progesterone concentration in the peripheral plasma is closely correlated with morphologic changes in the corpus luteum.

Similarities and differences in ovarian function observed between pregnant and hysterectomized mares suggest that, while PMSG does not appear to stimulate follicular development, it does prolong the life span and stimulate the secretory activity of the primary corpus luteum and induce ovulation and/or luteinization of secondary follicles in pregnant mares.

Foaling: The time of foaling, which usually takes place between nightfall and daybreak, seems to be influenced by photoperiod and quietness in the stable. It has been observed that 86 per cent of foalings occur between 7 P.M. and 7 AM. with a maximal incidence between 10 P.M. and 11 P.M. The imminence of foaling is suggested by the degree of mammary hypertrophy, waxing of the teats and possibly the discharge of milk from the udder. The best indication that the first stage has begun is the onset of patchy sweating behind the elbows and about the flanks. This sweating commences about four hours before foaling and increases as the stage progresses. The tail is frequently raised *or* held to one side.

Postpartum Oestrus (Foal Heat): Postpartum oestrus usually occurs 5 to 15 days after foaling. Some mares, however, may show oestrus as late as 45 days after parturition, but such oestrus might have been preceded by a quiet ovulation. The interval between postpartum oestrus and the following oestrus may be affected by the milk yield.

Breeding at the postpartum oestrus may cause increased percentage of abortion, dystocia, stillbirth and retained placenta. This may be due to the introduction of bacteria into the uterus before it is completely involuted and while it still lacks contraction ability. Involution of the uterus after normal foaling is rapid. Regression in size is almost complete by the first day of "foal heat". The relatively low conception rate from mating during this period appears to indicate that involution of the endometrium is not complete in all mares.

References:

1. Loy, R. G., Pemstein, R., O'Canna, D., and Douglas, R. H. Control of ovulation in cycling mares with ovarian steroid and prostaglandin. Theriogenology *15*:191-200, 1981.
2. Varner, D. D., Blanchard, T. L. and Brinsko, S. P. Estrogens, oxytocin and ergot alkaloids - Uses in reproductive management of mares. Proc. Am. Assoc. Equine. Pract., 219-241, 1988.
3. Lofstedt, R. M. Control of the estrous cycle of the mare. The Veterinary Clinics of North America - Equine Practice, 189-190, 1988.

Chapter 8

Specialized Management of Breeding Stock

Efficiency and success of the Stud depends on good care and management of breeding stock. The breeding stock in the Stud mainly comprises stallions and brood mares of various classes.

Specialized attention has to be given to the stabling, feeding and exercise of breeding stock. All stallions are given individual attention and the brood mares in a large stud, get collective attention in groups except on certain occasions when individual attention is needed for foaling mares and those running down in condition.

Care and Management of Stallions

The old saying that ***"sire is half of the herd"*** hold true in respect of the importance of breeding management of the stallion.

Whatever breed is used, the horse stallion (plate I) must have perfect and straight action, should stand and move gracefully. The stallion should move from the shoulder and not from the elbow, with limited knee action, carrying his toe well forward, reaching or passing the end of the nose.

Physiological Basis of Stallion's Fertility

Stallion's fertility is as important as the reproductive capacity of each individual mare in the breeding programme. The selection of the stallion is commonly done on the basis of pedigree and performance, with little consideration being given to the individual's reproductive capability. The most reliable measure of fertility in a stallion is the number and percentage of mares it settled in a season.

The sequence of events to produce normal reproductive function in a stallion are: a) sperm are produced in the tubule of the testes; b) they mature and acquire fertilizing capacity in the head and body of the epydidimis; c) sperm cells are maintained in a fertile state in the tail of the epydidimis; d) ejaculated by the contraction of the deferents ducts, accessory sex glands and muscles accociated with the penis. These processes depend on and are coordinated by the neuroendocrine system. The process from the start of the creation of the sperm cell to final maturation in the epydidimal tail is approximately 60 days. This means whatever a stallion ejaculates in February was begun in December. If an injury or infection, or any occurrence that would raise the temperature of the testes 2 degrees were to happen today, this stallion would still be fertile tomorrow, but would have the possibility of being infertile temporarily in 2 months. Many times when a stallion suddenly stops settling mares, after a number of successful months, breeding managers do not know to look back 60 days to seek a cause. Perhaps a kick, colic or cold with fever. The problem normally rectifies itself shortly as soon as new cells are available, assuming there were no complications or permanent damage to the testes

Accommodation

The stallion boxes should be roomy, airy and should have plenty of light. 4.25 x 5.00 m is ideal size for the stallion box. Earthern floors are usually preferable but these require frequent replacement and thorough ramming to keep them level. With a view to maintain proper hygiene and sanitation, the floor of the stallion boxes should be made with cement concrete, impervious and non-slippery by making grooves. The floors should have very gentle slope towards the rear so that urine can flow and drained away easily.

Each stallion box should be provided with an independent feeding and water trough with rounded corners to facilitate easy cleaning. There should be arrangements for proper cross ventilation and stallion boxes should have 3 m wide verandah (corridor) in front. Each box should be provided with electric ceiling fan, all windows and doors should be fly proofed and there should be arrangements for coolers/khas khas tattles to deal with the heat effect in summer months.

The stallion must be protected during winter from cold wind, by suitable wind protector. There should be open loose boxes made of pipe railings and posts, 7.25 x 7.25 m in size, well seperated from each other, for keeping the stallions at night during hot summer months.

Watering and Feeding

A horse takes 25-50 liters of water per day and this varies according to seasonal requirement. Provision of fresh and clean water should always be ensured. Each time horse drinks, some of its saliva mixes with the water in the trough and dust also contaminates water during windy day. Thus water becomes dirty and contaminated. This explains the necessity of careful and regular cleaning of water troughs every day.

The stallions are fed grain ration and fodder according to individual requirement. Main grain feeds comprise of gram, barley or oats and bran. All grains should be duly crushed.

The concentrate is fed to the stallions four times a day at evenly spaced intervals. Large quantity of finely chaffed hay should be mixed with the grain. The morning feed should be of a small quantity, not more than ½ kg per stallion, 2nd and 3rd feeds almost equal in amount and last feed should be the heaviest. Feeding troughs should be thoroughly cleaned before feeding. Sudden changes in the feeding routine and ration scale are bad and should be introduced gradually.

Fodder should be fed dry or green and given after chaffing. Bulk of the fodder is given at night and during mid-day break. Lucerne is the best feed for the stallions as it is rich in proteins and calcium content. Oats are fed dry as well as green. Best oat hay is when oats are cut in milky stage before the grain ripens. Oat hay should be fed after mixing with green fodder. Feeding of too much oat hay causes diarrhoea. Young' *doob'* grass is very good for stallions and should always be given without chaffing.

Bran mash has a laxative effect on the stallions and is recommended to be given once a week. For preparing bran mash, ½ kg of bran and 30gm of salt is added in a bucket and as much boiling water is poured over the bran as it will absorb. During the process, the bran is stirred continuously and later covered with a blanket and left to cool for 20 minutes. After that period, it is fed to the stallion. It becomes very palatable and if the stallion refuses, handful of chaffed green lucerne may be added to increase its palatibility.

Linseed is rich in oil and protein. It should be fed either crushed at the scale of 125-250 gm per stallions or in the form of oil at the scale of 60 gm per stallion per day. Linseed (boiled) is fed during winter months. It keeps the body warm and gives the coat a shining appearance.

Exercise

Exercise is by far the most important factor in keeping the stallions in tip-top breeding condition. The combination of over-feeding and idleness quickly leads to disaster. More vigorous exercise is required to be given during winter months and in summer, early exercise should be given to avoid profuse sweating. There are various ways of giving exercise to the stallions. Whatever method is employed, proper exercise during covering season is very essential. Ridden exercise is the best if it can be safely given to the stallions. For riding stallions, men trained in equitation should be employed. The stallions require 1 ½ hours exercise daily. It should be divided for an hour in the morning and ½ hour in the evening. The exercise should be alternatively changed into walk and trot at intervals. In winter, more time should be consumed in trot while in summer more time should be taken in walk. The stallions should be grouped together for exercise according to the temperament of the individual stallion. The stallions which resent the company of the other stallions should be given individual exercise. The area of exercise should be away from the brood mares stables and no brood mare should be visible while the stallions are being exercised. Enclosed exercising school with a wall all round is also used for exercising and grazing of the stallions. Exercising track is made all round and central area of the school is sown with lucerne for grazing. The track for exercise should be even, soft and at raised level from the ground. There should be no stone or hole on the exercising track. Dried dung or tan should be used on the track to keep it soft. Before the stallions are taken out for exercise, the exercising track should be inspected daily for its suitability. The stallions should be exercised under the supervision of a competent hand.

Stable Routine

Daily work of the stallion should be carried out according to set routine and daily stable routine be supervised by the Incharge. The work of the stallions must start early in the morning so that they have enough time for exercise, covering and grooming which should be completed during cool hours of the day. The first thing when an attendant enters the stable is to clean the water and feeding troughs, then a morning light feed is given to the stallions. While the stallions are busy in feeding, the bedding of the loose box is removed, the portions soiled with dung and urine are seperated and the remainder is laid outside systematically for aeration and drying, then the floors must be thoroughly cleaned by scrubbing. By this time, the stallion finishes his grain feed and he should be prepared for exercise. His feet are picked up and body lightly cleaned before saddling and taking him out for exercise. After return from exercise, stallion's girth is slackened, the stallion is allowed to cool himself for about 20 minutes before the saddle is taken off. The stallions are lightly groomed if the covering is done before grooming, otherwise thorough grooming is taken in hand straightaway.

Grooming

Regular and proper grooming is essential for health of stallions. The grooming ensures cleanliness, promotes blood circulation, keeps the coat short and shining and beautifies the appearence of stallions. Grooming must be done systematically as a routine. After grooming is over, all stallions should be checked. Slackness and faults in grooming should be pointed out on the spot and grooms warned to do their work properly. It is only the regular grooming which can bring shine to the coat. How hard one may groom in one or two days, his work is not likely to show up, if the grooming has not been carried out regularly.

After the grooming and the covering is over, the bedding is laid thick and spread evenly allover the standing. The sentries should be posted during mid-day break. They should ensure that the bedding is kept even and bare patches are covered with bedding. The dung should be removed from the stallion box immediately it has been voided. Sentries should also ensure that the 'jhools' (Rugs) are properly retained on the body of the stallions in cold weather and noticeable sickness is reported at once.

Winter 'jhools' should be properly fitted, surcingle and breast piece should not be very tight. The 'jhools' should be kept clean and free from dirty cakes. Summer 'jhools' are often used to protect the stallion from flies and to beautify its appearence. The stallions' sheath should be cleaned once a week with very weak disinfectant if they have not been used for breeding for more than a period of one week.

Breeding/Mating Management

Mating Systems: Vary from farm to farm, among breeds, and type of operation.

1. Pasture mating–natural mating. Stallion with groups of mares in pasture.
   - This method is used in special operations such as Pregnant mare Urine farms (equine estrogen preparations), pony herds.
   - Mares are examined at two week intervals for pregnancy diagnosis starting from a month after introduction of the stallion.
   - Experienced stallions are used in this method.

- If young stallions are to be used, they should be hand-mated first to assess their mating performance before introduction to pasture.
- The advantages of this type of mating is that the stallion does the teasing and breeding and saves labour input.
- The constant presence of the stallion stimulates better estrus expression in the mares, and finally conception rates are usually 80% over the season.
- The disadvantages of this method of breeding include loss of supervision of breeding; increased chances of spread of venereal disease (if one mare is infected) and difficulty of assessing fertility and source of fertility failure.
- Lastly, pasture breeding may lead to coital injury and loss of stallion power during critical breeding season.

2. Hand-mating Breedings—Method used most extensively in most breeding operations.
   - The stallion is brought to the mare and mating is supervised.
   - The use of this method allows for observation of mating; mating behaviour of stallion, libido, allows for mating under strict hygienic conditions, facilitates maintenance of accurate records of mating and fertility level in the stud farm, and decreases chances of coital injuries.
   - However, the foaling rates are lower, and the cost of housing, labour for observation and breeding, and cost of special facilities may be high.

Procedures During Natural Cover—Hand-mating.

- Preparation of mare: Wrap tail (bandage) and wash vulva and perineal region with mild soap and water.
- Restraint of mare: if necessary use breeding hobbles, twitch, blindfold the mare and tranquilize. Maiden mares are ap-

prehensive and unpredictable during breeding and they should be "test jumped" with experienced gentle teaser to assess their mating behaviour.

- Protection of mare should be ensured by using, neck padding to mare and felt boots to stallion.
- Preparation of stallion: Tease stallion and wash penis when erect. Remove dirt and smegma. Use mild soap and water; rinse with water and dry with a towel.
- Preparation for mating: An experienced handler should position mare for breeding.
    - The breeding shed/area should be at least 30'x 40' or larger, and have good footing and free of dust.
    - Finely ground gravel, tartan, concrete covered with peat moss are used to provide good footing.
- Handling of Stallion: Firm control of stallion is to be ensured at all times. Also, discourage biting, mounting without full erection; over eagerness, nuzzling around carpus or tarsus.
- Mating: Allow the stallion to approach mare, allow nuzzling, shoulder contact with hindquarters of mare, until full erection is achieved; allow to mount when penis fully erect. (maneuver move's tail out of the way and guide penis to vulva if necessary).
- In a few cases application of lubricant, such as KY jelly will facilitate intromission.
- Observe for signs of ejaculation: Signs of ejaculation include tail flagging, and palpable pulsations in urethra. After ejaculation the stallion's head droops, the whole body is relaxed, and there is an increased respiration rate.
- Collect and examine dismount sample.
- Walk mare: If signs of discomfort or bloody discharge is seen at vulva, examine for vaginal tear.

3. **Artificial Insemination**—Involves semen collection, extension and insemination. Fresh, extended or frozen semen can be used. The use of this method extends the breeding

capability of the stallion and conserves stallion power.

- Time or decision to mate/cover during estrus:
- When hand-breeding or AI is used, it is necessary to determine when to mate and how often to mate during estrus.
- The decision to breed should be based on the following findings:
  - Mare "hot" on teasing. Very receptive to stallion.
  - Large preovulatory follicle present.
  - Cervix relaxed, down and cervical os open
  - Absence of evidence of infection.
  - Factors determining optimum time to mate include:

Viable life of the ovum, which is believed to be up to 24 hours. Inseminations after ovulation result in a poor conception rate. Pregnancy rates of mares bred the day prior to ovulation are 80% and bred 24 hours post-ovulation are 50%. Maximum fertility is obtained when frozen-semen is used if the mare is inseminated 0-12 hours before ovulation. The survival of highly fertile spermatozoa in the mare's tract is from 5-9 days.

- In practice: The breeding practices employed include:
  - Matings should occur 24 hours before ovulation.
  - Breed Day 2 or 3 of estrus, tease daily and rebreed if in estrus on day 6.
  - Breed every other day until end of estrus, starting from Day 2 or Day 3 of estrus
  - Breed daily.

  The method used will depend on availability of stallion power; fertility of the stallions, number of mares booked to stallion and the breeding methods used, i.e. AI versus natural cover.

  - Amount of semen for AI: 10 ml - 25 million motile sperm/ml

Artificial Insemination Procedures:

- Wash vulva and perineal region.
- Collect and extend semen.
- Inseminate—introduce sterile gloved hand into vagina, locate cervix, introduce insemination pipette, guide—allowing index and middle finger within cervix, into the uterus and deposit semen in the uterus.

BREEDING :

The stallions are usually put to stud work at the age of four years, after they have retired from turf. However, animals which prematurely break-down at 3 years are retired to the stud and such stallions have to be initiated into service. These young stallions will be let down which means that his body conformation changes, the hard tight abdominal muscles relax and normal, belly contour is developed. The well developed hard muscles of galloping and propulsion become softer and more elastic. As such, the time taken for the process of letting a horse down is not less than 3 months.

Many stallions are awkward in their first attempt at service and all possible help, guidance and encouragement must be provided at this time. For its first service, the stallion should be kept well under control and a mare in proper heat should be selected for service. Maiden mares and mares for DHAMAN (Foal heat) covering should not be put to such stallions.

Some stallions have bad breeding habits and such habits usually develop during their first use in the stud. Some are slow in mounting and often have to mount several times before actual ejaculation. The others bite badly during service.

Normally 30-40 mares are allotted to a stallion and the stallion has to cover 2 to 2½ times per mare in order to get them in foal. The total covering quota of the stallion should be fixed and number of mares allotted according to the age of the stallion. The new stallions in their first year of service in the stud should not cover more than 15 mares and their covering quota should not exceed 25 during the whole year. In the second year, the number of mares as well as covering quota should be gradually increased which should be limited to 50 coverings during the whole year. It is during the 3rd year of the stud service that a stallion is fully utilized and the covering quota should not increase 80-100 in a year. Similarly, when the stallion gets older than 15 years, the 'covering quota' should be accordingly reduced.

Normally, one covering should be allowed in 48 hours as replacement of semen takes place in this period. During busy covering season, there is no harm in using a stallion daily but this should not be continued for a long time as excessive use has adverse effect on concentration of the semen and motility of the sperms. If daily covering has to be given for few days, it should be ensured that 48 hours rest is given after 2-3 days. Total covering in a month for a stallion should not exceed 20.

Semen Examination

The sample for semen examination should be truly representative and not the dripping of dismount sample. The volume of a stallion's semen varies very widely ranging from 50-150 ml in one ejaculation, concentration of sperms also varies widely from 50-20 millions per m1 of semen. In stallions which are breeding every day for a month, the total quantity of ejaculate is reduced to 30 ml or less. A few days rest of over-bred stallion is usually sufficient to restore total volume of ejaculate to normal.

The semen of the stallion shculd be examined every month and its records kept in the register. First sample after prolonged rest should be discarded and the semen collected for examination from a subsequent service within a day or two. A drop of semen is examined under the microscope and spermatozoa should be observed for motility. An estimate should be made of a number of motile sperms. In good sample, 90-95 per cent spermatozoa should be alive at the time of collection and their movement should be rapid and strong. The following standard should be used for grading of semen of stallions:

Grade - '0' - No motility.

Grade - I - Spermatozoa exhibit weak, stationary or rotatory motion, about 20% motility.

Grade-II – Spermatozoa exibit oscillatory and rotatory motion, less than 50% active and motile, no waves are founed.

Grade-III – Progressive and rapid motion of spermatozoa producing slowly moving waves, 50-75% spermatozoa active.

Grade-IV – Vigorous and progressive movement with waves, 75-90% spermatozoa active.

Vigorous and rapid forward motion with very rapid waves, close to 100% of sperms are motile.

CARE AND MANAGEMENT OF BROOD MARES

Selection

The brood mares must be wide and roomy, well ribbed up, broad and muscular over the loins and quarters in order to provide enough room for the foal to develop. Horse breeding mares should have good conformation. Mule breeding mares are generally heavy draught type and coarsely bred, should have a big bone and big round belly and hips. The brood mares must be genitally sound and free from hereditary defects and should preferably have dropped a foal.

Accommodation

Stables for brood mares must be airy, roomy and protected from draughts. Brood mares as a rule are kept in liberty and should be provided with covered as well as open dry paddock. covered accommodation is provided at the scale of 4.25 x 2.50 m per mare and the brood mares should be stabled in small batches if individual boxes are not possible. Ideal stable for a batch of 15 brood mares or 10 brood mares with foal at foot is 4.25 x 35.00 m covered standing and 35.00 x 75.00 m dry paddock. The feeding troughs should be provided in the covered standing and as well as in the open dry paddocks. The mares should be allowed to roam about at their will under cover or in the open. There should be a water trough, with running clean fresh water outside in the dry paddock. Fencing for dry paddock should consist of upright angle iron posts with four strands of wire.

Each dry paddock should have some trees to provide shade for the brood mares. The ground should be level, sandy, free from stones and holes and must have facilities for quick draining during monsoons. Each group of brood mares in the paddock should have an independent grazing paddock, easily approachable.

The foaling boxes should be roomy and spacious in order to provide enough room for the mare and the foal. An ideal size for foaling box is 4.25 x 5.50 m. It should have independent watering and feeding troughs inside, should have electric ceiling fan and be provided with fly proof windows for cross ventilation, so that it does not become stuffy during hot weather. The floor of the foaling boxes should be made of cement with gentle slope of 5 cm in 3 m for the drainage of urine and water. It should have few shallow grooves to prevent the mares from slipping, to take the liquid away and keep the bedding dry.

Feeding and Exercise

The brood mares are given grain feed 3 times a day. Brood mares with foal at foot and in light condition should be fed four times a day, of which two feeds should contain boiled barley. All grain should be fed mixed with plenty of chaffed hay. The chaff is essential for giving bulk, to ensure proper mastication and to improve peristalsis and digestion of brood mares. Out of total quantity of salt, half should be mixed with the grain after soaking in the water and the remainder half should be provided in the form of lumps for licking, if possible.

All water troughs for brood mares should be cleaned and white washed twice a week. During winter, it sometimes becomes necessary to drain out water from the paddocks of the in-foal mares daily in the evening to prevent abortions due to chilling effect of drinking cold water at night. The sides of the water troughs should be povided with concrete standing to prevent it from becoming muddy as a result of spilling of water from the troughs.

Brood mares in liberty get enough exercise and no special attention is necessary for their exercise. The mares confined to loose box should be turned out every day in grazing paddocks. Exercise, in whatever form it may be, is essential for brood mares for promoting health and preventing ailments.

Trying of mares and detection of heat

The mares are polyoestrous and heat varies according to the climate and the season. The breeding season is mainly confined twice a year. The spring breeding season commences from Febuary till the end of June and Autumn breeding season is confined to Sept-Oct and Nov. The breeding in spring season is considered to be best time because the heat in the brood mare is regular and invariably accompanied by functional ovulation, the stallions are most prolific and conception rate of the coverings is high. The maximum coverings should be aimed during this period as the foals are born after service in this season, at a time of the year when plenty of good fodder is available and the climate is favourable for their quick growth. Nearly 70-80 per cent of the mares should be covered in this season. Autumn breeding season may be used for breeding of problematic mares after their treatment.

One should start trying all maiden and empty mares from 1st Febuary. The main advantage of this preliminary trying is firstly to over come the natural nervousness of the mares in the presence of teasers and secondly to get a clue as to the likely date the mare will be in season from 15 Febuary onwards. It is better to miss covering of the mare in the first heat of the breeding season as percentage of ovulation is much less.

In the presence of the teaser at the trying bar (plate II), the brood mares in season exhibit the heat by raising the tail, by standing quietly, by winking i.e twitching of the clitoris, by squirting urine frequently, bending her hind quarters followed by contraction and relaxation of vulvar lips and passing of vaginal discharge, which subsequently becomes thick, scanty and hangs out like a thin string. The vulva gets swollen and becomes slack. These external signs of heat are the indication of what is happening inside the genital tract of the mare.

The mucous membrane of normal vagina is of pink colour, free from inflammation or offensive discharge and os uterus is seen projecting out in the vaginal passage, erect and rigid, like a piece of cartilage. In normal condition during dioestrus and pregnancy, the os is tightly closed. In heat, there is dilation and relaxation of vulva and the os and moistening of vagina to facilitate the passage of sperms. Taking an average period of heat as seven days, during first two days, there is no change in the condition of the os, next three days there is full dilatation followed by last two days rigidly increasing contraction.

To detect rigid or relaxed os, it requires long practical experience. A tight hard rose bud represents rigid os, the full bloom rose just past its prime, is the relaxed os. When examined by speculum, the cervix in mares not in heat is seen protruding into the vagina standing erect above the lower spoon of the speculum. In heat, the cervix folds will become slightly thicker and oedematous, cervix loses its tone, lies flat at the bottom of vagina. The orifice opens, upper portion hangs down to cover the orifice and lower portion fails to appear like a membrane. Such a state rapidly disappears after ovulation and cervix contracts.

A mare may be covered for 4 days in succession during heat, yet the conception is the fruit of one day of these services. The other three are drain on the stallion's vitality. Every service should be aimed at conception and mare should be covered when she is unmistakably willing to accept the mounting of the stallion.

Covering of the Mares

The mare being found in a complacent mood and the generative organs in ideal condition, she is given service by the stallion.

At this stage, the follicle should be ripe, reaching about 3-4 cm in diameter. Occassionally, two follicles may be present in one ovary. The ripening of the follicle is indicated by formation of a wedge like "Theca-Intema Cone" that serves as a path breaker for the growing follicle towards the ovarian surface. The presence of well defined cone of the follicle is an indication for approaching ovulation.

The service of the mare must be as close to the nature as possible. Hobbles may be used as a protection of the stallion against the injuries from the kicks. Use of twitch is not recommended unless mare is maiden or nervous at the time of covering. If twitch is necessary it should be used temporarily and for just so long as is necessary to keep her in place and to get the horse to mount her. After the stallion has mounted, the twitch can be quit safely and should be immediately released.

The mare should be prepared for covering by tying a bandage at the root of the tail to prevent loose hair being forced into vulva and causing subsequent laceration of the stallion's penis during service. The stallion is led out of the stable by two attendants and is kept well under control. Stallion should be walked round at a safe distance from the mare so that she may see him and get time to settle down and resign herself. Later the stallion is made to stand 1 to 1.5 m away from the mare, not in direct line behind her, but to the left side of her so that mare and stallion form two sides of a square. The mare then can see all stallion's movement and understand his intention. The stallion will begin by curling up his lips and smell the air which to him is full of alluring smacks. He will accordingly get ready for his work, sometime at once and sometime not quite so quickly. However, he must not be led up to the mare until he is quite ready and the penis is fully drawn and erect. The mare's head is held little high when she will not be able to kick quite so easily or so hard. The stallion is then led up to the left side of the mare to within a distance of a metre or so, when he will be left to jump her without any further interference and trouble. The impact of the stallion on the mare is considerable and her tendency quite naturally is to move a step forward before she has steadied herself and for the stallion getting a good grip on her flanks in order to cover her easily. Further, movement of the mare should be prevented by the attendants in front of the mare, one holding her head and the other pressing his shoulder against shoulder of the mare.

While mounting, the attendants holding the stallion should assist. The attendant on the right side pulls the mare's tail towards him with his left hand and places his right hand on the mare's hips, to keep her steady. The attendant on the left side places his left hand on mare's hip and guides the stallion's penis with his right hand into the vagina. Some stallions resent the holding of the penis by hand, the idea is only to help in penetration and the hand should be kept close to the penis to prevent it going to the side or entering into the rectum. Mares that have foal at foot, their foals must of course be separated from them temporarily when they have come to be tried and covered. It is further better that the mare should not hear the cries of her foal, which generally upsets her and distracts her attention from the stallion.

It will be ensured that the stallion has ejaculated which is indicated by flagging of the tail, contraction of the anus and rythmic pulsation in the urethra. Some stallions go through these false motions even without ejaculation, therefore the proper method of testing the discharge of the semen, is by placing a finger very tightly on the under side of horse's penis towards the close of the service. If the horse is ejaculating, the impulse throb will plainly be felt and all doubt be set at rest. The stallion normally ejaculates close to the cervix or directly into the os. The stallions which bite badly should be muzzled during service. Normally, one service should be enough but if the stallion is having slack time and the judgement for selection for covering has not been correct, second service may be given. At the fag end of the breeding season, in case of mares having been continuously breaking, a third service may be given in the hope of winding up the season satisfactorily.

Management of In-foal Mares

Each mare should be kept in very pink of breeding condition. Sole function of the brood mare is for the production and rearing of young and that the mare which everyone acclaims as "looking splendid" may for that very reason be in very worse condition for performing the maternal function, while the mare whose condition may draw uncomplimentary remarks from unthinking critics, may yet be in ideal state for reproducing her species with unthinking regularity.

Exercise is most important during pregnancy. Liberty stabling and grazing provides enough exercise for these mares and those confined to stables suffer ill effects of it. While grazing, the mares should be scattered all over and not allowed to stay in groups. Any mare isolating from others and standing alone may be examined for illness. Any mare showing signs of discomfort, should be taken out to prevent infecting the pastures by abortion.

Provided the mares are properly trained, there is no harm in riding or using them in cart during early stages of pregnancy but they should be worked at a slow pace and not more than 1½ hours daily. As the time approaches for the mare to foal, care should be taken to prevent sudden frights and violent galloping. It is good plan to divide the mares into convenient sized groups according to their expected date of foaling. Full benefits of this arrangement will be reaped after the mares have foaled and they and their young ones are turned out in pastures and paddocks, for if the mares have been running together, there will be little risk of quarrels and injuries to foals.

The mares generally bring forth their foals at an average 338 days after covering. Accordingly, the ready reckoner to find out the expected date of foaling is given in Table 8.1.

Table 8.1 Ready Reckoner of Foaling

Date of		Date of		Date of		Date of		Date of		Date of	
Cover-ing 1	Foal . ing 2	Cover-ing 3	Foal ing 4	Cover-ing 5	Foal ing 6	Cover-ing 7	Foal ing 8	Cove r ing 9	Foa l ing 10	Cover ing 11	Foal ing 12
1Jan	4 Dee	1 Feb	4Jan	1 Mar	1 Feb	1 Mar	Apr 4	1 May	3 May	Apr 1	Jun 4
2 .	5'	2 "	5 "	2"	2 "	2 "	5"	2 "	4"	2"	5"
3'	6"	3"	6"	3"	3"	3 "	6"	3 "	5"	3"	6"
4'	7"	4"	7 "	4"	4"	4 "	7"	4 "	6"	4"	7"
5 .	8 "	5 "	8 "	5 "	5 "	5 "	8"	5 "	7"	5"	8"
6'	9"	6"	9"	6"	6"	.6"	9"	6"	8"	6"	9"
7 .	10"	7"	10"	7"	7"	7"	10"	7 "	9 "	7"	10"
8'	11"	8"	11"	8 "	8 "	8"	11"	8"	10"	8"	11"
9'	12"	9".	12"	9"	9"	9"	12"	9"	11"	9"	12"
10'	13"	10"	13"	10"	10"	10"	13"	10"	12"	10"	13"
11'	14"	11"	14"	11"	11"	11"	14"	11"	13"	11"	14"
12 .	15 "	12 "	15"	12"	12"	12"	15"	12 "	14"	12"	15"
13"	16"	13"	16"	13"	13"	13"	16"	13 "	15"	13"	16"
14"	17"	14"	17"	14"	14"	14 "	17"	14"	16"	14"	17"
15 "	18 "	15"	18"	15 "	15 "	15 "	18"	15 "	17"	15"	18"
16"	19"	16"	19"	16"	16"	16"	19"	16 "	18"	16"	19"
17"	20"	17"	20"	17"	17"	17"	20"	17"	19"	17"	20"
18"	21"	18"	21"	18 "	18 "	18"	21"	18 "	20"	18"	21"
19"	22"	19"	22"	19"	19"	19"	22"	19 "	2}"	19"	22"
20 "	23"	20"	23"	20"	20"	20"	23"	20 "	22"	20"	23"
21"	24"	21"	24"	21"	21"	21"	24"	21"	23"	21"	24"
22"	25"	22"	25"	22"	22"	22"	25"	22 "	24"	22"	25"
23"	26"	23"	26"	23 "	23"	23"	26"	23 "	25"	23"	26"
24"	27"	24"	27"	24"	24"	24"	27"	24 "	26"	24"	27"
25 "	28"	25"	28"	25 "	25"	25"	28"	25 "	27"	25"	28"
26"	. 29"	26"	29"	26"	26"	26"	29	26"	28"	26"	29"
27"	30"	27"	30"	27 "	27"	27"	30"	27"	29"	27"	30"
28"	31"	28"	31"	28 "	28"	28"	31"	28 "	30"	28"	31"
29 "	1 Jan			29"	1 " Mirch	29	1 Apr	29 ..	1 "	May29	1 Jun
30"	2"			30"	2"	30"	2"	30 "	2"	30"	2"
31 "	3 "			31 "	3 "			31 "	3 "		

I	2	3	4	5	6	7	8	9	10	II	12
I Jul	3 Jun	I Aug	4 Jut	I Sep	4 Aug Nov	I Oct	3 Sep	I Nov	4 Oct	I Dee	3
2 "	4"	2 "	5"	2 "	5"	2"	4"	2 "	5"	2"	4"
3 ". 5"		3"	6 "	3 "	6 "	3"	5"	3 "	6"	3"	5"
4"	6"	4"	7"	4"	7"	4"	6"	4"	'7"	4"	6"
5"	7"	5 "	8 "	5 "	8 "	5"	7"	5 "	8". 5"		7"
6"	8 "	6"	9"	6"	9 "	6 "	8"	6"	9"	6"	8"
7"	9"	7"	10"	7"	10 "	7"	9"	. 7"	10"	7"	9"
8"	10"	8"	11"	8 "	Il"	8"	10"	8"	Il"	8"	10"
9"	Il"	9"	12"	9 "	12 "	9"	Il"	9"	12". 9"		Il"
10"	12"	10"	13"	10 "	13"	10"	12"	10"	13"	10"	12"
Il"	13"	Il"	14"	Il"	14"	Il"	13"	Il"	14"	II "	13"
12"	14"	12"	15"	12"	15"	12"	14"	12".	15"	12"	14"
13"	15"	13"	16'"	13"	16"	13"	15"	13 "	16"	13"	15"
14"	16"	14"	17"	14 "	17"	14"	16"	14 "	17"	14"	16"
15"	17"	15"	18"	15 "	18"	15"	17"	15"	18"	15 "	.17"
16"	18"	16"	19"	16 "	19"	16"	18"	16 "	19"	16"	18"
17"	19"	17"	20"	17"	20"	17"	19"	17 "	20"	17"	19"
18"	20"	18"	21"	18"	21"	18"	20"	18 "	21"	18 "	20"
19"	21"	19"	22"	19"	22"	19"	21"	19"	22"	19."	21"
20"	22"	20"	23"	20. ,.	23"	20"	22"	20"	23"	20"	22"
21"	23"	21"	24"	21"	24"	21",	23"	21"	24"	21 "	23 "
22"	24"	22"	25"	22"	25"	22"	24"	22"	25"	22"	24"
23"	25"	23"	26"	23"	26"	23"	25"	23"	26"	23 "	25"
24"	.26"	24"	27"	24"	27"	24"	26"	24"	27"	24 "	26"
25"	27"	25"	28"	25"	28"	25"	27"	23--"	28"	25"	27"
26"	28"	26"	29"	26"	29"	26"	28"	26"	29"	26"	28"
27"	29"	27"	30"	27"	30"	27"	29"	27"	30"	27 "	29"
28"	30"	28"	31"	28"	31"	28"	30"	28"	31"	28 "	30"
29 "	1 Jul	29"	I Aug	29"	I Sep	29"	I Oct	29"	I Nov	29"	'1 Dee
30 "	2"	30"	2"	30"	2"	30"	2"	30"	2"	30"	2."
31"	3"	31"	3"			31"	3"			31"	3"

Some mares invariably go overtime while others do the reverse. Mares with low condition exceed their time for foaling by about two weeks, while mares in good condition foal in time or several days in advance ont. All pregnant mares should be shifted to the foaling boxes about 3 weeks before the expected date of foaling. The mares foaling 20 days ahead of expected date should be considered as premature foaling, if the foal is alive. The birth of a dead foal before 20 days should be presumed as an abortion. The birth of a dead foal within the range of normal foaling i.e, 20 days either side may be considered as stillbirth.

Management of Foaling Mares

All infoal mares should be closely watched for signs of approaching parturition when they get within a fortnight of their expected date of foaling. As the foaling time draws nearer, the filling of udder increases, which becomes firm and of rather turgid consistency. Doughy swelling under the skin in front of the udder often appears in some mares. There is nothing to worry about it as it disappears when the flow of milk starts after foaling. The penultimate stage of foaling is marked by sinking of the quarter on each side of the croup, in the hollow on both sides of the root of the tail. The pelvic muscles between hip joints, croup and back to the root of the tail may feel slackened and depressed due to influence of harmone 'Relaxin' (which is produced during last days of pregnancy). The swelling and relaxation of the vulva is often seen. There is appearance at the end of the teat of little nodules of wax like substance produced by the secretion of clear thick serum like material from the teat canal. It is always better to get the waxing mare into foaling box at night and keep her under constant observation. It is a good plan to inspect the mare's udder each morning and evening for a week or so before due date of foaling and make a note when wax has appeared. Mare usually foals within 12 to 24 hours after the wax drops off and milk begins to drip away, soiling the lower part of the hind legs. Once this stage has reached, the mare may foal at any time. Some maiden mares may foal without previous waxing or letting down milk. There is an old saying:

"She bags her udder a few days before

She waxes and slackens some hours before

She sweats and she fidgets some moments before

She foals. "

Before foaling, all items of foaling kit including lubricant consisting of liquid paraffin should be kept ready and sterilized.

Arrangements for warm bran mash containing jaggery (Gur) should be made beforehand. After foaling, not only the foal but the mare herself is liable to get infection if a foaling box is not previously kept ready duly disinfected. Her bedding and surrounding should be absolutely clean and healthy. Bedding should be thick and consisting of good clean straw. Danger of infection to the foal and to a lesser degree to the mare, persists for considerable time after foaling and is at its height during the first nine days.

The usual symptoms of approaching labour are that the mare shows excitement, pacing uneasily round and round in the foaling box, breaks into profuse perspiration, paws the ground, gazes around her flanks, lies down and gets up again repeatedly and passes small quantity of urine frequently. At this stage, care should be taken to regulate the ventilation while the mare is perspiring and is in a heated state.

During actual foaling process, there are short spasms of straining and heaving to expel the foal. First, there appears the blind end of the membrane sac in which the foal is enclosed, then the forefeet with frogs downward, followed by nose and knees, each series of spasms bringing forth the head, neck, shoulders and finally the entire body. Slightest difficulty in dealing with a delayed parturition should be dealt with coolness, calculated judgement and prompt action. Experience and intelligence alone will teach when to act swiftly and when to wait patiently and confidently. Once the deepest part of the foal's body i.e. from top of withers to the elbow is through the pelvis, the most constricted part of the passage, the rest is comparatively easy. Most mares foal lying down and very rarely standing. The whole operation takes 15-20 minutes. During this period, the attendant should act as a mere passive spectator to foaling, closely watching without disturbance. In case of undue delay in foaling, thorough examination of the genital tract should be carried out.

It is advisable to be ready to deal with the foaling mares and following procedure is recommended:

(a) Prepare half a bucket of weak antiseptic 1:1000 savlon lotion by adding 1 ml of savlon/litre of water. Place in this, 4 or 5 large swabs of cotton wool.

(b) Scrub and wash hands, forearms in soap and water, scrub the finger nails which should be clipped short

(c) Quietly approach the mare, swab around her vagina, rectum, sides of buttocks and under surface of the tail with antiseptic lotion.

(d) Tie clean bandages at the root of the tail.

(e) Lubricate the hand with sterilised liquid paraffin or with a lubricating antiseptic jelly.

(f) Gently insert the hand along the roof of vagina with back of the palm towards rectum. Right hand is best when mare is lying on her right side and left hand is best when mare is lying on her left, for carrying out thorough examination of foal's position and using plenty of lubricant.

The desirablity of allowing the mare to foal by her own unaided efforts if the presentation of the foal is normal, cannot be over emphasized. However, if the delivery is being unduly prolonged, there is a risk of suffocation from pressure of mare's pelvis on the foal's ribs. Once the nostrils are uncovered, the foal takes in air through them, the lungs are expanded and the foal may be said to start its separate independent existence. The usual procedure is to leave the foal's hind legs within the vagina, then with the fingers swiftly slit the enveloping membrane, simultaneously freeing the nostrils and exposing the navel cord.

When the foal's hind quarters are through, there is then a natural pause from the labour pain the mare has undergone and the foal's hind legs are still in. At this stage, nothing should be done to disturb the mare or the foal. The foal is still attached by its umbilical cord to the membrane and is receiving oxygen from its mother. A substantial portion of foal's full complement of blood is still circulating in the placenta and the umbilical arteries can be felt pulsating. To cut or ligature the cord at this stage is to deprive the foal of the blood which may be pressed back into the foal's body through the veins in the cord by constriction of uterine wall during the pause period. In few minutes, foal's hind leg will be delivered free to the outside. During this time, the cord pulsation should have ceased to be perceptible and when the tension is great enough the cord will break at the normal breaking point. This is usually about I"-1½" (2.5 to 4 cm) from the skin of the navel and it is an area of weekness where cord easily breaks. A little blood may escape which is unimportant, the broken arteries will soon retract into mass of tissue and cease to bleed of their own accord. Immediate dressing with an antiseptic agent e.g. Tincture iodine should be done.

The lying down position is the one most conducive to efficiency in foaling operations for at least two good reasons:

(a) The navel, being the port of "entry" of infection, can be tightly ligatured before it is severed and the chances of organisms gaining entry to the foal's system are much less than when the navel is ruptured by foal dropping from the standing mare on an unclean bedding.

(b) In case of abnormally thick navel cord, the severe drag which will ensure before the weight of the foal ruptured the cord, would be highly conducive to an umbilical hernia. The mare in health lies down to deliver foal but in debility she stands up.

Dystocia Management

Dystocia in the brood mare is one of the few true emergencies that equine practitioners encounter, where minutes make a difference in the survival of one of the patients (the foal). Duration of dystocia also influences the degree of reproductive tract trauma that occurs during resolution of the dystocia. There are four procedures used to resolve dystocia in the mare

i) Assisted vaginal delivery (AVD), where the mare is awake and is assisted to a small or large degree in vaginal delivery of an intact foal;
ii) Controlled vaginal delivery (CVD), where the mare is anesthetized and the clinician is in complete control of delivering an intact foal vaginally;

iii) Fetotomy, where the dead fetus is cut into more than one piece for removal from the uterus per vagina in an awake or anesthetized mare;

iv) Cesarean section (C-Section) where the fetus is removed through an incision in the uterus.

Most dystocias are resolved at the farm by personnel experienced with foaling mares. If a dystocia is not resolved quickly, sending the mare to a referral hospital may be a better option for the mare than waiting for the farm veterinarian to come to the farm and help deliver the foal. The equipment and training of the personnel would usually make a referral hospital a better environment for CVD, fetotomy, Cesarean-section, and for neonatal resuscitation and care. The decision to refer the mare should be based on the position of the foal, duration of the dystocia, distance to and preparedness of the referral hospital, and the experience of the farm and referral hospital veterinarians involved.

When faced with dystocia, the goal should be to deliver a live foal in a manner that does not impair the career of a reproductively sound mare. If the foal is dead, the obvious concern becomes the mare. To achieve these goals, the approach to dystocia in the mare should follow a continuum of potentially changing strategies, providing the best method possible to resolve that particular situation. There is no one procedure that is right for every situation. Ideally, the AVD, CVD, Cesarean-section, and fetotomy procedures are employed as needed to yield the most favourable result. Financial concerns may influence which procedures are used.

Approach to Dystocia in Modern Hospital

Sedation is achieved with xylazine, and anesthesia is induced with diazepam and ketamine. Anesthesia is maintained with halothane and oxygen. Once the mare is recumbent, hobbles are placed on the hind pasterns and hooked to a hoist. The mare is hoisted upward until the pelvis is approximately three feet from the floor. The position and posture of the fetus is determined, and the fetus is then repelled and repositioned to allow vaginal delivery. Rotation of the fetus to resolve dystocia may be first tried. Copious amounts of lubrication are used to help the delivery. When the head and distal forelimbs are exteriorized, the mare is lowered into lateral recumbency and traction is applied to the foal until delivery is accomplished. The umbilical cord is clamped and transected. The foal is quickly placed on a nearby, well-equipped mobile neonatal bed for resuscitation and stabilization. The mare is placed on a thick foam mat for recovery. Occasionally, the placenta can be removed during recovery.

Simultaneously to the controlled vaginal delivery, the ventral abdomen is clipped and partially prepped for a C-section. The elapsed time from the start of CVD should be watched closely. If the foal cannot be delivered within 15 min, or if it is determined before 15 min that the foal is in a position to preclude delivery within 15 min, a C-section is performed. If the foal is known to be dead, the surgeon should use his best judgment regarding continued CVD, fetotomy or C-section. If a C-section is to be performed, the mare is quickly transferred to a surgery table, placed in dorsal recumbency, and the final sterile preparation is applied to the ventral abdomen. The C-section is performed through a caudal ventral midline incision, with the mare in dorsal recumbency, tilted slightly towards the surgeon. The foal's hind limbs are found within one of the uterine horns, and this horn is exteriorized. An incision is made through the uterine horn, the hind limbs are grasped, and the foal is extracted from the uterus as rapidly and safely as possible. The umbilicus is clamped and ligated. The foal is then transferred to an adjacent neonatal room for resuscitation. The chorioallantois is separated from the endometrium along the edges of the incision. Uterine hemorrhage is controlled by ligation of significant bleeding vessels and a hemostatic simple continuous suture applied to the incised edge of the uterus. It is uncommon to be able to remove the chorioallantois from the uterus during surgery. The uterine incision is then closed using two inverting layers with absorbable suture material. On completion of uterine closure, oxytocin is administered to assist in uterine contraction and placental expulsion. The abdomen is lavaged and closed in routine fashion. The placenta is usually expelled within 6 - 12 hour post-operatively, often requiring more oxytocin. Further, post-operative care is similar to that after an exploratory celiotomy.The duration of dystocia has a direct relationship with reproductive tract trauma, which in turn affects subsequent fertility in the mare.

After Care of Foaling Mares

The placenta of the mare should normally drop within one hour after foaling. In case of delay beyond three hours, it should be removed by administration of hormones and by manual interference. After foaling, a mass of tangled foetal membranes will be hanging from the mare and if these are inclined to get in the way and strangled or stampeded upon as the mare turns and moves about in the foaling box, then the membrane should be tied up by a string into more compact mass, a little above the level of hocks. Tying the weight to the placenta is not advocated as it might cause pull at the roots and cause injuries to the uterine walls. It should be ensured that the placenta is expelled as a whole and intact and no piece is left inside. The placenta is then examined thoroughly by spreading and opening it inside out. Any defect or abnormality should be noted. Before disposal, the placenta should be weighed and disposed of either by burning or by burial. The container and the attendant's hands should be thoroughly disinfected. Haemorrhages after foaling should be viewed seriously.

Retention of placenta(ROP) or Retained Fetal Membrane(RFM)

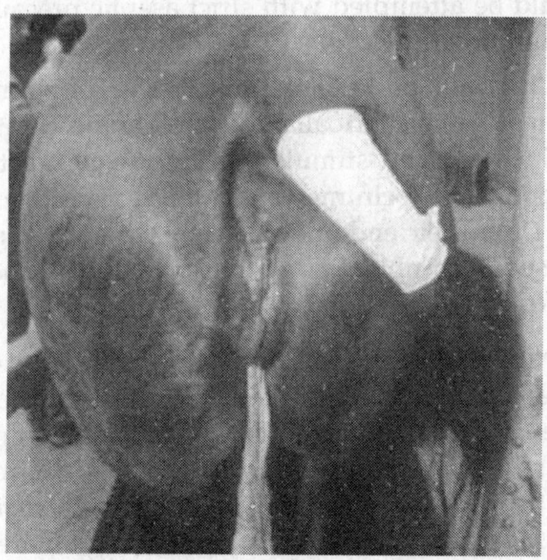

Fig .7.1 ROP

If the expulsion of placenta is delayed beyond three hours, it is liable to become infected with organisms and may lead to uterine infection and consequent sterility. Retention of the fetal membranes (RFM) is one of the most common peripartum problems in the mare, with an incidence in the range from 2% to 10%. Complications include acute metritis, septicaemia, laminitis and even death. RFM should be treated as emergency. The incidence much higher after dystocia. The thorough examination the fetal membranes is essential to determine which portion has been retained. The most frequently retained portion is the tip of the non-pregnant horn.

For treatment-

- Oxytocin can be given via the intramuscular route (20-40 iu), which can be repeated after one hour if the placenta has not been passed. Alternatively, use slow intravenous infusion of 50 iu oxytocin in 1 litre of physiologic saline during one hour. Symptoms of colic often follow injections of oxytocin and commonly precede natural expulsion so that pain-relieving drugs and sedation may be required.
- Only if this treatment fails and the placenta is almost detached but retained within the uterus the manual removal should be attempted with strict aseptic precaution and no undue force.
- Another method is placement of 10 L of warm, sterile saline inside the chorioallantoic membrane. Stretching of the uterine wall and stimulating uterine contractions via endogenous oxytocin may assist the separation of the microvilli from their endometrial crypts. This treatment should be used in combination with exogenous oxytocin administration.

Aftercare includes (depending on the severity of the case) regular general examination, checking the uterus (for involution and contents) and, if indicated flushing and siphoning the uterus with sterile NSS once or twice daily for a few days in combination with further injections of oxytocin. Tetanus antitoxin is recommended and if a risk for the mare developing a toxic metritis, she should be treated with broad-spectrum systemic and intrauterine antibiotics with antihistaminics. Cyclooxygenase inhibitors such as flunixin meglumine should be given to either treat or minimize the risk of development of endotoxaemia.

Provided treatment is begun at the correct time and no secondary complications develop the *Reproductive prognosis* for a case of retained placenta is good. Mares that have had RFM should not be mated at the foal heat as the chance of conception is reduced.

Feeding of Colostrum

The colostrum of the mare is rich in protein, minerals and vitamins and is heavily loaded with antibodies(gamma globulins) produced in the mare's serum against most of the common harmful bacteria. It has stimulating and slightly laxative effect on the meconium. The first secretion of colostrum only is rich and after 12-15 hours, its original antibody concentration is reduced to nearly half and in about 36 hours, the amount of antibody is very small and practically normal milk is secreted.

Dhaman (Foal heat) Covering

Foal heat or post parturient oestrus is a unique phenomenon in mares. The foal heat is invariably complete with follicle ovulating. This is possible as the ovaries of the mare in the later stage of pregnancy do not contain functional corpus-luteum so that new follicles begin to develop, as soon as level of the oestrogens and progesterone, by the placenta, drops low enough as to exert inhibiting effect on the pituitary ovarian activity and new follicles start developing before parturition. Furthermore, post parturient uterus of the mare is capable of involution in a short time, because of primitive loose non deciduate type of placenta of the mares, which permits separation of foetal placenta without major damage to the uterine endo metrium. If the restoration of the uterine epithelium after parturition is not complete, it may result in abortion. Foal heat is of about the same duration as cyclic oestrual periods.

Majority of foaling mares are ready for the stallions on the 9th day after foaling and in calculating 9th day, the day of foaling and day of covering are also counted. Normally, it is arrived at, by adding 8 to the date of foaling. Best general practice with foaling mares is to try every day from 7th day after foaling till satisfactory result is obtained upto 15th day.

If the mare has not shown heat after foaling and is not covered during 1st or 2nd post parturient heat, the dioestrus is unduly prolonged in heavy milkers, till after the foals are weaned. Presumably, this is due to the pituitary principally putting out lactogenic hormones at the expense of gonadotrophins. The experience has shown that some mares are a law into themselves and set all rules and regulations and date at defiance. The characteristics of individual mare have to be studied and recorded. The dates are very useful guides to probabilities and should not be rigidly followed.

The result of Dhaman (foal heat) covering has been found very satisfactory and certain precautions are necessary before enforcing this into an organized Stud. However, Dhaman (foal heat) covering should be avoided when the following conditions are encountered:

(a) When there is a difficulty in foaling and foal is taken out manually even if it is alive.

(b) When the foal is born dead or dies within 7 days after foaling.

(c) When placenta is retained for more than 3 hours in the uterus.

(d) When placenta weighs more than 6.5 kg.

(e) When the placenta is thick, oedematous and having ulcers on its surface.

(f) When foal is born a weakling.

(g) When the mare is continuing vaginal discharge more than 4 days after foaling.

(h) When the mare has sustained injury to the genital tract during foaling.

(i) When the uterus has not involuted to its normal size as detected by rectal examination.

(j) If the mare is weak in condition.

Management of Foal at Foot Mares

After foaling, the mare with her foal should remain in the foaling box for about 4 days. By this time, mare would have cleansed herself. The mare then is taken out of the foaling box in an open loose box and kept there with foal for about 15 days, by that time the foal starts recognizing its dam and is ready for mixing with the other foal at foot mares of approximately the same age.

The foal at foot mares should be kept in small groups of not more than 10 in the paddock, according to the age of the foals. The mares which foal in a month may be kept together, similarly other foal at foot mares should be grouped according to the month of foaling. A general rule to deworm a foal at foot mare, is the next day after her dhaman (foal heat) covering. As the foals start growing in age, the suckling of milk causes drain on the mares and some start losing condition due to the heavy drain on their health. Best care and management is required to keep foal at foot mares in reasonably good condition. They should be given extra grain feed, barley should be fed after boiling. Good grazing pastures have tremendous effect in maintaining the falling condition of these mares.

Management of Weanling Mares

The foals are separated from their dams when they are 6 months old. Early weaning of foal may be carried out on veterinary grounds if the foal is maintaining healthy condition and the mare is rapidly going down in condition. For 12 hours prior to separating mare and foal, the mare should be deprived of food and only small quantity of water is allowed to her. The foal's regular drain on milk supply and withdrawal of mare's food, combined, will ensure that the udder will be practically depleted of milk at the time of actual separation. After the separation has been completed, the mare can have small quantity of hay and after expiration of 4 hours, the udder should be fully relieved if distended. If small quantity has been secreted, it should not be milked dry but only a portion is drawn off. The object to be kept in view, is to dry up the milk supply as quickly as may be, while avoiding any risk of congestion or inflamation. Engorged udders are liable to cause damage to the tissues.

Management of Breeding Operations

Suitability of Breeding Stock

All breeding stock should be examined by the veterinary officer before using for breeding. The genital organs should be sound and the aru.mal should be fit for breeding and free from hereditary diseases. The stallion and the :mare are both equally potent in stamping their type and make upon the foal, which is to be the product of their mating and the foal will therefore be a brand of its parents in quality and defects. The influence of any high class stallion upon the improvement of an inferior breed may be quite enormous and in that respect, thoroughbred stallion is very potent. The potency of Arab stallion is still greater.

From breeding point of view, all the leading characteristics of the sire and of the dam are hereditary i.e. temperament, action, constitution and soundness and as a result of all of them combined, "the performance".

Precautions during covering

(a) The covering yard should be sprinkled with water to keep the dust down during covering.

(b) The brood mare's external genitalia should be washed with clean water.

(c) If the brood mare is bigger in size, she is made to stand in a dug out piece of ground.

(d) To dismount the stallion after covering, the mare's front should be moved a step towards her left side and stallion will dismount instantaneously.

(e) After dismounting, the stallion should be reined back and not allowed to turn round and kick the mare.

(f) The stallion's head should be pulled forward and down while mounting to prevent him falling at the back.

(g) The stallion's penis should be washed after covering with Savlon lotion 1 : 1000.

(h) Immediately after covering, the mare should be released from covering hobbles and led away from covering yard at a walking pace. Mare should not be allowed to stand, strain, urinate and throw away the semen from the vagina. "

Pregnancy Diagnosis of the Mare

After service, the sperms travel quickly through the genital tract and catch the ovum in the fallopian tube where the fertilation takes place. The sperms remain viable and retain their fertilizing power inside the genital tract for about 36 hours: The ovum can remain alive for approximately 6-8 hours in the genital tract. Taking these into consideration, the ovulation should take place at such a time, when the spermatozoa are already present in the genital tract. Therefore, the covering of the mare should be as close to the time of ovulation as possible.

The fertilized ovum takes 4-6 days to travel and to reach the uterus. Majority of pregnancy takes place in the right ovary though the ovulation is more from the left ovary. Fertilized ovum migrates into the right horn and implants there. The critical phase in the implantation and placentation of the foetus occurs in very 1st few week of the itritiated pregnancy. The mare, the fertilized ovum after it has entered the uterus does not imbed into endometrium by nidation, more so the developing foetal membranes anchor the embryo to the uterus as they are formed, instead the blastocysts remain free in the uterine cavity and eventually expand to fill the lumen. The attachment of the membrane remains very frail because they are held in position principally by pressure of the foetal fluid. At about six weeks, the just established Chorio-vitelline placental circulation changes to the chorio-allantois type and this period is regarded especially critical in the development when the embryo is more likely to "slip" than at other times, because at this stage the attachment is weaker than heretofore.

After covering, the mare should be tested the third day and if the mare has gone off heat, it is a good indication of conception and correct selection of the mare for covering. The covered mare should be kept away from the testing Pony for 10 days after the date of last covering. Thereafter, the covered mares should be shown at intervals to the testing Pony for next 15 days and if the mares do not show any signs of breaking the service, they should be presumed to be in foal. These mares should be kept in separate paddock as awaiting pregnancy diagnosis. The covered mares, therefore, should be grouped and paddocked in 3 lots (i) within 10 days after covering (ii) 10-25 days after covering and (iii) 25 days till the pregnancy diagnosis.

The pregnancy diagnosis per rectum of covered mares is better carried out early startitig from 30th day after service. The main advantages of early pregnancy diagnosis are firstly the mares going empty can be covered 2.3 times in the same breeding season and secondly to detect infection of uterine endo-metrium if the mare has not conceived. As there are more chances of early embryonic death during first two months of pregnancy, it is advisable to recheck these mares after completion of 60 days of pregnancy. This should be done regularly in the 2nd and 4th week of the month so that mares between 60 and 75 days of pregnancy are taken up for re-check every time.

While examining the uterus for early pregnancy, it is better to feel the uterine horn for uterine tone. The gravid uterus by 15 days becomes turgid and feels like a "rubber sponge roll", while non-plant uterine horn resembles a fold of "velvet cloth". In most mares, no uterine enlargement is detectable until 30 days but in small pony mares, an enlargement of 1½" (4 cm) in diameter, soft and resilient in consistency, may be felt just on side of the junction of the uterine horn and body at 25 days:

At 30 days, an isolated and clear enlargement can be felt at the same site and very similar in consistency, ovoid in shape 1½" x 2" (4-5 cm) in size (walnut to guava size) and there is a definite presence of tone in the horns and more on the pregnant side. Diagnosis at this stage is difficult in Dhaman mares. The foetus grow in size and at 5 weeks, enlargement has reached the size of an orange and the wall over the bulge is thinning and pemitting the examiner to feel the fluctuation. At six weeks, enlargement attains the size of a cricket ball and becomes slightly oval in shape. At 7 weeks, distinct oval enlargement of a grape fruit size is palpated. After 3 months, foetus. becomes quite big in size and it is not difficult to feel the complete enlargement. At this stage, the ovaries descend and move towards the centre. The foetal bumps are usually palpable after 5 months of pregnancy.

It is about 6 months after service that the mare's belly will drop and widen towards lower part of her flank. The infoal mare carries her belly more pointed and usually she shows rather large to one flank than to the other. The best way to view her is from behind and when in movement or often still better when she is made to take a step backward then slight swinging movement of the load, she carry is visible. In case of any doubt that the mare may have slipped a foal, she should be examined per rectum.

DIFFERENT STAGES OF EARLY EQUINE PREGNANCY

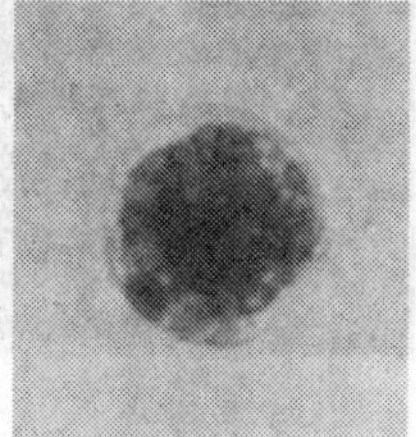

Fig : 8.2
The 32 to 64 cell stage of a developing embryo is the morula. This stage is seen up to about day 6 **post ovulation**

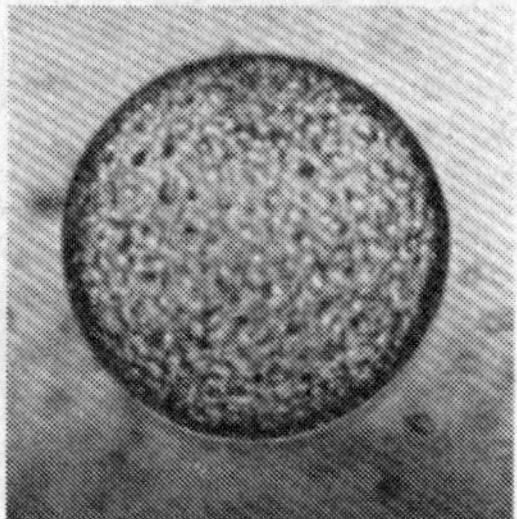

Fig : 8.3
This photograph is of an expanded blastocyst, highly magnified. Note the regularity of the circular shape. The blastocyst stage of development is considered to be reached when the blastocele cavity, or yolk sac, is seen to be developed within the embryo. It is at this stage of development that *embryo transfer* **is most commonly practised**

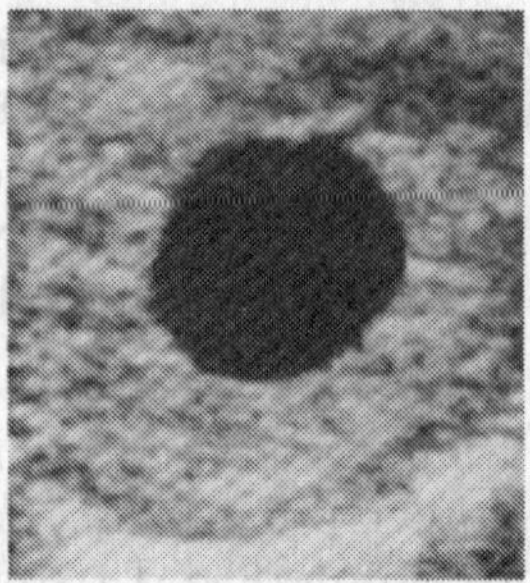

Fig : 8.4

A 15 day conceptus viewed by ultrasound. Note the regularity of the circular shape.

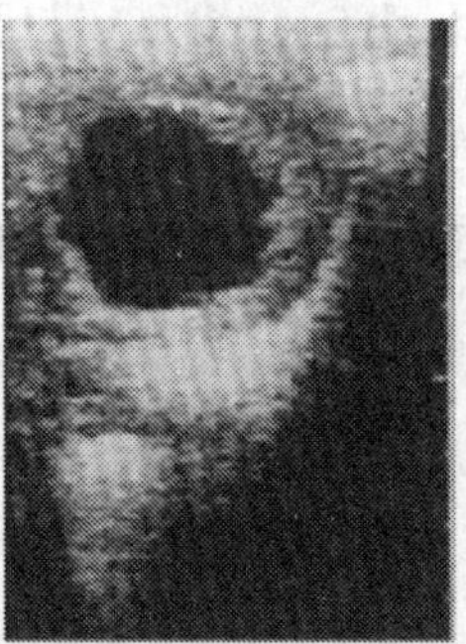

Fig : 8.5

By 18 days **the regularity of shape is starting to deteriorate - note the "ragged" edges**

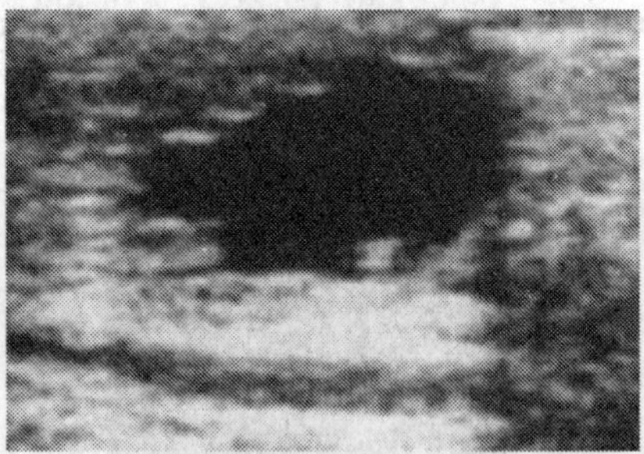

Fig : 8.6

By 22 days **the embryo itself can be seen with ultrasound - here it is visible between the red calliper marks on the image. The heartbeat can also start to be detected at this stage. Note here how the regular rounding has completely deteriorated, and the conceptus is appearing oval, and without "smooth" edges.**

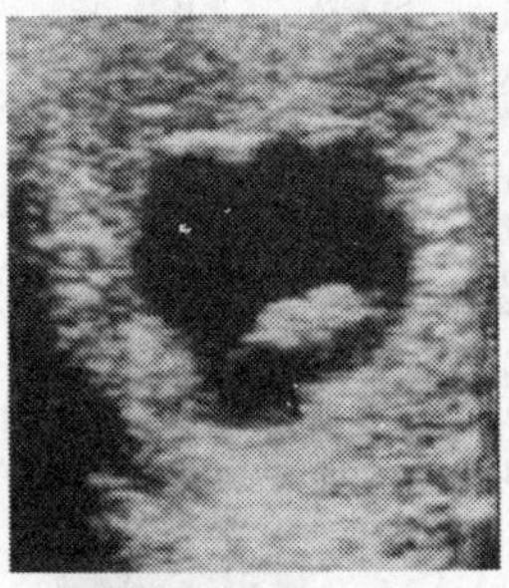

Fig : 8.7
25 days clearly visible embryo.

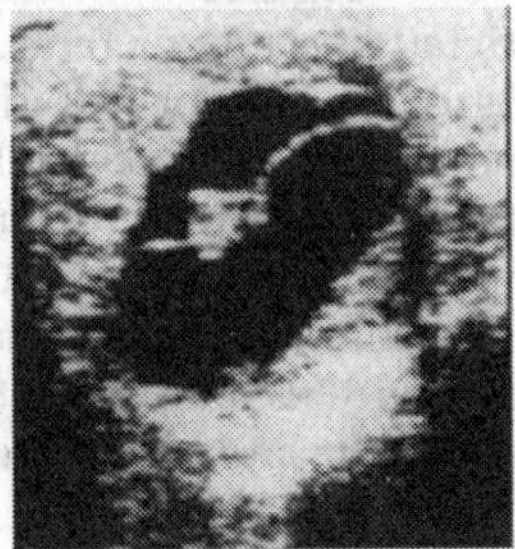

Fig : 8.8
At 29 days, the developing allantois (the outgrowth of the embryo's hindgut which forms the bladder, carries blood vessels in the umbilical cord, and later combines with the chorion to form the placenta) is visible, and the yolk sac (visible here as the upper portion of the dark section) is regressing. The apparent "division" in the conceptus at this stage is not to be mistaken for twin embryos - of which clearly only one is visible.

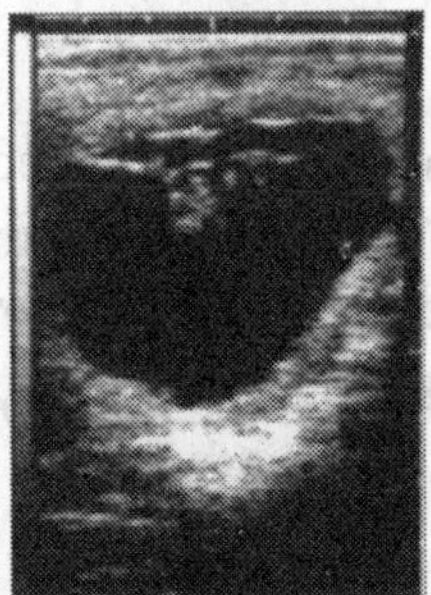

Fig : 8.9
By day 38 the yolk sac has almost completely regressed and is visible here only as the dark narrow "band" immediately above the embryo (compare this with the 29 day image).

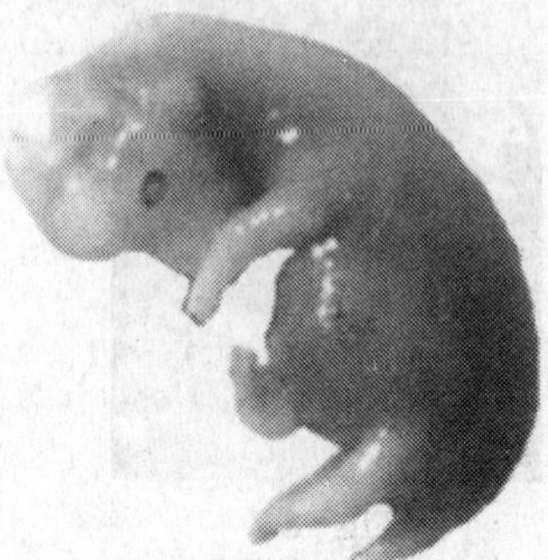

Fig 8.10

By day 50 the embryo officially becomes a fetus. As can be seen in this photograph of a 50-day fetus, the legs, head, tail and eye are all clearly defined externally. Internally organs and skeletal structures are in place. The overall size is a little deceptive with this image, and it is in fact about one inch in length. Within 10 days or so, the sex of the fetus can be determined using ultrasound, by establishing the direction of migration of the pedicle that will become either the penis or the clitoris. Upward migration towards the anus of course indicates a female.

Slow Covering Donkey Stallions

Donkey Stallions occasionally show signs of relative impotency, some stallions are slow coverers from commencement of their career, whereas others develop this trait during initial training after spending some time at a particular Stud. The causes of slow covering are :

Constitutional Causes

These may be due to the following reasons:

(a) *Excessive coverings.* The semen becomes thin and watery by using the stallion excessively for covering.

(b) *Masturbation.* Semen may be watery and not of sufficient viscosity, which is necessary for its retention and impregnation.

(c) *Excitable temperament.* The mere sight of a mare passing by the stable is enough to cause erection of the penis, masturbation and discharge.

(d) *Early discharge.* Some stallions naturally or as a result of over use, discharge very quickly. There is a lack of will-power in such stallions.

(e) *Infantile testicles.* Testicles may not be fully developed.

(f) *Shy stallions.* Some stallions are by nature very shy and require special training in the art of covering.

(g) *Age.* As far as possible, very old mares should not always be mated to young stallions. This practice if carried out on an extreme, is apt to make the stallion slow coverer.

(h) *Covering Donkey mares.* The practice of putting a donkey stallion to pony mares as well as Donkey mares, sometimes make the stallion a slow coverer.

(i) *History.* In some cases, slow covering is attributed to the stallion having at some time been kicked. Mares should always be properly hobbled before service. A sudden kick and the resultant fright makes the stallion shy. Injury of any kind to a stallion at the time of covering is likely to produce this result.

(j) *Size.* The practice of putting big stallions to very small mares and vice versa might make the stallions slow coverer. This practice should be avoided and a pit should be used to overcome the disparity in size.

(k) *Carelessness.* Carelessness on the part of the handler (groom) at the time of covering, by allowing the penis to go into the rectum instead of the the vagina might make the stallion a slow coverer for future use.

Indirect causes

These may be due to :

(a) *Feeding.* Under-feeding and over-feeding both lead to slow covering, in this direction perhaps over-feeding is more pernicious in its effect than under-feeding. Offering drinking water in the morning before covering during winter will induce the Donkey Stallions to have tendency of slow covering.

(b) *Exercise.* This is a very important factor in maintaining the covering capacity of a stallion. Grooms of Donkey stailions should ride them morning and evening without a saddle.

(c) *Service.* A stallion should have its full complement of mares for covering during the year. If he is allowed to cover either too few or too many, either factor may result in slow covering.

References

1*. R. M. Embertson (2003) Rood and Riddle Equine Hospital, Lexington, Kentucky, USA. In: 49th Annual Convention of the American Association of Equine Practitioners, 2003 - New Orleans,LA,USA, (Ed.)Publisher: American Association of Equine Practitioners, Lexington KY

Chapter 9

Artificial Insemination and Frozen Semen Technique

The earliest story of Artificial Insemination (AI) in equines dates back to 1322 AD. It is about an Arab, who had a good quality mare and wanted to breed her to a certain prominent stallion, whose owner was unwilling for the same. One night when his mare was in heat, the Arab saturated a cloth with the vaginal secretions, sneaked into the stable of stallion and rubbed the secretions under the nostrils. Eventually, this smell sexually excited the stallion enough to make him ejaculate. The Arab caught the ejaculate in cloth, hurried back to his mare and placed the cloth in the vagina of his mare. Although, it is almost inconceivable that such a procedure could have resulted in a pregnancy, yet according to the story, it did. 35 years ago, the average stallion covered 40 or so mares a year, but today, with the advent of ultrasound and better palpation techniques to pinpoint ovulation, instead of a mare needing to be bred "every other day until the end of her cycle", the stallion only needs to breed her once to achieve pregnancy. Consequently, we can see stallions breeding 200 mares a year by live cover.

In AI instead of the mare being bred "live cover" or "naturally" by the stallion, the semen is collected from the stallion, and introduced directly into the mare's uterus by means of a syringe and pipette. It is usual to add a diluent in the form of a "semen extender". This is a nutrient medium for the sperm, frequently containing an antibiotic. The nutrient will elongate the efficient life of the sperm, and the antibiotic, if added, should destroy any infective organisms present.

The need of artificial breeding is becoming an important factor for improvement of horses, both quantitatively and qualitatively. The artificial insemination in horses and its role in improvement of fertility is well recognized. AI in equines has been widely practiced in China, Russia and Eastern European countries. It is also in use in Japan, Germany, Poland, Holland, Scandinavia, America and Australia. The results from AI have been reported to be as high as 67 per cent to 70 per cent. Some workers have obtained conception rate (CR) to the extent of 60 percent by one single insemination done within one hour of collection of semen and stored at 30-35°C. Further, by three inseminations, the CR increased upto 92 per cent. Similarly, CR of 66.6 percent has been reported in mares inseminated with frozen semen within 12 hrs of estimated time of ovulation.

Lately, Thoroughbred Breeders Association has also advocated the introduction of AI with fresh or extended semen in thoroughbred breeding industry, to provide an effective means of national and international control of Contagious Equine Metritis and other infectious diseases. However, it stresses that AI in such animals would have to be under strict supervision of veterinary and stud farm authorities.

Stallions produce large volume of semen but it neither stores well nor is capable of being used for very many females. The sperms at the time of ejaculation are diluted to a great extent by the secretions from the accessory glands. Stallions of warm-blooded breeds in general, give a smaller ejaculate but it is of a higher sperm concentration than the voluminous ejaculate from draught stallions and jacks. The life of the sperm is limited by the sources of energy which it contains. Moreover, the contribution from accessory glands is rich in salts that interfere with sperm survivability by inducing more movements and causing exhaustion.

Semen Characteristics

It is a white, opalescent fluid. For practical purposes, the semen may be considered as consisting of two parts. The first ejaculate is watery in appearance and contains the main bulk of spermatozoa. It is much less in volume than the second portion. The second portion is thick, mucous secretion which comes from seminal vesicles and contains very few spermatozoa. Its main function is to carry spermatozoa into the uterus of mare.

The stallions expel a large number of sperms in each ejaculate and deplete the epididymal reserve quickly. As such, the collection should preferably be taken on alternate or third day. Fructose is present in negligible quantity in stallion semen, while ergothioneine and citric acid are present in relatively large amount. The phospholipids are much less than in bull semen which renders the stallion spermatozoa more sensitive to stress. The density of equine semen is low due to more vesicular secretions.

During a breeding season, the semen volume decreases gradually with the progress of time. After initial collection, it increases on 5th day, decreases again on following days, then increases from 12 to 16 days, followed by decreasing volume.

Constituents of Normal Semen

Volume per ejaculate	30 to 150 ml (40 - 320 ml)
Sperm Concentration (million/ml)	200 - 400 (30-800)
Total sperm/ejaculate	5 to 20 billion
Percentage motile sperm .	70 - 95 (Std. motility 80%)
Percentage morphologically normal sperm	70 - 90
pH	7.2 - 7.5 (7.0 - 7.8)
Viscosity	1.4 to 3.2 (Average 1.9)
Specific gravity	1.011 to 1.019

Animals either in too high a condition or in an unthrifty condition, produce inferior semen of low concentration and low viability. If stud animals are not used for a few weeks, the first discharge may contain large proportions of dead and stale sperms.

Semen Collection

The semen collection area should be spacious ,dust free, clean ,and free of distracting noises, animals, and people. One of the most important aspect of AI Programme is correct collection of semen. This involves proper scheduling and preparation of stallion, as well as the use of proper technique of semen collection. The collection can be done by the following 2 techniques in AI programme:

i) The Artificial Vagina

ii) Manual Manipulation

When young stallion is properly fed and managed, semen can be collected at the age of 24 months but to provide better quality, the semen should not be collected before the age of 30-36 months.

Live mounts such as teaser females or a castrated male are very good for routine semen collection. If some stallions can be trained to mount dummies, they will have extra advantage over other methods. The frequency should be 3 times a week.

The best known and widely used method for semen collection is with *artificial vagina* which stimulates natural conditions for evoking ejaculation. However, it requires skilled operator. During ejaculation, the end of the stallion's penis enlarges considerably, hence the AV for stallion is designed in such a way that one end of the cylinder is dilated. Accordingly, it is large and heavy to accommodate the stallion's erect, vascular, and muscular penis.

Prior to ejaculation, the penis should be washed with slightly warm soapy water and rinsed with clean water to remove smegma and other debris present on the surface of the penis. The dummy/mare should be hobbled for better restraint.

The Artificial Vagina for Stallion: It is made of one piece of rubber tubing 36 to 48 inches long and 7 to 8 inches in flat diameter. To provide for the water jacket, the rubber tubing is turned inside out, over a stiff rubber ring that forms the entrance. This ring is suitably made from an 18 inch long piece of rubber tube with ends jointed together by an inserted piece of wood. After the ring is manipulated into the proper position, it is fixed in place by cementing together the inner walls of the tube by two or three patches. A water inlet is provided by vulcanizing into the outer wall a stub of rubber hose that can be closed by a rubber stopper.

For the outflow of the ejaculate, a concentric hole of about 1.5" in diameter is cut into the outer and inner layer and the edges around the hole are cemented together. At the same time a stub of rubber hose is fitted into this hole to serve as the connector to the semen receptacle. Next, the edge of the outer and inner layer at the other end are cemented together so that the entire structure is a two walled tube, open at both ends. Two loops of rubber material are cemented to the outer wall, to serve as handles. The clamp for closing one end is simple, made from two strips of hard wood with two thumb screws. Russian, American and Japanese model of horse AVs are available and considered quite satisfactory for the purpose.

Before filling water in the jacket space, the clamp is put in place, later, the entire inside wall is covered with a sterilized non-spermicidal lubricant. A good lubricant can be made as follows:

60% cane sugar sol	100 parts
Refined starch	7 parts
Edible gelatin	3 parts
Glycerol	10 parts

It is mixed, heated and stirred up well. This is then diluted with equal amount of sterilized warm water just before use and is smeared on the inner surface of rubber tube.

AV is partially filled with water so as to give an internal temp of 54°C. About 1000 ml of water at 50°C-55°C is required to give correct tension. The air space connected to an expansion valve is provided to permit expansion of liner, when the penis engages the AV. The increase in pressure during thrusting stimulates the stallion to ejaculate. When pulsation at the base of the penis (characteristic of ejaculation) begins, the end of AV along with the attached collection bottle should be lowered sufficiently to allow the semen to flow into the collection vessel. Ejaculation is normally complete in 25 seconds.

A filter used to remove the gel of the semen is placed in the collection bottle and the tempered end of the inner liner is secured to the bottle neck by a clamp ring. An insulating bag is put over the collection bottle and secured to the distal end of the AV.

Type of AVs- There are several types of artificial vagina available commercially. Although there are differences, they all follow the same general design format of having a tubular inner liner, usually of latex, which is surrounded by a fillable water jacket encased in a harder outer shell. Attachable at the distal end is some form of collection apparatus to capture the ejaculated semen, this apparatus will often include a filter of some sort to remove the gel fraction of the ejaculate and any detritus such as smegma.

Each AV model has different advantages over another, and many technicians, and indeed stallions, develop a preference for one or another model. These are some of the commonest advantages to each model:

COLORADO STYLE

- Retains water temperature longer in cold weather
- Is more durable under extreme use
- Liner is cheaper to replace when worn or damaged
- If not too long, allows the stallion to ejaculate well clear of the heated liner, thereby avoiding danger of sperm damage by heat shock

MISSOURI

Manufactured by:
NASCO

- Is cheaper to purchase initially
- Is lighter and therefore easier to handle when filled with water
- Will allow for the addition of air to make the liner tighter
- Allows a less direct manual stimulation of the penis, which can be preferable with some stallions

FRENCH (INRA MODEL)
Manufactured by:
IMV International Corporation

- Extremely light weight - can be held with one hand
- Has 2 handles (second handle not visible) making it extremely easy to handle
- Holds marginally more water than the Missouri or Roanoke models, but not as much as the Colorado, making it lighter to handle, but maintaining good heat retention properties
- The removable/adjustable latex hood (seen at the right end of image) enables the use of a single AV for many different size stallions
- The latex hood also allows for the less direct manual stimulation of the glans of the penis during collection if required
- Liner is cheaper to replace when worn or damaged

ROANOKE
Manufactured by:
Roanoke AI Labs.

- Extremely light weight - can be held with one hand
- Allows for great bell pressure on penis glans, which is preferred by some stallions
- Shortness permits manual stimulation of the upper shaft of the penis at the sensitive pressure point located close to the preputial ring
- "Spit-off" pressure relief valve automatically adjusts water pressure to required level

---

Many farms and semen collection centres use a sterile liner in the artificial vagina. This liner is usually made of a thin plastic of some sort, and is especially useful if one is collecting semen from different stallions, as it pretty well eliminates any chance of cross-contamination of any kind, either bacterial or seminal. Even if not collecting multiple stallions, it is still extremely convenient, as it eliminates the need for removing and cleaning the latex AV liner after each use, and aside from the time savings, this will also assist in extending the length of time before the latex liner becomes worn out time of use, as this will prove a lot cheaper.

Semen Collection Using a Phantom Mare

The "phantom mare", or "breeding mount" is one of a simple design, and cheap to produce. It consists of three sections of power pole, two of which have been set into the ground for about three feet, one protruding about a foot further than the other. The third section of pole is secured over the top of the other two, with an overhang of about three feet at the lower end. This top section is then padded using something such as an old foam mattress, ensuring the end is well covered. The whole padded section is then covered with a durable non man-made material, such as canvas. The final height of the phantom should be considered during it's construction. Generally, the "rear" end (the lower end) should be slightly lower than the height of mare. Entire upper portion should be padded with atleast 4" of soft padding.

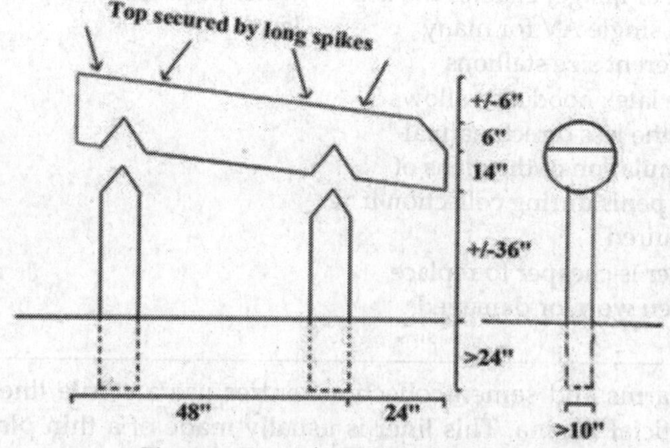

Fig. 9.1 : Power pole Breeding Phantom

Phantom Training to Stallion

Phantom training is not as hard as one might imagine it to be. It involves conditioned reflex response. The response is of course ejaculation. The condition the stallion must undergo to achieve that, is to mount the phantom mare (also known as a breeding dummy) and breed the AV.

Teaching to mount is achieved by the judicious use and placement of a mare in estrus. The stallion is first "teased", then the mare is placed in front of the phantom, slightly off to one side, usually the right, as it's commonest for the AV handler to work on the left. Initially, it is best to have the animals facing each other, however, if the stallion seems uninterested mare be turned should so that her rear faces him.

The stallion is led to the phantom mare, which should have had a little estrus mare's urine rubbed on the end nearest the stallion, and he should be encouraged to sniff this. Often, he will mount the phantom mare once he has sniffed the urine, but if he starts to lose interest, then the real mare is moved to regain his attention to the business at hand.

Usually, the stallion will mount after a little encouragement. At this point, his penis should be deflected into the AV, and he should be allowed to breed the AV. Stallions vary as to how much handling of the penis they will tolerate. Some one can be quite aggressive with, and really "work" the AV, others will not allow this, and will lose their erection, or dismount.

The AV handler can check to see if the stallion has ejaculated by feeling the base of the penis for pulsations at the time of the ejaculation. Visually, one can see if the tail is "flagged", and depending upon what collection method is used, in some cases one can see the semen filling the container attached to the AV.

It is important to note that although the phantom training process is not difficult, it is very essential to get the timing right, the degree of stimulation by the mare's proximity and the penis/ AV handling correct. Without all of these things coming together, there is a good chance the stallion will not ejaculate. If this occurs, then it is possible the exact opposite to that which is desired will happen, and the stallion will have learned that it is not desirable to mount the phantom. Some stallions will not mount a phantom, and/or ejaculate into an AV. Often these stallions are older stallions who have pasture bred or in-hand bred with minimum human intervention for many years.

Crump's Manual Semen Collection Method:-

Crump and Crump (1989) reported the use of a simpler procedure for collection of semen from stallions by manual stimulation of the penis while the stallion is standing and holding a disposable plastic bag over the end of the penis to catch the ejaculate. The manual pressure applied to the penis elicited pelvic thrusting and ejaculation, even before the stallion mounted the mare. This method may be an efficient alternative to traditional semen collection techniques using an artificial vagina and stimulus mare or dummy mount mare. Researchers who have tried the manual technique, suggest that both animals and handlers can be readily trained to use this method. Limited data suggests that semen samples obtained by manual stimulation are similar to those obtained using an artificial vagina.

Method: Once the stallion is washed, and an erection achieved, a plastic collection bag is secured around the penis by tape (don't secure the tape directly to the penis, and don't have the tape so tight as to interrupt circulation - the penis will become engorged just prior to and during ejaculation), and hot compresses are applied initially to the glans of the penis, once "thrusting" is seen, in the upper portion of the shaft. The thin compresses of (half-inch) man-made dishwashing "sponges" that are about 8 inches by 10 inches, are submersed in hot water (55 degrees Celsius), and squeezed out immediately before application. The first is held in the "flat" of the left hand, with the flat of the hand being applied against the end of the glans of the penis. The stallion should then drop his hindquarters slightly, and start a thrusting motion against the hand. Allow the hand to move with the thrusting, and at the same time use the other (right) hand to form a "U" of the thumb and index finger, with the other compress inside the "U", and gently apply pressure with this hand on each side of the penis shaft at the upper end. This pressure simulates the pressure applied naturally by the labia, whereas the left hand is simulating the pressure applied when pushing against the cranial portion of the vagina/cervix. No great amount of pressure is required, and in fact stallions will often resent excessive pressures.

After a short period of this stimulation (it varies with stallion, but considerably less than a minute would be "normal") the stallion will ejaculate, and the semen is collected in the bag. Not all stallions will respond to this method, but many will. Collections can be carried out on the ground, or on a breeding phantom. A good stallion handler is an important part of the team, especially the first few times this is done, as it is possible that the stallion unused to such handling may kick. For the same reason, suitable positioning of the collector is important.

Advantage: One of the advantages of this method is that it can be successfully used many more times in the course of a day than standard collection techniques, and can, therefore, be used to "clean out" a stallion, or establish a depleted value prior to checking TDSO (total daily sperm output), in a shorter time period.

Evaluation of Stallion's Semen

The evaluation of semen involves analysis of both sperm and seminal plasma. Phase contrast microscope with heated stage, an incubator/water bath, Semen Extenders, glassware and sperm counting device are required for evaluation of semen in a lab. There are a variety of commercially available counting devices to establish the concentration in millions per ml (*number* x 10^6/ml). some of which will also calculate the required volume to establish the correct insemination dose such as "micro reader" (*IMV International, minneapolis, MN*) and the "counterpoint sperm counter" (*Hamilton research inc., S. Hamilton, MA*). These devices all operate on the principal of a spectrophotometer, which is a machine that measures the light transference through some sort of medium. In fact, one can also use a spectrophotometer for this purpose. The "Spec 20" model of spectrophotometer is the standard which has to be calibrated for equine semen. Hemocytometer can also be used for same purpose but it is more time-consuming.

The process of evaluation should be rapid and effective. The semen should have a relatively uniform opaque appearance (indicating high sperm concentration). The sample should be free from dust, dirt, hair etc. As the stallion's semen contains gel, it should be well taken into account.

Good semen quality means the ejaculate which is with high population of spermatozoa, have normal parameter that together able to produce a normal rate of fertilization. A "good" sperm is one that is able to reach the site of fertilization and reach oocyte ,circumventing all the female barrier.

The sperms must have normal acrosome and plasma membrane, chromatin material that is able to form a normal pronucleus at decondensation, normal mitochondria to provide the sperm with ability to move, and a normal tail to provide the sperm with forward progressive motion. All these cell compartments must be in good working orders so that sperm is able to fertilize. And hence for proper evaluation, several parameter and cell components must be analyzed. The conventional as well as newer methods are available for the same which can be implemented by referral labs for detailed study.

Volume: Volume should be measured in the collecting bottle itself.

Motility: The percentage of progressively motile sperms should be estimated on a microscope stage incubator at 37-40°C for which a biotherm can also be used. Motility can be recorded easily in stallion's semen, as it contains more of seminal fluids. The rate of movements can be estimated microscopically on an arbitrary scale (fairly accurate). When the spermatozoa cease all the movements, there will be only the oscillatory motions. CASA(Computer Assisted Semen Analysis) system is commonly used in modern labs to evaluate sperm motility.

Live and Dead Sperms: The proportion of live cells to dead cells can be estimated by supravital staining with a stain mixture such as Nigrosine eosin. The dead cells stain red with eosin against the dark nigrosin background whereas the alive cells exclude the stain.

Concentration: Accurate determination of the number of sperms per millilitre of semen is extremely important. The semen volume and percentage of motile sperms give the number of motile sperms per ejaculate. The photoelectric colorimeter can be used for determining the density and the concentration, but the gel from the stallion's semen has to be filtered out.

Morphologic Evaluation: It is done by staining the semen smear slide with eosin nigrosin, aniline blue or Indian ink. The observation should be recorded for

(i) No. of normal sperms
(ii) Abnormal head or nucleus
(iii) Abnormal Acrosome
(iv) Abnormal neck
(v) Tailess head
(vi) Proximal droplet
(vii) Distal droplet
(viii) Abnormal midpiece
(ix) Abnormal tail - In Donkey's semen aboxial tail is considered as normal feature.
(x) Round spermatids (cell)

Preservation of Semen: For any work in artificial insemination, preservation has to be done and we require a special preservative for the horse semen. A good preservative should have the following properties:

(a) Should provide high nutrients as a source of energy.
(b) Should protect against the harmful effects of rapid cooling (for deep freeze only).
(c) Should provide a buffer to prevent harmful shifts in pH as a result of lactic acid formation.
(d) Should inhibit bacterial growth.
(e) Should increase the volume of pure semen.

Glucose is added as source of energy for spermatozoa. Egg yolk and milk can be used to protect against cold shock. Buffers like citrate, phosphate and TRIS etc. can be used to maintain a neutral pH and proper osmotic pressure. Penicillin, Strepromycin, Polymyxin B sulphate etc. are used to inhibit growth of micro-organisms in sperms. Glycerol is added to protect the sperm against the lethal effect of freezing.

It has been reported that sperm motility was significantly higher (40-58 per cent) at an osmotic pressure of 300-400 milli osmol/ kg than at other pressures (8-40 per cent).

The physiological function of the diluters is to counteract the effects of the semen constituents that impair sperm longevity. After they are deposited into the mare's uterus, spermatozoa suspended in the diluters are in a more favourable environment, than in the undiluted state, and live longer in this state, thus giving more chances for fertilization.

The following diluters are recommended for use by various workers :

(a) Egg yolk phosphate diluter:- To 100 ml of boiling distilled water, add 10 gm of chemically pure dextrose, 0.2 gm KH_2PO_4 (chemically pure) and 2.0 gm $Na_2HPO_4 \cdot 12H_2O$. Equal parts of this solution and fresh egg yolk are mixed together to make complete diluter.

(b) Milk based semen extender:

NFDMS	2.4 gm
Glucose	4.9 gm
Gentamycin sulfate	
(reagent grade)	150,000 units
8.4% NaHCO3	2 ml
Deionized water (sterile)	92 ml

(Mix liquids before adding NFDMS or gentamycin will curdle the milk).

(c) TRIS diluter for deep freezing the semen is prepared as follows :

Fructose	5.0 gm
Citric acid	6.8 gm
Hydroxymethylaminomethane	12.1 gm
Glycerol	32.0 ml
Distilled Water	368 ml

Before use, it is prepared in the ratio of 1:1:3 i.e. TRIS diluter I part, egg yolk I part and distilled water 3 parts.

(d) Lactose-EDTA-Egg yolk freezing extender

Lactose solution (11% w/v)	50 ml
Glucose-EDT A solution*	25 ml
Glycerol	5 ml
Equex STM	0.5 ml

*Composition of Glucose EDTA solution:-

Glucose	55.985 gm
Sodium citrate dehydrate	3.700 gm
Disodium-EDTA	3.699 gm
Sodium bicarbonate	1.200 gm
Polymyxin B sulfate	106 IV
pH	6.59
mOsm/kg	409

(To be diluted to 1000 ml with deionized water).

Commercially available Equine Semen Extenders

There are a variety of semen extenders available commercially, the majority of which are based on Dr. Bob Kenney's tried-and-true non-fat-dried-milk-solid **(NFDMS) "Kenney" formula**. The only variable in the majority of these is antibiotic which is added to it. It is always wise that when first time collecting the semen at start of the season, to split the ejaculate and store it in several different extenders (i.e. different antibiotics) to establish which seems to be most compatible with. There is usually a little variation, although sometimes it is negligible. The two antibiotics that favour the most are Amikacin Sulfate (**"EZ Mixin' CST" extender** from ARS is, as well as other commercially produced extenders), and Ticarcillin (in Canada this has now been replaced by "Timentin" which is a mixture of Ticarcillin and Clavulinic Acid). Using Polymixin B. Sulfate and Gentamycin in on-farm inseminations, seems to be more detrimental to longevity than others.

Another extender available since 2003 is - **INRA '96** (***IMV International, Minneapolis, MN***). This aerobic extender has some unique properties in that it can be successfully used at and up to 15° C with some stallions; at low extension ratios (as low as 1:1 semen : extender); and there is no need to remove all the air from the shipment.

Essentially, for the beginner, it is best to go with one of the many commercially available semen extenders, rather than attempting to mix your own.

Frozen Semen Technique

As long as semen is properly maintained in a liquid nitrogen storage tank, the viability is believed to be nearly unlimited (10,000 years has been suggested). Pregnancies have resulted from using semen that has been stored for ten to fifteen years. However, pregnancies have not been achieved with semen that has been re-frozen once thawed.

Advantage of Frozen semen include:

- There is no requirement to schedule shipments of semen to fit the mare's ovulation time;
- The market for semen is global, as there is little limitation on duration of delivery time;
- There is no requirement for the stallion to be taken out of competition for breeding, or to have his competitive attitude possibly disrupted by being bred;
- There is an "insurance factor" in case the stallion should become ill, die, or be unable for some other reason to fulfill

live covering/cooled semen breeding commitments;

- As the processing of frozen semen usually requires the involvement of a business that specializes in that processing, there tends to be better control over quality than is sometimes seen with cooled semen.

Disadvantages include:

- All stallions nay not have quality semen that will freeze;
- Mares require more intense estrus monitoring as frozen semen requires insemination within the 12 hours prior to or 6 hours following ovulation;
- Conception rates for artificial insemination with frozen equine semen are on average a little lower than those seen with fresh or cooled semen;
- To freeze semen is not initially as cheap as to prepare cooled semen, although in the long run it can be economical.

Stallion variability

Roughly 30% of stallions have semen that will be highly fertile post-thaw; 40% "average"; and 30% sub-fertile. In other words, 70% of stallions have semen that is capable of achieving pregnancies once frozen and thawed. The process must, however, be carried out, and pregnancies achieved, in order to know what percentage group any individual stallion falls into. Research is being continually carried out to attempt to overcome these problems, and as the use of frozen semen becomes more popular so the faster results will be achieved

The Freezing Process

Overview

A brief overview of the freezing process reveals that sperm are separated from the seminal plasma; a freezing extender is added at a certain concentration; the re-extended semen is packed into "straws" at a known sperm concentration; the straws are frozen using liquid nitrogen, and are then submerged and kept stored in the liquid nitrogen until they are needed for use. Semen is reputed to be viable for 10,000 years once frozen, but realistically pregnancies have been achieved with sperm that have been stored for 10 to 12 years.

Straw Size

Semen is collected from the stallion in the same manner as is normal for fresh or cooled use, usually using an AV, although other methods may also be used. Once collected, a basic semen analysis is performed identifying features as sperm concentration per/ ml,

total gel-free volume; total numbers of sperm present; and progressive motility. These figures are then used to establish the numbers of straws that may be frozen from that ejaculate. Different protocols call for different numbers of sperm per straw, depending upon both the straw size and the particular protocol being used. "Straws" are short tubes commonly made of PVC. The two sizes of straw most common are the half-millilitre (which is also seen in the cattle industry) and the "macro" straw which contains either four or five-millilitres. There are varied opinions as to which size straw yields the best results

Centrifugation

Once the concentrations are established, a centrifugation extender is added to the rest of the semen to afford it a degree of protection and it is centrifuged to remove the majority of the seminal plasma.

The seminal plasma is detrimental to sperm's livability over an extended period of time. Some horses' seminal plasma seems to be more of a problem than others, and it is hypothesized that this is one part of the reason for variability of success rates seen from stallion to stallion. A larger volume centrifuge is used, usually holding several 50-ml vials, and the semen is spun at a moderately high speed, usually producing G-forces in the region of 300 to 800 G. A soft pellet of sperm is desired, and once that has been produced, the seminal plasma is removed. Some protocols call for the removal of all the seminal plasma, and some for all but up to 10%.

Packaging Concentrations

The calculation of the total numbers of sperm in the ejaculate would provide the means to establish the correct number of straws to be frozen from the ejaculate. The half-ml straws are typically frozen at the rate of 400 million sperm per ml, and the "macro" straws are commonly packed to hold a total of 600 million sperm per straw. This would mean for example that an ejaculate containing a total number of 12 billion sperm would be capable of producing 60 half-ml straws, or 20 of five ml each straws. Ejaculates with a progressive motility pre-freezing of 50% or lower would not usually be considered worthwhile freezing, except under exceptional circumstances. Ideally, one would see ejaculates with progressive motilitiy in the 70-80% range pre-freezing being presented. The number of progressively motile sperm post-thaw will be evaluated, and it is this figure that will determine the numbers of straws needed for an individual insemination.

The actual number of straws capable of being frozen from a single ejaculate is entirely stallion-dependent, as the individual stallion will produce different numbers of sperm from ejaculate to ejaculate, and at different times of the year.

Freezing extenders

Once the number of straws to be frozen is established, it is easy to determine the amount of freezing extender that is required by subtracting the volume of the sperm pellets remaining after centrifugation from the total volume of re-extended semen required for the straws to be frozen.

Semen extenders are variable in actual ingredients, but all contain ingredients that serve a common purpose. There will be a nutrient, a buffer, a cryopreservant agent and antibiotic. A typical nutrient seen is a sugar, such as glucose or sucrose, which serves to provide energy source for the sperm. Buffers are added to balance pH and osmolarity of the solution, and the sugars also serve this purpose. The cryopreservant most commonly seen is glycerol, although others such as DMSO have also been used with varying success. The cryopreservant assists in stabilizing the cell (sperm) during the freezing and thawing process to prevent damage to cell orgenells.

The cryopreservant actually causes the removal including slight replacement of the water found within the cell, so that there is not the same expansion factor upon freezing, and the cell membrane does not rupture. Egg yolk, which is a common ingredient in a wide variety of frozen semen extenders, has nutrient value for the sperm during the freezing and thawing process; acts to some extent as a buffer; and also most importantly "coats" the sperm cell, and thereby prevents changes to and losses of some of the lipoproteins present in the cell membrane that can occur during the freezing and thawing processes. Various antibiotics are added to control bacterial content that may be present in the raw semen. It should be noted that the antibiotics will only protect against bacteria and not viruses, for which being frozen in liquid nitrogen is an ideal storage medium. For this reason it is desirable that stallions, whose semen is to be frozen, be tested EVA (equine viral arteritis) negative prior to collection.

Straw packing

Once the correct amount of extended semen is packed into the straws, an air bubble is introduced, and they are sealed. The air bubble prevent the "freezing glass jar" effect as it permits the expansion of the semen during freezing and prevents the rupture of the straw, or the "blowing" of the sealant at either end.

The half ml straws usually contain a "wick and powder" sealant at one end, which upon coming into contact with moisture (the semen) becomes solidified, and seals the top end (the "open" end of the straw is immersed into the semen and suction is applied, sucking the semen into the straw until the sealant at the top end prevents further suction by becoming solid). The bottom end of the straw is then sealed by using either polyvinyl alcohol powder (which is then dipped into water, and solidifies), or by inserting a small steel ball. The macro straws use steel or glass balls, and must have one end sealed prior to being filled. The semen is introduced into the macro straw by a pipettor that dispenses a pre-established amount. The open end is then sealed with another ball - often a glass one which are available in variety of colours which later aids in identification.

Straw Labelling

It is important that all the straws carry a variety of information written on the outside. The stallions name, registration number and breed; the date the freeze was performed; and the type of the extender used should be considered a minimum. Other information that may be considered suitable for inclusion would be the freezing location and company and the antibiotic used in the extender. This information is essential for identification of the straws prior to insemination, and should never be omitted.

Cooling and Freezing

Some protocols call for a slow cooling period for the packed straws, from room temperature to approximately 5° Celsius over the course of a couple of hours prior to the straws being exposed to the liquid nitrogen for the final freeze. If that is required, it is carried out in an especially programmed slow cooling machine. For the actual freezing process, two methods are commonly seen. A programmable freezer, and freezing in liquid nitrogen vapour.

The programmable freezing unit may also be capable of performing the slow cooling to 5° Celsius, and carries out the freezing process automatically once the straws are packed (some of the more expensive versions will even pack the straws).

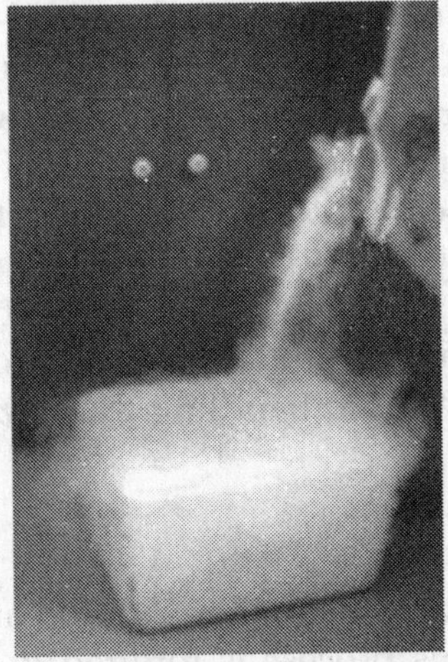

Fig 9.2 : Pouring Liq.N2 in freezing box

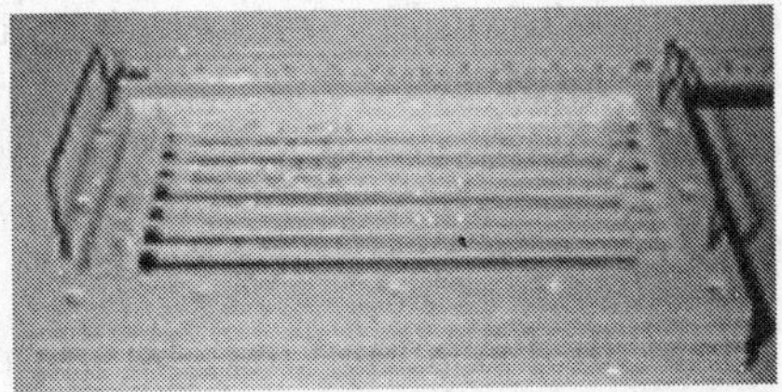

Fig 9.3 : Macrostraw in Freezing Rack

With the nitrogen vapour freeze technique, the straws are placed onto a freezing rack and lowered into a Styrofoam box (such as a picnic cooler) that contains at least 3 inches of liquid nitrogen. The freezing rack is designed to support the straws one inch above the liquid nitrogen, at which point the temperature is minus 160° Celsius. After being held in that position for 10 - 15 minutes, the straws are plunged into the liquid nitrogen (the temperature of which is minus 196° Celsius). There are variety of freezing racks available, but best are the floating racks, as this will result in an even freeze. Fixed racks are dependent upon the surface supporting the freezing box being leveled. If that surface is uneven as one end of the straw will be closer to the nitrogen than the other, it will result in both the air bubble within the straw floating to one end, and an uneven overall freeze, both occurrences of which are highly undesirable.

Transfer and Storage

Once the straws are frozen and have been submerged in the liquid nitrogen for 10 minutes, they are transferred to a liquid nitrogen storage tank, which is essentially an over size thermos container that holds liquid nitrogen. The half-ml straws must be first placed in a "goblet", (which is pre-cooled in liquid nitrogen), and they in turn are placed in a "cane", which is stored in a "canister" within the tank. Failure to place half-ml straws in such a storage apparatus within the tank will cause them to be exceedingly difficult to retrieve for use, as they will float out of the canisters and then be loose in the tank. The macro straws can be placed directly into the canisters for storage. There is only approximately four seconds available for transfer before thaw damage to the sperm occurs as a result of exposure to higher temperatures than the liquid nitrogen. From this it can be seen that care and respect in handling the frozen product is essential.

Transport of Stallion's Semen

The stallion's semen may be shipped to the mares' location and the mare bred by A.I. methods. This process is reffered to as "transported semen"(TS) or "shipped semen". This situation may be desirable if the mare lives a long way from the stallion, and semen does not ship well, or if she has a foal at foot, and the owner does not want to risk shipping them both. Other situations there may be several mares to be bred on one day.

The "Equitainer" (*Hamilton Research Inc.*) is one of the superior container for equine semen transport". It is most expensive initially, but durable. The Equitainer is reliable as far as insulation properties against heat or cold is concerned, and it's tough plastic shell is immensely durable and will handle the rough handling of courier companies and airline baggage handler. There are several "disposable" containers available for use with transported semen as well, such as the "Clipper" and "Equine Express II". These are constructed using a cardboard box with a Styrofoam type insulation.

Fig. 9.14 : Euitainer for Equine Semen Transport

England and Keane (1996) indicated that sperm exposure to x-rays does *not* reduce fertility. Therefore, semen transhipment and its X ray screening is safe. Frozen semen's longevity of fertility has been evaluated using x-ray exposure techniques which proved that x-rays do not reduce fertility.

Thawing of frozen semen

Transfer of the straw from the storage tank to the water bath for thawing must be facilitated as rapidly as possible. Thawing of the semen within the straw starts to take place at room temperature after only four seconds, and as a "rapid thaw" is critical to obtaining minimum damage to the sperm during the thawing process, damage will occur if the thaw takes place at room temperature. The name of the stallion should be checked prior to it's being thawed. The two sizes of straws require different thawing temperatures and times. The half-ml straws are typically thawed in a 37° Celsius water bath for 30 seconds. There is another protocol for the half-ml straw which is recognized as producing marginally better results, but it calls for 70° Celsius water for only seven seconds, followed by 35° water for at least 5 seconds, and timing is so critical that an error of only a couple of seconds or degrees can make a significant difference.

There are a variety of times and temperatures recommended for the thawing of the "macro" straw, ranging from 40 to 52 seconds, and 45° to 52° Celsius temperature water.

While minimum delay is essential from thaw time to insemination, it is recommended that a small sample of thawed semen from each straw be warmed and evaluated prior to its use. The insemination process when using thawed-frozen semen is no different from that performed for fresh or cooled semen.

Insemination

Insemination of semen in mares requires special attention. The semen cannot be deposited into the sperm life preserving area of the cervix because the cervix is not automatically equipped to serve as a holding space for the semen. It is deposited in the uterus, where the environment is not favourable for prolongation of life span of the sperm.

***Procedure for Insemination*:** Unlike artificial insemination in cattle, which involves guiding the insemination pipette through the cervix via manipulation per rectum, equine AI is carried out completely vaginally. The equine rectum is not as durable as a bovines', and it is for this reason that rectal palpation by the lay person is not encouraged by most veterinarians and teaching facilities. Insemination per vagina does mean that probably the most important part of the process is the preparation, during which the perineal area is cleansed as for surgery, most commonly using an iodine preparation such as "Betadine".To protect the inseminator from possible kicking, the mare has to be restrained by hobbles. She may be, preferably, put in a breeding chute. The area around the vulva should be scrubbed before insemination to minimize contamination. The arm, slightly lubricated, is passed into the vagina and the index finger inserted into the cervix. The inseminating catheter is then easily guided into the uterus (about 10 inches) and 20 to 50 ml of raw or extended semen is deposited. About 500-600 million motile sperms should be inseminated to get good results. More attention is to be paid to avoid shock caused to the semen by exposure to light or temperature change. Plastics have been used for inseminating equipments. The inseminating equipment consists of a wide mouthed glass bottle graduated to show 20 ml amount. The bottle is fitted with a rubber stopper having two holes. Through one hole passes a long tube reaching to the bottom of the bottle. The projecting end of this tube is connected by rubber tubing to a glass tube containing a cotton wool plug, which filters bacteria from the air passing through it. With a view to achieve best results, following precautions should be taken :-

(a) The apparatus is cleaned and sterilized by boiling for 10 minutes. Semen diluting fluid is used to rinse the apparatus and the semen already diluted for insemination is introduced into the bottle;

(b) The catheter is introduced by hand into the cervix and into the uterus (about 10 inches). The cervix is clamped off with the finger and the semen is now pumped into the uterus by the rubber bulbs;

(c) Only semen containing sperms with vigorous motility predominantly (not just with slow, weak or oscillating movement), should be used for insemination. When checking for motility of stored semen, the particular sample has to be warmed to a temperature to resuscitate the dormant sperms, particularly when the stiffening gelatin containing diluents are used;

(d) Before insemination, it is advisable to insert the hand into the vagina and to scoop out the accumulated mucus and urine etc. This is specially important in aged mares in which the position of pelvis has changed so that the floor of vagina is lower than that of vulva;

(e) Care should be taken when introducing the hand that no air flows take place into vagina, since stable air is always filled with bacteria and dust;

(f) Proper thawing of semen should be done before insemination as it has been reported that thawing of semen at 20°-25°C gives best results.

Optimum semen dose for successful pregnancy

If the mare is going to ovulate within the next 24 hours, and if the progressive motility of a single insemination dose yields more than 100 million progressively motile sperms, then insemination by just a single dose is optimum. The greater the volume of the insemination dose, the greater the possibility that a mare with a delayed uterine clearance problem may be incapable of clearing it - more commonly older or multiparous mares. A single insemination dose is calculated to be 1 billion sperms which will provide between 100 and 500 million progressively motile sperm at the time of insemination. As research has shown that inseminating greater numbers of sperm does not increase pregnancy rates, as such, if the mare is not likely to ovulate within 24 hours, then second insemination should not be performed until at least 24 hours after the first in order to avoid placement of sperm into a still-inflamed uterus.

Alghmdi and coworkers (2004) have suggested that sperm that are stored in extender rather than seminal plasma have an increased binding tendency to the inflammatory cells, therefore lowering pregnancy rates substantially. Extended semen does usually contain seminal plasma, but it may be diluted, so this effect, although not as pronounced as with all of the seminal plasma removed may still be apparent. It is important to note that the post-breeding inflammatory response is a perfectly natural occurrence, and indeed is essential for the successful establishment of pregnancy under normal circumstances. However - usually older or multiparous mares, at times, are unable to clear this fluid, and the result is an inhospitable environment in the uterus for the conceptus. Consequently the pregnancy is lost shortly after descent of the conceptus into the uterus about 5.5 days after fertilization. This problem can be very easily, cheaply and successfully managed with the use of oxytocin.

Fig. 9.5 : Liquid nitrogen Tank for semen storage

Usefulness of A.I. in Equines

Salient advantages of AI in equines are enumerated below:

(a) It reduces covering load on a Stallion, thus saving enormous stallion power. Normally, a stallion can cover only 40-50 mares per season but when AI is practiced, its genetic potential can be made available to many more mares;

(b) Mares suffering from or prone to chronic endometritis do have a chance to get impregnated;

(c) Semen can be transported to remote places and mares can be inseminated at required time on chosen site. Further, movement of mares from one stud to another can be avoided which in turn helps in prevention and control of various diseases;

(d) Synchronisation of oestrus is feasible and batch mating can be made possible;

(e) Mares with certain physical deformities can also reproduce;

(f) More than one mare can be covered with the same germ plasm in one day;

(g) A valuable stallion, even suffering with impediments to its efficiency, can be successfully used in the breeding programme;

(h) AI in horses can be used as an adjunct to the natural breeding;

(i) It can make possible to equalize the productivity between various proven stallions.

Short comings of AI

Artificial Insemination does not have any known adverse effect on the management practices, health and reproduction of equines. However, AI has been used to produce vast number of half sibs in the cattle industry, that too sometimes with accompanying genetic problems. This prospect also scares many in horse industry causing them to take a position against this concept of breeding. Further, if not properly controlled, AI obviously allows an opportunity for dishonesty and chicanery by manipulation of vials of semen which causes concern to breed registration authorities. In addition, there is a likelihood of predisposition to inherited defects and spread of low fecundity.

Factors Affecting wide scale implementations of AI in Equines

Several factors militate against the successful use of AI in horses. Amongst these are, large size of AV, ejaculation time longer, low fertility under small scale stud condition, the delicate nature of spermatozoa, poor transportability, poor low temperature storage and probable chances of introduction of infection etc. besides doubts about parentage by registration authorities. These factors should be taken into consideration while adopting artificial insemination in a stud farm.

References

1. Jim Crump, Jr. and Julia Crump (1989). Stallion Ejaculation Induced by Manual Stimulation of the Penis. The Journal of Theriogenology, Vol 31, Iss 2, pp 341-346
2. Alghamdi A. S., Foster D. N. and Troedsson M. H. T; (2004) Equine seminal plasma reduces sperm binding to polymorphonuclear neutrophils (PMNs) and improves the fertility of fresh semen inseminated into inflamed uteri. Reproduction 127 : 593-600.
3. Squires E.L., Brubaker J.K., McCue P.M. and Pickett B.W. (1999) Effect of sperm number and frequency of insemination on fertility of mares inseminated with cooled semen. Theriogenology 49: (4) 743-749
4. G.C.W. England and M. Keane (1996) The effect of X-radiation upon the quality and fertility of stallion semen Theriogenology, Vol. 46 (1)
5. JosMottershead, Frozen semen preparation and use Part1; published in "Canadian Morgan" Magazine, Nov/Dec 2000 issue.

Chapter **10**

Embryo Transfer Technology

Embryo transfer, in general, may be defined as collection of fertilized egg from the donor female and its transfer to the uterus of recipient females which act as its foster mother. The donor is an elite animal of high genetic value, while the recipient is any female with normal genitalia and reproductive functions.

In equines, embryo transfer was reported for the first time in 1972 by Japanese workers (Oguri and Tsutsumi). However, it has been met with reserve and scepticism by the owners and breed registries who consider this technique merely to procure pregnancies from old or problematic mares. In the late 1980's, a technique for cooling equine embryos was identified which led to the development of a practical method of short-term (24 hours) storage and transportation of equine embryos. That breakthrough allowed embryos to be collected in the "field" and then shipped to a centralized facility for transfer to suitable recipient mares. The ability to transport cooled embryos provided veterinarians with the opportunity to offer embryo transfer service without the onerous task of maintaining recipient mares, and eliminated the need to ship donor mares to a centralized facility. Presently, embryo transfer is the most widely used, assisted-reproductive technique for the mares.

The equines are seasonal breeders, having a well defined physiological breeding season. Further, the reproductive efficiency in horses is low as compared to that of other domestic animals, which may be due to hormonal dysfunction, genital infection, inadequate management and improper detection of heat etc. In the present scenario, the embryo transfer may be of great value in increasing the productivity of equines.

Various steps involved in embryo transfer are explained as follows:

Selection of Donor Mares

Selection of donor depends upon breeding history, breed society regulations, registration, age of the donor, cost of the mare and the foal etc. The ideal donor should be a proven brood mare having normal state of reproductive organs without any infection. Certain proven brood mares which are unable to carry the foetus till full term, due to physical constraints, and even habitual aborters, can also serve as donors. However, mares having residual infection which repeatedly return to oestrus, are considered to be a poor choice for donors.

Breeding management of the donor involves teasing to monitor reproductive behaviour, and the use of transrectal palpation and ultrasonography to monitor ovarian follicular activity during the estrous cycle. When in heat, the donor is examined daily to monitor follicular growth, which allows optimal timing of insemination with fresh, cooled or frozen semen. Ovulation is routinely "timed" using human chorionic gonadotropin (HCG; 5 IU/kg IV or IM) or the gonadotropin releasing hormone (GnRH) agonist Deslorelin acetate (Ovuplant 2.2 mg pellet SQ). The day ovulation is detected, is designated as Day 0. Currently, there is no practical and efficacious method of superovulating mares, which severely limits the efficiency of embryo transfer

Selection of Recipients

Recipient mare should have a proven record of producing live foals having normal genitalia. Size of the recipient mares is not a limiting factor for embryo transfer from a large donor. However, the size of the recipient may influence the final size of its off-spring achieved by the embryo transfer. The optimum age of recipient mares is 3 to 10 years. Synchronizing estrus between donor and recipient mares can be accomplished with routine protocols using prostaglandin F2 alpha (PGF2a) alone or in combination with exogenous progesterone. When in heat, recipients are examined daily with transrectal palpation and ultrasonography to monitor follicular growth and detect ovulation. The "window" of synchrony between ovulation in recipient and donor mares is +1 to -3 days (i.e., the recipient mare can ovulate one day before to three days after the donor mare). In an effort to eliminate the need for synchronizing recipient and donor mares, progestin-treated, ovariectomized mares have been used as embryo recipients, however, the success with their use has been variable, and has not been widely adopted.

Preparation of Animals

Mares are required to be aseptically prepared for Artificial Insemination, embryo collection and transfer, in order to avoid contamination and maintain maximum possible microbe free conditions. Mare's rectum is evacuated and the tail is bandaged. Buttocks and perineal region is washed with mild soap and water, then rinsed with 5 to 10 percent 'tamed' iodine solution and dried.

Synchronization of Recipients and Donors

Before transfer of an embryo, it is ensured that the 'recipient' is in the same reproductive stage as the 'donor'. The synchrony between the donor and the recipient is achieved with the help of prostaglandins and is considered to be a major factor in the success of embryo transfer.

Recipient and donor mares showing oestrus, at the same time, are palpated daily to determine the approximate day of ovulation. Once the follicle size is more than 25 mm, the donor mare is inseminated or covered on alternate days till the ovulation is confirmed by rectal palpation.

Selection of recipient is dependent on her ovulation, preferably occurring within 48 hrs to that of donor. Alternatively, 2000 IV of HCG can be used intravenously on either recipient or the donor, in order to improve the synchronization of ovulation.

Various workers have adopted different schedule of hormonal therapy for induction of oestrus and ovulation successfully.

Some of the methods successfully used for synchronization are as follows:

(a) Oestrus synchronization has been effected by prostaglandin ($PGF_2\alpha$) 100 to 600 mg when injected on two consecutive days for synchronization of oestrus beginning or after fourth day of dioestrus. The mares returned to oestrus within 4 days of the first injection of prostaglandin and ovulated at an interval of 7 to 12 days.

(b) Oestrus and ovulation has been synchronized when a single injection of 1.25 mg of prostaglandin was given on days 7, 10 or 13 after ovulation.

(c) Synchronization of ovarian cycle in the mare may also be achieved with a double sequential course treatment with $PGF_2\alpha$ and HCG when given in the order of prostaglandin on day 0, HCG on day 6, PG on day 14 and HCG on day 20.

(d) Synchronization of oestrus in mares is also practical by daily i/m injection of 150 mg of progesterone and 10 mg oestradiol for 10 days. In addition, 10 to 15 mg of prostagladin ($PGF_2\alpha$) is given on day 10. Ovulation of recipient mares was synchronized to occur 2 days after the donor's ovulation. 3000 IU of HCG has also been used for hastening the ovulation.

(e) The donors and recipients have been successfully synchronized by use of prostaglandins from selected mares between the 5th and the 13th day of dioestrus to induce luteolysis and combined either injection of Gluprostenol and HCG 3000 IU on day 7 to hasten the ovulation. Recipients were given 250 mg gluprostenol on day 14 and day 0 and HCG on day -8 and +7.

Hormonal synchronization is only successful in mares showing regular cyclical activity. Once regular activity is achieved/recorded, prostaglandin is the major means of synchronization. The response to prostaglandins is dependent on the presence of fully formed corpus luteum. Mares without corpus luteum or that have ovulated within the previous 5 days should not be considered for prostaglandin treatment. Recipient mares should receive prostaglandin one day after the treatment of the donor. Ovulation is determined by daily rectal palpation of the ovary for either insemination, covering or embryo transfer. It is advisable to observe atleast two consecutive oestrous cycles of mare before any embryo transfer programme is taken up.

Recovery Media Used for Embryo Collection

Modified Dulbecoo's phosphate buffer saline has been used as a recovery media which is supplemented with 100 mg crystalline penicillin and 10 ml (to prepare 1 percent) heat inactivated foetal calf serum for every litre of Phosphate Buffer Saline (PBS) just prior to collection. Heat inactivation of the complement which is embryo toxic is carried out by heating the serum to 56°C for 30 minutes. The recovery medium is kept in a water bath at 35°c.

Culture Media

Culture media for the embryo is prepared by pipetting 8 ml of PBS after addition of antibiotic into a sterile plastic tube. 2 ml of inactivated foetal calf serum is added to prepare a 20 per cent serum solution. The solution is sterilized by passage through a Millipore filter of pore size 0.22µ.

Day of Embryo Recovery

Equine embryos are selectively transported through the oviduct into the uterus on Day 5-1/2 to 6 post-ovulation at which time they are at the compact morula (Fig10. 1) to early blastocyst (Fig10. 2) stage of development. After entering the uterine lumen, the size of the embryo increases dramatically as it develops into an expanded blastocyst (Fig10. 3). Although, embryos can be recovered on Days 6 to 9 the optimal time of embryo collection is Day 7 or 8. The primary indication for recovering embryos on Day 6 is for freezing embryos. Embryos are not routinely collected on Day 9, because their transfer success rate is generally lower than Day 7 or 8 embryos.

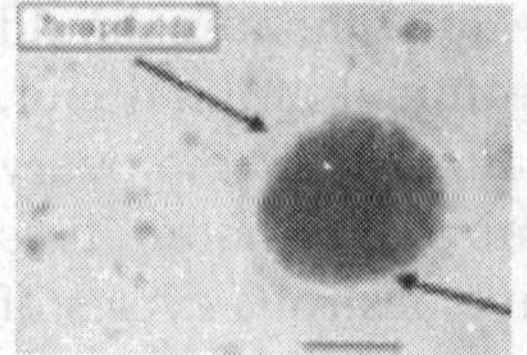

Fig 10.1

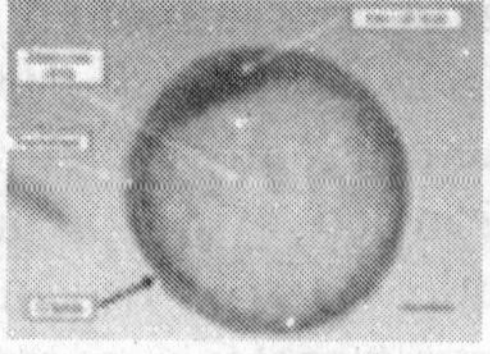

Fig 10.2

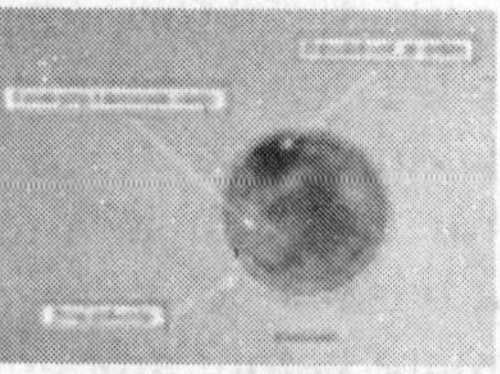

Fig 10.3

Two techniques of embryo recovery have been practiced:

(a) Surgical: Surgical method is of a more academic interest as it is expensive, time consuming and not without risk to the life of the mare. The mare is placed under general anaesthesia and incision is made in the ventral midline just anterior to the udder. The uterus is exposed, a pipette is inserted into one of the horns and flushing liquid is instilled into the body of the uterus. The uterus is gently massaged and the liquid is retrieved through the pipette. The process is repeated till embryo is recovered.

(b) Non Surgical: Embryo collection is performed using transcervical uterine lavage. This is preferred and is the popular method of embryo recovery. The mare is placed in stock and the external genitalia is cleaned as indicated in preparation of animals. The operator inserts a modified 2 way Foley's catheter (size 26 to 30) in the cervix (5 cms into the uterus) through vagina. The passage of the catheter may be enhanced by use of pre sterilized stainless steel stillette as a guide which can be withdrawn after the catheter is inserted. The catheter cuff is inflated and the catheter is then drawn back against the anterior end of the cervix so as to close the cervical passage. The recovery media is passed into uterus by gravity, the quantity of recovery media used, varies from 500-1000 ml. Uniform distribution of the recovery media in both horns is confirmed by rectal palpation. If only one horn is distended with the recovery media, the other horn is elevated per rectum for uniform distribution. Once the operator is satisfied as to the distribution and quantity of the media in both horns, the inflow tap is closed and the outflow is opened so as to collect the media in heat sterilized 100 ml glass cylindrical jars. The end of the outflow tube is kept in contact with the side of the jar just above the raising media level, to avoid fluid turbulence.

The contents of the jar is examined for the presence of an embryo. The process is repeated if no embryo is present. At least 95 per cent fluid is recovered and should be clear, free from blood and cellular debris. 20 IU oxytocin i/v can be given to flush out all the fluid. After the final flush, the cuff of the catheter is deflated and catheter is withdrawn. The fluid in the catheter is also checked for the presence of embryo, if it is already not detected in the cylindrical jars.

Identification of the Embryos

Recovery media after flushing is allowed to settle for 30 minutes before an attempt is made to locate the embryos. Since the embryos are denser than the media, they settle down to the bottom of the collecting jar. The top level of the fluid above 100 ml from the bottom is siphoned out and the remaining fluid is examined for embryo.

The remaining fluid at the bottom of the jar is poured into the grid marked search dishes and examined for the embryos. Detection of the embryo is best carried out at 15 x magnification under the stereo dissection microscope. Day 8 and 9 embryos can be seen with the naked eye but the embryos earlier than this period need the help of microscope. Once the embryo is located, it is moved, using a pipette, into a fresh culture media. It is rinsed 3 times in culture media dishes to dilute any possible contamination during recovery.

Preservation of Embryos

Once embryos are placed into the holding medium, they should either be expeditiously processed and packaged for transport or transferred into an appropriate recipient mare, since embryo viability decreases after storage in DPBS for more than 3 hours.

While awaiting packaging for transport or immediate transfer to a recipient, equine embryos appear to be quite tolerant of temperatures between room temperature (25°C) and body temperature (37ºC). However, efforts should be made to prevent rapid or extreme changes in temperature.

Packaging Embryos for Transport

Equine embryos are cooled and transported using methods developed by Carnevale *et al.*, which utilize Ham's F-10 nutrient mixture as the holding/cooling medium. Prior to use, Ham's F-10 medium must be buffered by diffusing a mixture of 90% N2, 5% O2, and 5% CO2 gas through the medium for three to five minutes, after which it is supplemented with 10% (v/v) fetal or newborn calf serum, penicillin (100 units/ml), and streptomycin (100 ug/ml). Because Ham's F-10 medium must be "gassed" prior to use with the help of an appropriate compressed gas cylinder and regulator. To package an embryo, Ham's F-10 medium is filter-sterilized into a 5 ml "snap-cap" tube, leaving a small air gap at the top of the tube. The embryo is then carefully transferred into the medium and the cap is securely snapped onto the tube. The tube is than wrapped with parafilm. A 50-ml centrifuge tube is then filled with F-10 medium (un-filtered), and the 5-ml tube containing the embryo is placed into the 50-ml centrifuge tube .The cap of the 50-ml centrifuge tube is closed eliminating as much air as possible, and it is wrapped with parafilm. The packaged embryo is then placed into an equitainer,which passively cools the embryo to 5ºC. Under these conditions, embryos can remain viable for at least 24 hours, during which time they can be transported via commercial airline or priority overnight delivery to the embryo transfer facility.

Embryo Recovery Rate

The recovery rate of embryos has been found to vary from 39 per cent to 90 percent. In barren mares, a recovery rate of 34 per cent has been reported. Further, no adverse effect has been observed on the oestrous cycle of the donor mares with repeated collection.

Embryo recovery rate is reported to be low from infertile mares whereas subfertile mares showing endometrial changes also affected the embryo recovery rate. Similarly, the recovery rate of embryos was low (35.3 per cent) in mares having endometritis as compared to the healthy mares (53.1 per cent).

Factors Affecting the Embryo Recovery Rate

Several factors have been identified that affect the embryo recovery rate such as reproductive state of the donor, barren mares, detection of ovulation and day of collection. Recovery rate is not influenced if collected on day 8 or 9 (0 is the day of ovulation) as compared to the embryo collected on day 6. The low recovery rate of embryos collected on day 6 may be due to the error on the part of technician to identify the small embryo or that the embryo is too young to arrive at the uterus since the exact time of ovulation is not possible to predict.

In aged mares, endometrial pathology and prolonged previous infertility causes reduction in embryo recovery. Embryo collection from maiden mares produced more embryos during the middle of the breeding season indicating that the follicles observed early in the season are non productive.

Method of Embryo Transfer

The embryo collected from the donor is locked with the culture media in between the air and media in the pipette or the straw before transfer. Frozen embryos are thawed and loaded in the insemination pipette similar to the freshly collected embryos. Embryo transfer can be carried out in two ways.

Surgical: Successful embryo transfer has been carried out by ventral midline or standing flank laprotomy using appropriate sedation/tranquilization in conjunction with local anesthesia. A small incision is made on the horn to facilitate the entry of transfer pipette. The embryo with the culture media is inserted into the lumen and the incision on the uterus is closed by compressing with a haemostat. Abdominal incision is closed layer by layer as done for any abdominal surgery. Although surgical technique of embryo transfer is successful, it is time consuming, expensive and not without risk to the life of the mare.

Non Surgical: Non surgical transfer has proved to produce more satisfactory results. The percentage of success achieved is similar to the surgical transfer and does not need the use of general anaesthesia. Non-surgical embryo transfer has generally been performed using a "standard artificial insemination pipette" and a disposable plastic "insemination gun", or a reusable stainless steel "insemination gun". Regardless of which instrument is used, an outer guard is generally placed over the transfer instrument. The mare is restrained in the stocks, she is prepared as for insemination/collection, to provide sterile condition and to avoid any contamination of genitalia while carrying out the embryo transfer. An insemination pipette containing the embryo is passed into the vagina similar to the methods used for AI in horses. To deposit the embryo in the uterine horn, the tip of the instrument is guided into the horn using transrectal manipulation. The operator guides the pipette into the cervix up to a distance of approximately 2 cms into the uterus, and the media with the embryo is expelled into the body of the uterus.

Pregnancy Rate of Embryo Transfer

The pregnancy rate up to 53 per cent by surgical embryo transfer and up to 54 per cent by non surgical transfer has been reported. However, some workers have observed that the pregnancy rate in recipient mares with normal endometrium was higher (63 per cent) than those with endometrial pathology (28 per cent).

It has also been reported that pregnancy losses between 35 to 50 days by surgical transfer, has been found to be 24 per cent and the pregnancy losses between day 24 and 100 after a non surgical transfer has been reported to be 35 per cent. Pregnancy rates were not affected if the recipient mare had evaluated +/- day of the donor mares, regardless of the method of embryo transfer technique adopted. It has also been found that the in-vitro maintenance or the embryo for more than 6 hrs was detrimental to pregnancy rates in non surgical embryo transfer. The factors responsible for pregnancy rates are embryo quality, embryo age, type and quality of media used, transfer technique, nutritional status of recipient and the seasionality.

Advantages of Embryo Transfer Technology

The advantages of adopting the Embryo Transfer Technique (ETT) for the propagation of equine species are many and they have been summarized below:

(a) Since the horses are seasonally polyoestrous and have an erratic oestrus behaviour, it is possible to collect 6 to 8 embryos from the normal healthy donors with the possibility of producing at least 3-4 foals in the recipients.

(b) ETT will increase the genetic influence of the herd without inhibiting the performance.

(c) A single stallion may provide as many as 100 foals in a breeding season.

(d) Technique of embryo preservation and splitting of the embryo may influence and extend the contribution of the donor to the gene pool even beyond its existence.

(e) ETT can be used for the study of hormonal and immunological problems associated with the pregnancy and can also be used for interspecies breeding.

(f) Mares which are not in position to carry the foetus to the full term of pregnancy, due to physical deformity, can be efficiently and economically utilized as a donor.

(g) Wild and exotic endangered equidae can be propagated in domestic horses with ETT.

(h) Selected female mules although infertile, can be used as surrogate mother/recipient to develop the intraspecies conceptus by embryo transfer.

References

D. Vanderwall (2000) Current Equine Embryo Transfer Techniques Recent. Advances in Equine Reproduction. In Ball, B.A. (Ed.)

Chapter **11**

Common Reproductive Disorders

Various reproductive disorders in mares can be grouped in two categories :

- Oestrous cycle irregularities
- Genital infections

Oestrous Cycle Irregularities

Prolonged oestrus: This is characterized by prolonged heat period ranging from 10 to 80 days with an average duration of heat period of 10-20 days. Such abnormal cycles are usually observed in the early breeding season. As the season progresses, the periods of oestrum become shorter, and subsequently even normal. To get satisfactory results, breeding should be delayed until the cycles becomes normal. However, majority of such mares eventually become barren.

Prolonged Dioestrus: In this condition, oestrus is not exhibited for prolonged period. However, whenever the mares exhibit oestrus, it is true period. In many cases, ovulation may be regular but may not be accompanied with oestrus. Further, the mares do not easily conceive and may be required to be mated with stallion repeatedly. However, if conceived, 50 per cent of them are likely to have normal cycles while the other half may continue to be of irregular type. These mares should be bred when they show good oestrus. In this type, only a small percentage of mares i.e. 10-15 per cent are likely to become barren mares.

Table 11.1 : Hormone Concentrations in the Normal Nonpregnant Mare

Hormone	*Normal Range*
Inhibin	0.1 - 0.7 ng/ml
Testosterone	20 - 45 pg/ml
Progesterone - Oestrus - Dioestrus	 - <1 ng/ml - >1 ng/ml

Irregular Periods of Oestrum: This group of mares is characterized by frequent prolonged periods of oestrum during dioestrus. Majority of mares may exhibit split oestrus in which mares are in heat for one or more days, then out of oestrum for one to two days and again back to oestrum for one or more days. Such mares may ultimately prove to be good breeders.

Anoestrus: In this condition, there is characteristic absence of manifestations of sexual desire. However, ovulation in such mares is usually regular. Such mares do not respond to teasing and are usually poor breeders.

Anoestrus cases are more commonly recorded in obese mares as well as in mares suffering with poor condition, inanition or starvation. On examination of reproductive organs, ovaries are generally small, hard, fibrous, inactive, and without follicular development. Treatment of such a condition with oestrogen and gonadotropins has not been found successful. However, administration of 500 ml of warm physiological saline solution intrauterine, preferably with antibiotics is reported to give good results. If required, such treatment may be repeated after a week when no oestrus is exhibited. Similarly, favourable results have also been reported by massage of the ovaries, provided this trait is not an inherited one, in the subject animal.

Silent Oestrus: In this condition the signs of oestrus are undetected or not shown by the mare during teasing testing despite the fact that ovulation does occur. It is common with foal at foot mare (lactational anoestrus) and in maiden mares in early breeding season. Some recently foaled mares will only show estrus in the absence of the foal and under heavy teasing. Many of these mares are having endocrinological oestrus - in other words, the hormones are doing what they should be doing, and the mare is producing a follicle and ovulating, but won't "stand" to be bred. Some of these mares will "break down" in the face of heavy teasing. In organized farm, failure to detect heat and bad teasing regime is more common than the actual problem. The diagnosis is based on careful vaginal examination and rectal palpation to detect follicle of ovulatory size. The treatment includes careful teasing and additional teasing of such mares and stabling such mares near stallion. There are mares that will not show any signs of oestrus except for the day they are ovulating, and even then only after heavy teasing. The breeding of these mares would probably be missed if they were not palpated. "Serial palpations" every other day are useful. Restraining such mares while covering is necessary. A dose of tranquilizer is also found helpful.

Anovulatory-Hemorrhagic-Follicles (AHF)

Also known as "Autumn Follicles" or "Persistent Anovulatory Follicles(PAF)". Unusually, the follicle continues to develop beyond the size at which normally ovulation occur in the mare, and the development seems to continue for an inordinate amount of time.

Cause : It is suggested probably low follicular estrogen levels [1]; insufficient gonadotropin stimulation (which can result in low follicle stimulating hormone - FSH - and/or luteinizing hormone - LH - levels) [2]; or hemorrhage into the interior (lumen) of the follicle [3]. There has been a degree of correlation between those animals that have received hCG or GnRH in an attempt to stimulate ovulation, but it should be noted that the condition will also develop in mares that have neither received stimulatory drug, nor is the incidence significantly high enough to be considered enough of a problem to prevent giving the drugs at all. The incidence of PAF's is also more common in the transitional phases of the year - both spring and fall, hence the name "autumn follicles" - as well as in older mares. The specks that appear on ultrasound are thought to be initially blood, and the subsequent strands fibrinous. PAF's have been shown as occurring in over 8% of oestrous cycles in a recent study [4] with age differentials recorded as below, and an overall recurrence of 43.5% in the same breeding season

6-10 years old	16-20 years old	mean age of PAF mares
4.4%	13.1%	15.4 +/- 5.5 years

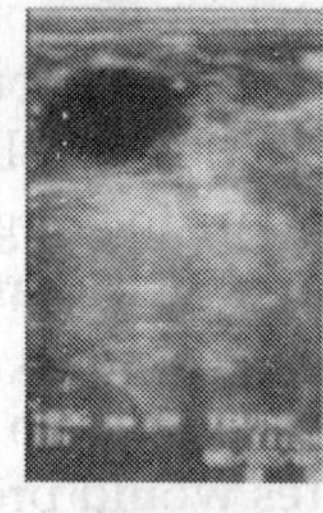
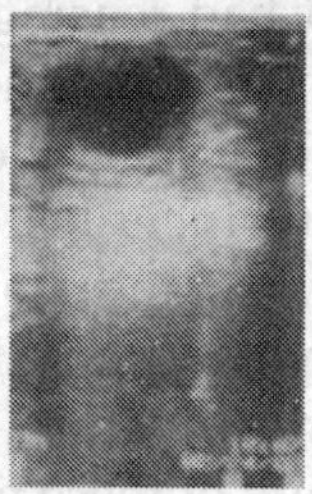

Normally Developing
Fig. 11.1 and 11.2

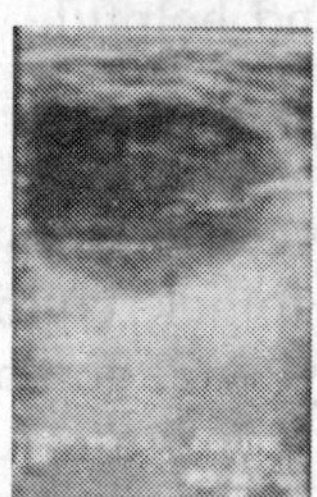

Developing Specks & Strand
Fig. 11.3 & 11.4

The frustrating aspect of these PAF's is that they are not fertile (as there is no ovulation), so the cycle on which they occur is lost, and many also result in a delay in return to subsequent oestrus, so future breeding may also be delayed. About 85% of PAF's do develop luteal tissue (the tissue which is present when a mare normally ovulates, that luteal tissue being contained within the corpus luteum) which is evidenced by the follicle showing a fully anechoic appearance on ultrasound, and elevated levels (more than 1 ng/ml) of progesterone. These may respond to treatment and resolve if a luteolitic dose of prostaglandin F2á is given. The remaining 15% however, which retain an anechoic appearance on ultrasound, will remain *in situ* despite all attempts to dislodge them (in some instances as long as 100 days). For years, the presence of a condition known as "cystic follicles" in the cow has been considered to be absent in horses, although there have been occasional incidences of such a diagnosis being made. The recent research work at Colorado State University suggests that there is a distinct correlation between the nonechoic equine PAF and follicular cysts in cattle, and the echoic equine PAF and bovine luteal cysts, and that perhaps the previous beliefs should be reconsidered

Abnormalities of Luteal Function

Persistent Corpus Luteum

The corpus luteum that forms after ovulation is usually functional for 14 - 15 days in the non-pregnant mare. Corpora lutea that fail to regress at the normal time post-ovulation are considered to be pathologically persistent . Luteolysis, or destruction of corpus luteum, occurs as a result of prostaglandin release from the endometrium. Occasionally, a mare may fail to regress the corpus luteum spontaneously at the normal time. The most common causes of a persistent corpus luteum are:

1. ovulations late in diestrus, resulting in corpora lutea that are immature (<5 days old) at the time of prostaglandin release;
2. embryonic loss after the time of maternal recognition of pregnancy;
3. chronic uterine infections, resulting in destruction of the endometrium and, therefore, diminished prostaglandin release, and
4. inadequate prostaglandin release at days 13 to 15.

If untreated, the corpus luteum may persist for 2 to 3 months. This syndrome may be suspected clinically in mares that are not expressing normal oestrus behaviour during the physiologic breeding season, and it must be differentiated from the syndrome of mares with silent heat. In addition, mares that have been bred and do not return to oestrus and are later diagnosed as not pregnant may also have a persistent corpus luteum. Diagnosis of a persistent corpus luteum is made by an analysis of plasma progesterone concentrations or a clinical response to prostaglandin administration. Progesterone concentrations more than 1 ng/ ml are indicative of the presence of luteal activity. Mares with a persistent corpus luteum will have good tone in the cervix and uterus on palpation, and the cervix will appear tight and dry on vaginal speculum examination because of the influence of progesterone.

Shortened Luteal Phase (Premature Luteolysis)

Dioestrus in the normal mare lasts approximately 14 to 15 days. Premature destruction of the corpus luteum (luteolysis) may be associated with an early onset of oestrus and a decrease in the inter-ovulatory interval. The most common cause of premature luteolysis in the mare is endometritis. Inflammation of the endometrium can result in sufficient synthesis and release of prostaglandins to cause luteal regression. Consequently, a mare that exhibits a shortened dioestrus should be examined for endometritis. A culture, biopsy and cytologic examination of the uterus may be indicated.

Luteal Insufficiency

Primary luteal insufficiency implies a deficiency in progesterone production. Luteal insufficiency has been suggested to be a cause of sub-fertility in mares, although data is limited. Maintenance of pregnancy in some habitually aborting mares following administration of exogenous progestogens offers circumstantial evidence that progesterone insufficiency may be responsible for some cases of pregnancy loss. Documentation of progesterone insufficiency as a cause of pregnancy loss would necessitate:

1. an accurate initial pregnancy diagnosis,
2. ruling out other potential causes of pregnancy loss, and
3. measurement of low progesterone concentrations in a series of daily blood samples. Minimum concentrations of

progesterone required to maintain pregnancy in the mare have been suggested to be 4.0 mg/ml

Genital Infections:

Vaginitis: Generally, vagina of mare is more resistant to infection than the cervix and uterus. However, this condition may occur as primary infection in pneumovaginic condition and also secondary to severe metritis and cervicitis. Similarly, trauma, laceration and severe infection of the vulva may result in chronic vaginitis which in turn may lead to pneumovagina and, even stenosis in-some cases. Incidence of this condition is reported to be quite low in mares.

Cervicitis: It is inflammation of cervical mucosa and characterized by dark red to purple coloured external os which may be oedematous, pendulous and greatly relaxed. Cervicitis may be a sequel of variety of infection as well as traumatic injuries during parturition. It may further lead to chronic cervicitis, scarring, malformation and incomplete closure of cervical canal. In some cases, permanent sterility with development of cervical seal has been reported. In very few cases, adhesions or false membranes develop which may even block the cervix.

Metritis: This condition is characterized by deep red haemorrhagic areas alternating with areas of whitish yellow coloured mucosa, scattered irregularly on the endometrium. In severe cases, the endometrium presents patchy denudation of mucous membrane with dull granulation tissue. The degree of inflammation and type of exudate vary from acute stage to chronicity. At times, accumulation of the several litres of mucopurulent material in the uterus has been reported which may even occlude cervix. There may be very severe erosion and degeneration of endometrium leading to thin and atonic uterine wall. In advanced cases, the endometrium is practically destroyed and the mucosa becomes tough, thick, yellowish white fibrous membrane. Incomplete involution of the uterus with patent cervix, diffused oedema and patchy areas of sloughing on endometrium has been reported.

Salpingitis: The inflammation of oviduct is termed as salpingitis. This condition, if not treated successfully may lead to early embryonic death, abortion and even sterility in some cases. In mares, it is usually of ascending type due to infection from the uterus and infected oviducts exhibiting catarrhal inflammation. In few cases, the inflammation is so severe that untreated cases may result in fibrosis of the oviduct and occlusion of the lumen with inflammatory exudate. The presence of papillae containing a smooth muscle sphincter, through which the oviduct opens into the lumen of the uterus, may be the possible explanation of rarity of salpingitis in the mare.

Control Measures: Most of the genital infections can be prevented by observing strict sex hygiene during breeding operations. In addition, broad spectrum antibiotics which are most effective against gram negative as well as gram positive organisms should be administered. However, the specific drug of choice is required to be selected by antibiotic sensitivity test. The selected drug should preferably be infused intrauterine during oestrus and the treatment should be repeated at least 2-3 times. Simultaneous parenteral administration of the same drugs helps to maintain proper blood concentration and promotes rapid recovery. After completion of therapeutic schedule, bacteriological examination of the cervical mucus should be undertaken to ascertain the infection free state of the uterus, before natural breeding artificial insemination.

Endometritis

Endometritis in the mare is a disease of great economic importance and one of the most important causes of infertility.

Persistent Mating Induced Endometritis:- In mares, spermatozoa are deposited directly into the uterus. Spermatozoa are rapidly transported to the oviducts; however, only a small number of spermatozoa ever reach the site of fertilization in the oviduct . The majority of the ejaculate remains in the uterus and is cleared by uterine contractions and an acute uterine inflammatory response. Fertile mares clear the inflammation within 24 to 36 hours of mating, well before the embryo enters the uterus at 5.5 days after ovulation. If the inflammation is prolonged it can be highly injurious to the endometrium. Breeding management and treatment strategies for mares with endometritis need to be tailored to each individual and depend on reproductive history, external and internal genital conformation, age, parity and results of endometrial cytology, culture and biopsy.

Treatment

LeBlanc(2003) suggested that treatment is directed at rapid removal of intrauterine fluids after breeding. A number of protocols have been proposed. Use a combination of uterine lavage performed between 4 and 12 hours after breeding in combination with oxytocin or cloprostenol. The uterus be lavaged with physiological saline or lactated ringers between 4 and 8 hours after breeding and the mare should be given 10 to 20 IU of oxytocin intravenously. The rationale for this protocol is to delay treatment until 4 hours after breeding so that viable sperm are not prematurely washed out of the uterus. Pregnancy rates were decreased when uterine lavage or oxytocin was given within 2 hours of breeding. Treatment is conducted within 8 hours of breeding to limit contact between inflammatory by-products and the endometrium, to "mimic" the inflammatory response of reproductively normal mares, and to prevent bacterial growth. The physiological inflammatory response to semen peaks between 8 and 12 hours after breeding in reproductively normal mares. Bacteria have been recovered from the uterus of susceptible mares but not from resistant mares approximately 9 hours after inoculation with *Streptococcus equi* sub-species *zooepidemicus* during oestrus . It is found that both resistant and susceptible mares exhibited a rapid rise and fall in bacterial numbers from 1 to 5 hours post-inoculation. No bacteria can be recovered after 5 hours from the uterus of normal mares; however, bacterial numbers began to rise steadily in susceptible mares at 9 hours and continued to rise for the 24 hour study .A clinical study indicates that timing of uterine lavage after breeding influences pregnancy rates. Twice as many mares that received a uterine lavage between 4 and 6 hours after insemination (6/9) were pregnant compared to mares that were lavaged 18 to 20 hours after insemination (3/9). The dose of oxytocin should be limited to 10 to 20 IU. Larger doses of oxytocin (25 IU) have been associated with a decrease in pregnancy rate.

Mares with persistent mating induced endometritis and lymphangectasia, are treated as recommended above and are administered cloprostenol (250 micrograms IM; Estrumate; Intervet) at 12 and 24 hours after breeding. The rational for the combined therapy is that oxytocin induces strong uterine contractions for 30 to 50 minutes and is associated with rapid clearance of intrauterine fluids. Prostaglandin F2á produces low amplitude contractions that persist for 4 to 5 hours. Their use is associated with a much slower uterine clearance of fluid than oxytocin. Prolonged uterine contractions may assist in lymphatic flow as they rely on myometrial contractions to induce lymph drainage.

Non-specific endometritis may be due to wind-sucking or to *iatrogenic* contamination during diagnostic procedures. The uterus may become contaminated with bacteria at coitus, but this infection is normally eliminated rapidly and usually does not interfere with either fertilization or implantation. In some cases however, the infection will persist leading to endometritis and infertility.

Some cases of metritis are caused by difficult parturition or retention of the placenta. In most mares, the uterus becomes infected at this time even if they have foaled normally, but as long as involution of the uterus takes place normally the infection is eliminated rapidly. Sometimes metritis may be a sequel to vaginitis.

It can also be related to the chemical irritation which accompanies urine pooling. However, recent evidence suggests that bacterial endometritis only becomes established in the uteri of mares that have impaired uterine defence mechanisms.

The bacteria most frequently implicated in equine endometritis are *B-haemolytic Streptococci, Escherichia coli, Staphylococcus aureus, Pseudomonas aeruginosa,* and both *Klebsiella pneumoniae* and *K. aerogenes.*

Diagnosis: The diagnosis of endometritis is based upon the history and clinical examination aided by the bacteriological and cytological examination of uterine discharge, the use of endometrial biopsy for histological examination, hormone assays to determine underlying endocrinological factors and possibly ultrasound technique.

Uterine bacterial cultures alone should not be used to diagnose endometritis because many of the bacteria that cause endometritis are also common commensals on the perineum and in the vagina, and contamination of uterine cultures is common despite the use of guarded culture swabs. Bacteria isolated from a single uterine culture should only be considered significant if there are accompanying signs of endometrial fibrosis of uterine biopsy, or inflammatory cells are present on cytologic evaluation of the endometrium. If bacterial culture alone is to be utilized to confirm a diagnosis of endometritis, the same organism should be isolated on at least two or three sequential cultures several days or an oestrous cycle apart. Uterine defense mechanisms may control general contaminants during oestrus and allow only the isolation of bacteria that are specifically involved in endometritis. Furthermore, the uterus is better equipped to cope with *iatrogenic* contamination during oestrus; therefore, it is preferable to perform diagnostic procedures during oestrus rather than dioestrus. It is also not advisable to culture the flora of the uterus within 48 hours after breeding because of misleading results that may arise from airborne contamination of the uterine lumen and natural contamination by the ejaculate.

Endometrial biopsy enables one to determine the significance of endometrial bacterial cultures and give prognosis on the reproductive potential of mares. Prognosis is based primarily on the degree of fibrosis present within the endometrial sample.

If endometrial fibrosis is severe, lymphatic lacunae may be present and there may even be transluminal adhesions and pockets of fluid accumulated within the uterus. Such advanced changes can usually be appreciated by transrectal ultrasonography or endoscopy and if these changes are extreme, they may even be palpable per rectum.

Treatment: Mares with a tendency towards pneumovagina should be treated surgically by Caslick's operation to stop aspiration of the air. After vulvar suturing, the vaginitis and endometritis may resolve spontaneously if the mare has normal ovarian cycles, but such mares are usually treated with intra-uterine antibiotics. The choice of antibiotic is dependent upon the type of organism present and its antibiotic sensitivity pattern.

When the mare is cycling normally, the normal phagocytic and self-clearing activity of the uterus will lead to resolution of endometritis in some cases without the use of antibiotics. Therefore, use of prostaglandin or oestrogens has been advocated when there is reduced follicular activity, and particularly if pyometra is diagnosed, or during the winter months when the mare is not cycling.

In practice, veterinarians often attempt to augment uterine defence mechanisms in susceptible mares by supplying opsonins in the form of immunoglobulins and complement derived from serum or colostrum. At this time, it is not clear how such augmentation of the immune system should relate to antibiotic therapy, because many antibiotics are known to inhibit cellular immunity and may even be contra-indicated when immuno-therapy is used.

Antibiotics can be administered to mares by local or systemic routes, but if the local route is used, sufficient saline or sterile water must be infused as part of the treatment to ensure adequate distribution of the antibiotic within the uterus. However, before antibiotic or immunologic treatment is initiated, any fluid or debris present within the uterus should be flushed out with hot (50°C) saline until the saline flush becomes clear. The flushing procedure should be repeated daily until the first flush of the day is clear. Hot saline flushes serve as mild irritants to the endometrium, stimulating uterine blood flow and neutrophil migration into the lumen; therefore, they may be beneficial even if there is no debris within the uterus. For augmentation of the immune system, 100-200 ml of autogenous, heparinized or citrated plasma is infused into the uterus for several days after the saline flushes and the mare is bred during the subsequent oestrus period. Plasma or serum can be infused again on the first and second day after ovulation. It is important not to heat-sterilize the plasma, used for these treatments because, complement and antibodies will be denatured at high temperatures.

Contagious Equine Metritis (CEM)

It is a highly contagious venereal disease of horses. It was described for the first time in mares at stud farms in the Newmarket area of England in 1977. The disease is characterized by a specific form of metritis in mares, referred to as Contagious Equine Metritis (CEM). It has subsequently been described in Ireland, France, the United States, Australia, Japan and in many other countries worldwide.

The causal organism for CEM is an unusual gram negative coccobacillus found in smears of cervical and Vaginal exudate which grows on heated blood agar in an atmosphere containing 5-10 per cent carbon dioxide in hydrogen. These findings were confirmed by transmission experiments in ponies.

The classification of the organism has been the subject of debate between bacterial taxonomists. Initially, it was found that hematin stimulated the growth of the organism and on this basis it was named *Haemophilus equigenitalis.* However, it is now recognized that it does not belong to the *Haemophilus* genus but to a new genus - *Taylorella,* and the name *Taylorella equigenitalis* has been proposed for the CEM organism. *Taylorella equigenitalis* is transmitted venereally to mares from asymptomatic carrier stallions. It causes suppurative endometritis and early embryonic death resulting in a repeat breeding syndrome until the mare becomes immune to the organism.

Symptoms: After mares have been covered by infected stallions, they may develop a profuse uterine discharge 2-6 days after service. The discharge may be frank pus or a bright, mucopurulent fluid. However, in some mares, the discharge is very slight and may not be noticed. There are varying degrees of inflammation of the vaginal mucosa. The result of the infection is a high prevalence of infertility due to interference with fertilization and implantation or to early foetal death. Abortion is not a feature of this disease. As the endometritis subsides, most mares become fertile again after several oestrous cycles.

Diagnosis: The diagnosis is confirmed by isolation and identification of the causal organism. Guarded or sheathed swabs are taken from either uterine discharge in acute cases or the clitoral fossa and the endometrium in early oestrus in suspected carrier mares. In the stallion, swabs should be taken from the sheath, the urethra, the urethral fossa and from pre-ejaculatory fluid. The swabs should be sent to the laboratory in a suitable transport medium such as Amies or Stuart's medium.

Smears should be prepared from uterine discharge and stained by Gram's method. Large numbers of polymorphonuclear leukocytes are indicative of an active endometritis and small gram negative coccobacillary bacteria may be causal organism.

In some cases, endometrial biopsy may be required, but it does not detect latent carriers. In other cases, where contamination by other bacteria or fungi has made cultural examination of stallion difficult, test mating or the collection of smegma and its direct inoculation into a susceptible mare have been used in attempts to demonstrate infection.

A variety of serological tests have been investigated for use in the diagnosis of CEM. If the Serum Agglutination Test (SAT) is used, titres of 1:80 are reached about 3 weeks after infection and may decline to insignificant levels after 6 weeks. With the Complement fixation test (CFT), although titres also peaked at about 3 weeks, they declined much more slowly. Thus the SAT may be of value in the diagnosis of acute cases, while the CFT could be used to detect chronically infected animals. Passive haemagglutination and ELISA tests are also useful diagnostic procedures.

Treatment and Control: A moratorium should be imposed on breeding activities and all the stallions on the farm treated systematically with penicillin or ampicillin for 10 days. In addition, their genitalia are washed with chlorhexidine scrub and the prepuce packed with furazolidone ointment. Non-pregnant mares are treated with crystalline penicillin via the intra-uterine route for 7 to 10 days, but once infected they are always regarded as potential carriers of CEM and should not be rebred naturally. Treated stallions can only be used again once they have had six negative penile and fossa glandis cultures taken at weekly intervals. It is also recommended that two to three maiden mares be bred naturally by a stallion that has undergone treatment, and that the uteri and clitoral sinuses of those mares should be cultured on three occasions within 14 days post-breeding.

Horses that have never been used for breeding can be imported from countries where CEM is endemic with only the usual quarantine restrictions. However, mares that have been used for breeding require clitoral sinusectomy, a course of intensive antibiotic treatment and at least three negative serological tests for CEM at the port of origin. For that purpose, either a passive haemagglutination test or an ELISA test for CEM should be used as these tests have been shown to be more accurate than tube agglutination or complement fixation tests. Imported mares are retested upon their arrival. Sexually experienced stallions should have negative serological tests in the country of origin and must also be retested, cultured and testbred to at least three mares. Female foals from mares which have been exposed to CEM should be tested for it when they reach puberty, by serologic testing and culturing of their uteri and clitoral sinuses. New regulations pertaining to the control of CEM include possibly withdrawing the need for clitoral sinusectomy because the CEM organism can be harboured, for long periods of time almost anywhere in the genital tract.

For routine culturing of the CEM organism, swabs should be placed in Amies transport medium and then placed into chocolate agar and incubated under 5 per cent CO_2, The organism is fastidious and slow growing; therefore, cultures are not regarded as being negative prior to 10 days of incubation.

The serious nature of CEM and the threat it posed to the equine production has led to strict control measures which include a series of three negative swabs taken in stallions from pre-ejaculatory fluid, prepuce, urethra and urethral fossa and in mares from the clitoral fossa and sinuses and an endometrial swab taken during oestrus. When CEM organism is isolated, the horse must be treated adequately, rested for a suitable time and resampled.

Treatment of stallions usually consists of thorough and repeated cleansing of the extended penis and sheath with chlorhexidine followed by the application of furazolidone ointment. In mares, although the condition often resolves spontaneously, latent infection remains and treatment is recommended.

Uterine irrigation with chlorhexidine, nitrofurazone, ampicillin or penicillin for 3-5 days has been used in addition to parenteral administration of penicillin or ampicillin. In symptomless carriers, the local cleansing of the clitoral fossa and sinuses with chlorhexidine is not to be recommended for treatment of either stallions or mares, or as a prophylactic measure at the time of covering. This can lead to the destruction of the normal flora and the establishment of pseudomonas infection, which may be then transmitted venereally leading to further trouble.

Although not widely used in thoroughbred horses, artificial insemination has considerable potential for controlling venereally transmitted infection in horses.

Fungal Metritis

If fungi are isolated from uterine fluid or identified in the sediment of such fluid, fungal endometritis should be suspected. Such cases are usually encountered where there is substantial fluid accumulation in the uterus, and fungi can be seen in this fluid but not in endometrial biopsies from these mares. Fungal elements stain well by the Periodic Acid Schiff (PAS) reaction but are more easily identified with Gomori's methanamine silver or Grocott's stain. The most common fungi isolated from these cases are *Candida* spp. and *Aspergillus fumigatus*. Many cases of fungal metritis appear to resolve spontaneously, but if the infection appears to be persistent, appropriate treatment with antifungal drugs, locally as well as parenterally should be undertaken.

Coital Exanthema ('Spots'): III infection. This is a vesicular, often ulcerative venereal disease that causes genital discomfort and reluctance to breed in both sexes. Secondary infection may complicate the condition occasionally but it usually heals spontaneously within 7-10 days. Infection is generally through a carrier mare and stallion helps in spreading the infection from one mare to another during coitus. Symptoms include swelling and red colouration of prepuceal mucosa in the beginning and pain is evidenced while mating, pruritis, frequent urination, flat, dull and opaque areas on prepuceal membrane which may develcp into vesicles, erosions and granulation. Later on, deep red patches that bleed easily are visible on prepuceal mucosa. In addition, white patches have been noticed on glans penis and vulva due to permanent loss of pigmentation. This condition is highly infectious and affected mares should not be bred till they are fully recovered. Complications due to secondary bacterial infection should be treated with appropriate antibiotics.

Pyometra

Pyometra is relatively uncommon in mares, probably because of the rarity of retained placenta in this species. This may be due to remarkable rate of postpartum uterine involution and the distensibility of the equine cervix. Mares with pyometra are seldom debilitated and do not have high circulating leukocyte counts. Therefore, pyometra is often discovered during a routine examination for infertility. Unless there is closure of the cervix by adhesions, mares with pyometra also tend to show a purulent discharge from the vulva, a strong indication of the disease. If the uterus is distended with fluid but no foetus is visible by trans-rectal ultrasonography, the mare is also likely to have pyometra because mucometra is so rare in horses.

In most cases, uterine lavage with large volumes of fluid is an effective treatment when the purulent material has first been siphoned from the uterus. The lavage should be supplemented by high doses of antibiotics administered by parenteral and intra uterine routes. The most frequent causative organism in equine pyometra is *Streptococcus zooepidemicus;* therefore, penicillin is the antibiotic of choice unless a culture and sensitivity test dictate otherwise.

Neoplasia

The most common forms of genital neoplasia in the mare are squamous cell carcinomas of the vulva, granulosa cell tumours of the vulva and granulosa cell tumours of the ovary. The former are not usually metastatic, but occasionally they cause deformity of the vulva with secondary wind sucking and consequent endometritis. Due to the fact that squamous cell carcinomas are locally invasive, they should be removed by radical excision if possible. Melanomas are also encountered in the perineal region but are usually benign and seldom cause genital complications.

Granulosa cell tumours(GST)or Granulosa thecal cell tumourr(GTCT) occur in young and old mares and usually disrupt ovarian cyclicity. Although they are benign, they produce a variety of sex steroids that exert a negative feedback effect on the hypothalamic pituitary axis. This results in quiescence of the unaffected ovary and long periods of infertility. Sexual behaviour at this time may be masculine, feminine or simply passive. Granulosa cell tumours are usually easy to diagnose on a presumptive basis because an enlarged ovary can be palpated per rectum on one side and small quiescent ovary on the other side. This is almost unique to this type of tumour because most other ovarian tumours in the mare do not produce sex steroids. Granulosa cell ally up to 30 cm in diameter. The measurement of serum testosterone may be of further diagnostic value in these cases because serum testosterone is often elevated significantly in mares with granulosa cell tumors (Table-11.1).

Behavioral symptoms: A GCT may also be suspected if the mare's attitude suddenly changes. For example, she may become very "studdy", displaying stallion attitudes and postures, and may become aggressive, and even start to develop the typical stallion cresty neck. This is as a result of the granulosa cell tumor secreting testosterone. Alternatively, she may display continuous oestrus ("nymphomania"), or even only very occasional oestrus.

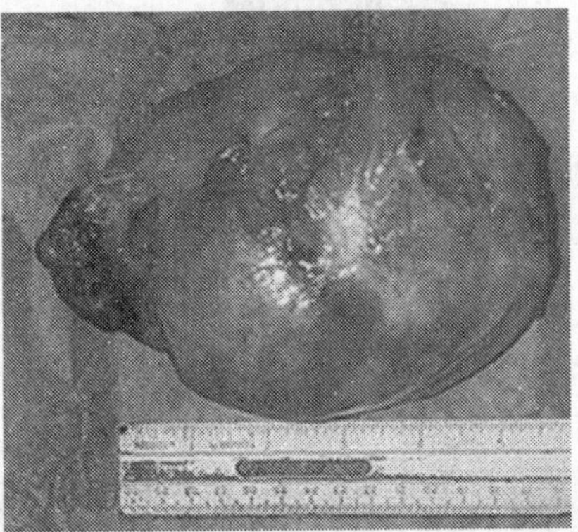

Fig 11.5 : GST 16 cm Appx

The tumours may be surgically removed trans-vaginally or through a flank incision. However, the owner should be warned that the mare may take several months to initiate normal ovarian cycles again because of the chronic nature of the negative feedback suppression on the unaffected ovary. On rare occasions, these mares never return to cyclicity.

The ovary (seen on the right) is roughly kidney-shaped, with the depression in the center of the lower side

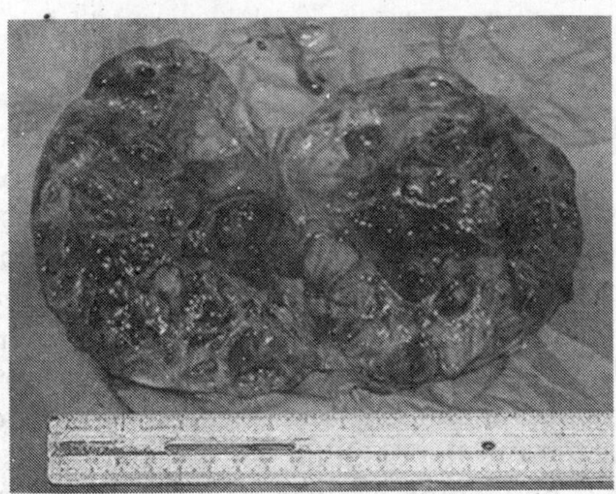

Fig.11.6 : TS of GST with Honey Comb Structure

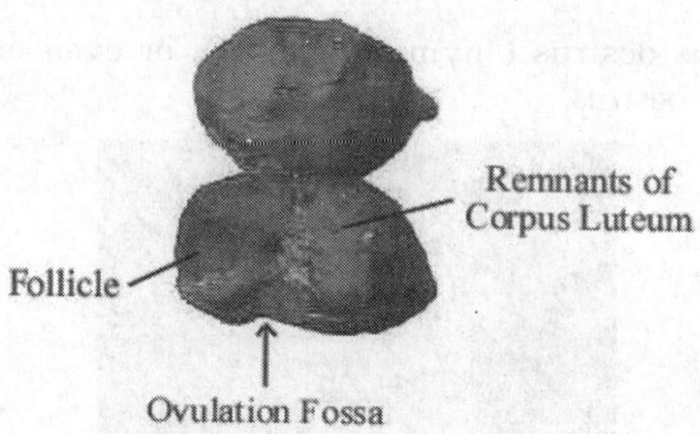

Fig.11.7 Normal Overy

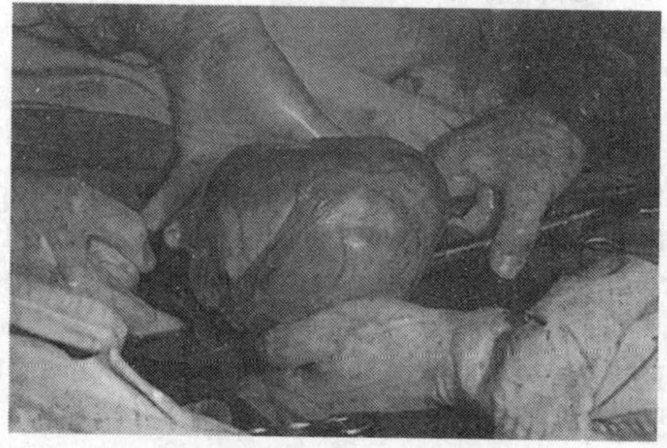

Fig.11.8 Surgical Removal of GST through Flank Incision

Placentitis

Bacterial placentitis may be diffuse because of haematogenous entry into the uterus, or local and ascending due to infection via the cervix. In either case, the foetus dies because of placental compromise and septicaemia and often pneumonia as well from inhaling contaminated amniotic fluid. *Streptococcus* spp, *Staphylococcus* spp., *Pseudomonas aeruginosa, Klebsiella pneumoniae* and other bacterial Species have been cultured from these abortions. In cases of fungal placentitis, the placenta may be characteristically thickened and severely inflamed. On the histologic sections of the placenta, the fungal organisms can be demonstrated by Gomori's silver stain, Grocott's stain or by the Periodic Acid Schiff (PAS) reaction. Fungi such as *Aspergillus* and *Mucor* spp., etc. are usually isolated from these cases, but recently a *Histoplasma* spp. has also been reported to cause abortion in mares.

Equine Viral Arteritis (EVA)

It has recently been shown that stallions can shed the EVA virus for prolonged periods of time and can transmit it venereally to mares. Mares that contract EVA in this manner will experience an acute febrile episode, 7-10 days later and can become chronic carriers, shedding the virus in their urine. These mares are positive for EVA by a serum neutralization test. Mares that are affected early in pregnancy probably abort occasionally, but abortion is more common in advanced pregnancy when mares contract the infection by inhalation of viral aerosol. The foetus is often autolyzed at the time of abortion but otherwise shows no pathognomonic lesions. There is no specific treatment for this disease. However, vaccination with killed vaccine has been advocated by many workers.

Equine Viral Rhino Pneumonitis (EHV 1)

Susceptible mares will abort a well-preserved foetus 1-2 months after exposure to the abortifacient form of EHV I virus. There is usually no evidence of placentitis, but signs of pulmonary oedema and fluid accumulation in the thoracic and peritoneal cavities are fairly common. A diagnosis is achieved through histopathology, virus isolation from the peritoneal and pleural fluids and fluorescent antibody examination of the adrenals and other organs. Sometimes abortion storms invoking several mares will be encountered. The foetuses are a significant source of virus and should be removed immediately. In addition, all the normal mares should be vaccinated against rhinopneumonitis. The general incidence of abortion due to EHV I can be reduced by vaccinating brood mares with a killed or modified live virus vaccine during the 5th, 7th and 9th months of gestation. This strategy is designed to stimulate maximum immunity and achieve protection during the last half of pregnancy, when mares are at maximum risk for abortion. However, protection is never absolute and despite diligent vaccination, mares may still abort due to EHV I. Weanlings should be kept separate from brood mares.

References

1. Pierson, R.A. Folliculogenesis and ovulation. In: McKinnon, A.O.and Voss, J.L. (ed). Equine reproduction. Philadelphia: Lea and Febiger, 1993. p 161-71.
2. McKinnon, A.O., Ovarian abnormalities. In: Ranaten, N.W., McKinnon, A.O., (ed). Equine diagnostic ultrasonography. Baltimore: Williams and Wilkins, 1997. p 233-51.
3. Ginther, O.J. Reproductive biology of the mare. Basic and applied aspects. Cross Plains,WI: Equiservices,1992.
4. McCue, P.M., Squires, E.L. Persistent anovulatory follicles in the mare. Theriogenology 58 (2002) 541-543.
5. McCue, P.M. Diagnosis of Ovarian Abnormalities Recent Advances in Equine Reproduction, Ball B.A. (Ed) (2000),.)
6. LeBlanc M. M. Persistent Mating Induced Endometritis in the Mare: Pathogenesis, Diagnosis and Treatment. Recent Advances in Equine Reproduction Ball B.A. (Ed) 2003;

Chapter **12**

Description of the Horse

Very often, the veterinarian is called upon to issue a certificate of Identity of a horse for varying purposes as to establish ownership, sale and purchase, registration, identification of strayed/stolen horse, reporting of lost/dead animal, inter-state/International move of horses and insurance purposes etc. The art of describing the identity of a horse is commonly known as description. The procedure of description has been standardized so as to ensure uniformity at all levels and with a view to include maximum detail pertaining to the horse. Accordingly, a format has been devised for the purpose by Royal Western India Turf Club, in which various details are described by the veterinarian in words as well as by figure drawing of various markings. The following order of description is adopted:

Colour

Breed

Sex

Name

Height

Age

Markings

  Marks on head including eyes

  Marks on limbs (fore first then hind).

  Marks on body

  Marks, if any on mane and tail

  Adventitious marks, congenital abnormalities, whorls or any other special features.

The details of body colours and markings are as follows :

Body Colours (plates V and VI)

The principal colours are black, brown, bay and chestnut. When there is any doubt as to the colour, the muzzle and eye lids should be carefully examined for guidance. Details are as under:

Black - Where black pigment is general throughout the coat, limbs, mane and tail, with no pattern factor present other than white markings.

Brown - Where there is a mixture of black and brown pigment in the coat, with black limbs, mane and tail.

Bay Brown - Where the predominating colour is brown, with muzzle bay, black limbs, mane and tail.

Bay - Bay varies considerably in shade from dull red approaching brown, to a yellowish colour approaching chestnut, but it can be distinguished from the chestnut by the fact that the bay has black mane and tail and almost invariably has black on the limbs and tips of the ears.

Chestnut - This colour consists of yellow coloured hair in different degrees of intensity, which may be noted if thought desirable. A "True" chestnut has a chestnut mane and tail which may be lighter or darker than the body colour. Lighter coloured chestnuts may have flaxen manes and tails.

Grey - Where the body coat is a varying mosaic of black and white hair, with the skin black. With increasing age, the coat grows lighter in colour. As there are many variations according to age and season, all of them should be described by the general term 'Grey'. In horses of this colour, any distinctive hoof markings may be useful for purpose of identification. Chestnut foals of grey parentage may become grey after 12 months of age. The flea-bitten grey may contain three colours or the two basic colours, and should be so described.

Roan - Roans are distinguished by the ground or body colours, all of which are permanent. Coat has a mixture of body colour and white hair.

Bay Roan - Where the body colour is black or brown, with admixture of white hair, giving a blue tinge to the coat.

Bay or Red Roan - Where the body colour is bay or bay roan with an admixture of white hair which gives a reddish tinge to the coat. On the limbs from the knees and hock down, the black hair usually predominate; white markings may be encountered.

Strawberry and Chestnut Roan - Where the body colour is chestnut with an admixture of white hair.

Piebald - Where the body coat consists of large irregular patches of black and white. The line of demarcation between the two colours is generally well defined.

Skewbald - Body coat consists of large irregular patches of white and any other colour except black. The colour combination should be described i.e. 'bay and white' or 'chestnut and white' etc.

Note - The term "whole coloured" is used where there are no hair of any other colour on the body, head or limbs.

MARKINGS

The variations in marking of horses are infinite and cannot be accurately described by a limited number of terms without certain arbitrary groupings. In some cases, a combination of the terms given below must be employed. It is stressed that all Certificates of Identity should be in conformity with later remarks accompanied by a diagram on which the markings are indicated accurately.

The description invariably begins with forehead. The presence and position of the whorl or whorls should be clearly specified, with reference to the midline and to eye level, and the position of white markings should be defined with reference to whorls.

HEAD :- (plates VII to IX)

Star - Any white-mark on the forehead. Size, shape, intensity, position and coloured markings (if any) on the white should be specified. Should the marking in the region of the centre of the forehead consists of few white hair only, it should be so described and not referred to as a star.

Stripe - The narrow white marking down the face, not wider than the flat anterior surface of the nasal bones. In the majority of cases, the star and stripes are continuous and should be described "Star and stripe conjoined" where the stripe is separate and distinct from the star, it should be described as "interrupted stripe"; where no star is present the point of origin of the stripe should be indicated. The termination of the stripe and any variation in breadth, direction and any markings on the white would be stated, (e.g.) "broad stripe" "narrow stripe", "inclined to left/right".

Blaze - A white marking covering almost the whole of the forehead between the eyes and extending beyond the width of the nasal bones and usually to the muzzle. Any variation in direction, termination and any marking on the white should be stated.

White Face - Where the white covers the forehead and front of the face, extending laterally towards the mouth. The extension may be unilateral or bilateral, in which cases it should be described accordingly.

Snip - An isolated white marking, independent of those already named and situated between or in the region of the nostrils. Its size, position and intensity should be specified (see flesh marks).

Lip Markings - Should be accurately described, whether embracing the whole or a portion of either lip (see flesh mark).

White Muzzle - Where the white embraces both lips and extends to the region of the nostrils.

Wall Eye - This term should be used exclusively where there is such a lack of pigment, either partial or complete, in the iris as usually to give a pinkish white or bluish-white appearance to the eye. Any other important variations should be noted.

Whorls - The location of the whorls or irregular settings of coat hairs on any part of the body especially so on the head and neck (plate X) should be precisely indicated on the diagram accompanying the certificate. Whorls should be shown by the use of small cross (x) and not by a circle or dot. Unless full advantage is taken of the whorl system, the scarcity or absence of white marks can make identification by written description very difficult. Whorls must be noted on head, neck and body. Whorls may also be found in throat region, over the trachea and in the jugular furrow. Head whorls are best described in relation to the eye level and it should be noted whether the location is median or to the right or left of mid-line. Position of whorl/whorls in relation to any white marks should be clearly stated e.g., 'contained in star', 'in crescent of star', 'irregular star above and to right of median whorl at eye level'.

BODY

Grey Ticked - Where white hairs are sparsely distributed through the coat in any part of the body.

Flecked - Where small collections of white hairs occur distributed irregularly in any part of the body. The degrees of flecking may be described by the terms "heavily flecked", "lightly flecked".

Black Marks - This term should be used to describe small area of black hairs among white or any other colour.

Spots - Where small, more or less circular collections of hair differing from the general body colour occur, distributed in various parts of the body. The position and colour of the spot must be stated.

Patch - This term should be used to describe any larger, well defined irregular area (not covered by previous definition) of hair differing from the general body colour. The colour, shape, position and extent should be described.

Zebra Marks - Where there is striping on the limbs, neck, withers or quarters (plate XII).

Mane and Tail - The presence of differently coloured hair in mane and tail should be specified.

LIMBS (Plate XI)

White Coronet - Where the hair immediately above the hoof is white. Describe the situation of the white marking as far as possible.

White heel - For the purpose of description of marking, the heel is to be taken as the back of the pastern extending to the ergot. Where the white is confined to one or both the bulbs of the heel, it must be so specified.

White Pastern - For the purpose of description of marking, the term "pastern" is to be taken as extending from immediately below the fetlock joint down-wards. Any variation of extent of the white should be specified e.g. half pastern, three-quarter pastern.

White Fetlock - For the purpose of description of marking, the "fetlock" is to be taken as comprising the region of the fetlock joint and downwards. Any variation of the extent of the white should be specified.

Higher white Markings - For the sake of greater uniformity and certainty, white markings extending higher than those already defined, the particular height to which the white extends should be precisely stated and variation in the upper margin noted e.g., white to middle of cannon (foreleg) or shank (hind leg), "white to knee (foreleg) or hock (hind leg)".

MISCELLANEOUS

Mixed - To be used to describe a white marking which contains varying amounts of hair of the general colour.

Bordered - To be used where any marking is circumscribed by a mixed border, e.g., "bordered star" "bordered stripe".

Flesh Marks - Patches where the pigment of the skin is absent should be described as "flesh marks".

Acquired Marks - There are many adventitious marks (i.e. not congenital marks) which are permanent, e.g. saddle marks, bridle marks, collar marks, girth marks, other harness marks, permanent bandage marks, firing and branding marks, surgical and injury scars, tattoo marks. Whenever these occur, they should be described. If horse should happen to be docked, this fact should be mentioned.

Congentical Abnormalities - Any congential marks or the abnormalities which can not be included in the description under other headings should be clearly described in the certificate and indicated on the diagram where possible.

The "Prophet's Thumb Mark" describes a fairly deep but very localised depression. It is most frequently found on the neck on the pectoral muscles or on the point of shoulder.

Projection of the upper jaw or "Parrot Mouth" or its opposite, "Sow Mouth" will never disappear and should be mentioned.

In addition to these markings, any characteristic marking shown by the animal should be included in the certificates of Identity. Further and to assist the Registeritig Authorities every Certificate of Identity should be accompanied by the appended diagram with the markings accurately filled in as described.

Language - As far as descriptive markings are concerned, the language used in description should be simple. After all, markings are also required for lay persons such as owners. "One third shank white, more posteriomedially" is technically correct but apt to confuse a layman.

And, finally, a few "Do's" and "Don'ts":-

- Do corroborate factual detail with notification of birth and return of mares.
- Do keep your description brief, simple and precise.
- Do make use of the "remarks" column to explain any discrepancies. Do mention any artificial marks such as scars.
- Do try and show the brand-marks in the diagram in as correct a position as possible.
- Do ensure that the address of the identifying veterinarian is clearly written.
- Do reply to queries raised as soon as possible so that the registration is speeded up.

- Don't leave any column blank. Fill in "nil", "no makings", etc. as appropriate.
- Don't use abbreviations such as Fet for "Fetlock", "ant" for "anterior", "c" for "with" etc.
- Don't over describe.
- Don't fill in factual information which is not supported by documentary evidence.
- Don't put a circle around the cross(x) used to denote the position of whorl.

CERTIFICATE OF IDENTITY

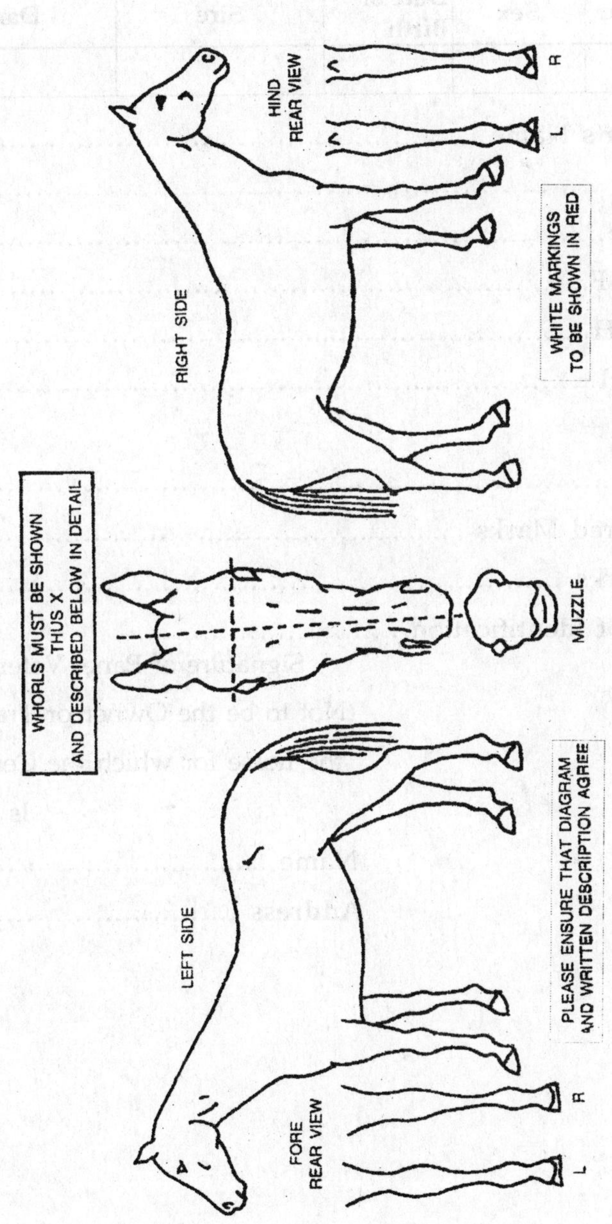

Colour	Sex	Date of Birth	Sire	Dam

Owner's Name ....

Head ....

L | L.F..

I | R. F..

M | L.H..

B | R.H..

S |

Body ....

Acquired Marks ....

Remarks ....

Date of Identification ....

Signature of Panel Veterinarian

(Not to be the Owner or Trainer of the horse for which the Certificate Is issued)

Name ....

Address ....

A Thoroughbred
Horse Stallion

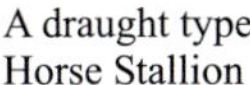

A draught type
Horse Stallion

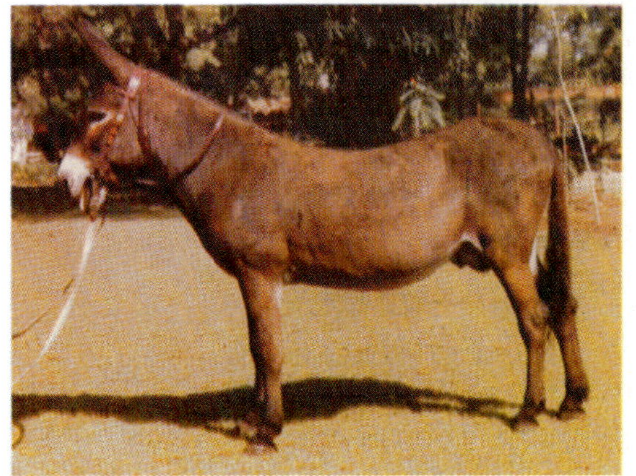

A Donkey
Stallion

Plate I

A Testing Pony

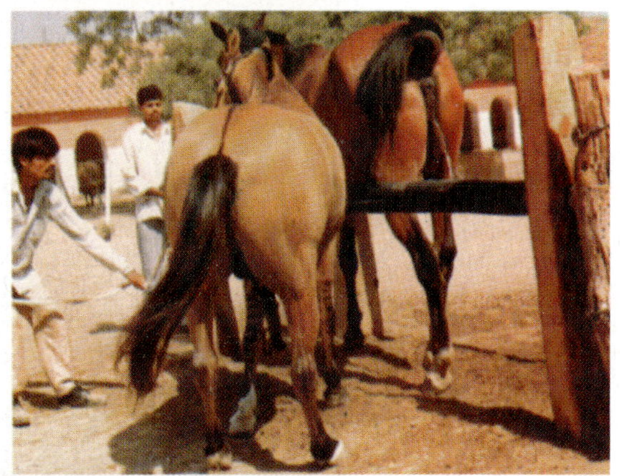

A Brood mare in heat at 'Teasing'

A mare with her two month old mule foal

Plate II

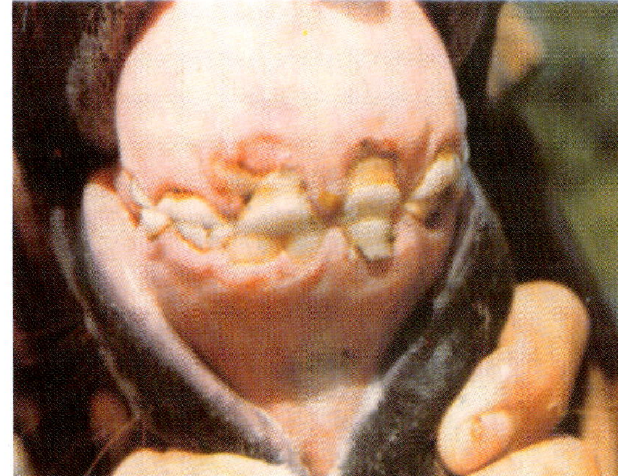

Two year old

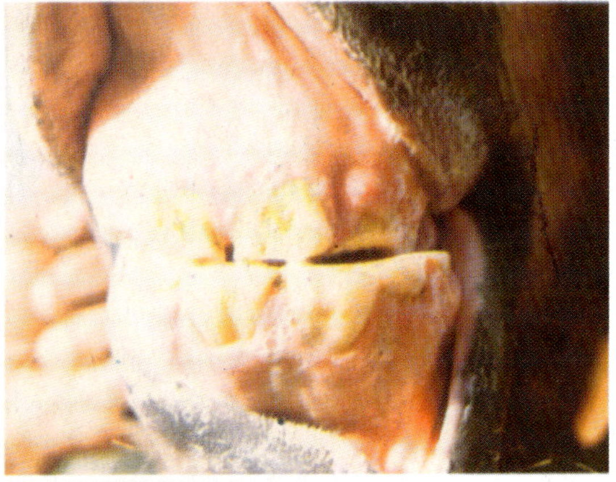

Three year old

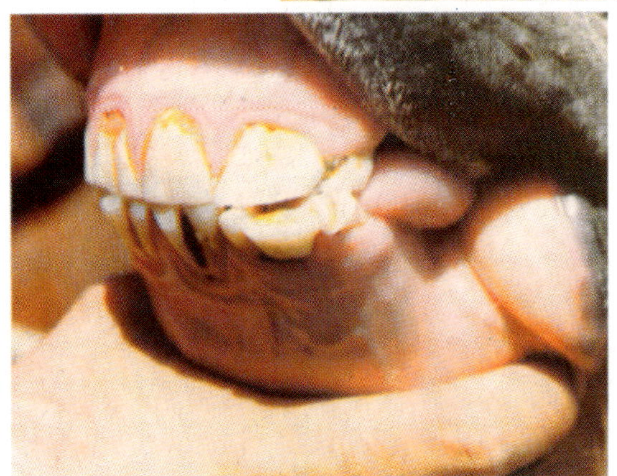

Four year old

Plate III

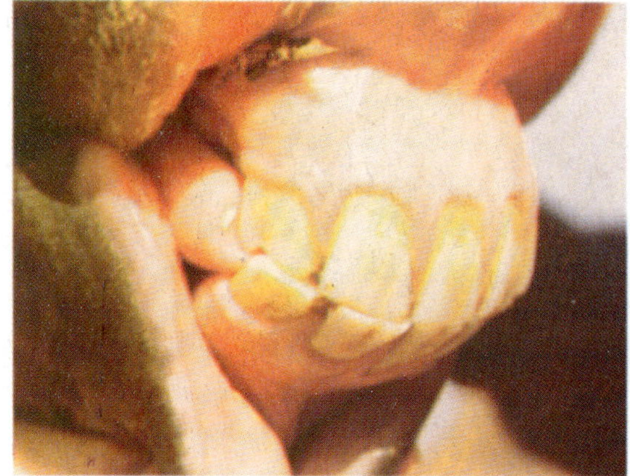

Seven year old

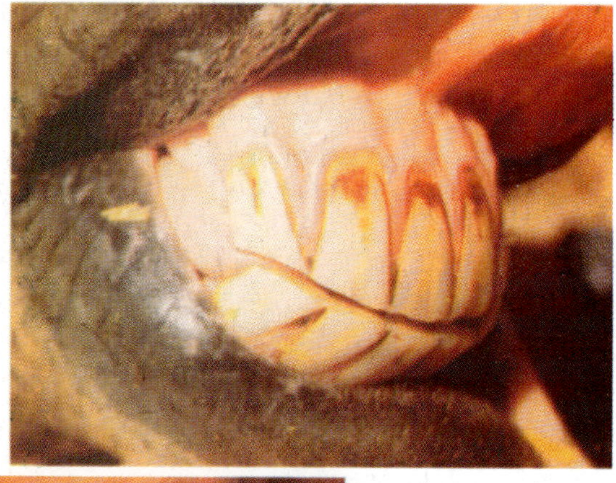

15 year old

Aged horse
(more than 20 years)

Plate IV

A Chestnut mare

A Boy Brown mare

A Bay mare

Plate V

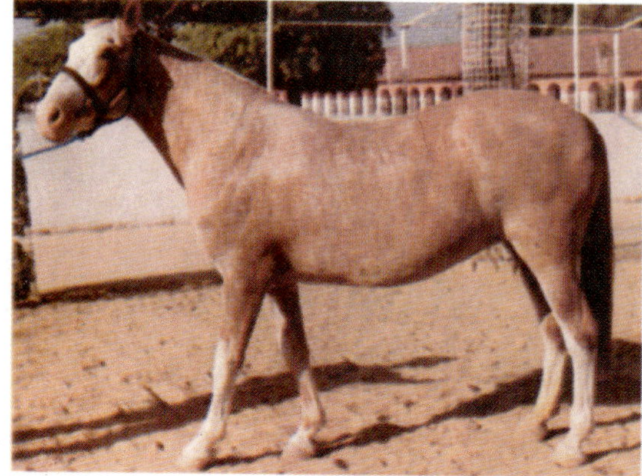

A Chestnut roan mare

A Grey mare

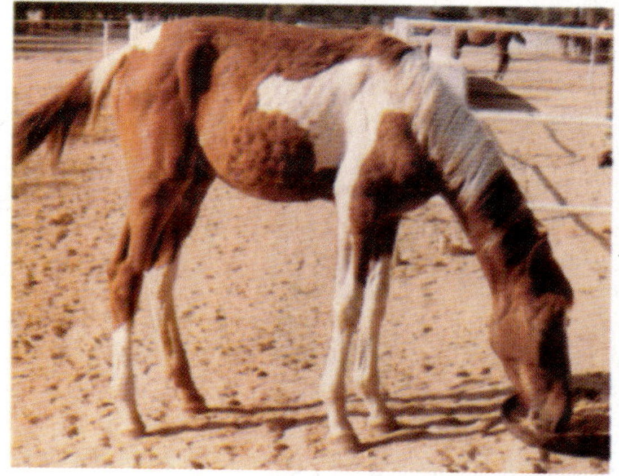

A Skewbald foal

Plate VI

Faint star, snip into left nostril

Broad star, conjoined ¼ stripe, snip

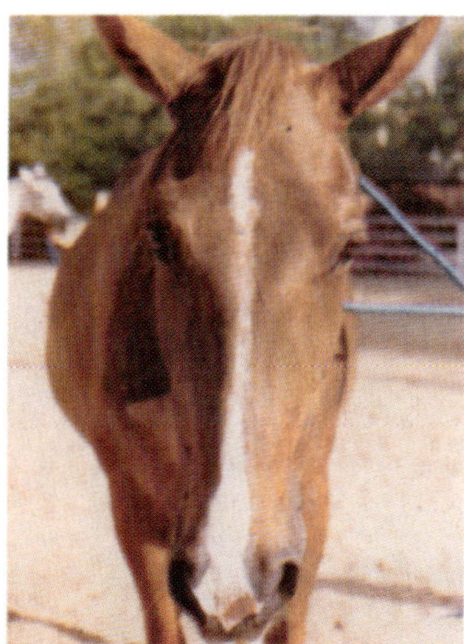

Linear star, conjoined stripe into right nostril

Broad, irregular star, blaze into both nostrils

Plate VII

Elongated star

White face into both nostrils

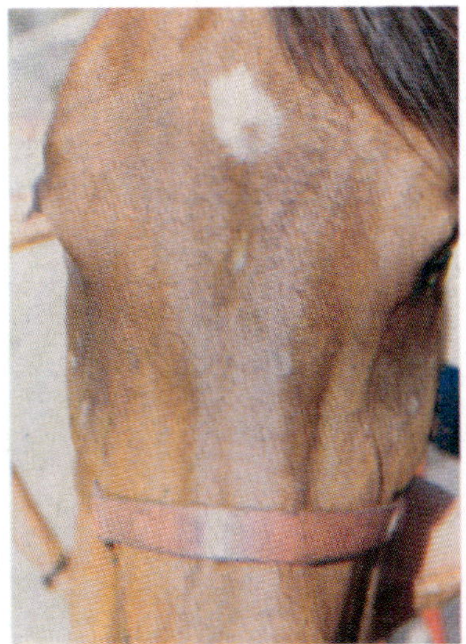

Broad circular star, whorl contained

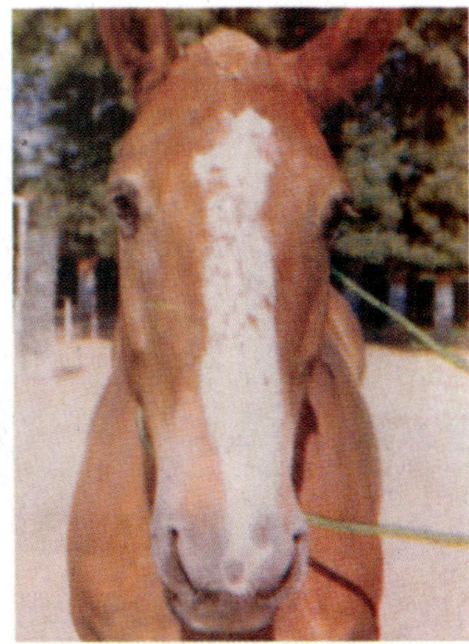

Broad, irregular star, conjoined blaze into left nostril

Plate VIII

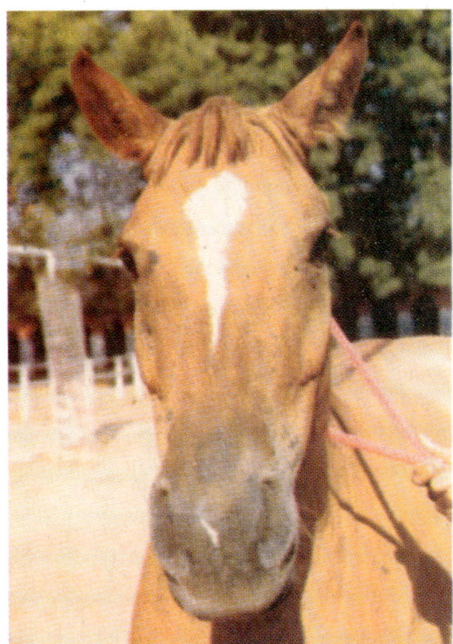

Broad irregular star, broken ½ stripe, faint snip

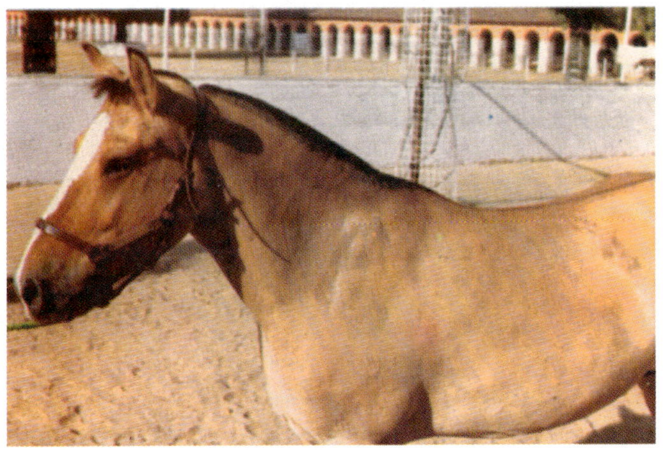

Mare showing List

Plate IX

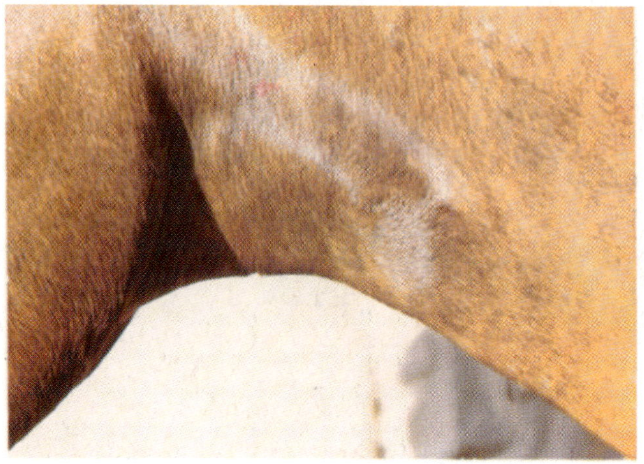

Whorl at neck

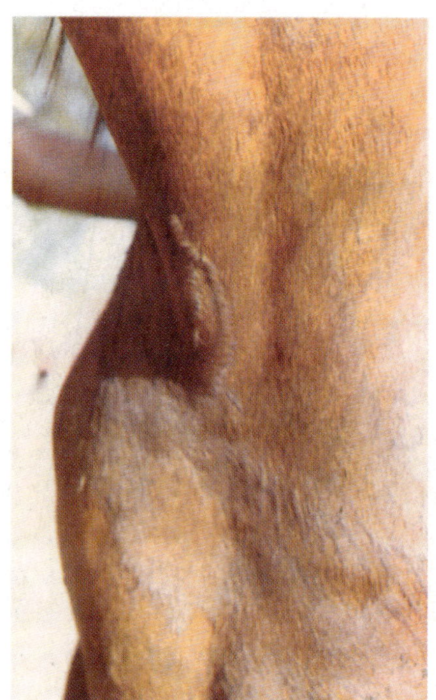

Whorl at base of neck
(throat region)

Plate X

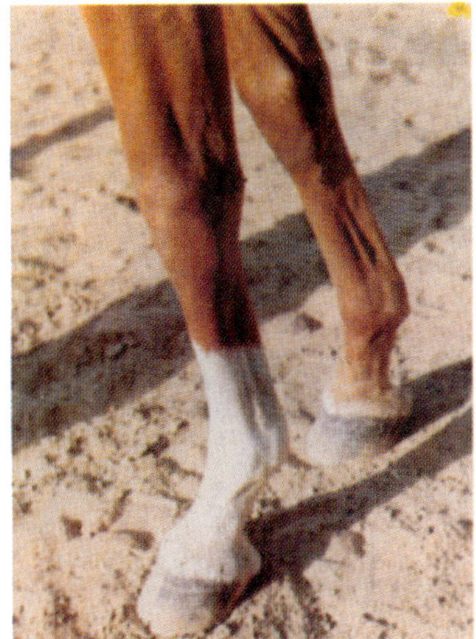

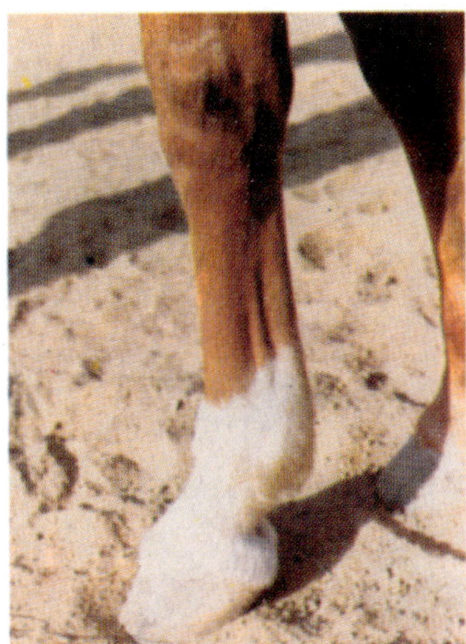

White leg partly

White fetlock

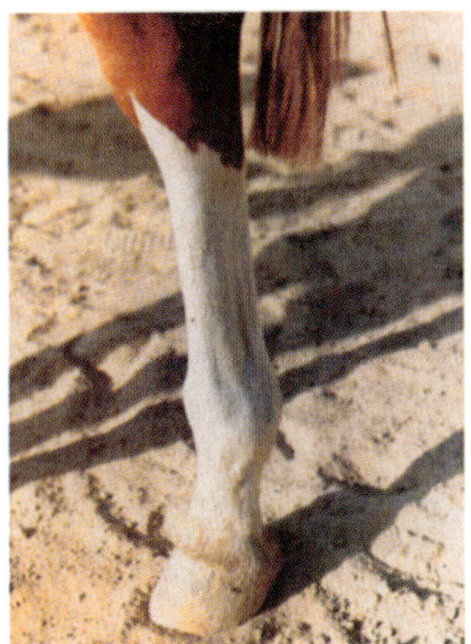

White Leg

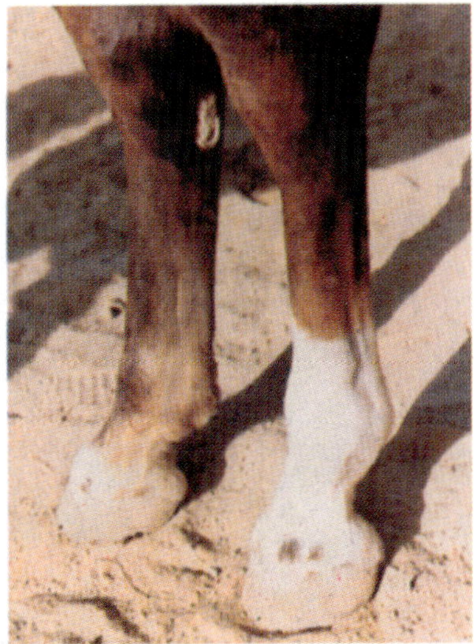

Leg partly with black spots at coronet

Plate XI

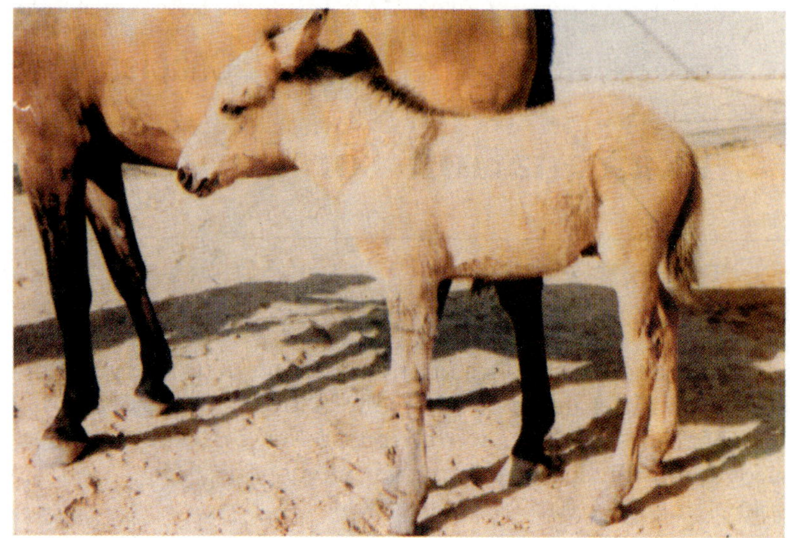

Mule foal showing list, cross and Zebra marks

Oat Hay stack in making

Plate XII

Chapter **13**

Examination for Soundness

Introduction

Soundness denotes absence of any condition that may interfere with natural usefulness of a horse in performance of its work. A sound horse is one which possesses no detectable or discoverable defects of abnormality, congenital or acquired, liable to interfere with its usefulness.

Soundness may be classified as:

(a) Working soundness, and

(b) Breeding soundness

A horse, sound for breeding purposes may not necessarily be sound for working or vice versa. For this reasons, all abnormal findings must be recorded in the original examination.

While recording the detailed observations on soundness of an animal, the words to the effect that "At the time of Examination" should precede, so that subsequent unsoundness cannot be construed as being present at the time of original examination. For whatever reason an examination is made, it must entail a record of description of the animal, for purposes of "Identification" in the future.

Working Soundness

A horse which is to be examined for working soundness must be closely checked for certain qualities needed for that particular job. A draught horse should have the qualities and conformation for the work it has to perform. Similarly, a polo pony should possess certain requisites. Before proceeding further, one must know the various conditions which can cause unsoundness.

Conditions which make the Horse Permanently Unsound

HEREDITARY	ACQUIRED
Spavin	Arthritis
Articular Ring Bone	Splint
Thoroughpin	Pedal ostitis
Stringhalt	Side Bone
Cryptorchids	Curb
Blindness	Bog spavin
Cataract	Shivering
Parrot Mouth	Hernias
Sesamoiditis	Roaring
Hereditary Multiple Exostoses	Nerve Paralysis
	(Radial, Prescapular, Tibial)
	Any form of Venereal disease viz
	Dourine,Vibriosis, Salmonellosis, Vaginal Papilloma, Contagious Equine, Metritis etc

Conditions which Attribute to Temporary Unsoundness

Sand Crack

Thrush

Quittor

Corns

Dropped Sole

Laminitis

Sweeny

Wind Gall

Leg Interference

- Scalping
- Forging
- Over Reaching
- Cross Firing
- Speedy Cutting

Conditions which Attribute to Breeding Unsoundness for Stallions

Roan Colour

Phymosis

Paraphymosis

Poor Sex Libido

Poor Fertility

Poor Semen Quality

Cryptorchid

Hernias (Scrotal or Umbilical)

Arthritis

Blindness (Aneurosis)

Cataract

Roaring

All other conditions mentioned in the list of permanent unsoundness.

Conditions which Attribute to Breeding Unsoundness for Mares

Tipped Vagina

Recto-Viginal Fistula

Umbilical Hernia

Pyometra

Muco Pululent Vaginitis

Vulvitis

Abnormalities of Ovaries

- Hard, Fibrous and Extensively Large
- Adhesion of Ovary to Fallopian Tube
- Nymphomania
- Abnormality of Uterus/Cervix
- Flabby Uterus
- Small Uterus
- Tumours in Uterus
- Thick Rigid Cervix

The conditions enumerated above may be congenital or acquired. If congenital, then the animal is not suitable for breeding. However, in some cases of acquired conditions, a horse may be considered for breeding.

Some of these conditions are quite common and at times may be considered only blemishes. As such, good judgement must be used to determine the importance of particular condition. For example, a splint unaccompanied by lameness, clear of vital structures and joints and in an animal with good conformation, is a minor condition and such an animal should not be classified as unsound. Take another condition for example, either Thoroughpin or Wind gall. First thing to decide in these cases is whether these conditions have been produced by sprains and are healed or whether they are due to poor conformation with consequent trauma to vital structures. If they are due to trauma and the animal has a sound conformation, then it is not a blemish. But if it is due to poor conformation, then the animal is definitely unsound. Declaring an animal sound or unsound should, therefore, be based on many factors and no hard and fast rule can be made applicable to all cases.

In addition, there are a number of vices that may render a horse unsound. Some of these are:

Biting

Backing

Crib biting/wind sucking

Kicking/lashing at stalls or attendants
Bolting
Shying
Weaving
Stall walking (excessive)
Tail wringing or swinging

These are not easy to be detected unless closely observed based on practical experience.

Procedure of Examination for Soundness

A soundness examination must always be followed as a rigid routine so that everything is checked and the possibility of overlooking defects is minimized. The following procedure is suggested while examining animals:

General Appearance

Visual Examination

The best thing to do first is to gain a general impression of the animal presented to you and have a visual examination from a distance. A definite routine must be adopted. The animal should be viewed from in front, from either side and from behind. Go through each part of the body you face minutely and make a note of the points you observe. If this is done systematically, many embarrassing mistakes could be avoided. A lame animal could be seen pointing one of the forelegs, if lame in front. All conformational defects, scars, torn ears, crooked tails and so on, could be easily detected in a static animal. A horse may be turned several times in a tight circle to check wobbler syndrome or for signs of incoordination.

Skin

Affections such as ringworm, galls, mange, cracked heels, and so on, may not respond to treatment and should be carefully assessed from soundness point of view.

Head

Examine for any bulging of bones of the face, for facial paralysis, cysts, openings discharging along the ventral border of the mandible indicative of alveolar periostitis or there may be unilateral nasal discharge. Horses with dental defects viz. Parrot mouth, Scissor mouth and so on, are unsound. Any cough should be regarded with suspicion and constitutes unsoundness.

Eyes

The eyes should always be examined for any changes that may have occurred and will affect good vision. Horses are not often presented for examination for soundness in which obvious eye changes have occurred. Corneal opacity and cataract are reffered to as unsoundness. In certain cases of Amaurosis, it escapes the eye of the examiner. A horse suddenly taken out of stable will lift its legs higher than normal indicating blindness.

Neck and abdomen

The jugular vein on each side of the neck should be distended to see if they are both patent. If only one is functionless, it is a blemish but if both are affected, it is an unsoundness. Pulse should be taken for any irregularity which, if noticed, would necessitate auscultation of the heart. Any defect of the heart or lungs constitutes an unsoundness. Observe for signs of emphysema.

Close-up Examination

A spavin test should be administered to both hind limbs, and the tuber-coxae should be checked for knocked down hip. Check for any signs of neurectomy having been done earlier in any part. If in suspicion, carry out the needle puncture test of the skin and the site checked for any post operative scars. See if the limbs do not drop further than their corresponding on the other side, indicating injury to the suspensory ligament or to the flexor tendons. Any atrophy of muscles, and exostoses of bones must be noted and critically examined when locomotory system is examined. During general close up examination, be on the look out for any sign of infectious disease. All palpable lymph glands should be examined for enlargement. All lacrimal discharges must be critically examined for any eye diseases or systemic condition. The conjuctival mucous membranes must be examined for anaemic condition and for icterus. If any signs of anaemia or icterus are found, further detailed clinical examination including laboratory tests must be caried out. After carrying out visual and close up examination, the animal should be subjected to critical system-wise examination.

Respiratory System

Check lungs with a stethoscope when the animal is at rest for any signs of emphysema indicating heaves, any consolidation or other pathological condition which could be determinable with a stethoscope.

Exercise an animal to check up roaring. Place your stethoscope over the larynx and palpate the larynx for muscular atrophy. While palpating trachea and larynx, watch out for any-previous tracheotomy or roaring operation. While the animal is at work, be on the look out for any abnormality in breeding.

Circulatory System

Using stethoscope, check the heart both while at rest and immediately after work for any abnormalities e.g., pericardial friction rub, tachycardia, partial heart block and so on. Jugular vein must be checked for excessive jugular pulse. A jugular pulse could mean a right atrioventricular leak. The characteristic of the pulse (femoral/sub-maxillary) should be noted.

Digestive System

Check teeth for dental caries, supernumerary teeth, parrot mouth and for any missing teeth. An examination of outer edges of incisor teeth can detect crib-biters. Examine tongue for lacerations, and cuts. A faecal worm check may be done. Rectal examination for any aneurysm may be carried out, if necessary.

Nervous System

Examination of locomotor system would reveal any incoordination, wobbly gait, shivering, stringhalt and so on. Raise the horse's head reasonably high with the hand and release it quickly to determine the horse's balance. If there is some disturbance in semicircular canals, vertigo will usually be seen after this test. While dealing with nervous system, the eyes should also be checked thoroughly for the following :

(a) Blindness

(b) Corneal opacities and ulcers.

(c) Iris adhesions - this is usually detected when determining the reaction of pupil to light.

(d) Cataract - can be due to senility, injury or periodic ophthalmia.

(e) Reaction of the pupil to light.

Locomotory System

The main consideration of course in judging soundness of an animal, lies in its locomotory efficiency. The animal may have every thing but if it does not have sound legs then it is of no use.

Lameness

Lameness is only an indication of some structural or functional disorder in one or more limbs which is manifested as pain either while in progression or in standing position. The causes of lameness can be :

(a) Trauma;

(b) Congenital or acquired anomalies;

(c) Surgical conditions including inflammatory processes, exostoses etc;

(d) Metabolic disturbances (Rickets, hypocalcaemia);

(e) Certain infectious diseases.

The diagnosis of lameness is a difficult job and requires a detailed knowledge of anatomy and physiology of the limbs. Even most experienced veterinarians differ in their opinion. Knowledge of theory is not of much use unless the vet has practically acquainted himself with various types of techniques to diagnose lameness, by closely observing lame animals in his daily routine.

Classification of Lameness

Lameness has been customarily classified as –

(a) Supporting leg lameness (weight bearing)

(b) Swinging leg lameness (non weight bearing)

(c) Mixed lameness.

Supporting Leg Lameness

This type of lameness is seen in a horse while supporting weight or landing on the foot. The extent and duration of weight bearing is reduced by taking a shorter step and elevating the body during the support phase of the stride. It is usually seen in case of injury to the feet, bones, joints, ligaments and motor nerves.

Swinging Leg Lameness

This type of lameness is spotted when the animal is in motion that is during the swing phase of the stride cycle when the limb is being brought forward. It is usually due to some pathological changes involving joint capsules, muscles or tendons.

Mixed Lameness

This type of lameness is seen when the leg is moving and is also supporting weight. This lameness can be a mixture of any combination of swinging leg and supporting leg lameness.

Majority of lameness cases are in the forelimbs and 99.0 per cent of forelimb cases are lame due to some conditions below carpus. Most of the hind limb lamenesses are in the hock. It must be remembered that a horse may be lame in more than one limb or may have more than one pathological condition in the lame leg. However, the type of work, a horse is put to, may also give an indication to the seat of lameness. A turf animal usually develops carpitis or injury to tendons and suspensory ligaments. A draught horse is more prone to ring bone, side bone, bone spavin. A polo pony develops usually tendon trouble or trouble from hind quarters and hock joints. In all cases of lameness, the foot must be examined for elimination. History of every lameness case must be obtained before an attempt is made on judging lameness.

Procedure for Lameness Examination

Visual Examination. Lameness is always an unsoundness and a horse should be carefully examined for it. It should be examined at rest, walk and trot. Move it on smooth hard surface as it might fail to show lameness on, turf or soft ground. The person leading the horse should have his hand 45 cm below the bridle, to allow free movement of its head.

Examination at Rest: A horse should first be observed after having been rested for an hour or more in a loose-box. It is more apt to show lameness following confinement than after exercise. Make a horse stand for a short while and see if it shows signs of supporting leg lameness. It can often give a clue to the location of pain and sometimes even about struçtures involved. The preliminary rest is very important since many forms of lameness, specially those due to lesions involving joints, tendons and ligaments become intensified after a rest. In some cases, symptoms can only be readily observed during the first few paces taken by an animal after an initial rest. It must be remembered that a horse will show less lameness while in gallop than in canter, less in canter than in trot unless lameness is really severe.

In certain cases it may be desirable to exercise a horse or make him work for an hour, then let it rest for another hour before making examination for lameness. This may not be possible when buying animals in shows and sales. In such a case, it is better to wait giving an opinion until facilities for proper examination are provided.

However, while examination of.a horse in a stable, the compensating effort will show the structures involved. The following table will give a rough indication. These parts have to be critically examined and then only final opinion formed.

Compensating-effort	Probable structures involved
If animal stands with carpus forward and heel raised.	The carpal, pastern, fetlock and heel areas.
Points affected foot.	Navicular disease, fracture of extensor Process of third Phalanx.
Forelimbs held posterior and carpus Flexed with the resting on the ground	The shoulder of the same side.
Forearm extended, knee flexed, foot Being on a level with or posterior to its Opposite member-dropped elbow.	Elbow joint.

One word of caution, always compare the above findings with the normal attitude of limbs. In normal forelimbs, the weight is borne equally on both the legs and they are exactly opposite to each other. If both forelimbs are involved, the weight will be shifted frequently from one foot to the other or both forelimbs may be placed too far out in front. In the hind limbs, it is normal for a horse to frequently shift the weight from one limb to the other. In case, a horse consistently rests on one hind leg and refuses to bear weight on the other for a length of time or cannot be forced to bear weight, the possibility of that hind leg being lame is to be explored.

Outside the stable, when a horse is taken outdoors, great care should be taken to observe how it backs or turns. Shivering or stringhalt may each be possible if there is an obvious disinclination to back or turn freely. Sometimes, definite symptoms of these can be seen.

On being brought out of loose box, carefully observe while standing in front, the general symmetry of the head, eyes, ears, nostrils, shoulders, forelimbs and feet. Any asymmetry should be noted down for a later careful study. After completing the study from the front, the veterinarian should move to the left of animal and examine the head, neck, limbs in profile. At this time, not particularly any errors in alignment of knees or fetlocks, any uprightness of shoulders, hollow backs, malformation of neck, jaws and so on. Similarly, any deviation from normal in hind limbs, with particular reference to hocks should be noted. Now the veterinarian should move behind the animal and compare the right and left sides of hips, buttocks, gaskins, hocks, hind cannons, feet and so on, note the way the tail is carried. Finally, go round the right side of the animal and repeat the examination as done for the left side.

Examination during Exercise: While at walking/trotting, for most horses and stallions, an exercising bridle should be put on. For others, a halter will suffice. The handler who is to walk/trot the animal should be on the left of the animal and he should be instructed to hold the reins/rope loosely so that the horse's head has the opportunity for free play. The first few steps should be carefully observed, note whether each foot comes freely off the ground, whether muscular movement is free and void of any jerks, whether each foot is lifted and carried forward to equal distance, and whether the sound made by putting the foot down is approximately same with each foot.

After walking for about 20-30 metres, the handler should turn the horse away from him to the right side. While turning, watch carefully how the animal turns. The animal then should be walked back straight towards the observer. It must be ensured that the horse is made to pivot round first on hind legs and then on his forelegs in each direction. These pivoting movements are important for detecting animals suffering from shivering or incipient stringhalt.

The horse then must be made to back half a dozen steps and then immediately led forward. Sudden change of direction of this nature may intensify latent lameness or expose slight shivering or commence stringhalt. Subsequently, the horse should be trotted, the procedure being the same as for walk. Most lamenesses are detected when the horse is moving at a slow and steady trot.

Forelimb Lameness. If the animal is lame from forelimb, the head will drop when the sound foot lands and when the weight is placed on the lame leg, the head will be raised in order to ease pain in the affected leg. If the animal is not acutely lame, then trot should be used for diagnostic purposes because any lameness evident at walk will be itensified at trot. Great caution must be exercised not to confuse a left fore lameness with right hind lameness and right fore lameness with a left hind lameness, because in the hind limb the head will be raised when weight is put on the sound foot and dropped when it is put on unsound. It is a sound policy to observe critically for forelimb lameness when the animal is trotted towards an observer and for hind leg lameness when the animal is trotted away. The following points may also be borne in mind and will be useful in diagnosing seat of lameness. In a normal gait, the heel is lifted first when advancing the limb and when a foot lands the heel, touches the ground just before the toe. Hence in case of :

- pain in heel, foot will land on toe.
- diffuse pain in foot (laminitis), foot will land with exaggerated effort on the heel.
- toe is involved, the foot will land as in (b)
- lame from shoulder, scapulo humeral joint usually remains semifixed during progression, with marked lifting of head. Sometimes the head may be pulled towards the affected side.

Hind Leg Lameness

Trot the animal away from the observer to detect any signs of hind leg lameness, watch critically the hip. When the sound limb strikes the ground, the hip drops on the sound side and head raised at the same time. The hip on the affected side is raised and the head drops when weight is put on the unsound limb. Pay special attention to hock joint because hock is the most vulnerable joint for lameness. The toe is excessively worn in involvement of hock or stifle.

Examination for Seat of Lameness by Palpation

After having done visual examination so far, it is now incumbent to carryout examination to pinpoint seat of lameness. This is usually done by manual palpation. This as usual must be done in a systematic way. There are two ways of doing it. Start either from foot and upwards or vice-versa.

Examination of Forelimbs

Examine the foot for

- contraction of heels;
- condition of frog and sole;
- carry out pincer test to detect any tender spot in sole; and
- any separation of white line and hoof. This must be explored in detail using a hoof knife.

Examine the hoof wall for :

- dryness;
- contraction; and
- cracks - sand cracks; wear and tear of ground surface will indicate any abnormal wear.

Examine the coronary hand for :

- excessive heat, best appreciated by using back of the hand; excessive heat may mean development of low ring bone - pain means developing signs of inflammation/abscess,
- drainage at heels may be due to punctured foot and
- drainage at quarters may mean quittor.

Examine lateral cartilage for :

- ossification,(side bone).

Examine pastern for :

- heat and inflammation and
- for developing signs of high and low ring bone.

Examine fetlock for:

- pain and inflammation,
- articular wind galls and
- arthritis.

Examine cannon bone area for :

- lateral, medial splints - usually seen on medial side;
- suspensory ligaments - this ligament is just posterior to cannon bone, injury mostly at the distal end where it bifurcates for attachment to sesamoid bones. Ligament should be examined both while the animal is standing and limb in flexed position; and
- flexors and extensors - for signs of inflammation, break down, blistering, firing, bowed tendons.

Examine carpus for :

- distention of synovial sheaths;
- swelling of tendons;
- hygromas;
- carpitis; and
- free movement

Examine elbow and shoulder joints for :

- pain and jnflammation;
- crepitation; and
- capped elbow.

Apart from the above, be on the look out for injuries, scars, suturing marks, any scars at the site of neurectomy.

Examination of Hind Limbs

Examination of hind limb from foot to just below hock is the same as for forelimbs. Examination of hock must be done very carefully as this is the most susceptible joint.

Examine hock for :

- bog spavin;
- bone spavin;
- occult spavin;
- curb and thoroughpin.

A routine spavin test must be done. This is done by holding the hind limbs in flexion for one or two minutes. Immediately following this flexion, the leg is released and the animal moved at a slow trot. If the lameness is exaggerated, the test is considered positive for occult or bone spavin.

Examine stifle for :

- presence of any upward deviation of patella and
- gonitis.

Examine hip joint for :

- dropped hip and
- involvement of the joint produces a supporting leg lameness with an accompanying swinging leg lameness.

Examine pelvis for :

- fractures of tuber coxae; tuber ischii; public symphysis; and
- fractures of sacro-iliac junction carried out through rectal examination.

Aids to Diagnosis of Lameness

While a thorough knowledge of musculoskeletal anatomy and physiology is essential for the diagnosis of lameness, it frequently is insufficient in itself and additional technique may be required as an aid of diagnosis e.g.; nerve block, which can be conducted without the help of expensive equipments.

Nerve blocks: Local nerve blocks are a great aid in determining the site of lameness. The most useful among them are nerve blocks involving posterior digital nerves (upper plantar, lower plantar). The other nerves that could be blocked are median, ulnar in the forelimbs, the upper and lower plantar, anterior and posterior tibial in the hind leg. But it must be mentioned that barring plantar nerve block, nerve block of other nerves is of limited use owing to collateral nerve supply leading to insufficient block.

Dentition

It is best to make a note of age of the horse while examining its digestive system.

Breeding Soundness

It is always preferable to have a horse working sound as well, when examining for breeding fitness but in many cases these animals are retired to stud owing to a breakdown or being unfit for racing. Whenever an animal is retired to stud, it must be ensured that the cause of retirement to stud is not inheritable in which case the animal should be declared unsound. The following points will be borne in mind while examining stallions and brood mares.

Stallions

Stallions should have a healthy and masculine disposition, both testicles should have descended, genitals normal, should have no vices or masturbatory habits. He should be clear of all inheritable conditions which would make his offspring unfit for the purpose they are bred for, if these traits appear in them. Semen must be subjected to a thorough test for knowing sperm percentage, motility, live and dead count, rate of movement, density and so on. Only animals with a semen graded 'good' should be selected as a stallion. Do not forget that a stallion must have a very sound hind quarters and a pair of healthy forelimbs. Otherwise, he will be unable to mount and do the covering properly. The following conditions are also cause of unsoundness:

(a) Any form of venereal disease at present or its history in past.

(b) Tumours, injuries, ulcers on penis.

(c) Scrotal hernia.

(d) Epididymitis.

(e) Monorchid/cryptorchid.

Examination of Brood Mares

The points to remember, while judging mares for breeding fit condition, are the same as for other animals i.e. should not possess any weaknesses which are inheritable. Apart from the normal deviations, genitals must be subjected to a thorough detailed rectal exploration, its ovaries, fallopian tubes, uterine horns and cervix must be examined.

The following conditions will be looked into during rectal examination:

Ovaries

- Ovaries should not be hard, fibrous, or excessively large. If one ovary is hard and other normal and active, it is not unsound.
- Ovulation fossa should not have adhesions with infundibulum.
- Both ovaries should not be small.

Fallopian tube

- No adhesions in the tube.
- No growth/tumour in and around the tube.

Uterus

- Should not be enlarged - enlargement could be pyometra, thickened walls due to previous infection.
- Should not be flabby especially during breeding season. Flabbiness could mean reduced breeding efficiency.
- Should not be infantile uterus.
- No haematomas/tumour.
- Must pick up tone during breeding season.

Cervix

- A thickened cervix, laceration, infection and cervical adhesions can make an animal unfit for breeding.
- Cervicitis.

Vagina

- Adhesions in vaginal wall.
- Adhesions of vaginal wall with cervix.
- Vaginitis and other vaginal infections.
- Recto-anal fistula.
- Anal/vaginal tears due to earlier foalings.
- History of previous sutures.

A cervical/uterine swab (preferably when the mare is in heat) taken aseptically should be subjected to cultural examination. Only a clean animal should be classified as sound. The mare should be trotted and seen whether she is a wind sucker (Pneumovagina). The external genitalia (Vaginal lips) should be vertical and straight. A slopy vaginal opening like a shrunken vagina is easily prone to infection owing to faecal material falling into the opening at the time an animal defecates. A sutured mare or an animal subjected to Caslick's operation should not be classified as Sound Breeder. It is not advisable to recommend mare beyond 10 years age for breeding, as the percentage of conception/fertility goes down beyond this age. If the owner insists, the animal may be examined and if found fit otherwise may be declared as breeding fit, but with the remarks that age may be a factor against it.

Conditions met with in horses which render them permanently/ temporarily unsound and those that render a stallion/brood mare breeding unsound are listed in the beginning of this chapter for ready reference.

Other Details to be Recorded

Description of the Animal

After having examined an animal for soundness, it will be necessary to issue a certificate as to the fact that the animal examined is sound or unsound. For this, an accurate and complete description of the animal is necessary. This description should include colour, breed, or class, sex, age, height and any defects, along with its identification marks where by the animal can be identified.

Issue of Certificate

The certificate is a signed statement by a veterinary surgeon that he has examined a particular horse on a particular date giving its full description, defects and expressing his opinion as to whether the animal is sound or unsound. There should be no room for doubt or ambiguity in this certificate. It must be stated clearly whether the animal is sound or unsound.

Form of Certificate

In the interest of uniformity the undermentioned form may be used:

CERTIFICATE OF SOUNDNESS

(Name and address of Veterinary Surgeon)

No : ________________ Date:

I have this day ________________ examined at the request of________________________ (description of the animal colour, breed, sex, age and height). The said ________(horse, mare, gelding, colt or filly) has the following unsoundness, if any :

(a)

(b)

(c)

(d)

In my opinion, the said animal is sound/unsound.

Identification Marks :

Marks on the head/eyes -

including whorls -

Marks on limbs -

Right fore -

Left fore -

Left hind -

Right hind -

Marks on body -

Remarks on mane and tail -

Adventitious marks -

Signed ________________

Qualifications ____________

and Registration No. with Vet Council_________

Chapter 14

Stabling

One should try to create an optimal environment in which the animal is content, healthy and comfortable. Ideally, the best housing environment for equines is a run-out situation in which the horse can choose to be inside or out. Except in the most extreme cold conditions, the horse is able to thermoregulate either behaviourally or physiologically. Keeping horses outside is probably the most natural, but may not have adequate shelter from the sun and no dry place for them to stand. Cold-dry weather can be tolerated well by horses who have grown adequate coats but cold-wet weather, when the horse must stand in mud, is a stress. Horses are reluctant to lie down in muck and prolonged exposure to mud may lead to "thrush". Skin problems *Dermatophilosis,* "rain scald" or "rain rot" can also develop in horses kept outside. There are several acceptable methods of stabling equines. The traditional box stall may not actually be the best accommodation even though it is the largest.

Fig. 14.1

Stable Site: The chief considerations in selecting a site for stables are: fresh air, good light, dry foundation, a good water supply, facilities for free drainage, prevailing winds and the position of surrounding buildings.

The nature of the soil is of vital importance and a sub-soil of gravel or deep sand, offering the best prospect for a firm base, with free drainage and consequent dryness is considered best. Similarly, self-drainage soils, any rocky formation, such as limestone, chalk or granite, are also suitable; but stiff clay, deep loam, peaty and marshy soils are not naturally favourable and should it become necessary to occupy them, sub-soil drainage must be extensively adopted.

Construction of Stable :-

Walls:-These should be made of vitrified bricks or stones as per the availability and plastered with good quality cement. The walls be made damp proof and strong enough to sustain the weight of the desired type of roof.

Roof:- should be at least 12 ft (3.66 m) high to the spring of the roof and should be damp proof. The roof can be flat or sloppy. However, sloppy roof without over head rooms are by far the best, as their construction secures adequate air space, light and natural roof ventilation. The pitch or slope of the roof which is necessary, varies somewhat with the material employed. However, it is not possible to get all the qualities required in an ideal roof out of any one material as the desiderata being: an equable temperature in both hot and cold weather, noiselessness, non-inflammability and durability.

Materials for Roofs:

(a) Tiles, either flat or pantiles, maintain an equal temperature and afford roof ventilation, but are easily broken or loosened and be come untidy and leaky.

(b) Slates are fixed to the woodwork of the roof by two nails driven through each, and are not easily displaced, but they are as liable to breakage as tiles. Both tiles and slates make excellent roofs if kept in good repair and they should have an under roofing of boards.

(c) Stone flakes are substituted for slates where stone is abundant, but are very heavy, and clumsy.

(d) Thatched and tarred felt roofs are also used in many areas but these are prone to fire, though they have the advantage of being noiseless, and warm in cold climates.

(e) Galvanized iron is prone to baking heat in hot weather and to freezing temperature in cold; it is also excessively noisy when vibrated, but it is comparatively cheap and easily transported, so that it is commonly used in those localities, where, in spite of its drawbacks, it is very acceptable. It should, in any case, have a wooden inner roofing.

(f) Reinforced concrete and cement (RCC) formulation. It is very strong, durable and withstand all types of geoclimatic variations. However, it needs walls made of stones/ bricks using cement as adhesive material. As such the cost of construction is slightly higher.

Covered accommodation for animals should preferably be in blocks to suit the individual needs. The stalls should be arranged either in single row or in two rows facing each other with 1.2 meter wide passage in between. Each stall should measure 4.3 metre x 2.3 metre x 3.66 metre. Manger and water point at the scale of 1.4 metre per horse, having two separate compartments, should be constructed in the stall with inner width 0.45 metre, depth 0.3 metre and height of 0.75 metre at front crub and 1 metre on rear wall. In addition, open standing measuring 3.7 metre x 2.3 metre for each horse along with manger and water point should also be provisioned.

In addition, tethering rings should be provisioned both in front and rear in the covered accommodation as well as in open standing which are required for tying the animals as and when required. Further, adequate water supply, lighting arrangements and drains along with soakage pits are essential to maintain proper hygiene and sanitation in the stable.

Floor:-

Floors should be laid on a solid foundation, raised above the outside ground; should slope from front to rear only so much as will admit drainage to the back of the stall; absolutely impervious to wet; smooth, but not at all slippery, and durable. In the endeavour to comply with these requirements, a bed of concrete 10 to 15 cm thick should be first laid and the slope from the front to the rear of the stall made about one in sixty, i.e. a slope of not more than 5 cm in 3 m. Any floor not laid on concrete will sink in places, and harbour pools of urine.

Materials for Paving:

(a) Cobblestones, set in cement, are uneven and never give the animal a good or level standing; they are rarely laid on a concrete foundation and consequently sink in parts; the supporting cement cracks and urine finds its way in between.

(b) Bricks are only suitable if thoroughly vitrified. Ordinary bricks are very porous, rapidly absorb moisture, wear quickly and unevenly, but are not slippery. They should be laid on their sides as they last longer. Vitrified bricks are impervious to wet, but some of them wear very slippery. There are, however, others which do not become too glassy, and these make excellent paving.

(c) Stone slabs wear smooth and require constant rechipping; they are liable to crack and cannot be called a good flooring.

(d) Cement and concrete is laid in several varieties, and is considered to be good, durable, non-slipping and safe. It should have gentle slope for the drainage of water and urine. Shallow grooves are made in such floors to prevent animals from slipping. This type of floor is most commonly seen in modern stables.

(e) Wood blocks or any other material, as wooden sleepers, which will absorb wet are quite unsuitable, although, when treated with creosote, the former may be very usefully employed in forges and outbuildings.

Ventilation:-

The object of ventilation is to change the air of a building frequently enough to keep it fresh without allowing a draught to strike the animals.

The effect of quality of the air is significant on various body functions and unless a full supply of fresh and clean air is constantly available, the body is not so well able to perform hard work, or to resist the attack of disease as it otherwise would be. A practical and reliable test for the purity of the air in a stable is the effect produced on the sense of smell when entering it. If there is no apparent difference from the air outside, it is satisfactory; but if there is any stuffiness, the ventilation is defective, and the air of the stable requires to be changed more frequently.

Draught and Chill:- A draught is a current of air passing through a confined space, like a building, at such a place that it produces a feeling of cold when it strikes the skin. The effect of such a draught on a warm skin full of blood is to drive the blood into the internal organs and produce chill and shivering. The hotter the skin when the animal is exposed to the draught, the greater is the danger of a chill. If the air has to be changed very often, its constant inrush will keep the animals in a perpetual draught, and as it is one of the chief objects of ventilation to avoid this, a considerable cubic space is necessary in order to keep the atmosphere pure without having to change it too frequently. Careful experiments have shown that although men require only three changes an hour, yet eight or ten changes an hour is not enough too often for the horse's comfort or health, and a calculation based on that, shows 33 cubic metres for each horse is sufficient, which is a convenient space in all respects.

It may be mentioned here that a stable ventilated to such a degree that it does not differ from the open air, will be extremely cold in winter, but the health of animals may still cope up from cold since they stand varying temperatures remarkably well, and chills from standing in a draught, particularly when heated and tired, are the only changes of temperature which are at all likely to produce sickness. In cold weather, the heat and condition of the body may, if necessary, maintained by extra food, bedding, or clothing and not by allowing the occupants of a stable to breathe an atmosphere heated by the emanations from their own bodies and the exclusion of fresh air. Similarly in hot weather, proper arrangements are essential to save the animals from the effects of hot winds so as to avoid excessive sweating and heatstrokes.

Means of Ventilation:-

Doors - Stable doors are valuable additions, but cannot be regarded as permanent means of ventilation. They should be kept open as much as possible, especially when the stable is empty, so that the floors may be well aerated. When there are doors at each end of the building, one may usually be kept open throughout the day, or where half-doors are fitted, the top half certainly kept open.

Windows:- These are the main inlets for fresh air, and to get the full benefit from them they should be arranged along both outer walls of the stable, one over each stall. Stable windows should be hinged from the lower edge, or centre so that they may be opened with an inward slant. With windows on each side of the stable, those to the leeward should always be kept open, and in calm weather those on both sides. The amount of inlet space required for each horse is not less than 0.9 sq m.

Drainage:-

The requirements for efficient stable drainage are quite simple: viz., a stall level from side to side, but sloping sufficiently (1:60) from front to rear. To allow urine flowing to the back of the standing; a shallow, open, surface drain is made behind the stalls so as to convey the collected fluid to the outside drain or sewer.

In order that the standing may be as level as possible, the stalls should not slope more because it will allow the urine to run off, and the drain at the back should be quite open and as shallow as the quantity of fluid to be carried will allow. If, in a very long stable, this drain may be made to slope from the centre towards both ends - a hog-backed drain. Closed and underground drains are more likely to become foul and choked from neglect.

A drain in the centre of the stall is also undesirable, as in addition to the faults just enumerated, it necessitates a standing which slopes to the centre, instead of a level one. All drains should be free of sharp angles, any change of direction being made by curved pipes or bends.

Stable Fittings:-

Stable doors should be 2.45 m high and 1.25 to 2.45 m wide, according to whether the men have to lead single horse or pairs through them. Too narrow a door has been the cause of many accidents The door may be hinged or made to traverse on rollers. Further, hinged doors should open outwards to permit free entrance if the animal stands in the doorway and also to guard against accidents from striking the half-closed door. The horizontal arm of the hinge should reach well across the door to support its weight, and a suitable swing-back stop should be fitted to prevent it banging to.

Half-doors, the top and bottom portions opening separately, are excellent for stables. The top half can usually be left open - on the lee side for ventilation; and when fitted to loose boxes, the occupant can look out. In the latter case, the lower part should be high enough to exclude the possibility of jumping over. Traversing doors should be hung on rollers from above and fitted with large smooth handles, on which a loose horse cannot get hung up.

Latches should be strong, easily turned and with large handles, which offer no projections for loose horses to get injured.

Windows should be hinged along their lower border so that they open with an inward slant. There cannot be too much light in a stable, and if possible each animal should have a window over its stall with its lower edge 2.45 m from the floor and should leave no projection for the horse to play with or get entangled in.

Mangers:- are made entirely of concrete and should be large, broad, with a perfectly smooth surface, and all corners well rounded. An overhanging lip to prevent food being wasted when the horse scatters it by blowing or muzzling in it, is sometimes found but it lends itself to accumulating dirt unless well attended to. Broad mangers are to be preferred to narrow ones, as the greedy horse cannot plunge his mouth deeply into the food and seize large mouthful, and deliberate mastication is more likely to be obtained. The rim of the manger should be sufficiently broad to prevent it being seized by the teeth, as this encourages crib-biting.

Hayracks:- should be on the same level as the mangers, and not as may be seen in many old-fashioned stables, above the horse's head. In this latter position, the animal is constantly exposed to the risk of getting dust and fragments of hay in his eyes, and in addition, an undue proportion of the ration is likely to be wasted by his pulling it down, when it tramples under feet and gets soiled as he reaches for more. Where all the hay is fed as chaffs, a hayrack is of course unnecessary, and a manger in the stall serves the double purpose.

The fittings, such as latches, window fastenings, etc, in a stable should not have projections on which a loose horse can injure himself. Horses which get loose during the night always appear to have the faculty of finding and wounding themselves on any rough or sharp projection in the stable.

Electric light fittings:- These should be well out of reach of the animal, and also protected from accidental interference.

Chapter **15**

Grooming and Stable Management

Grooming: The objects of grooming are cleanliness, prevention of diseases and improvement of the animal's condition and appearance and the results may be sufficiently attained for the horse by good brushing and wisping once a day. The necessity for and the amount of grooming required varies with the condition under which animals are placed, the better they are fed and the faster the pace expected of them when at work, the greater should be the amount of care towards getting the skin into perfect condition. Grooming may, therefore, be limited to the amount of care necessary for cleanliness and health, or it may be prolonged and amplified with the object of maintaining the skin in best possible condition even while work is at high pressure, and this is derived by hand rubbing and wisping i.e. massage.

The importance of grooming as preventive of diseases must not be underrated; whilst it is quite true that mange and many other diseases are not produced by dirt, it is nevertheless equally true that they are most frequently spread with greater rapidity, and are much more difficult to eradicate, where dirty conditions prevail. The regular brushing and cleansing of the coat is an undoubted preventive measure against various skin diseases.

The relation of regular exercise to the amount of grooming required is another matter which should be kept in mind. It is a well-known fact that an idle horse is always more difficult to clean than the one which is at work; indeed, it is almost impossible to keep some skins free from scurf and grease when the horse is idle. The idle horse, therefore, requires even more attention and thoroughness as regards grooming than his fellow at work. Accordingly, regular exercise is considered, in addition to its other benefits, a labour saving procedure.

Extra grooming, especially massage of any kind, has a great effect in improving the general condition, and it has always received the greatest attention from those who train animals for any form of severe and prolonged exertion. It must be borne in mind that all working horses are kept under purely artificial conditions. They receive an amount of food which is, far in, excess of their bodily requirements and which is converted into the extra energy enabling them to produce the work required; whereas in a natural state, they eat no more than to sustain them, take little more exercise that enables them to change posture and only carry their body weight. The extra food consumed and work done produce greater and more rapid changes throughout the body, as a result of which various systems of body are required to perform much more work. The work, which is rendered possible by the increased nutriment, creates a large amount of extra waste which is got rid of by the lungs, kidneys, bowels working at increased pressure and the skin throwing off more material in the sweat and dandruff. The amount got rid of by the skin is very considerable and increases enormously when exertion is severe and sustained, so that when the condition required is for the production of fast work, it is essential that the skin should be in as good fettle and as well trained as the rest of the body. Grooming, therefore, is one of the means which helps to make and keep the body fit as well as clean.

Grooming Equipments:- The grooming tools consist of body brushes, curry comb, dandy brush, mane or tail comb, sweat scrapers, sponge, rubber and wisp. Body brushes are made of stout bristles or vegetable fibre and have a broad hand-loop of webbing across the back to prevent the brush slipping from the grasp. The use of the body brush is to remove scurf and dirt from the coat, and for this purpose, the bristle brushes are superior to those made of fibre. Fibre, however stiff at first, ultimately flattens down from the continued pressure on the brush. Bristles, on the other hand, though more expensive, do not bend, but simply wear shorter, and retain their upright position till worn down to the back. It is well to remember that as bristles get shorter, they become less pliant and stiffer, so that a half-worn brush is a very prickly article and should be used with consideration.

Fig. 15.1

Curry Combs - The curry comb consists of several straight, blunt toothed blades in a metal back, with a broad loop of webbing for the purpose of securing it on the back of the hand. It is essential that the teeth should be smooth and blunt, though may be rounded at the top and bottom. This prevents the bristles being unduly worn away when the comb is used to clean the body brush, and also guards against injury to the skin when used for the removal of dirt. Other patterns have wooden handles, and some have a series of curved springy blades, instead of the straight rigid ones usually met with. At the sides, small projections of the blades are seen on many patterns for the purpose of knocking on the ground when dislodging dirt from the back.

Use of the Curry Comb - The use of curry comb on the skin should generally be restricted as its utility is confined to cleansing the body brush of scurf. To effect this, only an occasional rub on the brush is necessary, but its use is much abused by animal attendants who make a great show of cleaning the brush and do little work with it on the skin, the result being that the brush is quickly worn out. The dirt should be dislodged by knocking the side of the comb on the floor behind the horse, where it can be seen and swept up, and is evidence of the man's diligence. Blowing the scurf out of the comb should not be practised as it results in the dust being inhaled by the horses or settling again on the coat from which it has just been removed. In light horses, use of curry comb is limited to the removal of caked dirt and mud. However, in some commercial stables, generally the animals are groomed all over with it, and subsequently brushed with a dandy brush.

The method has a good deal to recommend it where time is an object; it is quick, effective, does not in any way injure the skin, and seeing that this is the case, some discretion may be allowed in its use.

Water Brushes - These are made of longer, finer, and softer bristles than body brushes. They are intended for damping the mane and tail, and washing the feet and legs. They are also often used dry for grooming fine coated, ticklish horses, and are certainly very useful for grooming the head and face. When employed for washing feet, their use should be confined to the hoof only; wetting of the legs should be avoided as a routine.

Dandy Brushes - These are made of stiff whisk fibre. They are, in general, use as a grooming brush, and as a matter of fact, are most useful in any stable. On light horses, their use is limited to the removal of hard caked dirt, the rest of the grooming being performed with the body brush. However, in commercial stables, these are often used, in conjunction with a free use of the curry comb. Their use saves time and labour and they are most efficient instruments of grooming.

Mane or Tail Combs - These are made of horn or metal, with deep, broad teeth; though convenient, they are not actually necessary and, if not very carefully used, they tear out and break the hair considerably.

Sweat Scrapers - These are long flexible blades of smooth metal with a handle at each end by means of which the lather of a sweating horse may be conveniently and quickly removed. Another variety has a central handle with a rigid curved blade, but the pattern is not so good as the flexible one, since the rigid blade does not adapt itself to the curves of the body so well.

Sponges - These are commonly used during grooming for cleaning the eyes, lips, nostrils, and dock. Though the convenience of sponges for this purpose is undoubted, they should invariably be prohibited on the appearance of any contagious disease, as they are one of the commonest means by which infection is spread.

Rubbers - These are generally used to give the coat a final polish after the rest of grooming is completed, and a damp rubber may, with the advantage, take the place of a sponge whenever possible, since it can be easily disinfected and cleaned by boiling, a process which ruins sponges.

Wisp - It is a pad of hay or straw, made by twisting the material into a rope and doubling it into a convenient-sized pad as described below. Its proper use, which is really a form of massage, is a most valuable method for improving the condition of the skin and coat. To make a wisp, soft hay or straw should be twisted into a convenient-sized rope about 2.5 to 3.0 m long; two loops are then formed at one end, one being very slightly longer than the other. Each of these loops in turn is then twisted beneath the remainder of the rope until the end is reached, when it is passed through the extremity of each loop and tucked under one of the twists. A really good wisp should be no wider than can be conveniently grasped by the hand. A little practice is necessary to make one really well.

Time for Grooming - As a matter of appearance and cleanliness, horses should be "quartered" (lightly groomed) before going to exercise, but the "strapping," i.e. thorough grooming is best carried out on return from work, unless it has been of a very exhausting nature, when horses are better left alone until recovered from fatigue. As a practice, it is advisable to pick out and inspect the feet before commencing to groom the horse, in order that the feet are not overlooked.

Method of Grooming to be adopted - The horse must be cool and dry. Commencing at one side of the neck immediately behind the ear, the coat should be thoroughly brushed out, the brush moving the way the hair lies *as* a rule, though in order to get rid of hard dirt or scurf, it is sometimes necessary to brush in a circular direction. To use the brush with the best effect, the man should stand well away, keep his arm stiff, and lean the weight of his body on the brush, which should be placed gently on the skin and not brought down with a bang, especially on a thin-skinned, ticklish horse. If the man stands close, with a bent elbow, and brushes with his arm only, he could not force the bristles or fibres through the coat so well, or remove the scurf so effectively. He should use the brush in the left hand for most part in grooming the left side, and for hind-leg. He should grasp the hamstring with his free hand. The horse is now turned round in the stall, the head and mane brushed and eyes, nostrils, and the dock cleaned. Finally, he is put about again, the tail is brushed out and the whole coat wisped and given a final polish with a rubber.

In grooming the head, it is well to use a soft brush if one is available, and for this purpose, a dry water brush is frequently requisitioned; it is further to be noted that a good groom is careful not to knock the skin with the wooden edge of the brush when going over the bony projection of the head and legs.

Wisping - As previously stated, it is a form of massage. It stimulates the skin, increases blood supply into it, great effect on the oil glands of the hair, increasing their output, and thereby giving a marked gloss to the coat. The wisp should be brought down with a bang on the skin, in the direction of the hair, and the process repeated all over the body, care being taken to avoid delicate parts.

Hand-rubbing is another excellent form of massage, and is specially useful for removing the loose hair of the coat as well as stimulating the skin. The hands are slapped on the body one after the other, and the weight of the groom's body leant upon them and the forearms, whilst both are moved over the skin with firm pressure. In the case of the legs, brisk but gentle rubbing with the fingers and palms in the direction of hair is an excellent stimulant to the circulation of the limbs. For the removal of loose hair by rubbing, the hands and arms should be kept slightly damp. Length of time occupied is no criterion of the quality of work done and quick, hard - grooming should be encouraged in every way.

Brushing the Mane - If the hair is at all damp, matted or kinked, it should be brushed till well separated and then, commencing at the highest point of the withers and keeping the horse's head low, so as not to spoil the part already cleaned, it should be taken as a lock at a time and brushed out from the roots.

To Thin the Mane - This should only be done when the hair is so thick as to be intractable, and is accomplished by taking a few hairs at a time from the under surface, freeing them from the rest, and pulling them out quickly. The hairs on the upper surface should not be touched. When sufficiently thinned, the mane should be brushed out and the ends made level by simply plucking them with the fingers. On no account should they be cut with scissors, or the appearance will be spoiled.

To lay the Mane - As a rule, water brushing the mane when cleaned and tying a rubber cornerwise over it, is all that is requisite to make it lie tidily, but when this is insufficient, it may be wetted, plaited in locks, and small weights tied along the ends of the plaits. Very intractable manes can be made to lie by plastering down with wet clay, which easily brushes off when dry, and after a few repetitions, leaves the hair in the desired position.

Hogging the Mane - When "hogging" is practised, the hair should be cut from each side and carefully edged off to avoid a sharp clipping line against the hair of the neck. A well developed forelock is a protection against flies, and if it is removed, an eye fringe should be worn whenever necessary. If a mounting lock is required, it should be a large one, or it will rapidly pull out and look untidy.

Grooming the Tail - The hair of the tail should be treated like the mane, brushed out from the roots, lock by lock for cleanliness, and finally straight down for appearance.

To Bang the Tail - Place the hand under the dock to raise it into the position in which it is carried when the animal is moving, and having determined the right length, an assistant should gather the hair firmly together with a double grasp, holding it quite straight, with the portion to be cut showing between his hands. The cut should then be made with the shears inclined a trifle upwards, so that the outer hairs *of* the tail may be a little longer than those nearest the legs. Under hairs are to be pulled out and not cut.

Wet and sweating horses should be dried before being groomed. If they are wet from rain, wisping with handfuls *of* loose straw and brisk friction with the rubber subsequently, is a good method of making them warm and dry.

A sweating horse should be led about till dry, scraped and wisped as above, or allowed to roll in a sand bath. Further, if the weather permits, he should not be brought into the stable till he is quite cool. Seat patches under the saddlery should be dried immediately after the saddle is removed, or have some covering left on the back till they are cool.

"Breaking out", that is, sweating in patches, is occasionally observed after drying or grooming in hot weather; the patches should be again dried, and if they recur, the animal may be led out into the open for a little while. The condition occurs most frequently in horses which are not fit, but some animals constantly exhibit it; a good practice is to place a layer of straw lengthways along the horse's back under a rug.

To judge the cleanliness of a horse, the hand may be passed the reverse way of the hair, to get a view of the skin, and the points of the fingers run firmly against the set, of the coat. The grooming is not proper when lines of grey are left on a dirty skin and the points of the fingers are likewise covered with scurf. Similarly, places between the branches of the under jaw, under the crown piece of the head collar, the bends of the knees and hocks, under the belly, between the forelegs and thighs and the tail are usually scamped when the work is not thorough.

Other stable details which may be included under "grooming" are washing of the mane, tail, and sheath, and picking out the feet.

The mane and tail may be washed with soap and water when necessary to remove greasy dirt. Rubbing the tail is not uncommon, and is generally due to its dirty condition, the irritability being in such cases removed by a good washing and subsequent brushing.

The sheath should be washed occasionally with mild antiseptic solution. Some horses require it often than others, especially those that stale without drawing the penis, a habit which is generally induced by the accumulation of dirt. At certain season of the year and in hot climates particularly, the prevalence of maggots from the attacks of flies renders a close attention to this detail very desirable. Soft soap should not be used for washing the sheath.

The feet should be picked out thoroughly while grooming, and on return from work. It is a detail which does not always receive the care it should, as apart from the necessity of cleanliness, the sole of the hoof is so liable to injury, from accidents at work, that very frequent inspection of it should be made. The most convenient form of hoof picker is a strong, blunt iron spike or hook, and in use its point should not be forced down the sides of cleft of the frog with more vigour than is necessary to remove the dirt. Any sharp pointed instrument is unsuitable for this purpose. While washing the stable, the legs should not be wetted during the operation.

Washing Stable Brushes - It is occasionally necessary to thoroughly wash stable brushes, to get rid of accumulated grease. The usual method by which this is accomplished, namely boiling the brush or soaking it in a tub of hot water, ruins the article by separating the back, and causes avoidable waste. The brushes should have the backs scrubbed with soap and water and whipped dry, the bristles should be "dipped" in hot, strong soda water till free from grease, and then similarly dipped in strong brine. The latter process is essential to re-harden the bristles which become soft in water or soda water. After cleaning they should be stored, bristles down, till dry. Instead of "dipping" they may be allowed to stand in shallow trays of soda and salt water, but the backs should not be immersed.

Washing

The washing of horses, as a general practice, is to be strongly condemned. In cold and changeable temperate climates, it may very easily lead to sickness, and even in warm and equable temperatures, its practice is not always without adverse effects. The only purposes for which the use of water or soap and water is necessary on the body of the healthy horse is for the removal of dirt stains which will not groom off, and for the occasional cleansing of the mane, tail, and hooves. The dangers which washing may give rise to are not, however, due to the wetting of the skin, but to want of attention to the subsequent drying; and in all cases where it is found necessary to wash, too much care cannot be bestowed on making sure that the animal is thoroughly dried and the warmth of the skin kept up, or a chill results. The use of soap removes a great proportion of the usual greasiness of the coat and consequently some of nature's protection and until this is restored, an unusual liability to chills is present, which can only be guarded against by thorough drying and protection from draughts. From the same cause, i.e., removal of the natural grease, the coat of washed horse is dull and lacks the glossiness which it would otherwise carry. Washing of the body, then, should be avoided as a rule, except for the special purposes mentioned, and should it be necessary at any time to break the rule, greatest care should be taken to dry the skin thoroughly, clothe the animal warmly for the time, and keep it out of draughts.

Washing the legs and belly on return from work in order to get rid of mud is frequently followed by stiffness and cracking of the surface, This is more likely to happen if warm water is used or when the weather is cold, and especially when there is a *keen* wind; it is most common in the heels, legs and bellies of horses which are washed on return from work. When confined to the hollow of the heel, the condition is called "cracked" or "greasy heel", the latter term originating from the fatty nature of the discharge from the oil glands of the skin which collects around the injury. On the legs and belly, it is commonly attributed to the irritation of mud.

The condition is a serious one and may incapacitate horses for long periods, but it may be practically banished from the stable by prohibiting the routine washing of legs and feet. Mud should be left till dry, and then brushed off.

It has been stated that animals with white legs are more frequent sufferers from cracked heels than others and this is no doubt the case; but it is not on account of weakness or peculiarity of the white skin, but owing to the fact that it is more frequently washed.

There must, however, be occasions on which it becomes necessary for the sake of appearance to wash white legs, and if they are thoroughly dried, no harm results. The drying must, however, be quite thorough and the circulation of the part well maintained by brisk rubbing. Washing the hooves, both round the wall and on the sole is occasionally required as a matter of cleanliness after the feet have been picked out. It is not necessary to do it as a matter of routine, and whenever possible it should be done outside the stable.

Horses at work take no harm from rain and may be ridden through water with impunity, because the natural greasiness and subsequent exertion of the journey keep up the circulation and warmth of the wetted skin till it is dry again.

Clipping

Under natural conditions, the horse's thick winter coat provides him with an extra warm covering during the time when the weather is cold. The extra warmth of the long, thick hair, added to the increased greasiness always found under a heavy ungroomed coat, keeps the body warm and so helps considerably to maintain the weight and condition.

If, however, horses are required to work hard, the coat becomes a positive drawback, adding considerably to the exhaustive nature of the labour, keeping the animal in a constant sweat and preventing rapid drying of the skin after exertion, as a result it is found that a loss of condition is inevitable. On the other hand, a clipped horse not only works with less distress and it is, moreover, dried and cleaned with much less labour and risk of chills. An argument which is sometimes advanced for not removing the hair from the back of the fetlock is that it acts as a natural drain for water when the animal sweats or is wet.

Altogether, apart from its beneficial effect on the horse's condition and working power, clipping enables the groom to dry and clean wet and dirty animals better, more quickly, and with less labour.

Whether the hand or power clipper is used, some little skill is necessary to produce the best results, and as the tooth blades of all cutters are hard tempered and very accurately adjusted, they are easily broken and frequently found out of order unless carefully handled.

In using the hand clipper, the pressure exerted on the skin should be quite even throughout or the result will be "ridgy", and the right hand, which operates the blades, should do so without any pressure whatsoever. Care must be taken not to cut any of the mane and tail hair, and when the legs are left unclipped, the appearance is enhanced by slanting the boundary line from the back of the elbow upwards to the front of the forearm, where there is a natural dip in the limb, similarly in the hind limbs, the line should slope downwards and backwards from the point of the stifle.

If the power clipper is used, the driving machine should be worked at an even pace and should be placed in such a position that it cannot be knocked over by any unexpected movement of the animal, or a barrier should be erected to protect it. With either variety, the blades must be kept free from accumulating scurf and dirt, occasional brushing and wiping with a little paraffin oil being all that is required.

Singeing - With modern clippers, singeing is unnecessary, but as a matter of appearance, a lamp may be run over the animal occasionally to keep down rapid growing hairs which give a ragged look to the coat.

Period for Clipping - Horses may be clipped with advantage from the time their coat thickens in the autumn until summer coat shows signs of coming in the spring. The frequency of the operation will probably depend on the time and labour available. If there is no limit to these, the machine should be run over the coat every time it shows at all long, and frequent clipping certainly keeps animals smart in appearance, as well as giving the other advantages already enumerated. Where, however, labour and machines are limited, it is found most advantageous to clip at the beginning of winter. This period varies with the severity of the season, and the individual animal. Some animals are, in fact, clipped all the year round and carry quite good coats.

Further, following points with regard to clipping of animals must be considered:

(a) The nature of the work.

(b) Environment.

(c) Supply of food.

(d) Supply of clothing

(e) Clipping as a means of cleanliness to control parasitic diseases.

The benefit which animals voyaging from a cold to a hot climate at a time when their coats are thick, derive from clipping en route is evident. It is true that the long coat falls off naturally under these circumstances, and the hair rapidly adapts itself to changes of climate, but its removal by the machine at once relieves the animal of an unnecessary blanket and should be carried out when possible.

The use of clothing during the winter months for working horses which have been clipped is practically universal, and where horses are called on to work up to their rations, it is beneficial to the animal's condition, and economical to the owner. A sharp line of distinction must, however, be drawn between the legitimate use of clothing as a compensation for the loss of a thick warm coat, and its abuse. At times, in order to preserve a sleek appearance, several rugs are placed on the animal and the stable is closed against all ventilation in order to keep the atmosphere warm. This procedure, although attaining its object, namely, fat and sleekness, but it is at the risk of impairing the constitution, rendering the animal more liable to serious disorders.

Observation leaves no doubt that the use of a rug in winter and after clipping, helps to maintain condition, and in turn working ability, without an increase of ration. The modern stables are comparatively cold when properly ventilated, and although this is right and healthy, yet the temperature of the body must be maintained, and if no artificial substitute for the coat is provided when the animal is at rest in a cold atmosphere, more of the food will be utilized for the maintenance of the body heat, and less will be available for the work than would otherwise be the case. Economy and efficiency combined, therefore, point to the use of a rug whenever the horse is worked up in cold climatic conditions, otherwise his condition must be maintained by extra rations. The comfort and appearance of the animal are both added to by the use of a rug.

Clothing

The term "clothing" as applied to horses comprises a hood, pad, roller, breast piece, and quarter sheet. With the exception of the hood, all these articles are combined in a shaped rug which fastens across the chest and has a surcingle stitched on. Some rugs fasten centrally on the breast, whilst others have a flap which buckles on the side, the latter being the better plan, as it prevents the front being blown up. For a similar reason, a well fitting "fillet string" should be fastened round the quarters to prevent the wind blowing the rug over the back; or the rug may be fastened to the flap of the rug.

The fit at the neck is another point which should be looked into. Very often the opening is much too large and as a consequence, the rug gradually works back over the shoulders till the top is drawn tightly across the withers and may cause a sore from pressure. When surcingles are stitched on, a space of four inches (10 cm) should be left free where the web passes over the backbone or shrinkages from wet may cause injury by tight pressure. A well fitting rug should embrace the neck like a collar, but in rather looser fashion, cover the body down to the level of the elbows and extend as far back as the dock; the fillet string should be capable of adjustment and the buckle of the surcingle sufficiently high up to prevent the horse lying on it when down.

Rugs are made of thick woollen blanketing or of jute sacking, lined with stout woollen cloth, and both are quite lasting, though the latter perhaps shows dirt least.

If the roller is not stitched to the rug, it should have a pad on each side of the spine, sufficiently thick to prevent the webbing coming down on the centre of the back when it is drawn tight. These pads are frequently so badly designed and stuffed that they do not prevent pressure on the backbone and a sore is the result. They should be thickest near the spine and thin off to nothing at their lower edges, pieces of felt laid on each other, then skived off, and covered with leather or serge, make a very serviceable pad.

Cleaning the Clothing - The rug should be well shaken and brushed every morning, and not wetted if it can be helped. If, however, it becomes necessary to scrub it, as little water as possible should be used, and the material well stretched when drying to prevent shrinkage. When rugs have to be disinfected by soaking, the fluid should be used cold for the same reason.

Bandages - Bandages are generally used on the legs of horses either to keep the legs warm and the circulation active or to protect them from injury whilst at the work. To keep the legs warm, a bandage should not be any tighter than to prevent it slipping down. It should cover as large a surface as possible and be applied without wrinkles and with even pressure throughout.

Stable bandages are usually about 2.15 or 2.45 m long and should be put on as follows - starting just below the knee or hock, enough should be unrolled to make one turn round the leg, at a slight downward slope; keeping the bandage close to the leg, allow it to unroll itself round and down the limb in the same direction it was started, until it reaches the coronet. Now it will naturally take an upward direction and its unrolling should be continued till the point from which it started is reached, where the tapes are to be tied in a bow on the outside of the leg, and the end should be tucked in neatly. In this position, they will be out of the way and not likely to be rubbed or undone. As an additional security, the corner of the loose end first applied may be turned down so that the next turn of the bandage will pass over and fix it. The nice adjustment of a bandage can only be acquired by practice, but the above directions will enable a correct method to be adopted. The usual errors are starting to unwind at too great a slope and then endeavouring to correct this by pulling the material in the required direction; and failing to get the bandage over the fetlock without altering its direction.

Warm bandages put on too tightly, defeat their object by stopping the circulation, and wrinkles are very likely to cause injury to the skin from the pressure of the folds which lie over them, for the same reason, knots, or bows should not be tied either on the back of the tendons or on the front and readjusted. All precautions should be taken to prevent any injury from pressure. The legs should be hand-rubbed after removing bandages.

Bandages put on for work should reach from below the knee to above the fetlock and should not in any way interfere with either joint. They should be fastened with a double strap and buckle stitched on the material, or if tapes are used, by a knot and should be removed as soon as the work is done. These bandages should not be put on too tight to prevent injury from pressure.

Material of bandages should be pure woollen for warmth, and some are now made with a fleecy side for this purpose.

Bandages which are put on to protect the legs from injury while at work should be made of stockinette, an elastic material which permits some pressure being applied when they are put on.

To roll a bandage, fold it by the end of which the tapes are attached i.e. the side on which they are stitched must be facing you. Double the tapes into a small bundle about the width of the bandage and lay them across the place they are stitched to, then roll the tapes inside. When the bandage is applied the tapes will then be outside in the most suitable position for fastening.

Knee caps to protect the knee in case of a fall at exercise, are generally used in sports horses. They are made of stout woollen cloth with thick leather bosses on the front, which are shaped to prevent them interfering with the bending of the joint. The top strap, which must be soft and padded on its inner face, should be tight enough to keep the knee cap in position, whilst the lower one should be quite slack, so that the lip may be freely bent when trotting. If these precautions are not observed, knee caps may lead to the very accident, they are designed to prevent.

Methods of Securing Horses in Stables

A head collar, chain or rope and log are usually used for this purpose. These are generally made of leather, but webbing is occasionally employed. The throat lash may be sewn on each side of the cheek piece, or be a separate strap passing over the poll and attached to the crown piece by a loop. The fit of a head collar is matter which does not invariably receive the attention it should, for one which is so loose as to be easily got rid of teaches the habit of "slipping" the head collar, which is often difficult to overcome. The nose band must be sufficiently loose to admit the free movement of the jaws in mastication and yawning which is the utmost extent, the animal requires to open his mouth. The brow band should be just long enough to allow the cheek pieces to pass from the crown down, without rubbing the bones on each side of the temples or cutting the base of the ears. The throat lash should not be slacker than admits of easy swallowing. The cheek pieces should end just below that prominent knob of bone which is seen half-way between the eye and the comer of the mouth, so that when side ropes or pillar chains are fitted, these will be out of the reach of the lips.

Slipping the head collar is a trick at which some horses become very expert, and they accomplish it either by getting the head rope over the head and then leaning back, or rubbing the poll under the edge of the manger. In either case, the crown piece is pulled forward over the ears and the head collar drops off. To prevent it, following points may be considered:

(i) If the throat lash is stitched on to the cheek piece, leave off the brow band, the crown piece will then ride further back on the neck and admit of the throat lash being tightened;

(ii) If the throat lash is a separate strap, lengthen the loop by which it is attached to the crown piece or slip it out of the ear loops of the brow band;

(iii) Discard the head collar and substitute a broad neck strap which should be fitted with only enough looseness to allow the animal to swallow.

The proper length for a head collar rope, strap or chain is the distance from the lower ring of the back strap of the head collar to the ground when the horse is standing upright. As compared to chain, ropes and straps are noiseless, much lighter, and not so likely to be a source of accident, as their lightness causes the slack to run back more easily. However, rope is considered the best as the horses are less likely to chew it.

Double ropes are sometimes attached to each side of the head collar, instead of the usual single one from the back strap, and this method is useful if it is desired to confine the horse to one side of the stall, as by shortening one of them, he will be compelled to stand on that side.

Pillar reins or chains are attached to the back of the stall post and are very useful for cribbers and windsuckers. They should not be longer than to reach each side of the head collar. If kept loose they are likely to be seized by the animal, and when the horse has a bit in his mouth, accidents are the occasional consequence.

Bedding

The provision of a good bed is an important detail in the economical management of working horses. It is quite possible for them to take a considerable amount of rest while standing. However, there are some which at times lie. The more rest they can be induced to take, the longer their legs will probably last, and they are more likely to keep good condition. A good bed has a marked effect in inducing horses to lie down for long periods, and frequently, during both day and night, and it also prevents injury to the elbows and other parts from contact with the hard stable floor. An ideal bed should provide a level elastic surface, be dry and warm, should either completely absorb and deodorize all urine, or allow it to drain away immediately, and have no injurious action on the hooves. The various articles which may be used for bedding are, straw of several varieties, sawdust, shavings, sand, and peat moss etc.

Straws - Straw of any variety, which is to be used for bedding, should be long, dry, clean, free from mould, bright in colour, and not much bruised in threshing. This description applies, of course, to first class grass straws. Excellent beds may be made from inferior qualities, but they do not last so long and are more wasteful, and should only be used when the price admits of a larger issue than it is possible to make of better straw.

To examine straw in the truss, note whether the stems are much crushed and split. This detracts from its value, as once the outside varnish like coat is broken, urine does not drain off completely but is partly absorbed by the stalk, which becomes soaked and, on subsequent drying, brittle. The truss should be opened, and the interior examined for any damaged portions. Mouldiness may be detected by smell, and by the presence of discoloured spots and patches; dampness by the feel, and probably by accompanying mouldiness also.

Bale Straw - It is less economical than truss, owing to the extensive crushing which is inevitable and which lessens its wearing quality.

As a bedding, straw is undoubtedly the most attractive material on account of its bright, clean appearance, and the comfortable elastic bed it provides; but unless a sufficient amount can be supplied for frequent change over and thoroughly dried, it becomes dirty, damp, urine soaked mass, particularly in wet weather, which is neither comfortable nor sanitary.

Management of Straw Bedding - Old bedding, when removed from the stalls, should be well shaken up, and only the dung and short refuse taken to the dung heap. In fine weather, it should be spread in the open till thoroughly aerated and dried, then placed in wind rows till required. In hot climates, it may become too dry and brittle if exposed to the sun for long periods, and should, when sufficiently dry, be stacked in large heaps. In wet weather, it should be spread out under cover, outside the stable if possible, to get well aired and as dry as can be. The fresh straw should be well mixed with old before bedding down, and kept towards the rear of the stall where it cannot be reached and eaten by the animals. Under no circumstances should the bedding be stacked in the front of the stall, under the manger, where a greedy horse can eat it, and where he is compelled to breathe the ammonia which rises from it.

In making a bed, the litter should be tossed so that it lies evenly over the stall, the straws criss-crossed and not all one way. This will ensure its being elastic, and not easily disarranged. The rear of the bed should have the loose ends of the straw neatly turned, which is done by placing the handle of a fork near the edge, pressing one foot on it to steady it, and twisting the straggling ends beneath it. As horses usually lie well back to the extent of their head chain or rope, the bed should not be made right up to the front of the stall.

Wheat Straw - Wheat straw is the best; it is long, stout and sufficiently tough. Also it is not so sweet as oat straw, and therefore, not so readily eaten. It should be of a bright but pale yellow colour and if it has been much weathered, becomes discoloured and greyish.

Oat Straw - Oat straw is not so hard and tough. It is more easily crushed and does not wear so long; but as it is more digestible and sweeter to the taste, it makes excellent chaff either alone or when mixed with hay. In colour, it should be a bright golden.

Barley Straw - Barley straw is not suitable for bedding, may cause an irritation of the skin, and, if eaten may lead to colic.

Rye straw - Rye straw is the toughest of all, and wears longest, but it is scarce and dear, there being another market for the limited supply as a stuffing for collars. The straws are finer than wheat, and the colour not so bright.

Rice straw. Rice straw is used in some places and it makes good bedding and is very durable.

Sawdust - Sawdust may be utilized when it can be obtained in plenty but owing to its liability to rapid fermentation, it cannot be successfully employed unless the supply is ample. In any case, only sawdust from well seasoned wood is suitable. Green sawdust becomes hot as soon as it is pressed together in the bed and soiled by the urine. As with all absorbent litters, stable drains should be stopped before the bed is laid, or it will fill and choke them; the soiled portions must be removed at every opportunity and turned and aerated daily. If these precautions are not observed, the sawdust gets hot, and rapidly becomes fly-blown and full of maggots.

Wood Shavings - Shavings are occasionally used in the neighbourhood of factories which produce them in quantity. They make a fair bed, are not so liable to get hot as sawdust, but are not so absorbent, and often contain small blocks and chips of wood which must be carefully picked out before use.

Sand - Sand under favourable conditions makes most excellent bedding, but is unsuited for damp, cold climates. In hot, dry weather and especially where the stable floors are not impervious to wet, it makes a comfortable sanitary bed and is much liked by horses. Sand free from any trace of salt must be used, or horses will eat large quantities and will suffer from serious sand colic. If sand is used in cold weather, a layer of straw on the top makes a very comfortable bed.

A sand bath i.e., a large circular bed, several inches deep, is an excellent addition to any stable and horses thoroughly enjoy a roll on it when they return hot from work. Further, it dries them at once. It is occasionally stated that sand spoils the coat, but the objection has no foundation, in fact.

Peat Moss - Peat moss makes excellent bedding; it is very highly absorbent, gives a firm but elastic surface, sufficiently warm, yet cool to the feet, and is a deodorizer of the urine. To this last quality, some of the faults of which it has been accused of can be traced, for there being no smell in the stable, sufficient attention may not be paid to the litter, with the result that horses' feet suffer. Peat moss requires the same attention as any other absorbent litter, and if this is not given, it will have the same effect as any other urine saturated material, namely, to rot the horn of the foot, and cause an eruption on the skin from contact with it when lying down. These conditions are likely to occur if the so-called "continental" system of allowing bedding to remain down for long periods without any sanitary attention is adopted. This can be prevented if the initial bedding is 20 cm deep and laid with a heavy-roller; as occasion arises fresh peat moss is scattered over the top so that there is always a dry surface. The beddings should not be raked up but only the droppings and wet patches removed.

Good peat moss should contain no earthy matter, but consist of close fibred limps of moss, which can be easily broken by the hand, but held closely together by interwoven threads

General Notes on Bedding - Before using any absorbent litter, block all stable drains; if this is not done, the material will get down, gradually choke them, and render them very troublesome if they are required at any future time.

A wooden or brick ledge, or, in hot climates, a mud rim, at the back of a sand, sawdust, or peat moss bed helps to keep it tidy.

Dung should be removed from the beds as soon as passed, if

possible as it is otherwise trodden into the litter and increases wastage.

In order to induce horses to take plenty of rest, it is a good plan to keep them bedded down as much as possible. A comparatively simple matter with peat moss but straw bedding requires more management and in order to check waste as far as possible, the litter should not be put down until the horses are groomed.

STABLE TRICKS AND VICES

Horses should be kept out of the stable as long as possible daily, for long hours of work is a distinct preventive of stable tricks and vices as well as beneficial to the general health and condition.

Weaving : It is nervous habit acquired by many wild animals in captivity, and occasionally by horses; the animal rocks itself to and fro continuously, sometimes lifting each forefoot in turn as the body is swayed to the opposite side. As the collar chain, when worn is drawn through the manger ring at motion, the habit is often accompanied by a good deal of noise, and while some do it constantly, other practise it at intervals only. A constant weaver gives himself no rest, and as the habit is incurable, it must necessarily take a great deal out of animals which practice it, though no special accident or disease can be directly attributed to it. Nevertheless, It is advisable that they should be kept apart, so that others are not disturbed, and do not learn the trick from observation. It is also well to provide weavers with a bedding e.g., peat moss, which will not readily slip from under the feet, and to give a head rope or strap instead of a noisy chain. Divide the animal's ration into many small feeds to keep them occupied when in the stable.

Windsucking and Crib-biting. A windsucker is an animal that swallows air by arching its neck, drawing its head towards its chest, and giving a gulp. A crib-biter achieves the same end but leans on or catches hold of the mangers with the teeth in order to get a firm purchase, and at the moment he gulps, a characteristic "grunt" is emitted. Horses are prone to learn these two vicious habits from their neighbours; once acquired they are never forgotten, and are incurable, though much may be done to prevent horses indulging in them until they learn to outwit the preventive. For both windsuckers and crib biters, a broad strap, fitting tightly round the top of the neck, with a small wooden or metal gullet plate stitched on, so that it projects on each side and sticks into the throat when the head is bent. It will stop both habits whilst the discomfort is sufficiently great. A "flute" bit may be worn which is a hollow tube snaffle perforated with several holes throughout its length like a tiny whistle, so that when it is adjusted, suction cannot be exerted owing to the impossibility of completely closing the mouth. It is an effective preventive measure when worn, but unfortunately it is not always replaced immediately after work or feeding, and so the animal gets an opportunity to fill himself with wind, of which the animal takes full advantage. A piece of thick rubber with a strap passing through it, fastened around and just behind the lower jaw prevents the teeth grasping or leaning against the manger, but is not very successful to warrant its adoption. Crib-biter may be put into a loose box with four blank walls and nothing to lay hold of, until they learn to windsuck, or they may be turned about in the stall and kept constantly on the pillar reins; but no means of effecting a permanent cure has yet been found.

The effect of the constant pressure of the incisor teeth of the crib-bitter against the manger or other hard objects, results in the fronts of the teeth of both the upper and lower jaws getting worn away, and in bad cases, they may be down to the level of the gums.

Indigestion and colic also frequently result due to windsucking and crib-biting, and as the habits, are easily acquired by others, and so horses that practise them should be separated as far as practicable.

Biting - It is a vice, more common in stallions than in mares or geldings. However, all three may suffer. A playful habit of snatching at the man whilst being groomed which some horses display, may not come under the head of viciousness, but as the results are equally painful, it should not be encouraged by unnecessary tickling. A wicked biter, when being groomed or otherwise handled, may be rendered safe for the time, by a thick wooden bit which prevents the teeth being closed; or otherwise handled. Similarly, a short stick reaching from the cheek piece of the head collar to the rollers and tied to each will allow only vertical but not lateral motion of the head. Tearing the clothing is another bad stable habit which is very persistent when once acquired and can only be absolutely prevented by the use of a stout leather guard fixed on the head collar. This should be fastened to the back strap of noseband and sufficiently deep to reach well below the level of the lips. This will render it impossible for the clothing to be reached by the teeth and as it is permanently attached to the head collar, it is always in place when required.

Kicking ; It may be due to want of work, the remedy for which is obvious; or a persistent vice which is always troublesome, and frequently dangerous. It is more common in mares than in the geldings. Some animals kick constantly in the dark, and a light in the stable keeps them quiet, but others will continue the habit in spite of every precaution. To overcome this problem, the bails and stall posts may be padded or wrapped with straw to prevent the noise and hence the chances of the injury lessened. It appears in some cases that the noise produced is stimulus to repetition, and, if deadened animals occasionally stop.

Alternatively, kicking boards may be slung from the bails. These should be thick, heavy boards, extending at least half-way up to the stall from the rear stall post, reaching within a couple of inches of the ground and hinged to the bail so that they swing when hit. They may be padded with sacking loosely filled with peat moss to deaden the sound. Although, they do not cure the evil, they are one of the best palliatives.

Similarly, kicking blocks of wood or rubber may be made to fit closely into the hollow of the heel, and being fastened there prevent very accurately, because if they slip from the heel, they are useless and may even increase the trouble. Another variety of kicking block is a shackle with a few links of heavy chain which may be attached sometimes to a smooth wooden bail. When the horse kicks, the chain or block hits him on the leg and in some cases stops the habit.

Attaching heavy weights to the legs by means of shackles e.g., bags of sand, or hanging these behind the animal so that they swing back when struck, are harmless and sometimes quite efficacious expedients, and the legs may be shackled together if other means fail.

It will be noted that some of the methods given above are likely to cause considerable damage to the animals if the kicking is persisted as such, they should be carefully supervised when employed. Horses which are not cured of the habit by one method, will sometimes yield to another, and none should be practiced if they do not at once check it.

Gnawing the walls and eating their own droppings are instances of depraved appetite, occasionally observed in horses. The former is usually ascribed to a craving for lime salts, but it is by no means proved that it is anything but a bad habit. The presence of a lump of rock salt in the manger will suffice to distract the attention till it is forgotten. If the habit continues, that portion of the wall within reach may be covered with tar varnish (tar 1 part, naphtha 3 parts). Eating dung is a dirty habit which once acquired seems to be very difficult to stop. The animal will even try to slip its head collar in order to get at its own faeces. As indigestion may be a possible cause, in both the above cases, a careful veterinary examination of the animal and an equally thorough revaluation of the food, should be undertaken.

To prevent animals eating off the ground, a baggage strap passed behind the poll, is looped to another baggage strap passing over the nostrils in the position of the noseband. Every time a horse attempts to lower its head, there is a pressure on the muscles of the neck and nostrils which prevents an extension of the head.

Daily Routine of Stable Duties

The usual hours for stables are morning 6 to 7 am in summer, 6.30 to 7.30 am in winter, subsequently, on return from work or exercise in the evening 5 to 5.30 PM.

In the morning, the stable is to be cleaned out, the bedding placed in wind rows and the stable aired. Every horse should then be lightly groomed, the feet picked out, and manes and tails brushed down.

The horses should then be watered. The saddle or harness may be put on, leaving the girth loose and the horse left to feed. However, in cold weather, it is preferable to replace rugs and should not be saddled up until actually required.

Immediately on return from work, the horses should be watered and the bridles should be taken off. The saddle or harness should be removed, the blanket being put outside to dry and the horse carefully examined for possible injuries. The feet should be picked, examined and cleaned. Any injuries or loose shoes should be noticed. It should be followed by thorough grooming. After grooming, the horse is inspected carefully to examine every part of the body, paying special attention to the tail, mane, throat, ears, knees, belly and insides of the things and hocks.

No horse is well groomed unless he is groomed vigorously and the horses should always be inspected as soon as they are groomed. It should be followed by trotting if required and then feeding. The stable head collar should be cleaned and bedding should be provided to the horse. Before horses are fed, it should be ensured that all gutters are swept clean, barrows emptied, utensils conveniently placed, buckets filled with clean water, and the ventilation suitably arranged.

One should make a point to visit stables at various times of the day. Horses' habits and peculiarities may be much better studied when they are alone in the stable.

A stable guard should invariably be available all the times at the stables. The stable man should not leave the stable unattended. It is his duty to unrack the horses when all have finished their feeds, tie up those horses that may get loose, straighten rugs, remove droppings, and report any case of injury or animal off its feed. He should be responsible for the safety of the saddlery and utensils, and that the ventilation is not interfered with. A horse that lies down in the day should not be disturbed unless there is danger of injury. However, if any injury is noticed at any time, it should be properly attended to.

Smoking or striking a light in the stables or near any forage should be prohibited. If the stall is slippery, sand or litter is to be sprinkled on the flooring.

Horses are particularly terrified by fire, and should a fire occur in the stables they must be led, backed, or ridden out of the stable. If they are unwilling, a coat or cloth should be thrown over their eyes. Care should be taken that they do not break back to their stables.

Condition and Exercise

"Condition" as applied to animals, means muscular fitness of body for the work required. When using the term "condition", the picture of a racehorse with each muscle outlined, and strung up, and capable of undertaking the greatest possible exertion. Although, this type exemplifies "condition" in its highest degree, it may not truly represent the bodily state required for the particular work in hand. The condition of the racehorse, when optimal, represents highest level of nutrition, maximum work, and a concentrated nervous energy which cannot be maintained at constant pitch indefinitely. However, such a high strung, nervous state is not required in work horses still thorough fitness is absolutely essential. A well regulated stable of hunters during the first part of the season exhibits the quality of condition which should be looked for at the commencement of a campaign i.e. the body well covered with flesh, without any sign of running up light towards the flank. The animal is full of spirits, capable of long continued exertion without fatigue, and with a healthy appetite. Such a state of bodily health can be almost indefinitely continued when once attained, and allows some reserve of flesh and animal spirits to draw on when the pinch of hardship comes. This class of condition is the criterion of a work horse. Further, condition of this description must not be confounded with fatness. A young horse from the dealer's yard is fat but may not be fit if his muscles are soft and flabby, unable to stand severe exertion and rapidly fatigued. Not only his muscles, but every other structure of his body is in the same state. The blood vessels soon lose their elasticity; his heart fails in driving power; his lungs cannot sustain rapid breathing, nor his joints constant bending; and although he is jumping out of his skin at the beginning of the day; a very moderate amount of work makes you wonder if he is the same horse that started so well.

To get horses into condition, sufficient good food and healthy exercise judiciously combined, and continued over a long period, is the sole recipe. The transformation of fat, flabby flesh into hard and tough muscles is a gradual process. It cannot be forced and a regular course of graduated exercise is the only way to accomplish it. This work should never be so severe as to fatigue the animal; the soft muscles will suffer from the reaction of over exertion to such an extent that an actual loss of flesh will result in. Working with tired animals may lead to accident and disease as this is the time when they sustain bad falls and severe sprains. The muscles do not act in absolute unison, and extra weight is thrown on the tendons, which naturally suffer. However, once good, hard, muscular development has been attained, any work within reason will not only be performed without great effort but will continue to add to the quality of the condition already acquired. It is important to recognize this "cumulative" power of condition which means that you cannot only demand a good amount of work from a seasoned horse, but it actually does him good. At the same time, there is less and less risk of accident and disease; that may throw him entirely out of work for any considerable period. The conditioning process is required to be repeated over again, though not perhaps to quite the same extent. This must be particularly borne in mind when horses are again taken into work after a run at grass or a long bout of sickness.

Amount and Class of Work - At first, the work should be light, but spread over a considerable time, and indeed the longer the time which can be spent outside the stable, the better will be the condition of horse. However, when it is not possible to devote so long period with the animal, a minimum of 2 to 4 hours daily work schedule must be enforced. The conditioning and exercise should be carried out at the walk and trot, the proportion being about four or three to one respectively. The exercise of a racehorse should include two or two and a half hours constantly on the move in the morning, with 3000-5000 metres trot and canter and one to one and a half hours walk in the evening, get the animal fit to commence the faster part of his preparation. Even when this is in progress, long walking with a moderate amount of trotting should constitute the "healthy exercise" for getting into working condition and for maintaining it. Any attempt to try and crowd extra work into less time under the impression that it will have the same effect should be specially avoided, as it does not harden muscle of the animal in the same way, and make him tucked up in the belly, perhaps irritable in the temper, as well as unduly heated on return from work and more liable to chills.

The exercise should not follow the same route every day. Horses have a wonderful memory in such matters, and as soon as they think they are on the direct road home, will often hurry, fidget and sweat till they get there. This nervous effect may usually be avoided by taking a different direction daily, breaking the work a little by an occasional halt, grazing and leading.

The exercise should include walking steep hills and should utilize any soft level road sides for trotting. The first 1000 metres should be covered slowly, so that the horses can feel their feet, stretch their legs and empty their bowels before they are called upon to trot, and the last 1500 metres should also be walked so that they return to stables cool.

The amount of weight which a horse is to carry or draw should be frequently loaded, especially in the case of saddle horses and pack animals, to ensure that the skin and muscles of the back are accustomed to the pressure of the load for hours at a stretch.

Effect of Feeding on Condition - To produce the best results, the policy of full feeding and fair work must be adopted. No other combination will get the best out of a horse. A small ration and little work will keep him round in appearance but plenty of food and sufficient work, judiciously combined, is the only routine which will really make him fit for the desired purpose. This adjustment of ration to work is a practical point and is one of the hallmarks of a good horsemaster and must be gained by observation and experience. When the work is light e.g., at the beginning of a young horse's training, half ration is generally accepted as a standard on which to begin feeding, but a rule of thumb method should be avoided and each horse's needs considered on its own merit. In no case, the ration be so small, or the work so hard, that the colt's bloom i.e, his round and glossy sleekness, disappears.

Thirst and sweating are very prominent features of the early stages of training and are to some extent dependent on each other. Apart from the sweating which may naturally be expected as a result of work, some young horses are liable to sweat very profusely from purely nervous causes, and more especially when the work is conducted in a confined atmosphere.

It is not always possible to prevent every young horse sweating from the excitement of new lessons, particularly in the case of highly bred or excitable colts; but such outbreaks take more out of a horse than a far greater amount of quiet work and should be avoided in every way.

Working in the open air in preference to a roofed school, absolute quietness of methods, the avoidance of long monotonous lessons, and the example of older, well behaved animals, doing the same things quietly, are all valuable in keeping horses cool in body and temper. There are instances, as stated above, where sweating can not be prevented, and thirst is a natural result. Thirsty horses are to be allowed to drink their fill. It is best that they should not be sweating, but the fact of their being hot need not be a bar to their drinking, if care is taken to keep them on the move till cool, which also prevents risk of chills. As the condition improves, the keenness of thirst will diminish.

The quantity and quality of the sweat is very generally taken as an index of condition, and rightly so. When the body is soft and flabby, slight exertion produces a copious sweating of a soapy lathery nature, which dries slowly, and frequently breaks out again. As the condition improves, the amount of work required to make the skin damp increases, and the sweat itself is less greasy and more watery in consistency. It dries with rapidity, and does not recur. There are, however, some free sweating horses which lather freely even when in good condition. Weather has great influence on sweating as on a cold, clear day, it takes a lot of exertion to turn a hair, whereas a damp muggy morning will make them sweat freely.

It has been observed that horses will not retain hard condition for an indefinite period of time. Condition is best maintained by those horses which sweat sufficiently.

It is noticed, particularly in hot climates, that many horses lose their condition and at the same time cease to sweat. They are then commonly known as 'non sweaters'. This may and very frequently does occur, to horses that have previously been quite good doers, but from the time sweating ceases, they become bad doers and will remain so, as long as they remain non sweaters.

Chapter 16

Care of Feet and Shoeing

In a state of nature, the hoof is sufficiently hard, and grows with rapidity enough to withstand the wear caused by the animal's weight when travelling over natural country. The shape of the hoof and quality of its horn differs according to climate and soil, and in hot countries where it becomes hard and dry, animals may be worked to a considerable extent without shoes. On roads, however, the natural growth of the hoof is not sufficiently hard, or rapid, to keep pace with the extra wear entailed by carrying or drawing a load, and to prevent them getting footsore, it is necessary to shoe working horses by some substance harder than horn.

A rim of iron has been found the best for the purpose up-to-date, and our object when attaching it to the hoof (shoeing), is to cause as little damage to the natural structure as possible, and yet secure it firmly.

Structure of the Foot

The bones - buried in the centre of the foot and surrounded by the soft, sensitive structures which produce the horn of the hoof, are the small bones which form the last joint of the leg. They are the 3rd phalanx, earlier called as "coffin" (pedal) bone, and the navicular bone; and with the lower extremity of the 2nd phalanx, earlier called as short pastern (coronet) bone, which reaches below the level of the coronet, they form the foot (pedal) joint.

The 3rd phalanx may be described as a pyramid, the back of which has been hollowed out, and the ground surface slightly arched. It is a remarkably porous looking bone, an appearance due to the large number of blood vessels with which it is provided, each of which is accommodated in one of the minute holes covering its surface. Its actual position in the hoof is clearly shown in Figs. 16.1 and 16.2. It is wedged into the toe of the foot, and although its sides (wings) extend some distance further back than the central portion, it leaves the back half of the foot practically free from any bony foundation.

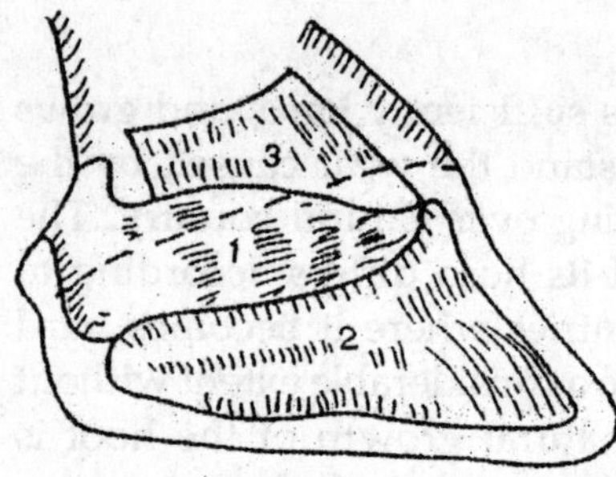

1. Lateral Cartilage
2. 3rd Phalanx
3. 2nd Phalanx

Fig. 17.1

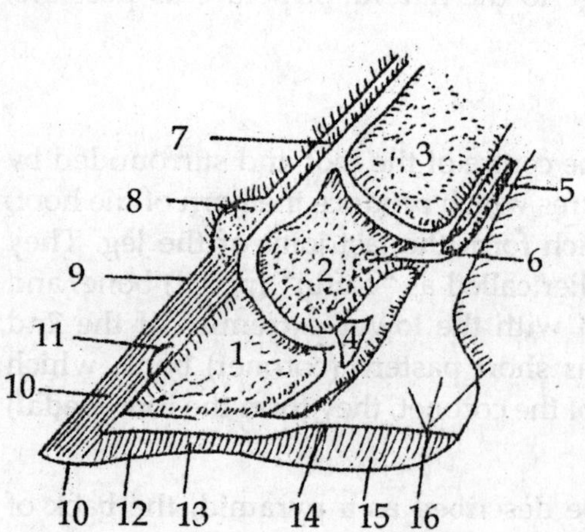

1. 3rd Phalanx
2. 2nd Phalanx
3. 1st Phalanx
4. Navicular Bone
5. } Perforans Tendon
6. }
7. Extensor Tendon
8. Coronary Bond
9. Wall
10. White Line
11. Sensitive Laminae
12. Fleshy Sole
13. Horny Sole
14. Fleshy Frog
15. Horny Frog
16. Frog Pad

Fig. 17.2

The Navicular Bone - The small, shuttle, or boat-shaped bone is placed across the back of the central part of the 3rd phalynx where a narrow, smooth surface for it to lie against may be seen.

The rounded end of the 2nd phalanx meets the large, smooth surface on the top of the rear slope of the 3rd phalanx, and rocks to and fro on it as the foot is moved.

A highly polished layer of tough, elastic substance covers those parts of the bones which meet each other, and the whole joint is bathed in synovial fluid to make it work smoothly.

The Cartilages - Attached to and extending from near the top of the 3rd phalanx on each side, continued all along its edge, and curving round the heel beyond, there is a large springy structure called as the lateral cartilage. In a fine-skinned horse, its outline can be clearly seen, extending along the sides of the coronet (Fig. 16.1), and its spring may be easily demonstrated by pressing hard on its edge at the heels.

Ligaments of considerable strength pass from bone to bone holding them firmly in position, yet permitting all necessary movements.

Tendons - Starting from muscles in the arm above, these run down the limb, both in fore and hind, and are attached firmly into the bones (Fig. 16.2). In front there is only one, which is spread out on the pastern and the top of the 3rd phalanx, behind there are two, one reaches under the 3rd phalanx and the other is fixed to the sides of the 2nd phalanx.

The Fleshy Structures - At the back of the foot, filling up the space which lies between the wings of the 3rd phalanx and lateral cartilages, is a thick tough, elastic pad which converts the whole of the back of the foot into a firm, soft cushion, sometimes called the 'frog pad' or 'cushion of the heels'.

Round the coronet, and forming the bulge which is noticeable in this region, is another thick but narrower strip of the same nature known as the coronary band (Fig. 16.3). Beneath the 3rd phalanx also there is a similar though thinner layer known as the fleshy sole.

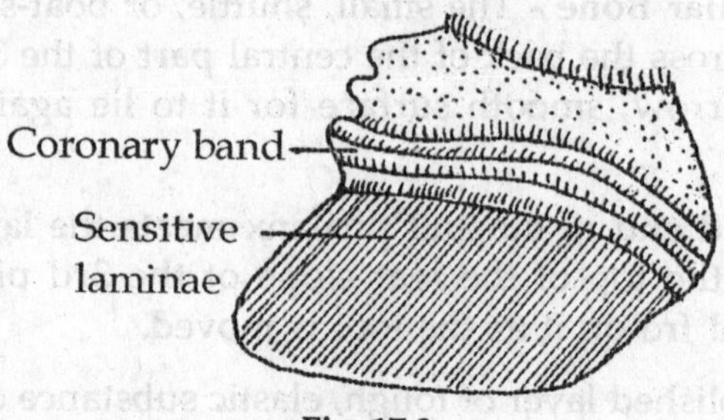

Fig. 17.3

The surfaces of the coronary band, the fleshy sole and fleshy frog are covered by innumerable small finger-like projections, which give them a velvety appearance, and it is from these little points that the horn of the hoof grows.

The outer surface of the 3rd phalanx is covered by a series of fleshy leaves known as laminae which are five to six hundred in number and the edges of which running from top to bottom of the bones. These laminae form the chief bond of union between the fleshy and horny parts of the hoof.

The blood vessels of the foot are extremely numerous, they permeate the bones and fleshy parts to such an extent that, in the living animal, the foot may be said literally to swim in blood; and it is a matter of common knowledge that trivial wounds in this part bleed with the greatest freedom.

The nerves of the foot are distributed with equal profuseness, and although the hoof itself is not sensitive, the slightest touch on its surface is felt by the animal.

The Hoof - Horn, wherever it grows, is the same in structure, and consists of a hard, tough, gluey substance, in which are embedded a number of hair-like tubes. It may differ considerably in consistence, some varieties being almost as hard as a brick; and others as elastic as rubber; a difference largely due to the amount of moisture which the individual specimen contain. This moisture is contained in the tubes; the horn has a certain quantity in its composition, and its presence produces that toughness which always characterises a healthy growth. The horn of the hoof, whether originating from the coronary band, fleshy sole or fleshy frog, grows in the same direction, namely; sloping downwards and forwards, at the same angle that the toe makes with the ground.

The Wall - It is that part of the hoof which is visible when the foot is on the ground. At the extremity of the heels it bends sharply back, and runs forwards for a short distance, this recurved portion being called the "bar". The upper edge of the wall, at the coronet, is thin and soft, and its inner side is hollowed into a groove which accommodates the coronary band. Below this groove, the wall is uniformly thick from top to bottom at any given point, whether toe, quarter (side of hoof), or heel be examined. From the toe, however, the horn gets gradually thinner towards the quarters and heels, but where it turns round to form the bars, it again suddenly thickens and then gradually thins off to nothing as it runs forward (Fig. 16.4). The inner side of the wall, including the "bar" is lined by a number of horny leaves, corresponding in arrangement with the laminae which cover the 3rd phalanx. The outside horn of the wall is extremely hard, but it gets softer and lighter in colour as the laminae are approached, and on the ground surface of the foot, the relative position of these i.e., the junction of the wall and sole, is marked by a distinct "white line". Around the upper edge of the wall is a thin, rough-looking band which runs all around the hoof to join the horn of the frog; it is very prominent and white when the foot has been soaked in water.

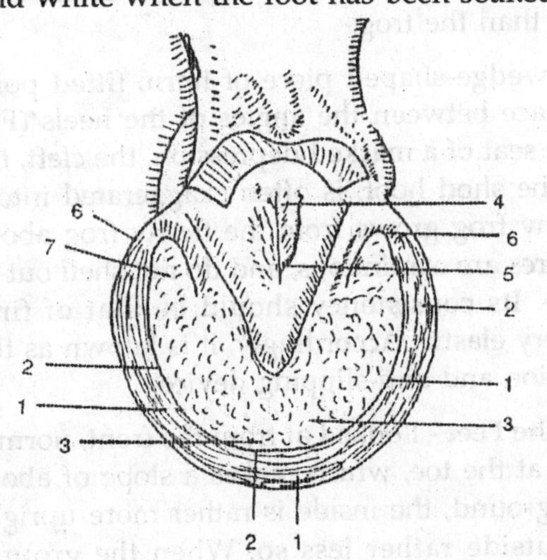

Fig. 17.4

The wall grows from the coronary band; and if untouched, being neither worn nor cut, the horn of the wall will grow on indefinitely, and the rate of growth at the toe being greater than at the heels, it will soon become disproportionately long and may then be a cause of stumbling.

The sole conforms in shape to the under surface of the 3rd phalanx, its outer edge resting on the ground, from which it is slightly arched towards the centre. Viewed from the ground surface, it is roughly crescent-shaped; the circumference being embraced by the wall, the points clasped and held firmly in position by the bars, and the space between them filled by the frog. In the living foot, the sole and wall appear firmly united, but a prolonged soaking of the dead hoof will cause complete separation at the "white line," which is then clearly seen to be a continuation downwards of the horny leaves. The horny sole grows from the fleshy sole, its fibres slanting in the same direction as those of the wall, but, unlike the latter, on attaining a definite length varying from 0.5 to 2 cm, they separate from the parts above, and shell out of the hoof. This natural provision prevents overgrowth of the sole, which, therefore, requires little attention from the farrier. The horn of this part is softer than the wall, but harder than the frog.

The frog is a thick, wedge-shaped piece of horn, fitted point foremost into the space between the angles of the heels (Fig. 16.4). Its centre is the seat of a marked depression, the cleft, the depth of which, in the shod hoof, is often exaggerated into a deep crack. The horny frog grows from the fleshy frog above it, like the wall its fibres are continuous, and do not shell out as do those of the sole. Its consistency should be that of firm rubber, tough and very elastic. Accordingly, it is known as the nature's anti-concussion and anti-slipping device.

Make and Shape of the Feet - Looked at from the front, normal forefeet are rounded at the toe, which makes a slope of about 50 degrees with the ground, the inside is rather more upright than this and the outside rather less so. When the ground surface is viewed, the outer edge makes a rather bolder curve than the inner, the heels are wide and the frog big and full, with its point perhaps slightly turned to one side from hard thrusting on the ground. Both feet are alike in size and shape, any deviation being rare, except as an index of disease. The hind feet are not so round as the fore, they are more pointed at the toe, which is also more upright, and they are narrower all over. The feet are placed quite straight and square when the horse is standing naturally. A hind foot is often rested, but a forefoot never, except when painful, it is then stuck out in front of the other to relieve it of the body weight, commonly known as 'pointing'.

'Flat' feet are large in circumference, very sloping, with as a rule, low heels, flat soles which are sometimes thin, and a large, prominent frog which alone saves them from rapid destruction. When such feet are marked by 'ridges' or rings of horn from unequal growth, they are sometimes called 'oyster' feet.

In mules, boxy, narrow or club feet are the opposite of flat, and are characterized by smallness, uprightness of the wall, high heels and small frogs.

'Long,' 'fleshy' feet are those in which the toe is unduly long and cannot be reduced to normal proportions without risk of injury.

Weak heels are those in which the rate of horn growth is very slow, a feature often found in flat feet.

The thickness and rate of growth of horn varies within the widest limits in different animals. Nine months can be taken as an average time for newly formed horn at the coronet to reach the ground. Some walls grow so rapidly that a considerable amount must be removed punctually every month, others scarcely require touching. As the horn grows forwards at the same slope as the toe, this part usually gets unduly long sooner than the heels, but in exceptional cases, the latter may show a quicker growth. The thickness of soles may vary considerably, some being like a board and others so thin that pressure with the thumb will 'spring' them.

In hot climates, if the work is mostly on unmetalled roads and the horn of the hoof is hard and dry, animals may be worked without shoes. Mules work well under these conditions. However, as a general rule it is not advisable to work draught animals without shoes.

When animals are worked unshod, great care must be exercised and the following points should have careful attention:

- The feet inspected regularly by the farrier and the ground surface of the wall slightly rounded off with the rasp to prevent breaking and splitting of the horn.
- The heels lowered or the toes shortened, if required, in order to keep the hoof to its proper proportions.
- The animals trotted up periodically to ensure that "they are not foot sore". If the action is pottery, shoe up for a time to allow the feet to grow. After sufficient growth has taken place, the animals may again be worked without shoes.
- Special care is necessary during wet weather when animals are worked on macadamized or gritty roads, as the horn wears down very rapidly under these conditions.
- A set of shoes fitted for immediate use should be maintained for every animal.

Preparation of the Foot

Farrier's tools are classified as 'shoeing tools', for preparing the foot and nailing on the shoe, and 'Forge tools' for use at the fire and anvil, in shoe turning.

Shoeing Tools - *The shoeing hammer*, for driving nails and twisting off their points when driven through the hoof, has a very strong, curved claw for this purpose. The make of this claw is of importance, it must be able to grip and easily twist off the point of the nail, which may, by a sudden movement of the horse, wound the smith's leg unless bent over or removed.

The buffer made of steel about 14-15 cm long, has a blunt chisel at one end for cutting clenches, and a point at the other for punching out stubs, or broken nails.

The rasp three-quarter coarse cut and quarter file cut, should be about 40 cm long and of the best quality. With a good rasp, the farrier can do nearly everything required in the preparation of the foot for shoeing.

The drawing knife has a curved blade with a bent over end. It was originally designed to pare out the sole when that was considered a correct method, but its use is now limited to cutting off rags of horn and taking out small pieces of wall for the clips. Beyond this, in regularly shod feet, it is rarely necessary.

Pincers with wide opening, sharp jaws, are used for levering of the shoe, drawing nails and to assist in clenching up. Overgrown feet, such as may be found in batches of horses running unshod for long periods on soft soil, are lowered by special hoof cutting pincers or a toeing knife.

Forge tools. These include the anvil, fire tongs, shoe tongs, turning hammer, the sledge, fuller, stamp and pritchel. All these tools are required for making/forging the various types of shoes.

Preparation of Foot for Shoeing - Presuming that the hoof is of normal proportions and regularly shod, the shoe is removed and as much horn as has grown since the last shoeing is rasped off, the comparative length of toe and heel being accurately preserved and the bearing surface for the reception of the new shoe kept quite level. Any flakes of horn which are evidently just coming away from the sole may be pulled out, and any markedly ragged pieces of frog cut off, but no paring of the sole, or slicing of the frog, should be practiced. The most vulnerable part of the foot lies between the wings of the 3rd phalanx and embraces the navicular bone and it is imperative in preparing the foot that the wall at the heels is not weakened by undue rasping. In the past, this has sometimes been advocated in a fruitless attempt to get the frog of the shod foot on the ground, however practically it seems quite impossible.

Faults of Preparation:

Overlowering of the Wall - skill and experience are the only safeguards against this, and, as in other details, the farrier has to trust his eye and hand.

Uneven Bearing Surface, from overlowering one side as compared with the other. A fault only found among learners or due to carelessness.

"Stumping up" or "Dumping" the Toe. This is a serious fault. If the toe requires shortening, it should be done by rasping the ground surface and not the front of the wall. If the latter is practised, it narrows the bearing surface of the foot, and by rasping away the hard, outer horn, exposes the softer, moister layers beneath, which then become brittle. When an attempt is subsequently made to drive nails into the brittle horn, this splits and breaks off, so that the shoe may be lost. However, dumping may be occasionally necessary with flat feet, in order to get the nails high enough up the wall to give a secure hold.

Paring the Sole - This was formerly considered a correct procedure. The horn was carefully pared until it sprung under the pressure of the farrier's thumb. That naturally thick, protective sole was thought to be detrimental to the elasticity of the foot and was, therefore, pared until it yielded on pressure. The soft horn of the pared sole rapidly became brittle and dry just like that of the dumped toe, and a mixture of clay and cow dung was then plastered into it at night, to keep the foot cool. A continuance of the two last practices resulted in the horn becoming so brittle that a run at grass or standing in clay was sometimes necessary to make further shoeing possible. The practice is now, altogether discarded, and with the best results.

Paring the Frog is another relic of the past, now prohibited. The frog was, for some reason, regarded as a delicate organ which would be injured from contact with the ground. The result was disastrous, and resulted in shrivelled, thrushy frogs which gave no assistance in distributing concussion, and were themselves liable to bruise from any unevenness of the road.

Opening the Heels is another term for cutting away the bars, in order to make the heels look wider. It weakens the heels, ultimately causes them to contract, and is rightly prohibited.

Over-lowering the Heels is a common fault due on the one hand to an exaggerated idea of frog pressure and on the other because the inexperienced farrier finds it easier to rasp away the horn at the heels than at the toe. By over-lowering the heels, not only are the heels weakened but more weight is thrown on the tendons and ligaments and lameness may result.

There is no doubt that to the unthinking observer, a neatly dumped foot with a smoothly pared sole, opened out heels and symmetrically trimmed frog, has a more attractive appearance than the natural, strong, somewhat rough looking hoof, with its flaky looking sole and rather ragged, prominent frog, and for this reason such practices flourish. The insidious nature of these evils also aids in their continuance, for so strong is the hoof that it is only after a year or two of persistent abuse that their effects are apparent. Then, however, the dry brittle wall, into which nails can be driven with greatest difficulty, the high-arched easily bruised sole, the thrushy, shrivelled frog, and ultimately shortening the animal's useful life. It is worthy of note in this connection, that all unnecessary cutting and paring of the hoof increases the farrier's difficulties, and only the most skilful workmen can shoe persistently ill treated feet with some success.

In speaking of the structure of horn, it was noted that the moisture contained in the tubes gave it the quality of toughness. This moisture is most abundant in the young, soft horn, and becomes less and less in the outer and older portions. Rasping the outside of the wall, paring the sole, and cutting the frog, nails unskilfully driven necessitating withdrawals, permits its escape and produces brittleness. These operations should, therefore, be confined to the narrowest possible limits.

Materials Used in Shoeing

Shoes - The shoes of horse and mule are generally made of wrought iron and are available in various sizes, keeping in view varying size of feet. These are symmetrical and interchangeable and not made specially for the right or left foot. As both branches of the shoe must be regarded as potentially inner ones, the nail holes are fine and less pitch is given to them at the quarters. Each shoe should conform exactly to its specification and the bearing surface - must be perfectly level, or slightly seated in fore shoes and free from all irregularities, as protuberances will burn their way in hot shoeing and in cold shoeing, will prevent close apposition between shoe and foot.

Nail-Holes - must be stamped clean through the web and of correct pitch and size for the shoe. Similarly, web should be slightly narrow at the heels so that projecting edges liable to cause the shoe to be trodden upon, are avoided and also to give room for the bulbs of the frog.

Machine made shoes, when set to a specification, are always repeated with accuracy and are considered better than hand made shoes in which uniformity is difficult to secure than those being made in different forges by farriers of different degrees of ability and where the work may be hurriedly carried out.

Different Types of Shoes

The following types of shoes are normally used for the purposes as indicated against each (Figs. 16.5 to 16.9).

Plain Shoe - They are plain on both surfaces with one clip in the fore and two clips in the hind. Hind shoes may have calkins at the heels. They are manufactured in various sizes.

Seated out Shoe - The bearing surface of the shoe touching the sole is hollowed out, so that pressure is exerted on the wall only. This is used in cases, where the sole is flat, and must NOT be pressed by the shoe. It is used in bruised sole, flat sole, burnt sole and dropped sole (after-effects of laminitis).

Saucer Shoe - Extra wide and seated web, useful for dropped sole which follows chronic laminitis.

Fullered Shoe - Fullering is, making a groove in the ground surface of the shoe, in which nail holes are placed. This shoe is used on racehorses and on snow covered ground to prevent feet from slipping. It is not good for holding nails and wears quicker as it is lighter in weight. Should be plain at the toe and heels.

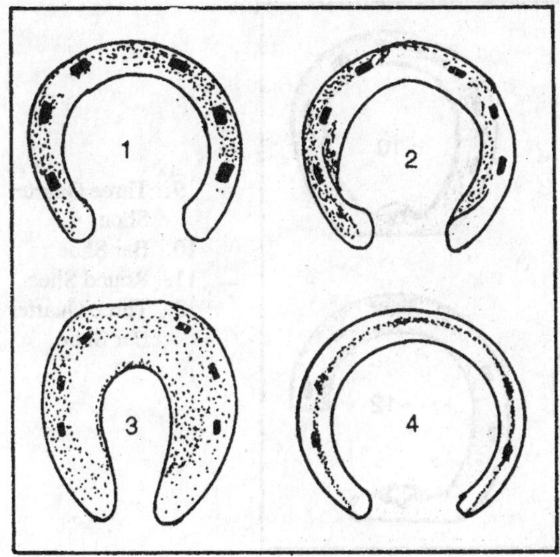

1. Plane Fore Shoe
2. Seated Out Shoe
3. Saucer Shoe
4. Fullered Shoe

Fig. 16.5

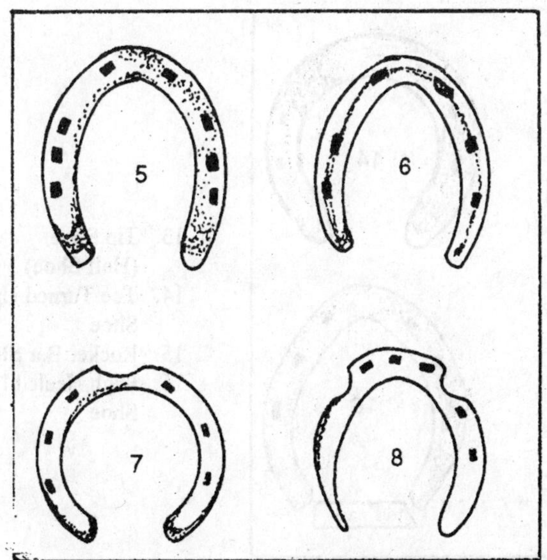

5. Calkin Shoe
6. Wedge Heel Calkin Shoe
7. Concave Shoe
8. Knocked Up and Feather Edged Shoe

Fig. 16.6

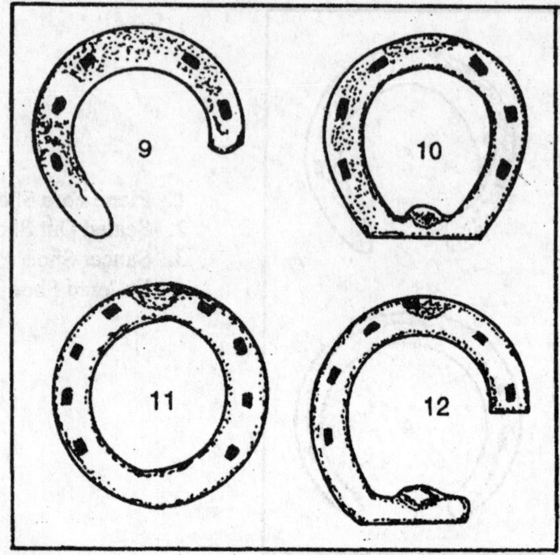

9. Three Quarter Shoe
10. Bar Shoe
11. Round Shoe
12. Three Quarter Bar Shoe

Fig. 16.7

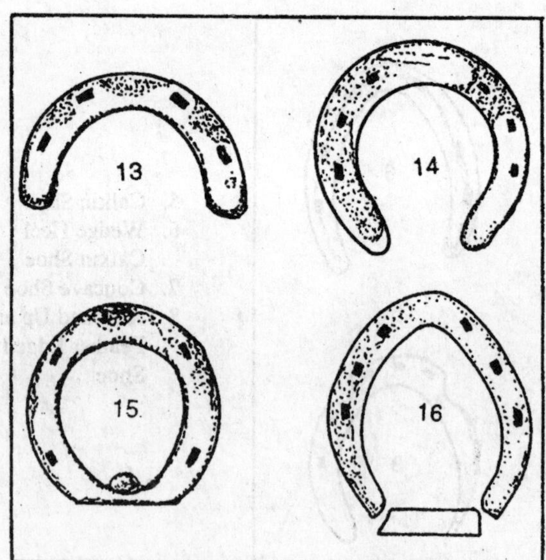

13. Tip Shoe (Half Shoe)
14. Toe Turned Up Shoe
15. Rocker Bar Shoe
16. High Heeled Bar Shoe

Fig. 16.8

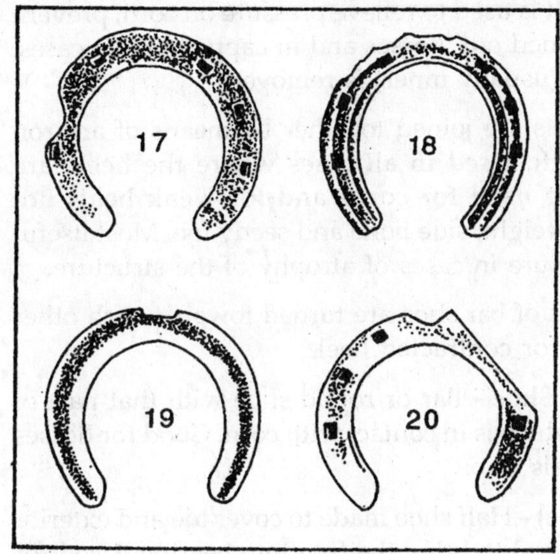

17. Anti Brushing Shoe
18. Rodway Shoe
19. Martin Shoe
20. Anti Speedy Cutting Shoe

Fig. 16.9

Calkin Shoe - Calkin is a projection of the heel by turning down the heel at right angles. The projection is forced into the ground by the animal's weight, giving a good grip. Used in hind legs for draught horses, polo ponies and animals working in hilly and snowy terrain.

Wedge Heel Shoe - The heels are narrowed and thickened. May be used in combination with calkins. It serves the same purpose as calkin shoe, and lessens chances of brushing.

Concave Shoe - Inner edge of the ground surface is rounded off. Reverse of 'seated out shoe' in that the ground surface is narrower than foot surface. Used for hunters and also to avoid 'over reach'. Lighter than the ordinary shoe and not so likely to be sucked off in heavy going.

Knocked up and Feather-edged Shoe - The inner branch of the shoe is considerably narrowed from toe to heel and at the same time slopes inwards under the hoof. Used for horses which 'brush'.

Three Quarter Shoe - Is one from which an inch or two of heel has been removed. It is used to relieve pressure on corn, prevent brushing in 'toe turned out' horses and in capped elbow cases. Half of the branch (usually inner) is removed.

Bar Shoe - The heels are joined together by means of an iron plate of same width. Used in all cases where the heels are contracted. May be used for corns and for weak heels not capable of bearing weight, side bone and seedy toe. Most useful to ensure frog pressure in cases of atrophy of the structure.

Round Shoe - Heels of bar shoe are turned towards each other and welded. Used for contracted heel.

Three Quarter Bar Shoe - Bar or round shoe with that part of one heel removed which is in contact with corn. Good for horses with contracted heels also.

Tip Shoe (Half Shoe) - Half shoe made to cover toe and exterior portion of quarters and to bring the frog into bearing. Used for corn cases, capped elbow cases, and to give pressure to the frog.

Convex Shoe - The inner edge of the ground surface of the web of the shoe is thicker than the outer edge. Used for horses which wear their shoes abnormally quickly.

Toe Turned-up Shoe - The toes of the fore shoes are sharply set up at an angle of 22 degrees from the centre of the web, replacing the clip. Used for horses which stumble.

Rocker Bar Shoe - Is a bar shoe in which the ground surface at the middle of both the quarters is thickened and slopes gradually towards toe and heel. Used in Laminitis cases. Animal can throw himself back on his heels as this position affords great relief.

High Heeled Bar Shoe - Used for severely sprained tendon cases.

Anti-brushing Shoe - In this the inner branch is rasped and comes under the hoof. It is used in forefoot to prevent brushing.

Rodway Shoe - Has a double fuller, the outer of which carries the nail holes. There are three ridges on the ground surface which increases the foothold by breaking the plain surface and also by collecting grit and small stones etc. in the grooves between them.

Martin Shoe - Has a double fuller like the Rodway shoe but the inner groove is wider and into this rubber is fixed by beating the grooved rim inwards. This is an anti-slipping shoe.

Nails - Nails are made of best quality iron and are available in sizes numbered from 2 to 16. The size of a nail implies that the size number is equal to the weight in pounds of 1000 nails of that size e.g., a No. 5 nail is one of which a thousand of that size would weigh 5 lbs. Therefore, the higher the number, the larger the nail. The front of a nail i.e., the side which forms the outer circumference of the shoe is flat from head to point. The inner side of the point is bevelled to bring it out of the hoof when driven. If a nail is driven the wrong way, it is sure to cause injury.

The qualities of a good nail are:

(a) Head should not be too broad at the top - it may become fixed in the nail-hole only by its upper edge and when the shoe has had a few days' wear, the nail will lose its hold and the shoe become loose.

(b) Neck should not be too thick - is liable to press on the sensitive foot or to break the wall.

(c) Shank should not be too wide or too thick.

(d) Point should not be too long or too tapered - this will leave insufficient metal to form a good clench, and is liable to bend, or turn in driving.

(e) Nail should be stiff and solid enough to drive without buckling or splitting.

Systems of Shoeing

Two systems of shoeing are recognized viz. *'hot shoeing'* and *'cold shoeing'* .

Hot Shoeing - the shoe is specially made to fit the foot, it is tried hot, and adjustments are made before it is finally nailed on. A visit to the forge is necessary for this. This system is generally adopted because it is the best way to ensure a perfect fit. The farrier can see at a glance from the brown appearance of the burnt horn where the web of the shoe touches the hoof and by rasping these parts down till perfect contact of the whole is assured as proved by a complete brown rim, he is certain to get an accurate fitting of the shoe to the foot.

Cold Shoeing - In this system, a ready made shoe is employed which is fitted and altered cold as far as possible. Cold shoeing cannot be carried out for heavy horses because of the impossibility of altering the shape of large shoes when cold. As a rule, shoes to be fitted cold, are stamped with several extra nail holes and these are placed close together. This allows a wider choice when nailing the shoes on the horses. In cold fittings, a nicer appreciation by the eyes of the surfaces to be joined is required. Cold fitting is, therefore, not as accurate and solid as compared to the hot and the result is a greater proportion of loose or lost shoes from the shoe rocking and the clenches rising. Although not so accurate and satisfactory, cold fitting may at times be a necessity where facilities of hot shoeing are not available.

Advantages of Hot Shoeing

(a) Shoe can be put on in half the time as hot metal can be altered with ease.

(b) Exact juxtaposition between iron and hoof can be obtained.

(c) Bearing surface of wall and sole is rendered impervious to water.

(d) Charring of the horn renders hoof, less liable to split when the nails are being driven.

Method of Shoeing

The procedure of shoeing/reshoeing falls into six definite stages:-

(a) Removal

(b) Preparation of the Foot

(c) Fitting of the Shoe

(d) Nailing On

(e) Finishing

(f) Inspection

Removal

It is the method in which old/slightly worn shoes are replaced with new/repaired shoes. The foot is taken between the knees and all the clenches are cut by means of the buffer and driving hammer. Each branch of the shoe is raised with the pincers so that the nails are partly drawn out. Care being taken not to twist the shoe on the foot as this may result in the breaking of a portion of the wall of the toe or the quarters. The raised shoe is knocked down with the closed pincers, each nail drawn out with the pincers and the shoe removed and after removal, shoe of same size is fitted again.

Preparation of the Foot: It has been described in detail earlier in this chapter. In short, it comprises reduction of the overgrowth of horn and the adjustment of the foot for the fitting of the new shoe. Both foot and shoe must fit each other and neither is more important than the other. The primary object is an even level bearing surface on sound horn and as wide as can be obtained.

The sole and cleft of the frog are first cleaned out with the drawing knife. Any stumps of nails are removed with the buffer and pincers or by punching them out with a new nail which has had its sharp point cut off. Loose chips of horn from the lower outside edge of the wall are cut off with the drawing knife. The over growth of wall is reduced by the drawing knife. Ragged parts of the sole and frog are trimmed away. Undue cutting of sole and frog is avoided. The rasp is then used to provide the foot with a level bearing surface.

Signs of a Well Prepared Foot

(a) When horse is standing on level ground:

(i) From the front - both sides of the wall should be of equal height and the transverse plane of the coronet should be parallel to the ground.

(ii) From the side - toe, quarters and heels should be proportionate i.e. in fore hoof the height should be in ratio of 3:2:1 and in hind hoof 2:1½:1.

(iii) From behind - frog should touch the ground and heels should be of equal height.

(b) When the foot is lifted

(i) Level bearing surface from one heel all round the circumference of the hoof to the other heel.

(ii) Sole should be concave and rough i.e., not pared out.

(iii) Bearing surface should consist of the whole thickness of the lower edge of the wall, the beginning of each bar, the horn of the 'white line' within the wall and a small margin of the sole should be brought to the same level.

Fitting the Shoe

This is carried out when the shoe is still hot. The searing of horn which results, reveals exactly the extent to which foot and shoe are in perfect contact. Any adjustments necessary in the shape of the shoe or the length of the feet are then made.

The two conditions to be fulfilled are :

(a) Fit the shoe to the surface of the foot.

(b) Fit the shoe to the circumference of the wall.

A well fitted shoe should have a perfectly level even bearing on the whole of the wall, the base, the white line and outer line of the sole.

The hot shoe is carried to the foot on a pritchel and is fitted to the prepared foot. It should be of such a temperature as to sear the horn without causing a burst of flame. If too hot, it can be dipped for an instant into water. The shoe is held sufficiently long in contact with the foot to sear the horn and burn it down where it touches. If the horn chars unduly at one place, the shoe is removed, laid down nearby, the heavily charred portion is rasped off and the shoe replaced for a second fitting. If the shoe is 'true' in all respects, the whole of the bearing surface in a well, prepared foot should char evenly to a dark honey colour. The position of the clip should also be noted. The height of a clip should be about the same as the breadth of the web. The breadth of the base should be about the same. The free edge should be rounded, not sharp pointed. If any alterations to the shoe are needed e.g. correction of an uneven bearing surface, widening or narrowing the shoe, changing irregular curves, lengthening, shortening or bevelling the heels, these are carried out. When the fit is quite correct, the shoe is cooled by being plunged repeatedly into cold water as it is apt to become brittle if held for sometime in cold water. When the shoe is cold, it is held in the vice and robbed over with the file to remove any loose flakes of iron from the surface. It must be ensured that the shoe is not bent during the process. Similarly, shoes should not be back pritchelled as the nails will not be gripped properly in back-pritchelling with the result the shoes will get loose.

Faults in Fitting the Shoe

(a) Overlowering of the walls
(b) Excessive burning of the horn
(c) Dumping
(d) Shoes too wide
(e) Shoes too long
(f) Shoes too short

Nailing On

Nails should be chosen carefully so that they will give sufficient grip in the nail holes. It is important that the right size nails are used. If too large, the head will project and wear away too soon. If too small, the head will not properly fill the nail hole. One fault is as bad as the other for both result in early loosening of the shoe. The head must not project more than about 3 mm from the ground surface of the shoe, as otherwise it would wear and the shoe would become loose. This projection of 3 mm is, however, necessary for tightening the clenches. Normally, five nails are sufficient for small shoes, three on the outer branch and two on the inner. Medium-sized shoes have six or seven nails and heavy shoes have eight or more.

Fine or Shallow Nailing - where the nail penetrates too little of the wall so affording an insecure hold.

Coarse or high nailing - where the nail comes out too high up the wall. The risk from the above is that the nail may be driven too close to the sensitive structures i.e., 'Nail binding' or actual penetration into the sensitive structures i.e., 'pricked foot'.

The first nail to be driven is either the outside or inside toe nail. The shoe tends to shift slightly to the opposite side when the first nail is driven and it must, therefore, be tapped back into position. Provided the shoe is properly fitted to the foot, it probably does not matter much what actual sequence of nailing is followed. The nails are driven alternately on the outside and inside branches, so that each is evenly secured and of the same degree of tightness. The flat side of the nail is always placed to the outside of the foot so that the pitch of the nail is directed outwards. The correct course of the nail through the horn is judged by the feel and sound of the blows. A hollow sound indicates that it is not being driven through hard horn. The point of the nail is entered in the neighbourhood of the white line and is sloped at such an angle that it comes out of the wall at such a height as to give the shoe a secure hold. The end of the nail where it penetrates the wall is turned over and twisted off leaving a small piece projecting called the 'clench'. When all the nails have been driven, the closed jaws of the pincers are put against the end of the nail on the wall and the head is driven well home into the nail hole; this causes the clench, to rise and to turn over slightly. A portion of the horn is next removed with the rasp from under each clench just big enough to form a bed for it and with the closed jaws of the pincers against the head of the nail, the clenches are tapped down with the driving hammer. The size of the clench should be such that it leaves a square piece of metal visible. Clenches provide a means of preventing the nail from being drawn out of the wall or becoming loose. Clips, generally, one toe clip for a fore shoe and two quarter clips for a hind shoe, assist in keeping the shoe in position and also afford greater security.

Finishing

The clenches are tidied up with the rasp. The toe clip is tapped lightly back into position. The rasp is run around the extremity of the wall where horn and shoe meet to reduce any risk of cracking. Clenches rise and get loose when:

(a) the shoe rests upon a bearing surface so weak or narrow that the horn yields.

(b) nail-heads do not fit the nail-holes.

(c) instead of a notch being made in sound horn for the clench, the end of the nail is turned over on the broken horn caused by the exit of the nail.

Faults in Nailing and Finishing off

(a) Nail pricks - nails driven into sensitive structures.

(b) Nail presses or Binds - nails driven so close to the sensitive structures that they bruise them or press upon them. Lameness may occur only a day or two after shoeing.

(c) Drawn Nail - nail in driving is misdirected and then withdrawn after having pricked the sensitive structures. Pus production may result if the nail has carried infection into the sensitive matrix.

(d) High nailing.

(e) Shallow nailing.

(f) Injuries from clips.

(g) Injuries from clenches rising.

(h) Rasping outside of wall.

Inspection of a Shod Horse

(a) When horse is standing on level ground

  (i) Shoe made to fit the foot and not the foot to fit the shoe i.e., toe not 'dumped' and wall not rasped away to meet the iron.

  (ii) Foot suitably reduced in length at both toe and heel and evenly to both inside and outside.

(iii) Frog in contact with the ground.

(iv) Clenches well formed (even, flat and broad), in line, the right distance up the wall and not driven into old nail holes.

(v) Place for clip has been neatly cut and clip well drawn (low and broad) and well fitted.

(b) When the foot is lifted

(i) Shoe should be suitable for the purpose intended. Should be as light as possible consistent with its being able to withstand wear for a month.

(ii) No abuse of the knife on sole or frog or bars.

(iii) Sufficient nails have been used, neither too many nor not too few.

(iv) Right size of nails used, heads driven home and fill the nail holes.

(v) No daylight shows between shoe and foot, particularly at the heel.

(vi) Heels of the shoe should neither nor too long and not too short.

(vii) Shoe should be properly finished off.

(viii)Shoe does not interfere with the functions of the frog.

(ix) Shoe must fits the foot.

(c) Trot up the horse for signs of lameness. If the animal is not lame, the shoeing is perfect.

Corrective Trimming

If a horse is to maintain a normal gait, its foot must be balanced and in alignment with the body at the moment the foot leaves the ground. Faults in the gait of a horse may occur if the rider is unskilled or the horse's equipment is not properly adjusted. Each horse must be considered individually in order to select the trimming procedure that will improve a faulty gait. Even though two or more horses have the same fault in gait, each may require a separate method of trimming for correction.

It is also important to realize that faulty gaits in the mature horse can rarely be totally corrected, but rather an attempt is made to modify and improve them with sound trimming and shoeing principles. With time and persistence, these modifications, although slight, can allow the horse to achieve its potential.

In most cases, horses with a faulty conformation and gait will have to have their feet balanced with each trimming even if they have been shod. The reason for this is that concussion and uneven weight-bearing can alter the rate of hoof wall growth enough to create an imbalance. A good example of this is a base-narrow horse; even with the foot balanced it will tend to bear more weight on the lateral aspect of the hoof wall. The lateral side of the hoof wall will have a reduced rate of growth compared to the medial side. Consequently, it will be necessary to rebalance that foot with each trimming.

Although, all of the methods of correction may be recommended for a particular condition, as a general rule it is best to use the least severe and most economical corrective measure that will produce a functional gait. Radical changes may produce pathologic changes in the limb. Corrective shoeing follows physical laws, and keen observation of the gait, and way of travel of a horse will give the necessary clues to correcting the problem. Some defects, however, are so bad that they cannot be corrected. Corrective measures should start with corrective trimming in the young horse, when possible. Faulty gaits in mature animals cannot be corrected; they can only be modified and improved.

In general, one must remember that the horse will perform best when he is trimmed and shod with his own angulation of hoof wall and toe length, keeping the pastern and hoof axis unbroken. This will vary from horse to horse, and each individual must be given due consideration, even when it varies from what are considered to be normal ranges. Occasionally, a horse will show a type of gait interference such as over-reaching or scalping that will require change in angulation for correction. Angle changes not greater than 2° can be made in an attempt to correct the problem and will lesson the likelihood of damage to the limb. At subsequent shoeings, additional changes of angle not exceeding 2° can be made.

When considering corrective shoes, it is important to realize that increased weight on the distal limb of a horse with a gait abnormality often exaggerates the abnormal flight of the foot which potentially can create more damage and increase fatigue.

The object of corrective trimming is to trim the foot until it is level in balance, and has a normal foot and pastern axis for the horse. The theory behind trimming a horse so that it wears its foot or shoe evenly, is to reduce uneven concussion to the foot. The foot should be observed in flight from both front and rear to determine where the foot lands. The wall on which the foot lands will be low, and the opposite wall is trimmed to level the foot. The hoof should be trimmed so that there is no break in the foot and pastern axis.

If a horse is base-narrow and toes-in, or is base-narrow and toes-out, the outside wall and heel are usually worn too low, and a compensating portion must be removed from the inside wall from toe to heel to level the foot. If the horse is base-wide and toes-out, the inside wall and heel may be worn down, and the outside wall must be trimmed to bring the foot near a normal foot level. It is important to observe the gait of the horse carefully and to watch where the foot lands from both the front and rear, before deciding where to correctively trim the foot. Squaring the toe and levelling the foot of young horses helps them break over the centre of the toe. If a horse is shown at halter, squaring the toe may cause a judge to mark the horse down. By watching the horse walk, one can determine how the foot lands. If the foot is put down unevenly, that region of the wall that takes most of the weight when the foot lands will be low, while other regions of the wall will be high and, therefore, must be lowered. Any portion of the wall that has begun to flare outward as the result of poor conformation must be rasped down on the outside of the wall and trimmed to the proper level. If the wall is rasped on the outside, the hoof wall tends to regain a more normal shape.

Chapter 17

Principles of Equine Feeding

The wild horses due to domestication, are now offered feeds and fodder which vary widely in physical form, nutrient-concentration and their digestibility. Even the times of feeding have been generally restricted. Although, some sort of feed consumption occurs throughout the day and night but intense feeding occurs at predetermined intervals and in required quantity. Man has also introduced unfamiliar materials particularly starchy cereals, protein concentrates and dried forages to meet the varied requirements of horses without causing metabolic and digestive disturbances.

It will be prudent to discuss the characteristic features of the gastrointestinal tract of the horse before attempts are made to lay down the principles for feeding the horses.

Mouth: Mouth of the horse has lips, tongue and teeth for prehension, ingestion and grinding the feed ingredients so that it acquires a suitable form for propulsion through the alimentary tract and permits the adequate action of digestive juices. Horses use upper lips to put the feed between the teeth to grind it further. Lips are also used as funnel for sucking the water. The presence of incisor teeth in upper and lower jaws enable the horse to shear off the forage and masticate the feed by lateral and vertical movements of jaw. Salivation helps to pulverize feed during the mastication process. As horses are monogastric animals, the grass and hay consumed by them must be ground to particles of less than 1.6 mm in length before swallowing. On an average, about 3000 to 3500 movements are required to chew one kg of hay whereas only 800 - 1200 chewing movements are sufficient for one kg of concentrate. Saliva secretion is stimulated by the presence of feed material and as much as 10-

12 litres is secreted daily. The saliva is devoid of any enzyme but it has lubricating effect.

Stomach: Stomach alone makes up for just about 10 per cent of the total volume of gastrointestinal tract. The ingesta is held for a very short time in the stomach which is about 2-3 hours. The entrance of the stomach is guarded by a strong muscular valve called cardiac sphincter and does not permit regurgitation or vomition. Ten to thirty litres of gastric juices are secreted into the stomach which is stimulated by physical presence of the feed and not by sight of the feed. The pH of stomach varies in different regions of stomach. It is 5.4 in fundic region and 2.6 in the pyloric region. Some amount of fermentation does take place in stomach especially in saccus caecus region, releasing some lactic acid. The pH of stomach falls due to HCl secretion which converts inactive pepsinogen to active pepsin enzyme which has proteolytic activity. Presence of food in stomach stimulates, through vagus nerves and hormones - the secretion of pancreatic juice in the duodenum. This juice has low enzyme activity but contains sodium, potassium chloride and bicarbonate ions. Continuous secretion of bile juice also takes place as the horse does not have a gall bladder. The brush border of the small intestine and pancreatic juice contain enzymes which cause the degradation of carbohydrates, protein and fats which results into their absorption as glucose, amino acids and fatty acids. The fat is mostly absorbed through the lymphatic system. The small intestine is about 21 m long. Much of the digesta is propelled through it very fast. It is as fast as approximately 30 cm per minute. The material that leaves small intestine is made up of fibrous feed residues, undigested feed, starch, protein, micro-organisms, intestinal secretions and cell debris.

Large Intestine and Caecum: The large intestine is made of the right and left segments of dorsal colon and right and left segments of the ventral colon. The large intestine is 3-4 m long and its capacity is more than double the caecum. The caecum is located at the distal end of the ileum which is present in the form of blind sac about 1 m long in the adult horse. It has a capacity of 25-35 litres. The caecum and colon are enlargements of the gastrointestinal tract to accommodate fermentation of digesta by micro-organisms. Faeces contains bacteria which is more than half of its dry weight. The bacteria are able to secrete enzymes capable of breaking down cellulose, hemicellulose, pectin and lignin into their component parts suitable for absorption. However, it is a slow process as compared to digestion of protein and starch which warrants arrest of flow of digesta for adequate time so that the microbial fermentation can take place. Most of the digesta reaches caecum and ventral colon within 3 hrs of a meal. It takes about 24 hrs to void 10 per cent of the waste material, 36 hrs for 50 percent and 65 hrs for 95 per cent of waste material, which indicates that large intestine is the place where unabsorbed material spends the greatest proportion of time. Passage time is also influenced by the physical form of the diet such as pelleted diets have a faster rate of passage than chopped or long hay and fresh grass moves more rapidly than hay. The walls of large and small intestine contain both longitudinal and circular muscle fibres which are essential for peristalsis through admixture of digesta with juices, absorption of the products of digestion. The intestinal contractions increase during feeding.

Microbial Digestion

Microbial digestion is a very important type of digestion in the herbivorous animals besides the mechanical enzymatic degradation. It results into hydrolysis of cellulose, glucose and synthesises indispensable amino acids and B complex group of vitamins alongwith Vitamin K_2. The microbial population inhabited in the caecum and colon of the horses is made of bacteria and ciliate protozoa. The dietary constituents and the ratio of grain to hay or forage, greatly influence the number of micro-organisms and their species distribution. Frequency of feeding may not affect the digestibility of nutrients but it has a large impact on the incidence of digestive disorders and metabolic upsets.

The microbial fermentation results in formation of large quantities of short chain volatile fatty acids (VFAs) of which, acetic acid, propionic acid and butyric acid are the principal

VFAs using dietary starch and fibre as the substrate. Continuous absorption of VFAs takes place from the large intestine. In addition to this, water and electrolytes are also absorbed from caecum and colon. The digesta of the small intestine contains 87-93 per cent water, whereas water content in faeces of healthy horse is approximately 58-62 per cent. The water content is not much influenced by the type of diet, however, some difference may occur.

The microbial population and species distribution is greatly affected by the type of diet. Bacteria adapted to grain digestion are poor digesters of hay and a similar situation has been noticed for hay-adapted caecal microbes. Abrupt changes in the diet may lead to impactions leading to colic, laminitis, or swollen legs. Microbial degradation occurs at a higher rate in caecum and ventral colon than in dorsal colon. Further, the rate of degradation is higher when diet is starchy as compared to one with more of cellulose material. These changes of the diet also affect the yield of the various volatile fatty acids and their ratio. Increased starch levels form more propionate whereas structural carbohydrate gives rise to more of acetic acid. Microbial activity also produces gases principally, carbon-di-oxide, methane and small amounts of hydrogen sulphide which are further absorbed, ejected or utilized for further metabolism.

Most of the energy in horses is provided by the dietary sugars and soluble carbohydrates. The nitrogen is also absorbed more in the form of amino acids and very less of dietary nitrogen is converted to microbial protein. Young growing horses particularly, respond to supplementation of poor quality dietary protein with lysine.

Principles for Feeding Horses

- The individual variation of feed requirement and body condition must be given due consideration for planning the feeding regimen of the horses. Some horses perform best while being trim or empty stomach whereas others exhibit their best when their body condition is optimum.
- The growth, development and expectations from the horse

regarding its performance will determine the extent of feeding especially, in early days.

- Both over-feeding and under-feeding are harmful for horses, therefore, the diet has to vary as per the requirement of the horse and its physiological status. Feeding habits must be given due consideration when feeding horses.
- All feed ingredients of horses should be free from extraneous substances such as weeds, dust, mould etc. The hygiene of feed box should also be maintained.
- The time of feeding the horses should be strictly adhered to. Also no abrupt changes in the diet should be permitted. However, if a change is required, it should be progressed slowly.
- Well being of horses depends a lot on the exercise. It helps to keep them in shape for riding, racing, work and performance besides it improves their appetite, digestion and overall condition.
- A clear, wholesome and fresh water source should always be available to the horse.
- A source of salt or complete mineral mixture should always be available for horses at all times which gives them an opportunity to take extra minerals depending upon their requirements.
- The feed of the horses must contain roughages, otherwise the heavy feed concentrates are likely to pack the stomach. However, feeds too high in fibre may also cause discomfort or digestive disturbances, especially in racehorses.
- The feed of the greedy eaters should be thinned out in the feed box.
- Oral hygiene and dental care should receive due attention as teeth problems limit the horse's ability to chew.
- Weighing of horses to find out gain or loss in the condition is a valuable parameter to decide the response of feed and effect changes in the feeding schedule, if required.

- Horses should be fed in groups according to their age, growth or development stage to prevent over-feeding or under-feeding which may occur if horses of varying sizes and age are fed together.
- Foals should be allowed access to creep feed so that they achieve the maximum for their growth and bone development as the mare's milk falls short of almost all essential feed nutrients.
- Regular deworming and health inspections are important to keep horses healthy. The stables should be kept cleaned and manure-removed to reduce parasitic infestation as they decrease feed intake, feed efficiency and body weight.
- The digestive tract of horses is limited in size and feeding large quantities of grain or concentrate feeds at one time results in higher frequency of colic and grain founder. Therefore, high performance horses, which require large amount of energy from grain or concentrate sources, should be fed three to four times daily instead of two times. More frequent feeding with less portions in each one, will reduce grain founder, colic and other digestive problems.
- The grain portion of the diet of high performance horses should be reduced if they are not being exercised. The roughage portion can be suitably increased. This is essential to prevent azoturia or Monday Morning Sickness, which causes muscle spasms or tetany.
- The diet of horses must contain roughage to provide fibre or bulk. This will reduce vices such as wood chewing, tail and mane biting. It will also decrease the incidence of digestive disorders.
- The horses should not be exercised after feeding as the stomach contents are likely to cause pressure on the diaphragm, leading to laboured breathing due to restriction in the lung expansion. Secondly, the absorption of nutrients is also affected as the blood circulation is diverted from splanchnic bed of blood vessels around the intestines to vital organs, reducing the absorptive process.

Table: 17.1 Expected Feed Consumption by Horses

Physiological Status	*Forage % of Bodywt*	*Diet*	*Concentrate % Bodywt*	*Diet*	*Totalfeed intake as %ge of Bodywt*
Mature Horse					
Maintenance	1.5-2.0	80-100	0-0.5	0-20	1.5-2.0
Mares Late Gestation	1-1.5	65	0.5-1.0	35	1.5-2.0
Mares Early Lactation	1-2.0	45	1.0-2.0	35	1.0-3.0
Mares Late Lactation	1.0-2.0	60	0.5-1.5	40	2.0-2.5
Working Horses					
Light Work	1.0-2.0	65	0.5-1.0	35	1.5-2.5
Moderate Work	1.0-2.0	40	.75-1.5	60	1.75-2.5
Intense Work	.75-1.5	30	1.0-2.0	70	2.0-2.5
Young Horses					
Nursing foal-3months	0	20	1.0-2.0	80	2.5-3.5
Weanling foal-6months	.5-1.0	30	1.5-3.0	70	2.0-3.5
Yearling foal-12 months	1.0-1.5	45	1.0-2.0	55	2.0-3.0
Long yearling -18 months	1.0-1.5	60	1.0-1.5	40	2.0-2.5
2 year old-24 months	1.0-1.5	40	1.0-1.5	60	2.0-2.5

Roughage vs Concentrate Feeding

The level of concentrate and roughage required to be fed to various classes of horses has been included in Table 17.1. These should be adopted as per guidelines which can vary depending upon the condition of horse, its level of performance and physiological status.

The forage level can be from 0.5 to 1 per cent of the body weight. Higher level of forage reduces the chances of digestive disturbances, colic and other disorders. Level of activity is very important to determine the level of concentrate and forage feeding. High level performance horses need more energy and, therefore, their diet cannot contain more roughage which can cause distended digestive tract resulting into discomfort when they are exercised or worked heavily. It may also cause quick tiring and laboured breathing. Therefore, forage in the diet of such horses should be maximally fed in the evening when the horses are at rest and some part can be given in the morning and noon diet. The forage quality is another very important factor which determines the level of forage in the diet.

Lactating mares, nursing foals, weanlings and horses undergoing intense work consume the least amount of forage. As such, the concentrate levels are higher in the diet to meet high requirement of energy. Idle horses require least amount of concentrate in their diet and can do well on high quality of forage alone. The pregnant mare can do well on half forage and half concentrate. During the last one third of gestation, the level of concentrate needs to be increased to take care of foal's development in the uterus. Similarly, during lactation also, the percentage of concentrate in the diet needs to be increased further to take care of milk production.

The forage to concentrate level in the diet also depends upon the condition of the horse. The level of activity determines the ratio of forage to concentrate in the diet. Therefore, the following considerations besides the physiological status of the horse, will determine the level of forage relative to concentrate:

(a) Individual needs (b) Level of activity

(c) Response to diet (d) Condition of the horse.

The levels can be altered or modified to meet the specific requirement of the individual horse.

Water, its Role and Requirement

The body of animal in general, contains about 70 per cent water but its level varies in various tissues of the body. Water is not an inert material or solvent but is an active and structural constituent, therefore an adequate intake of water at all times is very important. It is possible to survive for longer without feed but not without water. Loss of 10 per cent of body water results in disorders and 20 per cent water loss may result in death. Lack of water in diet can also lead to digestive disturbances.

A number of mineral elements such as sodium, chloride, potassium, calcium etc. are lost in sweat and urine during physical activity. Loss of electrolytes increases with degree of physical activity, increased temperature and humidity. The replacement of water and electrolytes is a must to prevent the occurrence of fatigue, muscle weakness and decreased feed intake. Caecum and colon are the main sites for water absorption. Water is also obtained by the body through metabolic water formed during the oxidation or breakdown of carbohydrates, protein and fat. For example, 100 gm of protein, carbohydrate and fat results in the formation of 41, 107 and 60 gm of metabolic water respectively.

Role:

- Water is an ideal dispensing medium because of its solvent and ionizing powers which facilitates cell reaction and because of its high specific heat, it is able to absorb the heat of these reactions with a minimum rise in temperature. The latent heat of vaporization also plays an important role in regulating body temperature.
- It aids in digestion, in the transport of metabolic products and excretion of waste products.
- It is a constituent of cells and body fluids. Surplus water is excreted via urine, faeces, perspiration and vapours from the lungs via breathing.
- Water as a constituent of synovial fluid lubricates the joints and as cerebrospinal fluid, it acts as a water cushion for the nervous system.
- In the ear, it transports sounds and in eye, it is concerned with sight.
- It provides cushion to the body organs and system.

Factors affecting Water Requirements

The younger the animal, more is its water content. It is believed that the growth process requires more of it. Water intake is affected by the composition of the feed, or kind of hay or grain that is fed. Horse needs about 2-4 litres of water per kg of feed. Water intake is also affected by climate or temperature in the area. Rise in environmental temperature increases the water requirement. Composition of faeces affects the water requirement e.g., diarrhoea is the most common cause of dehydration. The work and exercise performed by the horse also considerably influences the water needs.

In mares, lactation increases the water requirement by 50 to 65 per cent depending upon milk yield. Highly digestible feeds such as grains require less water for its excretion. Faecal water is highest in feeds such as hay.

The amount of water excreted in the urine is correlated with total amount of dry matter digested because water is required for the absorption of digested nutrients from the intestinal tract. This explains why there is more water excretion with legume forages as compared to grass forage.

Under conditions of water scarcity, the horse may concentrate its urine to some extent by resorbing a greater amount of water than usual, thereby lowering its requirement of water.

A lack of water lessens feed consumption which in turn decreases growth, feed efficiency and productivity. During exercise and extended work, there is an immense loss of water and electrolytes. In a horse weighing 450-500 kg, which contains about 300 litres as water, the losses can be as high as 8-14 per cent. Dehydration through sweating also entails a loss of both water and electrolytes. Sweat consists principally of Sodium and Calcium with lesser quantity of Potasium and a smaller proportion of Calcium and Mgnisium. The total concentration of electrolytes in sweat is higher than that in blood plasma so a decline in blood plasma concentration, despite considerable dehydration, is readily understandable.

Thirst, is in part controlled by the osmotic pressure of the blood and, therefore, it is frequently necessary to rectify electrolyte loss before dehydrated horses drink adequate quantity of water. Horses during endurance ride and extended work, should be given at least 2 minutes to drink water. Hard work diverts much of the blood supply to the skeletal muscles, away from the splanchnic bed of blood vessels serving the gastrointestinal tract. It is thought that this inhibits the efficient absorption of water so that the amounts consumed on any one occasion should be relatively small. After work, very dehydrated animal should be given about 4.5 litre every minute preferably containing 30 gm of electrolytes. Dehydration. is frequently accompanied by coldness and fatigue, muscular tremors, colic, thumps, lack of appetite and low ratio of pulse and respiration. When the absorption from the gut is in doubt, the dehydrated animals should be given 5 per cent glucose-electrolyte solution intravenously.

After normal hard work, a horse should be cooled by gentle exercise of the muscles through walking but access to grazing or hay should not be ruled out. After this relaxation of 1-1½ hours, tepid water should be given before a light meal of concentrates.

Chapter 18

Types of Feed and Fodder

Formulation of a balanced diet is one of the most important consideration for feeding equines. Further, it is equally essential to know the nutrient value of various feeds in terms of protein, energy, vitamins and mineral contents which help in selecting the ingredients for formulating the required quality of feed. In addition, various other factors which need to be considered include, the purpose for which feed will be used, such as, growth, lactation, gestation, training, high performance or just for maintenance and whether the horse will be pasture-fed or stall-fed. Due consideration to all the above factors alongwith the availability of feed stuffs is important in planning the nutritional requirement of various classes of equines as well as to meet the specific requirement of individual animal.

The feeds of the horses can be divided in two broad categories:

- Concentrates
- Roughages

The concentrates are composed of cereals, grains, cakes, meals and other industrial by-products which are rich sources of energy and proteins besides minerals and some vitamins. The roughages include hay, silage, grasses or pasture which may be succulent or dry. These are essential to satisfy the volume receptors of the stomach and form the bulk. In addition, hay provides important nutrients also and when fed even alone, can meet the nutrient requirements of the horse at maintenance level. The structural carbohydrates which get fermented in the caecum and colon provide about 25 per cent of the energy requirement of the horses through generation of volatile fatty acids. Composition of various feed stuffs used for equine feeding, is given in Table 2.1.

Individual feed ingredients with their nutrient value are discussed below.

Cereal Grains

Oats - Oats have traditionally formed a very important component of horse diet. It is known for low density and high fibre contents which helps to avoid over-feeding and at the same time its grain size is more appropriate for chewing. As such, it does not require any processing for horses aged over 1 year, if the teeth are sound. There are very less chances to produce grain founder or other digestive disturbances as a result of feeding excess quantity of oats as compared to the other cereals.

Normally heavy bright oats which contain a small percentage of hull are preferred and heavier ones can be obtained by screening. The best quality oats may contain just 25 per cent hulls whereas it may go up to 50 per cent in poor quality. Mouldy oats should never be used since they may cause colic as well as heaves. Oats may be fed whole, crimped or rolled which may improve its digestibility. Many prefer to feed steam rolled oats.

Barley - It is another grain which is enveloped in a hull and constitutes 10-14 per cent of the total grain weight. It is relatively smaller and more tightly apposed to a grain which is larger as compared with oat hull. Therefore, barley grain should be crippled or lightly rolled to rupture the hull before feeding. Because of higher starch content and weight of the barley, it may cause digestive disturbances when fed alone, hence mixing barley with more bulky feeds such as 15 per cent or more wheat bran or 25 per cent oats may minimize the occurrence of colic. It is normally fed in combination with oats, brewer's dried grains, citrus or beet pulp or any other bulky feeds. Barley protein is of slightly lower nutritional quality than that of oats, being relatively deficient in lysine. Also oil content is generally low.

Corn - It is widely used in feeding of horses and ranks second to oats. As the grains are very hard, they should be cracked before feeding. Corns contain twice the energy per unit volume of oats and therefore, it is fed at higher level in cool weather and its level is decreased during warm weather. It contains about 65 per cent starch and the crude protein levels range from 8 to 10 per cent. Its protein is deficient in tryptophan and lysine. However, corn is best utilized by the horses, if it is balanced with other feeds to offset its shortcomings. Heavy/bulky feed (wheat bran, brewer's dried grain, citrus or beet pulp) can be fed to horses along with the corn. Sometimes, whole ear-corn is coarsely grounded and fed to mature horses. The cob weighs about 20 percent of the whole ear of corn and supply bulk in the diet. Maize has two varieties i.e. yellow or white. The yellow maize contains pigment cryptoxanthin which is a precursor of Vit A.

Sorghum - The kernel of sorghum is naked like that of maize and wheat. It is more spherical in shape and smaller in size than that of wheat. When compared to corn, it contains more crude protein but less oil. The sorghum protein is deficient in lysine as such it should normally be fed in combination with heavy feeds. The size and shape of sorghum warrants that it should always be rolled, cracked, coarsely ground or steam flamed before feeding to horses. Since it is a high energy cereal, it should form only a portion of the cereal intake to avoid digestive disturbances.

Wheat - It is not commonly used in feeding of horses, as it contains gluten, which is a sticky substance. When wheat is ground, it is rather doughy and tends to ball up moisture and poses palatability problems. If it is to be fed, it should be mixed with other bulky feeds. It should be cracked, coarsely ground or steam flaked before use. Wheat protein is deficient in lysine. Its level in feed should not increase above 10-20 per cent of the concentrate diet.

Gram - It is reddish or yellowish brown, rather shrivelled pea, roughly pyramidal in shape. The kernel is bright yellow. It is fed as crushed and mixed with other grains. It is a good source of protein and can provide the requirements of protein alone at maintenance level when good quality roughage is not available. For better utilization, it can be soaked in water preferably for 5-6 hours. However, excessive soaking is likely to cause fermentation.

Rice - The hull covering the grain is thick fibrous but can be easily removed. It constitutes about 20 per cent of the total weight. Feeding of hull alone can cause problems as it contains silica and also its edges are sharp which can cause irritation. Rice is a reasonable source of lysine and the grain can be fed without removal of the hull.

Agro Industrial By-products

Wheat Bran - It contains about 8.5 to 11 per cent crude fibre and 14 to 16 percent crude protein. Wheat bran is an expensive source of nutrients but it can form as a mash, a palatable vehicle for oral administration of drugs and has the capacity to absorb much more than its weight of water. Thus, it has a laxative effect on the intestinal tract. It is a rich source of phosphorus and contains more than 1 per cent phosphorus of which most is in the form of phytates. Bran is deficient in calcium. Further, the phytates are known to depress the utilization of dietary calcium and zinc, as such, its use in larger quantities accelerates the onset of bony abnormalities in young and adult horses. It is generally used 5-20 per cent of the concentrate Wheat Middlings

They are derived from wheat milling and are of two types, that is coarse middlings and fine middlings. Coarse middlings are similar to bran and contain about 6-8.5 per cent crude protein. Fine middlings contain less crude fibre. The protein content is about 20 per cent. In addition, it contains about 5 per cent fat. Wheat middlings are rich source of energy and the level should not increase 5-20 per cent of the concentrate diet.

Brewing and Distilling By-products

These are the major by-products derived from brewing. Malt culms are the sprouted embryonic radical (Root) and plumule

(Stem) which remain after the process of malting. They are dried to form the malt culms. The remaining sprouted grain is meshed to remove the sugar, leaving the grain which is dried to form brewer's grain.

Brewer's grains are good source of protein and are rich in lysine also. They contain about 25 per cent protein, 5-7 per cent fat and 16-18 per cent fibre. Since the palatability of these products is low, mollasses can be added. These can be used upto 40 percent to replace oats and soyabean without affecting the digestibility of the other nutrients. Accordingly, these may be considered as another source of bulk. In young horses, dietary level of these products should not exceed 10-20 percent of total diet. If used at 20 per cent level, lysine supplementation is essential. Older horses can use upto 20-40 per cent but attention should be paid to lysine level.

The most coveted and expensive by-product of brewing is yeast which in dry form contains 420 gm of high quality protein per kg and is a rich source of a range of water soluble vitamins and phosphorus. When required, yeast may be fed to horses in poor condition, at a rate of 30-50 gm daily.

Mollasses

The cane mollasses or black strap mollasses obtained from sugar is an excellent energy source for horses. It results as a by-product of sugar industry consequent to crystallization and separation of sucrose from the water extracts of the sugar beet and sugar cane. The residual thick black liquid, termed mollasses, contains 75 per cent dry matter, of which about two third is sugar. The nitrogen is present mostly as non proteinaceous nitrogen and is of significant nutritive value. It is used as a binding material in feed industry. It also increases palatability and reduce dustiness. Cane mollasses is a rich source of calcium, potassium, pantothenic acid and niacin. It should be added only upto 5-10 per cent of the diet especially in hot and humid areas where it might cause wetness in the feed and result in mould growth.

Beet mollasses can also be used for feeding to horses but cane mollasses is normally preferred, although, both have similar nutritive value.

Pulps

Citrus and beet pulps are used for feeding to the horses. The citrus pulp contains about 6 per cent crude protein and 3.5 percent fat. It is a bulky feed and a good energy source. It can be added upto 5-15 per cent of the diet depending upon the age of horse. Lower level is preferred for younger ones.

Citrus pulp consists of the pulp and residue of oranges and grape fruit, being processed for juice. The palatibility and feeding will depend upon processing conditions and the percentage of the various citrus fruits it contains. It can replace oats in pelleted feeds and can be included upto 15 per cent. Beet pulp can also be used in a similar way as citrus pulp for feeding horses and should be limited to 15 per cent of the concentrate diet.

Rice By-products

Rice meal and rice bran are the two by-products of rice industry. Rice by products are rich source of fat which is made up of more unsaturated fatty acids and, therefore, it is likely to get rancid very rapidly. Removal of fatty acids is essential to improve its keeping quality. Rice bran is also rich source of silica and phosphorus. The Phosphorus is mostly in the form of Phytates. Its level in diet should not exceed 5-10 percent. Rice bran contains approximately 12 per cent crude fibre, 13 per cent protein and about 14 per cent fat, which after extraction is brought down to 1.5 to 2 per cent.

Hominy Feed

It consists of a mixture of corn germ, corn bran and a part of the starchy portion of the kernels and is a by-product of process used for producing corn meal for human use. It resembles corn in nutritive value and is rich in unsaturated fatty acids which becomes easily rancid. Therefore, it should be kept in a cool and well ventilated storage area. The crude fibre level is 7-8 per cent whereas protein level ranges from 8 to 23 per cent. Though the nutritive value of protein is not good, yet, the feed is quiet suitable as a supplement in horse rations and is a good source of water soluble vitamins.

Vegetable Protein Sources

Oil seeds residues are the richest source of protein. Other sources include peas, beans and yeast and high quality of dried forages such as lucerne meal or alfalfa meal. Microbial protein is likely to be a new source in the days to come. Protein supplements for feeding to horses should be selected on the basis of total protein level, balance of amino acids and requirement of correcting protein and amino acid deficiency in the energy feeds commonly used in horse's diets. The mineral and vitamin content is also to be given due consideration while deciding their inclusion levels. Protein supplements that contain a high level of the indispensable amino acids, especially lysine, are preferred for young growing horses. Plant protein supplements are preferred in horse diet but small levels of animal protein concentrates such as, fish meal, meat meal and bone meal are sometimes used. Dried skim milk can also be used as protein source in horses especially for young horses. Oil seed meals are much richer sources of protein than the cereals. However, linseed meal is a poorer source of lysine-when compared with soyabean meal. Sunflower seeds are rich in the sulphur containing amino acids, cystine and methionine.

Soyabean Meal

It is a plant protein source with highest level of lysine and is commonly used in horse feeding. Its protein levels range from 44-48 per cent and usually fed to horses in combination with other protein source.

Raw soyabeans contain allergenic and anticoagulant factors as well as protease inhibitors. The correct toasting and cooling of the beans destroys these factors without detracting from the protein quality. However, over heating soyabean meal destroys lysine whereas under heating soyabean meal makes it methionine content less available.

Whole uncooked soyabeans should not be fed to horses since they contain trypsin inhibitor which inhibits the enzyme trypsin from digesting protein.

Linseed Meal

The unique feature of linseed is that it is a source of relatively indigestible mucilage which can absorb large amount of water and produces a thick soup during the traditional cooking. The lubricating action of soup regulates faecal excretion and sometime overcomes constipation without causing looseness. Linseed meal is a popular protein supplement for horse feeding. It is low in lysine content, as such should not be fed alone as a protein source.

The cooking of linseed destroys enzyme livase which is responsible for the release of hydrocyanic acid. The low temperature removal of oil during the production of linseed meal, implies that product may be toxic if fed as a gruel. Linseed products are rich in phosphorus and relatively good sources of thiamin, riboflavin, niacin and pantothenic acid.

Cottonseed Meal

It ranks next to soyabean meal in feeding of horses. Although, it contains relatively good quality protein yet suffers from the presence of yellow toxic pigment called gossypol. Heating during processing partly inactivates the toxin in the raw material but excessive temperature binds gossypol with lysine thus depressing protein quality. Cottonseed meal cannot be fed as a sole protein source since it contains half the level of lysine as compared to soyabean meal.

Sunflower Seed Meal

It is produced from the seeds of sunflower plant and is considered poor source of lysine. Horses can be safely fed this meal but it may be unpalatable in higher quantities. As such, sunflower seed meal should not be fed as the only plant protein source and is preferred in combination with other protein sources. In addition, lysine should be supplemented. Sunflower meal on an average has 32 per cent of crude fibre and approximately 20 per cent protein, if undecorticated. However, the protein percentage is 40-45 if decorticated. Although, its lysine level is low but methionine level is double the soyabean meal's level of the amino acid.

Groundnut Meal

It is a very palatable protein supplement for horse feeding but is deficient in lysine and methionine. It should not be fed alone as a protein source to growing foals. Its level should not increase more than one third of the total protein supplement. If groundnut meal is being used, it should be fed fresh as its storage is likely to lead to rancidity owing to the presence of unsaturated fatty acids.

Rapeseed Meal

It is high in fibre content and contains about 36 per cent protein and 2.1 per cent lysine. Inclusion of rapeseed meal does not pose any problem of acceptability of feed by horses. Similarly, there is no effect on daily gain and feed efficiency in growing horses when fed diets containing 15 per cent rapeseed meal and 15 per cent soyabean meal.

Animal Protein Sources

Dried Skim Milk - It is highly palatable, digestible and a good source of protein, minerals and vitamins alongwith high level of lysine. It also contains lactose as the carbohydrate. However, it is too expensive to be used as protein supplement for horses. It is primarily used in foal's diet to supplement mare's milk or as a part of milk replacer given to weanlings. It is deficient in fat soluble vitamins as its fat percentage is low.

Cow's Milk - It contains on an average 12.5 per cent dry matter with 3.7 per cent fat, 3.3 per cent protein and 4.7 per cent of lactose. It can be used for feeding the orphan foals. It is highly deficient in magnesium and iron, but rich in vit. A. Milk protein contains adequate lysine.

Fish Meal - It is an exceptionally good source of protein and indispensable amino acids-lysine and methionine. It is also rich in minerals such as calcium, phosphorus, manganese, iron and iodine and several water soluble vitamins including vitamin B_{12} (only found in animal products and bacteria). Inclusion level of 5-10 per cent in creep feed or milk replacer is quite satisfactory for foals. Fish meal is expensive which limits its use. In addition, it may be contaminated with pathogenic organisms especially *Salmonella* species or other enteric organisms which can cause digestive disturbances.

Meat Meal/Bone Meal - They can be supplemented to concentrate diets in small amounts and are good source of protein, lysine, calcium, and phosphorus. However, utilized meat meal/bone meal should never be fed to horses as it may be contaminated with *Salmonella* sp., leading to diseases which become difficult to eradicate.

Single Cell Protein - With the industrial production on a commercial scale of microbial protein, a new high quality protein source has become available to the horse industry. The crude protein level of bacteria and yeasts being used as protein source, ranges from 34 to 72 per cent and 40 to 45 per cent whereas fat percentage varies from 2-21 for bacterial and 2.5-5.5 for yeasts.

Roughage

Lucerne Hay - An excellent and well balanced feed for horses and can be exclusively used for feeding. It is a good source of protein, vitamins, minerals and other nutrients. The alfalfa hay is a good source of calcium of which 20-30 per cent is present as oxalic acid. It is not only a fair source of phosphorus but rich source of vit A. It is also a good source of vit D and quite rich in riboflavin and niacin. In completely pelletised feed, alfalfa hay has been seen to increase the digestibility of cellulose and energy.

When fed in pelletized diet or as wafers, it may develop certain vices in horses as wood chewing and coprophagia. It has about 15 per cent protein, though its protein content varies greatly depending upon how well it was cured and on the stage of maturity at which it was cut. A considerable loss of nutritive value occurs due to shattering of leaves which are rich in protein, minerals and vitamins. The cutting of lucerne in full bloom is best for horses as early cut may be too laxative. After full bloom stage, the value of the alfalfa hay falls considerably.

Oat Hay - It is considered most ideal roughage for mature horses. Oat hay is commonly fed in bundles without threshing. The nutritive value is best when cutting takes place at the soft dough (milky) stage. It is low in protein and calcium and can not be fed alone without supplementary protein and mineral source.

Silage - Silage is highly susceptible to moulds and may get spoiled because of low moisture and on exposure to oxygen. It is not usually fed to the horses. However, when considered essential, silage should be fed mixed with hay maximum to the extent of one third to one half of the hay, on dry matter basis. It should not be fed to valuable horses used for racing, high level performance and hard work, as it may cause digestive disturbance and distention of stomach resulting in poor performance.

Yeast Culture - Feeding of live yeast culture to growing horses has been reported to enhance nitrogen retention and hemicellulose digestibility. The horses undergoing training have been found to have better conditioning effect which is depicted by increased aerobic capacity.

The increased nitrogen retention has been reported primarily by improving the effective biological value of feed protein. It may also be associated with positive effects on both protein synthesis and protein degradation in young growing horse.

Table 18.1 : Composition of Feed Stuffs used for Equine Feeding

Feeds	*DM*	*TDN*	*Crude Protein*	*EE*	CF	*NFE*	*Ash*
Dry Roughages							
1. Alfalfa Hay	90.5	50.3	14.8	2.0	28.9	36.6	8.2
2. Oat Hay	88.1	47.3	8.2	2.7	28.1	42.2	6.9
3. Soyabean hay	88.0	49.0	14.4	3.3	27.5	35.8	7.0
4. Timothy hay	89.0	48.9	6.5	2.4	30.2	45.0	4.9
5. Wheat Strand	92.5	40.6	3.1	1.5	37.5	42.1	8.3
Green Roughages							
1. Alfalfa Green	25.3	14.7	4.5	0.9	7.2	10.4	2.3
2. Berseem green	18.4	11.8	2.5	0.6	3.8	8.6	2.9
3. Cow pea	16.3	10.8	3.0	0.5	3.8	7.0	2.0
4. Oat	26.6	16.9	2.6	0.8	7.5	13.7	2.0
5. Soyabean forage	24.0	15.2	4.1	1.0	6.6	9.9	2.4
Concentrates							
1. Barley	89.4	77.7	12.7	1.9	5.4	66.6	2.8
2. Corn	90.7	88.6	11.5	7.9	2.4	67.1	1.8
3. Cotton seed	92.5	72.6	42.7	6.4	10.6	27.0	5.8
4. Cow pea	89.0	76.0	3.4	1.4	4.0	56.7	3.5
5. Gram	89.0	-	20.0	3.5	9.5	63.5	3.5
6. Linseed meal	90.9	77.4	38.0	5.9	7.7	33.7	5.6
7. Milk (mare)	9.4	10.1	2.0	1.1	0	5.4	1.0
8. Mollasses (cane)	74.0	54.0	2.9	0	0	62.1	9.0
9. Oat grain	91.4	86.6	15.8	5.2	3.3	64.6	2.4
10. Rape seed oil meal	89.5	68.1	33.5	8.2	10.8	30.2	6.9
11. Rice Bran	90.9	67.0	12.5	13.5	12.0	39.4	13.5
12. Sunflower seed	93.1	86.8	16.3	29.8	26.6	17.5	2.9
13. Soyabean seed	90.0	87.6	37.0	8.0	5.0	24.5	4.6
14. Wheat bran	90.1	67.2	16.9	4.6	9.6	62.9	6.1
15. Yeast Brewer's dried	93.8	70.5	49.3	1.0	3.7	31.9	7.9

DM - Dry Matter NFE - Nitrogen Free Extract
EE - Ether Extract TDN - Total Digestible Nutrients
CF - Crude Fibre

Chapter 19

Feeding Standards and Nutritional Requirments

Feeding standards are tables showing the amount of nutrients which should be provided in ration for animals of various ages and classes depending upon their physiological status, in order to secure the best results.

The history of feeding standards goes back to as early as latter half of eighteenth century when **German scientist, Albrecht Thayer (1752-1828),** evolved the concept of hay equivalents as measure of relative value. It was based on determining the materials in feeds extractable with water and other solvents. Subsequently, other workers in Germany and England conducted feeding trials to compare value of hay with turnips, Carrots, cabbage and oil meals. In 1827, Pront recognized protein, fat and carbohydrate as essential organic nutrients. Simultaneously, simple techniques for analysis were developed and based on analysis of nutrients, feeding standards for farm animals were formulated for the first time by Grouven in 1859.

In **1864 Wolff** devised a standard based on digestible protein, digestible ether extract and digestible carbohydrate, derived from results obtained in feeding trials. Later on, the Wolff standards were somewhat modified in **1866 by Lehmann,** another German scientist. These standards were known as **"Wolff Lehmann Feeding Standards"** and were widely used for many years in Europe and United States. In 1890, At-Water, proposed a feeding standard based on the available fuel values of feed. These values applied to digested nutrients and were obtained by the use of 'Rubned factors' (4.1 K Cal/gm for carbohydrate, 9.3 K Cal/gm for fat and 4.1 k/Cal/gm for protein).

The first book entitled "Feeds and Feeding" was published by Henry in 1898. It contained, Wolff Lehmann Standards alongwith tables showing average composition of various feeds, digestion coefficients for protein, crude fibre, nitrogen free extract, ether extract as well as intake of dry matter, digestible protein, digestible carbohydrate and digestible ether extract. In 1907, Kellner presented feeding standards, based on net energy. He added pure carbohydrate, protein and fat to a basal maintenance diet and separately determined the amounts of these pure nutrients required to produce a unit of body fat. He took starch as the standard and assigned values of fat producing power to various nutrients. Accordingly, Kellner standards were expressed in starch values. During the same period, Scandinavian Feed Unit system was also advocated in which nutritive values of feeds were expressed in terms of commonly used feed stuff instead of a specific nutrient like, starch. Since Scandinavian feed units were determined by actual feeding trials, they were considered to be more practical and realistic.

In 1915, Armsby set forth a feeding standard based on digestible true protein and net energy. This system, however, did not gain much acceptance. The book entitled "Feeds and Feeding", was published again in 1915, and contained, nutrient requirements based on dry matter, digestible protein, TDN (Total digestible nutrients) and nutritive ratios. In the subsequent years, digestible nutrient system was used almost exclusively in the United States. The total digestible nutrient system has certain inherent limitations as this takes into account only faecal losses in assessing the nutritive value of a feed stuff. The digestibility figures reflect only the apparent digestibility, as the metabolic faecal losses are not taken into account. This system treats roughage of different types and concentrates at par while evaluating their nutritive values, without considering the variability amongst them with regard to heat increment or gaseous losses which are more for poor roughages than for hay and much less for concentrate. Thus, this system had the drawback to over-evaluate roughages and under-evaluate concentrates.

The feeding standards so far described, dealt with feed stuff as physical quantities and suggested the requirements in terms of weighing units such as pounds or kg. However, it was felt that largest purpose served by food in the body is to furnish energy, therefore, describing a feed in terms of energy content provides a common basis for comparing it with other feed stuffs. Accordingly, the existing feeding system was studied indepth and it was emphasized to evolve a system by which the nutritive value of a feed can be assigned under particular circumstances of maintenance and production and by which productive performance of the animals would become more predictable. In his recommendations, he suggested that basic tabulations of nutritive value of feed stuffs must be expressed in terms of ME (Metabolizable Energy) determined at maintenance level and expressed per kg of feed stuff. Such values enable compilation of the ME of total ration. In the light of these developments, National Research Council of National Academy of Sciences of USA formed a Committee on Animal Nutrition in 1942 to undertake the task of setting forth a statement of quantitative needs for all the recognized nutrients. Keeping in view various developments in the field, sub-committees of experts for each class of stock were accordingly set up to review the literature. Initially, the term 'allowance' was used to provide a margin of safety, but in 1953, the Committee on Animal Nutrition, decided not to include such margins in future but to set forth intakes considered adequate for normal growth, production and health. Since the report of NRC represented pooled judgement of a group of experts in the field of species in question, it was considered to be most authoritative statement of nutritional needs of farm animals for feeding practice in USA. With very little work done in the nutritional requirements of the horses depending upon their physiological status, age, sex, class and climate, the recommendations of NRC are followed with slight modification depending on availability of various feeds and fodders in the region and the economics of feeding.

Limitations of Feeding Standards

Though NRC tables of nutrient requirements are designed to

be the best general guides for practice but these should be considered subject to modification in special cases. Practical feeding factors such as feed costs, rate of grain, milk yield of lactating mares, are considered to be of utmost importance. Similarly, palatability of feed and physical nature of the feeds are also required to be taken into consideration. As such, no standard can be a complete guide. However, these considerations help in planning of experiments and interpreting the results so obtained. In addition, environment is also known to change the nutrient requirement for which little data is available.

Nutrient Requirements of Various Classes of Equines

The requirements of various nutrients stated herein indicate the minimum amounts needed to sustain normal health. However, horses are required to be treated as individuals and, therefore, should be fed as individuals. The nutrient requirements of various classes of equines are given in Tables 18.1 to 18.7. Similarly, expected feed consumption by horses on the basis of percent body weight is given in Table 18.3. However, while applying these recommendations, consideration should also be given to the following factors:

(a) Digestive and metabolic differences among horses.

(b) Variation in production and performance capabilities of the animal and expectations of the owner.

(c) Health status of the animal.

(d) Variation in the nutrient available in feed ingredients.

(e) Interrelationship among various nutrients.

(f) Previous nutritional status of the horses.

(g) Climatic and environmental conditions.

Table 18.1 : Daily Nutrient Requirements of Ponies (200-kg mature weight)

Animal	weight (kg)	Daily gain (kg)	DE (kg)	Crude Protein (Meal)	Lysine (g)	Calcium (g)	Phosphorus (g)	Magnesium (g)	Potassium (g)	Vitamin A (10^3 IU)
Mature Ponies										
Maintenance	200		7.4	296	10	8	6	3.0	10.0	6
Stallions (breeding season)	200		9.3	370	13	11	8	4.3	14.1	9
Pregnant Mares										
9 months	200		8.2	361	13	16	12	3.9	13.1	12
10 months	8.4		368	13	16	12	4.0	13.4	12	
11 months	8.9		391	14	17	13	4.3	14.2	12	
Lactating mares										
Foaling to 3 months	200		13.7	688	24	27	18	4.8	21.2	12
3 months to weaning	200		12.2	528	18	18	11	3.7	14.8	12
Working Ponies										
Light work	200		9.3	370	13	11	8	4.3	14.1	9
Moderate work	200		11.1	444	16	14	10	5.1	16.9	9
Intense work	200		14.8	592	21	18	13	6.8	22.5	9
Growing Ponies										
Weanling, 4 months	75	0.40	7.3	365	15	16	9	1.6	5.0	3
Weanling, 6 months										
Moderate growth	95	0.30	7.6	378	16	13	7	1.8	5.7	4
Rapid growth	95	0.40	8.7	433	18	17	9	1.9	6.0	4
Yearling, 12.months										
Moderate growth	140	0.20	8.7	392	17	12	7	2.4	7.6	6
Rapid growth	140	0.30	10.3	462	19	15	8	2.5	7.9	6
Long yearling, 8 months										
Not in training	170	0.10	8.3	375	16	10	6	2.7	8.8	8
In training	170	0.10	11.6	522	22	14	8	3.7	12.2	8
Two year old, 24 months										
Not in training	185	0.05	7.9	337	13	9	5	2.8	9.4	8
In training	185	0.05	11.4	485	19	13	7	4.1	13.5	8

Table 18.2 : Daily Nutrient Requirements of Horses (400-kg mature weight)

Animal	*weight (kg)*	*Daily gain (kg)*	*DE (kg)*	*Crude Protein (Meal)*	*Lysine (g)*	*Calcium (g)*	*Phosphorus (g)*	*Magnesium (g)*	*Potassium (g)*	*Vitamin A (10^3 IU)*
Mature Horses										
Maintenance	400		13.4	536	19	16	11	6.0	20.0	12
Stallions (breeding season)	400		16.8	670	23	20	15	7.7	25.5	18
Pregnant Mares										
9 months	400		14.9	654	23	28	21	7.1	23.8	24
10 months	15.1		666	23	29	21	7.3	24.2	24	
11 months	16.1		708	25	31	23	7.7	25.7	24	
Lactating mares										
Foaling to 3 months	400		22.9	1,141	40	45	29	8.7	36.8	24
3 months to weaning	400		19.7	839	29	29	18	6.9	26.4	24
Working Horses										
Light work	400		16.8	670	23	20	15	7.7	25.5	18
Moderate work	400		20.1	804	28	25	17	9.2	30.6	18
Intense work	400		26.8	1,072	38	33	23	12.3	40.7	18
Growing Horses										
Weanling, 4 months	145	0.85	13.5	675	28	33	18	3.2	9.8	7
Weanling, 6 months										
Moderate growth	180	0.55	12.9	643	27	25	14	3.4	10.7	8
Rapid growth	180	0.70	14.5	725	30	30	16	3.6	11.1	8
Yearling, 12 months										
Moderate growth	265	0.40	15.6	700	30	23	13	4.5	14.5	12
Rapid growth	265	0.50	17.1	770	33	27	15	4.6	14.8	12
Long yearling, 18 months										
Not in training	330	0.25	15.9	716	30	21	12	5.3	17.3	15
In training	330	0.25	21.6	970	41	29	16	7.1	23.4	15
Two year old, 24 months										
Not in training	365	0.15	15.3	650	26	19	11	5.7	18.7	16
In training	365	0.15	21.5	913	37	27	15	7.9	26.2	16

Table 18.3 : Daily Nutrient Requirements of Horses (500-kg mature weight)

Animal	*weight (kg)*	*Daily gain (kg)*	*DE (kg)*	*Crude Protein (Meal)*	*Lysine (g)*	*Calcium (g)*	*Phosphorus (g)*	*Magnesium (g)*	*Potassium (g)*	*Vitamin A (10^3 IU)*
Mature horses										
Maintenance	500		16.4	656	23	20	14	7.5	25.0	15
Stallions (breeding season)	500		20.5	820	29	25	18	9.4	31.2	22
Pregnant Mares										
9 months	500		18.2	801	28	35	26	8.7	29.1	30
10 months			18.5	815	29	35	26	8.9	29.7	30
11 months			19.7	866	30	37	28	9.4	31.5	30
Lactating mares										
Foaling to 3 months	500		28.3	1,427	50	56	36	10.9	46.0	30
3 months to weaning	500		24.3	1,048	37	36	22	8.6	33.0	30
Working Horses										
Light work	500		20.5	820	29	25	18	9.4	31.2	22
Moderate work	500		24.6	984	34	30	21	11.3	37.4	22
Intense work	500		32.8	1,312	46	40	29	15.1	49.9	22
Growing Horses										
Weanling, 4 months	175	0.85	14.4	720	30	34	19	3.7	11.3	8
Weanling, 6 months										
Moderate growth	215	0.65	15.0	750	32	29	16	4.0	12.7	10
Rapid growth	215	0.85	17.2	860	36	36	20	4.3	13.3	10
Yearling, 12 months										
Moderate growth	325	0.50	18.9	851	36	29	16	5.5	17.8	15
Rapid growth.	325	0.65	21.3	986	40	34	19	5.7	18.2	15
Long yearling, 18 months										
Not in training	400	0.35	19.8	893	38	27	15	6.4	21.1	18
In training	400	0.35	26.5	1,195	50	36	20	8.6	28.2	18
Two year old, 24 months										
Not in training	450	0.20	18.8	800	32	24	13	7.0	23.1	20
In training	450	0.20	26.3	1,117	45	34	19	9.8	32.2	20

Table 18.4 : Daily Nutrient Requirements of Horses (600-kg mature weight)

Animal	*Weight (kg)*	*Daily gain (kg)*	*DE (kg)*	*Crude Protein (Meal)*	*Lysine (g)*	*Calcium (g)*	*Phosphorus (g)*	*Magnesium (g)*	*Potassium (g)*	*Vitamin A (10^3 IU)*
Mature Horses										
Maintenance	600		19.4	776	27	24	17	9.0	30.0	18
Stallions (breeding season)	600		24.3	970	34	30	21	11.2	36.9	27
Pregnant Mares										
9 months	600		21.5	947	33	41	30	10.3	34.5	36
10 months			21.9	965	34	42	31	10.5	35.1	36
11 months			23.3	1,024	36	44	33	11.2	37.2	36
Lactating mares										
Foaling to 3 months	600		33.7	1,711	60	67	43	13.1	55.2	36
3 months to weaning	600		28.9	1,258	44	43	27	10.4	39.6	36
Working Horses										
Light work	600		24.3	970	34	30	21	11.2	36.9	27
Moderate work	600		29.1	1,164	41	36	25	1304	44.2	27
Intense work	600		38.8	1,552	54	47	34	17.8	59.0	27
Growing Horses										
Weanling, 4 months	200	1.00	16.5	825	35	40	22	4.3	13.0	9
Weanling, 6 months										
Moderate growth	245	0.75	17.0	850	36	34	19	4.6	14.5	11
Rapid growth	245	0.95	19.2	960	40	40	22	4.9	15.1	11
Yearling, 12 months										
Moderate growth	375	0.65	22.7	1,023	43	36	20	604	20.7	17
Rapid growth	375	0.80	25.1	1,127	48	41	22	6.6	21.2	17
Long yearling, 18 months										
Not in training	475	0.45	23.9	1,077	45	33	18	7.7	25.1	21
In training	475	0.45	32.0	1,429	60	44	24	10.2	33.3	21
Two year old, 24 months										
Not in training	540	0.30	23.5	998	40	31	17	8.5	27.9	24
In training	540	0.30	32.3	1,372	55	43	24	11.6	38.4	24

Table 18.5 : Daily Nutrient Requirements of Horses (700-kg mature weight)

Animal	*Weight (kg)*	*Dailygain (kg)*	*DE (kg)*	*Crude Protein (Meal)*	*Lysine (g)*	*Calcium (g)*	*Phosphorus (g)*	*Magnesium (g)*	*Potassium (g)*	*Vitamin A (10^3 IU)*
Mature horses										
Maintenance	700		21.3	851	30	28	20	10.5	35.0	21
Stallions (breeding season)	700		26.6	1,064	37	32	23	12.2	40.4	32
Pregnant Mares										
9 months	700		23.6	1,039	36	45	33	11.3	37.8	42
10 months			24.0	1,058	37	46	34	11.5	38.5	42
11 months			25.5	1,124	39	49	35	12.3	40.9	42
Lactating mares										
Foaling to 3 months	700		37.9	1,997	70	78	51	15.2	64.4	42
3 months to weaning	700		32.4	1,468	51	50	31	12.1	46.2	42
Working Horses										
Light work	700		26.6	1,064	37	32	23	12.2	40.4	32
Moderate work	700		31.9	1,277	45	39	28	14.7	48.5	32
Intense work	700		42.6	1,702	60	52	37	19.6	64.7	32
Growing Horses										
Weanling, 4 months	225	1.10	19.7	986	41	44	25	4.8	14.6	10
Weanling, 6 months										
Moderate growth	275	0.80	20.0	1,001	42	37	20	5.1	16.2	12
Rapid growth	275	1.00	22.2	1,111	47	43	24	5.4	16.8	12
Yearling, 12 months										
Moderate growth	420	0.70	26.1	1,176	50	39	22	7.2	23.1	19
Rapid growth	420	0.85	28.5	1,281	54	44	24	7.4	23.6	19
Long yearling, 18 months										
Not in training	525	0.50	27.0	1,215	51	37	20	8.5	27.8	24
In training	525	0.50	36.0	1,615	68	49	27	11.3	36.9	24
Two year old, 24 months										
Not in training	600	0.35	26.3	1,117	45	35	19	9.4	31.1	27
In training	600	0.35	36.0	1,529	61	48	27	12.9	42.5	27

Table 18.6 : Daily Nutrient Requirements of Horses (800-kg mature weight)

Animal	Weight (kg)	Daily gain (kg)	DE (kg)	Crude Protein (Meal)	Lysine (g)	Calcium (g)	Phosphorus (g)	Magnesium (g)	Potassium (g)	Vitamin A (10^3 IU)
Mature Horses										
Maintenance	800		22.9	914	32	32	22	12.0	40.0	24
Stallions (breeding season)	800		28.6	1,143	40	35	25	13.1	43.4	36
Pregnant Mares										
9 months	800		25.4	1,116	39	48	36	12.2	40.6	48
10 months			25.8	1,137	40	49	36	12.4	41.3	48
11 months			27.4	1,207	42	52	39	13.2	43.9	48
Lactating mares										
Foaling to 3 months	800		41.9	2,282	81	90	58	17.4	73.6	48
3 months to weaning	800		35.5	1,678	60	58	36	13.8	52.8	48
Working Horses										
Light work	800		28.6	1,143	40	35	25	13.1	43.4	36
Moderate work	800		34.3	1,372	48	42	30	15.8	52.1	36
Intense work	800		45.7	1,829	64	56	40	21.0	69.5	36
Growing Horses										
Weanling, 4 months	250	1.20	21.4	1,070	45	48	27	5.3	16.1	11
Weanling, 6 months										
Moderate growth	305	0.90	22.0	1,100	46	41	23	5.7	18.0	14
Rapid growth	305	1.10	24.2	1,210	51	47	26	6.0	18.6	14
Yearling, 12 months										
Moderate growth	460	0.80	28.7	1,291	55	44	24	7.9	25.4	21
Rapid growth	460	0.95	31.0	1,396	59	49	27	8.1	25.9	21
Long yearling, 18 months										
Not in training	590	0.60	30.2	1,361	57	43	24	9.6	31.3	27
In training	590	0.60	39.8	1,793	76	56	31	12.6	41.2	27
Two year old, 24 months										
Not in training	675	0.40	28.7	1,220	49	40	22	10.6	35.0	30
In training	675	0.40	39.1	1,662	66	54	30	14.5	47.6	30

Table 18.7 Daily Nutrient Requirements of Horses (90O-kg mature weight)

Animal	*Weight (kg)*	*Daily gain (kg)*	*DE (kg)*	*Crude Protein (Meal)*	*Lysine (g)*	*Calcium (g)*	*Phosphorus (g)*	*Magnesium (g)*	*Potassium (g)*	*Vitamin A (10^3 IU)*
Mature Horses										
Maintenance	800		22.9	914	32	32	22	12.0	40.0	24
Stallions (breeding season)	800		28.6	1,143	40	35	25	13.1	43.4	36
Pregnant Mares										
9 months	800		25.4	1,116	39	48	36	12.2	40.6	48
10 months			25.8	1,137	40	49	36	12.4	41.3	48
11 months			27.4	1,207	42	52	39	13.2	43.9	48
Lactating mares										
Foaling to 3 months	800		41.9	2,282	81	90	58	17.4	73.6	48
3 months to weaning	800		35.5	1,678	60	58	36	13.8	52.8	48
Working Horses										
Light work	800		28.6	1,143	40	35	25	13.1	43.4	36
Moderate work	800		34.3	1,372	48	42	30	15.8	52.1	36
Intense work	800		45.7	1,829	64	56	40	21.0	69.5	36
Growing Horses										
Weanling, 4 months	250	1.20	21.4	1,070	45	48	27	5.3	16.1	11
Weanling, 6 months										
Moderate growth	305	0.90	22.0	1,100	46	41	23	5.7	18.0	14
Rapid growth	305	1.10	24.2	1,210	51	47	26	6.0	18.6	14
Yearling, 12 months										
Moderate growth	460	0.80	28.7	1,291	55	44	24	7.9	25.4	21
Rapid growth	460	0.95	31.0	1,396	59	49	27	8.1	25.9	21
Long yearling, 18 months										
Not in training	590	0.60	30.2	1,361	57	43	24	9.6	31.3	27
In training	590	0.60	39.8	1,793	76	56	31	12.6	41.2	27
Two year old, 24 months										
Not in training	675	0.40	28.7	1,220	49	40	22	10.6	35.0	30
In training	675	0.40	39.1	1,662	66	54	30	14.5	47.6	30

Note: Mares should gain weight during late gestation to compensate for tissue deposition. However, nutrient requirements

Table 18.8 Expected Feed Consumption by Horses (% body weight)[a]

	Forage	*Concentrate*	*Total*
Mature Horses			
Maintenance	1.5-2.0	0-0.5	1.5-2.0
Mares, late gestation	1.0-1.5	0.5-1.0	1.5-2.0
Mares, early lactation	1.0-2.0	1.0-2.0	2.0-3.0
Mares, late lactation	1.0-2.0	0.5-1.5	2.0-2.5
Working Horses			
Light work	1.0-2.0	0.5-1.0	1.5-2.5
Moderate work	1.0-2.0	0.75-1.5	1.75-2.5
Intense work	0.75-1.5	1.0-2.0	2.5-3.5
Young Horses			
Nursing foal, 3 months	0	1.0-2.0	2.5-3.5
Weanling foal, 6 months	0.5-1.0	1.5-3.0	2.0-3.5
Yearling foal, 12 months	1.0-1.5	1.0-2.0	2.0-3.0
Long yearling, 18 months	1.0-1.5	1.0-1.5	2.0-2.5
Two year old (24 months)	1.0-1.5	1.0-1.5	1.75-2.5

Accordingly, the nutrient requirement of horses will be dealt with under the following heads:

(a) Energy

(b) Protein

(c) Minerals

(d) Vitamins

Energy - The energy in the body of horses is provided by carbohydrates and lipids.

Carbohydrates - The horse being a non ruminant herbivore, uses dietary carbohydrate as the primary source of energy. After ingestion, these are subjected to pancreatic and intestinal enzymatic digestion. The non structural carbohydrates such as starch, maltose and sucrose are hydrolyzed and absorbed as monosacharides proximal to the caecum. Glucose derived from this digestion enters the portal vein and contributes in a major way to the energy budget of horse. Non structural carbohydrate that escapes precaecal digestion and structural carbohydrate such as cellulose and hemicellulose, are subject to anaerobic microbial fermentation, largely in the caecum and colon. This fermentation produces volatile fatty acids i.e. acetic, propionic, isobutyric, butyric, isovaleric and valeric. These volatile fatty acids are absorbed and constitute important source of energy particularly for horses which are fed high forage diets.

Lipids - These are concentrated source of energy that can be readily utilized by the horse. However, in unconditioned horses, fat is not as efficiently utilized as in conditioned horses. Triglycerides of dietary origin, mobilized from the adipose tissue, are hydrolyzed to fatty acids and glycerol. Most of the fatty acids are metabolized by the liver to yield energy and ketone bodies. Alternatively, they can be re-esterified to triglycerides. The energy requirements are expressed as digestible energy (DE). If the use of total digestible nutrients (TDN) is preferred, 4.4 M Cal of DE is assumed to be equivalent to I kg of TDN. Numerous factors such as individuality, body composition of the animal, environmental temperature, humidity and weight of the horse etc influence the energy requirement of horse for maintenance. Therefore, the following energy requirements should be considered as general guidelines. The use of metabolic body weight for purpose of calculating energy requirement does not fInd any advantage over the actual weight.

Protein - Protein accounts for about 22 per cent of the fat free composition of the mature horse and it is 80 per cent of the animal's structure on a fat free, moisture free basis. Amino acids are the building blocks of protein, muscles, enzymes and many hormones. The dietary protein requirement of the horse is a function of the needs of the animal which is related with the quantity of protein available and the digestibility of that protein. Mature horses at maintenance are less sensitive to protein quality than growing horses. The digestibility of the protein is low on a low protein grass hay and high on a high protein hay - concentrate mixture. The diet formulation for horses are based on crude protein basis. Moderate excesses of protein have no detrimental effect on horses.

Minerals - Minerals are involved in a number of functions in the body including formation of structural components, enzymatic co-factors and energy transfer. Some minerals are integral parts of vitamins, hormones and amino acids. Horses obtain most of the necessary minerals from pasture roughage and grain. The mineral content of feeds and the availability of minerals vary with soil mineral concentration, plant species, stage of maturity and condition of harvesting. There are seven macro minerals (Calcium, Phosphorus, Potassium, Sodium, Chloride, Magnesium, Sulphur) and eight micro-minerals (Cobalt, Copper, Fluorine, Iodine, Iron, Manganese, Selenium, Zinc) which are essential in diet. The requirement of macro minerals has been listed in Tables 18.1 to 18.8 for various physiological functions.

Calcium - It makes up about 35 per cent of bone structure and is involved in other body functions including muscle contractions and blood clotting mechanism. Its absorption, which declines with age, is as high as 70 per cent in young horses and 50 per cent in mature horses. The Calcium absorption is also affected by dietary concentration of Calcium, Phosphorus, Oxalates and Phytate, besides vit-D levels in the body. Higher levels of these interfere with the absorption of Calcium. Similarly, lower levels of Phosphorus and vit-D also decrease the absorption of Calcium.

If the absorption efficiency of dietary Calcium is 50 per cent, a 500 kg horse would require 20 gm of dietary Calcium.

Phosphorus - Phosphorus makes up 14-17 per cent of the skeleton. It is also required for energy transfer reaction system of phospholipids, nucleic acids and phosphoproteins. In mature horses, the endogenous phosphorus loss has been estimated at 10 mg/kg of body wt/day. The true phosphorus absorption ranges from 30-35 per cent and varies with age of the animal with source and concentration of dietary phosphorus. Phosphorus in the form of phytate is purely absorbed but some phytate phosphorus may be partially available because there is some phytase in the lower gut of equines. Oxalates in higher amount too depress the phosphorus retention. With phosphorus absorption efficiency of 35 per cent, the requirement of phosphorus for maintenance of a mature 500 kg horse would be 14.3 gm/day. Inadequate dietary phosphorus will, like inadequate calcium and vitamin D, produce ricketic changes in growing horses and osteomalacic changes in mature horses. Excess phosphorus reduces the rate of calcium absorption and leads to chronic calcium deficiency and nutritional secondary hyper parathyroidism which is also known as Big Head, or Miller's disease, or Bran disease. Nutritional secondary hyper parathyroidism is characterized by a shifting lameness and in advanced cases, by enlargement of the upper and lower jaws and facial crest.

Potassium - Potassium is the major intracellular cation which is involved in maintenance of acid-base balance and osmotic pressure. Forages/grasses are rich sources of potassium. Mature horses require 0.06 gm of Potassium/kg of body wt/day or approximately 0.4 per cent of the diet. Since forages usually constitute a significant portion of the diet, the potassium requirement of the horses is easily met. Excess dietary intake of potassium is excreted readily primarily via urine, provided the water intake is adequate. The daily potassium requirement for maintenance is estimated to be 0.05 g/kg of body wt or 1.52 gm/M cal of DE/day.

Sodium - It is also one of the major extracellular cation and the major elecrolyte involved in acid-base balance and osmotic regulation of body fluids. The sodium concentration of natural feed stuffs for horses is often lower than 0.1 per cent. Sodium chloride (common salt) is often added to concentrates at rates of 0.5 to 1.0 percent or fed as free choice in the form of plain iodized or trace mineralized salt. Endogenous sodium loss in the idle adult horse has been estimated at 15 to 20 mg/kg of body wt/day. If sodium is 100 per cent absorbed, then a 500 kg horse will require 7.5 gm of sodium to meet the daily requirement. This amount would be provided by 19 to 25 gm of sodium chloride/day.

Gestation, lactation and exercise increase the requirement of sodium. Chronic sodium depletion results in decreased skin turgor, a tendency for horses to lick objects, a slowed rate of eating, decreased water intake and eventually a cessation of eating. In acute sodium deficiency, muscle contraction and chewing are uncoordinated and horses have an unsteady gait.

Chloride - It normally accompanies sodium, and is an important extracellular anion involved in acid-base balance and osmotic regulation. Chloride is an essential component of bile and is important in the formation of hydrochloric acid, which is a component of gastric secretions necessary for digestion. The chloride requirements have not been specifically established. Its deficiency results in blood alkalosis because of a compensatory increase in bicarbonate during the chloride deficit. Clinical signs may include decreased food intake, decreased milk production, dehydration, constipation and depressed appetite. Horses are considered tolerant to high levels of salts in their diets, if they have free access to fresh drinking water.

Magnesium - Magnesium constitutes approximately 0.05 per cent of body mass of which about 60 percent is associated with the skeleton. In addition, magnesium is an activator of many enzymes. The absorption of magnesium varies from 40 to 60 per cent. *Dudogeneous excretion* of magnesium by the mature horse is estimated at 6 mg/kg of body wt/day. The daily magnesium requirement is approximately 15 mg /kg of body wt or 0.46 gm/M cal of DE. Hypomagnesemia in foals results in nervousness, muscle tremors and ataxia followed by collapse, hyperpnoea, sweating, convulsive paddling and sometimes even death.

Sulphur : Sulphur, in the form of sulphur containing amino acids, biotin, heparin, thiamin, Insulin, and chondroitin sulphate makes up about 0.15 per cent of the body weight. Non ruminant animals like horse must meet their sulphur amino acid requirements from organic sulphur form such as preformed cysteine and methionine. Although some dietary inorganic sulphur is incorporated into sulphur containing microbial protein in the equine hind gut, however, amino acid absorption from this region is limited. Inorganic forms of dietary sulphur are used in the synthesis of some sulphur containing substances such as chondroitin sulphate, heparin and insulin. Adequate high quality dietary protein usually provides at least 0.15 percent organic sulphur which is adequate to meet the sulphur requirements of the horse.

Trace Minerals

Cobalt - It is an integral part of vitamin B_{12} molecule. Caecal and colonic microflora of horses use dietary cobalt in the synthesis of vitamin $B_{12.}$

Copper - Copper is essential for several copper dependent enzymes involved in the synthesis and maintenance of elastic connective tissue, the mobilization of iron stores, preservation of the integrity of mitochondria, melanin synthesis and the detoxification of superoxide. The efficiency of copper absorption is inversely related to the dietary copper concentration. Availability of 10 mg of copper / kg of diet for all ages of horses regardless of degree of work or stage of reproduction is considered sufficient. Copper interacts with many other minerals including molybdenum, sulphate, zinc, selenium, silver, cadmium, iron and lead. Horses are relatively tolerant to high dietary copper concentration but its deficiency leads to osteochondrosis and osteodysgenesis.

Fluorine - Fluorine is known to be involved in bone and teeth development, however, its dietary necessity for horses has not been established. Horses appear to be more tolerant than cattle of excess fluorine. Excess intake results in discoloured teeth (Fluorosis), bone lesions, lameness and unthriftiness. Horses can tolerate 50 mg of fluorine/kg of diet for extended periods without detrimental effects.

Iodine - Iodine is essential for the synthesis of thyroxine (T_4) and triodothyroxine (T_3) thyroid hormone that regulates basal metabolism. The dietary requirement of horses is estimated to be 0.1 to 0.6 mg/kg of diet which can be met by feeding supplemented iodized salts. Foals born out of iodine deficient dams may be stillborn and have difficulty in standing or suckling even though dams may not show sign of clinical deficiency. There is thyroid hyperplasia (simple goitre) due to iodine deficiency. Iodine deficient mares may exhibit abnormal oestrous cycle but usually do not have thyroid enlargement. The maximum tolerable dietary concentration of iodine has been estimated to be 5 mg/kg of dry matter equivalent to 50 mg of iodine/day for a horse consuming 10 kg of dry matter daily.

Iron: A 500kg horse contains approximately 33 gm of iron in its body. This is distributed in haemoglobin (60%), myoglobin (20%), storage and transport forms (20%). Forage and by-product ingredients commonly contain 100 to 250 mg of Iron/kg, whereas, grains usually contain less than 100 mg/kg. However, the dietary iron absorption in non-ruminants, fed adequate iron is likely to be one percent or less. Daily endogenous losses of iron have not been reported for horses and their dietary iron requirement have not been researched specifically. The iron requirement is estimated to be 50 mg/kg of diet for growing foals or pregnant and lactating mares and 40 mg/kg of diet for mature horses. Common feed stuffs therefore, meet the iron requirements. The primary signs of iron deficiency are microcytic and hypochronic anaemia. Although young milk fed foals are most susceptible to this anaemia, iron deficiency is not a practical problem in foals or mature horses at any performance level. This is because body efficiently salvages and retains iron derived from the catabolism of body constituents. High concentrations of supplemental dietary iron (500 and 1000 mg/kg) fed to ponies had no effect on feed intake, daily gain, red blood cell count, haemoglobin concentration, packed cell volume or serum iron, calcium, copper, manganese. The higher dietary iron level, however, depresses both serum and liver zinc.

Manganese - It is essential for carbohydrate and lipid metabolism and for synthesis of the chondroitin sulphate. It is necessary for cartilage formation. The manganese requirement of horses has not yet been studied but based on the data of other species, 40 mg/kg of manganese in diet, is considered adequate. Roughages contain 40 to 140 mg of manganese per kg and concentrates except corn contain 15-45 mg/kg. Abnormal cartilage development is the main symptom of manganese deficiency. This is mainly due to failure of chondroitin sulphate synthesis which results in bone malformation.

Selenium - It is an essential component of selenium dependent glutathione peroxidase which aids in detoxification of lipo and hydrogen peroxides that are toxic to cell membranes. Selenium is absorbed quite efficiently (77%) in non-ruminants. It is about 29 per cent for ruminants. The selenium requirement of the horse is estimated at 0.1 mg/kg of diet. The clinical and morphological manifestations of selenium deficiency are affected by the concomitant vit. E status. Nutritional myopathy (White Muscle disease), involves skeletal and cardiac muscles. The myopathy results in weakness, impaired locomotion, difficulty in suckling and swallowing, respiratory distress and impaired cardiac function. The maximum tolerable level of selenium in horses is estimated at 2 mg/kg of diet and the LD50 for orally administered selenium is considered to be approximately 3.3 mg of selenium/kg of body weight. Acute selenium toxicity (Blind Staggers) is characterized by apparent blindness, head pressing, perspiration, abdominal pain, colic, diarrhoea, increased respiration and heart rate. Chronic selenium toxicity (Alkali Disease) is characterized by alopecia, especially about mane and tail as well as cracking of the hooves around the coronary band.

Zinc - It is present in the body as a compound of many metalloenzymes such as carbonic anhydrase, alkaline phosphatase and carboxy peptidase. The biochemical role of zinc is related largely to the functions of these enzymes. The highest concentration of zinc occurs in the choroid and iris of the eye and in the prostrate gland. Intermediate concentrations are present in the skin, liver, bone and muscles, whereas less concentrations are found in blood, milk, lungs and brain. Zinc absorption is regulated by the zinc status of the animals and may be in 5-10 per cent range. Common equine feed stuffs contain 15-40 mg/kg of zinc. Mare's milk contains 1.8 to 3.2 mg of zinc/kg of fluid milk and it is assumed to be highly available. Its deficiency in foals is accompanied by inappetence, reduced growth rate, parakeratoid alopecia and tissue zinc concentrations. Horses appear quite tolerant to excess dietary zinc. It also helps in proper functioning of taste and smell receptors.

Vitamins - Vitamin requirement like those of other nutrients are affected by age, stage of production and a variety of stresses such as gastrointestinal infections and intense muscular exercise. The need for supplemental vitamins depends on the type and the quality of the diet, the amount of microbial vitamin synthesis in the digestive tract and the extent of vitamin absorption from the site of synthesis. Horses grazing on high quality pastures are likely to need only little or no vitamin supplementation because forages are rich sources of most fat and water soluble vitamins.

Classification - The vitamins are classified as fat soluble or water soluble depending upon their solubility in fat or water respectively (Table 18.9). Fat soluble vitamins include vitamins A,D,E and K, whereas water soluble group of vitamins is composed of vitamin B complex and vitamin C and some other metabolic substances which are like vitamins eg., Inositol. Fat soluble vitamins are absorbed alongwith dietary fats via mechanisms similar to fat absorption, and their absorption is favoured by factors which favour the absorption of fats. Any metabolic abnormality or disease which interferes with fat absorption also adversely affects absorption of these vitamins. Fat soluble vitamins are excreted out through faeces. Water soluble vitamins are excreted primarily through urine. These are non-toxic when used at reasonable levels: However, vitamins A and D can be harmful if used in excess.

Table 18.9: Classification of Vitamins

Fat Soluble Vitamins		*Water soluble Vitamins*
Vit A -	A_1 – Retinol	*- Vit B Complex*
	A_2 - Dehydroratinol	B_1 - Thiamine
		B_2 - Riboflavin
		B_3 - Niacin
Vit D -	D_2 – Ergocalciferol	Pantothenic acid
	D_3 – Cholecalciferol	B_6 - Pyridoxine
Vit E	- Tocopherol	Biotin
		Folacin
Vit K -	K_1 – Phylloquinone	B_{12} - Cyanocobalamine
	K_2 - Menaquinone	Choline
	K_3 - Menadione	- Vit C - Ascorbic acid

Fat Soluable Vitamins

Vitamin - A: Vit-A is important for vision and specific photoreactive metabolites are found in visual pigments within the retina. This vitamin also plays a basic role in cell differentiation. In vit A deficiency, epimedial cells that would normally be of a transitional, cuboidal or columnar type, may develop as keratinized squamous cells. Bone remodelling in the growing animal is also modulated by vit-A.

Carotene is found in highest concentration in green forage but is also present in yellow corn. Carotenes are destroyed gradually by light and heat therefore, carotene concentration in sun cured hay is lower than in fresh forage from which the hay was made. If the hay is stored, the carotene concentration declines gradually and after 2 years, less than 10 per cent of the original carotene level may remain. Field curing also decreases the carotene content of the forages.

Much of the conversion of dietary carotene to vit A occurs in the wall of small intestine. This conversion, however, is not very efficient in horses. Carotene in alfalfa hay appears to be more available as a source of provitamin A activity than carotene in grass hays. Carotene intake from alfalfa hay is approximately 24.5 mg/kg of dietary dry matter or 400 to 500 μg/kg of body weight.

Supplementation of carotene in the diet has been seen to increase semen production and libido in stallions and tends to improve ovarian activity, stronger heats and improved conception and tendency to reduce embryonic mortality in pony mares.

Deficiency of vit. A is characterized by night blindness, excessive lacrimation, hyperkeratinization of the cornea and skin, anorexia, poor growth, respiratory infections, sublingual salivary gland abcesses, impaired conception, elevated cerebrospinal fluid pressure, progressive weakness and decline in plasma, liver and kidney vit-A concentration. Prolonged vit-A feeding in excess quantity may cause bone fragility, hyperostosis, exfoliated epithelium and teratogenesis. NRC has recommended an upper safe level of 16000 IU of vit-A/kg of dry feed for prolonged administration.

Vitamin - D: Two primary vit D active compounds are found in nature. Vit D_2 (Ergocalciferol) results from ultraviolet irradiation of ergosterol which is synthesized from plants, but only after they have been cut and exposed to sunlight. The chlorophyll screens out the necessary wave length of the ultraviolet light of sun required for the irradiation and synthesis of vitamin D_2 and D_3. It is primarily from ultraviolet irradiation of 7-dehydrocholesterol synthesized by the tissues of the horse and is present in the skin. Dietary vit-D requirements for the horse have not been established and deficiency on a practical diet are not likely. Although limited experimental data suggests that for early growth, ponies deprived of sunlight may require 800-1000 IU of vit-D/kg of dry diet.

Deficiency of vit-D causes rickets but such symptoms have not been noticed in horses. However, it has been found that there is loss of appetite and slower growth as well as decreased ash. Excessive intake of vit-D is characterized by calcification of blood vessels, heart and other soft tissues and by bone abnormalities.

Vitamin-E: Vit-E is a generic description for the natural or synthetic compounds that are qualitatively equivalent in biological activity of alfatocopherol.

Vit-E activity of feeds and feed stuffs depends on the chemical forms and the condition of storage. Moisture in feeds sufficient to permit fermentation and mould growth results in rapid decline of the activity of natural vit-E compounds. The studies on vit-E requirement have revealed that vit-E supplements should be provided daily rather than at less frequent intervals. To ensure nutritional adequacy, adult horses should receive an oral supplementation of 600 to 1800 mg of d, 1 - á-tocopheryl acetate. This would be equal to 1.5 to 4.4 mg/kg of body weight. Exercise tends to increase the Vit-E requirements. Vit-E and selenium supplementation are also required for optimum immune function.

Myodegeneration is the common deficiency symptom with pale, diffuse or linear areas in skeletal and cardiac muscles. Signs of vit-E toxicity in horse have not yet been produced. The NRC has proposed a safe upper level of 75 IU/kg of body wt/day.

Vitamin K : The function of this vitamin is expressed through the activity of a vit-K dependent carboxylase found in the microsomal fraction of horse liver, spleen, kidney which promotes the post translational conversion of specific glutamyl residues in vitamin K dependent plasma protein to ã-Carboxyglutamyl residues. These residues are essential for the ca^{++} dependent interaction of vit-K dependent clotting factors with phospholipid surface. Dietary vit-K requirements have not been determined but good quality hay/pasture feeding and menaquinones synthesised by intestinal bacteria presumably meet the requirements.

The deficiency of vit-K produces decreased thrombin production which in turn results in fibrin clot formation and increased susceptibility to haemorrhage. Presence of mycotoxins, dicoumarol and confinement feeding have caused increased vit K requirement.

Water Soluble Vitamins

Good quality forages supply the adequate amount of vit B complex with the exception of vit B_{12} as it is synthesized only by anaerobic bacteria, provided sufficient cobalt is present. Abundant synthesis of other B complex vitamins also occurs by intestinal microflora, thus the food supply will meet the vit B requirements of most adult horses. Mare's milk generally meets the needs of the nursing foal, till it starts consuming forage and feeds.

Thiamine: Thiamine synthesized in the intestinal tract of horses may not meet all the requirements of the horse therefore its dietary supply is essential. 2.75 mg/kg of dietary dry matter is sufficient to meet the requirement of the horses. Exercise increases the thiamine requirement of the horses. Presence of antithiamine compounds and thiaminase in dietary plants such as bracken fern may increase the thiamine needs.

Its deficiency causes anorexia, loss of weight, ataxia,

bradycardia, missing heart beats, and periodic hypothermia of hooves, ears and muzzle.

Riboflavin: It is synthesized in the intestine of adult horse by microflora. Although, riboflavin deficiency has not been demonstrated in horses, but since it is involved in as an essential constituent of enzyme system needed for the utilization of fats, carbohydrates and proteins, its deficiency causes a decreased growth rate and lowered feed utilization. There is atrophy of epidermis, hair follicles and sebaceous glands, dermatitis, vascularization of the cornea, photophobia and excess lacrimation. Earlier, it was considered that periodic opthalmia (Recurrent Uveitis or Moon Blindness) is a consequence of riboflavin deficiency. Invasion of the cornea by leptospira or microfilaria have also been implicated in periodic ophthalmia.

Niacin: It is synthesized by the microbial flora in the caecum and colon of the horses and forms the amino acid tryptophan in the horses' tissues. No dietary niacin requirement nor its deficiency has been described in horses. In other species, inflammation of lingual and buccal surfaces is common followed by necrosis, ulceration and foul breath odour. Dematitis . and haemorrhagic enteritis may also be seen.

Effects of niacin excess have also not been described in horses and very little niacin storage occurs in the body.

Pantothenic Acid : It appears to be synthesized in the intestinal tract of adult horses. Its dietary requirements have not been established. Similarly, its deficiency has not been described in the horses. In other species, dermatitis, achromotrichia, enteritis, neuritis, degenerative changes in the peripheral motor nerves leading to impaired adductor muscle function have been noted due to its deficiency.

Vitamin B_6: It is a generic name for three metabolically interconvertible compounds pyridoxine, pyridoxal and pyridoxamine. It appears to be synthesized by microorganisms in the intestinal tract of horses. Neither dietary vitamin B_6 requirements have been established, nor vit-B_6 deficiency has been described in the horses. In other species, deficiency signs include scaly dermatitis, alopecia, microcytic hypochromic anaemia, impaired immune function and neurological abnormalities resembling epilepsy.

Biotin: It appears to be synthesized by micro-organisms in the intestinal tract of the adult horse. No control studies have been reported regarding requirement. However, clinical reports claim an improvement in hoof quality in adult horses when 10 to 30 mg of biotin/day is fed for atleast 6 to 9 months. No evidence of biotin deficiency in the horse has been reported. Signs in other species include, inflammation and cracks on the plantar surface of the feet.

Folacin : It is a generic name for folic acid and related compounds with similar biological activity. It is synthesized by micro-organisms in the intestine of the adult horse. There is no experimental information on the folacin requirement of the horse. Folacin functions as a coenzyme for several enzymes involved in body metabolism.

Vitamin B_{12} : It is generic term for compounds that exhibit qualitatively the biological activity of cyanocobalamin. It is synthesized by anaerobic micro-organisms in caecum and colon for which adequate supply of cobalt is required. Vit-B_{12} contains about 4 per cent cobalt and it is absorbed from the lower digestive tract of the horses. No studies have revealed requirement for additional dietary supply of vit-B_{12}. Similarly, its deficiency or toxicity has also not been reported in horses. This vitamin is unique being synthesized only by micro-organisms in nature However, animal product feeds are good source of this vitamin. It is required for propionic acid utilization, therefore a diet involving increased volatile fatty acid production would require vitamin B_{12} adequacy. It is stored principally in the liver and is metabolically related to other nutrients such as methionine, choline and folacin. Its absorption in the ileum is facilitated by intrinsic factor which is released in gastric juice.

Choline: Choline was previously known as Bilineurine or lipotropic factor. It is involved in transportation of excess fat from the liver. Its deficiency causes fat to accumulate in the liver which results in fatty liver. Choline requirement of horse has not been studied. However, it serves as a source of labile methyl group, and can be completely replaced by methionine for this function. Accordingly, it is not treated as vitamin in the strict sense of the word.

Vitamin C (Ascorbic Acid) : Tissues of horses can synthesize ascorbic acid. A deficiency of vit C results in symptoms of Scurvy characterized by bleeding, swollen and ulcerated gums, weak bones, loosening of teeth and fragility of the capillaries that result in haemorrhages throughout the body. Ascorbic acid is stored to a limited extent in the body thus needs to be supplied regularly.

Ascorbic acid tends to get destroyed in feed with pelleting and the stress of heat and moisture.

Vit-C is also required for hydroxylation of lysine and proline which are required for collagen synthesis which is subsequently required for cartilage and bone growth. Vit-C is related with Riboflavin, Folacin, Vit-B_{12} and its deficiency may affect utilization of other B complex vitamins.

Chapter 20

Practical Feeding of Various Classes

Brood Mares

Optimum feeding of brood mare is one of the most important aspect of management of any breeding stud, to achieve higher conception rate, growth of foetus through in utero *nutrient,* birth weight of foal and its further development of bones, body growth and protection through passive immunity gained through colostrum. The level of feeding can be gauged from the condition of horse and its response to it. It is advisable to avoid any extreme condition of fatness or thinness. The suggested nutrient concentrations in total diets of horses and ponies has been included Tables 18.1 to 18.7.

Breeding Season

Maximum breeding activity in both mare and stallion takes place from April to November, which can, however, be artificially changed by manipulating daylight length and diet. The oestrous cycle of mares is of 22 days long during which the oestrus lasts for 6 days. The fertility is low initially in the season but as day length increases and greener pastures are available, the fertility rate is improved. Infoal mares should be kept fit to minimize difficulties during foaling and to provide greater freedom for controlling milk secretion by feeding during lactation. Conception rate, of mares who are in good condition at foaling but lost weight during lactation, are as good as those mares who are in good or thin condition at foaling that maintained or gained weight in lactation. However, there are reports of reduced conception rate, longer post partum intervals and more cycles per conception in thin mares. The foal heat occurs within 9 to 14 days of foaling and subsequently heats occur at 22 days interval in unbred mares. The gestation period of mare lasts for 335 to 345 days which depends upon season of breeding, day length, sun rays, humidity and temperature during last three months of pregnancy. Conception is maximum during April to June and least during January and February.

A mare is capable of considerable adjustments but in the extremes, excesses or deficiencies of energy will reduce her reproductive efficiency. There will be poor expression of oestrus and ovulation and even death of embryo in energy deficient mares. On an average, there are 1. 71 oestrus periods per mare per year and 2.75 services per mare yearly. The maximum conception has been recorded in mares from 9 to 15 years of age which slowly declines with age. Twinning is rare in mares.The average foal crop range between 50 to 65 per cent. Some mares may breed one year and skip next year. Abortion during early 90 days of gestation is more in energy deficient mares. Conception rate is low at foal heat and pregnancy losses which occur between fertilization and 150 days post ovulation, are reported to be between 11 to 13 per cent.

Feeding

The most important period of feeding of a pregnant mare is the last 90 days of gestation. 60-65 percent of weight of foetus gets deposited during these last 90 days as growth rate of embryo is the greatest during this period. The products of conception i.e., foal, fluid and placenta etc are about 12 per cent of the body weight of mare weighing 450 kg or less, whereas they are 10 per cent or more in mares weighing more than 450 kg.

Lactating mares are estimated to produce milk equivalent to 3 percent of body weight daily during early lactation (1-12 weeks) and 2 per cent of body weight during late lactation (13-24 weeks). Therefore, a lot of body energy of mare is utilized for synthesis of milk energy and this process of conversion of digestible energy of feed into milk energy is about 60 per cent efficient.

The dietary requirements of the breeding mare can be arbitrarily divided into three stages:

(a) Requirement upto 8 months of gestation,

(b) Requirement during last 3 months of gestation,

(c) Lactation and 0-4 months post-parturition.

The first 8 months of gestation have no practical impact on the nutrient needs of the mares. It neither necessitate increase in the maintenance levels nor enhances the already high nutrient requirement of lactating mares.

During the ninth, tenth and eleventh months of gestation, the digestible energy(DE) requirment is formulated by multiplying the maintenance requirements by 1.11, 1.13 and 1.20 respectively. The protein requirements also increase during this period and with a protein utilization efficiency of 60 per cent, a 500 kg gestating mare requires 127, 130, 178 gm of digestible protein (DP) per day for foetal deposition above maintenance levels, thereby increasing the total DP requirement to 427, 430 and 478 gm daily. Further, presuming the digestibility of protein to be 55 per cent, a 500 kg mare would need 776 gm in 9th month, 782 gm in 10th month and 869 gm of crude protein (CP) daily in 11th month. Similarly, assuming the efficiency of calcium absorption to be 50 percent, the requirement of calcium would be 11, 25 and 11 gm/day for ninth, tenth and eleventh month of gestation. During the same period,the phosphorus requirement has been estimated to be 7, 12 and 6.7 mg/kg of body wt/day. In addition, the requirement of other macro and micro minerals and fat soluble as well as water soluble vitamins too increases considerably.

The requirements of energy, protein, minerals and vitamins are the maximum for a mare during the first phase of lactation i.e. from 1 to 12 weeks post-parturition. The energy requirement of lactating mares depends upon the composition and amount of milk produced. The requirement of energy is 792 K Cal of

DE/kg of milk produced above the maintenance level. The protein content of milk is highest immediately after parturition and it decreases gradually as lactation progresses. Crude protein requirements are calculated presuming that mare's milk contains 2.1 and 1.8 per cent protein in early and late lactation respectively. Utilisation of digestible protein for milk protein formation is 65 per cent and digestibility of protein in the digestive system is 55 per cent. The requirement of calcium for lactation, ranges from 1.2 gm/kg of milk during the first post partum week to 0.8 gm/kg of milk during 15 to 17 week post partum, above maintenance requirement, whereas requirement of phosphorus ranges from 0.75 gm/kg of milk in early lactation to 0.50 gm/kg of milk in late lactation.

The detailed requirement of all nutrients for various classes of animals has been given in Tables 18.1 to 18.8.

In the last quarter of pregnancy, foetus occupies an increasing proportion of mare's abdominal cavity. Accordingly, her capacity for bulky feeds declines during the period in which nutrient requirement increases. The quality of hay and concentrate should improve during the last 3 months of gestation. The diet in this period should contain concentrate mixture with 16 per cent protein upto 25 to 35 per cent of the diet which can increase or decrease depending upon the condition of the mare, its response to feed and quality of the hay and pasture used. The suggested concentrate is given as Table 19.1 for gestation. It is recommended that the total diet fed during gestation contains at least 12 per cent protein which means that hay or pasture should contain atleast 10 and preferably, 11 to 12 per cent protein. The higher level of protein should provide a safety factor for hay and pasture which may have protein of low digestibility depending upon kind of pasture used and its stage of maturity when consumed or harvested.

Table 19.1 : Suggested Concentrate Diet for Gestation Period of Mare

*Feed***	*Percentage in Diet*
Oats	30
Corn	10
Barley	13
Wheat Bran	10
Soyabean Meal	11.5
Linseed Meal	04
Alfalfa Meal	10
Black Strap Molasses	07
Dicalcium Phosphate	02
Limestone	00.5
Salt trace Mineralised	01.0
Vitamin Supplement	01.0

** The concentrate diet should contain 16 per cent protein, 1 per cent calcium and 0.9 per cent phosphorus.

A study on pony mares has revealed that protein percentage in diet does not affect general reproduction parameters such as oestrus or ovulation but it affect progesterone concentration which in turn may be responsible for the differences in conception rate which is low with low level of protein and high with optimum protein levels. The pregnant and lactating mares also require high quality of protein for proper foetal development and milk production.

Feeding of Mare During Lactation

The mare suffers maximum stress owing to parturition followed by lactation and rebreeding. Therefore, Inadequacy in energy, protein, vitamin and mineral contents of feed will lead to decreased milk production, poor rebreeding performance, delayed post-partum intervals, low conception rates and increased embryo mortality.

During first 3 months of lactation, feed intake increases by 37 percent over feed intake during the last quarter of the pregnancy which is approximately 1.5 to 2.0 percent of body weight. In this phase, concentrate diet should form 45 to 55 per cent of total feed intake of the mare. However, the amount of concentrate intake can vary depending upon the quality of hay and pasture, milk production, general condition and other such factors. The total diet of mare should contain at least 12.5 to 14 per cent protein including good quality hay/pasture which should contain at least 10 per cent protein. Minerals should be self fed to mares especially if they need more than that is supplied in the concentrate mixture and when the milk production is high. Inclusion of soyabean meal has been shown to improve the protein content of early lactation mare's milk and it is considered to be accompanied by faster growth of the foal. The suggested concentrate mixture for first phase of lactation is given in Table 19.2.

Table 19.2 : Suggested Concentrate Diet for Lactation

*Feed***	*Percentage in Diet*
Oats	15
Corn	30
Barley	10
Wheat Bran	07
Soyabean Meal	15
Linseed Meal	05
Alfalfa Meal	07
Black Strap Molasses	07.0
Dicalcium Phosphate	01.25
Limestone	00.75
Salt	01.00
Vitamin Supplement	01.00

**The nutrient level in the concentrate diet should be adjusted to 16 per cent protein, 0.8 per cent calcium and 0.7 per cent phosphorus.

In the second phase of lactation that is from 13 weeks to 24 weeks, the milk production decreases to about two third. Accordingly, there is 30 to 40 per cent decrease in quantity of concerates and total feed intake.The foal also starts supplementing its nutrient requirement from creep feed and hay/pasture feeding. The average protein requirement during this stage should be 11 to 12.5 per cent and the concentrate level should be about one third of the total diet.

Table 19.3 Nutrient Concentrations in Total Diets for Horses and Ponies (dry matter basis)

	Digestable (Mcal/kg)	Energy[a] (Mca/lb)	Diet Proportions Conc. (%)	Hay (%)	Crude Protein (%)	Calcium Lysine (%)	Phosphorus Lysine (%)	Magnesium (%)	Potasium (%)	Vitamin A (IU/kg)	(IU/lb)	
	1	2	3	4		5	6	7	8	9	10	11
Mature Horses												
Maintenance	2.00	0.90	0	100	8.0	0.28	0.24	0.17	0.09	0.30	1830	830
Stallions	2.40	1.10	30	70	9.6	0.34	0.29	0.21	0.11	0.36	2640	1200
Pregnant mares												
9 months	2.25	1.00	20	80	10.0	0.35	0.43	0.32	0.10	0.35	3710	1680
10 months	2.25	1.00	20	80	10.0	0.35	0.43	0.32	0.10	0.36	3650	1660
11 months	2.40	1.10	30	70	10.6	0.37	0.45	0.34	0.11	0.38	3650	1660
Lactating mares												
Foaling to 3 months 2.60	1.20	50	50	13.2	0.46	0.52	0.34	0.10	0.42	2750	1250	
3 months to weaning2.45	1.15	35	65	11.0	0.37	0.36	0.22	0.09	0.33	3020	1370	
Working Horses												
Light work	2.45	1.15	35	65	9.8	0.35	0.30	0.22	0.11	0.37	2690	1220
Moderate work	2.65	1.20	50	50	10.4	0.37	0.31	0.23	0.12	0.39	2420	1100
Intense work	2.85	1.30	65	35	11.4	0.40	0.35	0.25	0.13	0.43	1950	890
Growing Horses												
Weanling, 4 months2.90	1.40	70	30	14.5	0.60	0.68	0.38	0.08	0.30	1580	720	
Weanling, 6 months												
Moderate growth 2.90	1.40	70	30	14.5	0.61	0.56	0.31	0.08	0.30	1870	850	
Rapid growth	2.90	1.40	70	30	14.5	0.61	0.61	0.34	0.08	0.30	1630	740
Yearling, 12 months												
Moderate growth	2.80	1.30	60	40	12.6	0.53	0.43	0.24	0.08	0.30	2160	980
Rapid growth	2.80	1.30	60	40	12.6	0.53	0.45	0.25	0.08	0.30	1920	870
Long yearling, 18 months												
Not in training	2.50	1.15	45	55	11.3	0.48	0.34	0.19	0.08	0.30	2270	1030
In training	2.65	1.20	50	50	12.0	0.50	0.36	0.20	0.09	0.30	1800	820
Two year old, 24 months												
Not in training	2.45	1.15	35	65	10.4	0.42	0.31	0.17	0.09	0.30	2640	1200
In training	2.65	1.20	50	50	11.3	0.45	0.34	0.20	0.10	0.32	2040	930

[a]Values:- Assume a concentrate feed containing 3.3 Mcal/kg and hay containing 2.00 Mcal/kg of dry matter

Feeding the Foal

Neo-natal feeding of the foal depends upon how well the mare has been fed during the gestation. A well balanced diet supplies all nutrients needed for development of foal and also enables the mare to produce optimum milk after foaling. The foal should receive adequate nutrients post-natal, and pre-weaning, to have a good bone development and optimal growth.

Colostrum Feeding

The mare has to pass adequate passive protection to foal which is provided through colostrums. Besides, colostrum has laxative substance that promotes bowel movement and elimination. Mare has to, therefore, be in foaling area preferably a month before foaling so that she confers immunity to microbial strains peculiar to her environment, especially those causing scours, joint ill and septicemia etc. Immunoglobulins do not pass through dam's placenta and are absorbed only through first part of intestine during first few hours of life. The immunoglobulins get concentrated in the udder of mare during last two weeks of gestation. The mare's colostrum contains protein upto 19 per cent immediately after parturition which falls to 3.8 per cent after 12 hours and to a fairly constant level of 2.2 per cent, after 8 days.

The foal absorbs gamaglobulin as intact undergraded molecules throughout first 12 hours of life which gets reduced to a great extent in next 24 hours. Amounts of these specific antibodies so acquired by foal, start to decline from 24 hours of age. With in 3 weeks, the values are halved and by 4 months, the titre of specific immunity provided by the mother is barely detectable. The foal's own system of building active immunity in the form of autogenous gamaglobulins first provides detectable products at 2 weeks of age in the blood of colostrum deprived foals and at 4 weeks in colostrums fed foals. By 3-4 months of age, the gamaglobulins attain adult plasma concentration. Thus, the foal is more susceptible to infection than an adult in the same environment, particularly when it has received inadequate quantity of colostrum.

The foal may at times be deprived of colostrum because of premature birth of foal, small intestine malabsorption, delayed suckling, premature leakage of milk through teats or death of the mare. In case of colostrum deprivation, it is necessary to give colostrum from another mare preferably one accustomed to the same environment or failing this, cow's colostrum can be given. The foal should receive about 500 ml of colostrum by nipple or stomach tube every hour for three or four feeds before 12 hours of age. After 18 hours, the colostrum has little systemic immune value, however, it does have some beneficial local effects within the intestinal tract. If the plasma concentration of immunoglobulins falls below 400 mg per 100 ml blood then foal may be given blood plasma from another horse at the rate of 22 ml/kg body weight over a period of 1-2 hours which is approximately I litre per foal.

Feeding of Mare's Milk

A healthy foal nurse with in 30 to 45 minutes and adiquate quantity of mare's milk which contain 2.1 MJ of groos energy per kg, meets the nutrients needs of the foal during first 2 to 3 weeks of life. However, supplementation of other feeds is essential after 2-3 weeks to meet the increasing energy needs of the foal.

Moreso, mare's milk is deficient in energy, protein, vitamins and minerals and it alone is insufficient for foal to sustain at this age. On an average mare's milk production is 3.1 percent of her body weight at 11 days post-partum, 2.9 per cent at 25 days and 3.4 percent at 39 days which meets the requirement of dry matter (DM) to the exent of 3.1, 2.1 and 2 per cent of the foal's body weight. Mare's milk contain 2.1 MJ of groos energy per kg. The nutrients in mare's milk and requirement of the foal are given below :-

Table : 19.4. Milk and Nutrient Production by Brood Mare

Month of Lactation	*Milk Production (lt/day)*	*Digestible energy (Kcal/day)*	*Digestible Protein (gm/day)*	*Calcium (gm/day)*	*Phosphorus (gm/day)*
0-1	30.6	7256 (8153)	375 (450)	17.4 (18)	5.9 (14)
1-2	32.3	7276 (10411)	330 (500)	14.7 (18)	4.4 (15)
2-3	37.2	7909 (12747)	319 (546)	13.5 (17)	4.5 (15)
3-4	33.2	6795 (14161)	292 (535)	10.0 (17)	3.5 (15)
4-5	24.0	4905 (15372)	196 (522)	6.5 (16)	2.2 (15)
5-6	16.5	3375 (16351)	135 (510)	4.5 (16)	1.5 (15)

However, the milk yield is markedly influenced by the mare's innate ability, by feed consumption during the later stages of pregnancy and more importantly, by water availability and intake of energy and nutrients during lactation:

Creep Feed

At about 7-15 days of age, the foal starts to nibble on the feed given to the mother. To meet the inadequacy of nutrients in mare's milk and avoidance of imbalance diet to the foal, horse owners prefer to feed well balanced creep feed to the foals. It is usually recommended that creep feeding be started after 1-2 weeks of foaling. The creep should be located where the mare goes periodically during the day for water or shade. The use of creep feed helps to ensure that inherited potential of growth and development is realized and it is one of the important factor in avoiding set backs when the foal is weaned from its mother. Creep feeding also accelerates anatomical and physiological maturation of the gastro-intestinal tract.

At 5-6 weeks of age, a foal should be given 0-1 kg of creep feed per 50 kg of body weight daily. By weaning time, the foal should be consuming at least 2-3 kg of creep feed per day. Creep feed also help in conditioning of the foal to the change over from mother's milk to a man made diet. However, If the mare and foal are doing well during the first 6-12 weeks of age, creep feeding may be deferred until the mare's milk production starts decreasing and unable to meet foal's requirements.

Table 19.5 : Suggested Creep Feed for Nursing Foals

Feed	*Percent in Diet*
Oats	35
Corn/Barley or combination	35.4
Soyabean Meal	15
Dried Skim Milk	5
Black Strap Molasses	5
Dicalcium Phosphate	2
Limestone	0.8
Salt trace mineralized	1
Vitamin Supplement	0.8

Growth Rate of Foals

Foals weigh about 8-10 per cent of the mare's weight. The size and weight of foal at birth are influenced by the nutrition of the mare and heredity. Usually, the colt is heavier than filly. The new born foal will have a wither height of about 60 per cent of its mature height. Foals double their weight in first month of life which is again doubled after 3-5 months of age. However, rate of growth starts to decrease after that.

The wither height reaches about 80 per cent of expected mature height in 3-5 months and indicates high rate of bone growth and development necessitating proper nutrition including vitamins and minerals.

The following table shows the pattern of expected growth rate in horses in terms of weight gain and mature height.

Table 19.6 :- Growth Rate in Equines:-

	% of mature weight	*% gain* in *weight*	*% of mature height*	*% gain in height*
At birth	9		60	
At 3 months	30	37	77.6	24
At 6 months	46		84	
At 12 months	65	19	92	8
At 18 months	80	15	95	3
At 24 months	90	10	97	2
At 30 months	95	5	98	1
At 36 months	98	3	99	1
At 42 months	99	1	100	1
At 48 months	100	1	-	-

Nutrient Requirements for Growth

The digestible energy requirement increases with age of the foal. However, very high energy intake is associated with developmental orthopaedic disease. Starch feeding causes significant changes in serum insulin, thyroxine and triidothyronine which retards cartilage maturation. The protein requirement for growth have been found to be 50 and 45 gm/MCal of DE/day for weanling and yearling respectively. Lysine is the first limiting amino acid in the diet of growing foals which is 2.1 and 1.9 gm/MCal DE per day for weanling and yearling respectively. The growing foals deposit approximately 16 gm calcium per kg of gain whereas phosphorus requirement is 8 gm/kg of gain. The requirement of vit A to support normal growth has been estimated to be 20 IU/kg of body weight or 1760 IU/kg of feed, whereas requirement of vit-D has been calculated to be 275 IU/kg of feed. Alternatively, 6.6 IU of vit-D per kg body weight is sufficient in most circumstances.

Feeding Growing Horse / Young Stock

Foals are normally weaned at 6 months, however, it may be at times early in special circumstances. During this period the growing horse achieve 65 per cent of mature body weight and 92 per cent of mature height Therefore, the most critical time in the life of a growing horse is between weaning and up to 1 year of age. Second and third year are, however, important for achieving full growth, maturation of bone, muscles and other parts of body.

Feeding of the Weanling

Weaning of foals is preferably at the age of six months. Weaning before six months is practised where the owner can supplement the feed of the foal with creep feed, starter diets which are excellent substitutes to supplement mare's milk. Delayed weaning is preferred by some in order to take advantage of the nutritional value of the mare's milk especially when availability of good quality feed for the weaned foal is limited. Early weaning, however, requires excellent diet fortified with minerals, vitamins, amino acids, protein besides superior managerial ability.

Weanlings grow rapidly and develop bones and muscles considerably, therefore, diet has to be well balanced in terms of energy, protein, minerals and vitamins. It is important to note that fastest gains are made during the first year and horses with heavier mature weights, gain faster than horses of lighter mature weight. Thoroughbred foals have been seen to attain 46, 67 and 90 per cent of their mature weight at 6, 12 and 18 months of age respectively. However, ponies attain 55, 75 and 84 percent of their mature weight at 6, 12 and 18 months of age which indicates that lighter breeds attain mature weight at an early age. Thoroughbred foals attain 83, 90 and 95 percent of their expected mature height at 6, 12 and 18 months of age which indicates that during the first few months after birth, the fastest growth and elongation of most of the bones occurs. It, therefore, warrants a balanced feeding for mare to produce plenty of milk for the foal and a well balanced creep feed to supplement the mare's milk for high level performance.

The creep feeding to foal before weaning is given at an approximate rate of 0.5 to 0.75 per cent of the body weight which after weaning should be increased to 1 to 1.5 per cent of body weight. In addition, the foal should be given forage at least at the rate of 1 kg per 100 kg body weight. The individuality of horse, its likes and dislikes, eating habits, quality of concentrate feed, quality of hay/pasture are some of the factors which determine the roughage to concentrate ratio of the weanling's feed.

Table 19.7 : Suggested Concentrate Mixture for Weanlings

Feed	*Percentage in Diet*
Oats	25
Corn	31
Milo	7
Soyabean meal	2.3
Dehydrated alfalfa meal	5
Black Strap Molasses	5
Vitamin Supplement	0.75
Dicalcium Phosphate	2
Limestone	0.25
Salt trace mineralized	1.00

Above table gives the suggested concentrate mixture which can be fed to weanling foals being developed for high level performance. Oats and corn are the energy sources whereas soyabean meal is plant protein source which is rich in lysine, the indispensable amino acid, required for growth. The molasses is added for palatability and to help control dust. The vitamin supplement is used to reinforce the diet and make sure it is adequate in all the vitamins needed whereas salt trace mineralised ensures essential mineral elements required by the horse. The concentrate diet should be about 70 per cent of total dry matter intake and should have 18 per cent protein whereas remainder should be high quality hay or pasture which should contain at least 12 per cent crude protein. The total diet should have 16 per cent crude protein. The feeding of weanling should be individually carried out so that aggressive ones do not dominate the timid weanlings. The concentrates should be fed at least twice daily whereas pasture or good quality hay should be provided on a free choice basis. Regulated exercise is a must for weanling to help develop sound bone and fitness. However, forced and excessive exercise may lead to development of joint inflammation, soreness, lameness, pulling up on their pasterns, bending over on the knees etc. These external disorders represent a variety of internal skeletal problems and are inaccurately put together under epiphisitis. There are three factors which are known to cause skeletal disorders in horses:

(a) Genetic predisposition associated with large size at maturity,

(b) Nutrient imbalance or deficiencies in the total diet,

(c) Confinement coupled with forced exercise.

Feeding Yearling and Long Yearling

Weight gains and development of long bones decrease during the second year of foal's life but since it is still growing, it should, therefore, continue to be fed on a high quality diet. During this stage, the roughage to concentrate ratio should be 50 per cent each with total DM intake ranging from 2-3 per cent of body weight. If the yearling is being developed for the racing or performance then higher level of concentrate i.e. 75 per cent or more, should form part of their diet.

The total diet of yearling should provide about 13-14 per cent protein. The concentrate portion should contain 16 per cent protein whereas forages should have at least 10 per cent. The long yearlings require a little less of protein, calcium and phosphorus than the yearling and the forage portion of the diet also increases to 60 per cent or more depending upon whether the long yearling is developed for performance or pleasure riding. The long yearling being developed for pleasure riding can be fed exclusively on good quality pasture but should be shelf fed a mineral supplement, adequate in all essential minerals.

Feeding of Performance Horses

Very little research information is available to guide the feeding schedule of horses for high level of performance. Both overfeeding and underfeeding can lead to dietary imbalances and therefore, can seriously hamper the performance of the horses. Most of the studies on the nutritional requirement have been conducted in stalls or under experimental conditions but the stress of heavy exercise and the weight of the rider on the horse undoubtedly increases the need for certain nutrients over that of a horse kept idle in a stall. Oxygen needs and nutrient requirements due to muscular wear and tear increase in performance horses.

The racehorses are required to be treated as individual and should be catered and fed as individuals. They vary in their likes and dislikes for certain feeds, time of eating, level of feed intake, proportion of forage to concentrate and response to difficult handlers.

Energy availability during exercise

The energy requirements for heavy exercise are approximately 70 times greater as compared to walking since the racehorse has to perform at a high speed for a small duration, the maximum energy availability and utilization should occur during this stage. Muscle glycogen and free fatty acids play dominant role in supplying energy to the muscles for work in both conditioned and unconditioned horses. The conditioned horse adapts itself to utilize fat in addition to glycogen, to meet the increased energy requirements of exercise and training. The unconditioned horse is, however, not able to oxidize or utilize fat as efficiently as the conditioned horse and uses more muscle glycogen for exercise. The fat in the muscle is used as free fatty acid to provide energy. It has been seen that adding 5-10 per cent fat in the diet of racing horses has a sparing effect on muscle glycogen reserves which can be subsequently used to defer fatigue in the exercising horse. Addition of fats to diets increases requirement of protein as amino acids are directly related to calorie level in the diet. Increased fat level in diet increases vitamin and mineral requirement in the diet of horses. Addition of vitamin E has been seen to have a desirable response in blood packed cell volume, haemoglobin and glucose after exercise.

Calcium retention in the body increases during the exercise period which is largely due to decreased urinary excretion of calcium. Exercise also increases rate of calcium deposition in the bone by 15-20 per cent. Excessive sweating that occurs during exercise increases the requirement of minerals especially sodium and chloride, since sweat contains 0.7 per cent salt. Sweat losses are influenced by temperature and humidity. Excess sweating causes exhaustion and fatigue and extra salt is required to be taken to avoid exhaustion fatigue and collapse. Therefore, salt should be self fed to horses besides it being fed through feed. Moderate work alone causes loss of 50-60 gm of salt in the sweat and 35 gm in urine of horses. Excessive heat that is generated during exercise is dissipated by sweating which may lead to electrolyte imbalance and adversely affect thirst mechanism and failure to replace water loss may affect feed intake.

Blood picture after endurance rides, reveal an elevated pH and a tendency to develop alkalosis. Respiration rate also becomes quite high which returns to normal within 30 minutes of resting period. The energy requirements of performance horses are difficult to quantify as it is influenced by condition and training of the horse, ability and weight of rider, degree of fatigue, environmental temperature and diet composition.

The light, medium and intense work increase the energy requirement by 25, 50 and 100 per cent above maintenance. The protein requirement for a working horse has not been adequately elucidated. Increased nitrogen retention has been reported due to increased muscle protein content related to muscle hypertrophy. As such, feeding high protein diets to working horses is not advantageous.

Feeding Racehorses

The racehorses must not be allowed to become fat. They need to be kept in trim and thrifty condition for which it is important that they are fed protein, energy, vitamins and minerals in adequate amount to develop their body and perform to the maximum of their inherited potential.

The concentrate diet should be upto 50 percent of the total diet, however, it will vary depending upon condition of the horse and quality of the hay and/or pasture used. The concentrate feeding can increase or decrease depending upon whether the horse is under light training or heavy performance. The condition of the horse can serve as a guide as to whether too much or too little concentrates are being fed in relation to forage intake.

Table 19.8 : Suggested Concentrate Diet for Racehorse

Feed	*Percentage in Diet*
Oats	30
Corn	10.75
Barley	9.50
Wheat Bran	7.0
Alfalfa Meal (dehydrated)	8.0
Soyabean Meal	23.0
Black Strap Molasses	7.0
Dicalcium phosphate	2.0
Limestone	0.75
Salt trace mineralized	1.0
Vitamin Supplement	1.0

The racehorses should be fed high quality hay/pasture and should always have access to mineral lick and fresh clean water.

The energy level in the concentrate diet could be increased by replacing some of the oats with corn and decreasing wheat bran and alfalfa meal. Excess of high energy grain in feed is to be avoided since it may cause digestive disturbances because of carbohydrate overloading.

Many horse trainers prefer to add 5-10 per cent fat to the concentrate diet for high level performance. Fat increases the energy density of the diet and may allow reduction in total feed intake required to meet energy requirements which is important as it is difficult to take enough total feed during intense work. Moreover, it minimizes the possibility of colic, founder and other digestive disturbances occurring from too heavy concentrate consumption during intense activity. Addition of fat also increases the muscle glycogen of exercising horses. If fat is used, it needs to be a high quality product and it has to be protected against rancidity by a proper antioxidant, which can cause digestive disturbances and decrease in the palatability of the diet. Increased fat level in the diet also calls upon to increase the protein and calcium phosphorus levels.

The concentrate diet of high performance horses should supply about 18 per cent protein which will allow the use of hay and/ or pasture with a protein percentage of 7 to 10 and the diet will have a overall protein percentage of 12 to 14 per cent. It is always better to supply protein on higher side rather than run the risk of a lack of protein.

Feeding of the Stallion

The feeding and nutrition of stallion has not attracted much attention of the research workers probably because of paucity of stallions for the purpose of research. However, stallions are subject to the same seasonal influences as affect the breeding cycles of the mare, i.e., fertility is greatest in summer and least in the winters. Improved fertility in stallions can also be obtained by subjecting them to artificial light and richer food in winter months. At no time, should the stallion be allowed to fatten or lose condition. The energy requirements of the stallion rise during the breeding season.

Feeding During Non-Breeding Seasons

When the stallion is not being used for breeding purpose, a high quality pasture will supply a large part of the nutrients needed. Stallion should always have access to adequate minerals, vitamins and fresh clean water. Green and leafy hay can also be fed if pasture is not sufficient. Concentrate feeds should be fed in small amounts to supplement the forage used and to keep the stallion in a trim and thrifty condition.

Feeding During the Breeding Season

Breeding season imposes increased activity on the stallion and will, therefore, need more energy, protein, minerals and vitamins which can be accomplished by feeding a higher level of concentrate in the diet. During this period, the concentrate and roughage can be in equal proportion, however, level of concentrates can increase or decrease depending upon the quality of forage, condition of stallion and number of services required per week.

Chapter 21

Storage of Feed

Storage or preservation of feed for equines is a very important aspect of economical farm management as horses are specifically very sensitive to any mould or growth of any obnoxious contaminant in the feed. Besides, it leads to heavy losses of nutrients. Storage of feed, whether it is roughage or concentrate, is carried out during the stage when it is available in excess so that it can be utilized when there is dearth of the feeding material. The roughages are normally preserved in two forms:

- Hay
- Silage

Hay : Hay is the single most important harvested roughage for livestock and considerable losses can occur if hay is not cured and stored improperly. As such, appropriate knowhow and proper implementation of good farm practices is essential for proper hay making and its storage.

Characteristics of high Quality Hay

Hay should be made from plants harvested at a sufficiently early stage of maturity. It should be leafy and green in colour with stem soft and pliable. If the harvesting of hay crop is delayed to advanced stage of maturity, the percentage of protein, digestibility, minerals and vitamin content will decidedly decrease. The hay should be free from foreign material, weeds, mould and mustiness. It should have an attractive fragrance that adds to its palatability.

For work horses or light horses, hay crop is to be harvested when in bloom because when cut at very early stage, hay is apt to be laxative. Similarly, when hay is cut very late in the seed stage or even later, it will have low nutrient value for all classes of animals.

Moisture Content

The hay kept safely in barn or stack (plate XII) should not contain more than 15 per cent moisture and the baled or chopped hay should contain even less. Hay containing too much moisture, when stored, will undergo pronounced fermentation and become very hot. The nutritive value may be greatly decreased because of mould or the losses of nutrients which occur in the extensive fermentation. Also there is always a danger of spontaneous combustion when hay is stored with high moisture content. However, slight fermentation or sweating that occurs in properly cured hay, when it is stored, does not cause any marked loss of green colour or nutrients. It even seems to improve the aroma and palatability of the hay. The practical methods to check the moisture content is to twist a wisp and if the stems are slightly brittle, the hay can be stored safely.

Losses of Nutrients in Hay Making

The losses that occur in hay making are:

(a) Losses of leaves and other finer parts by shattering.

(b) Losses by fermentation and bleaching.

(c) Losses of soluble nutrients by leaching in case of heavy rains

Losses by Shattering: If legume hay becomes too dry, there will be considerable loss of leaves by shattering when the hay is raked or loaded. The leaves contain 2 to 3 times more protein as compared to the stems. Also the leaves are much richer than the stems in minerals and vitamins and are lower in fibre. Proper hay making is, therefore, one of the important factors in determining its feeding value.

Losses by Fermentation and Bleaching: Curing of hay in the field is not a simple process of drying. During this process, fermentation takes place in which some of the organic nutrients, especially the sugars and starch, are oxidized to carbon dioxide and water, thus get lost. Fermentation has a very destructive effect on the carotene in hay. If hay is cured by proper methods without undergoing pronounced heating, the losses by fermentation will be relatively small but if extensive fermentation takes place, as in brown hay, a heavy, loss of carbohydrates will occur and also the carotene and other vitamins will be destroyed. Similarly, if hay is bleached by long exposure to sun, nearly all the carotene will be lost. Generally, the greenness of the hay is directly proportional to its carotene content. Loss of nutrients also occurs when the hay is under cured and results in moulding of hay.

Loss by Leaching: Hay, when exposed to heavy and prolonged rain, severe losses may occur through leaching. During this process, considerable amount of protein and carbohydrates are lost. Severe leaching also results due to heavy rain when the hay has dried out considerably and still not fit for storage. However, hard rain, soon after the crop is cut, may not cause much loss of nutrients.

Storage of Hay

There are many ways in which hay can be processed and stored i.e., Loose hay, Baled hay, Pelletized hay, and Wafered hay etc. The hay should be free from dust or moulds otherwise it is likely to cause respiratory difficulties including heaves. Horses consume more hay when fed as wafers or cubes than when it is fed as baled hay. Wafers size should be such that it breaks readily on consumption and should not cause choking. Size of pellets is usually about 1 to 2 cm for mature horses and smaller pellets for the young horses. Pellets should not be too hard or too soft. One of the advantages of wafers and pellets is that they reduce dust and also save loss. It also saves storage space, reduces transportation cost and increases forage intake by the horse. Also use of pellets allows addition of minerals, vitamins and other nutrients.

Silage

Silage does not have much role as a nutrient for equines owing to its contamination with moulds and larger in volume because of high moisture content.

It can, however, be used to some extent for idle horses duly mixed with hay. The silage making has following advantages:

- At low expense, silage furnishes high quality succulent feed in any season of the year.
- More stock can be kept per unit area of land.
- Ensiling of crops may be carried out when weather does not permit curing them into hay or dry fodder.
- Smaller loss of nutrients especially carotene when a crop is ensiled than when it is cured in the field as hay or dry fodder.
- Even stem, coarse stalks can be eaten by the animals.
- Weedy crops which make poor hay may produce satisfactory silage.
- Fodder crops after harvesting can be stored in less space as silage than as forage.
- It permits early removal of crop from the field thus enables the land for further agricultural operations.

Biochemical Changes in Silage Making

When green forage from a suitable crop is placed in compact mass, the following changes take place which convert it into silage. The living plant cells continue to respire or breathe rapidly using up the oxygen in the air entrapped in the mass and giving off carbon dioxide. Approximately within five hours, almost all oxygen is completely utilized and this prevents the development of moulds which fail to grow under anaerobic conditions.

During fermentation, there is a rise in temperature which should not exceed 37.7°C. Acid forming bacteria multiply enormously in the silage and these bacteria attack the sugars in the green forage producing organic acids, chiefly lactic acid, some acetic acid and alcohol. This activity prevents the growth of undesirable bacteria which can cause rotting or putrefaction.

Enough Acid Formation Checks

fermentation and silage can be kept for long periods. If air does penetrate as on the top of silo, adjacent to the crack in the wall, mould will grow and destroy the acid. Putrefactive bacteria can thus develop and cause further spoilage. The dry matter content of the crop meant for ensiling should not be less than 30 per cent. Lesser dry matter is likely to lower the quality of silage and there may be considerable loss of juices. Also, there is formation of more of butryic acid as compared to lactic acid and acetic acid. If the forage is too dry, it is apt to mould. Sugars are the chief compounds acted upon by the bacteria in the acid fermentation of the starch and pentosans may be attacked to limited extent. Acid production is proportional to sugar content of the forage. Too much presence of sugar leads to a greater loss of nutrients due to fermentation. In silage, proteins are broken down or digested to a greater extent. There is some formation of ethanol and alcohol also during the process of fermentation which gives characteristic smell to the silage.

Nutrient Preservation During Silage

The loss of dry matter and digestible nutrients is less and the carotene content is also generally preserved. The main loss is of sugars which are oxidized to CO_2 and H_2O and thus lost. However, such loss should not amount to more than 5-10 percent of the dry matter of the crop. Losses may be more, if the silo is not compactly filled and also due to spoilage of silage at the top of the silo. If forage is too high in moisture content then a loss of nutrients occurs through juices that run out. This should not exceed 1-3 per cent of the dry matter in case of corn. However, it may increase, if the water content is too high.

Crops Suitable for Silage

A green forage must have certain qualities to make a good silage. It should neither be too dry nor too high in water content. If it is too dry it will not pack well and enough air will remain, which will permit the development of moulds. If moisture level is too high, the silage is apt to be very sour or it may even be spoilt. It is essential that the pH of the silage should be acidic to prevent the growth of the undesirable bacteria that cause rotting or putrefaction. Presence of sufficient amount of sugar is a must to lower the pH. The forage must be thoroughly trampled with special care, to force out as much air as possible. Corn and Sorghum are ideal silage crops as they contain enough sugar so that sufficient acid is produced in silage fermentation. With these crops, there is no need to add preservative, minerals or molasses. Legume forages are lower than grass forages in sugars and they are more alkaline in nature than corn or sorghum. Also, they generally have less than 25 per cent dry matter, therefore, wilting of the forage crop for 2-3 hrs to bring the dry matter to 30-40 per cent level, is essential. It will also improve the percentage of sugar per unit of forage. However drying for much longer periods will result in loss of nutrients.

Feed Storage

Storage process, if not given due attention, is likely to affect the nutritive value of feed, forages, cereals and compound feeds. The feeds contain saturated and unsaturated fat, fat soluble vitamins and other various labile and readily oxidizable substances. However, the loss of nutrients during storage will depend upon degree of protection, environmental conditions, their propensity to oxidation and presence or absence of catalytic substances. All fat soluble vitamins are subject to oxidation alongwith saturated and unsaturated fatty acids. Rancidy of fats also decreases the overall acceptability of feeds. However, some anti oxidants can be added to reduce the rancidity and provide stability to the feeds. Artificially added fat soluble vitamins also do have more stability as compared to their natural counterparts. B-complex vitamins are generally resistant to destruction.

The rooms/silos meant for storage of feeds should have low and uniform temperature, low humidity, good ventilation, absence of direct sunlight and free from rodents and insects. Such rooms, should be devoid of windows and should be insulated. The roof of the building should be leak proof and the floor should be impervious and rodent proof. The stacked feed should be sufficirntly above the ground and approachable from all sides. High moisture level can lead to mould growth which can affect the acceptability of the feed. Further, the fungus can grow in stored feed with relatively low moisture and high osmotic pressure, which is technically known as conditions of low water activity. Such conditions cause heating, mustiness, caking, lack of acceptability and eventually decay of stored fodder as well as grains. Fungal toxins that are produced in this process, affect the feed stability and nutritional value. *Aspergillus* and *Pencillium* species are considered to be the main culprits where moisture content give water activity of 0.73-0.78 at temperature ranging between 5 and 40°c. Most storage fungi have minimum temperature for growth i.e. 0-5°C, grow optimally at 25-30°C and do not grow at temperature above 40-45°c. However, *Aspergillus flavus* grows vigorously at 50°C and *Penicillium* grows slowly at temperature down to 2°C. Moulds growth in the feeds leads to formation of metabolic water which further helps the growth of fungi.

Insects accelerate deterioration of feed and grain and also generate heat and metabolic water besides acting as vector for fungal spores. These insects and mites grow in dirty and badly stored grain by hatching their eggs and multiplying further. Mites multiply even at 4°C and moisture level of 12.5 per cent. Insects, however, require higher combination of temperature and moisture.

It, therefore, implies that cleanliness, fumigation of stores, hygienic storage of grain and feed at low temperature and in dry conditions, without pockets of high moisture, are the greatest assurance for maintaining the feed quality for long term.

Mites can be detected in feed by observing for a minute during which movement of feed particle is apparent. Mites produce sour smell with moulding, discolouration of the grain dust and a fungal smell can be readily detected. Rodent infestation not only causes feed loss but also introduces the risk of enteric diseases, principally, Salmonellosis.

Propionic acid, sorbic acid, calcium propionate, hydroxquinoline are some of the preparations which can be used for coating the grain. However, these preparations are not generally effective when included in mixed feeds.

which then affect the acceptability of the feed. Further, the fungus can grow in stored feed with relatively low moisture and high osmotic pressure, which is technically known as conditions of low water activity. Such conditions cause heating, mustiness, caking, lack of acceptability and eventually decay of stored fodder as well as grains. Fungal toxins that are produced in this process affect the feed stability and nutritional value. *Aspergillus* and *Penicillium* species are considered to be the storage fungi where moisture content give water activity of 0.7-0.78 at temperature ranging between 5 and 40°C. Most storage fungi have minimum temperature for growth i.e. 0-5°C, grow optimally at 25-30°C and do not grow at temperature above 40-45°C. However, *Aspergillus flavus* grows vigorously at 50°C and *Penicillium* grows slowly at temperature down to 2°C. Mould growth in the feeds leads to formation of metabolic water which further helps the growth of fungi.

Insects accelerate deterioration of feed and grain and also generate heat and metabolic water besides acting as vector for fungal spores. These insects and mites grow in dirty and badly stored grain by hatching their eggs and multiplying further. Mites multiply even at 4°C and moisture level of 12.5 per cent. Insects, however, require higher combination of temperature and moisture.

It therefore implies that cleanliness, fumigation of stores, hygienic storage of grain and feeds below temperature and in dry conditions, without pockets of high moisture, are the greatest assurance for maintaining the feed quality for long term.

Mites can be detected in feed by observing for a minute during which movement of feed particle is apparent. Mites produce sour smell with moulding. Accumulation of the grain dust and a fungal smell can be readily detected. Rodent infestation not only causes feed loss but also introduces the risk of enteric diseases, principally Salmonellosis.

Propionic acid, sorbic acid, calcium propionate, [illegible] any one of the preparations which can be used for coating the grain. However, these preparations are not generally effective when included in mixed feeds.

Chapter 22

Saddlery

Various types of saddles are used for riding and carriage of load. These may differ in various details but their construction is based on the same principles. Hence, they have similar frame work, known as 'saddle tree' consisting of a 'front arch' and a 'rear arch' secured by two 'side bars' placed parallel to each other. The purpose of using two arches is to ensure that spine of the horse is not pressed. Similarly, the side bars not only distribute the weight equally on the back but also keep the arches in their place. The description of important parts of most commonly used riding saddle (see Fig. 22.1), is as under:

Saddle Tree :- It consists of a front and a rear arch made up of steel. Both the arches are secured by two side bars, placed parallel to each other. The front arch forms the 'pommel', the rear arch forms the 'cantle'. The side bars rest on the back of the animal and distribute the weight of the rider along the animal's back. The side bars are made of wood and are slightly twisted to enable them to conform to the shape of animal's back. The ends of the side bars are slightly curved upwards and outwards. That part of the side bar which projects in front of the saddle is called the "burr" whereas the one projecting behind the saddle is called the "fan". Just behind the front arch, the side bars are fitted with a steel bar and a roller through which the stirrup leather passes.

Numnah/Felt Panels: Side bars are fitted with detachable numnah/felt panels. The leather pockets at both ends of the numnah panel are fitted in the fan and burr. The front leather pockets are provided with straps and buckets for securing them on to the side bars. The object of numnah panels is, firstly to provide extra padding without filling up the channels of the saddle and secondly to provide a surface which grips the blanket and prevents slipping of the saddle. They also afford protection to the side bars.

'V' Girth Attachment: It consists of front and rear straps which connect the 'sweat flap' to the side bar, meeting in a 'V' shape on the sweat flap to which they are rivetted. The front strap has two parts, the upper part secured to the side bar has a buckle and the lower part secured to the sweat flap is punctured with three holes for adjustment to suit the conformation of different animals. The tear strap whose upper part is screwed to the side bar and the lower part rivetted to the sweat flap does not require any adjustment. The sweat flap consists of an oblong piece of leather to which the straps of 'V' attachment are secured and on this are also sewn the girth straps. The sweat flap prevents the girth straps becoming saturated with sweat and protects the animal's sides from being pinched by the girth buckles.

The Seat: It is made of leather and covers the frame of the saddle between the front and rear arches which are connected by a sling of webbing. The webbing takes off the strain from the leather.

The Flap: It is a leather covering on the sides of the saddle. The shape of the flaps suits the bend of the rider's legs when his feet are in the stirrups.

The Stirrup Leather: It is to hold the stirrup iron. It has a buckle at one end and is punched with holes at the other end for adjustment.

The Stirrup Iron: These are made of steel. The top part is of semi-oval shape with a slot at the top through which the stirrup leather passes. The tread is the flat portion on which the rider's foot rests.

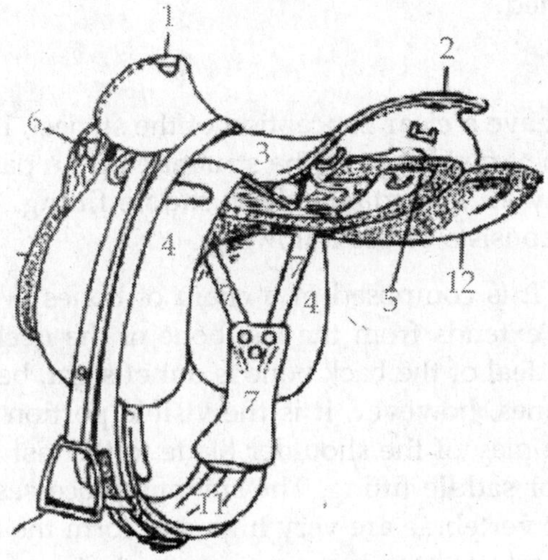

Fig. 22.1 : Riders Saddle

1. Pommel (Front Arch)
2. Cantle (Rear Arch)
3. Seat
4. Flap
5. Fan
6. Burr
7. "V" Attachment
8. Surcingle
9. Stirrup Leather
10. Stirrup Iron
11. Girth
12. Numnah Panels

The Surcingle: It is a plain leather strap, 5 cm in width, tapering to 2.5 cm width towards the buckle. At the other end, is attached a strap 2.5 cm wide, punctured with holes for buckling.

Girth: It is made of leather or cord with split openings and varies from 0.75 to 1 metre in length. There are two buckles at one end to hold the girth straps. At 7.5 cm from each end, is sewn a leather loop, through which the surcingle is passed before being fastened.

Fitting

In order to have a clear conception of the subject, it is essential to have some knowledge of the structure of the parts involved as these play an important role in saddle fitting. The back of the animal consists of the following:

The Spine: It is composed of a chain of bones (Vertebrae) in which back extends from the last bone of the neck to the last rib. A great deal of the back bone is out of sight, being covered by blade bones, however, it is the visible portion of the back i.e. from the play of the shoulder blade to the last rib which is important for saddle fitting. The spinous processes of the first few thoracic vertebrae are very high and form the withers and the upper part of these bony processes of the vertebrae form the ridge of the back bone.

Ribs: There are 18 pairs of ribs in equines, out of which 8 front ones are called true ribs as they are fixed into the breast bone (sternum) whereas the remaining are called false ribs as they are lashed to each other and not to the sternum. The true ribs are strong and straight and can carry weight not only on their upper surface but also on their sides. False ribs on the other hand, are comparatively thinner and more curved and can carry weight on the upper surface only and not on their sides. When a saddle is placed on the back, it rests on the ribs and it is the ribs and not the spine that actually carry the weight.

Loins: It is composed of five lumbar vertebrae. They have thin and long transverse processes. The width of the loins depends on the length of transverse processes. There are no ribs supporting the lumbar vertebrae, hence they can-not take any weight.

Movement of Shoulder Blade: The speed and ease with which an animal moves depends on the unrestricted movement of its limbs. The forelimbs of the animal are fixed to the body by means of strong thick muscles. The muscles which fix the forelegs to the body are firmly attached over the sides of the ribs and inner surface of scapula which moves alongwith the foreleg. Its movements are forward and backward. Therefore, no weight/ saddle should interfere with the free movement of the shoulder blade, otherwise animal will not be able to move with ease.

Back Muscles: In a healthy animal, the space between the processes of the vertebrae and the ribs is filled up with back muscles. A well developed back muscle runs the whole length of the back. From the saddle fitting point of view, it is the most important muscle of the body, as it is on this muscle that the saddle rests and it acts as a cushion under the weight.

Fundamental Principles of Saddle Fitting

From the brief anatomical description of the back, we are in a position to form some idea as to where the weight is best carried. The facts can be summarized as under:

(a) The withers must not be pressed or pinched upon.

(b) The spine (central line of back) must have no pressure imposed upon it.

(c) The shoulder blades must have free and unimpeded movements.

(d) The weight must not be placed on loins.

(e) The weight must be evenly distributed over the weight bearing surface which extends from the play of the shoulder to the last rib.

(f) The weight must be imposed on the ribs through the medium of muscles covering them.

Procedure of Saddle Fitting

No saddle has yet been made which will fit every type or shape of equine back, just as no one pair of shoes will fit all human feet. Hence, each animal should have his own saddle. There are three sizes of saddles for horses. Having selected the size of saddle which approaches the nearest to the shape of the horse, bare saddle tree is first placed on the horse's back so that the front arch is above the hollow behind the shoulder. The saddle tree should conform to the shape of the horse's back. Following points are then attended to:

(a) That the front arch is wide enough to admit the hand on

either side and also sufficiently high to clear the withers.

(b) That the width between the side bars is sufficiently great to enable them to come well down over the ribs, and not to press into the sides of the withers.

(c) That the side-bars bear evenly on the horse's back from the play of the shoulder to the last rib. Rear fans should be clear off the loins.

(d) That the arches and seat are clear of the spine.

(e) That the length of the saddle corresponds to the available length of the back.

The saddle is then taken off, fitted with numnah panels and replaced on the horse's back. Now the saddle tree will be considerably raised and proper thickness of the blanket can be estimated. The addition of blanket, however, reduces the width of the front arch and narrows the saddle across the top of the side bars.

The blanket is then folded and placed on horse's back and the saddle on the blanket. The blanket must be well pressed up into the front arch and before the girth is tightened, it should be ensured that the burrs are off the shoulder and fans off the loins. If they are not, the thickness of the blanket beneath the side bars must be increased by turning it up on either side. The girth is now pulled up and a man is placed in the saddle. The fit of a saddle cannot be determined until the saddle is inspected with a man sitting on it as some parts which appear well clear off the back when there is no weight on the saddle, may be brought dangerously close to it by the pressure of a man's weight.

The first thing to be checked now is the freedom of the withers from any pressure. The hand should be readily introduced beneath the blanket over the top and along both sides of withers. If there is any difficulty in inserting the hand, then the saddle is not properly fitted over the withers.

Thereafter, it is seen that the shoulder blades are free from pressure. This is done by passing the hand beneath the blanket to the play of the shoulder. If there is pressure, the hand will only be introduced with difficulty. Assuming that the hand can find its way in, the horse's foreleg should be advanced to its full extent by an assistant. This should be possible without the examiner's fingers being pinched between the shoulder blade and side bar, even when the man in the saddle is leaning forward. If the fingers are pinched, the shoulder blade will also be pinched, therefore to correct it, saddle must be raised by fitting thicker numnah panels on the side bars or by making an extra fold in the blanket. The above test should be carried out on both sides.

After this, fans should be tested for loins pressure, with a man leaning back in the saddle, the flat of the hand should find ready admission under the fans.

In order to ascertain whether the pressure on the side bars is evenly distributed, the animal is ridden for half an hour and the saddle is carefully ungirthed and lifted from the blanket without disturbing it. The imprints of side bars on the blanket will show at a glance whether they are pressing evenly from top to bottom and from front to rear. The examination of the side bar impressions should be made immediately as the elasticity of the blanket soon causes it to lose the impressions. The commonest places to find excessive pressure are the top edge of the side bar behind the front arch and the bottom edge in front of the rear arch. If a deeper impression is formed at places other than mentioned above, then the pressure is not distributed evenly and the corresponding part of the horse's back is receiving an undue amount of weight. This may not necessarily cause a sore back in an animal in good condition or with a good blanket and numnah, but it will certainly do so should the horse lose condition or the blanket or the panel be thin as these conditions bring the tree nearer to the bony framework of the horse.

Saddling

Even a well fitted saddle may cause sore back if it is not properly saddled up. There is a marked distinction between bad saddling and effective fitting. A horse sustaining a wither gall due to the blanket resting on the spine and not by pressure of the front arch is an injury by bad saddling. The following points should be stressed while saddling horses:

The folded blanket should be placed on the centre of the horse's back. There should be no grass or grit sticking to it. It should project about 5 cm in front of the burr and behind the fans. Double fold method is the one normally used for folding the blanket. In this method of folding, the blanket is first doubled lengthwise, then it is doubled again crosswise. It is then placed lengthwise across the horse's back with the selvedged edges on the left side and to the rear. The folding of the blanket may be modified to suit special conditions. For instance, in the case of a horse which has lost condition, a useful method is the channel fold. In this method, the blanket is folded lengthwise in three equal parts, each end is then turned over and folded towards the centre.

Two or three folds may be taken as required to suit the horse's back, leaving the channel in the centre. In those cases, which require an extra thickness of blanket under the front arch, the envelope fold will be found useful. In this method, the blanket is folded in three folds of equal width in the length of the blanket. A fold of 60 cm is then made at one end, the other end is turned over, forming a pocket, into which the opposite end is tucked. It is then placed on the horse's back with thick end near the withers. When this method is used, a second blanket is necessary to prevent rubbing of 'V' attachment.

The front of the saddle should not be so far forward that it interferes with the play of the shoulder. The panels of the saddle should lie flat on top of the horse's ribs. The burrs and fans should bear no weight when stuffed panels are attached. The front arch should clear the withers to the breadth of not less than two fingers when the rider is in the saddle.

The girth should be placed about 10 cm behind the point of the elbow. It should be sufficiently tight to keep the saddle in its place. It should be tightened gradually, and not with violence, care being taken that the skin is not wrinkled.

The surcingle should lie flat over the girth and should not be tighter than the latter.

To attach the stirrups to the saddle, pass the end of the stirrup leather through the stirrup iron, then through bar on the side bar of the saddle from below, inwards to outwards then fasten to the tongue of the buckle. The buckle should be then pulled up close to the bar on the side bar, the point of the stirrup leather passed under the two leathers from the front, then passed under the surcingle.

Adjustment of the "V" attachment (Fig. 22.2) : The normal position of the attachment is with the buckle in the central hole 16 cm from the rivet; this position will suit a very large number of horses. The upper and lower holes are provided for the adjustment; additional holes must not be punched. On animals with straight shoulders that carry the saddle too far forward, the front strap should be shortened by buckling it in the lower hole; on those that have deep chests and sloping shoulders and are thick infront of the saddle, the front strap should be lengthened. In no case will it be worn as a true "V' i.e. the front and rear straps of equal lengths; this would depress the rear part of the saddle and cause other difficulties. Care should be taken in all cases to buckle the left and right straps in corresponding holes.

1. Pommel (Front Arch)
2. Cantle (Rear Arch)
3. Seat
4. Side Bars
5. Fan
6. Burr
7. Numnah Panels
8. "V" Attachment

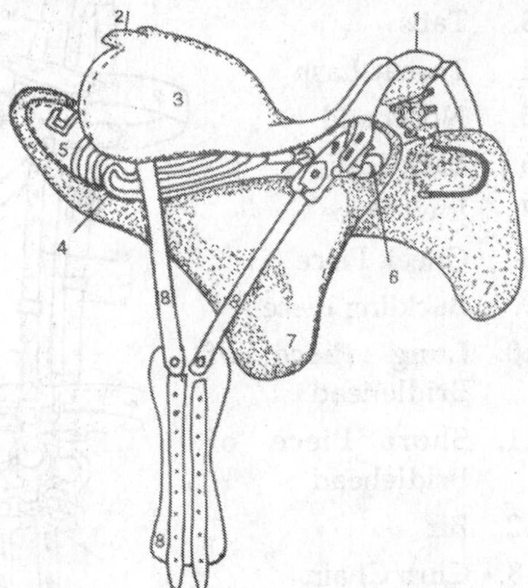

Fig. 22.2 : Adjustmet of V-attachment

Common Faults in Saddling

(a) The blanket not properly folded and raised off the back bone.

(b) The loose end of any strap getting in between the blanket and skin.

(c) The sweat flap of the girth, or in panelled saddles, the panel flap getting turned in when putting the saddle on in a hurry, thus forming a thick ridge which gets pressed into the side and produces injury.

(d) A horse which has either a loose girth or a tight surcingle is considered to be badly saddled.

The Head Collar - Description and Fitting

General Description

The head collar (Fig. 22.3) is constructed in such a way that it can be used either as a bridle or as a head collar in the stables and for rests while on move. It consists of the following parts:

1. Crown Loop
2. Brow Band
3. Tabs
4. Throat Lash
5. Noseband
6. Back Stay
7. Jowl Piece
8. Cheek Piece
9. Buckling Piece
10. Long Piece of Bridlehead
11. Short Piece of Bridlehead
12. Bit
13. Curb Chain
14. Cheek Rein
15. Curb Rein

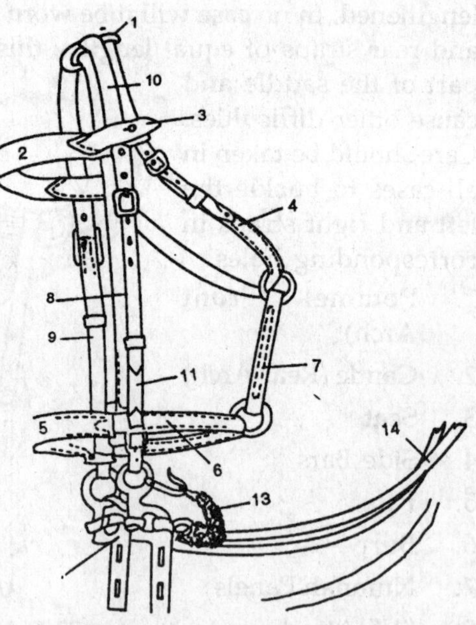

Fig. 22.3 : Head Collar

Crown Loop: It is a small piece of leather, consisting of two loops which connect the cheek piece and throat lash at the top of the bridle on the animal's poll.

Brow Band: It consists of a leather strap with the two loops at each end, through which both, the cheek piece and throat lash pass, and over these loops lie the tabs, which are small leather straps stitched on to the brow band and fastened by a brass stud which is sewn into the loop of the brow band, through which the bridlehead passes. The object of the brow band is to prevent the cheek piece and throat lash from slipping backwards. The object of the tab is to hold the bridlehead in position.

Cheek Piece: It consists of a strap of leather sewn on at one end of the square which connects the noseband and back stay together on the left side. At the other end, it is punched with holes for securing to the buckle of the buckling piece.

Buckling Piece to the Cheek Piece: It consists of a strap sewn on at one end to the square which connects the noseband and back stay together, but on the opposite square to that which holds the cheek piece. At the other end of the buckling piece is a buckle to which the cheek piece is fastened. The cheek piece and buckling piece, when fastened together, support the noseband and back stay in position.

Throat Lash: It consists of a plain leather strap with a buckle at one end and punched with holes at the other for adjustment. The throat lash secures the bridle on the animal's head.

Noseband and Back stay: These are two leather straps connected to each other by two square links. On the back stay runs the lower ring of the jowl piece.

Jowl Piece: It consists of a short piece of double leather with a ring sewn on to each end, connecting both the throat lash and back stay.

Bridlehead : It has two parts:

- The long piece has a buckle and leather billet at one end

for securing to the bit, and punched with holes at the other end for adjusting with the short piece.

- The short piece has a buckle and leather billet at one end for securing to the bit and at the other end is buckle for engaging with the long piece.

Bit Reversible: It is made of steel and is of two patterns, namely, one with a smooth mouthpiece and the other with the mouthpiece "twisted" on one side. The bits are available in three sizes large, medium and small. The parts of the bit marked in Fig. 22.4 are as follows:

- *Eye:* It is the loop at the top of the cheek through which the billet of the bridlehead is passed.
- *Upper, Centre and Lower bars:* These are the ring and slots through which the leather billet of the rein is passed.
- *Mouthpiece with port mouth and canons:* It is the steel bar which joins the cheeks of the bit. The straight parts are called canons, the bend in the centre is called the port mouth; the object of which is to give the rider greater leverage on the animal's mouth, if required.
- *Curb Chain:* It is the steel chain of 19 links secured to the eye of the bit on one side and to the curb hooks on the other eye.

Fitting

Brow Band: The brow band should be just long enough to allow the cheek piece to pass from the crown down, without rubbing the bones on each side of the temple or cutting the base of the horse's ears.

Cheek Piece and Budding Piece: The cheek piece and buckling piece should be parallel to and behind the projecting cheek bone.

Throat Lash: The throat lash should fit loosely, being only sufficiently tight to prevent the head collar from slipping over the horse's ears, thus in no way interfering with the

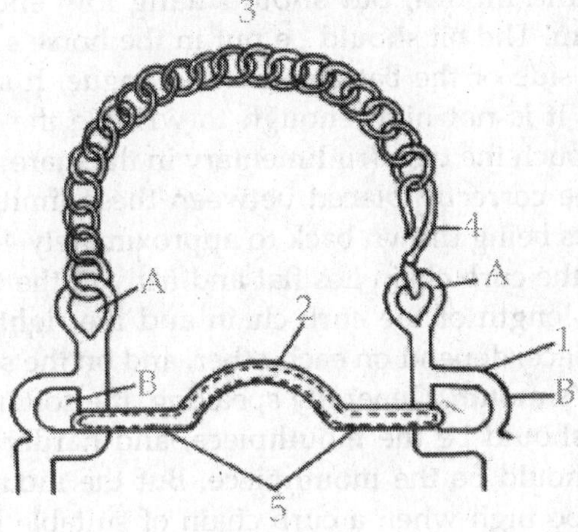

Fig. 22. 4 : Parts of the Bit

1. Cheek Piece
   A-Eye
   B - Upper Bar
   C - Centre Bar
   D - Lower Bar
2. Mouth Piece with Port Mouth
3. Curb Chain
4. Curb Hook
5. Canons

breathing or swallowing. A good guide is to allow the breadth of the hand between the throat lash and the horse's cheek. The buckle of the strap should be in line with the horse's eye on the left side.

Noseband and Back Stay: The noseband and back stay should fit so as to admit the breadth of two fingers between the horse's nose in front and the noseband, and between the horse's jaw and the back stay. The noseband and back stay should hang so as to allow two finger breadth below the projecting cheek bone.

Bridling

The bridoon (used for training young horses) should touch the corners of the mouth, but should hang low enough not to wrinkle them. The bit should be put in the horse's mouth with the smooth side of the bar against the tongue. It should be so placed that it is not high enough to wrinkle the lips, or low enough to touch the tush (rudimentary in the mare). The mouth piece will be correctly placed between these limits when, the lower cheeks being drawn back to approximately 45 degrees to the mouth, the curb chain lies flat and truly in the chin groove. The proper length of the curb chain and the right position of the mouthpiece, depend on each other, and on the sensitiveness of the horse's mouth. Generally speaking, the softer the mouth, the higher should be the mouthpiece, and harder the mouth, the lower should be the mouthpiece. But the mouthpiece will always be too high when a curb chain of suitable length, rises above the chin groove.

The curb chain should be fixed permanently on the right side of the bit. The adjustment to the left hook should be made by twisting the chin to the right until it is quite flat, putting the last link on the hook and then taking up as many more links as may be necessary. Generally speaking, the "greener" the mouth, the longer should be the curb chain.

Care should be taken to fit each horse with a bit of the correct size. A narrow bit pinches the horse's lips; a wide bit moves from side to side and bruises them and also causes uneven pressure on the bars. When a bit with a straight bar is used, most of the pressure is taken by the tongue. The use of a bit with a port brings pressure on the bars, because the tongue tends to fit into the port. The tongue, by moving, is able in effect to alter the position of the spot on which the pressure is exerted in the case of a straight barred bit; but when a port-mouthed bit is used, the latter always bears on the same portion of the bars. A bit with a straight bar, therefore, has an effect on the horse very different from that caused by a bit with a port. Whether a bit with a straight bar or one with a moderate port will suit a horse better, depends on individual idiosyncrasy and many other factors, amongst which the following are important:

(a) Previous training of the horse.
(b) Temperament of the horse.
(c) The rider.

The greatest care should, therefore, be taken to fit a horse with the mouthpiece which suits him best and when it is first used, care must be taken that its pressure on the tongue is not such as to induce the horse to try to get his tongue over the bit.

A bit with a very high port is severe because the port presses on the roof of the mouth when brought into play. The effect is increased, and may be made cruel, by a tight noseband which prevents the horse from opening his mouth. A very narrow port is also severe because it pinches the tongue. The use of very narrow or very high ports should never be allowed except in special circumstances and for particularly a good horseman. When a bit with a sliding bar is used, care must be taken that the horse's lips are not pinched between the cheek piece and the bar owing to the holes in the latter having become too large from wear.

The reins should be of such a length that, when held by the middle in the full of the left hand, with a light feeling of the horse's mouth, they will touch the rider's waist.

The Breastplate and Martingale

The breastplate is not as a rule required. It is only necessary on horses whose conformation is such that the saddle is continually slipping back. When used, it should be so fitted that the upper edge of the rosette or leather is three finger-breadths above the sternum. It should admit the breadth of the hand between it and the flat of the shoulder.

The martingale should be used only for exceptional horses. It should never be necessary for a horse which is well trained and is of reasonable good conformation. Its use is justifiable in the following cases:

(a) For a horse which naturally carries his head so high and whose head and neck are so badly placed that it is no effort to him to evade the bit raising his head.

(b) For a horse which has been badly trained and has learnt to evade the bit by throwing his head up. A martingale gives the rider a certain amount of control by preventing this evasion.

(c) For a horse which, because he is afraid to face his bit, or as a result of bad riding and being jobbed in the mouth, has developed the habit of jumping with a hollow back. A martingale, by preventing getting his head up, may cure this by inducing him to round his back and jump in better style again.

The martingale should be fitted of such a length that there is no strain on it until the horse has got his head higher than the normal position. Its action is automatic and independent of the rider's hands. It does not interfere with the recovery of a horse which makes a mistake at a fence, except when he drops his hind legs into a ditch or water.

Care and Maintenance of Saddlery

Care and maintenance of saddlery is very essential. It not only prolongs the life of the article but also prevents injury to the animals. It also increases the efficiency, as well maintained, pliable leather goods are easy to handle. To preserve the original shape, proper storage is essential. Leather goods demand regular care and maintenance and if it is not attended to, they are adversely affected and begin to rot. Water, heat and neglect are the three enemies of leather.

Leather used in manufacture of harness and saddlery is of two types:

Tanned Buff Leather: It has considerable degree of stiffness to retain its shape. It is mostly used for saddle seats, leather panels of back saddle and leather parts of web girth. To prevent cracks, this leather is treated with soft soap on its upper surface (grain side). No dubbin is to be used on this type of leather.

Curried Leather: This is soft and pliable leather. Parts of saddle made from this type of leather include straps, girths, reins and leather stirrup etc. To keep it soft and pliable, dubbin and soft soap is applied.

Criteria for Use of Soap and Dubbin

Soap laundry is the best preservative where it is important to maintain the stiffness or rigidity of shape of the store e.g., articles made from tanned buff leather. Any good quality soft soap can be used.

Dubbin is the correct preservative where softness is desired and the articles have to be maintained in a soft condition such as curried leather stores. Dubbin containing 50 per cent tallow (animal fat) and 50 per cent castor oil.

The application of soap as a preservative, and of dubbin to maintain pliability, is only of value when these agents enter the fibres of the leather. Only a certain quantity can be absorbed so the use of excessive quantities is not only useless and a waste of material, but produces a sticky surface on the leather to which dirt and grit will adhere.

Leather must be free of dust and mud before soap and dubbin are applied. All articles should, therefore, be thoroughly brushed and rubbed over with a cloth before soap or dubbin are used. No leather article should be washed or soaked in water. This destroys its vitality, and causes it to crack easily when it dries. Soap or dobbin are more readily absorbed when the surface of the leather is lightly damp; after the removal of dust or grit by brush and dry cloth, the surface should be rubbed over with a damp cloth, and soap or dubbin then applied with a rag or the hand. Those parts of saddlery which come into contact with the animal's body, and consequently absorb sweat, should be rubbed over with a cloth dipped in warm water, care being taken that the leather is not made too wet, but only damped, and that all caked dirt and sweat are removed.

Soap or dubbin must be thoroughly worked into the leather. When possible, the preservative should be left on for two or three days to allow it to penetrate the leather thoroughly, but this may not be practicable under conditions when the saddlery is likely to be immediately required for use. In either case, after working thoroughly into the leather, all preservative remaining on the surface should be removed by polishing with dry cloth.

Stitching should not be scrubbed, as this removes the wax and causes the tread to rot and break.

Leather work should never be dried by a fire, or by exposure to direct sunshine. This destroys its durable properties and cause rapid deterioration. Leather work that has become wet from rain etc, should be cleaned and treated with soap or dubbin while wet, and dried as gradually as possible.

The best method of testing the conditions of leather is by feeling it between the fingers; and by its appearance. No leather should appear obviously dry, and when felt, should be smooth and springy. Articles which should be pliable, should be passed between forefinger and thumb and slightly bent; lack of grease will then be evident to the touch.

No definite rule can be laid down as to how often leather work should be soaped or dubbined. This will depend on the particular article, the extent to which it is being used, and climatic conditions. Articles exposed to the fumes of ammonia, which is given off by animal's urine on standings and in stables, require very frequent treatment with soap and dubbin to enable them to resist these fumes which rot leather rapidly. Those parts of saddlery which are in contact with the animal, require more frequent treatment because of the harmful effects of sweat. Leather if used in a damp climate, or exposed to frequent rain must be cleaned regularly to enable it to withstand the adverse effects of constant damp.

The following is the correct method and sequence of cleaning leather articles :

Tanned Buff Leather: Examples of this are the leather backs of panels, the parts of web girths; seats and flaps of riding saddlery. Remove dust and dirt from both sides of the leather with brush and dry cloth. Rub over with damp (NOT wet) cloth, on grain side only. Work in soap, by means of a damp rag or the hand, on the grain side only. Remove all surplus soap and polish with dry cloth. One exception to the above is in the case of tanned buff leather which comes into contact with the animal, e.g., the bottom edge of the flesh side of the flaps of a riding saddle. If these become discoloured and caked with sweat, they should be well rubbed with a soapy rag to remove the sweat and dirt, and then thoroughly dried with a clean cloth.

Curried Leather: Remove dust and dirt with brush and dry cloth. Dampen slightly, preferably with a cloth wrung out in warm water, work dubbin into the flesh side, and yellow soap into the grains of the leather. In the case of straps which require to be kept particularly pliant, and shackle leathers, a small quantity of dubbin should be worked into both sides of the leather.

Metal Work

Steel or brass buckles, dees, chains etc. need NOT normally be polished. They should be cleaned by rubbing with bath brick, or, if this is not available, ordinary earth is effective, but sand or grit should NOT be used. Care should be taken to remove all rust, and, in the case of brass fittings, the verdigris, which forms on them in damp climates and if not, properly dried after leather work is cleaned. Both rust and verdigris are harmful to leather. After cleaning, all metal parts should be oiled lightly by rubbing over with an oily rag.

Felt, Webbing and Blankets

The felt linings of panels must be kept clean by thorough brushing. If these linings are allowed to become caked with sweat and dirt, they will rapidly cause sore backs. When saddles are removed they should be made to rest on the front arch, with the panels well apart and facing the wind or sun. When dry, they should be brushed and beaten with the flat of the hand to remove grit and dust and keep them soft. If the linings are wet through exposure to rain or dampness, every opportunity must be taken to dry them. Saddles should be put or hung where there is a maximum flow of air.

Girths, and other components made from webbing require attention to prevent them becoming caked with sweat and dirt which makes them hard and will cause galls. Web articles should be dried after use and well brushed. Periodically, it is necessary to scrub the webbing with soap and water. This should not be done more frequently than is essential to keep the webbing soft as it hastens wear. When girths are scrubbed, care should be taken to avoid wetting the leather parts, should be well soaped, and buckles oiled. The articles should be dried by hanging out in the air.

Blankets must be kept free from dust and dirt by thorough shaking and brushing.

Repairs

Regular inspection, timely repair, and use of correct methods go a long way towards prolonging the life of saddlery. Stitching which shows signs of wear or weakness should be re-sewn at once, not left until it breaks. Particular attention must be paid to parts of leather articles which are in contact with metal. Also to straps which are punched for the buckle-tongue. If one hole is always in use and shows signs of wear, the strap should be shortened at the buckle end to bring a fresh hole into use. Experience will quickly teach the user which components are subjected to the most wear. Such parts should receive particular attention.

Preservative Mixture

The best method of cleaning, preserving and softening of saddles is to use following preservative mixture: -

Ingredients

Soft soap	14 parts
Dubbin	7 parts
Turpentine oil	1 part
Linseed oil	2 parts

Method of Preparation: Cut the soap into long thin pieces and place in a large tin or drum. Add dubbin in small pieces. Pour in the turpentine oil and the linseed oil. Mix well and boil over a fire; stirring the whole for a while, until all is mixed into a thick paste. Mixture is ready for use when cold.

Method of use : Rub well into all leather work, both on the top and lower surfaces. If this is done well, new saddlery will be rendered soft immediately. It is much better to use preservative mixture than to use soap and dubbin separately.

Daily Maintenance

(a) Articles under constant use need daily application of soap and dubbin.

(b) Steel and iron material, specially the bit should be wiped over with an oil rag.

(c) If exposed to water, saddlery should be dried before storing.

(d) Numnahs should be brushed and dried in the sun.

Periodical Maintenance

(a) Strip off all parts into pieces once a month.

(b) Inspect the wear of each part.

(c) Clean and treat with preservatives.

(d) Following require more frequent treatment;.

Girth, Sweat flaps, Stirrup leather and Brow bands

(e) Ensure that holes of girth straps are not worn out.

(f) Examine every part for pliability.

Sore Backs (Saddle Galls) and their Prevention

The term 'sore backs' includes all injuries inflicted on animals by the use of saddlery. Sore backs are preventable injuries and are caused by a definite cause. By having a look at a sore back, it is possible to trace the actual cause operating in causing it. Hence, if we remove the cause there will not be a sore back. It should also be kept in mind that if the cause remains to continue, it may lead to disastrous results. As a matter of fact, in most of the cases, the fault lies with the saddle.

Cause of Sore Backs

Sore backs or injuries to various part of the body due to saddlery are caused by one of the two undermentioned means or a combination of the two, viz:

(a) By friction.

(b) By pressure.

The former causes injury by rubbing and the latter by partly or entirely cutting off the blood supply. Some power of resistance to both friction and pressure does exist in all animals, and the power of resistance is much more in hard working animals compared to the animals in soft condition. Therefore, the condition of an animal has an enormous influence on the production of sore backs. Condition of the animal may be one of the three undermentioned types:

Hard Condition: Seen in well fed and hard worked animals.

Poor Condition: Seen in animals which are under-fed and over worked.

Soft Condition: Seen in fat animals which are well fed but not sufficiently exercised.

The power to resist friction and pressure is much less in animals belonging to last two categories mentioned above.

Sore backs can be produced by any part of the saddle. In order to have a better understanding of the various causes operating in producing sore backs, each part of the saddle is taken separately and its injury producing potential and the remedial measures be described as under:

Front Arch Injuries: The front arch causes injury to the withers when it is too low or too narrow. The shape of an animal also pre-disposes him to injuries due to front arch. High and thick fleshy withers are particularly susceptible to front arch injuries. Injuries caused by low front arch are due to the loss of condition and muscle wastage. In such cases, the remedy is to use the saddle blanket. For high and thick withers, have a saddle with a higher or wider front arch. Another alternative is to use the blanket folded in such a way so as to keep fewer folds under the front arch, and thus increase its width.

Rear Arch Injuries: Injuries caused by rear arch are not very common. However, the blanket may cause inflammation if allowed to come down on the back which gets tightly stretched over the spine.

Injuries from Side Bars: The injuries produced by side bars are numerous and extend from front to rear. They are caused by irregular pressure, viz., the curves in the bars do not correspond to the curves of the back, and undue pressure is exerted at certain points instead of being distributed evenly all over the saddle. As we know that the whole secret of saddle fitting lies with the fitting of side bars, they must conform to the shape of the back in such a way that the most perfect adaptation between the two surfaces results, if possible as perfectly as that obtained by placing one sheet of paper over another.

- Injuries from side bars result when certain portions of the bars are resting on the back while the others have no bearing whatsoever, and easily admit the fingers underneath. There are two places in side bars which do not fit well, viz, the lower edge of the side bars just behind the front arch and the upper edge of the side bars just behind the rear arch.
- Injuries from burrs or fans are met with by folding the blanket shorter and putting more folds under the side bars.
- Injuries from the upper edge of the side bar pressing into withers can only be prevented by obtaining a larger saddle tree. If this is not possible and same tree has to be used, strips of numnah along the lower edge of the bar in sufficient quantity may be placed to raise the upper edge of the back.
- Injuries due to the lower edge of the side bar pressing into the back can be prevented by placing strips of numnah along the upper edge of the side bar and also by increasing the number of folds of blanket.
- Injuries due to side bars being too curved, occur about the middle of the back. Since the curve cannot be reduced, the only thing that can be done is to fill up both ends of the side bar with strips of numnah.

- Injuries produced by the side bars are aggravated by defects in balancing the weight carried. Some personnel ride with one stirrup leather longer than the other (generally the left one). This leads to a defect in the balance of the weight on the back.
- The position of the injury on the back indicates whether the side bar is at fault or not. To discover the exact position of the defect, the bare tree is placed on the back but it is held at such a height above it as will correspond to the thickness of the numnah panels and blanket. If this precaution is not adopted, the side bars will occupy a lower position on the back and the localization of the cause of trouble will be wholly wrong.

Injures Produced By the Seat: The seat produces injuries by sinking under the weight of the rider and resting on the spine. This especially happens when the horse has lost condition. This can be prevented by lacing up the webbing tighter.

Injuries Produced by Numnah: A numnah injures a horse either on top of the withers or on the middle of the spine over the ribs. These injuries can be avoided by careful saddling. The numnah of the saddle should be placed well up in the fork before gjrthing. Animals working with numnah resting on the withers or spine always have the hair over the spine standing erect, like a paint brush. Injury over the loins is produced by the numnah pulled too tightly over the spine in girthing up, aggravated by heavy weight in the saddle and loss of condition. It can be prevented by strapping the numnah higher up to the rear arch. Caked mud on numnah can also cause galls.

Girth Galls: Girth galls result from bad conformation, bad saddling and sudden loss of condition of an animal. An animal in soft condition is especially susceptible to girth galls. An animal with shallow uprunning brisket and bulging curved ribs is predisposed to girth galls as his saddle moves forward. Sometimes elbow also gets galled from the friction of the edge of the girth.

Girths that have become hard, inelastic and rigid from sweat or water, are liable to cause gall from their rigidity.

A horse that gets galls from bad saddling, is due to not tightening up of the girth sufficiently. Several animals learn the trick of distending their chests with air when they are being girthed up. The object is to avoid being tightly girthed up. The girth of such animals be tightened after they have walked for some distance. A loose girth allows the saddle to oscillate and move forward on to the neck, with the result that the girth catches behind the elbow and chafes them.

The girth of leather gets hard from sweat and looks unsuitable for the purpose but no trouble arises from a leather girth as it soon softens up under the warm skin and is kept well dressed from the grease from horse's skin.

Girth galls arising from mal-conformation, viz., shallow brisket and arched ribs can be prevented by strapping the girth back by means of a surcingle placed under the seat towards the rear arch.

Many devices have been used to prevent galls such as splitting the girths or introduction of hide or string girths. All these give the girth, a better grip on the skin.

When a thin blanket and short numnahs are worn, the buckles on the girth cause injury to the sides from the pressure which they exert. The remedy is to put a piece of numnah under the girth buckles. The buckles of girths that are too long will ride under the weight of rider and can cause pressure galls. Similarly, if the girths are too short, the buckles will be under the bottom edge of the panels and will cause pressure galls.

Injuries to Shoulder Blade from Burrs. Injuries to shoulder blade bone are caused by saddles that are too large. Where blanket is used, we may raise the 'burrs' off the shoulder by increasing the folds under the bars.

Injuries from Exposing Hot Backs to Air. Backs immediately exposed to air by removing the saddle, while they are still wet and hot, is a time honoured source of injury. By sudden exposure, small swellings erupt all over the back. To avoid these swellings, backs should not be exposed and saddles be taken off after half an hour or so, though girths should be loosened.

Injuries from continuous pressure. It is a well known fact that if continuous pressure is applied to a part for sufficient time, the part dies for want of blood supply. When animals are over worked and underfed, their vitality and power of resistance is lowered and they are likely to be pre-disposed to sore backs arising from continuous pressure.

Chapter 23

Transportation

General Conditions

Animals to be transported should be healthy and in good condition. The animals need to be examined by a veterinary officer for freedom from infectious diseases and their fitness to undertake the journey. The transportation should be comfortable and animals should reach it's destination in fit condition. Care should be taken for animal welfare chiefly in terms of water and feed provisioning, extreme environmental temperatures and injuries. The attention should be paid to avoid aggression among the animals due to transportation stress and reaction to new environment. During summer months, the equines are heat stressed while being transported and may loose up to 10% of their body weight in a day, if not properly rehydrated.

Following guidelines should always be considered:

(a) Pregnant and very young animals should not be mixed with other animals.

(b) Different classes of equines should be kept separately.

(c) Diseased animals, whenever transported for treatment, should not be mixed with other animals.

(d) Troublesome animals should be given tranquillizers before loading, especially when being transported by aircraft.

(e) Tame/quiet animals should be loaded first and troublesome animals last.

(f) Entires (stallions) should not be carried with brood mares in the same vehicle/wagon.

(g) Animals should be loaded after proper watering and feeding.

(h) Watering arrangements *enroute* should be made. Small quantities of water may be carried for emergency.
(i) Sufficient food should be carried during the journey.
(j) Animals should, as far as possible, be given some exercise during journey.
(k) All vehicles should be inspected for safety, suitability and cleanliness before loading the animals. These should be properly disinfected and sprayed with disinfectant before loading.
(l) Adequate arrangements should be made for the care and management during the journey.
(m) Veterinary first-aid equipment with an attendant, trained in rendering first-aid should accompany the animals.
(n) Seriously sick and injured animals should be given veterinary treatment as early as possible.
(o) To prevent injuries, stable and tail bandages should be used in long journeys.
(p) A temperature that is normally comfortable for animals should be maintained during transportation. The animals should be protected from sun and rain.
(q) Adequate ventilation should be ensured.
(r) Dung should be removed as frequently as possible, but not later than every 8 hours. Place occupied by the animals should be kept clean and free from decaying fodder.
(s) Animals should be given prophylactic vaccination/inoculation against contagious diseases as insisted upon by the importing countries and states. A valid certificate issued by a qualified veterinarian should accompany the consignment.
(t) Animals should be marked or tagged securely with requisite particulars. The tag should be of thick cardboard of 6 cm x 8 cm size with metal eye and tied securely to the head collar. The tag should carry the following information:
    (i) Name and address of the consigner,
    (ii) Name and address of the consignee,

(iii) Number and types of animals being transported, and

(iv) Scale of rations and food provided for journying days.

(v) Where suitable ramps and platforms are not available, improvised ones should be used for loading/ unloading animals from carriages. The minimum width of the ramps should be 90 cm and the top should be in level with the flooring of the vehicle. The ramps should have side protection and anti-slipping device.

(u) Wagons should be provided with sand, saw dust or straw bedding to prevent slipping of animals. The layer of saw dust or sand should not be less than 3 cm thick and the thickness of straw bedding not less than 10 cm.

(v) Fire precautions should be strictly observed. Smoking should be strictly prohibitted. Fire fighting equipment should accompany the transport.

Transportation by Rail

Animals should be transported as far as possible by passenger trains only. In areas where such trains are not run, the equines may be transported by goods trains provided that special precautions are taken.

Valuable animals like horse and donkey stallions, racehorses and brood mares should be transported in horse box. These boxes are specially designed and are provided by the railways on firm demand. However, when horse weagon are not available, ordinary cattle wagon can be used for transportation of six horses/brood mare along with their foals per wagon on broad gauge, 4 on metre gauge and 3 on narrow gauge. Attendants should be allowed to travel along with the animals in each wagon. In extreme summer, water should be sprinkled over the wagons by the railway authorities to bring down temperature. Ice slabs in specially made containers may be placed inside the wagon, if recommended by veterinarian. Every wagon should have two attendants if the animals are more than two in number. Animals should be loaded parallel to the rails, facing each other. Two breast bars should be provided on each side of the wagon, one at a height of 60 to 80 cm and the other at 100 to 110 cm.

Material for padding such as paddy straw should be placed on the floor to avoid injury if an animal lies down. This should not be less than 6 cm thick. Rations for the journey should be carried in the middle of the wagon.

To provide adequate ventilation, the upper door of one side of the wagon should be kept open and properly fixed. This door of the wagon should have wire gauge welded to it to prevent burning cinders from the engine entering the wagon and leading to the outbreak of fire.

Transportation by Road

Specially fitted vehicles with a special type of tail board and padding around the sides should be used. Ordinary lorries when used, may be provided with anti-slipping material on the floor. The superstructure, if low, should be raised. Bamboo poles of at least 8 cm diameter between each animal and two stout batons at the back should be provided to prevent the animal from falling.

To prevent horses being frightened or injured, their heads should face left of the vehicle, away from the passing traffic. Each lorry should carry 4 to 6 animals along with one attendant.

The speed of the truck in which equines are transported should not exceed 40 km per hour. All starting, stopping and turning should be done slowly. While transporting the animals, the truck should not be loaded with any other merchandise.

Fig. 22.1 Horse Float

Transportation by Air

In modern aircrafts, animals are either secured in crates of 2 to 3 horses each or kept tied in pens, 4 to 5 to each pen. The floors of aircrafts are protected by a thick layer of wood shavings and covered with polyethylene sheets and the sides of the aircraft body are well padded. All aircrafts for transporting animals shall be inspected for fittings, etc. and animals shall be administered tranquillizers before loading.

In addition, special attention should be given to the following points :

- Entires (stallions) and brood mares should not be accommodated in the same crate.
- Loading should be effected through ramps or lifts.
- An attendant should accompany the animal consignment.
- A veterinary first-aid kit with a veterinarian should always be available in the aircraft.
- Coir matting should be placed on the floor, so that loaded animals do not produce any sound during the journey.
- Hay bundles should be placed in between the hind legs and the sides of the aircraft.

Transportation by Sea

All ships to be used for conveying animals should be inspected for fittings. The ship may preferably be of shelter dock type with ample mechanical ventilation, good drainage and arrangements for exercising of animals.

Horses may normally be accommodated in single stalls and mules in pens, each pen holding 4 to 5 mules. Ample ventilation should be ensured by providing port holes and permanent air trunks or electric blowers on all decks. Exhaust fans should be installed to blowout foul air.

The pens should be mucked out twice a day and decks scrubbed once every 24 hours. This should be done when animals are being exercised. All standings should be thwart to the ship with heads facing inwards.

Length between breast rail and back lining should be 2 metres. Breast rails should be 1.10 m from the platform. Passage between two rows of pens should be not less than 1.5 metres. Parting boards between pens should be 3 metres.

To avoid distress, specially during hot weather, the ship may sail immediately after embarking. Disembarking should be done as early as possible after anchoring.

Entires (stallions) and brood mares should not be accommodated on the same deck. A pharmacy and spare stable for 5 per cent of animals should be provisioned.

Chapter **24**

Antimicrobial Therapy

In recent years, the problems that threaten the effectiveness of antimicrobials have appeared with increasing frequency. These problems include antibiotic resistant bacteria, transfer of drug resistance among organisms, effects of the host environment on antibiotic action and drug toxicity. Antimicrobial agents, whether administered singly or in combination, should not be considered "magic shots" but as adjuncts to the host's natural defence mechanisms. Accordingly, before administration of an antimicrobial agent is considered, attention should be directed towards maximizing the animal's natural defence mechanisms, and establishing the patient's nutritional, and other allied requirements.

Antimicrobial Agents

Any chemical substance inhibiting the growth or causing the death of a micro-organism is known as an antimicrobial agent. Most of the antimicrobial agents originate either as natural products of micro-organisms or are synthesized in the laboratory. Further, the words antibiotics and antimicrobial drugs are generally used synonymously for chemicals of natural, semi-synthetic, or totally synthetic origin that are used clinically for their action against pathogenic micro-organisms.

Antibacterial agents are usually classified bactericidal or bacteriostatic. A drug that causes the death of bacteria is termed bactericidal and the one that inhibits the growth of bacteria is referred to as bacteriostatic. Antibiotics that inhibit a single or only a few species of micro-organisms are said to have a narrow-spectrum of activity. The drugs against a variety of micro-organisms are said to have a broad-spectrum.

The antimicrobial agent must meet the following important criteria before being considered for use:

(a) It must be relatively non-toxic to the host.

(b) It must exhibit antimicrobial activity at low concentration when introduced into the body of an infected animal.

(c) Leave unaltered the host's natural defence mechanisms, such as phagocytosis and production of antibodies.

Choice of Antibacterial Drug

The selection of an antimicrobial agent for the treatment of an infection depends upon several factors including the patient's general physical condition, the aetiologic agent, site of infection or the organ system infected, host immuno-competence and the properties of antimicrobial drugs. Bactericidal drugs are preferable to bacteriostatic drugs whenever the immune defences of the host are compromised. Bactericidal drugs are also preferred in severe infections and also in the treatment of long standing infections so as to eliminate a pathogen to prevent relapses or carrier states. The site of infection is particularly important in selection of an antimicrobial agent as the antibiotic used should be able to penetrate the infected organ system.

The probable causative organism and its sensitivity is the most important factor in making the choice of an antibiotic. Because most infections are treated on an empirical basis, chemotherapy may be guided by a knowledge of the probable infecting organism although it may not be possible to isolate and identify it. Though, the best strategy for selection of drug is to determine the microbiological status (including sensitivity test) in the actual case, however, when this is not possible, the choice of drug can be based on microbiological profile of the stock.

Sometimes several different drugs may be effective against the same micro-organism and the choice of drug is determined by the ease with which it can be administered, its distribution in an effective concentration to the site of infection, the risk of producing undesirable side effects and cost of the antimicrobial product.

Antimicrobial Sensitivity Test (AST)

Susceptibility

The words susceptible and resistant are used somewhat indiscriminately. These are relative terms, as within an animal a micro-organism may be susceptible in one situation or at a specific site of infection and resistant in another. The most important parameter is the concentration of antimicrobial that inhibits the growth of the infection and organism or kills it outright. The concentration of antimicrobial agents that must be attained in the serum, body fluids or tissues to achieve the desired effect can be measured *in vitro* by the use of the sensitivity tests. Basically, all the tests presently in use, measure the minimal concentration necessary to inhibit growth (Minimal Inhibitory Concentration or MIC). However, if the worked out MIC of the drug cannot be achieved at the site of infection, the antimicrobial agent will ultimately be ineffective.

Collection and Handling of Specimens for AST

For the isolation of micro-organism and its worked out susceptibility to be reliable, it is important that the specimens for microbial culture must be collected and handled in a way that they are not altered by bacterial cell death, bacterial overgrowth or contamination with extraneous bacteria. It is essential to obtain such specimens before start of antimicrobial therapy. Material collected on sterile swabs should be despatched to laboratory in a suitable transport medium that prevents overgrowth or death of bacteria during transport. A word of caution: improperly collected and handled specimen will result in isolation of wrong organism whose AST results will be misleading.

Dosage Schedule and Route of Administration

The objective of an antimicrobial dosage regimen is to deliver a sufficient concentration of drug to the site of infection for an adequate period so that the infecting organisms are reduced to a number that will allow the host's defence mechanisms to eliminate those remaining organisms. The dosage regimen must at the same time, avoid the production of drug concentration toxic to the host. Most of the times, it is necessary to administer multiple doses of a drug to control an infection. Conventional dosage regimens for commonly used antimicrobial drugs in horses are presented in Table 23.1. However, several other factors e.g., route and frequency of administration, duration of therapy and bio-availability may influence the dosage schedule of a particular drug.

The main factors which influence the choice of route of administration are the forms available, the drug of choice, the infection site and the species of animal. Other factors include cost of preparation and convenience of administration.

The most satisfactory technique for maintaining therapeutic plasma concentrations at a steady state/level, is to administer the drug by continuous intravenous (I/V) infusion. Though there are practical limitations in use of this technique in veterinary practice, yet the use of this technique can be considered wherever possible. Of the extravascular parenteral administration, intramuscular (I/M) injections are by far the most frequently used. The local routes like intra-articular or sub-conjuctival injection and intra-mammary or intra-uterine infusion aim at directly placing high concentrations of antimicrobial agent close to the site of infection. These routes differ from the major parenteral routes because of the fact that the systemic availability is not a prerequisite for delivery of drug to the infection site. The combined use of systemic and local delivery of drug to the site of infection represents the optimum approach to treatment of conditions where the infection site may be relatively inaccessible, such as in a case of mastitis.

As for the oral administration, the oral preparations which are mostly in solid dosage forms, must dissolve before it can be absorbed. The ingredients of the dosage form can have a profound effect on dissolution of the active ingredients and thereby control its rate of absorption which can influence the effectiveness of therapy.

Table 23.1 : Conventional Dosage Regimens and Route of Administration for Some Antimicrobial Drugs in Horses

Name of drug	*Dosage/kg B.W.*	*Frequency of Administration*	*Route of Administration*
Ampicillin	7.5 to 10 and upto 22 mg	8 hourly	I/M, I/V
Chloramphenicol	30 - 50 mg	8 hourly	I/V, I/M
Erythromycin	10 mg	12 hourly	I/V
Gentamycin	5 mg	8 hourly	I/M
Kanamycin	10 mg	12 hourly	I/M
Neomycin	10 mg	12 hourly	Oral
Oxacillin	25 mg	12 hourly	I/V, I/M
Oxytetracycline	4 - 10 mg	24 hourly	I/V, I/M
Penicillin G Procaine	40,000-100,000 IU	12-24 hourly	I/M
Penicillin G Procaine Benzyl	15000 IU	12 hourly	I/M
Streptomycin	10 mg	12 hourly	I/M
Sulphamethylphenazole	100 mg initially	24 hourly	I/V
Sulphamethoxypyredazine	followed by 50 mg		
Griseofulvin	55 mg	24 hourly	Oral
Amikacin sulfate	(a) 7 mg	8 hourly	IM, IV
	(b) 22 mg	24 hourly	IM, IV
Amoxicillin sodium	11-50 mg	6-8 hourly	IM, IV
Amphotericin B	0.3-0.6 mg	4-8 hourly	IV (dilute, slow)
Cefazolln sodium	10-20 mg	6-8 hourly	IV
Cefotaxime sodium	20-30 mg	6-8 hourly	IV
Cefoxitin sodium	20 mg	4-6 hourly	IV
Ceftiofur sodium	2.2-5 mg	12-24 hourly	IM, IV
Ceftriaxone sodium	25-50 mg	12 hourly	IM, IV
Cephalexin	25-33 mg	6 hourly	Oral
Cloxacllin, sodium	10-30 mg	6 hourly	IM, IV
Erythromycin estolate, ethyisuccinate	25-37.5 mg	6-8 hourly	Oral
Fluconazole	4 mg	24 hourly	Oral
Furazolldone	4 mg	8 hourly	Oral
Metronidazole	20-25 mg	12 hourly	IV, IM, Oral, PR,,
Neomycin	2-6 mg	6-12 hourly	Oral
	4.4 mg	8-12 hourly	IV
Nitrofurantoin	2.5-5 mg	8 hourly	Oral
Spectinomycin	20 mg	8 hourly	IM
Sulphadimethoxine	55 mg	24 hourly	IV
Sulphadoxine/trimethoprim	15 mg	12-24 hourly	IM, IV (slow)
Sulfonamide/trimethorprim	15-30 mg	12-24 hourly	Oral, IV, IM
Vancomycin	20-40 mg	6-12 hourly	IV

Combination Therapy

Though a much debated subject, the combined use of antimicrobial drugs is advocated under certain circumstances in order to achieve a more effective or less toxic therapeutic regimen. There are several reasons for use of combination therapy which are summarized as follows:

(a) To achieve a synergistic effect when this is possible.

(b) To deal with those mixed infections which are not susceptible to one antibiotic.

(c) To delay the development of bacterial resistance.

(d) To reduce the risk of toxic effects by giving smaller doses of each antibiotic.

(e) To treat urgent cases before bacteriological diagnosis has been made.

Combined therapy is best carried out with therapeutic agents which attack entirely different chemo-receptors in the organism. There are, however, only very few instances where synergism between antibiotics has been demonstrated clinically. Some examples of potentiation of the antibacterial effect of some drugs or synergism are:

(a) A combination of Sulphamethoxazole and Trimethoprim acts against different pathways in the bacterial metabolism and together they are active against a wide range of bacterial pathogens.

(b) Greater effectiveness of a combination of Penicillin and Streptomycin compared with the use of each antibiotic alone.

(c) Combination of Sulphonamide and Colistin has been shown to have a synergistic effect *in vitro* upon *Pseudomonas aeruginosa*.

However, all combinations of antimicrobial drugs may not be synergistic and some can be even antagonistic. In addition, improper drug combinations may lead to alteration of the expected antimicrobial effect. Further, mixing of antimicrobial drugs with each other is required to be considered keeping in view their synergistic/antagonistic characteristic so as to avoid physical, chemical and pharmacological incompatibilities.

Side Effects of Antimicrobial Drugs

Various side effects develop in animals with the use of certain antimicrobial drugs. These side effects, which at times may even result into death of animals, limit the usefulness of antibiotics in treatment of certain diseases. For example, Penicillins may cause hypersensitivity, colitis-x syndrome, anaphylaxis and at times central nervous system disorders. Similarly, amino glyceride groups of antibiotics are known for their side effects leading to ototoxicity and cardiovascular depression. Tetracyclines may also cause diarrhoea, colitis-x syndrome and anaphylaxis. Other antimicrobial drugs containing trimethoprim may also result in anaphylactoid reaction whereas erythromycin administration at times may cause intense local reaction.

view their structure/antagonistic characteristic so as to avoid physical, chemical and pharmacological incompatibilities.

Side Effects of Antimicrobial Drugs

Various side effects develop in animals with the use of certain antimicrobial drugs. These side effects, which at times may even result into death of animals, limit the usefulness of antibiotics in treatment of certain diseases. For example, Penicillins may cause hypersensitivity, Coombs syndrome, anaphylaxis and at times central nervous system disorders. Similarly, aminoglycoside groups of antibiotics are known for their side effects leading to ototoxicity and neuromuscular depression. Tetracyclines may also cause diarrhoea, Coombs syndrome and anaphylaxis. Other antimicrobials like sulphonamides, trimethoprim may also result in anaphylactoid reaction whereas erythromycin administration at times may cause intense local reaction.

Chapter **25**

Important Diseases and their Prevention

BACTERIAL DISEASES

GLANDERS

Glanders is one of the most ancient of all diseases recognized. A scourge of solipeds, glanders was frequently seen in an acute form in the ass, in a sub acute form in the mule and in a chronic (or even latent) form in the horse. Because the causal organism, Burkholderia (Pseudomonas) mallei, survives so poorly outside these hosts, the disease was always most prevalent in horses massed for military purposes or in the growing cities and towns.

Burkholderia (Pseudomonas) mallei can produce glanders in a wide range of species including humans and carnivores.

History

The first recorded description of glanders is from the third century from *Aristotle*. In 1664, glanders was recognized as a contagious organism and in 1830, it's zoonotic potential was suspected. In the late 1800's, the Mallein test was developed for diagnosis of glanders. At the turn of the century the U.S., Canada and Great Britain all implemented glanders-control programmes.

During World War I, glanders was believed to have been spread deliberately to infect large numbers of Russian horses and mules on the eastern front. This affected the troops and supply convoys as well as artillery movement because of their dependence on horses and mules. Human cases of glanders also increased in Russia during and after World War I. It is widely held that the Japanese deliberately infected horses, civilians, and prisoners of war with glanders during World War II.

The United States studied glanders as a possible biological weapon in 1943-44 but did not weaponize it. The former Soviet Union is also believed to have been interested in *Burkholderia Mallei* as a potential biological weapon agent after World War II.

Glanders was eliminated from U.S. domesticated animals in the 1930's. Six unrelated cases of glanders occurred in 1945 among laboratory workers on a biologic-weapons programme at Camp Detrick, Maryland. One recent human case of glanders in a laboratory worker occurred in 2000. A microbiologist at USAMRIID (U.S. Army Medical Research Institute of Infectious Disease) contracted glanders in March 2000. He became febrile and presented with a mass in his left axilla. Despite the fact he received aggressive antibiotic therapy, he developed multiple splenic and hepatic masses and eventually respiratory distress. With continued antibiotic treatment he eventually recovered. A diagnosis of glanders was not confirmed until 2 months later, though a tentative diagnosis was suspected due to his work history. This was the first human case reported in the US since 1945. Despite the efficiency of spread in a laboratory setting, glanders has only been a sporadic disease in humans. No epidemics of human disease have been reported.

During the year 2004 and 2007,several cases of glanders have been detected amongst the local horses,mules and donkeys in various parts of Maharashtra and UP in India.

Aetiology

1. Burkholderia mallei share few bacteriological features in common with other members of the genus and its taxonomic position has always been problematical. It is Gram-negative aerobic bacteria.
2. Burkholderia mallei is an obligate parasite which does not

survive for more than about 6 weeks. Outside, it is very sensitive to sunlight and drying even when partly protected by the purulent exudates, it produces in its host. Horses usually acquire the infection by ingestion or inhalation. Transmission is through discharges from actively infected animals, although succinctly affected carriers are known to play a role in the dissemination.

3 After penetrating the mucosae passively, the organism, like the tubercle bacillus, has a marked propensity to travel and deposit itself in lymphatic tissues. It also infects pulmonary tissue where it is associated at first with microscopic inflammatory foci. These foci enlarge to from microscopic nodules and ultimately larger, chronic granulomata. A diffuse interstitial pneumonia can accompany this process. At any point during these events exudates containing the bacilli from the nodules can be discharged into the airways and so reach the upper respiratory tract. They can be seen in the congested and even haemorrhagic mucus membrane of the nasal cavity.

4 The bacillary organism may also infect the lymphatic tissues of the limbs where they give rise to farcy. Farcy comprises of a chronic lymphatic tract. As in the nasal cavity these lesions rupture to discharges purulent exudates. The exudates contaminate stables, tack, harness and utensils with Burkholderia (Pseudomonas) mallei and, is thus, a major source of infection for other animals and humans. The clinical and pathological events that follow inhalation (or cutaneous inoculation) of Burkholderia mallei are similar to those that occur after its ingestion.

Although, horses that have apparently recovered from the disease are resistant to further infection, they may suffer from the disease. In occult (latent) glanders, the pulmonary lesions are quiescent but can be provoked by stress into renewed development, leading to dissemination of the infection in the body and its release to the exterior. The reactivation of these quiescent lesions in the infected horses explains why in the past the severe strain of military operations was often associated with major outbreaks of the disease in the cavalry.

Although, humans are much more resistant to Burkholderia (Pseudomonas) mallei than Equidae, the organism can produce disease, which chronically affects the skin and subcutaneous tissues and can generalize with fatal consequences.

Diagnosis

Clinical glanders is distinctive once the nasal and cutaneous lesions have formed and Burkholderia (Pseudomonas) mallei is easily recognized in smears from such lesion. It is a Gram – negative, beaded rod about 1.5 μ to 2.0 μ in length and 0.3 μ to 0.5 μ in width. An affected horse can also be detected by serological methods and the complement fixation test (CFT) is generally regarded as the most reliable.

However, counter immune electrophoresis with appropriate antigen is fast and simple and is said to be as reliable as the technically more complicated CFT. The mullein test can also be employed to detect infected horses. Mallein is a protein produced by Burkholderia (Pseudomonas) mallei during growth. When it is inoculated Intradermally into the eyelid or instilled into the conjunctival sac, it gives rise to swelling of the eyelid and the formation of a purulent exudates in the eye of a glanderous animal within 24 hours. This test is indispensable for control of glanders.

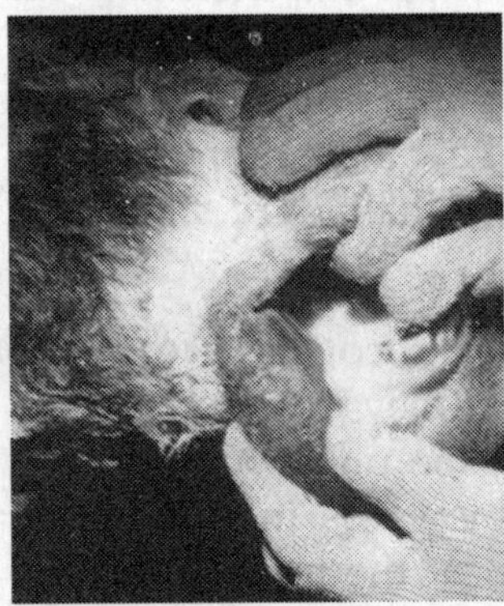

Fig. 24.1 A granulomatous lesion in the lip of a donkey in glander

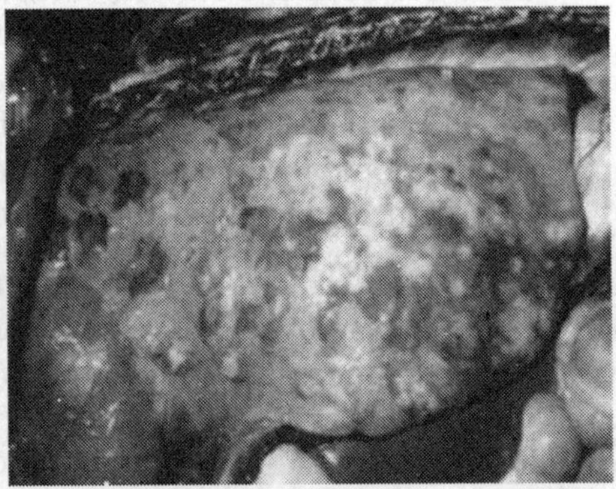

Fig. 24.2 Firm rounded miliary nodules in Lungs in glanders

Treatment and Control

The horse is essential to the persistence of Burkholderia (Pseudomonas) mallei. Consequently, no convincing case can be made for treating a horse with the confirmed disease or infection. The destruction of infected animals has eliminated the disease from the horse populations of many areas of the world.

STRANGLES (STREPTOCOCCAL INFECTION)

Introduction

Streptococci are probably the most frequently isolated pathogens of Equidae. The species and subspecies usually encountered are *Streptococci equi, Zooepidemicus* and *S. equisimilis* are the most host adapted and causes strangles, a suppurative lymphadenitis of the head and neck of horses of all ages. Streptococci equisimils is the least commonly isolated equine group "C" streptococcus and is occasionally isolated from uterine or placental samples and from abscessed lymph nodes and arthritic variation.

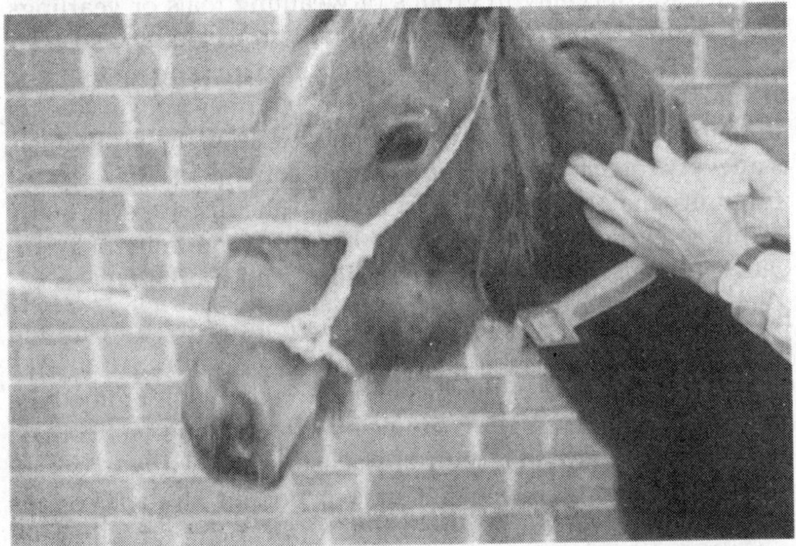

Fig. 24.3 Strangles in Horse : Swellon Submundibular lymph Node

Strangles is a highly contagious and serious infection of horses and other equids caused by streptococcus equi. While usually occurring in young equine, equine of any age lacking immunity from previous infection or vaccination may succumb. The disease is characterized by severe inflammation of the mucosa of the head and throat along with extensive swelling and often rupture of the lymph nodes, which produces large amounts of thick, creamy pus.

Aetiology

Strangles is caused by streptococcus equi which can be isolated from the nose or lymph nodes of affected animals, and is usually readily identified in the laboratory.

Epidemiology

The highly host-adapted Streptococcus equi maintained only in horse populations in which clinical disease is occurring. Survival is brief in the environment unless the organism is protected in moist discharges. Horses of all ages are susceptible, though strangles is most common in animals of less than 5 years of age and especially in groups of weanling foals or yearlings. Foals under 4 months of age are usually protected by colostrum derived passive immunity. Streposoccus equi is maintained in the horse population by carrier horses but does not survive for more than 6-8 weeks in the environment. Although the organism is not very robust, the infection is highly contagious. Pre-existing immunity may ameliorate expression of the disease. Morbidity in this age group may be up to 100% with a mortality of 1-5 %. Older animals show a lower morbidity and mortality.

Equine strangles is highly contagious and easily transmitted through bacteria found in discharges from an infected animal. Coughing will aerosol the bacteria throughout the immediate air stream. Transmission is either by direct or indirect contact of susceptible animals with a disease horse. Direct contact includes contact with a horse that is incubating strangles or has just recovered from the infection, or with an apparently clinically unaffected long-term carrier. Indirect contact occurs when an animal comes in contact with a contaminated stable (buckets, water trough, feed, walls, doors) or pasture environment (grass, fences), but almost always the water trough and flies. The incubation is typically 3 -12 days and the normally runs its course in 2-4 weeks. However, equine may shed the bacteria from 4 weeks to as long as 8 month after clinical signs resolve. Therefore, affected animals should be isolated from unexposed equines for prolonged periods. Convalescing animals can become chronic carriers. Immunity may last from 5-8 years after recovery., however, some equine may not develop immunity post – infection and are susceptible to reinfection.

Strepococcus zooepidemicus occurs widely as a mucosal communal of the nasopharynx and external genitalia of the horse and other host animals. An opportunist pathogen, it invades mucosal and epithelia surfaces damaged by virus infection or injury. It is the most commonly encountered pathogens in the horse and is isolated frequently from infected wounds and infection sites of older horses and from umbilicus of foals in the first few days of life.

Pathogenesis and Clinical Findings

The incubation period varies from 3 to 14 days after exposure. Any equine with abscessed lymph nodes of the head and neck and a high fever should be considered a strangles suspect. Common clinical include.

- Thick yellow discharge from nostrils and eyes.
- Swollen lymph nodes of the head and neck, often draining pus.
- Difficulty in swallowing, often with an extended neck.
- Fever up to 106°F
- Depressed with no appetite
- Coughing

Animals show typical signs of a generalized infectious process (depression, in appetence, sudden onset of fever (39.5- 40°C), loss of appetite, and halitosis) with nasal discharge (initially mucoid, rapidly thickening and purulent), a soft cough and slight but painful swelling between the mandibles, with swelling of the submandibular lymph node. Horses are often seen positioning their heads low and extended, so as to relieve the throat.

The occlusive effect of the node enlargement may result in suffocation unless emergency tracheotomy is performed. In most cases abscesses in affected lymph nodes rupture in 7-14 days after the first clinical signs. Suprapharyngeal lymph node abscesses usually drain the pharyngeal area resulting in a copious nasal flow of purulent material.

Although the disease process described above is classic, some horses (especially older animals) will develop a mild, short lasting disease without or with minor lymph node abscessation. This is thought to be the result of partial immunity. Streptococcus equi of relatively low virulence may also cause similar signs. Nearly 100 % of the animals in an exposed herd may be infected. but the mortality rate of strangles is usually less than 2%. Death generally occurs due to nervous system infections, pneumonia, or abscesses developing in the internal organs. **Strangles gets its descriptive name because swollen lymph nodes may cause airway obstruction and death due to asphyxiation.** The main and often fatal complications of strangles are.

- Bastard strangles, which describes the dissemination of infection to unusual sites other than the lymph nodes draining the throat. For example, abdominal or lung lymph nodes may develop abscesses and rupture, sometimes weeks or longer after the infection seems to have resolved. A brain abscess may rupture causing sudden death or a retro pharyngeal lymph node abscess may burst in the throat and the pus will be inhaled into the lung.
- Purpura Haemorrhagica, which is an immune-mediated acute inflammation of peripheral blood vessels may occur within 4 weeks of strangles, while the animal is convalescing. It results from the formation of immune complexes between the horse's antibodies and bacterial components. These immune complexes become trapped in capillaries

where they cause inflammation, visible pinpoint hemorrhages in the mucous membranes. These haemorrhages lead to a widespread severe oedema of the head, limbs, and other parts of the body. Purpura can also be a complication of routine vaccination.

Minor, non–fatal complications include:

- Post strangles myocarditis, may follow strangles in a small proportion of horses. An electrocardiogram (ECG) can determine such condition and whether horse can return to heavy work or to training after an episode of strangles.
- Purulent cellulites (inflammation of the subcutaneous tissue), which is an unusual occurrence where infection speeds locally in the subcutaneous tissues.
- Laryngeal hemiplegia (roaring) may follow abscessation of cervical lymph nodes.
- Anaemia may develop during the convalescent period because of immune–mediated lysis of red blood cells.
- Guttural pouch emphysema may be concurrent with classic strangles, or follow the immediate convalescent period. The 2 guttural pouches are large mucous sacs., each is a ventral diverticulum of the Eustachian tube, situated between the base of the cranium dorsally and the pharynx ventrally. They open into the nasal pharynx and each has a capacity of about 300 ml. Persistent infection in the guttural pouch may lead to inspissations (drying) of pus and, in some cases, the formation of a solid, stone–like, concretion called a chondroid. Animals that have persistent infection of the guttural pouches become the carriers, the major source of infection to spark outbreaks in susceptible horses with.
- Apart from long–term guttural pouch carriers, recovered horses may shed Streptococcus equi from their nose and in their saliva for up to 6 weeks following infection. Therefore, isolate all horses that have had strangles from susceptible animals for 6 weeks following infection.

Approximately 70 % of animals develop a solid, enduring immunity to the typical disease following recovery from strangles. This immunity is associated with mucosal Ig G and Ig A, and serum Ig G opsonic antibodies to the M protein.

Strepococcus zooepidemicus is a constant secondary invader of the upper respiratory tract mucosa as a sequel to influenza or herpes viruses. Many small purulent foci are produced in the lymphoid follicles of the mucosa and the resulting nasal discharge is mucopurulent. The draining lymph nodes often become enlarged and hardened and may become abscessed in some animals but abscessation is much less frequent. Affected animals have nasal and ocular discharges, cough, may be slightly febrile and lose body condition. Secondary pneumonia due to Strepococcus zooepidemicus occurs in a portion of foal populations infected with influenza virus and is responsible for much of the morbidity in this age group.

Strepococcus zooepidemicus is occasionally isolated from lesions of pleurisy or peritonitis. It is a common cause of joint ill in foals which may acquire infection in the birth canal. The organism enters the umbilicus and the ensuing bacteraemia result in sensorial infection, pyoarthritis, and permanent damage to the joints.

Diagnosis

Diagnosis can be confirmed by culturing pus from the nose. From abscessted lymph nodes or from the throat of clinically affected horses. Although Strepococcus equi isolates are thought to be genetically identical, isolates may vary in virulence (atypical isolates) which differ in their sugar tests from typical S. equi. **PCR** is more sensitive test and can detect 90% carriers but it is more expensive. A series of 3 nasopharyngeal swabs (e.g., swabs introduced through the nose to collect material from the back of the throat), evenly spaced over 2 or 3 weeks, will result isolation and identification of the organism and can detect 60% of carriers. For the detection of carriers, the laboratory should use a selective medium (Columbia blood agar with nalidixic acid and colistin).

Treatment

The equine group C streptococci are very sensitive to penicillin, erythromycin, chloramphnicol, cephalosporins and tetracyclines. Where appropriate, strangles is usually treated with doses of penicillin administered intramuscularly up to 10 million units. Since most cases recover uneventfully and develop enduring immunity, antibiotic administration is usually reserved for relief of life-threatening lesions that are intruding on the airway or for Strepococcus zooepidemicus infection in foals complicated by pneumonia. Similarly, penicillin is very effective for prophylaxis of in-contact animals.

However, antibiotics should be used with careful consideration as they may delay maturation and draining of abscesses and ablate the protective immune response.

There is argument that treatment in strangles will impair the development of immunity and may predispose an animal to prolonged infection and to bastard strangles. Treatment of a horse in the early stages of strangles is usually effective and is not associated with untoward effects. The causative agent is highly susceptible to penicillin G. If the disease is more advanced, then use of antibiotics may be avoided and nursing care be strengthened. Hot packs applied to abscess may expedite healing. Antibiotics may, however be used if complications arise.

Prevention

Strangles can be prevented from spreading by taking the following precautions:

- Vaccinate equine if strangles is endemic in the herd or on the farm. Both killed and a live vaccine are available for the control of strangles.
- Killed vaccines in general, are administered with an initial series of intramuscular injections followed by an annual booster. There may be adverse reactions at the injection site (marked pain, frank abscesses). Some animals may developed purpura Haemorrhagica following vaccination. The killed vaccines do not provide complete protection

but they do reduce the severity of clinical illness should it occur.

- An intranasal live attenuated vaccine is available in some countries for the prevention of strangles. The vaccine is administered twice, at an interval of 1-2 weeks. This approach to vaccination is more attractive than a killed, vaccine since it produces the nasopharyngeal antibodies necessary for protective immunity. Because the vaccine is a live but attenuated (using a low virulence organism) Strepococcus equi, take care to avoid contamination. Concurrent injection of other vaccines may result in Strepococcus equi abscesses at these sites, presumably through inadvertent contamination.
- Isolate new arrivals for two three weeks before introducing them to the herd. Check rectal temperatures twice daily for evidence of fever. Because fever usually develops two days before bacteria shedding, early detection of fever may prevent further transmission. A veterinarian should examine isolated equine having nasal discharge. Prompt diagnosis is important to prevent spread of the disease. Stop movements of equines on and off the infected premises.
- Disinfect stalls, water troughs, tack, and grooming utensils. Do not mix equipment between infected equine and other groups.
- Handle infected equine only after handling non infected animals. Wash hands, arms, footwear, etc. after handling infected animals.
- Thorough disinfection of the stables should be done. Bedding associated with infected equine should be burned. If burning is prohibited, the bedding should be composted under cover.
- Implement strict fly control measures by installing screens, electronic fly killers and using insecticides.
- Drying and sunlight can kill the Strangles bacteria. Phenolic disinfectants are recommended in equine facilities. Bleach and quaternary ammonium compounds quickly

become inactivated with organic matter, so it is important to thoroughly clean surfaces prior to disinfections. Effective disinfectants are povidone iodine, Chlorohexidine glutarldehyde, and phenol (1: 200).

- Investigation of carriers: It should be done either before a new animal introduced into a stable or at least 30 days following recovery of a horse from strangles. If an animal is positive, endoscopic evaluation of the guttural pouch is recommended, chondroids removed, and guttural pouches treated by flushing and infusion of million units of penicillin G in 3% gelatin. In addition, these horses should be treated with penicillin G intramuscularly for 7 days, isolated for 30 days, and then retested with the 3 consecutive series of nasopharyngeal swabs and culture. PCR is not usually recommended in these animals because it is so sensitive that it may identify dead bacteria and so give a "positive" reaction. Animals that remain positive should go through a repeat treatment and culture cycle.

ANTHRAX

The horse, like humans and the pig, is less susceptible to anthrax than ruminants. Nevertheless, when a horse is infected with Bacillus anthraces the course of the disease is acute and death usually occurs within days.

Aetiology

Bacillus anthraces is a large, non-motile, Gram-positive rod. The capsule is always formed in vivo by virulent strains but only in special circumstances in vitro.

Vegetative cells sporulate in the presence of air. Buffering and carbon dioxide inhibit the production of spores in the diseased animal. Unlike the vegetative forms, the spores are resistant to most disinfectants unless they are applied for prolonged periods at comparatively high temperatures.

Epidemiology and Pathogenesis

The persistence of Bacillus anthraces as a threat to animal health depends on a combination of environmental factors. There are well-recognized enzootic zones in the world (e.g. parts of the Indian subcontinent, Africa, North and South America) in which circumstances regularly favour the organism . In these areas the existence of alkaline and calcareous soils with suitable amounts of nitrogen and combination of a warm temperature (frequently < 15ºC), with periodic wetness promotes abundant multiplication of the vegetative bacilli. Decrease in the humidity and temperature in these enzootic areas promote sporulation and the extensive contamination of the soil and vegetation is further augmented by spores from the carcasses of animals dying from the disease. The spores can survive in soil for more than 60 years.

Sometimes in the subtropics or tropics biting flies inoculate Bacillus anthraces into the skin, but in general, anthrax is contracted by ingesting or inhaling the spores. When ingested, the spores lodge in the pharyngeal or enteric mucosae, and encapsulate. The capsule prevents phagocytes and destruction of the cell. The vegetative cells begin to produce toxin. The complete toxin is a complex of substances, which are encoded by a plasmid. Anthrax infections results only if the bacteria produce a capsule and exotoxins both of which are encoded on plasmids. Three factors which induces pathogenesis are oedema factor, protective antigen and lethal factor. Factor I, also known as Oedema factor is due to one component of the toxin (adenycyclase) which provokes massive oedema at the site of invasion. This event favours further multiplication and dissemination of the vegetative cells into the lymphatic system. Factor II is a substance for promoting the binding of factors I and III (a lethal substance) to mammalian cells. The lethal substance cause bacteraemia and Septicaemia when the lymphoid tissues can no longer contain the agent. Death usually follows within a few hours. The circulating toxin also produces general impairment of phagocytes, capillary permeability, irreversible damage to the clotting mechanism, and shock with renal failure. It is important to appreciate that in acute anthrax, the production of lethal amounts of the toxin precedes Septicaemia by several hours.

Clinical and Pathological Findings

The onset of the disease in the horse is sudden and course shows prodromal indications. Marked, subcutaneous swellings develop in the more dependent parts of the neck, thorat, abdomen and genitalia. Fever and extreme depression accompany severe colic and dysentery. Death follows these signs in a day or two. Rigour mortis is incomplete and uncloted, tarry blood oozes from the orifices of body. The pathological picture is one of haemorrhagic oedema and vascular damage throughout the body. There is haemorrhagic necrosis and gross swelling of all lymphoid organs.

Diagnosis

Diagnosis in a freshly dead animal is by microscopic examination of blood smears. The blood should be collected from a small superficial vein that is likely to ooze little when opened. Swabs of this blood are also normally required. Any leakage from the vessel should be stanched with swabs soaked in strong disinfectant or the vessel should be cauterized. The smears slides should be handled with caution because spores are likely to be present. The presence of blue, square-ended bacilli surrounded by large pink capsules which frequently have frilly edges is conclusive diagnosis. These bacilli are often in short chains.

Treatment and Control

Bacillus anthraces is very sensitive to a wide range of antibiotics, including penicillin and the tetracyclines. These drugs are curative if administered in massive doses to an animal before the toxin has produced irreversible damage. They also prevent the development of the disease in other animals within a group deemed to be at risk from exposure to a common source of infection.

In areas where the disease is known to constitute a more or less continuous threat, annual vaccination with anthrax spore vaccine (a non encapsulated strain with low virulance) should be done 30 to 60 days in advance of the usual anthrax season.

TETANUS

Aetiology

Clostridium tetani is a Gram - positive rod, about 0.5 μ in diameter and 2-5 in length micron μ and is typical of the toxigenic, speculating bacteria that comprise this genus of anaerobes. When sporulating, the vegetative organism develops a spherical spore at one end of the cell, giving rise to the characteristic morphological appearance of "drumsticks" in smears. The spores are very resistant to chemicals., even acidified phenol takes 2 hours or more to kill them under the most favourable circumstances. Oxidizing disinfectants, such as solutions of iodine, are faster and more reliable but steam, under pressure, is the surest method of destroying spores.

Epidemiology and Pathogenesis

Clostridium tetani is often abundant in equine faeces but it occurs in the gut of other herbivores and in the soil. The numbers in soils vary greatly, but the organism is especially abundant in warm areas with rich, well cultivated soils.

Tetanus occurs sporadically throughout the world, the prevalence in unprotected populations correlating with the numbers of spores in the soil. Mammals in general are susceptible to tetanus but, for reasons yet to be determined, the horse is the most susceptible animal and hence at greatest risk of developing the disease.

Clostridium tetani cannot excoriate or multiply in normal blood. In damaged tissues where necrosis and lowered oxygen tension combine to create a sufficiently anaerobic state, the organism multiplies and toxin is released. So although deep, penetrating and heavily contaminated wounds produce the most favorable circumstances for the organism to flourish, tetanus can develop after even minimal superficial damage provided an anaerobic state develops in the infected area.

In addition, one component of tetanus toxin, the haemolysin, is itself a necrotizing substance which contributes to the development of the conditions necessary for the replication of the agent and release of the neurotoxin, tetanospasmin, the major component of the toxin. The interaction between, tetanospasmin and its action on the nervous tissues and the way it is distributed in nerves, is responsible for the development of the clinical signs of tetanus.

To produce tetanus, tetanospsmin must be adsorbed by the gangliosides that are present in nervous tissues. Once this has occurred the binding is virtually irreversible, which explains why tetanus antitoxin is much more effective prophylactically than therapeutically, even when given in large doses.

When tetanospasmin is released by the organism multiplying in a wound, it enters the local motor and sensory nerves. If the production of toxin is abundant, free toxin also enter the capillary vessels and lymphatic channels. The organism itself does not spread from the site of injury. Tetanospasmin can reach the CNS via the nerves or through the blood. These two possible routes of distribution of the toxin in vivo give rise to ascendic tetanus, in which the movement of the toxin is along the motor nerve trunks to the cord or descending tetanus, in which toxin distributed by the vascular system, affects the voluntary muscles of the head and subsequently those of the trunk, forelimbs and then hind limbs. The skeletal muscles of the side of the body with the wound are affected before those of the opposite side. The action of tetanospasmin in nervous tissues is multiple contractions of muscles simultaneously when stimulated, in contrast to the normal state where contraction of one muscle is accompanied by relaxation or inertia in its counterpart.

Clinical and Pathological Findings

The incubation period of tetanus is very variable. It generally ranges from 1 to 3 weeks after the injury, although some cases have been attributed to wounding that occurred a few months previously. Usually the longer the incubation period the more favourable the prognosis

The horse suffers from descending tetanus, which is marked by an inability to retract the nictitating 'membranes and spasms in the facial muscles, producing in the an appearance resembling the lockjaw. Premonitory signs include continuously pricked ears, stiffness, trembling and increasing difficulty in eating chewing, and making other natural movements. As the disease develops all muscular responses become exaggerated. Hyperesthesia increases so that the slightest sensory stimulus provokes violent contractions of the skeletal muscles. The limbs are rigid, the fore limbs stick out forward and the hind limbs back in a "Sawhorse" stance. Sweating is profuse, the heart rate increases and the repeated, uncontrollable spasms interfere with breathing. The body temperature rises in the later stages of the disease when the horse experiences spontaneous convulsions. Eventually, the muscular contractions are violent and continuous and can be provoked by the the most minor external stimulus.

Diagnosis

The clinical disease is remarkably distinctive. Only eclampsia in the mare and laminitis, in which there is no prolapsed of the nictitating membrane, are likely to be confused with tetanus.

Treatment and Control

Despite the virtually irreversible effect of the toxin on nervous tissue, large doses (300,000 IU/kg IV every 12 hours for 36 hours) of tetanus antitoxin parentrally prevents more nervous tissue being drawn into the pathological process and neutralizes the entire toxin that is in the vascular system. Any good effect obtainable from antitoxin is likely to be limited to the earlier stages of the disease. If antitoxin (50 000 IU) is injected into the subarachnoid space the outcome may be more successful. The precipitating wound, if found, should be drained and infused with penicillin. Penicillin should also be given repeatedly in large doses (22000 IU/ kg IV q.i.d. or IM m.i.d.) to kill the organism and prevent yet more toxin being released.

The risk of tetanus is so great after wounding or surgery that immunoprophylaxis against the disease is essential in horses. Boosting dams with tetanus toxiod about 6 weeks before parturition enhances the immunity acquired by foals in the colostrum. Foals can also be protected passively by giving antitoxin (approximately 3000 IU) parentrally which protects for about 2 weeks and can be repeated until the foal is competent enough immunologically to respond actively to tetanus toxoid, as they are when 2-3 months old.

Tetanus toxoid with adjuvant is a highly immunogenic antigen, which induces a durable, active immunity even if given simultaneously with antitoxin, provided separate sites are used for the respective injections. Despite the marked immunogenicity of tetanus toxoid, two doses about 4-6 weeks apart are needed to produce an adequate active immunity against the tetanospasmin. Solid immunity is usually established in about 2- 4 weeks after the course is completed.

The immunity created by a course of toxoid also needs to be reinforced at regular intervals, as per the degree of risk and the immunological responsiveness of the individual horse. One year after the primary course, a boosting dose of toxoid should be given and followed by further doses every 18-36 months, the timing being dependent on the perceived risk

ULCERATIVE LYMPHANGITIS

Ulcerative lymphangitis is a mildly contagious disease of horses characterized by inflammation of the lower limbs. Classical disease is caused by *Corynebacterium pseudotuberculosis,* but similar lesions can be produced by other phylogenic bacteria.

Epidemiology

The disease is primarily seen in horses, but may also affect cattle. Ulcerative lympangitis is widely distributed in regions where horses are found and tends to be sporadic. Infection occurs through abrasions in the lower limb and most likely when horses are crowded in unhygienic conditions . The disease is due to infection of skin lesions with phylogenic bacteria and is not highly infectious.

Clinical Signs

The disease is due to infection of skin wounds, which is followed by infection of lymphatic vessels and the development of abscesses along their course. The following signs are seen:

- Infected wound on the lower limb
- Swelling and pain
- Lameness
- Subcutaneous nodules particularly around the fetlock
- Ulcers
- Initial ulcers may heal, but secondary ulcers are common. The disease can persist for up to several months.

Post-mortem Findings

Nodular abscesses in the sub-coetaneous tissues that may rupture and discharge creamy green pus. Lymphatic draining the area are enlarged with secondary ulcers along them.

Diagnosis

Ulcerative lymphangitis may be confused with other disease such as:

- Glanders
- Epizootic lymphangitis
- Sporotrichosis

As the first two are important to confirm the diagnosis. Samples and swabs of the pus from discharging lesions should be collected for bacterial culture.

Control

Local treatment of ulcers is usually sufficient to control the disease. Parenteral antibiotics may be necessary in severe cases. The disease can be prevented by good hygiene in stables and disinfection of lower limb injuries.

EPIZOOTIC LYMPHANGITIS

Epizootic lymphangitis is a contagious disease of equines due to fungus, *Histoplasma capsuatum farciminosum.*

Epidemiology

Equines, mainly horses suffer from this disease. Rarely it can affect camels, cattle and humans.

Currently it is reported from many African regions. However, in the past it has been pesent in several countries of Europe, Asia and America.

The disease is transmitted by contamination of skin wounds or direct abrasions by flies or grooming objects. The fungus could survive in the soil as a saprophytic organism.

Clinical Signs

Initial lesions take few weeks to 3 months to appear and consist of a painless swelling and ulcer at the site of entry. The nodule is intradermal and is freely moveable over the subunits. Oedema progresses in the region and the nodule gradually enlarges and ultimately bursts. The surrounding tissues become hard, variably painful and swollen.

The infection spreads along lymph vessels and causes cord-like lesions, leading to diffuse and irregular involvement of an area of skin. After the initial lesion increases in size, additional cycles of eruption and granulation lead to progressively smaller areas of ulceration. Spontaneous recovery usually occurs in 3-12 months and leave scars. Occasionally severe arthritis where lesions are closed to joints, conjunctivitis or keratconjunctivitis, and a serous or purulent nasal discharge may be observed.

Rarely cause death, lesions are confined to external tissues, lymph nodes and vessels.

Differential Diagnosis

- Ulcerative lymphangitis
- Glanders
- Cryptococcosis
- Sporotrichosis

- Strangles

Diagnosis

7 Swabs of pus, smears or histological sections of the lesion can be used to demonstrate presence of the fungus by coloration, culture or PCR. Serological tests are available and include FAT (fluorescent antibody), ELISA and passive haemagglutination tests.

Treatment and Control

Treatment with Amphotecin B can be efficient. Killed and live vaccines exist but are not readily available. Eradication of the disease on a particular farm may be achieved by slaughtering of chronic cases not responding to treatment coupled with strict hygiene practices.

MELIOIDOSIS

Melioidosis is a bacterial disease caused by *Burkholderia (Pseudomonas) pseudomallei.* It is primarily a disease of rodents that can spread to many species of animals, including humans. Heavy mortalities have been reported in sheep.

Epidemiology

Many species of animals are susceptible including birds, goats, sheep, pigs, horses, rodents and humans. There are also reports of infections in dolphins, tropical fishes and non-human primates. It is potentially fatal in humans.

Meliodosis occurs mainly in tropical countries. It is present in South East Asia and also occurs in Australia.

In subtropical regions the main sources of infection are contaminated soil, mud and water.

Insect bites and cutaneous abrasions, ingestion and inhalation can also be a source of Infection. Rodents appear to be the main reservoir of the organism. Goats' milk has been found to be infected and drinking raw goats' milk is a potential hazard. Direct animal to human transmission is rare.

Clinical Signs

The disease may be acute or chronic, and clinical signs vary according to the location of lesions. Cases tend to be sporadic. Symptoms in horses are

- Metastasis pneumonia
- Fever
- Colic and diarrhoea
- Lymphangitis on the legs
- Affected horses may survive for months with emaciation and oedema.
- Rare cases of nervous disorders have been described.

Post-mortem Findings

The major finding is multiple abscesses that can occur in most organs, particularly the subcutaneous tissues, regional lymph nodes, lung spleen and liver. The pus is tick or caseous, and green-tinged similar to infections with *Corynebacterium pseudotubercuilosis.*

Differential diagnosis

Other conditions producing multiple abscesses in various organs include:

- Tuberculos
- Caseous lymphadenitis
- Actinobacillosis

In horses meliodosis could be confused with ;

- Strangles
- Glanders

Diagnosis

Swabs of nasal discharges and abscesses should be submitted for culture and bacteriological examination. Blood samples should also be sent for ELISA and immuno-fluorscence tests.

Control

Attempts to treat cases by giving antibiotics have been disappointing. Because of the risk to humans, It is preferable to slaughter affected animals and destroy the carcass. The premises should also be disinfected thoroughly.

VIRAL DISEASES

EQUINE RABIES

Equine rabies is a sporadic, but highly fatal, zoonotic disease caused by a Lyssavirus. The incidence of rabies in horses compared with that in many other animals, is low but the disease is of importance because rabid horses may serve as a source of infection for humans as infected horses may become aggressive and attack humans and other animals.

Aetiology

Rabies is caused by a neurotropic rhabdo virus of Rhabdoviridae family that belongs to genus Lyssavirus. The virus is quite fragile and is readily destroyed by heat, desiccation, ultraviolet light and most disinfectants. It can, however, survive in a refrigerated carcass for several days.

Epidemiology

Horses are moderately susceptible to rabies and usually become infected by the bite of a rabid animal that is acting strongly and may bite on the muzzle, face and/ or lower legs.

Infection by inhalation, which may occur in a cave inhabited by rabid bats, or by the oral or tran placental route is unlikely to play a significant role in the epidemiology of the disease in horses. Rabid dogs and cats are a threat to horses and other domestic animals but wild animals are the most likely source of virus in many countries.

Pathogenesis

Rabies virus infect the body by salivary contamination of a bite wound. The virus replicates in the muscles at the site of the bite before invading the axons of the peripheral nerves and Spreading centripetally to the brain stem and spinal chord. Once the virus enters the spinal cord it spreads rapidly throughout the Central nervous system (CNS). It is thought that the cerebrospinal fluid may be involved in the spread of the virus at this stage. The virus replicates in the CNS and spreads centrifugally along peripheral nerves to other parts of the body. High concentrations of virus are shed in the saliva.

As the virus is present in the nervous system for much course of the disease, the immunological response to infection is often minimal. The virus infects the central nervous system and destroys nerves, causing paralysis and death.

Clinical Signs

The incubation period usually varies from 2 to 9 weeks but can extend up to 5 month. The clinical signs are extremely variable and rabies should be considered in the differential diagnosis when a horse is presented with rapidly progressive neurological disease, especially in countries where rabies is endemic.

Terminally, the signs are those of diffuse CNS disease but documented cases indicate that the early signs differ greatly between individuals. They include lameness, pyrexia, anorexia, muscle tremors, colic, ataxia, profuse salivation, teeth grinding and frequent whining. The disease usually progress to death within 4 to 5 days, although some horses will survive up to 15 days.

Two clinical forms of rabies are recognized in the horse as in other species: the dumb or paralytic and furious form. Horses, which develop the dumb form often depicts ascending paralysis, ataxia and faecal and urinary incontinence. Muscle tremors were the most frequently observed (81%) and most common initial sign. Other common signs included: difficulty in swallowing (71%), in coordination or paralysis (71 %) and difficulty in standing. Horses become recumbent, make paddling movement with forelegs and dig in the floor.

Horses, which develop the "furious form" show excitement,

become vicious, kick, exhibit blind staggers, suddenly fall and may salivate profusely and chew themselves or foreign objects. Horses may behave erratically at a particular site of the body. Such cases usually deteriorate rapidly and paralysis, convulsions and death ensue.

Diagnosis

Ante–mortem laboratory examinations are of limited diagnostic value. Measurement of antibody tires against rabies in serum or cerebrospinal fluid, or examination of skin biopsies or corneal smears by immunfluorescence test may give diagnostic positive result but a negative result does not preclude rabies as a possible diagnosis. If an animal is only suspected to have rabies and is not showing clinical signs, strict isolation can be attempted for up to 3 month.

The post-mortem diagnosis of rabies can be made from examination of the brain using FAT (Fluorescent Antibody Test). Histological examination for the presence of ***Negri's bodies,*** the characteristic large eosinophillic cytoplasm inclusions, which occur in ganglion cells and neurons, is reported to identify 85 % of positive cases.

Prevention and Control

The elimination of stray dogs and cats together with the immunization of pets, plays a major role in the control of the disease in developing countries. It is recommended that horses receive a single 2 ml dose of vaccine starting at three months of age, repeated at one year of age, followed by annual re-vaccination.

EQUINE INFLUENZA

Equine influenza is a major virus disease that causes flu like symptoms in horse and donkeys. The virus affects respiratory epithelium from the nose to the lungs.

Aetiology

The influenza virus (RNA virus) belong to the family

orthomyxoviridae genus influenza virus. There are two distinct strains of this virus i.e. A/Equi 1 and A/Equi 2. The latter A/ Equi 2 is move severe and vide spread than A/Equi 1. A with the subtypes H7 N7 and H3 N8 . They are categorized on the basis of the antigenicity of their internal proteins and are divided into two subtypes on the basis of the antigen city of the surface proteins i.e. haemagglutinin (H) and neuraminidase (N).

Epidemiology

Equine influenza is contracted by inhalation. There is no evidence that horses become chronically infected with the virus. Epidemics often start at equestrian events where horses congregation period varies from 1 to 5 days and depends primarily on the size of the virus challenge. The virus into the atmosphere contribute to the rapid spread of the disease.

In a susceptible group of horses, morbidity can be as high as 100%. Mortality is usually low but can be as 10% depending upon the immune status of the horses at the time of exposure, the environment and the animals that are subjected to be disease.

During the year 1987 the severe outbreak of the disease was reported in India with heavy morbidity and mortality. Over 83000 equines suffered from the disease. A high morbidity (80-100%) was observed in horses donkeys and mules at various places. The disease involved all categories of horses, and donkeys without any variation due to age, sex or breed.

Secondary complications like strangles, purpura haemorrhagica, chronic bronchiolitis, chronic alveolar pulmonary emphysema were noticed in some of the sick equines which were either not given sufficient rest, adequate therapy or were kept under poor stable hygienic conditions.

The entry of equine influenza in India was attributed due to the importation of large contingent of horses from France. These landed at Delhi in the last week of December 1986 and January 1987 and were distributed to some of the farms in Northern India. Subsequently, equine sports events held at Delhi during January/February resulted into the spread of the disease to

Madhya Pradesh, Uttar Pradesh, Delhi, Haryana, Punjab, Chandigarh and Jammu & Kashmir.

The causative virus A/Equi-2 (H3 N8) type was isolated by NRCE, Hissar, India and were designated as A/Equi-2/ Ludhiana/87 and A/Equi-2/Bhiwani/87 as per place of their origin.

Pathogenesis

The virus infects the ciliated epithelial cells of the upper and lower airways.

The cells then damaged by the virus, which leads to:

- A decreased ability to clear bacteria and foreign substances from the lungs
- Bronchitis and pneumonia can then develop if bacterial infection occurs
- When the body tries to rid itself of the virus, the horses gets a fever and may become sick, stop eating, and cough a lot.

Clinical Signs

Both subtypes of equine influenza viruses produce similar clinical signs in horses, but A/Equi 2 infections are usually more severe. The first sign is an elevation in body temperature (up to 41 °C which is usually biphasic). This is followed, within a few hours to a maximum of 2 days, by a dry deep cough. The other most commonly observed clinical signs are serous nasal discharge, which may become mucopurulant. Oedema of the legs and scrotum is sometimes observed. Spasmodic and impactive colic have also been reported in some cases.

Horses usually recover clinically from uncomplicated influenza within 10 days but coughing may persist for long. Secondary bacterial infection prolongs the recovery period. Pneumonia may occur in foals, horses that are stressed by tenuous exercise and donkeys which are more susceptible to influenza than horses.

A/Equi 2 virus is more pneumotropic than A/Equi 1 virus and

have also been associated with myocarditis. Pregnant mares may abort the foetus as a result of fever. Sequelae of equine influenza can include chronic pharyngitis, chronic bronchiolitis, alveolar emphysema which can contribute to COPD, sinusitis and guttural pouch infections.

Equine influenza may be mild even asymptomatic in horses protected by recent or regular vaccination or by previous exposure.

Pathogenesis

The virus infects the ciliated respiratory epithelial cells, which become vacuolated, oedematous and loose their cilia before being desquamated. This impairment of the clearance mechanism increases the susceptibility of the respiratory tract to secondary bacterial invasion. Damage to the respiratory epithelial cells can occur within 1 day after the onset of symptoms. Regenration may begin a few days later but complete resolution may take up to a month, long after the horse appears clinically normal.

Diagnosis

The classical signs of influenza that are seen in unvaccinated horses are easy to recognize. The two major features of the disease are its rapid and dry deep cough. Diagnosis of equine influenza in a vaccinated population is more difficult as the clinical signs may resemble more closely than those caused by other pathogens such as equine rhinovirus, equine herpes virus or bacterial infection than classical influenza. A presumptive diagnosis of influenza based on clinical signs should be confirmed with appropriate laboratory confirmation.

- Virus Isolation - Nasal swab samples are taken by passing a swab as far as possible into the horse's nasopharynx to absorb respiratory secretions. Immediately transfer swabs to a container with virus transport medium and transport the sample on ice to the lab.
- Serological Testing - Pared serum sample collected in early stage of the disease and 3 weeks later showing a four fold increase of antibody titre is confirmatory.

- HI test, CF test and ELISA are also used for serological diagnosis. 1
- Other test – a wide range of laboratory tests are available that allow more rapid diagnosis of influenza. There are now commercial influenza detection kits available devised for diagnosis of human influenza, which can be used by the vet to detect equine influenza. Nasal swabs are taken and virus can be detected in only 15 minutes to obtain a result.
- If horses are vaccinated in the face of infection, it is not possible to determine whether the increase in antibody levels is due to vaccination or infection.

Management

The standard recommendation for the management of equine influenza is complete rest and administration of a course of antibiotics or sulphonamides to prevent bacterial infections. A non –steroidal anti- inflammatory drug (NSAID) can be used in cases of high fever to prevent excess pulmonary inflammation and abortion in mares.

There is no cure for the flu, but steps should be taken to decrease the severity of the illness

- Horses should get one week of complete rest for every day they have an elevated temperature.
- Return to work should be gradual
- Resting the horses will :
  - ☐ reduce the severity of the clinical sign
  - ☐ reduce the recovery period
  - ☐ minimize chronic dIseases after the horse recovers
  - ☐ decrease virus shedding, thus reducing the risk of transmission to other horses
  - ☐ Adequate fresh water should be provided with electrolytes
- Clinical signs should be monitored daily for signs of secondary bacterial infection

- If secondary bacterial infection occurs, obtain samples for bacterial culture and antibiotic sensitivity test for appropriate treatment.

Previously healthy adult horses usually recover from uncomplicated **influenza** within 10 days, however,

- Coughing may persist for long
- If secondary bacterial infection occurs it can prolong the recovery period
- Complications from bacterial infections may cause death in adult horses.
- *Complications include*:

  Pleuritis

  Pneumonia

  Purpura haemorrhagica
- Increased risk of heaves, sinusitis and guttural pouch infections
- Relatively high death rates have been recorded in foals, animals in poor condition and donkeys.

Vaccination

Vaccinated horses are less susceptible to the disease than unvaccinated or inadequately vaccinated horses. The equine influenza vaccines, currently available are inactivated. Safe live attenuated vaccines have proved very difficult to develop because of the inherent mutability of the virus. Current vaccines contain either whole or subunit viral antigens, usually combined with an adjuvant such as aluminum hydroxide.

Intra nasal vaccines use a modified live equine influenza virus that can grow only at the cooler temperatures found in the horse's nasal passages and upper airways, where it induces a potent immune response. Because the vaccine virus cannot grow at the higher temperatures found in the lungs and the lower airwards, it does not cause respiratory disease. The Vaccination Protocol for horses are as follows:

Performance Horses

- Annual vaccination for racehorses and competition horses is mandatory in several countries.
- Timely additional booster vaccinations to be given prior to such events where horses will be exposed to the virus.

Recreational Horses

- Recreational horses are at less risk of contracting influenza if they are not commonly exposed to other horses.
- If your horse will be mixing with other horses at non - competitive events, it is at higher risk of getting the flu.

Breeding horses

- Brood mares should be vaccinated in the later stages of pregnancy, but not later than 2 weeks prior to foaling.
- This will ensure the foal receives a good supply of maternal antibodies in the colostrums.

Foals

- Vaccination of foals when they still have high levels of maternal antibodies (From the colostrum) is not recommended as it may lead to the induction of tolerance.
- Vaccinate foals after maternal antibody titers have declined to negligible levels, usually at around 6 month of age. Foals from non–immunized dams should be vaccinated earlier, at about 3 months of age.

FEI Vet Regulation for Equine Influenza Vaccination

The FEI requires all horses competing in FEI competition to provide evidence of sufficient vaccination against equine influenza. Vaccination against equine influenza is an important deterrent to equine respiratory disease amongst FEI competition horses and is essential for health regulatory reasons. The vaccination protocol involves regular six monthly booster vaccinations following a primary vaccination course. The primary course is essential to stimulate initial immunity and for an optimal effect of subsequent booster vaccinations.

All horses and ponies for which an FEI passport or a national passport approved by the FEI has been issued, must have the vaccination section completed and endorsed by a veterinarian, stating that it has received two injections for primary vaccination against equine influenza, given between 21 and 92 days (i.e., 1-3 months) apart. In addition, a booster vaccination must be administered within each succeeding 6 months (± 21 days) following the second vaccination of the primary course. None of these vaccination must have been given within the preceding 7 days including the day of the competition or of entry into the competition stables.

The above are the minimum requirements for influenza vaccination. The primary course and subsequent booster vaccinations should be given according to the manufacturer's instructions that will fall within the stipulation of the FEI ruling. If a horse is not competing in FEI competitions for an extended period, at least the manufacturers' recommendations for booster vaccinations should be followed.

EQUINE VIRAL ARTHRITIS (EVA)

Introduction

Equine Viral Arteritis (EVA) is a contagious respiratory disease of equines, so named characteristic inflammatory lesions induced by the causal virus in the smaller blood vessels, of the acutely infected animal. However, clinical disease is a relatively rare occurrence. It is the abortigenic potential of the virus which cause international concern and often leads to restrictions on movement of seropsitive horses.

Aetiology

Viral arteritis of horses, donkeys and mules is caused by toga virus. EVA is an enveloped spherical RNA virus. It was formerly classified as a non–arthropod born toga virus but now recognized as a member of corona virus–like super family. One serotype is recognized although there are various strains and considerable genome variations.

Serological surveys indicate that the equine viral arteritis virus is widely distributed throughout the world. Considerable diversity is present between geographically isolates of the virus. Similarly, there is variability in pathogenicity among strains with some strains capable of causing the range of clinical signs collectively referred to as EVA, and others eliciting nothing other than a low to moderate febrile response.

Equine arteritis virus is not a resistant virus outside the body and is readily inactivated. It is sensitive to sunlight, high temperatures and low humidity and various disinfectants and lipid solvents. However, viability of the virus is preserved at refrigeration and freezing temperatures. Equine arteritis virus can remain infective in frozen semen for very lengthy periods of time, extending to many years.

Epidemiology

In spite of the apparent world wide distribution of EVA, disease outbreaks appear to be infrequent and sporadic in nature.

The virus is transmitted by the respiratory and venereal routes and to a lesser extent by indirect contact with fomites. The greatest concentration of virus is usually shed via the respiratory tract: shedding can last for up to 16 days. Aerosol transmission is the most significant means of spread of EVA either on breeding farms or wherever horses come into close contact with one another, for example, at racetracks, shows, sales etc. Aborted foetuses are heavily contaminated with virus and are a source of infection. It is transmitted in two ways.

(a) Horizontal Transmission: Predominantly by nasal fluid, but also by urine faeces, Lacrimal fluid and vaginal discharge. Aside from virus spread by direct contact, it can also, though infrequently, be transmitted indirectly by means of apparel, breeding shed equipment, etc. contaminated with infective secretions/ excretions.

(b) Venereal Transmission: Mainly from stallion to susceptible mares. Carrier stallions play a critical role in the spread of the virus. A high proportion of EVA-infected stallions (1:3) may become long-term carriers and shed virus constantly in the sperm-rich portion of their semen. The carrier state has only been identified in the stallion and not in the mare, gelding or sexually immature colt. Equine arteritis virus is localized in certain accessory sex glands in the chronically infected stallion. Establishment and persistence of the carrier state has been shown to be testosterone dependent.

Transmission of virus may also occur by the congenital route, resulting either in abortion or in the birth of a congenitally infected, live but diseased foal. In such instances, the placenta, placental fluids and the foetus are plentiful sources of virus. Initial venereal transmission is followed by lateral spread of virus via the respiratory route. The incubation period after venereal exposure is usually approximately 1 week . The incubation period after respiratory exposure to virus is from 3 to 14 days. The mortality rate in natural outbreaks is very low.

Clinical Signs

Clinical signs of EVA infection are extremely variable and the majority of the cases are clinically in apparent. Onset of clinical signs is preceded by an incubation period of 3 to 14 days, which varies with the route of infection. It is shorter in the case of aerosol exposure and longer where transmission occurs by the venereal route.

The most common clinical signs are:

(a) Upper respiratory disease with systemic signs including oedema and respiratory distress.

- Fever up to 41 °C that can last for 2 to 9 days;
- A variable degree of anorexia and depression;
- Leucopenia;
- Limb oedema which is most pronounced in the lower hind limbs but may involve all four limbs;
- A serous to mucoid nasal discharge associated with a variable degree of rhinitis;
- Supraorbital or paraorbital oedema;
- Conjunctivitis of varying severity commonly referred to

as "pink-eye";

- Photophobia, most frequently observed in cases with severe conjunctivitis;
- Oedema involving the scortum and prepuce of the colt/stallion and the mammary glands of the mare;
- Urticarial rash which may be localized and occur as small, discrete lesions usually on the cheeks, sides of the neck or pectoral region, or it may be generalized and present as popular rash over most of the body.

(b) Other clinical signs that may be observed less frequently include:

- Oedematious swellings in the intermandibular space, beneath the sternum, the shoulder region or other parts of the body;
- Respiratory distress, including tachypnoea, coughing, and dyspnoea especially in young foals;
- Diarrhoea;
- Posterior paresis and ataxia;
- Sub maxillary lymphadenopathy;
- Popular eruptions on the mucous membrane inside the upper lip, these are usually found in association with skin rash.

- Gingival and buccal erosions.

(c) Abortions – Not necessarily associated with clinical disease and occur 12 to 30 days after exposure during the 3 rd to 10th months of gestation.

(d) Oedema of mammary gland is frequently seen in mares and the majority of stallions develop scrotal oedema.

(e) Mortality in natural cases of EVA infection occurs infrequently in neonatal foals that are usually congenitally infected with the virus, these succumb from interstitial pneumonia within 48 to 96 hours of birth. Deaths have also been reported in foals, a few weeks to months of age, that develop a rapidly progressive pneumonia and enteritis.

Clinical Pathology

No characteristic changes in serum biochemistry and haemogram.

Diagnosis

The diagnosis of EVA cannot be made, based solely on the clinical signs without corroborative virus isolation. Serological diagnosis of EVA is based on seroconversion. If the first serum sample is collected during the acute stages of the disease the convalescent serum sample should be taken 14-28 days later. The Serum Neutralization Test, and CFT are probably the most popular test for EVA detection.

Diagnostic confirmation is by virus isolation from blood, sperm-rich fraction of semen, nasopharyngeal swabs or tissues. Histological lesions of arteritis in small arteries are the characteristic signs of this disease and serve to differentiate it from E/A which is also accompanied by petechiation of mucosa and joindice in acute cases.

Post Mortem Findings

The gross and microscopic lesions associated with EVA are consistent with the predilection of the virus for the media of the arteries and the prominent microscopic lesion widespread necrotizing arteritis of small arterities. Pathological examination of the aborted fetuses revealed oedema of the eyelids, oedema of lungs, increased pleural fluid and petechial haemorrhages of the pleural and peritoneal surfaces. Haemorrhages and infarction in the spleen and degeneration in liver and kidneys. There are characteristic histological changes in the small arteries.

Management and Control

The spread of EAV can be limited by restriction of movement of horses from affected premises, strict quarantine and hygiene measures.

Two vaccines have been developed against EVA, a modified live virus vaccine (Arvac, Ft. Doage Animal Health) and an inactivated adjuvant virus vaccine (Artervac Ft. Dodge Animal Health). Vaccination with a modified live EAV vaccine, especially of stallions, foals and seronegative mares results in good protection. The vaccine manufacturers advise against its use in pregnant mares and foals less than 6 week of age. The inactivated vaccine, though safe for use in pregnant mares, is not as strongly immunogenic as the modified live virus vaccine. Two or more vaccinations are frequently required to stimulate a detectable neutralizing antibody response.

Seronegative mares should not be mated with seropositive stallions because of risk of transmission of infection. Seropositive mares, or mares that have been vaccinated at least 3 weeks, can be bred to seropositive stallions.

EQUINE INFECTIOUS ANAEMIA

Introduction

Equine Infections Anaemia (EIA) occurs in horses populations worldwide. It is characterized by antigenic variability of the causal virus and by persistent infection. Affected animals remain viraemic and often suffer irregularly recurring episodes of disease. They become lifelong carries of the virus. EIA is sometimes referred to as " swamp fever" as most outbreaks occur in warm wet areas where haematophagous insects, that transmit the virus, are abundant.

Aetiology

Equine Infections Anaemia (EIAV) is a member of the Lenti (Lanti) virus subfamily of retroviruses and possesses many of the characteristic features of that subfamily including a complex genome organization, tropism for cells of the monocyte/ macrophage lineage, and establishment of a persistent, lifelong infection. EIAV has the genetic RNA material, which it uses to produce DNA. This DNA is then incorporated into the genetic makeup of infected cells. The virus has been found in blood, milk, saliva, faeces and semen of diseased horses but rapidly loses its infectivity outside the body. Clinically, sick horses have higher titers of virus in their blood and tissues than in apparent carriers. The virus is readily destroyed by sunlight, and by most chemical disinfectants. The virus is stable in refrigerated serum but is inactivated by heat (56ºC), detergents and organic solvents such as ether. Persistent replication of the virus within the cells leads to periodic emergence of novel antigenic stains of EIA.

Epidemiology

Identified in France, in 1843 and first tentatively diagnosed in the United States in 1888, has commanded a great deal of attention over the years. There is no cure for EIA. Although most infected horses show no symptoms, they remain infectious for life, endangering the health of other horses. Despite testing and measures to eradicate the disease approximately 2000 new cases are identified each year in the U.S.A.

EIA is significant historically because it is the first disease of horses proven to be caused by a "filterable virus " i.e. one that can survive a special laboratory filtering procedure and remain infectious. EIA is the first lenti virus induced disease proven to be transmitted by insects. Lanti and has a defined antigenic drift was defined (Antigenic drift is the virus ' ability to change its from sufficiently so that it is no longer vulnerable to existing antibodies).

Transmission

The virus is mechanically transmitted by biting flies or by contaminated needles, teeth rasps, stomach tubes and any other instruments, which may cause abrasion. All infected horses serve as a potential source of virus for other susceptible horses. Viraemia peaks when horses are pyrexic and is usually low when horses appear healthy, thus the role of inapparent carriers in perpetuating the disease may not very significant.

House flies (Tabanus spp), stable flies (Stomoxys spp) and mosquitoes transmit the virus but because of their large mouth parts, house flies are the most effective natural vectors of EIA. Transmission of EIA is dependent on the interrupted feeding of the vector because the virus does not remain viable in the arthropod for more than 4 hours. Natural outbreaks of EIA usually occur during the summer and early autumn in low-lying marshy areas and river valleys.

Transmission of EIA can occur translucently but is more likely if mare is clinically ill during the gestation period than if it is an apparent carrier. Foals may become infected after birth by ingesting virus through contaminated colostrums or milk.

When conditions are ideal for spread, the morbidity of EIA can approach 100 % in horses and the mortality may be as high as 30%. The incubation period for EIA following the subcutaneous inoculation of infective blood into a susceptible horse is usually about 14 days but it may be up to several months. The initial illness is commonly acute or sub acute with definite clinical signs, and lasts from 3 to 20 days followed by cycles of febrile periods and death or apparent recovery.

EIA affects the horse's immune system. The virus reproduces in blood cells and circulates throughout the body. The horse's immune system, via antibodies, attacks and destroys the infected red blood cells. The reduced blood count causes anemia, and associated inflammation damage vital organs, such as the liver. Because the horse's immune system is impaired, the horse may also become susceptible to secondary infections, such as bronchopneumonia. EIA-infected horses can die from the virus infection as well as from related secondary infections.

Clinical Signs

EIA is difficult to diagnose because the symptoms vary from horse to horse and can mimic other disease. Additionally, some individuals may demonstrate no obvious signs. Signs may include one or more of the following:

- Fever and/ or sudden fluctuations in temperature (temperature may even exceed 105° F)
- Depression
- Decreased appetite
- Fatigue or reduced stamina
- Rapid breathing

- Sweating
- Rapid weight loss
- Bloodshot eyes with watery discharge
- Swelling of legs, lower chest, and abdomen
- Weakness characterized by wobbly or rolling gait
- Pale or yellowish mucous membranes
- Irregular heartbeat and / or weak pulse
- Colic
- Abortion in mares

Degrees of Infectiousness

Acute: When horses are exposed to EIA virus, they may develop severe, acute signs of disease and die within 3 to 14 days. This from of the disease is the most damaging and the most difficult to diagnose because the signs appear rapidly, and often only an elevated body temperature is noticed.

During an acute attack, a severe anaemia develops due to the destruction of red blood cells and reduced haemopoiesis. This is characterized by a low haematocrit, low hemoglobin value, low red blood cell count, and a high sedimentation rate. However, immature red cells are usually not observed, the white blood cell picture may show a Leucopenia or be normal. Death is usually related to the severity of the anaemia.

The *sub acute* form of EIA is reported to be the most common from of the disease. It is characterized by a sudden onset, a high fever of 104 to 108° F, severe depression, depressed appetite and a rapid loss of physical condition. A profound weakness may result in incoordination, recumbency or prostration. Jaundice and oedema of the ventral abdomen, sheath and limbs may develop, with or without petechial haemorrhages of the mucous membranes at the base of tongue and on the conjunctivae. The heart rate and intensity of heart sounds are greatly increased especially with moderate exercise. A yellowish or bloody nasal discharge may be present. An enlarged spleen may be palpated on rectal examination.

Chronic: If the horse survives first acute bout, it may develop a recurring clinical disease with following signs:

- Fever – temperature rise suddenly to about 105 °F or, rarely, as high as high 108° F. Then it may drop back to normal for an indetermitant period until the onset of another episode.
- Petechial haemorrhages – Minute blood – tinged spots appear on the mucous membranes.
- Depression – The horse appears more or less dejected (head hangs low) and generally listless.
- Weight loss – The horse may refuse feed or may eat an inordinate amount but still continues on an obvious decline from normal weight.
- Dependent oedema – The horse's blood may experience a marked drop in its red corpuscle count and appear thin and watery. The animal may also have an irregular heartbeat, and a jugular pulse may become evident.

The horse with chronic EIA is the classic "swampier" who has lost condition, is lethargic and anorexic, has a low haematocrit, and demonstrates a persistent decrease in the number of blood platelets, especially coincident with fever induced by EIA virus. One fifth of a tea spoon of blood from a chronic case during a feverish episode contains enough virus to infect 10,000 horses.

In-apparent: By far the majority of horses are in-apparent carriers, they show no overt clinical abnormalities as a result of infection. They survive as reservoirs of the infection for extended periods. In-apparent carriers have dramatically lower concentrations of EIA virus in their blood than horses with active clinical signs of the disease. Only 1 house fly out of 6 million is likely to pick up and transmit EIA virus from such horse. All horses infected with EIA virus are thought to remain virus carriers for life. The in-apparent form may become chronic or acute due to severe stress, hard work, or the presence of other disease.

It should be recognized that the classification of acute, sub acute and chronic are arbitrary and only represent EIA infection with varying degrees of severity. Our present knowledge indicates that most horses with persistent clinical signs of EIA, sooner or later, die from the disease or are euphonies because of impending death.

Pathogenesis

The virus appears to have a predilection for macrophages and monocyte, which provide a vehicle for dissemination to a variety of organs including the liver, kidney, adrenal, brain and heart. The infection causes febrile reaction and virus localizes in spleen, liver, kidney and lymph nodes. It cause damage to the intima of small blood vessels, recticnloendothelial system and results in excersive destruction of erothrocytes and haemolysis leading to anaemia. These complexes may also be responsible for damage to the reticuloendothelial system leading to haemorrhage and oedema.

Diagnosis

The successful adoption of the agar-gel immunodiffusion (AGID) test to the diagnosis of EIA by Dr. Leroy Coggins and co-workers at the N.Y.S. Veterinary College, Cornell University, has provided a reliable and economical diagnostic tool. The agar–gel immunodiffusion (AGID) or Coggins test was shown to correlate with horse incubation test results for EIA and, therefore, could be used to identify EIAV carriers. The antigen used in Coggins test, is the p 36 viral core protein, which is very stable and reacts with serum from horses infected with different variants. Although, other serologic tests have also been defined and approved for the diagnosis of EIA, the AGID test is recognized internationally as the "gold stranded" serologic test. By law, EIA is a reportable disease. All positive cases must be filed with the state veterinarians and the Animal Husbandry Department. The virus can be isolated in equine macrophages or equine dermal cells. More recently developed tests include ELISA, which appears to be more sensitive than the coggins test. However, Coggins test is still regarded as the most reliable serological test for EIA.

Management and Control

The antigenic variation of the virus presents a major obstacle to the development of an efficacious vaccine. No vaccine of proven efficacy is currently available. Antibodies are produced in response to disease infection. Consequently, it is impossible to distinguish between vaccinated and infected animals.

Blood transfusions and fluid therapy may assist in recovery from clinical disease but there is no effective means of eliminating EIA. Management and control is based primarily on the detection of infected horses by the coggins test and their isolation from other horses. Since infected horses are the only known reservoir of the virus, it is quite feasible to eradicate EIA from an area by testing and slaughter of reactors. The testing of all incoming horses will help to maintain the disease – free status. Control of vectors by drainage of swampy areas and strategic use of insecticides may help to limit the spread of the disease.

There is no effective treatment for EIA. There is no vaccine to prevent it. There is no cure. However, good management can reduce the potential of infection. The following guidelines will help:

- Use disposable needles and syringes, when administering vaccines and medications
- Sterilize dental tools and other instruments before using them on another horse.
- Test all horses for EIA at least annually.
- Stable owners should require negative Coggins certificates before introducing any new horses to the farm.
- New horses should be quarantined for 45 days and observed for any signs of illness, including elevated temperatures, before introducing them to the herd. They should be retested, if exposure to EIA is suspected.
- All stable areas should be kept clean, dry, and waste – free. Good pasture management techniques should be practiced. Remove manure and provide adequate drainage to discourage breeding sites for insects.

- Horses that are at greater risk, being in frequent contact with outside horses or who live or travel in geographic regions known for EIA outbreaks, should be tested more frequently i.e. every 4-6 months.
- Horse show and event managers should require and verify current negative Coggin's certificates for all horses entering the premises.

ARBOVIRAL ENCEPHALITIS

Togaviral And Flaviviral Encephalitides

Aetiology

The toga viruses are small enveloped RNA viruses. Within the family Togaviridae, viruses of the genus Alfa virus Eastern Equine Encephalitis (EEE) Virus Western Encephalitis (WEE) virus and Venezuelan Equine Encephalitis (VEE) Virus are associated with encephalitis in horses.

The family Flavivirdae contains only one genus i.e. which include Japanese B Encephalitis (JE) Virus. It causes encephalitis in horses. The toga viruses and flaviviruses are classified biologically as arboviruses because they are transmitted by arthropods.

Epidemiology

The viruses of WEE, EEE, VEE and JE have sylvatic life cycles, involving bird and rodent reservoirs and insect victors. Transmission of the these viruses to the horse is nearly always by the bite of an infected Culex mosquito. The mosquito ingests infected blood from the amplification host. The virus replicates in the cells of the mid - gut and travels via the haemolymph or nerves of the salivary glands. The extrinsic incubation period varies from 3 days to 2 weeks. The mosquito remains infected for life and its longevity does not appear to be affected by the presence of the virus. Horse and people are dead-end hosts for WEE virus and EEE virus.

Clinical Signs

It is not possible to differentiate between EEE, WEE, VEE or JE on the basis of clinical infection with any of these viruses. Sub clinical disease, is characterized by a generalized febrile illness with depression anorexia and tachycardia or encephalitic disease which can be fatal. The initial signs may go undetected and sudden death of apparently healthy horses has been reported in VEE.

The typical signs of the encephalitic disease begin with fever and depression. In appetence and reluctance to drink can result in dramatic weight loss. Hematological examination will often reveal a severe leucopenia. It may take from 12 hours to 5 days before the neurological signs develop. Some horses exhibit transient excitement and restlessness. They may walk in circles, press their head against fixed objects and chew aimlessly. Intense pruritis have also been recorded. Such horses can be aggressive. This period of hyperactivity is followed by a period of profound depression. Typically the horse is unwilling to move and stands with its legs apart, its head drooping or supported on a fixed object. The lower lip becomes pendulous and the tongue may hang out. There may be tremors of the facial muscles and dysphasia. The horse appears to suffer from faulty perception and has difficulty in maintaining its balance. Progressive ataxia and weakness result in recumbence. Seizures may occur with spasmodic movements of the legs.

Pathogenesis

The virus replicates at the site of infection and in the regional lymph nodes. This is followed by a period of extra neural amplification, when the virus spreads via the blood to organs such as the liver and spleen, the horse may experience a generalized febrile illness and in many cases the disease is self-limiting. If the virus is not successfully cleared by the reticulo-endothelial system, it may cross the blood brain barrier and encephalitis ensues. The gray matter including the bones, medulla, spinal cord, cerebellum, thalamus and olfactory bulbs are most often affected. The most common post mortem findings are oedema and haemorrhage of the brain and spinal cord. Histological examination reveals neuronal lyses, glosses, and focal per vascular round cell infiltration. However, these lesions are not patho gnomonic for any of the encephalitis viruses.

Diagnosis

Serological diagnosis is based on a specific rise in antibody titre in paired, (acute and convalescent) serum samples. Tests used for this purpose include HIT, CFT, virus neutralization (VN) immunodiffusion and ELISA. Because the antibody titers against these viruses rise quite quickly VN antibodies are often detectable within 7 days post-infection. It may however may take several days, for the horse to exhibit signs of neurological disorder in VEE. Recently, an Ig M capture ELISA technique has been developed for some of the encephalitis viruses, which permit diagnosis with a single serum sample.

Treatment

Before imitating intensive nursing and treatment, it is wise to evaluate the chance of survival and the possibility of residual CNS damage. The prognosis for a horse with EEE and VEE is poor. The prognosis for a horse with JE or WEE is better and with intensive nursing, many affected horses may recover.

In the absence of antiviral agents, supportive measures and symptomatic therapy are the primary modes of therapy. Throughout the therapy, it is important to minimize self-inflicted trauma by using heavily padded bedding, leg bandages and a padded helmet. Every effort should be made to maintain the horse in sternal recumbence. Slinging will restrain the affected horse and prevent the problems associated with prolonged recumbence. If it is not possible to maintain the horse in sternal recumbency or in slings it should be turned on the opposite frequently.

Supportive measures include feeding by stomach tube, Administration of balanced fluid solutions and cold water or alcohol baths to decrease pyrexia. It may be necessary to catheterize the bladder and also to empty the rectum manually.

Secondary bacterial infections should be treated with appropriate antibiotics. Corticosteroids are sometimes administered to decrease inflammation of the CNS but may make the animal more susceptible to secondary bacterial infection. Osmotic diuretics may decrease intracranial oedema in cases with severe progressive depression. The administration of barbiturates, chloral hydrate or diazepam may be indicated to control seizures

Control

Control of alpha virus and flavi virus can be achieved by vaccination and vector control. Mosquito habitats destroyed by proper drainage and elimination of stagnant water. Individual horses can be protected using insect repellents and screens. The insidence of alpha virus and flavi virus flagitious encephalitis is much lower in stabled horses than in horses on pasture. Major epizootics sometimes necessitate massive aerial spraying of insecticides.

EQUINE HERPES VIRUS INFECTION

Equine Herpes Virus (EHV) is endemic in equines. Equine Herpes viruses abortions result in significant financial loss to horse breeders each year and herpes virus respiratory disease is a major cause of loss of performance in racehorses and in competition horses.

Aetiology

Herpes viruses are enveloped DNA viruses. There are four Equine Herpes Viruses.

(a) Equine Herpes Virus-1 (EHV-1) is associated with respiratory disease abortion and neurological Syndrome.

(b) Equine Herpes Virus-2 (EHV-2) has not been conclusively implicated in a disease syndrome.

(c) Equine Herpes Virus-3 (EHV-3) cause coital exanthema.

(d) Equine Herpes Virus-4 (EHV-4) formerly known as EHV - 1 subtype 2, is a respiratory pathogen which has occasionally been associated with abortion.

Respiratory Disease

The immune response elicited by respiratory EHV–4 infection is not very durable, but repeated exposure does lead to a gradual build–up of immunity. Clinical disease is most prevalent in young stock. The spread of the disease in a group of yearlings in a farm can be rapid (within a weak) with a morbidity rate of up to 100%. EHV-4 may circulate in a training yard for several months with a few different horses becoming infected each week. In order horses, virus spread is slower and is often subclinical, but can result in a loss of performance.

EHV-1 is more virulent than EHV-4, and respiratory disease caused by EHV-1 is usually more severe. The virus spreads more rapidly. The morbidity rate is higher and infection can result in neurological disorders.

Abortion

Both sporadic and multiple abortion due to EHV-1 infection occur each breeding season. It is widely accepted that abortion is usually preceded by a respiratory infection which is often sub clinical or so mild that it is not readily observed. Mares in mixed yards are most at risk as horses or ponies can be exposed to the virus at race meetings, shows, hunts or sales and serve as a source of infection for brood mares.

The average incubation period is 3 weeks but it has been shown to vary between 9 days and 4 month. Stress factors such as transport over long distances or illness may induce a reactivation of latent virus and precipitate abortion.

Although, abortion as a result of EHV-1 infection usually occurs during the last third of pregnancy, it has been recorded as early as 4 months and a foal may even be carried to term and born alive but infected.

Neurological Disease

EHV-1 neurological disease is uncommon but since it was first recognized in 1966, it has been recorded in all parts of the world where large numbers of horses are maintained. A few cases occur annually in many countries. The disease has occurred in association with respiratory disease and / or abortion in competition yards, in training yards and on stud farms. Outbreaks have been recorded on stud farms with no concurrent cases of EHV-1 abortion. Horses of all ages and both sexes can be affected but recently foaled mares seem to be most susceptible. Morbidity may be as high as 100% in some groups of horses. The disease can be fatal and severely affected cases necessitate euthanasia. Direct contact seems to be necessary for transmission of virus. Affected horses may remain viraemic for extended periods and in some outbreaks new cases arise over several months.

EHV-4 has only rarely been isolated from cases of neurological disease.

Coital Exanthema

Outbreaks of coital exanthema caused by infection with EHV-3 are frequently observed during the breeding season. Transmission is primarily by the venereal route. Clinically, stallions are less severely affected than mares but reactivation of latent virus tends to infect the mares they cover each season. Lesions are sometimes observed on the mammary glands of mares and the muzzles of foals.

EHV-2

EHV-2 is endemic world–wide and is commonly isolated from healthy horses. Although, sick foals shed large quantities of EHV–2. It has not been conclusively linked to any disease.

Clinical Signs

Respiratory Disease

Respiratory disease caused by EHV-1 and EHV-4 are characterized by a transient elevation off temperature to 38.9–40.0ºC, in appetence, nasal discharge, pharyngitis, depression and sometimes limb oedema. Affected horses usually give a few coughs but coughing is not a major feature of uncomplicated EHV respiratory disease. There may be slight enlargement of the mandible and retropharyngeal lymph nodes. Horses frequently suffer from secondary bacterial infections, which prolong the recovery time.

Abortion

Abortion usually occurs without any premonitory signs and the placenta is not retained. The mare's subsequent fertility is unimpaired. Foals which are infected in utero but survive to full term are usually abnormal from birth and show signs of acute reparatory distress. Their mucous membranes are often jaundiced. They usually die before 2 weeks of age.

Neurological Syndrome

Neurological syndrome usually occurs 7 -10 days after an episode of respiratory disease. At the time when the nervous signs are evident, the horse usually shows no signs of respiratory disease and its body temperature and appetite are normal. Nervous signs vary from mild ataxia followed by complete recovery to fatal paralysis. Early signs may include stiffness, posterior incoordination and urinary incontinence. Uveitis, hypopyon, subcutaneous oedema of the hind limbs, colic, diarrhoea, scrotal oedema and prolapsed of the penis in males are sometimes encountered. These may be followed by sternal and then lateral recumbence, dyspnoea, convulsions and death. Sudden death with no prior clinical signs has been recorded.

Coital Exanthema

Coital exanthema is manifested by vesicles, which become pustule and ulcerate. Scabs develop which persist for 2-3 weeks and may leave white scars. Mares develop lesions on the perineal skin around the anus. In severe cases the lesions may extend to the hindquarters and hind limbs. The mare may experience extreme irritation on urinating. Stallions tend to be less susceptible than mares but lesions may occur on the prepuce and penis resulting in an unwillingness to cover. The lesions usually heal within 2 weeks.

Diagnosis

Respiratory Disease

Upper respiratory tract infection caused by EHV must be differentiated from equine rhinovirus, equine influenza virus, equine arteritis virus, bacterial infections and allergic rhinitis. Serological diagnosis can be made on the basis of a significant rise (4–fold or greater) in antibody titer, which requires the collection of blood samples during the acute phase of the disease and 10- 14 days later. The majority of diagnostic laboratories routinely use the complement fixation test (CFT). However, it is less reliable indicator of recent exposure. Because of close antigenic relatedness, infection with EHV-1 and EHV-4 can not differentiated on the basis of serology. Virus isolates can be typed by immunofluorscence with specific monoclonal antibodies or by the more time–consuming DNA restriction end nuclease analysis.

Neurological Disease

As the nervous signs do not manifest for about 10 days post-infection, the majority of horses suffering from EHV neurological disease have high antibody titers against the virus. Thus the examination of a single serum sample is often a useful diagnostic aid.

Coital Exanthema

EHV -3 can be isolated from swabs of the ulcerative lesions.

Management and Control

Both killed and live attenuated EHV-1 vaccines have been widely used many years to protect horses against equine herpes virus respiratory disease, but their use met with only limited success. Recently, vaccines containing inactivated EHV-4 have been introduced and since the majority of outbreaks of equine herpes virus respiratory disease are caused by EHV-4, it is reasonable to anticipate that they will offer greater protection than those products which contain only EHV-1.

VESICULAR STOMATITIS

Vesicular stomatitis is characterized by the development of vesicles on the feet and mouh. In horses it is associated with a very painful lameness.

Aetiology

Vesicular Stomatitis Virus (VSV) belongs to the same family as rabies virus i.e. Rhabdoviridae.

Epidemiology

Horses, cattle and pigs are susceptible to vesicular stomatitis. Sheep and goats are much more resistant. The disease may be transmitted to humans beings.

The mode of transmission of the virus is not fully understood. The virus cannot penetrate intact skin but can enter through abrasions, wounds and mucous membranes, thus the feeding of poor quality rough forage which causes abrasions in the mouth facilitating virus spread . Transmission may occur by direct contact of saliva and vesicular fluid from clinically affected animals. However, several outbreaks have occurred in horses which have had no contact with infected animals and it is widely believed that the virus is transmitted by insect vectors.

Pathogenesis and Clinical Signs

Following a 1 to 3 day incubation period, there is pyrexia and inflammation of the mucosa of the mouth and tongue with the formation of vesicles. The vesicles rupture and leave ulcers. The resultant irritation leads to salivation and a reluctance to eat. This can result in considerable loss of condition. In severe cases, ulcers may develop on the nasopharnx, larynx and nasal turbinates which result in epistaxis and respiratory distress. Lesions found on the coronary band is common and results in lameness which in severe cases may culminate in the sloughing of the hoof. Unless complicated by secondary bacterial infection the oral lesions usually heal within a couple of weeks . Lesions on the horses develop a severe coronets and cracked hoof walls. Mortality is rare but may occur if there is severe secondary bacterial infection of the mouth which prevents the animal from eating or drinking.

Diagnosis

A definitive diagnosis of vesicular stomatitis can be made by isolating the virus from the vesicular fluid or by serological examination of two blood samples collected at 10 -14 days apart. Seroconversion can be detected by the CFT or SNT.

Management and Control

Infected horses should be isolated and supplied with ample water and soft palatable feed. The use of systemic antibiotics may be indicated if the horse has secondary bacterial infection. Fluid therapy and nasogastric tube feeding are indicated if the horse is unable to eat or drink. Involvement of the feet may necessitate treatment similar to that employed in cases of laminitis. If the disease is present in an area, insect control and the removal of animals from wooded pasture and their confinement in stables will help to curtail the spread of the virus.

LEPTOSPIROSIS AND DERMATOMYCOSIS

LEPTOSPIROSIS

Introduction

Leptospira is a bacterial organism that is found commonly throughout the world and the organism can persist for many years in soil where animals have been housed. Leptospirosis can cause abortions, still decreased milk production, recurrent uveitis and death.

Aetiology

Leptospira are divided into six major serographs and these are then further divided into over 500 serorities. Of these are seven main ones that are found in horses. These are L. autumnalis, bratislava L. grippotyphosa, L. hardjo, L. icterohemmorhagica and L. pomona.

Epidemiology

Leptospirosis is very common in domestic and wild animals and can also infect humans. In particular regions, there will be one more maintenance hosts which serve as the reservoir for the infection. Leptospira will be transmitted to incidental hosts by shedding into the environment from a maintenance and / or damaged skin and migrate to various body organs of an incidental host. The contamination comes from contacting the urine of the infracted animal through water, mud, bedding or food. Cattle and swine can shed leptospira in their urine for over a year and horses may shed for four months. The maintenance hosts can be wildlife such as deer, raccoons, and rodents.

Leptospiral bacteria like warm, moist conditions and are found in many animals. Horses get it from drinking water that has been infected or they may pick it up from grass, hay or grain contaminated by the urine of infected animals. Horses can catch it from other horses, although the majority have most likely contracted it from infected cattles rats or wildlife. The frustrating thing about leptospirosis and uveitis in horses is that the uveitis may not occur for 18-24 or more months after the leptospirosis infection. In addition, while some horses are very ill with the disease, others may show no obvious signs of infection. Testing for leptospirosis at the time uveitis occurs may confirm that the disease was active at one time but it is too late to do anything about the leptospirosis for that horse.

Clinical Signs

Signs of leptospirosis include fever, anorexia, conjunctivitis, and decreased milk production.

Recurrent Uveitis is an immune-mediated reaction and a sequel to a Leptospira pomona infection, which occurred few months or years previously. Acute signs include varying degrees of blepharosphasm, lacrimation, photophobia, aqueous flare, hyphema, miosis, a swollen dull iris, hypotonia, vitreal inflammation, and retinal vaculitis or papillary inflammation. No single case shows all these signs. Clinical signs will often disappear followed by recurrence. Severe attacks can lead calcific band keratopathy (calcification of the cornea), permanent blindness, atrophy of the eye and / or glaucoma.

Pregnant mares can also have leptospira localize in the uterus/ placenta and, subsequently, in the foetus, resulting in death of the foetus. Equine abortions are most frequently associated with L. pomona infection. The horse is probably an incidental host. L. bratislava is thought to be "host adapted " to the horse and can exist without causing disease in the horse.

Diagnosis

A paired serum taken three weeks apart is essential for diagnosis. A four fold change in titre to the organism in the paired sera would provide a presumptive diagnosis.

Treatment

Streptomycin and penicillin are used to treat leptospirosis.

Equine Recurrent Uveitis: Steroids, either topically or subconjunctivaly are often used to reduce the inflammation. Caution should be exercised, due to the possibility of corneal ulceration following their use. Atropine (1-4%) will dilate the iris and relieve the ciliary spasms, blepharospasm, lacrimation and photophobia. Extended use of 1% atropine or use of 4% atropine can lead to colic due to its effect on gut motility. Flunixin melanamine is sometimes used in acute cases and can quickly bring relief thereby facilitating an examination of the eye. Cyclosporine may be used when corneal ulceration is present and steroids would be contra-indicated. Antibiotics have only been indicated when there is evidence of an acute infection or secondary bacterial infections. It is important to realize that medical treatment is usually lifetime, even if the uveitis is controlled. If medication is discontinued or decreased the horse will likely have a repeat attack, and the attack will probably be a severe one. Each attack of uveitis is cumulative, that is, the damage from each attack adds on to the damage from all previous attacks, and brings the eye that much closer to blindness and potential removal. The goal is to keep the inflammation controlled from starting. Long-term treatment will often consist of a daily or every other day dose of NASID (nonsteroidal anti-inflammatory drug). Some horses may respond better to phenylbutazone.

Management

Leptospira can survive in water for up to 20 days and in manure up to 61 days. It is, therefore, very important to keep animals away from drinking stagnant water, have good management of manure, and practice good sanitation. Human hands can spread infection which wildlife can access. Draining wet muddy areas where horses are pastured, thoroughly disinfecting stalls and areas where animals who have active leptospirosis and washing hands and clothes when in contact with the infection will help in controlling the disease. Vaccination of herds or individual animals in areas where leptospirosis is prevalent, is also usually recommended although there is still much discussion regarding vaccinating horses. Moreso, there is no approved vaccine for horses at this time.

DERMATOMYCOSIS

Dematomycosis (Ringworm) is a skin infection caused by a dematophyte fungus. The fungi which causes ringworm in animal species and humans, includes the Microsporum and Trichophyton species. The skin lesions start as small raised spots with loss of hair. These spots usually become scurfy or a dry crumbly scab may form. If spread by grooming, the condition can become extensive. The infection is highly contagious and whole groups can become affected in an outbreak.

Aetiology

Ringworm is a common contagious skin disease of horses. Caused by various Microsporum and Trichophyton spp. *Trichophyton equinunm, Trichophyton mentagrophyte, Microsporum gypseum, Microsporum canis* are the most frequently associated.

Epidemiology

Infection is transmitted among horses by direct contact with an infected animal (including humans) or by indirect contact via contaminated tack, clothing, covers, or fungal spores within the environment and contact with infested stables or trailers. The fungi are quite resistant to environmental factors and can remain on fence railings and timber structures for long period. The fungi can remain on the skin for up to three weeks before clinical signs develop so the disease can be spread before there are signs of infection. Very often it is a new animal which introduces the condition to an establishment. Younger animals are more likely to be affected than older ones, although very old or debilitated animals are also susceptible. Infection produces immunity which is quite long-lasting. It is important to note that handling infected horses and contaminated tack can infect humans. Illness, poor nutrition, overcrowding, age and stressful environment predispose horses to infection. Young and elderly horses are more susceptible to infection. Continuous wetting of the horse's skin e.g. sweating, washing-down can decrease the skins protective barrier therefore, enabling infection to occur.

Clinical Signs

The classic ringworm lesion is a circular patch of hair loss with stubbly hairs on the margin. The skin can appear to be crusted and / or scaly. Ringworm lesions usually begin as small raised lumps that progress to the typical ringworm lesion. Some horses can become itchy and may also show evidence of pain. The presence of the pathogenic fungi and dematophyte are observed in horses with hoof lesions. Fungal infection should be considered in cases of hoof disease that do not respond to improved management and nutrition.

Control

Ringworm is usually a self-limiting disease and most horses recover within 1-6 months. Treatment is usually advisable as it decreases the transmission of disease between horses and other animals including humans. Antifungal shampoos (e.g. ketaconazole shampoo, Selenium shampoo) and/ or washes e.g., 3% Captan, povidone iodine and lime sulphur are useful for decreasing the transmission of disease but do not alter the course of infection. Systemic treatment with antifungal drugs like Griseofulvin for the treatment of ringworm infections caused by *Trichophyton equinum and Microsporum gypseum* are effective but this is very expensive and its use is usually limited to small animals. The usual dose for a 400 kg horse is 2.5 grams once daily by mouth for a minimum of 10 days. Topical applications like Miconazole and Ketoconazole can be tried.

PIROPLASMOSIS AND TRYPANOSOMIASIS

EQUINE PIROPLASMOSIS

Aetiology

The protozoan genus Babesia is member of the piroplasmida, a constituent group of the Apicomplexa. In the vertebrate host they form intraerythrocytic pyriform, round or oval bodies, which multiply by budding. When a tick, intermediate host, ingests infected blood, the parasite Babesia enter the gut epithelium and multiply by schizogony forming organisms known as vermicules.

Equine piroplasmosis is caused by two species of haemoprotozoan piroplasms viz Babesia equi and Babesia caballi. The organisms occur into trophozoites, which grow and divide.

Babesia equi trophozoites occur as a round, oval elliptical or spindle structures, measuring between 1.0 - 3.0 μ in diameter. This species has a tendency to divide into 4 merozoites in the form of a cross in erythrocytes called the Maltese cross.

Babesia caballi is relatively larger species with pyriform stages measuring 2.5 - 4.0 μ in length. Rounded or oval (1.5 - 3.0 μ) forms may also be seen in erythrocytes.

Babesia equi behaves rather differently as Transovarian transfer of the organisms rarely occurs. The mature merozoites infect new RBCs and the division process is repeated. However, in equi, it has been demonstrated that the sporozoites inoculated into horses through the tick bite invade the lymphocytes. They undergo development in the cytoplasm of lymphocytes resulting in formation of Theileria like schizonts. The merozoites released from these schizonts enter the RBCs. Therefore, the taxonomic position of Babesia equi is controversial and has been redscribed as Theileria equi.

Transmission

Horses acquire Babesia organisms when parasitized with ixodid ticks harbouring sprozoites in their salivary secretions. The organisms are transmitted transstadially by various genera of ticks like Dermacentor, Rhipicephalus and Hyalomma spp.

Epidemiology

The incidence of equine babesiosis is closely related to the geographical distribution and seasonal activity of tick species responsible for its transmission. Babesia caballi is found in Asia, Africa, America, Southern Europe and Russia while Babesia equi is prevalent world-wide including India.

In areas with a high transmission rate, the immune status of the horse population is maintained at a high level and the incidence of disease is low. Disease will, however, be inevitable in animals introduced form a non-infected region. A zone of endemic instability occurs if the number of infected ticks is insufficient to ensure immunity in a high proportion of the animals at risk. In these circumstances, babesiosis will occur sporadically at the time of year in which ticks are active. A new endemic focus is likely to be formed when an infected horse is moved into a locality with a "clean" tick population.

Babesia equi is more pathogenic than Babesia caballi. An incubation period of 6-10 days and 10-21days has been recorded for Babesia caballi and Babesia equi infections, respectively. The exact mechanism of pathogenesis in equine babesiosis is not completely known; still, sledging of blood in capillaries of various organs is mainly responsible for pathogenesis in peracute infections.

In acute infections, there is large-scale destruction of erythrocytes resulting in anaemia. In addition, intravascular haemolysis, indiscriminate phagocytosis of infected / non-infected erythrocytes by activated macrophage system also contributes to anaemia in babesiosis. Intravascular haemolysis results in marked hyperbilirubinaemia and icterus. There is leucocytosis with neutrophilia.

Clinical Signs

Equine babesiosis can occur in acute, sub acute and chronic forms. Peracute form of the disease is rare in which the animals die within 24-48 hours of the onset of clinical signs. The major symptoms with Babesia caballi infection are fever, anaemia, icterus, highly coloured urine (hemoglobinuria is rare) gastroenteritis and sometimes paralysis of hind quarters.

Hemoglobinuria is more common in infection with B equi. The animal exhibits colicky symptoms, pawing, high (intermittent fever, incoordinated gait and circling movements). There are reports on cerebral form of babesiosis in equines. The animal shows oedema of dependent parts like fetlock and ventral aspect of abdomen, petechial haemorrhages on mucous membranes of nostrils and nictitating membranes. The animal may pass hard faeces covered with yellow mucous. Pregnant mares may abort.

Diagnosis

It is based on history of prevalence of ticks, manifestations and identification of Babesia organisms in stained blood smears (Maltese cross in Babesia equi). Hematological values like reduced hemoglobin and TEC and increased ESR, help in diagnosis. There is fall in platelet count and fibrinogen content of blood. Serological tests like CFT and ELISA are also employed for diagnosis of equine babesiosis.

The National Research Center on Equines (Hisar) has developed a simple, sensitive, cost-effective CFT based diagnostic kit named 'COFEB - kit' for detection of Babesia equi infection in equines. The indigenously developed diagnostic kit can give results in 3 hours. However, more sensitive and rapid methods using PCR have also been developed for detecting Babesia equi and Babesia caballi infections, especially when routine stained blood smears and serological tests fail to do so.

Treatment and Control

Imidocarb @ 2 mg / kg body weight intramuscularly twice at 24 hours interval is effective against Babesia cablli infection. However, a dose of 4 mg / kg body weight four times at 72 hours interval is effective against Babesia equi. Antitheilerial drugs like Buparvaquone @ 5 -6 mg / kg body weight parentrally can be administered for treating Babesia equi infection. Diaminazene acetuate @ 3-5 mg/kg body weight injected deep intramuscularly can eliminate Babesia caballi infection.

Control can be attained by destroying tick vectors using acaricidal drugs. Eaterogenic transfer of infected blood using contaminated needles and surgical instruments should be avoided. Strict quarantine measures must be adopted.

TRYPANOSOMIASIS

Introduction

Trypanosomiasis or surra, caused by Trypanosoma evansi, is one of the most important haemoprotozoan infections of the horses. The livestock all over India particularly in Rajasthan, Haryana, Punjab, Madhya Pradesh, Uttar Pradesh, Maharashtra, Tamil Nadu, Kerala and Andhra Pradesh have been reported to suffer from Trypanosoma evansi infection.

Transmission

T evansi is transmitted mechanically by biting flies, particularly of the genus ***Tabanus***. Transmission occurs only when the feeding is interrupted. There is no development of the trypanosome in the Tabanus. The successful transmission can occur if the transference of the parasite takes place within a few minutes after bite and the chances are great that it is transmitted almost instantly. Lyperosia, Stomoxys and Haematopota spp can also transmit the disease.

Typically, the life- cycle also involves a bloodsucking arthropod in which acyclic development takes place. After initial multiplication, development to the eqimastigote stage, where the kinetoplast is anterior to the muscles, takes place at various sites in the arthropod gut.

The feeding activities of biting flies that visit two or more animals in quick succession, e.g., tabanids, can lead to the mechanical transmission of trypomastigotes into susceptible vertebrate host without the intervening metabolic cycle.

Some species, e. g. the T. equiperdum has dispensed with arthropod vectors altogether and is transmitted by physical contact during coitus.

Epidemiology

The incidence and the severity of disease vary in different localities according to the strain of Trypanosoma evansi.

In the Indian subcontinent, an increase in surra has been associated with monsoon months, reaching the climax in October and November when the fly breeding is at it's highest. The incidence is lowest in April and May when water resources have dried up and fly breeding is greatly reduced.

Pathogenesis

Period of incubation is variable and depends upon the intensity of infection and the species and health of the animal. Symptoms usually appear 1-2 weeks after infection.

(a) *Pyrexia Stage*: Corresponding to the appearance of large numbers of trypanosomes in the peripheral blood the body temperature is raised by 4 °C to 5 °C above normal. The animal is dull depressed and shows irregular appetite. Depending upon the species of the animal the pyrexial stage may continue from 2 days to 3 weeks. Then temperature returns to normal and the animal starts feeding normally, although it continues to develop weakness and shows loss of condition. During this period the trypanosomes disappear from the peripheral blood to reappear again in the subsequent pyrexial paroxysm. Intermittent fever is characteristic of Trypanosoma evansi infection in animals.

(b) Anaemic Stage: Most noticeable pathological change is the progressive anaemia, erythrocytes are reduced to 25 per cent of the normal value and haemoglobin concentration falls. Whether the severe anaemia is due to the destruction of red cells or inhibition in their production is not definitely known, but it is presumably due to an inhibitory effect of the toxin liberated by the trypanosomes. There is increased weakness and as a sequel to severe anaemia, oedema develops on the dependent parts of the body. Oedema is conspicuous in the scrotal region, on the sheath of the penis, the fetlock and pastern joints, urticaria, loss of hairs, conjunctivitis and petechial hemorrhages under the memrana nictitans are common in horses and camels.

(c) *Nervous Stage* : Though the nervous stage is not a common feature of Tryponasoma evansi infection in horses, it may be exhibited in certain cases. During this stage the animals show great weakness in the lumbar region, in coordination of muscular movements, staggering gait, paralysis of the hind quarters, prostration, inability to feed and drink, and finally death. Although, majority of animals die of exhaustion and anaemia in the anemic stage, but symptoms of nervous disorder have been observed in horses in the last stage of the disease.

Causes of Death

(a) Sugar consumption theory: Trypanosomes consume large quantity of blood sugar resulting in the breakdown of the liver function and the resultant hypoglycemia and fatal intoxication.

(b). There is an increase in the blood, which interferes with the normal absorption of oxygen by the haemoglobin resulting in asphyxiation. Mechanical blocking of the lung capillaries by the obstruction of the agglutinated trypanosomes result in asphyxiation with fatal termination.

(c) Trypanosomes liberate toxins or proteolysis enzymes, which result in the formation of toxins which cause severe anaemia and death.

Clinical Signs of surra in Equids

A prominent feature of trypanosomiasis is the relapsing nature of the disease. Each remission marks a successful reduction in parasite numbers by host immunity. The recurrence of disease correspond with period of increasing parasitaemia, which occur when the trypanosome population circumvents the previous immune response. This the parasite can do by periodically expressing surface - coat glycoprotein of a differing antigenic nature and the phenomenon is known as antigenic variation. Multiplication continues until the host mobilizes an immune attack against the new antigenic form.

The main symptoms are high rise of temperature, anaemia, general urticaria eruptions and petechial hemorrhages and the mortality is usually 100%. The disease is characterized by two kinds of period:

a. *Paroxysm* when the trypanosomes are seen in the blood.

b. *Intermission,* when the flagellates are absent from the blood.

Diagnosis

Microscopic Examination

In pyrexial phases when trypanosomes are present in large numbers in the peripheral blood, both the fresh blood film and stained preparations may reveal trypanosomes but detection of light or chronic infection is almost impossible with a microscope.

Microscopic examination of fluid from superficial lymph glands, i.e. prescapular or prescural, taken on a slide, fixed and stained may show presence of trypanosomes.

Treatment

The latest and most satisfactory remedy for surra is Qunapyramine sulphate (Antrycide). It is synthethetically prepared drug and has been shown to have consistently good results against surra. It is administered subcutaneously and a single injection of 3 to 5 mg / kg body weight is very satisfactory against various trypanosomal infections. Antrycide methylsulphate is a curative and Antrycide chloride is a prophylactic salt. The prophylactic properties of the drug are due to persistence in the subcutaneous region of the site of infection from where it is slowly absorbed by the body.

Various other drugs used are different Dramamines, Phenthridinium compounds and Antypol complexes. Dramamines including Pentamidine and Stilbamidine have been used with little success.

Berenil (Diminazene aceturate) has proved useful in sterilizing infections providing resistance to other drugs. The drug is primarily curative and not prophylactic.

METAZOAL DISEASES

HELMINTH PARASITES

Helminth parasites are ubiquitous in horse. Regular deworming is necessary to effectively control these parasites. However, anthelmintics resistance in some of the most important parasites of the horses has become widespread. Excellent worm control can be achieved by using knowledge of parasite life cycles, good pasture and stable management coupled with strategic dosing where necessary.

Major Internal Parasites Of Horses

Type of parasite	Species involved	Predilection sites	
		Adults	Larvae
Cyathostomins (Small strongyles)	About 50 species known , 4 are common	Large intestine	Intestinal wall
Roundworm	Parascaris equorum	Small intestine	Liver, Lungs
	Strongyloides spp.	Small intestine	Foals infected by the larvae in their dams' milk
Large strongyles	Strongylus spp. Triodontophorus	Large intestine	Cranial mesenteric Artery or visceral Arteries
Tapeworms	Anoplocephala spp.	Ileocaecal junction	Invertebrate Intermediate host (Forage mites)
Lungworm	Dictyocaulus arnfieldi	Airways	Lung parenchyma
Pinworm	Oxyuris equi	Large intestine	Intestinal wall
Bots	Gastrophilus spp.	Female flies lay eggs on hairs	Stomach
Apicomplexa	Various, including Sarcoystis, Neospora,	Various tissues	N/A

Although, in mixed infection as rule, a number of specific disease syndromes may emerge

- Stongyloidoses (*Thread worm*) - Young foals
- Parascariasis - Older foals and yearlings
- Strongylosis and Cyanthostominosis - All ages

Three classes of anthelmintics are available for control (Ivermectins., Pyrantel., Benzimidazoles). With the rise in Benzimidazole resistance among the cyathostomins, it is essential that development of further resistance be slowed through strategic anthelmintics use together with maximal use of complementary control methods such as pasture management and dung removal. Hence it is advisable to treat horses only when indicated by faecal egg counts and to rotate drug family used twice a year.

STRONGYLOSIS

Equine Strongylosis is usually due to mixed infection of strongyle species but dominated by cyathostomes. Large strongyles, especially Strongylus vulgaris now rarely detected (<5% prevalence) in countries where modem anthelmintics widely used. Strongylosis occurs in horses, ponies and donkeys of all ages but young animals (between 1 and 3 years of age) are more susceptible.

Aetiology

There are 40 species of strongyles represented in the horse. Most are relatively small i.e. less than an inch length. The species of the genus Strongylus are referred to as large strongyles, sclerostomes, palisade worms, red worms and bloodworms. The smaller ones are commonly know as small strongyles or cyliocostomes or cyathostomes.

There are two subfamilies of parasites, the strongylinae, and the cyathostominae.

Superfamily	Family	Subfamily	Genus examples
Strongyloides	Strongylinae	Strongylinae (large strongyles)	Strongylus
			Triodontophorus
			Cyathostomes
		Cyathostominae (Small strongyles)	Cylicostephanus
			Cylicocyclus
			Cylicodontophorus
			Poeteriostomum
			Gyalocephalus

The large strongyles are members of the subfamily strongylinae which includes two genera in domestic horses and donkeys, the genus strongylus and the triodontophorus. Although some strongyles occur in every horse, these three species are the most important pathogens.

- **Strongylus vulgaris** - *"Two tooth strongyle"*
- **Strongylus edentatus** - *Toothless strongyle"*
- **Strongylus equines** - *"Large strongyle"* (has 3 teeth)

Strongylus vulgaris is the most important of the three due to the larval migration. It is smallest of the red worms and bores through intestinal wall, enters the mesentric vessels, espacially to the cranial mesentricantory and develops there which leads to occlusion of artery and aneurism. The females measure 20-24 mm.

S. edentatus : This worms bores through and undergoes part of its develpment in the peritoneal cavity. It is often found mature in the tunica vaginalis at castration, and at times free in abdonal cavity.

S. equinus : This worms also bores through the intestine and wanders in the pertoneal cavity, and it frequently found encysted in the liver, lungs and pancreas. Its female measure 38-47 mm.

Triodontophorus measure 10-25 mm, and have 3 pair of teeth. This genus overlaps with Strongylus vulgaris in size, but has life cycle typical of the small strongyles.

- **Triodontophorus serratus** - "Large small strongyles"
- **Triodontophorus tenuicallis** "Large small strongyles"

Small Strongyles or "Cyclostomes" or "Cyathostomes"

The small strongyles, or cyathostomes, are the most abundant helminth (or nematode) parasites of these hosts.

Large numbers of adult cyathostomes reside on the surface or within the luminal contents of the large intestine of Equids, where the different species have preferential developing sites. As an example, cylicocyclus nassatus, cylicostephanus minutus, C. calicatus and Cyathostmum catinatum predominate in the ventral colon whereas the predominant species in the dorsal colon are Cylicostephanus longibursatus, C. goldi and C. insigne. Coronocyclus coronatum and Petrovinema poculatum preferentially develop in the caecum.

Epidemiology of Equine Strongyle Infections.

The large and small strongyles are cosmopolitan parasites. They appear to have adapted to a wide range of climatic conditions and, in the absence of good parasite control programmes, are common in horses, donkeys and mules throughout the world. The biological characteristics of the periphrastic stages of the small strongyles and of strongylus vulgaris are well known and are presumed to be similar to the other two important species of large strongyles in equines viz. strongylus equinus and strongylus edentatus.

Life Cycle of Large Strongyle:

The life cycle is direct. Eggs passed in the faces are typical strongyle and develop on the ground before hatching. They may hatch in as little as two hours to release first larval stage (L_1) which then molts to second stage (L_2) and then infective third larval stage (L_3) on pasture. Larvae develop to the infective stage within 5 to 6 days. The third stage larvae are very resistant and may live many years (at least 4 years) on the pastures in fecal masses.

The horse becomes infected per os. The larvae go to the large intestine and burrow into the wall (muscular coat) where they undergo as short period of growth and molting. The exact time that they remain in the muscular coat of the intestine is not known because nodules are formed by their presence. But it is possible for the 4th stage larvae (11 days) to migrate through peritoneal cavity to liver (6-7 weeks) and pancreas and back again to caecum. A hepatic–pulmonary type of migration is also possible.

- Strongylus vulgaris migrates towards the heart within the media of the arteries.
- Strongylus edentatus may be similar to that of strongylus equines or may reach by portal vessels or may stay in wall of intestine for 3 months and return to lumen without migration.

Life Cycle of Small Strongyle

The adult female worms lay their eggs, which are deposited in the external environment with the host's faeces. The morulated eggs develop into first stage larvae within days of being deposited into a suitable external environment. These eggs are very resistant to environmental factors.

The larvae migrate to the grass surrounding the foecal pat, which maximizes their chances to be acquired by a suitable host. The highest numbers are found during the late summer and early autumn when the temperatures are more favourable for their development.

Development of the Life Cycle in the Host

Upon ingestion, the larvae exsheath on their migration through the gastrointestinal tract. The exsheathed larvae burrow into the glands of **Lieberkuhn,** where the majority of the species invade the mucosa, and may migrate deeper into the sub mucosa of the large intestine. Once in the wall of the large intestine the larvae continue to develop to the next larval stage or arrest their development as a hypobiotic third stage larvae. Some species of **cyathostomes** are able to undergo hypobiosis (arrested development) as escheated, encysted early third stage larvae (EL3s) in the intestinal mucosa of infected horses. Hypobiosis has been defined as the arrest, retardation, and inhibition, on suppression of parasitic larvae that have not completed development in the host within the commonly accepted development interval for the species. Synchronous emergence of large numbers of previously arrested L4s occurs in early spring and is the cause of the clinical syndrome known as larval cyathostomes. It is suggested that the escheated third stage larvae become surrounded by fibroblasts that form a capsule, the host's reaction to the invasion, thereby the inflammation seen around the larvae is minimal. But it is noted with a marked eosinophillic infiltration in the sub-mucosa directly underneath of the encapsulated larvae. The larvae are quickly encapsulated upon invasion, and elicit an inflammatory response that is granulocytic in nature. The larvae developing in the mucosa or submucosa of the large intestine begin to molt to the fourth stage before or after entering the lumen of the large intestine. The adult worms found in the faeces after each phenothiazine treatment develop from larvae encysted in the mucosa of the intestine, and that removal of the adult worms population acted as a cue for the encysted larvae to emerge.

Only two factors are known to trigger resumption of third stage larva development in cyathostomes infections.

- The elimination of adult parasites from the intestinal lumen by using an anthelmintic compound.
- The natural synchronized senescence of adult cyathostomes during the late winter or early months.

Pathogenesis

Larval stages rather than adults are responsible for the main pathogenic effects. Weight loss is due to protein losing enteropathy (intestinal damage). Colic may be due to either intestinal motility changes and/or disrupted intestinal blood flow and/ or irritation of the gut lining. Large strongyles may cause incidental blood loss when feeding on the gut lining resulting in anaemia. Diarrhoea is a feature of larval cyathostomins arising at times of synchronous mass emergence into the lumen of larvae arrested in development within the large intestinal lining.

Effect of Strongylus vulgaris

The larvae of Strongyle vulgaris are important because of their location in the artery – primarily the anterior mesenteric artery that supplies blood to the large intestine. Their attachment to the lining of the vessel causes.

- Roughened lining of vessel - produces an ideal site for fibrin and leukocytes to be taken out of the blood stream thrombi. These tend to block the vessel.
- Weakened arterial wall – In addition to sucking blood the worms may have a secretion, which weakens the epithelium.

- Verminous aneurysm - The weakened wall of the vessel results in an aneurysm which is quite common and which may rupture.
- The aneurysms tend to thromboses quickly and throw off emboli when the animal is overworked. These aneurysms interfere with the circulation of the blood. This produces a lack of blood supply to the intestine which becomes predisposed to colic (severe abdominal pain).
- Death may occur in severe cases.
- If an embolus lodges in the vessels, which supply the muscles of the hind legs, sudden lameness occurs. It goes away as the circulation gradually improves in the affected areas, but repeated lameness is common.
- As a result of the larvae and adults feeding on epithelium and blood, typical signs of parasitism occur. The condition is called Stongyloidosis or Strongylosis.

Both large and small strongyles damage the lining of the intestinal wall at the point of attachment. As they wander from place to place, abandoned areas may ulcerate, haemorrhage or become infected by bacteria.

The massive emergence of the developing larvae is termed as larval cyathostomins. If massive infestations occur, a more generalized widespread catarrhal or haemorrhagic inflammation is seen. Animals with heavy infestations show oedmatous enteritis, with large areas of epithelial erosion and numerous ulcers that indicate the presence of emergent larvae.

Postmortem Findings

May be anaemia, emaciation, oedema and/or ascites. Erratic strongylus larvae may be found in main organs and tissue, i.e. spleen, kidney aortic valves, etc. Nematodes may be usually red in colour, ranging between 1-30mm. These parasites are recoverable from faeces after anthelmintic treatment.

- Normal locations: nodules in small intestine and large intestine, liver, beneath peritoneal surfaces of body wall, (especially in right flank area) in the cranial mesenteric artery, ileac arteries, abdominal aorta, also found in the thrombi and in initial proliferations in vessels.

- Aneurysms: Thrombus: Emboli, Infarcts and gangrenous enteritis and fibroitic arterial lesions (healed) in the thrombi and in intimal proliferations in vessels in 50% of the horses. Haemorrhagic nodules on serosal surfaces. Ulcers in large intestine, colon and caecum.

Clinical signs

- Weight loss, poor coat condition and thriftiness
- Colic maybe severe or recurrent bouts
- Lethargy, poor performance
- Diarrhoea (cyathostomiasis only)

Diagnosis

Surprisingly difficult and usually presumptive, faecal and blood tests may help.

Anthelmintic Group	Examples	Mode of Action
Macro Cyclic Lactones (Marcrolides)	Ivermectin Exprinomectin Doramectin Moxidectin Milbemycin oxide Selamectin	Bind to glutamated chorine channels causing paralysis
Benzimidazoles	Thiabendazole Mebendazole Fenbendazole Oxfendazole Oxibendazole Albendazole	Interfere with energy Metabolism by inhibition of Polymerization of microtubules
Pro – benzimidazoles	Febantel	Same as benzimidazoles
Imidazothiazoles	Tetramisole Levamisole	Cholinergic agonists
Tetrahydrophrimidines	Morantel Pyrantel	Cholinergic agonists
Organophosphates	Dichlorvos Haloxon Trichlorfon	Inhibitors of cholinesterase
Piperazines	Piperazine Salts	Ant cholinergic action – block Neuromuscular transmission

Antehelmintics Efective Against the Small Strongyles

Drug	Route	Dose
Oxibendazole	Oral	10 mg / kg
Fenbendazole	Oral	10 mg / kg daily for 5 days
Oxfendazole	Oral	10 mg / kg
Febantel	Oral	6 mg / kg
Pyrantel Pamoate	Oral	6.6 mg / kg
Pyrantel tartrate	Oral continuous feeding	14.4 mg / kg
Ivermectin	Oral	0.2 mg / kg
Moxidectin	Oral	0.3 mg / kg

Control

Although, control programmes on different horse establishments will vary as per their conditions, the following measures will dramatically reduce the level of infection :

- Treat all animals with a broad spectrum anthelmintic.
- Treat new arrivals and isolate for 72 hours before allowing them to join resident animals.
- Change to unrelated anthelmintic compounds once yearly to avoid drug resistance problems.
- At the end of the grazing season, if the animals are to be housed, treatment with Ivermectin, Oxfendazole, or a high dose Fenbendazole will reduce the numbers of developing cyathostomes larvae and prevent disease in the spring.
- Stress management factors such as good stable hygiene, clean pasture, proper disposal of manure and under crowding conditions.
- Several sanitary and management practice will add in the control of strongyles. These are;
- Clean, dry stalls
- Protection of feed and water from paddocks and pastures.
- Manure composting
- Chain harrowing
- Clipping of pastures
- Rotation of animal species in pastures.

- The low phenothiazine system functions in a prophylactic or preventive way by markedly reducing or preventing the contamination of pastures with infective larvae . The low level system consists of the daily feeding in the grain ration of 2 gm. of phenothiazine for the first 21 days of each month, followed by a rest period for the remainder of the month during which no drug is fed. The intermittent periods of dosing are repeated, month after month, on a year round basis in herds with permanent pastures, where re exposure is heavy. It results in
- Practically a complete cessation of egg production by adult female worms.
- Inhibits the development of infective larvae in the faeces from the eggs that are produced.
- This system is thought to bring about the slow removal of the adult worms from the digestive tract.
- Hinder the development of infective larvae after they have been taken into the body.

With the advent of more effective medicinal agents, there is a tendency to neglect the hygienic aspects. Medication should supplement rather than replace wholesome food and water and clean surroundings.

NEMATODES OF THE SMALL INTESTINE

PARASCARIS EQUORUM - HORSE ASCARID

Heavy infections with the roundworm Parascaris equorum are extremely common in foals and yearlings; the main clinical sign is unthriftiness. Parascaris equorum is a large conspicuous worm. The females may be as large as 50 cm in length and 8 mm in diameter. Males are smaller, ranging from 15 to 28 cm long.

Its predilection site is the small intestine of equines, including zebra. In heavy infections, Parascaris may be responsible for gut impactions and ruptures leading to a fatal peritonitis.

Epidemiology

Parascaris equorum has a cosmopolitan distribution. Female worms are prolific egg layers and as a result infected foals may pass millions of egg daily in their faeces. These thick- shelled eggs are resistant to freezing and drying and can, therefore, survive for long periods in the environment. The outer layer is sticky and ensures that eggs will be present almost everywhere in a foal's environment. The sticky outer coat enables the egg to adhere to stable floors, fittings, etc., and may facilitate passive spread of infective eggs.

Infection is primarily a problem in young horses. Suckling and weanlings are more susceptible than yearlings, while in mares this infection is uncommon and the infections are characteristically light. This decreased susceptibility as age increases, is credited to an acquired immunity resulting from the earlier infections. Horses undoubtedly continue to pick up infective acrid eggs in contaminated food and water throughout their lives, but the worms are generally unable to establish and maintain themselves in the older immune animals.

Life cycle

The adult male and female parasites (15-50 cms in length) live in the small intestine and produce circular, sticky eggs, which are passed in the faeces. These develop to the infective stage, which infect the egg containing the larvae, in a minimum of 10-14 days and foals are infected by ingesting these eggs. Parascaris equorum larvae migrate through the liver and lungs to their final site in the small intestine. The prepa tent period in the horse is 10-12 weeks.

Parasitic Phase

Infection and Migration to the Lungs

Foals become infected by ingesting eggs containing L2s. These hatch in the gut and L2s migrate through the wall of the small intestine (A) to the liver (B) via the hepatic portal system. Most

L2s reach the liver. Within 24 hours after infection. The molt from L2 to L3 appears to occur between the mucosa of the small intestine and the liver within 7-14 days after infection, the majority of larvae have migrated to the lungs (C) via the heart and pulmonary arteries.

Migration from Lungs to the Gut

L3s break out of the alveolar capillaries into the alveoli and migrate up the bronchial tree to the trachea and pharynx. They are coughed up and swallowed. The final two parasitic molts (L3s Immature adults) take place in the small intestine. The period ranges from 12-16 weeks.

Clinical Signs

The clinical signs of parascariosis include fever, a white/gray nasal discharge, coughing, unthriftiness, colic and rarely, intestinal rupture with subsequent peritonitis. The injury produced by acaroids covers a wide range, from light infections producing moderate untoward effects to heavy infections, which may be the essential cause of death. Death from ascarid infection is usually due to a ruptured intestine. Serious lung damage caused by migrating ascarid larvae may result in pneumonia. More common and probably more important, is a retarded or impaired growth and development manifested by potbellies, rough hair coats and digestive disturbance in colts (2 to 5 months old often). A thousand or more worms are associated with clinical signs of disease.

Diagnosis

Ante mortem diagnosis can be made by findings characteristic eggs (brown, thick – shelled, spherical) in the faeces. The large nematodes are often seen in the faeces, particularly after anthelmintic treatment. Recovery of adults during a post mortem examination is common.

Prevention and Control

Good sanitation and sound management practices can play an important role in the prevention and control of this infection.

Actually, sanitation in the control of acaroids, as with the strongyles, is essentially the proper disposal of manure. The same general procedures apply to both infections. However, in comparison, acaroids are more difficult to cope with because of the extreme resistance to environmental conditions exhibited by the ascarid larvae enclosed in their tough eggshell.

Treatment

All classes of anthelmintic have good efficacy against adult stages but much less effective against migrating / immature acaroids. Proven regimens for larval stages are Fenbendazole and Ivermectin. No known agent can be employed prophylactically against acaroids in the way small doses of phenothiazine are used against strongyles. Then treatment is limited to the administration of therapeutic doses at intervals. Periodic removal of the worms by treatment interrupts the contamination of the environment with eggs for the dam or succeeding crops of foals.

Control

Since it is extremely difficult to remove infective material already present, control measures should be aimed at preventing further contamination of the environment. This will be achieved by 4-6 weekly anthelmintic treatments of foals from 1-2 months of age onwards to remove developing parasites and thus reduce the number of infective eggs, which would otherwise become available for foals of the same or succeeding generations. Where possible mares and foals should avoid for several years the pastures previously grazed by young animals.

PINWORM INFECTION

Oxyuris equi is common in young foals. The female worm lay eggs around the anus, which causes a perineal pruritis. Broken hairs and occasional bare patches on the tail, are caused by rubbing in response to the itching. On lifting the tail the egg masses are seen as grayish/yellow streaks on the perineum.

Pinworm is susceptible to all of the modem broad-spectrum anthelmintics.

ECTOPARASITES OF HORSES

Ectoparasites are agents that live on or close to the surface of its host – generally, skin. They are important for two reasons.

(a) They are a direct cause of disease and annoyance. Some cause illness through blood loss (lice) and severe dermatitis (mange mites., biting midge dermatitis (sweet itch")). Others are unsightly and /or complicate existing conditions (maggots in wounds – "fly strike").

(b) Arguably, more important is their role as **vectors** (transmitters of diseases). As a general rule, ticks are the most versatile vectors since they parasitized all vertebrate groups, transmit some of the most significant animal pathogens, and survive for up to 3 years, permitting them to assume dual roles as disease **vectors** and **reservoir hosts.**

Vector	Disease agent	Disease
Biting midge (*Culicodes* spp.)	West Nile (WN) Virus	West Nile virus encephalomyelitis
	Equine Infectious Anemia (EIA) virus	Equine infectious anemia ("Swamp fever")
Mosquitoes (Multiple species)	Eastern Equine Encephalomyelitis (EEE) Virus	EE encephalomyelitis
	Western Equine Encephalitis (WEE) Virus	WE encephalomyelitis
	Japanese Encephalitis (JE) Virus	Japanese Encephalitis
Forage mite	Tapeworm	Colitis
Flies	Equine Infectious Anemia Virus (EIA)	Equine infectious anemia
Ticks	Babesia Equi	Equine babesiosis
Biting flies e.g. tabanids	Trypanosomes	Trypanosomiasis
Culicine Mosquitoes	Setaria spp. (microfilaria)	Cerebrospinal nematodiasis

Ectoparasites of horses

Flies: There are several kinds of flies that suck blood from horses. These may include horn flies, deer flies, stable flies and in some cases, black flies. The main damage that flies do is annoyance to the horse. Flies transmit various diseases, as well as cause annoyance, hypersensitivity reactions, and myiasis.

Horse flies (Tabanus sp) and Deer flies (Chrysops sp) are serious pests of horses. These heavy-bodied, brown or black flies are swift fliers and vicious biters. They have clear or striped wings and range from 1/3 to 1 inch in size. These insects feed by piercing the skin of the horse and sucking the blood as it wells up in the wound. Only the adult females are blood feeders and they only feed during the day light hours. Horse flies and deer flies are usually found feeding on the head, neck, shoulders and back. Horse flies and other blood-sucking insects have been implicated in the transmission of "swamp" fever (equine infectious anemia) in horses.

Most horse flies and deer flies have only one generation per year. The female lays her eggs on vegetation around moist, swampy places. The larvae burrow into the mud where they spend the next year feeding on small animals. They pupate in the spring and emerge as adults by early summer. Control of horse flies and deer flies is very difficult. Some control can be achieved by draining wetlands or by using approved insecticides for larval control. Pyrethrum sprays, organophosphate and synthetic parathyroid insecticide sprays give limited control of these pests. These flies do not normally enter structures. Providing pastured horses space and structures for sanctuary during heavy attacks helps alleviate the control problem.

Stable Flies (Stomoxys calcitrans) : are the most injurious flies that attack horses. This insect is about the same size of the common housefly, but it is a blood feeder, both sexes feed on blood. Stable flies are usually found feeding on the lower legs or flanks of the horse. Due to the painful bite, horses will stamp and kick trying to get rid themselves of these pests. When present in large numbers, stable flies can cause considerable blood loss as well as severe irritation. The flies stay on the animal only while feeding, after which they seek a sheltered area to digest their meal. Females must have meal each time they lay eggs. These flies may contribute to the transmission of swamp fever and are victors of "summer sores" weeping wounds that are difficult to heal.

Stable flies breed in decaying organic matter. A fermenting mixture of straw, manure and urine is ideal. Although, horse manure is usually too dry to support their development, it become an adequate breeding medium when allowed to accumulate in stalls or barns where it becomes moistened with urine or water. Decaying straw, grass clippings, hay or silage are also suitable breeding materials for stable flies.

The life cycle of stable flies from egg to adult takes 21 to 25 days. Females can lay up 20 batches of eggs. High populations can build up under optimum conditions. Control of stable flies. Insecticides may be applied to the animal especially to the legs of the horse. They should be reaplied when they appear to be losing their effectiveness. Under heavy populations, pasture horses away from wooded areas and treat with insecticides every day or two.

House Flies (Musca Domestica), are not serious pests of horse, but they are important disease carriers. These flies transmit stomach worms and have been incriminated in the transmission of over 60 vertebrate pathogens by body part contamination, regurgitation and defecation. The horse fly can cause considerable irritation to the horse when feeding on secretions around the eyes. These flies are ¼ inch long and dull black or dark gray. House flies feed on a broad range of food and filth including rotting organic matter, garbage, all types of excrement, wet and rotting hay, grass, straw grain or silage but seem to prefer horse manure.

They have a short life cycle of 6 to 14 days and build up high populations around stables, if not controlled.

Summer Sores (Cutaneous Habronemiasis): As the name suggests, this is a seasonal skin disease caused by larvae of three nematode species {Habronema muscae, H. micro stoma and H. megastoma. The eggs of all the three species are passed out in the faeces, and development takes place as a result of ingestion of the eggs or larvae by the larvae of domestic flies. In case of H. microstoma. The host is stable fly (stomokys calcitrans) and in case of other two, common house fly (Muscadomestica) is the intermediate host. Flies become infected from faeces. The parasites develop in house and stable flies. The normal life cycle is completed when infective larvae escape from the probosis of the adult flies and are deposited on the skin around the horse's lips, and are then swallowed. Further development takes place in the stomach of the horse.

Cutaneous habronemiasis is a from of aberrant parasitism in which larvae gain access to deeper layers of the skin via wounds. The larvae may escape from the fly when it is resting on small abrasions on the body. In case of H. microstoma, the larvae may be actually planted in uninjured skin by the probosis of stomoxys. This further leads to development of summer saves, bursati and conjunctivitis. The disease is seasonal, first appearing in spring and, in most cases, regressing in winter. The occurrence of the disease is sporadic, only a few horses in a given area are affected, supporting the hypothesis in winter that it is hypersensitivity. Once the disease develops it recurs each succeeding summer unless preventative measures are taken. The disease can be controlled by fly control and wound care. Ivermectin can be used to kill newly deposited larvae.

Sweet Itch (cutaneous hypersensitivity to Culicoides spp.): Biting midges, particularly species of the genus culicoides, are incriminated in the transmission of multiple viral, protozoal, and filarial agents. Only female culicoides feed, usually in early evening and early morning hours. Culicoides are active during hot, humid and still environmental conditions. Sweet itch is a common skin disease of horse throughout the world and is known by various names. It is an allergic reaction to the bites of culicoides, and usually only one horse in a group will be affected. It is rare or nonexistent in horses under one year of age. The age of onset is 2- 4 years. Initially, the disease is seasonal and appears in spring.

EQUESTRIAN SPORTS

Chapter 26

Historical Background

The 'horse' has been used all over the world over the centuries; ranging from a pack animal, conveyor of man and material into battle field, travelling over land and in many other different forms.

The Egyptian tomb paintings give vivid pictures of how the horse was used and the decorative scenes on early Chinese vases indicate that people were riding and driving horses at that time. In many parts of the world, the horse is still the mainstay to the life and the livelihood of many families. The only means of travelling the more remote parts of the world is still by horse and many a modern war could not have been fought without the use of horses, when even the most up-to-date machinery could not cope up with the rough terrain encountered. It may seem a relatively recent development that the horse has been considered primarily for sport, but hunting has taken place worldwide for centuries. Perhaps, it was through this that man first realized what tremendous speed and jumping ability, the horse possessed. Chariot races in Roman times were an exciting but dangerous sport and races of speed and endurance have been recorded in various parts of the world in ancient times. One of the first organized horse races in England is thought to have been held as far back as A.D. 210 and there is historic evidence that subsequently various equestrian contests took place all over the world.

The precise date of first equestrian sport may be difficult to state but one knows that horsemen pitted their skills against one another in sporting contests hundreds of years before christ. Contests on horseback and chariot racing were very popular in ancient days. Equestrian games were included in the Olympic

Games at Paris in 1902, including long (6 m 10 cm) and high jumps (1 m 85 cm). The first three day event was conducted at Stockholm Olympics in 1912 under the Name MILITAIRE (only military officers with chargers competed). It covered a 55 kilometre course of which five kilometre was cross-country across obstacles, 3.5 kilometre steeplechase and dressage. The modern day three day event was introduced in Paris Olympics of 1924, open to military officers and also civilians under FEI (The International Federation of Equestrian Sports). Non-commissioned army officers were permitted to enter in 1956. Women riders were permitted to compete in Olympics in 1964.

History of Federation Equestre Internationale (FEI)

1 An international equestrian federation was constituted on 28th May 1921 under the name of Fédération Equestre International. (FEI).

2. The FEI was founded when the National Equestrian Federations of Belgium, Denmark, France, Italy, Japan, Norway, Sweden and the U.S.A. signed the first statutes at a congress in Paris on 24th and 25th November 1921. The first President was ***Baron-Du-Teil (France).*** Ever since, it has brought under its control, all international equestrian competitions and FEI is progressing horsemanship in the world. It has now over 120 member countries.

3. Membership in the FEI is open to the one national governing body from each country which is effectively in control of or is in a position to effectively control at least the Olympic equestrian disciplines, preferably the one body recognized by its National Olympic Committee, and which is prepared to accept the obligations contained in and abide by the statutes, regulations and rules. National governing bodies with membership in the FEI are referred to as "National Federations". India took membership of FEI in 1971 and Pakistan in 1982. English and French are the official languages of the FEI. The FEI is located in Switzerland, as an incorporated body under the Swiss Civil Code. In all matters of civil litigation involving the FEI Swiss law shall apply. All civil actions (litigation) shall be brought before

the Swiss courts of the city in which the FEI is located, subject to requirements regarding arbitration under the statutes. In case of war, the FEI should continue its activity in its present headquarters for as long as possible.

4 Presently the Honorary Presidents of FEI are H.R.H. The Prince Philip, Duke of Edinburgh and H.R.H., the Princess Royal, GCVO

Asian Equestrian Federation (AEF)

The Asian Equestrian Federation (AEF) was formed during the meeting of 8th Asian Games Federation held at Bangkok (Thailand) in December 1978. General O.P. Malhotra, PVSM from India was elected as the founder President with 18 member countries. Four prominent persons of the equestrian field from Iraq, Japan, Philippines and People's Republic of China, were elected as Vice Presidents. The executive members were elected from Indonesia, Hong Kong, Iran and Singapore.

Equestrian Federation of India (EFI)

EFI was born in 1967. It took up the membership of FEI in 1971 and ever since it is inculcating a love for the horse flesh and has been actively engaged in improving the standard of equestrian sports in the Armed Forces, Police, Para Military Forces and Civil Riding Clubs in India.

Equestrian Sports

Dressage

The word 'dressage' is derived from the French verb 'Dresser' which described the training and schooling of a riding horse. This is exactly what is understood by the word today but perhaps it has become associated with the more advanced training of horse on the flat.

The training of horses has fascinated man since the earliest times, but dressage became particularly fashionable in the 1700-1800s. Covered riding schools appeared and Europe became the centre of dressage and schooling particularly, Germany and

Switzerland. Simultaneously, Denmark and Russia also, excelled in dressage. In Olympic sport since 1912, dressage is governed at the top level by the FEI (Federation Equestre International) for international competitions. Each country adopts its own rules for national competitions adapted from those of the FEI and sets it own dressage tests to be performed in one of the two recognized arenas, a small one measuring 20 x 40 metres (66 x 131 feet) or of the size 20 x 60 metres (66 x 197 feet). The various tests are designed to suit horses of different levels of training, from novice to advanced.

Types of Competition

The international tests start at an advanced level and progress to include all the movements required at Olympic standard, for the ultimate competition - the Grand Prix test.

Dressage to music has recently been introduced at all levels and is proving tremendously popular with spectators and riders alike. Judged on similar lines to skating, there are two marks, one for technical merit and the other for interpretation of the music. Competitions are held for all age groups and standards. Every year, there is a major international championship for juniors, young riders and seniors as well. The Olympic Games are held every fourth year and the World Championships two years later. Every fourth year, European and American championships are also held slotted in between every two years. Germany is undoubtedly the champion nation in the field of dressage but Switzerland, Denmark and Russia have always produced good teams and Britain is now taking great strides to close the gap.

Show Jumping

Jumping competitions have been taking place since the turn of the century, but it was not until after the Second World War that international championships took place. It appears that the first organized class for show jumping took place in Paris in 1866. At that time, the riders disappeared after an initial parade, to jump some fences outside. Presumably, these were more like cross-country jumps but this did not appeal much to the spectators who were left watching an empty arena. Since that time, obstacles are being placed within the arena.

In 1912, show jumping was included in the Olymplc Games for the first time. In 1921, eight countries got together to draw up some guidelines on rules for show jumping (Belgium, Denmark, France, Italy, Norway, Sweden and the United States of America). This group effectively standardised regulations on the sport. This was the start of the FEI (Federation Equestre Internationale), now joined by all equestrian nations which is governing body of all international equestrian sports, including the equestrian events at the Olympic Games.

Types of Competition

The pattern of competition has been established around the Olympic Games, for world as well as European and Pan-American Games. Presently, there is major championship every year and numerous special championships at all the leading equestrian shows worldwide. These competitions are held for junior and senior riders as well as for children on ponies.

Jumping Derbys, where the horse is expected to jump a much longer course of more natural fences, demand special types of horses and clear rounds are relatively few. The Hickstead Derby with its famous bank and the Hamburg Derby are among the best known in the world.

Eventing

Horse trials originally started as a military sport for soldiers (in fact eventing is still known as the military sport in Europe). It was considered an ideal way to test the stamina and versatility of the chargers. It was not until after the Second World War, that civilians started participating in it.

Eventing has now become the fastest growing equestrian sport and international competitions are held regularly in the Americas, Europe, Australia, New Zealand, England, India and many other countries.

Types of Competition

The world of eventing combines dressage and show jumping with a speed and endurance section which at the top level, includes steeplechase, roads and tracks and the cross-country course with three phases being performed over three days. Dressage on day 1, speed and endurance and cross-country on day 2, and the show jumping on the last day. The whole competition being called a three day event. A condensed form of this competition without the speed and endurance section is used as the training ground for three day events, in the form of a one day event. Eventing is a tough sport. Whereas pure show jumping and dressage are specialist sports, eventing is more for the all round rider and horse. Accordingly, every rider's ambition is to compete in a three day event. Because of the demands on skill and fitness involved in eventing, a horse is generally not expected to do more than two three day events a year, but it may compete in several one day events depending on the severity and standard of the competition itself. These events often act as qualifying rounds for the three day event but these are designed for the different standards and experience of horses. The events are usually divided into a novice, intermediate and advanced grade. Many countries have a lower level even to help and encourage the young horse over smaller courses.

Veterinary Inspection And Horse Examination For Equestrian Sports

The object of the **Veterinary Examination** is to:

1 Verify the identity of each horse from its passport;

2 Check that the vaccination status of the horse is in accordance with the current veterinary regulations;

3 Verify whether all other details are correctly recorded in the passport;

4 Check that the animal has not been in contact with other animals suffering from infectious or contagious disease (e.g. strangles) or has come from an establishment that is not free of such disease;

5 To check that the Official Measurement Certificate for Ponies is in order at a FEI events for ponies;

6 Carry out a clinical examination to ensure that the horse is not suffering from any infectious or contagious disease. This examination may include the palpation of limbs and body, monitoring heart and respiratory rate, body temperature and any other pertinent clinical parameters necessary. The limbs may be palpated or lifted to examine a suspected abnormality. However, an examination for any lameness (i.e. flexion tests or a trot-up) is not part of this examination. A record of the clinical findings must be made which should follow the horse through successive examinations and inspections.

If the veterinarian's opinion is that the horse should not be allowed to be in contact with the other participants or should not take part in the event, the case must be referred to the Ground Jury and the Veterinary Commission/Delegate for a final decision

Horse Inspections

1. The aim of the standardized Horse Inspection protocol is to ensure the 'fitness to compete' of horses, taking part in Equestrian competitions by providing the same objective protocol for all disciplines except Endurance Riding.
2. Horse Inspections are not intended to be of an equivalent standard to a veterinary examination for soundness or a pre-purchase evaluation.
3. The specific level of fitness required to pass horse inspections which may vary between disciplines and even within some disciplines (e.g., 1st and 3rd Horse Inspections in Eventing).

4 The implementation of the 'fitness to compete' principle is essential to the fairness and objectivity of these inspections.

5 The decisions involved (i.e. accept/not accept or referred to the Holding Box) must be made by a panel of judges and veterinarians (i.e. the Inspection Panel).

The general lay out of horse inspection as per FEI rule is given in Fig 26.1

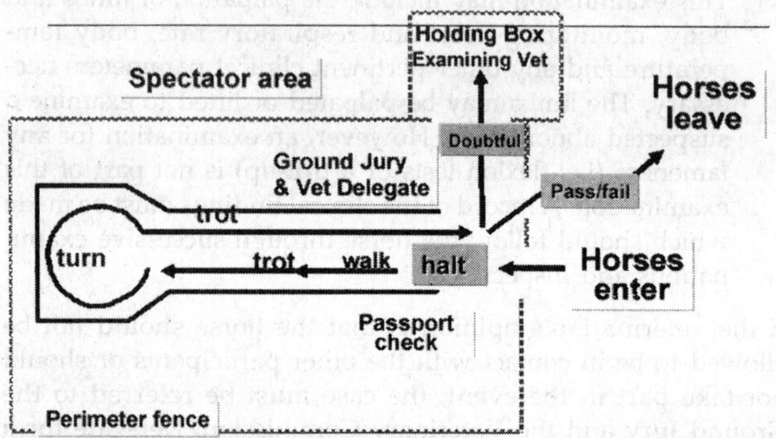

Walk 10 metres
Trot on loose rein 40 metres
Turn to the right (clockwise)
Trot back on loose rein 50 metres

Fig 26.1

Code of Conduct For Equestrian Sports

Those involved in equestrian sport should adhere to the FEI's Code of Conduct and acknowledge and accept that at all times the welfare of the horse must be paramount and must never be subordinated to competitive or commercial influences.

1. At all stages during the preparation and training of competition horses, welfare must take precedence over all other demands. This includes good horse management, training methods, farriery, tack, and transportation.
2. Horses and competitors must be fit, competent and in good health before they are allowed to compete. This encompasses medication use, surgical procedures that threaten welfare or safety, pregnancy in mares and the misuse of aids.

3. Events must not prejudice horse welfare. This involves paying careful attention to the competition areas, ground surfaces, weather conditions, stabling, site safety and fitness of the horse for onward travel after the event.
4. Every effort must be made to ensure that horses receive proper attention after they have competed and that they are treated humanely when their competition careers are over. This covers proper veterinary care, competition injuries, euthanasia and retirement.
5. The FEI urges, all involved with the sport to attain the highest levels of education in their areas of expertise.

Chapter 27
Dressage

Object and General Principles

The object of Dressage is a harmonious development of the physique and ability of the horse. As a result, it makes the horse calm, supple, loose and flexible, but also confident, attentive and keen, thus achieving perfect understanding with his rider. These qualities are revealed by:

(a) The freedom and regularity of the paces;

(b) The harmony, lightness and ease of the movements;

(c) The lightness of forehand and the engagement of the hind quarter originating in a leverly impulsion;

(d) The acceptance of the bridle, with submissiveness throughout and without any tenseness or resistance.

Some basic movements of Dressage

The Halt - At the halt, the horse should stand attentive, motionless and straight, with weight evenly distributed over all four legs, being in pairs abreast with each other. The neck should be raised and poll high and head slightly in front of the vertical.

The Walk - The walk is a marching pace of "four time", the sequence of hoof beats being, left hind, left fore, right hind and right fore. There are four recognized walks i.e. walk, medium walk, extended walk and free walk.

The Trot - The trot is a pace of "two time" on alternate diagonal legs (left fore and right hind leg and vice versa) separated by movement of suspension. There are four recognized trots i.e. collected trot, working trot, medium trot and extended trot.

The Canter - The canter is a pace of "three time" where at canter at the right, for instance, the foot falls follow one another as follows - left hind, left diagonal (simultaneously left fore and right hind), right fore, followed by a movement of suspension with all four feet in the air before the next stride begins. The Canter is always with light cadenced and regular strides, should be moved into without hesitation. There are following types of canters i.e. collected canter, working canter, medium canter and extended canter.

The Rein Back - The rein back is an equilateral, retrograde movement in which the feet are raised and set down by diagonal pairs.

Half Pass - The horse slightly bent round the inside leg of the rider, should be as close as possible parallel to the long sides of the arena, executed on the diagonal instead of along the wall.

The Pirouette and the Half Pirouette - The pirouette (half pirouette) is a circle (half-circle) executed on two tracks, with a radius equal to the length of the horse, the forehead moving round the haunches.

Execution of the Test

Test must be carried out entirely from memory, and all movements must follow in the laid down sequence. Every error of the course is penalized -

First time - 2 points

Second time - 4 points

Third time - 8 points

Fourth time - Competitor is eliminated

Marking

Dressage event is marked from 0 to 10 by each judge, 0 being the lowest and 10 the highest mark. The scale of marks is as follows:

10 - Excellent 4 - Insufficient

9 - Very good 3 - Fairly bad

8 - Good	2 - Bad
7 - Fairly good	1 - Very bad
6 - Satisfactory	0 - Not executed
5 - Sufficient	

Open Dressage

The competitor performs a set pattern of movements in an Arena, where he is evaluated and marked for each movement. In addition, collective marks are awarded on overall performance based on the horse's pace, impulsion, lightness and submission and on the rider's seat as well as his correct use of aids. A diagramatic sketch of dressage arena is shown in Fig. 27.1:

Open Dressage Test

		Movements	*Mks*	*Pts*	*Cor*	*Remarks*
1.	A	Enter at collected trot				
	X	Halt Salute Proceed at collected trot				
2.	C	Turn right				
	R	Circle right 8 Mtrs diameter				
3.	RF	Shoulder-in				
4.	FAK	Collected Trot				
	KXM	Change reins in medium trot				
	MCHS	Collected trot				
5.	S	Circle left 8 Mtrs diameter				
6.	SK	Shoulder-in				
7.	KAF	Collected trot				
	FXH	Extended trot				
	HCMB	Collected trot				
8.	B	1 ½ Circle right 10 Mtrs diameter				
	XM	Half Pass				
9.	MCHE	Collected trot				
	E	1 ½ circle left 10 mtrs diameter				
	XH	Half pass				
	HC	Collected trot				
10.	C	Half-Rein back 4 steps and immediately proceed in collected walk				
11.	M	Turn right Between G and H				
		Half Pirouette right				
12.	Between G and M	Half Pirouette left				

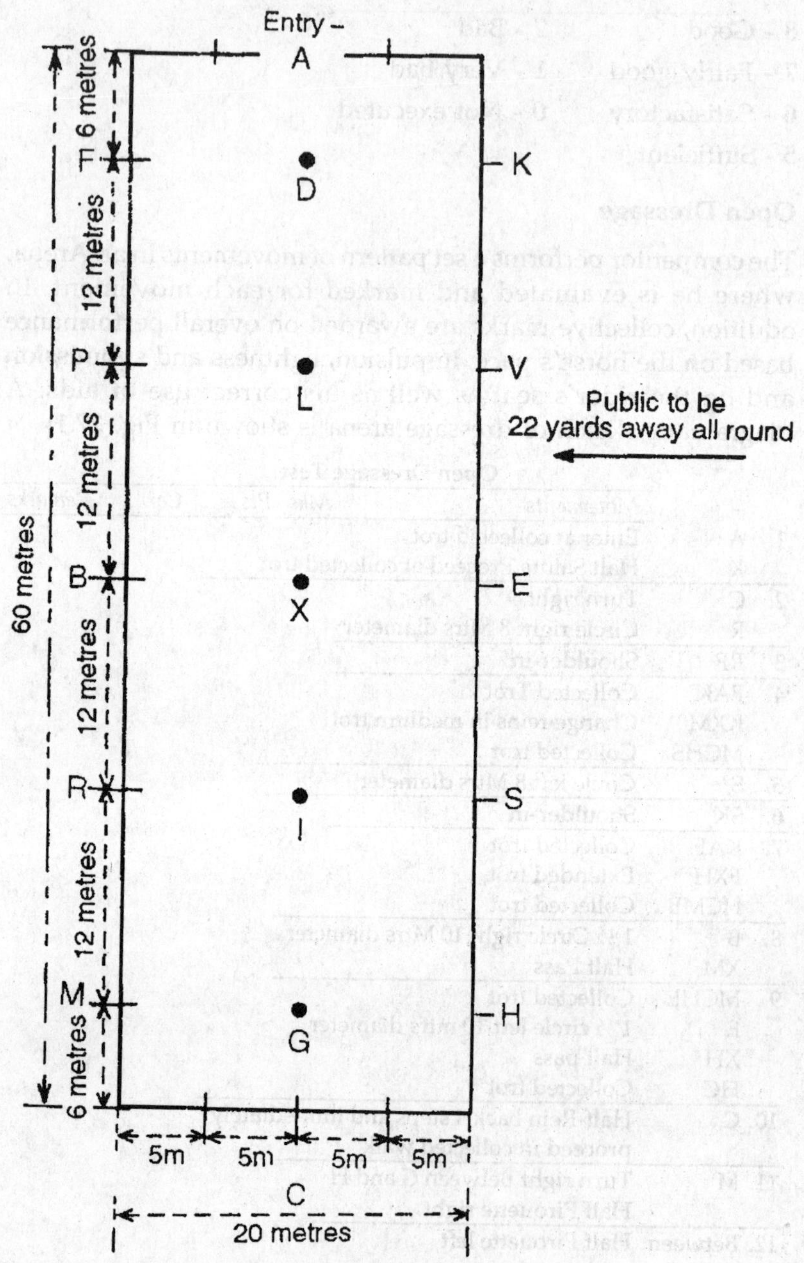
Entry –
A
K
D
V
L
Public to be
22 yards away all round
E
X
S
I
H
G
T
P
B
R
M
60 metres
6 metres
12 metres
12 metres
12 metres
12 metres
6 metres
5m
5m
5m
5m
C
20 metres

Fig. 27.1

13.	HXF	Extended walk
	F	Collected walk
14.	A	Proceed in collected canter right
	V	Turn right
15.	L	Simple change of leg (Through walk)
	P	Turn left
16.	R	Turn left
	I	Simple change of leg (Through walk)
	SHC	Collected canter right
17.	CA	Serpentine 3 loops without change of leg
18.	A	Circle right 10 Mtrs diameter
19:	KXM	Change rein with simple change of leg at X
20.	C	Circle left 10 Mtrs diameter
21.	HXF	Change rein in medium canter
	FAX	Collected trot
22.	X	Half-Immobility Salute
		Leave arena in free walk at A
		Total
		Total (Carried over)

Collective Marks

1. Pace (Freedom and regularity)

2. Impulsion (Desire to move forward, elasticity of the steps, suppleness of the back and engagement of the quarters)

3. Submission (attention and confidence, harmony, lightness and ease of the movements, acceptance of the bridle and the natural equilibrium)

4. Rider's position and seat:
   Correctness and effect of the aids:

TOTAL

To be deducted
Errors of the course and omissions etc. are penalized :
1st time - 2 points, 2nd time - 4 points
3rd time - 8 points, 4th time - Elimination

TOTAL

Dress Rule

1. **Civilians**: A black or dark blue tail coat (other colours may be approved by the FEI Dressage Committee by application), with top hat*, white or off white breeches, stock or tie, gloves, black riding boots and spurs must be worn. Dark blue jacket with a bowler hat or hunting cap is also permitted. This dress is also desirable for all other international dressage events, unless otherwise stated in any special rules. For safety reasons, a rider wishes to wear an approved protective headgear, this is permitted. National colours may only be used on collars of competitors' jackets and must be registered with the FEI.
2. **Military, Police**, etc. may wear civil or service dress at all international events. Service dress does not only apply to Members of the armed forces and police, but also to members and employees/students of military establishments and national studs /schools/institutes.
3. Spurs must be made of metal. The shank must be either curved or straight pointing directly back from the centre of the spur when on the rider's boot. The arms of the spur must be smooth. If rowels are used, they must be smooth and free to rotate. Metal spurs with round hard plastic knobs are allowed ("Impuls" spur). "Dummy" spurs with no shank are allowed.

Saddlery Rule

1. The following are compulsory: Dressage saddle, which must be close to the horse and have long, near-vertical flaps, double bridle with cavesson noseband, i.e. bridoon and curb with curb chain. A cavesson nose band may never be as tightly fixed so as to harm the horse. Lip strap and rubber or leather cover for curb chain is optional. Padding is allowed on bridles. No saddle covers are allowed.
2. *Bits*. Bridoon and curb must be made of metal or rigid plastic and may be covered with rubber (wrapping of bits and flexible rubber bits are not permitted). The lever arm of the curb bit is limited to 10 cm (length below the mouth

piece). If the curb has a sliding mouthpiece, the lever arm of the curb bit below the mouth piece should not measure more than 10 cm when the mouth piece is at the uppermost position. The diameter of the mouthpiece of the bridoon must be such that it should not hurt the horse.

3. **Whips**: At all international events, it is, under penalty of elimination, forbidden to carry a whip of any kind while competing in the arena. However, the use of one whip, with a total maximum length of 110 cm, in the practice area is allowed. The whip must be dropped before entering the space around the competition arena or the rider will entail a penalty of 4 points per judge. Upon arrival on the showground, only the rider when riding, walking, leading or lungeing a horse (lunge whip allowed), is allowed to carry a whip (maximum 110 cm) anywhere on the showground. The groom may also walk, lead and lunge a horse as above. Other parties are allowed to carry a whip, provided it is not in connection with the training of the horse.

4. **Gadgets** : Martingales, breast plates, bit guards, any kind of gadgets (such as bearing, side, running or balancing reins, nasal strips etc.), any kind of boots or bandages and any form of blinkers, including ear muffs, and any others, are, under penalty of elimination, strictly forbidden. Any decoration of the horse with extravagant items, such as ribbons or flowers, etc. in the tail, etc., is strictly forbidden. Normal plaiting of the horse's mane and tail, however, is allowed.

   False tails are permitted only with the prior permission of the FEI. False tails may not contain any metal parts, except for hooks and eyelets. Fly hoods will be permitted solely in order to protect horses from insects.These will be permitted in extreme cases only and at the discretion of the President of the Ground Jury/Technical Delegate. The fly hoods should be discreet and should not cover the horse's eyes.

5. **Checking of Saddlery**: A Steward must be appointed to

check the saddlery of each horse immediately he leaves the arena. Any discrepancy will entail immediate elimination. The checking of the bridle must be done with the greatest caution, as some horses are very touchy and sensitive about their mouths. The Steward must use disposable surgical/protective gloves when checking the bridle (one pair of gloves per horse).

6. **Warming-up and Training Areas**. Paragraphs 1 and 4 above are valid also for warming-up arenas and other training areas where, however, snaffles with a cavesson or a normal dropped noseband, Mexican noseband or a flash noseband, running martingales (with snaffle only), boots, bandages and single direct side reins (the latter solely when lungeing only with one lunge line) and ear muffs are permitted.
7. **Identification Number**: Each horse keeps the same identification number provided by the organizer on arrival throughout the competition. It is compulsory that this number be worn by the horse while actively competing and at any time while working in the exercise and schooling areas or being hand walked (from the time of their arrival until the end of the Event) so that they can be identified by all officials including the stewards. Failure to display this number incurs first a warning and, in the case of a repeated offence, a fine imposed on the competitor by the ground jury.

Show-Jumping

Of all equestrian sports, show-jumping competitions are the most popular. They test the rider's ability to present his well-trained horse at each jump correctly and accurately so as to clear it. They are easier to organize than cross-country events, since less space and fewer officials are required. The judge, course-builder and a time-keeper are necessary, and at least two active helpers must be available to rebuild fences and replace poles when competitors dislodge them; a steward in the collecting ring is needed to send riders in to jump in the right order.

Riders find show-jumping competitions exciting and often fascinating; also, since each rider is in the arena for little more than one minute, hundreds get the opportunity to compete in one day.

Although, most show-jumping competitions are held in outdoor arenas, indoor competitions are becoming increasingly popular in most countries, partly because the event can be held despite bad weather or unsuitable ground conditions outside.

Courses and Jumps

The length of a show jumping course will vary between 450 m and 2,000 m. The arena should be large enough to contain 10 to 12 jumps, including at least one combination. The start and finish must be clearly marked and the jumps should be numbered at one side, against the wing. They may also be flagged; a red flag on the right, white on the left. The ground should not be rough or uneven, nor boggy or hard. A small collecting ring at the entrance to the main ring is used for competitors to await their turn, and there should be a steward to control the order of jumping.

Show-jumps should have a strong and solid appearance, to encourage bold, confident jumping, and thus to avoid constant rebuilding. All show-jumps must knock down easily, but without bringing the wings with them, which means the cups holding the poles must not be too deep. Round poles should be held in round cups, not more than half the diameter of the pole; planks should rest on flatter cups so that they can slide off when hit. Similarly, an octagonal pole must only be used on an angled cup which allows it to fall.

Course-builders will provide a variety of jumps which are interesting for the riders, and also less repetitive for the horses, as well as making the competition visually more exciting for spectators. The first two jumps on a course should be sloping, with a good ground-line, the second could be a small upright. Spreads and uprights should alternate round the course to provide variety and interest.

To encourage a flowing style with no breaks in stride, a minimum of 18 m should be allowed between each fence (the distance will be shorter in indoor arenas) so that one can rebalance his/her horse before the next jump. In combination jumps, the distance is measured from the back of the first element, or part of the jump, to the front of the second. Equally, the turn on a show-jumping course should follow a smooth route, with enough space to straighten and balance the horse in front of a fence (particularly before a combination, big spread, or water jump). An experienced course builder who understands jumping, can build a variety of good courses and get a fair result without resorting to tricks. He will position each obstacle at a suitable distance in relation to the next, so that a minimum-adjustment to the canter stride of the horse should be necessary, "wrong" distances between jumps will upset the horse's rhythm and balance and may make him lose confidence.

A typical selection of jumps will consist basically of uprights and spreads, they can vary in appearance. The water jump, for instance, can be used with a small hedge, or similar object, placed in front of it as take-off guide (known as "open" water), or may have poles over it.

A hedge can be a useful "filler" in a fence to make it look substantial and inviting to jump whether artificial or a permanent planted one, it should not be higher than any pole placed beyond it. The pole should be clearly visible to the horse, so that he can judge the height and width of the obstacle. A brightly painted, or white pole is more obvious than a rustic, brown or green pole.

Combination can be either doubles or trebles. A double consists of two jumps spaced at one or two strides apart. The gap between the jumps should not exceed 12 m and this is only suitable between very big wide jumps. A treble is a jump with three elements, again with each one spaced either one or two strides apart. The distance between the jumps will vary according to the height and whether the jumps are uprights, spreads, or a combination of both.

On a show ground where competitions are held frequently, special permanent jumps may be built to make the arena interesting and attractive to riders and spectators. However, under wet conditions, the ground around the take-off and landing areas can become very cut up, taking a long time to recover and therefore, permanent fences should not be used too often, particularly if the course has to be used again soon afterwards.

The water jump must be sited so that it can be avoided easily when not in use. Smaller water jumps, or water-filled ditches, can be used under or in front of poles, as variation.

Ditches add variety to a show-jumping course as long as they are dug deep enough to be well defined, but not so deep that a horse could become stuck in them. Slopes are also popular, but banks are controversial. Many riders consider it unfair to ask a horse to jump on to, then off, a bank, when they have been schooled always to clear every obstacle without touching it. Others argue that a horse jumps a bank naturally and will not be confused if well presented at an attractive-looking bank which is obviously too big to be cleared in one leap (known as an Irish bank).

There are many permanent combination-type fences which can be built such as pens and boxes, ramps, etc. but there must always be an exit, in case the horse refuses and cannot extricate himself. Alternatively, the top rails must knock down.

Jumping at a Show

Before competing, make sure that the horse is fit, and able to cope up with what is required of him. As in dressage contests, one should begin by competing at a grade slightly below the standard of training he has achieved at home. When one is jumping clear rounds at this level, he can progress to more advanced competitions.

Before going to a show, check that you have all the equipments you will need and a haynet for the return journey. Work out your schedule to allow enough time on arrival to check in with the officials, collect your number, and study the layout of the show ground; meanwhile, your horse can stand quietly after his journey.

Remove any travelling gear from your horse, and tack up. Next, prepare yourself, making sure you are correctly and tidily dressed, with boots, spurs (optional), hard hat, jacket number (if worn), gloves and whip, if used, walk the course, then warm up your horse with a series of exercises at the trot and canter. When you feel he is ready, you can take him into the practice jumping arena and spare time by watching others jump and noting which jumps present particular difficulties.

Walking the Course

You just walk the course before the class is due to commence, in order to study both the jumps and the route you will take between them. Make sure you know the rules under which a particular class is to be run. A plan of the course is often available in the collecting ring, or near by. Study this first for the layout, and note which fences will be jumped in the jump-off and whether or not this will be against the clock, so that you can plan ahead to clear first round. The importance of speed in the timed jump-off makes it essential to work out the shortest route possible around the course.

When walking, plan each approach, noting the state of the ground, and decide how you will tackle any problems on the course. Walk any combination jumps with care, measuring the distance between each element, to judge the number and length of strides required. If the jump follows a turn, you should allow at least four strides of straight approach in the first round, particularly before spread fences, which should be jumped straight and with stronger impulsion. Plan exactly where to turn to allow a perfect approach to each jump (This may be more of a consideration in indoor arenas, where the jumps are often set more closely together). Upright jumps will require greater collection and accuracy, especially when following soon after a spread or combination.

The Practice Jumping Area

It is used to help supple your horse in preparation for first round. Approach a low jump (approx. 0.8m high) at the trot, to encourage your horse to jump off-his hocks. Then canter slowly at a slightly larger jump say, an upright with an inviting ground-line pole. Then, at your normal pace, jump the upright at the approximate height it is built in the arena, and a spread of similar dimensions. Vary your practice to keep your horse interested. Finish up over a lowered practice fence to boost his confidence before entering the ring.

Jumping the Course

You may be sent in before the previous competitor has finished jumping, in which case walk quietly along the side of the arena so as not to distract him. It is polite to salute the judges just before starting your round.

After the bell rings to indicate you should start, you have a minute to prepare yourself. Do not rush as you may tense up or change rhythm. If you have decided to approach the first jump on the right rein, pick up a right lead at the canter and settle into your rhythm.

Half-halts to balance the horse and control his impulsion may be necessary after every jump: These may have to be stronger after a big spread or water jump to recollect him, transferring the horse's weight back towards his hindquarters, if he has become too low or heavy on the forehand.

If your horse refuses, knocking down or moving the jump as he does so, the bell will ring. While it is being rebuilt, get into position ready to approach again as soon as the bell goes. The clock is stopped from the time the first bell rings, until it sounds again. After three refusals, the bell will signal your elimination. On completing your round, your horse should remain on the aids until you have left the arena.

Judging

Most competitions are judged under standard rules or speed rules. All jumping classes have a pre-arranged time allowed to complete the course. This begins from the moment horse and rider cross the starting line to the time they pass the finishing post or flag. If the time allowed is exceeded, they will be penalized with time faults and if twice the time allowed is taken, they are eliminated. When a horse refuses and displaces a fence, the clock is stopped to allow the jump to be rebuilt before the rider re-presents his horse at the jump. The winner is the one with the fewest penalties or faults.

If more than one competitor has a clear first round, there will be a "jump-off' over a slightly raised and shortened course. The first jump-off may or may not be "against the clock" (ie. the fastest wins). In the event of equality of faults after the second round, there will be a further, timed jump off. To jump both fast and accurately, demands great skill. It is not necessary that the horse which looks the fastest wins, but, rather, the well-trained, balanced, accurately ridden horse, which can take the shortest route, turn quickly and respond to the finest of aids exactly, is the winner.

In some jumping classes, speed is the deciding factor in the first round.

Faults

The horse is penalized for disobedience when he refuses to jump by stopping in front of the fence; runs out by veering off to the side of the jump(s); resists by, for example, napping (turning away, rearing or going backward) or refusing to even approach the fence; or if the rider has to make a circle, thus crossing his tracks. He is penalized for a knockdown if, as a result of touching the fence, any part of it is lowered in height. The numbers of faults incurred for each mistake are shown below:

Penalties table

Mistake	*No. of faults*
1st disobedience	3
2nd disobedience of the whole round	6
3rd disobedience of the whole round	elimination
Knockdown	4
Fall of horse/rider	8
Exceeding time allowed for each commenced second	1/4
Exceeding time limit	elimination

Eventing

The eventing is a complete test of horse and the rider. The essential requisites of an eventer are courage, stamina, jumping ability, good temperament and absolute soundness. The varied nature of eventing calls for a special test, he must be an all-round athlete, completely obedient to the rider's commands, and a pleasure to watch. For the cross-country, the steeplechase and the roads and tracks phase, he must have great stamina and agility. Lastly, as a show jumper, he must possess the right blend of caution and courage.

Eventing is the ultimate test of the partnership of horse and rider, for not only must the horse be at the peak of fitness, but also the rider must be physically and mentally equipped for the strenuous build-up required for the competition.

Show-jumping and dressage events give the rider an idea of what to expect in the latter without going further. Nevertheless, it is success in the three-day event that is the pinnacle of achievement in this equestrian pentathlon.

Three Day Event - Team and Individual

Three Day Event consists of four distinct and independent phases, which follow one another without interruption, performed at a stretch and with no allowance for any halt. Each competitor carries out the whole test alone.

Dressage (first day)

In the Three Day Event Dressage Test, certain movements are laid down and for each movement, he is allotted marks. In addition, bonus marks are allotted for regularity of pace, impulsion and lightness, freedom and submission of horse.

Cross-country (second day)

This test is to prove the speed, endurance and jumping ability of the true cross-country horse when he is well trained and brought to the peak of condition. It extends over a course of 21,400 m. At the same time, it demonstrates the rider's knowledge of pace and the use of his horse across country.

The test consists of four distinct and independent phases, which follow one another and are performed at a stretch with only one halt of 10 min to allow for a veterinary inspection after Phase 'C' and start of Phase 'D'. Each competitor carries out the whole test alone. The four phases are:

Phases	Roads and tracks, normally carried out at the trot and slow canter.
A & C	To cover 14,000 metres at a speed of 240 metres per minute (60 minutes).
Phase B	Steeplechase - Over a course of 1600 metres with 6 obstacles, to be carried out at a speed of 600 metres per minute (2 minutes).
Phase D	Cross-country - About 5400 metres with 20 natural obstacles to be run at a speed of 450 metres per minute (12 minutes).

Jumping Test (third day)

The third day begins with a final veterinary examination carried out by the ground Jury, assisted by the official veterinarian. This is followed by the Jumping Test. The object of this test is often mis-understood. The international rules define it as 'not an ordinary show-jumping competition nor a test of style and endurance'. Its sole object is to prove that on the day after severe test of endurance, horses have retained the suppleness, energy and obedience necessary for them to continue.

The jumping course may appear to be fairly simple but the track of the course is irregular and winding with changes of direction, constituting a test of handiness and obedience. Here again, the rider is able to familiarize himself with the course beforehand, but the horse sees the jumps for the first time when it enters the arena. Refusals and falls are penalized as in the speed and endurance test but not as severely. However in this test, knocking down an obstacle is also penalised. The test is over a course between 750 to 990 metres with 10-12 obstacles carried out at a speed of 400 m per minute. Maximum height of jump will be 1.20 metres, spread a maximum of 1.80 metres and water jump with a minimum width of 3.50 metres.

The jumping test is significant as a sequel to the arduous test of the previous day, often exerting a considerable influence on the competitor's final placing in the competition.

To obtain the final placing, competitor's penalty marks for each of the tests i.e. Dressage, speed and endurance, and jumping are added together, the winner being the competitor with the lowest score. In team competitions, the scores of the three best riders in each team, i.e., those with the lowest scores, are counted.

The Event Horse

Eventing puts a unique combination of demands on the horse. He needs to be a good all round athlete capable of a supple, obedient and pleasing performance in the dressage test, a good mover, tough enough to gallop round a steeplechase and a cross-country course in cold blood, having proved his stamina on miles of roads and tracks, and then be able to come out on the third day to jump a round to show-jumps, proving that he is a courageous but careful and sound performer in that area too.

Thoroughbred Influence

Event horses come in all shapes and sizes, but what they have in common is "class". The thoroughbred or three-quarter to seven eighth thoroughbred is definitely the ideal type. A little bit of native pony, somewhere along the line has proved very successful, as has a bit of Irish breeding, but whatever the horse is, he needs to be brave and of a reasonable conformation with good limbs and feet.

A balanced outlook with good depth, a broad chest, sloping shoulders and a strong behind are what most people look for when choosing an event horse. A well-muscled back and neck with a good, natural head carriage are also desirable. The way the horse moves should be straight, to prevent knocks when seen from behind. He should have rhythm and look good to the dressage judges when seen from the side. The head should be workmanlike, with a generous; bold eye that looks as if he will work for rather than against you.

The horse must be a good ride and suggest power and scope. He must be able to gallop and jump, and show an athletic ability and boldness that will take you over those daunting fences, when trained adequately to do so. It is always difficult to assess a young horse's potential, but he must have that something that says to you 'This is the One'. Everyone has particular likes and dislikes but it is what will suit you that is important when choosing the horse. Is he the right size and will you be able to handle him when he is fit and ready to go? Has he a calm temperament so that he will perform a sensible dressage, yet enough 'spark' to be motivated round the cross-country. You can teach a horse most things, but he needs the basic essentials before you can train him to cope with the sport.

Demands on the Rider

The rider's attitude is also very important. You need to be tough both mentally and physically to cope with the tension of competition and the build-up to it. You must be strong enough to ride a super-fit horse over big fences and through a dressage test, with all the problems such as walking the course in between. You also need a cool head, and the fitness and strength to ride and successfully too, in competition. Equally important is the competitive spirit. There are many competitive riders who appear to be on only average ability when they are riding at home. However, in competition their will to win becomes so strong that they really rise to the occasion and produce outstanding results. These are the riders who succeed where others fail.

One Day Event

The one day event is a prelude to three day event. It acts as introductory and includes show jumping, dressage and cross-country jumping for giving experience to rider and its ride. One day event is conducted on the same day by same rider on same horse. Dressage is conducted in the morning, cross-country 1 – 1 ½ hrs after dressage and jumping test in the afternoon.

Classification:

Individual classification: The final classification is determined by adding together all the penalty marks incurred in the different tests. The winner is the competitor with lowest total of penalty marks. In case of tie, the classification is determined according to the best cross-country score. If there is still a tie, the winner is the competitor whose time on the cross-country is closest to the optimum time in the cross-country.

Team Classification: The winning team is the one with the lowest total of penalty points after adding together the final score of the three highest placed competitors of the team. In case of a tie, the winning team is the team whose third competitor has the best score.

Tent Pegging

Tent pegging is a popular equestrian sport in India, Pakistan, Iran, Iraq, Afghanistan and Australia. It demonstrates the energy, skill and obedience of the horse and the physical power and aiming skill of the rider. Surprisingly, tent pegging did not originate as a sport but as a very effective Asian warfare tactic. In the days of the Cavalry, the soldiers mounted on their Steeds would make a pre-emptive strike on the unwary enemy camp, and in a charge across the sleeping soldiers in their tents. They used to pull out the pegs of the tents with their lances, causing them to collapse and putting the enemy soldiers into complete disarray and confusion. Accordingly, to keep the cavalier fit and trim, Chengez Khan introduced tent pegging as a competitive sport. Wooden pegs were used to simulate the pegs of tents. Since then, this competition is held to test the skill of the rider to pick up the wooden peg embedded in the ground, by striking with the point of his lance. Presently, we have two variations of this competition, i.e. Individual Tent Pegging and the Team Tent Pegging. In the Individual Tent Pegging, the competition is based on the individual skills of the horse and its rider. While in the team event, 3 riders compete as a team with other teams. As of today, the Tent Pegging is competition in which the combination of horse and rider with lance is tested on a marked track, with prescribed speeds, to pick up the peg with the lance. It is a competition to exhibit the horse's energy, skill and obedience to gallop on the marked track, when the rider is aiming and picking up the peg. It is, therefore, both the rider and his mount together, which contribute towards the successful results.

Each competitor is allowed four runs in round 'A' (two rounds at 6 cm wide pegs and two rounds at 4 cm wide pegs) and similar runs in round 'B'. The gallop should not be at a speed less than 800 m per minute.

Scoring

Pegs carried clear 15 meters - 5 points

If the peg is lifted out of the ground

but falls within 15 meters - 3 points

If the peg is struck by the point of
lance but not lifted out off the ground - 1 point

In the event of a competitor dropping his lance during a run, he or his team will be disqualified for that run, unless the spear drops after the 15 meter line. In the event of a spear breaking during a run, the run will hold good and points will be scored as laid down in the rules for scoring.

If the rider or horse or both fall

- Within the 15 m line after the peg, the competitor will get no points for that run
- Outside the 15 m line, points will be scored as laid down in the rules for scoring.

Only riders using the right hand for carrying the lance are permitted. It is essential that lance used is not less than 2.5 meter in length with clear point and not having jagged or serrated edges. The horse used for this competition should not be less than 6 years of age.

The Pegs

The dimensions of the peg are 30 cm long, 2.5 cm thick and 6 cm wide, 4 cm wide and 3 cm wide (in case of equality). These are driven into a specially prepared furrow, at an angle of 60 degrees from the horizontal, the sloping side facing the start line with exactly 17 cm of peg showing above the surface. The face of peg is painted white. The pegs are driven into the ground 50 cm apart, one behind the other. The first peg is 70 meter from the start line. The pegs are made of wood of date palm or any other fibrous material of similar weight that will not break up when pierced by the lance. The pegs are soaked in water before the competition, to prevent them from splitting.

Polo

Polo is undoubtedly the king of games. Being a sport full of thrills, risk and contact at high speed, it has its share of glamour and glory. The mounted ball game that was played 2,500 years ago in Persia spread to China, Japan and Tibet, and thence to Manipur (India). It was from the Manipuris, the soldiers of the British Army in India, learned to play in the 1850s. The crude version of the game that they enjoyed was not exported to Britain, but instead soldiers in Britain read of the contests between their fellow countrymen and the Manipuris and were inspired to play themselves. When those soldiers were posted to India, they refined the game and thereafter its success was assured. The world's first polo club was established in London in 1873 and only six years later, the USA began to set up its own network of clubs. Polo was introduced to Argentina by British ranchers in 1877, and that country soon became a centre for the sport, largely because of the outstanding horsemanship of the Argentinians and the abundance of very suitable ponies. Nowadays, polo is played allover the world. Although to play the game remains the privilege of the fortunate few, polo is becoming ever more popular as a spectator sport, for it provides the wonderful spectacle of horse and rider working together as a partnership, and each pair contributing to the efforts of the whole team.

Since the first records of a mounted ball game originate from Persia some 2500 years ago, we may assume that this was the cradle of what would become the highly sophisticated game of modern polo. Known then as 'Chaugan', the word means a mallet. The sport was essentially royal and aristocratic, and expressly designed to promote equestrian and cavalry skills. Sometimes played six-a-side, sometimes with eight players and even more. The Persian game gave rise to a good deal of noisy ceremony. Poet Firdausi wrote in the Book of Kings (AD 1010), "Then the band began to play and the air was filled with dust. You would have thought there was an earthquake, so great was the noise of trumpets and cymbals. Then the king started the game by throwing the ball in the correct manner".

Similarly, during the reign of Queen Elizabeth I, the three Sherley brothers, travelling in India and visiting the court of Akbar (1542-1602), witnessed that greatest of the Moghul emperors at play. There were twelve horsemen. Sherley's secretary George Manwaring, wrote "so they divided themselves, six on one side, six on the other, having in their hands long rods of wood about the bigness of a man's finger, and at one end of the rods, a piece of wood nailed like a hammer. After they were divided and turned face to face, there came one in the middle and threw a ball between the companies and having goals made at either end of the plain, they began their sport, striking the ball with their rods one to the other in the fashion of our football here in England" .

From Persia and other parts of the near East, the game was introduced into China and Japan, where it was known as "Daiku" meaning "strike the ball'. Polo almost died out in Japan during the rebellion that ended the feudal system, but by the 1880s, it had been revived. Its career in China continued unbroken and from there it went to Tibet, where it was known as "Pulu", the Tibetan word for ball.

It was almost certainly from Tibet that the people of Manipur, that mountainous state sandwiched between Assam and Burma, adopted the game. The Manipuris called it "kan-jai-bazee", but they know it too as Pulu, the word that so comfortably adapted to provide our name for the sport. Many of the Manipuri villages established simple polo clubs, and during the 1850s and after, these were joined by some of the European tea planters. Lieutenant Joseph Sherer, a subaltern in the Bengal Army, played his first game with the Manipuris in 1854. After the Indian Mutiny, he and his friend Captain Robert Stewart, Superintendent of Cachar, founded the first European Polo club in Manipur in 1859.

The Birth of Modern Polo

Considering the germ of the Manipuris', game entered the British Raj during the 1850 and then spread rapidly through the Indian Army, what in fact happened was that in the summer of 1869, officers of the 10th Hussars camping at Aldershot, in England, having been impressed by an account of the Manipuris' game in the field, sent for their chargers, fashioned some sticks and a ball and began knocking it about in imitation of the magazine's description. They then acquired from Ireland, some ponies of 13-14 hands and organized friendly matches between themselves. They called the game 'hockey on horseback' The number of players on each side was according to whim. Eight-a-side seems to have been the popular number. The first inter-regimental challenge was held between the 10th Hussar and the 9th Lancers, that autumn.

In 1872, the 10th Hussars were posted to India, being followed there a few years later by the 9th Lancers, and the game, which they had developed in England, soon superseded the rough-and-tumble sport which the Manipuris had shown to the British Raj. The outstanding player of those early years was Captain John Watson, who was the first man to demonstrate the usefulness of the backhand shots which he had practised assiduously. When Lord Roberts took command of the Madras Army, he recognized at once what an important element in army life polo had become. But it was obvious to him that the play was too loose and the rules too haphazard. John Watson was the officer whom Roberts selected to recommend future guidelines for the safety and discipline of the game.

Polo in India, where the game could be played the whole year round, added immensely to its vigour and standard back in Britain. Owing largely to the encouragement given to the Army and the much easier economic situation, the game was far more generally available in India.

The Game Goes World-wide

British ranchers in Argentina were used to play polo soon after its birth in India. Mr Shemnan being the prime mover in 1877. By the end of the 1880s, three clubs - including the renowned Hurlingham - were firmly established around Buenos Aires.

Promoted by the Englishmen and Americans, polo was also played by the turn of the century in Chile, Uruguay, Columbia and Brazil. The Royal Navy carried polo to New Zealand, Gibraltar, Tangier, Tunis Bizerta, Algiers; Crete, Egypt, Rome, Cannes, Madrid, Barcelona, Salonika, Constan-tubioke and the China station.

Polo - The game

Polo, like any other field game, has its own peculiarities according to its requirements. As such the size of the ground which is 300 yards X 200 yards seems to be rather too big when compared to other games like, Hockey, Football, Basketball and even perhaps Cricket. This has to be so because of the pace of the ponies (normally horses used in polo are called ponies) and the distance of a long shot. Basing on these two facts, the number of players that forms a team is limited to four only unlike 11 in most of other games. Like-wise these four players of a team cover their own half of the ground between them by positioning themselves at Back, Centre and Forward positions and are called No.1, 2, 3 and 4. Nos. 1 and 2 are Forwards, No. 3 is the so called pivot or Centre-half and No. 4 is Back. These positions they maintain both in attack and defence and, of course, they interchange these as and when demanded by a situation. Similarly, because of the fast pace of the game, its duration is divided into four *Chakkars* (Rounds) of 7-1/2 minutes each, taken from the fact that both the ponies and the players cannot last more than this and that particularly the ponies have to be changed. Three minutes are allowed for a quick change of ponies after each *chakkar* and there is 5 minutes interval at half time after first two *chakkars*. Thus, the total duration of a game is 30 minutes play. Normally, these days, due to lack of ponies, all matches are played for four *chakkars* but on certain special occasions some tournaments are played for six *chakkars*. The goals are 8 yards wide and the goal posts at least 10 feet high, light enough to break if collided with.

The game is administered in a match by two umpires who are mounted to enable them to keep close to the play and a Referee who sits off the field in a central position from where he can watch the entire game. In case where the two umpires disagree on certain breach, they come to the referee whose decision is final. At either goal, judges are appointed each of whom gives testimony to the umpires at the latter's request in respect to goals or other points near his goal. A time-keeper is positioned off the ground with a bugler standby who sounds the bugle at the conclusion of each *chakkar* as directed by the former. In the event of a drawn game, goals are widened to 16 yards by moving goal posts 4 yards outwards and the game resumed. After an interval of 5 minutes, the teams change ends and the game continues in periods of usual intervals until one side obtains a goal which determines the winner.

Handicaps : The players are graded annually by the National Federation based on their playing form and are awarded handicaps ranging from 2 to 10.

Start of the Game: To start off a game, the two teams line up in middle of the ground, each team being on its own side of the half way line. One of the umpires bowls the ball underhand and throw between the opposing ranks of players, from, a distance of five yards and the game starts. From then onward, the time-keeper starts functioning for timing the *chakkars.* When ball is hit behind the back line by the attacking side, a hit in is taken by the defenders from the spot where it crossed the line but atleast 4 yards form the goal posts with none of the attacking side within 30 yards of the back line. When the ball is hit over the side line, it is bowled underhand and hard by the umpire into the ground from a point just inside the line where it went out and both sides forming up as for the start off facing the umpire. On every score of a goal, the sides change ends, most unlike any other game.

Infringements and Fouls: These have been exacted so as to avoid accidents during the game and the causes that lead to a possible collision, called "Rules", are summarised as under :

(a) **Crossing - The Right of Way**:

During a game there exists at each moment a 'Right of Way' which is considered to extend ahead of the player entitled to it and in the direction in which he is riding. No player shall enter or cross this Right of Way except at such distance that not the slightest risk of a collision or danger to either player is involved.

(b) **Checking:**

No player may check or pull up either on or across the 'Right of

Way' if by so doing he runs the slightest risk of collision, with the player entitled to it.

(c) **Dangerous Riding**:

A player may ride off an opponent but he may not ride dangerously, as for example :

(i) Bumping at an angle dangerous to a player or his pony.

(ii) Zig-zagging in front of another player riding at a gallop, in such a way so as to cause the latter to check his pace or risk a fall.

(iii) Pulling across or over a pony's legs in such a manner as to risk tripping the pony etc.

(iv) Riding an opponent across the 'Right of Way'.

(v) Riding an opponent so as to intimidate and cause him to pull out, or miss his stroke.

(vi) Sandwiching i.e. two players of the same side riding off an opponent at the same time.

(d) **Rough Handling:**

No player shall seize with the hand, strike or push with the head, hand, forearms or elbow.

(e) **Misuse of Stick**:

(i) No player may hook an opponent's stick unless he is on the same side of the opponent's pony as the ball or in direct line behind and his stick is neither over or under the body or across the legs of an opponents' pony, nor may he hook or strike an opponents' stick above shoulder level.

(ii) No player may use his stick dangerously or hold it in such a way as to interfere with another player or his pony.

(iii) No player may intentionally strike his pony with his polo stick.

(f) **Carrying the Ball**:

A player may not catch, kick or hit the ball with anything but his stick.

Penalties: There are degrees of dangerous play and unfair play which give an advantage to the side fouling. The penalty to be inflicted is left to the discretion of the umpire. Depending on the gravity of the infringement, penalties are awarded to the side fouled. In all there are six penalties in order of the gravity of the foul committed and these are as follows:

Penalty No.1 (a) & (b)

This is the severest penalty i.e. a penalty goal. In this case, if in the opinion of the umpires a player commits a dangerous or deliberate foul in the vicinity of goal in order to save a goal, the side fouled is allowed one goal. In a slightly milder case, Penalty 1 (b) is awarded wherein a free hit is taken by the side fouled from a spot 10 yards from the middle of the fouler's goal and none of the fouler's side behind the goal but away on either side of it.

Penalty 2 - 30 yards Hit:

This is less dangerous and unfair breach than for penalty 1 and in this case a free hit is awarded to the side fouled from a spot 30 yards from the goal line of the side fouling opposite the middle of the goal, all the side fouling to be behind their back line until the ball is hit but not between the goal posts.

Penalty 3 - 40 Yards Hit:

This is for still lesser dangerous breach than for penalty-2 and in this case, a free hit is taken from a spot 40 yards from the goal line of the side fouling instead of 30 yards.

Penalty 4 - 60 Yards Hit:

In this case, breach is much less dangerous than earlier ones and a free hit is taken from a spot 60 yards from the goal line of the side fouling and none of the side fouling to be within 30 yards of the ball, the side fouled being free to place themselves where they choose.

Penalty 5 - Spot Hit :

This is a breach all right but not dangerous enough for a penalty.

In this case a free hit is taken from the spot where the foul took place and none of the side fouling to be within 30 yards of the ball.

Penalty 5(b) - Free Hit from the Centre:

In this case a free hit is taken from the centre of the ground, irrespective where the foul took place.

Penalty 6 - 60 yards Hit :

It is like a long corner in hockey/football. When the ball crossed the back line by the stick or pony of the side defending the back line, a free hit is awarded to the attacking side which is taken from a spot 60 yards from the back line opposite where the ball crossed it.

In order to enable the umpires to find a spot according to the penalty awarded from where the ball is to be hit i.e. 30, 40 and 60 yards from a goal line, flags are placed on both side lines at 30, 40 and 60 yards from the comer flag towards the Centre line flag. Thus, when an umpire has given penalty 2, i.e. a 30 yards hit he places himself on the line between the 30 yards flags of the side lines and in front of goal and drops the ball. Likewise in other cases he drops the ball at 40 or 60 yards spots.

The game finishes when the ball goes out of the ground after bugle of the last *Chakkar* is sounded and not at the sound of the bugle.

Chapter 28

Drug Abuse and Dope Testing

Drug abuse in sporting is called **doping**; the international word dope has its origin as Dutch word "*Doop*" which means Christian baptism. Any substance that could affect performance by its action on skeleto-muscular system, CNS, CVS etc., and giving unfair advantage in the competition by clandestine administration to an animal which is a normal constituent of diet and which could influence the athletic performance.

The equestrian sports and commercial horse races are vulnerable for drug malpractice owing to money and reputation at stake. Therefore, most of the controlling bodies have devised strict predication rules to maintain integrity by promoting equine welfare and by discouraging the possibility of unfair competition.

As per the regulation of Federation Equestre Internationale (FEI) the use of any substance or method that has the potential to harm the horse or to enhance its performance is forbidden. The precise rules concerning prohibited substances and medication control are laid down in the EADMCRs (Equine Anti-Doping and Medication Control Rules) which were formulated and adapted in meetings of FEI governing bodies (Bureau and General Assembly) held on 6-10, April 2005 in London, as per the task force on anti-doping and medication policy in conjunction with the ***World Anti-Doping Code***. The rules are effective from *01 June, 2006*. Equine anti-doping rules, like *Competition rules*, are sport rules governing the conditions under which sports are performed. The rules seek to prevent any attempt to alter a horse's performance or to mask an underlying health problem by the administration or application of prohibited substances to the horse's body. Anti-doping programmes seek to preserve what is intrinsically valuable about sport.

This intrinsic value often referred to as ***"the spirit of sport";*** is the essence of Olympism; it is how we play true. The spirit of sport is the celebration of the human spirit, body and mind. Doping is fundamentally contrary to the spirit of sport.

Categories of Doping:

Doping can be mainly of two kinds:

(a) **Doping to Win: -** To improve speed and performance. Stimulant doping of this type is usually considered an 'inside job'.e g.,
   (i) Xanthines - Caffeine, Theobromine, Theophylline.
   (ii) Sympathomimetic amines - Amphetamine, Adrenaline, Ephedrine.
   (iii) Steroids - Anabolic steroids.

(b) **Doping to Lose:** To reduce the speed and performance. It is usually considered an 'outside job' undertaken by outsiders seeking to influence the outcome of a race. e.g.
   i) Tranquilizers - Diazepam, Acetyl promazine
   ii) Hypnotics - Morphine
   iii) Sedatives - Xylazine.

The ways in which medication can be used in horse vary. Various categories of medications used to influence the performance of horse:

(a) **Medication to win** - Always illegal
   (i) Acute: Short-acting stimulants - e.g. Amphetamines, Cocaine (analgesic)
   (ii) Chronic: Repeated dosing for weeks - Anabolic steroids.
   (iii) Washy Horses : Doping with a very small dose of a depressant or tranquilizer to "take off the edge" of an excitable horse.

(b) **Medication to Lose** : Always illegal

  (i) Depressants: large doses of a tranquilizer, sedative or depressants.

(c) **Medication to Restore Normal Performance:**

  (i) NSAID: Phenylbutazone, Flunixin-often permitted under controlled medication rule.

  (ii) Corticosteroids : Intra-articular-occasionally permissible

  (iii) Fluids and Electrolytes: Often permissible.

(d) **Accidental or Inadvertent or Technical Doping:**

  (i) Procaine from procaine penicillin

  (ii) Caffeine from coca husks

  (iii) Botanical positives or false positives.

e) **Medication to Mask Other Drugs:** The masking agents concurrently given with prohibited drug before competition in order to reduce the risk of detection that drug. e.g. Administration of dipyrone and thiamine, thought to interfere with the detection of illegal medication.

f) **Medication to Dilute Other Drugs:** e.g. Diuretics: Furasemide

g) **Miscellaneous Mechanisms** : e.g. Blood Doping.

Prohibited Substances Under the Rule of Horse Racing

Many horse racing authorities now define a 'dope' by its pharmacological action. If any drug in any of the listed categories is found in a sample of body fluid taken before and after the competition from a horse constitutes an offence.

The FEI General Regulation (*2006*) states that any horse found to have a prohibited substances in any of its tissue, body fluid or excreta at an event as the result of medication test is disqualified together with the competitor, from all competitions at that event.

Equine Prohibited List

The Equine Prohibited List includes three classes of prohibited

Substances:

- Doping;
- Medication Class A; and
- Medication Class B.

SUBSTANCES AND METHODS PROHIBITED IN-COMPETITION

Prohibited Substances (Doping)

Agents, cocktails or mixtures of substances that may affect the performance of a horse; masking agents; substances with no generally accepted medical use in competition horses; substances which are usually products prescribed for use in humans or other species; agents used to hypersensitize or desensitize the limbs or body parts, including but not limited to:

- two or more anti-inflammatory drugs (steroidal and/or non-steroidal) or other combinations of anti-inflammatory substances with similar or distinct pharmacological actions;
- anti-psychotic, anti-epileptic and antihypertensive substances including reserpine, gabapentin, fluphenazine, and guanabenz;
- anti-depressants such as selective serotonin reuptake inhibitors (SSRIs), monoamine oxidase inhibitors (MAOIs), and tricyclic anti-depressants (TCAs);
- tranquilizers, sedatives (including sedating anti-histaminics) commonly used in humans and/or non-equine species, including benzodiazepines, barbiturates and azaperone;
- narcotics and opioid analgesics; endorphins;
- amphetamines and other central nervous system (CNS) stimulants including cocaine and related psychotic drugs;
- beta-blockers including propranolol, atenolol, and timolol;
- diuretics and other masking agents;
- anabolic steroids (including testosterone in mares and geldings) and growth promoters;

- peptides and genetically recombinant substances such as erythropoietin, insulin growth factor and growth hormone;
- hormonal products (natural or synthesized) including adrenocorticotropic hormone (ACTH) and cortisol (above the threshold);
- substances designed and marketed primarily for human use or use in other species and for which alternative and generally accepted products are available for use in horses;
- hypersensitizing or sensitizing agents (organic or inorganic or other substances likely to have been applied to body parts or to tack to influence performance);
- oxygen carriers; and other substances with a similar chemical structure or similar biological effect(s).

Prohibited Substances (Medication Class A)

Agents which could influence performance by relieving pain, sedating, stimulating or producing/modifying other physiological or behavioural effects, including:

- local anaesthetics;
- sympathomimetic cardiac stimulants;
- central and respiratory stimulants;
- clenbuterol and other bronchodilators and products used for the treatment of recurrent airway disease (RAD);
- a single non-steroidal anti-inflammatory drug ± metabolite(s);
- a single corticosteroid;
- sedatives or tranquillizers indicated for equine use including anti-histamines; thiamine; valerian and other herbal products other than those listed as prohibited substances (doping);
- muscle relaxants including methocarbamol and propantheline;
- anti-coagulants including heparin or warfarin; and other substances with a similar chemical structure or similar biological effect(s).

Prohibited Substances (Medication Class B)

Substances that either have limited performance enhancing potential or to which horses may have been accidentally exposed, including certain dietary contaminants.

These are listed below:

- isoxsuprine;
- dimethylsulphoxide (DMSO) when above the threshold;
- mucolytics and cough suppressants: bromohexine and other substances with a similar chemical structure or similar biological effect(s);
- hyoscine (n-butyl-scopolamine); Atropine and other anticholinergic substances with a similar chemical structure or similar biological effect(s);
- methylxanthines: caffeine and theophylline; theobromine when above the threshold;
- plant or animal derivatives: bufotenine, hordenine, tyrosine, gamma-oryzanol and other substances with a similar chemical structure or similar biological effect(s);
- terpines and inorganic contaminants (other than those detected on skin or tack swabs);
- evacuants: magnesium sulphate and other substances with a similar chemical structure or similar biological effect(s).

Marker. The marker is a compound, group of compounds or biological parameters that indicates the *Use* of a *Prohibited Substance* or a *Prohibited Method.*

Anti-doping and Medication Control Rule Violations

Where *doping, prohibited substances* or *prohibited methods* prohibited medication A or prohibited medication class B are involved, the following constitute anti-doping rule violations and medication control rule violations;

(A) The presence of a *Prohibited Substance* or its *Metabolites* or *Markers* in a *Horse*'s bodily *Sample*

(i) It is personal duty of each responsible person to ensure that *prohibited substance* is not present in his or her Horse's body during an *Event*. *Persons Responsible* are responsible for any *Prohibited Substance* found to be present in their Horse's bodily samples. Accordingly, it is not necessary that intent, fault, negligence or knowing use on the Responsible person part be demonstrated in order to establish an anti-doping or medication control violation.

(ii) Excepting those substances for which a quantitative threshold is specifically identified in the Equine Prohibited List, the detected presence of any quantity of a Prohibited Substance in a Horse's Sample shall constitute a rule violation.

(iii) As an exception to the general rule of (i), the Equine Prohibited List may establish special criteria, including but not limited to specific thresholds or extenuating circumstances, for the evaluation of Prohibited Substances that can be produced endogenously and/or be ingested from the environment or as a result of contamination. If such special criteria or circumstances apply, the detected presence of a Prohibited Substance in a Horse's Sample shall not automatically constitute a rule violation. Where thresholds have been established forth presence of a given Prohibited Substance, detection of a concentration above the applicable threshold shall constitute a rule violation.

(B) *Use* of a *Prohibited Substance* or a *Prohibited Method*

The success or failure of the *use* of a *prohibited substance* or a *prohibited method* is not material. It is sufficient that the *prohibited substance* or *prohibited method* was *used* for a rule violation to be committed.

(C) Refusing, or failing without compelling justification, to submit to Sample collection after notification or otherwise evading Sample collection.

(D) Tampering or attempting to tamper with any part of *doping control* or *medication control*

(E) *Trafficking* in any *Prohibited Substance* or *Prohibited Method*.

(F) Administration of a *Prohibited Substance* or *Prohibited Method* to any *Horse*, or assisting, encouraging, aiding, abetting, covering up or any other type of complicity involving a rule violation.

Burdens and Standards of Proof:

The organization or body shall have the burden of establishing that an anti-doping rule violation or medication control rule violation has occurred.

THRESHOLD SUBSTANCES

Horses may compete with the presence of certain substances in their tissues, body fluids or excreta for which threshold levels/ ratios are listed below, provided the concentration of the substance is not greater than the threshold level/ ratio indicated. Thresholds only apply to:

- substances endogenous to the horse;
- substances arising from plants traditionally grazed or harvested as equine feed; or
- substances in equine feed arising from contamination during normal cultivation, processing or treatment, storage or transportation.

The following constitutes an exclusive list of substances for which a threshold has been established. For each substance, a concentration level beneath that indicated is not a rule violation:

Available Carbon Dioxide (CO_2): 36 millimoles per litre in plasma

Boldenone (other than geldings): free and conjugate boldenone 0.01micrograms per ml in urine from male horses

Dimethyl sulphoxide: 15 micrograms per ml in urine or 1 microgram per ml in plasma

Estranediol in male Horses (other than geldings) : Free and conjugated 5E-estrane-3F,

17E- diol 0.045 micrograms per ml in urine

Hydrocortisone : 1 microgram per ml in urine

Salicylic acid : 625 micrograms per ml in urine or 5.4 micrograms per ml in plasma

Testosterone: 0.02 micrograms free and conjugated Testosterone per ml in urine from Geldings or 0.055 micrograms free and conjugated testosterone per ml in urine from fillies and mares (unless in foal).

Theobromine : 2 micrograms per ml in urine

Controlled medications:

Horses, however, may compete with the presence of certain substances in their body fluids provided the concentration of the substance is less than the maximum permissible concentration laid down by FEI. e.g.

(a) Phenylbutazone - 2mg/ml of plasma

(b) Oxyphenbutazone - 2mg/ml of plasma

(c) Salicylic acid - 750mg/ml of urine

(d) Theobromine - 2mg/ml of urine

(e) Dimethyl Sulfoxide - 15mg/ml of urine.

The misnomer "permissive" medication is often incorrectly used for controlled medication. The concept of controlled medication is not intended to allow unfit, unsuitable diseased or injured equine athletes to race or compete in the competition but rather to treat the disease.

Vitamins, Amino Acid preparations, intra- articular therapy are other normal medications allowed as therapeutic medications.

Treatment of horses suffering from gastric ulceration by the oral administration of ranitidine, cimetidine or omeprazole is currently permitted under FEI rules.

Common Drugs Misused in Equine Sports

The most common drugs used in atheletic horses are

(a) Anabolic steroids: To masculinize gelding and mare; to improve appetite.,e.g.,nandrolone(Dianabol),Boldenone, Trenbolene, Testosterone.

(b) NSAID: They block cyclo oxygenase pathway and suppress mediators of inflammation like prostocycline, prostaglandin etc., to reduce the heat, swelling and pain, for example.

(i) Flunixine - to reduce visceral pain

(ii) Meclofenamic Acid - to treat laminitis

(c) Corticosteroids: It stabilizes cellular lysosomal and mitochondrial membrane and inhibits phospholipase to reduce production of arachidonic acid and intern prostaglandins. Hence, it is used as anti-inflammatory agent, intra articular medications eg., prednisolone, hydrocortisone, dexamethasone, Betamethasone.

(d) Stimulants: Caffeine, Theobromine, Theophylline.

(e) Diuretics : used to eliminate other prohibited substances from blood or plasma.

(f) Miscellaneous drugs:

- (i) Amorphine - Marked effect on locomotor activity.
- (ii) Camphor - Respiratory stimulant
- (iii) Dimethyle Sulfoxide
- (iv) Polyethylene Glycol - General solvent of steroids, presumptive evidence for steroids.

Food Contaminants

As per *Vet Reg 2006* of FEI all riders and horse owners are warned that Stable management and feeding practices can have important consequences for testing of horses during competition. Occasionally, horses test positive for substances, which can be administered, but have also been reported as a result of stable or feed contamination. Examples are:

1. **Caffeine/Theobromine**: In the majority of horses testing positive for these substances it appears that the drugs were ingested via manufactured feed. Several feed producers have been approached during the legal follow-up of these cases and in some instances the contamination could be traced back to certain batches of feed. However, feed contamination does not diminish the responsibility of the rider

for the test result. In addition, if a horse is to be disqualified due to a positive analysis, it is of little help if afterwards it becomes clear that feed contamination was the cause. It is, therefore, strongly advised to check with the feed manufacturer or supplier whether the feed is routinely controlled for the presence of prohibited substances. If stable competition horses are stabled adjacent to horses receiving uncontrolled feed, a risk for medication control may be the result. Moreover, it is recommended that small samples of the different batches of feed are being kept in clean plastic bags or glass jars. By storing the feed samples and identifying date and batch number with a marker, it is possible to go back and check the feed afterwards if a horse proves positive.

2. **Isoxsuprine:** This substance, also known under the brand names of Duviculine, Vascuprin and Navilox have been used in the treatment of navicular disease and laminitis. However, it is a prohibited substance under the FEI Regulations and must, therefore, not be present at the time of competition. This medicine is often mixed with feed and sticks very easily to stable walls, feed bins, bedding, etc. After prolonged use in horses isoxsuprine is detectable in the urine for an extended period. It is advised that, if one of the horses is on isoxsuprine treatment, it should be separated from other horses, especially if competition horses are stabled at the same time. The horse under treatment should be fed as the last and should have its own feed bucket. It is strongly advised to make sure that the provider of this drug to the horse cannot spread the substance to other boxes (i.e. footwear, coveralls, buckets, hands etc.), thereby causing untreated horses to test positive.

Herbal or Natural Medicinal Products

1. Riders, trainers, grooms and veterinarians should be cautious against the use of herbal medications, tonics, oral pastes and products of any kind, the ingredients and quantitative analysis of which are not known in detail. Many of these products can contain one or more prohibited substances.

2. Persons administering a herbal or so-called natural product to a horse or pony for health reasons or to affect its performance, having been informed that the plant origin of its ingredients do not violate the regulations.
3. The use of any herbal or natural product to affect the performance of a horse or pony in a calming (tranquillizing) manner or an energizing (stimulant) manner is expressly forbidden by the regulations. The use of a calming product during competition may also have important safety consequences.
4. Most of the equestrian federations do not test or approve herbal or natural products to verify a possible violation of the Equine Anti-Doping and Medication Control rules and regulations. Therefore, a claim that the product does not violate the FEI rules or is undetectable by drug testing is the sole responsibility of the manufacturer or individual making such a claim.
5. The use of a herbal or natural product may result in a positive test result, contrary to the claim by the manufacturer or marketing agent. Many prohibited substances (e.g. salicylatels, digitalis, reserpine) have their origin in plants and may be regarded as serious rule violations.
6. As the analytical techniques in the testing laboratory become more refined, the fact that these products have not been detected by testing in the past does not hold any guarantee for their safe use in competition.

Doping Control. The process including test distribution planning, *sample* collection and handling, laboratory analysis, results management, hearings and appeals aimed at preventing any attempt to alter a Horse's performance (or to mask an underlying health problem) by the administration or application of *Prohibited Substances* in or on the Horse's body.

Testing For Drugs In Horses

Racing has one of the oldest and technically most elaborate systems for drug testing. The practice of drug testing started in horses in 1910; the first positive call was reported in 1912.

Analytic chemical analysis has made major strides and is now remarkably accurate, yet the area of pharmacology or drug effects is still wide open to interpretative differences.

Obtaining Sample:

The basic tool used in drug testing is the urine sample, with blood testing increasing in popularity. Sample collecting procedures must take into consideration both scientific and legal aspects. Incorrect labeling, contamination or sample switching must be avoided. The samples should be sealed with evidence tape duly signed by owner of the horse or his representative and shipped in a secure container. The sample can be divided into two portions at the time of sampling so that the second portion can be used for defence purposes. This is to be opened only after the first sample has been found to contain the banned substance and after the competitor has been notified and invited to attend the second analysis with his own expert if he so wishes. The thrust of the process at this point is to identify the urine sample correctly and to transfer it from the bladder of the horse to the testing lab with no possibility of contamination or confusion with other sample. This process is called establishing *the chain of evidence,* and it must be validated in the court if medication violations are to be successfully prosecuted.

Urine: This is the most preferred body fluid in all species, its collection is non-invasive; it is generally available in sufficient quantity and the drug or their metabolites tend to be present in relatively large proportions.

The horse groom may be allowed to collect urine sample in a sample jar held in a wire basket on the end of a long handle. Usually, urine is voided within 30-60 minutes after the competition. Switching of sample is common in race courses. Racing cyclists have reported to have carried a rubber bladder of negative urine under their arm connected by a rubber tube to the appropriate discharge point. There are instances of horse handlers substituting their own urine in the sample jar. Hence veterinary officer in charge should have a continuous observation on the groom.

The presence of appreciable quantities of nicotine, caffeine and uric acid in urine provide good evidence of human source.

Blood: The principal advantage of blood sample is that its integrity is easier to safeguard because it is usually collected by the veterinary surgeon in charge. The drug concentrations in blood are more easily interpreted than those in urine, and certain drugs, which are not excreted in urine in detectable quantities (eg., reserpine) can be deducted in blood. But it is used only as a second choice when urine is not obtainable.

Saliva: The principal disadvantage of saliva are that it is difficult to obtain a useful volume and few drugs are present at a concentration higher than that in plasma. The principal value of saliva is in the detection of topical concentration resulting from fairly recent oral ingestion.

Three pieces of surgical gauze are used, folded lengthwise to 8-ply thickness and a width of about 4.5 inches. Each of the two pieces are soaked in 1% acetic acid and holding with a uterine forceps, the gauze is held on both side of the horses mouth. The horse chews it and the saliva starts dripping and those absorbed on the gauze are collected in stainless steel pan. It is placed in a sample jar and sealed.

Technical difficulties in testing drugs:

The technical complexity in detection of drugs is manifold:

(a) Number of compounds: There are around 63000 chemicals in use which makes for an enormous number of substances likely to turn up in a race horse. At least 400 drugs are in common use. The sheer number of agents likely to be detected in horse urine is remarkable. Less amount is virtually undetectable.

(b) Dose of drugs: The dose of drugs given to horse can vary upto one million fold; ie., from few mg (millionth of a gram) of very potent substances such as Etorphine to few grams of a substance such as Naproxen (narcotic and stimulant-elephant juice). Large differences in dosage account for large differences in detection capabilities.

(c) Detection time: It is the time that passes until the analyst can detect the drug. The half life of the drug in the horse vary about 300 fold, from about 30 minutes for certain drug to about several days for drugs that are slowly eliminated. Reserpine can be detected even for about a year. The ability to detect a drug depends on the amount of the drug administered to a horse. For example, the drug phenlybutazone administered in more amount is relatively detected for longer periods than Fentanyl, which is administered in less amount, virtually undetectable.

(d) Sensitivity of testing procedure

(i) The sensitivity of testing procedure should reflect the duration of action of the drug tested. For eg., Flunixine, which is given in lower doses, than phenylbutazone is cleared rapidly from blood and is inherently a more difficult drug to detect than phenylbutazone.

(ii) The differences between individual horses in the speed of elimination are also quite variable and affect the detection duration. The concentration on urine of phenylbutazone on 5th day varies in the range of 30 fold between horses. This is due to the differences in the plasma concentration, the way in which individual horses handles the same drug and the variations in the pH of the horse urine, which markedly affect the elimination of the drug.

(iii) The modern analytical methods have tremendously improved the sensitivity but the criticism is that it leads to false positive results of very minute quantities of the drug, which was administered long before for some treatment purposes.

Clearing Rates:

Following are the clearing rates of certain drugs:-

(a) Methyl xanthines

(i) Caffein -03days

(ii) Theobromine -12days

(iii) Theophilline -04days

(b) Sympathomimetic drugs:

(i) Amphetamine -48hours

(ii) Methylamphetamine -48hours

(iii) Adrenaline -20hours

(iv) Ephidrine -24hours

(c) Anti-inflammatory drugs

(i) Salicylates -24hours

(ii) Ibubrufen -48hours

(iii) Flunixine -48hours

(iv) Naproxen -60hours

(v) Meclofenamic acid -96hours

(vi) Phenylbutazone -150hours

(d) Diuretics

(i) Hydrochlorthiazide -30hours

(ii) Furosemide -52hours

(e) Tranquilizers and hypnotics:

(i) Pentobarbitone -20hours

(ii) Accetyl promazine -32hours

(iii) Chloral hydrate -48hours

(iv) Phenobarbitone -72hours

(v) Promazine -72hours

(vi) Chlorpromazine -96hours

(f) Corticosteroids:

(i) Prednisolone -3days

(ii) Flumethasone -4days

(iii) Dexanethasone -6days

(g) Miscellaneous:

(i) Procaine -4days

(ii) Procaine Penicillin -13days

(iii) Pentozocine -5days

(iv) Nikethamide -9days

Screening and Identification of Drugs:

Different procedures used for screening and identification are:

(a) Colour Tests

(b) Microcrystal Tests

(c) Thin Layer Chromatography (TLC)

(d) Gas Chromatography(GC)

(e) High Performance Liquid Chromatography (HPLC)

(f) Mass Spectrophotometry

(g) UV Spectrophotometry

(h) Radio-immuno Assays

(j) ELISA Technique

Analytical detection levels and irrelevant concentrations of certain substances and Screening Limits of Detection (SLODs) are established on the basis of risk management to control the sensitivity of the screening method for a specified substance in a horse's urine or blood sample to ensure the integrity of the sport. Where SLODs have been established they are universally applied by standard laboratories of federations.

The Detection Time (DT) is the period of time during which a drug remains in a horse's system such that it can be detected by the laboratory. The detection time is influenced by numerous factors including the size of the horse, the route of administration, the drug formulation, the number of doses administered, individual horse factors (e.g., metabolism, disease, etc.) and the detection limit of the screening method used to detect the drug (unless a quantitative threshold has been adopted by the regulatory authorities). The Withdrawal Time (WT) for a drug is decided upon by the treating veterinarian and includes the detection time plus a safety margin, chosen with professional judgment and discretion of the treating veterinarian, to allow for individual differences between horses.

However, it shall always be kept in mind that a Horse, as a biological entity, does not necessarily follow the scientific modeling used to provide indicative information.

Chapter **29**

Welfare Requirement of Horses in Equestrian Sports

Introduction

The **Guidelines for Welfare of the Horses'** are issued by the *Equestrian Federation of India* to provide an outline of the principles of husbandry, management and handling for the horses used as riding animals in clubs, schools or other similar educational institutions where riding is taught.

The Guidelines do not replace the need for experience and commonsense in horse husbandry, and the use of veterinarian advice when necessary. The overriding theme and principles of these guidelines are that the well being of the horse must at all times be considered above the demands of owners, trainers, riders, sponsors, officials or spectators.

The Guidelines aim to establish and document guiding principles which are already well accepted by those experienced with horses and emphasize the importance of good horsemanship and husbandry practices.

The intent and principles of the guidelines shall apply to all horse owners/ clubs / institution members. It is brought out that persons in charge of horses have a legal liability to care for horses under their control. If a violation of these principles is presented to the EFI with credible evidence, EFI will refer the matter to the Animal Welfare Board or SPCA as deemed fit.

All clubs, educational institutions and horse owners are also required to be familiar with Prevention of Cruelty to Animals Act, 1960 (59 of 1960) and its regulations. The act has been enacted as law that a person shall not, without reasonable excuse, commit an act of cruelty, or deliberately causing unnecessary pain to an animal, or fail to provide it with appropriate and adequate food, water, shelter and exercise. The Animal Welfare Board of India has been set up by the Ministry of Environment and Forests under the Prevention of Cruelty to Animals Act, 1960 (59 of 1960), as a body to keep the law in force.

Responsible Ownership

The owners are responsible at all times for the welfare of their horses unless that responsibility has been given to another person or persons under an agreement. Evidences must exist in writing, signed by the owner and the person or persons taking that responsibility.

Owners, handlers, trainers and breeders of horses should be aware that proper feeding, maintenance and training of horses represent long-term responsibilities and considerable expense. Many welfare problems are created when owners or handlers neglect animals on economic grounds. Responsible ownership also entails disposing of an unwanted horse in a humane way or selling it to a suitable new owner.

General Husbandry

Horses are kept under a variety of conditions, from outdoor grazing to housing in individual boxes or stables. The basic needs of horses are as under:

(a) Readily accessible food and water to maintain health and vigour;

(b) Freedom of movement to stand, stretch and lie down;

(c) Regular exercise;

(d) Social contact with other horses and/or people;

(e) Shelter and accommodation that provides adequate protection;

(f) Protection from disease, and regular inspections to assess the need for attention to feet, teeth and parasite control;

(g) Rapid identification and treatment of injury and disease.

Behavioural Needs.

The design of facilities, the stocking density, and the composition of groups of horses must ensure that each horse has a sufficient area to prevent undue stress and/or injury. Subordinate horses must have an opportunity to escape from bullying by dominant animals in the group. Colts, stallions, weanlings, pregnant and sick animals require segregation from other groups of horses, to reduce the risk of injury and disease.

Supervision

Horse kept under intensive management in stables and paddocks should be inspected and fed at least twice a day. They should have free access to water at all times.

Horses grazing under more extensive conditions require variable supervision, according to the density of stocking and availability of suitable feed; nature and disposition; age and pregnancy status; and the nature of fencing and reliability of water supply. Mares in the last month of pregnancy should be closely observed for signs of foaling.

Steps must be taken to ensure that horses are attended to promptly in the event of fire, flood, injury or sickness. Constant observation for injury, change in eating/drinking pattern and any signs of ill health must be reported to a vet and assistance taken.

Food and Water

Water

Horses require free access to an adequate supply of good quality water. If fed in buckets, bucket supply of water should be replenished at least twice a day. Requirement for water vary widely depending on age, body weight, air temperature and humidity, level of work, state of health and type of diet of the horse (**Appendix 1**). If fed in buckets, bucket supply of water should be replenished early in the morning before each of the feeds and before putting the horse away for the night.

Food

Horses need food for maintaining their health, vitality and welfare. Food for horses should meet the appropriate requirements of growth, pregnancy, lactation and work (**Appendix 2**).

If there is insufficient pasture for nutritional needs for horses, kept under extensive conditions, they should be given extra feed on a regular basis. Regular supervision should be provided to observe behaviour patterns and response to feed. Feeding troughs for horses should be spaced to minimize bullying and allow subordinate animals assess to feed. Less thrifty horses require segregation and special feeding if they lose condition and vitality.

When a horse fails to thrive, the quality, quantity and availability of feed and the health of horse (including the state of its teeth and the extent of parasitism) should be evaluated. If there is any doubt, veterinarian advice must be sought. Horse owners must at all times take account of seasons and precautions should also be taken to protect horses from foods harmful to health; e.g., poisonous plants, uncontrolled access to grain or pellets.

Horses should not be overfed. Overfeeding can induce laminitis or founder expressed as lameness. Animals at risk should be exercised and their intake of food reduced to minimal maintenance requirements. Affected horses should be moved to supervision and not exessively fed (dry feed, grain or other concentrated high-energy feed). However, all components of diet essential for growth, health, work and vitality should be readily available to horses.

Excessive amounts of high-energy grain feeds may affect the reactions of horses to restraint and training. Inadequate or excessive feeding may result in ill-health and affect horses' attitude and movement.

In the stables, feeding and water troughs generally should be raised and placed in a corner. They should be smooth and free of protrusions, resist tipping and be easy to clean. Food should be stored in containers with close fitting or hinged lids to prevent entry of vermin. Unconsumed feed if any should be suitably disposed off and feed adjusted accordingly to prevent wastage.

Premises

General Requirements

Premises should be designed to minimize the risk of injury to horses. Horses must not be kept overcrowded as the risk of injury increases where horses are overcrowded and the competition for food, water and space leads to fighting. The premises should afford/shelter from heat, cold, rain and wind. Should be adequately spacious, comfortable with no sharp protruding edges with the close visibility of other horses/ humans and provide protection from wild/ stray animals.

Fencing

Fencing should be of suitable height and be sufficiently sturdy to prevent escape. Suitability of fencing varies according to the size, sex and disposition of the horses, stocking density and paddock size. Fences should be properly maintained and, when horses are in close confinement, should be readily visible.

Barbed wire, prefabricated wire fencing, and high tensile wire are prone to cause severe injury to horse and are, therefore, not recommended for use in small areas. Electric fencing, properly fitted and maintained, provides a safe and effective barrier to horses, when used with conventional post-and-wire and post-and-rail fences, or if erected alone in a highly visible form.

Gateways should be designed to give easy and safe passage of horses and they should not be too narrow. Gates should be fastened with a secure chain or catch, to prevent escape of horses and possible injury.

Accommodation

Healthy horses can tolerate extremes of heat and cold if they are acclimatized and have adequate feed, water and shelter. However, steps should be taken to minimize the effects of climatic extremes and other factors producing either heat or cold stress. Young foals, very old or sick horses are most susceptible. Horse owners should ensure that adequate shade or protection is provided, depending on prevailing weather conditions.

Horses must be clipped in summer months. Horses that are clipped during winter should be rugged, except when working or when weather conditions are very mild. Rugging should be seasonally appropriate and protective for the horse. During warm conditions, summer weight rugs to avoid heat stress should replace winter rugs.

Yards or stables including looseboxes and shelter-sheds provided for horses should not restrict their freedom to stand, lie down, stretch and groom themselves. Stables should be constructed and maintained to provide adequate security and minimize risk of injury and disease. Paddocks and yards should be free of objects likely to cause injury.

The floors of yards and stables should have surfaces that permit adequate drainage and allow horses to stand and walk normally. Stabled or yarded horses should be given adequate exercise every day.

Stables should have adequate natural ventilation to prevent the accumulation of ammonia, stale air and moisture. Air vents on the roof and/or on opposite sides of the box are preferred. Horses owners should ensure that adequate shade or protection depending on prevailing weather condition is provided to horses confined in yards.

Stables or yards for individual horses should be fit for the purpose. For horse of 14.2 hands in height or more, the suggested floor area should be at least 13.5 square metres, with each side being a minimum of 3 metres in length. For ponies the area should be at least 9 square metres with each side being a minimum of 2.5 metres in length. The height of the stable should be in all cases a minimum of 60 cm above the height of the poll of the horse or pony with its head in a normal position. The roof should provide adequate shelter from the elements, including adequate insulation for both hot and cold weather.

Guttering and down pipes should be provided to drain storm water away from stables. Horses kept in stables should be accommodated singly unless accustomed to shared accommodation, e.g., mare and foal.

The walls should be capable of withstanding damage. They may be lined with plywood sheets or rubber or belting etc. to prevent injury to horse and also to protect the walls from pawing and kicking. The doorways should be at least 1.2 m wide and 2.4 m high with no protrusions. Hinged doors should open outwards.

Fire-fighting equipments must be available and there should be ready access to horses to enable them to be released quickly in case of fire. Smoking should be strictly forbidden in the stables with a "NO SMOKING" sign displayed next to stables.

Provision should be made for storage of food, bedding, stable equipment and saddlery. Horses must not be able to gain access to food stores.

Clean bedding such as hay, straw, sawdust, wood shavings, shredded paper or rice hulls, should be provided for warmth, insulation and protection from abrasion. Wood shavings/paper shaving or any other material which has strong pungent vapours irritating the eyes and respiratory system should be avoided.

Dirty bedding and stale or contaminated feed and water should be removed each day. Disposal of washings urine and dung should be made hygienically away from the stables to avoid fly menace. Where possible, fly proofing door/window mesh be used to avoid discomfort to horses. Use of flycatchers is recommended.

When horses are accommodated for short term period in stalls, the stalls should provide adequate ventilation and shelter. The floors should have a surface that permits adequate drainage.

Special Husbandry Requirements

General Management

Persons responsible for the supervision of horses should be able to recognize signs of ill-health and may need to call a veterinarian to diagnose and treat any illness, injury or parasite infestation. Healthy horses show the following signs:

(a) are active, move freely, eat and drink well;

(b) have clear eyes and nostrils, clean skins and coats, and

(c) are neither very thin nor over fat.

Sick horse may show the following signs:

(a) Dullness and loss of condition, these signs being frequently associated with an inadequate diet, internal parasites or teeth problems;

(b) Digestive upsets – seen as diarrhoea with soiling of tail and hind legs, or constipation or colic (abdominal pain) with restlessness, pawing, looking and kicking at the stomach or rolling, often accompanied by straining, teeth –grinding and patchy or generalized sweating;

(c) Lameness due to injury, laminitis or founder, foot abscess or improper hoof maintenance;

(d) Discharges from eyes, nostrils, or swollen glands under the throat - these are indications of respiratory disease and may be accompanied by a cough, fever, and loss of appetite.

Injuries and infectious diseases occur more frequently where horses are over-crowded and facilities are not maintained adequately.

Horses should not be allowed to suffer for want of attention. Persons responsible for the welfare of horses should seek urgent veterinarian attention for horses showing symptoms:

(a) Acute abdominal pain, colic or abdominal distension;

(b) Respiratory distress;

(c) Serious injuries, including deep wounds, severe hemorrhage, suspected bone fractures, or eye injuries;

(d) Straining for more than 30 minutes by a mare that has not foaled;

(e) Inability to rise or stand;

(f) Loss of appetite;

(g) Marked lameness or injuries not responding to treatment within 24 hours;
(h) Persistent signs of respiratory disease (cough);
(i) Diarrhea;
(j) Weight loss;
(k) Dry, harsh coat;
(l) Any other unresolved signs of ill health.

When horses are seriously injured or sick, if proper care and attention cannot be provided they should be removed to suitable facilities to permit adequate treatment, supervision and continuing after-care. If such an arrangement is not feasible and the state of the animal is beyond treatment, a licensed veterinarian should take the decision for the animal to be killed humanely. Horses belonging to riding clubs and taking part in organized sports must undergo a mandatory immunization programme as per National policy and have the same endorsed on their passports. Periodic test for Glanders and EIA must be carried out.

Training and Performance

Persons engaged in training and using horses should be experienced, or under direct supervision of an experienced person.

Horses should not be broken to ride until they are aged at least 18 months. Horses should be of the appropriate type, be adequately fed, housed and trained to the degree of fitness for the task to be performed.

Persons involved in the training of horses should be familiar with average requirements for age, suitability and fitness levels of horses used for the purpose for which the animal is being trained.

Abnormal physiological and behavioural responses to training and confinement should be recognized and measures taken to correct them. These responses may include aggression, biting pawing, kicking, weaving pacing, crib–biting, wind sucking etc.

Training methods involving cruelty or repeated pain 'insults' must not be used. Horses must not beaten or abused while loading/unloading.

All saddlery, harness and other equipments such as bandages, boots, plates, tongue ties and bits used with horses should be non-injurious of sound condition, well-fitting, correctly adjusted, and regularly cleaned, so that the risk of injury and disease to horse is reduced. Supportive or protective elastic bandages may be used on joints and tendons during training competition and racing. Bandages must be securely fixed used during work. Animals to be treated in case of saddle/girth/ bridle galls or spur injuries. Strong cognizance to be taken by EFI officials, event veterinarians and jury whenever such incidents come to notice.

In equestrian sports, the use of the whips and spurs should follow the guidelines of the particular discipline as laid down by FEI.

Horses require regular exercise for a period of weeks before they are adequately conditioned for more strenuous exercise.

Inexperienced persons training or riding have an obligation to use the horse in accordance with its fitness and, if in doubt, should seek advice from an experienced horseperson. Veterinary attention should be sought if there is any doubt about the fitness of a horse for training or competition.

Foot care

Shoeing should be practiced only by experienced persons or farriers. Horse's hooves should be trimmed regularly as required to permit normal mobility. Horses ridden or driven on roads and tracks or hard surfaces should always be shod. Shoeing should not provoke an abnormality of gait or conformation.

Hooves of horses in work should be inspected each day for signs of injury, loose shoes or impacted stones or infections. Shod horse should be inspected at least every six weeks for replacement or adjustment of shoes. Shoes should be removed or inspected regularly when horses are not in training or regular use. Due veterinary care be taken of horses when they develop sand cracks, thrush, canker, quittor or any foot ailment.

Treatment Procedure: General Guidelines

Effective management and treatment of horse involves using various forms of restraint. These will vary with the temperament, disposition and previous learning experience of the particular horse, the nature of the management procedure and the skill of the handler.

Restraint methods used on horses should always be the minimum necessary to carry out routine management procedures. Prolonged or over-zealous use of restraints, such as nose and ear twitches, may cause severe reaction from many horses. Adequate facilities to provide a safe environment, and suitable equipment, should be available when horses are subjected to any procedure or treatment.

Treatment procedure should only be performed by competent persons. Treatment practices causing pain should be performed only under the influence of suitable analgesic prescribed by a veterinarian and/or anaesthetic administered by a veterinarian.

Identification

Skin branding, lip tattooing and micro chipping are the accepted methods of identifying horses. Hot iron or freeze branding are the usual methods of permanent identification. Horses should not be branded using corrosive chemicals. Horses should be branded before weaning and as early as management practices will allow. Branding should be performed only by experienced persons.

Surgical and Medical Procedures

Surgical procedures should be performed and anaesthesia given only by a veterinarian. Horses of any age should not be castrated without the use of appropriate anaesthetic agents.

Practices such as firing, kicking (cutting the skin or ligaments of the tail to ensure the tail is held high) and limb neurectomy for the purpose of performance enhancement are not acceptable.

Medication such as vaccines, food additives, liniments lotions should be used strictly in accordance with the manufacture's instruction. Over-dosing may be harmful; under dosing may be ineffective.

Treatments should be administered in a hygienic manner. Medical wastes, syringes and needles, etc should be disposed of in accordance with clinical waste disposal requirements.

Protection from Disease

Routine vaccination of horses against tetanus is recommended. Owners should seek veterinarian advice about vaccination against other diseases. Prompt appropriate preventive treatment should be given to horse for diseases that may be common in a district. Routine treatment for internal parasites and early treatment of external parasites should be practiced. The effectiveness of treatment must be evaluated by veterinarian examination if the response to routine treatment is poor.

Good hygiene and cleanliness in and around stables, including disposal of effluent and litter, will reduce the risk of parasitism and disease. Control of flies and vermin can be aided by use of proper storage bins and prompt removal of spillage, daily cleaning of stables and surrounds and proper disposal of waste. Suitable pest control measures such as fly baits and surface residual sprays should be used, if necessary. Safety precautions are essential to protect both users and horses when using such chemicals. Horses diagnosed with a contagious disease must be immediately isolated from other horses.

Paddocks used for grazing horses should be managed in such a way that contamination by parasites or other disease-producing agents is minimized. Good management practices include spelling paddocks for interval, grazing with other species such as sheep and cattle, collection of droppings where size of yard makes it feasible and avoidance of overstocking.

Humane Death

When it is necessary, the method of humane killing (Euthanasia) should be effective and should cause sudden and painless death for any horse. It should be performed only by veterinarians.

Euthanasia should be performed behind appropriate protective screens to shield from public view. Disposal of the carcass should meet with hygiene regulations. Postmortem of a dead horse should be carried out by a licensed veterinarian. In case of highly infectious diseases like anthrax, the carcass should not be opened. The most acceptable way of disposing of the carcass is by burying it deep with adequate lime and salt. Graves should be marked.

Transport

Appropriate training and conditioning reduces the risk of injury to horses during transport. Horses unaccustomed to being transported should be transported in the company of other horses already exposed to travel. Young or unbroken horses frequently travel best when loose-penned in small groups in trucks. Horses should be fitted with suitable head-stalls and the leads should be secured to the vehicle using a quick release knot, so as not to endanger the animals. It is recommended that horses should be transported in separate compartments of a truck or trailer as under:

(a) Horses significantly different in size of type, for example, weanlings and adults, light or heavy horse, etc.

(b) Stallions - separately with high dividers

(c) Mares in advanced pregnancy - double width compartments

(d) Mares and foals –double width compartments

(e) Un weaned foals should be transported with their mothers.

After 24 hours of road travel, a rest period of 12 hours should ideally be provided, before starting the next stage of the journey.

Special precautions should be taken to provide water, shelter and ventilation during extremely hot weather. Horses in transit should be fed and watered at intervals of no longer than 8 hours. Provision should be made for foals to suckle their dams during transit.

Horses should have adequate leg supports, eg bandages, boots knee and hock caps, etc, fitted to minimize tendon, ligament joint and bone damage. Bell boots may be used to protect the coronet and hooves. Hoods, blankets and sheets are desirable to protect part of the body that is likely to suffer abrasion or bruising during transport. Extra tall horses should be fitted with poll protectors to ensure injury does not occur to the head.

Lame and sick horses should not be transported except to or from a place for veterinarian treatment. Mares more that 10 months pregnant should not be transport for more than 8 hours. Mares with foals at foot should not be transported within 7 days of foaling unless it is to or from a place for veterinarian treatment, or is for a journey of two horses or less. Mares foaled fewer than 14 days should not be transported for more than 8 hours.

The design and construction of vehicles should be suitable for horses. All transport vehicle doors and ramps should be fitted with secure latches, and should be close-fitting to reduce the risk of injury and/or escape. Loading facilities should be constructed so that they are unlikely to cause injury to animals. Floors of transport vehicles should be of solid construction and provide a non slip footing for horses. Horses should not be transported in double decker transport vehicles.

Inspection of horses should be carried out by either the driver or attendant not later than 30 minutes after commencement of the journey, and thereafter at intervals of at least every 2 hours. Horses should be unloaded as soon as possible after arrival at the destination.

Transport vehicles should be thoroughly cleaned and inspected regularly for faults. Faulty vehicles must be repaired before further use.

Appendices

Appendix 1 - Water Requirements

1. The basic maintenance requirements of water for ponies and horses are about 52 ml/kg body weight/day. A rough guide is as below:

Ponies	200-300 kg bw	10-15 litres daily
Horses	300-450 kg bw	15-25 litres daily
Horses	450-500 kg bw	25-30 litres daily

2. These requirements are significantly increased with growth, work and lactation. Two or three times as much water as shown above is needed by horses in work or lactation. Water requirement is closely related to dry matter intake of food. Horses need 2-4 litres of water per kilogram of dry matter intake. This requirement increase as air temperatures rise (15-20% increase for 13^0 C to 25^0 temperature change).

3. Water troughs and containers should be inspected regularly for function, replenishment, cleanliness and freedom from contamination. Water should always be clean.

Appendix 2 - Feed Requirements

Horses should be fed according to body condition and work. It is undesirable for any horse to be overweight or underweight. The efficiency of food utilization will vary between particular horses. Thoroughbred horses require substantially more feed per kilogram of body weight than other breeds. Most horses kept in smaller areas require supplementary feed for some part of the year, depending on stocking density and their requirements for growth, pregnancy etc.

Approximate minimum feed requirements of ponies and adult horse are shown in the table. Horses in hard work may have special feeding requirements.

Body weight of horses (kg)	Idle horse (maintenance only hay* (kg)	Moderate work (jumping, evening). Horses need both hay and grain	
		hay* (kg)	grain (oats) (kg)
300	5.0	4.0	1.0
400	7.0	5.0	3.5
500	8.0-9.0	5.5-7.5	4.0-6.0

* good quality pasture hay rich in clover, or Lucerne hay

Inexperienced people should consult a veterinarian or an experienced horse-person about selection of suitable foodstuffs for horses used for training and racing.

Protein, mineral and vitamin supplements should be provided when required.

Adequate, good quality food is necessary for the growth of young horse. At six months of age horses require much energy – rich foods and more protein than idle, adult horses.

Lactating mares require about 70% more energy foods than idle adult horses.

Appendix 3 - Excessive Use of Whip, Spurs, Bit

1. WHIP

The use of a whip must be:

- for a good reason;
- at an appropriate time;
- in the right place;
- with appropriate severity.

Type

Whips with raised seams, metal interior, projections, metal rivets etc. are not allowed.

Reason

The whip must only be used either as an aid to encourage the horse forward or as a reprimand. Thus, it must never be used to vent a rider's temper - any use for such a reason is automatically excessive and, therefore, a breach of these rules.

Time

As an aid, the appropriate time is when the horse is reluctant to go forward under normal aids of seat and legs. As a reprimand, the only appropriate time is immediately after a horse has been disobedient, e.g. refusing (but not after elimination, when it will always be excessive). The whip should not be used after a horse has jumped the last fence on a course.

Place

As an aid to go forward, the whip may be used down the shoulder or behind the leg. It must never be used 'over-arm', e.g. a whip in the right hand being used to the left flank. The use of a whip on a horse's head or 'over-arm' on the neck is always excessive use.

Severity

It should never be hit more than once after disengaging the hand from the reins for any one incident; and if the horse is marked by the whip, e.g. the skin is broken or there is a weal, its use is excessive. Horses with evident whip abuse signs may not be allowed to start at the discretion of the President Ground Jury.

2. SPURS

Spurs must not be used to reprimand a horse. Such use is always excessive, as is any use that results in a horse being marked by a spur. Horses with evident spur abuse signs may not be allowed to start at the discretion of the President Ground Jury.

3. BIT

The bit must never be used to reprimand a horse. Any such use is excessive. Horses with evident bit abuse signs may not be allowed to start at the discretion of the President Ground Jury.

IT IS AT THE DISCRETION OF THE PRESIDENT GROUND JURY TO ELIMINATE THE RIDER

Chapter **30**

Conservation of Indigenous Equine Species

India has a rich biodiversity of equines in the form of six distinct indigenous horse (*Equus caballus*) breeds, namely Kathiawari, Marwari, Spiti, Zanskari, Bhutia and Manipuri, in addition to indigenous donkeys and wild asses. These horse breeds are well adapted to different agro climatic regions and possess certain unique characteristics

The Food and Agriculture Organization of United Nations has cautioned the world community about the diminishing biodiversity which also includes equines and, therefore, it is a dire necessity and high time to conserve this precious germplasm.

At present there are not less than 200 breeds of horses in the world. Horses have entered into human heart through their common sense, and excellence in both work and sport. In the days of yore, horses left their glorious imprints in the field of warfare. Mechanization in the modern days has deleteriously affected the growth of equine rearing. It is well worthwhile to note that India possesses some valuable stock of indigenous breeds, which are capable of further development and propagation. Most of the Indian breeds are well adopted for the specialized type of work they are required to perform. The livestock census has revealed a significant decrease in equine population in our country. Uttar Pradesh, Madhya Pradesh, Bihar and Punjab had the largest number of horses among various states of India, in decreasing order. Rajasthan, U.P., Gujarat and Tamil Nadu have the largest population of donkeys in decreasing order. It should be the endeavour of the Government and every citizen of this country to ensure that this noble animal is conserved against this temporary lull in its breeding. The duty of veterinary professionals in this regard should be considered very high.

Horse Breeding in India Through Ages

Horse breeding carried out by private or government agencies help in conserving the equine population and it's up gradation, through encouragement of the government. Horse breeding in this country dates back to 1779 when British Army created the stud department (**the present Remount Veterinary Corps**) for breeding horses in India with a view to meet their requirement of horses. About 7 stud units were set up at different parts of this country, of which those in south were closed later. As the breeding bases located in Northern India, were found to more productive and hence the first Horse Breeding Area was established in Meerut district with HQ at Babugarh in the year 1875 and the first District Remount Officer was appointed in 1901. Later for Indian soldiers of World War-I, who left army, three-bound system of breeding areas were set up at Shahpur, Chenab and Montgomery districts and one unbound system breeding area in Pindi District for breeding horses and mules. The breeding operations went on well till the partition of India in 1947. In the post-Independent India, all these establishments went to Pakistan by virtue of their location and hence the Meerut breeding area was revived at Babugarh in 1948, and breeding operations were started in various centers of UP, Punjab and Rajasthan. For Punjab and Rajasthan, seperate breeding area operated from Jalandhar Cantonment. Later on with a view to achieve self sufficiency and to meet the increasing demands of horse and mules **Army Equine Breeding Studs** were established at Babugarh in 1957 and at Hisar in 1965. Since ponies purchased in 1962 from high mountains performed well, breeding from hill ponies at a height of 9000 feet and above with suitable stallions as *Haflingers* from army studs was considered worth trying.

During the year 1966,when production of both breeding areas (*Babugarh and Jalandhar*) reached the peak, the produce of army studs also started maturing for issue. It was then decided that both the breeding areas should drastically reduced and only few selected/ more productive stables of breeding areas were retained. Subsequently, both the horse and mule breeding areas were closed.

Present Status of Thoroughbred Breeding in India:

Private breeders to meet the demand of racing horses are carrying out breeding of thoroughbred horses in India. India stud book is being maintained by Stud Book Authority of India, which is a part of *Royal Western India Turf Club Ltd.*, that undertakes registrations of individual thoroughbred stallions and brood mares. The studs are registered with Ministry of Agriculture. Thoroughbred horses are used for riding, hunting, polo and other equestrian events. The Remount Veterinary Corps of Indian Army is carrying out in large scale breeding of thoroughbreds to meet its requirement as also meets the specific requirement of para military forces and police. Over the years the high pedigreed stallions have been imported from UK, France, Germany etc. to improve the thoroughbred stock of Indian origin.

Native Breeds:

Native breeds are bred within themselves to improve their breed quality. They are improved in their performance by cross breeding with various foreign breeds. The emphasis in the native pony world is now very much on performance, to produce good performance lines based primarily on conformation and temperament.

Each breed has got its typical movement. In the chosen breed, long stride, carrying head and neck high, a well-laid-out shoulder and not too short a back are important while selecting a performance pony.

The difficulty in carrying out breeding operations with native ponies is that these breeds often do not have pedigree or performance records of "families" for picking up. Priorities in selection can only be temperament, movement, and conformation including good feet, durability and soundness. The success of selection will be related to good management and initial training.

Judicious mixing of native, Arab and thoroughbred blood can evolve good riding ponies. The effort in breeding is to create a strong gene pool, containing genes for performance and the resulting modern competition horse is basically a type of equine cocktail.

Besides the Indian breeds of horses, Pakistani breeds of horses i.e. Baluchi, Hirzai and Unmol are also maintained and bred in India. Some horses of Connemara breed were imported at Himachal Pradesh and used for improving the local breed.

Some foreign efforts in improving the native breeds:

Some successful foreign experiences in developing their native breeds are worthwhile to be considered here.

The Peruvian Paso horse is one of the oldest and purest breeds in the world. It has a highly individual four beat lateral gait which is inbred and inherent as a result of 450 years of selective breeding. The Trakehner breeds of horses is one of the oldest in Europe with a history reaching back over 400 years. It originated from a small horse in East Persia renowned for versatility and stamina. English thoroughbred is used to cross Trakehner either way.

In earlier days the Shetland breed of horses were just suitable rides for tiny tots or harness ponies. But now they are genuine performance ponies. The sire 'Jack' of Londonderry stable contributed greatly for improvement of this breed in that of 490 foals entered in stud book at that time 248 were of Jack and 160 of his eight grandsons.

The Mongolian horse, descended from Tarpan, has been developed through regular selection in the last about 1000 years. In modern days Mongolian mares are cross bred with Don and Trotter stallions imported from Russia. Also these are cross bred with Budenny and Thoroughbred stallions as part of programme to evolve a 3-breed new horse that can hold its own against the best of the world in Olympics.

Donkeys:

It is the most simple and unselfish member of equine family. It is a very hardy animal which can work incessantly on poor forage. It is mainly used as a pack animal and is sure-footed. The Nubian ass is the parent of our present day donkey. Donkeys were domesticated at about 4000 B.C. in both Mesopotamia and Eqypt.

There are two types of donkeys - small grey and large white which are commonly seen in India. The small grey donkey is seen throughout the country and is dark grey with Zebra stripping on limbs, neck and quarters. The large white is seen mostly in the Kathiawar region of Gujarat state. It is light grey to white in colour. Large white asses (Khol) are an endangered dwindling species. The strength of which has fallen down to just 2000 from the 30,000 a few decades back. Presently, these animals are kept confined in a sanctuary.

Conservation of Indian Germplasm:

Efforts at protecting our indigenous equines are being undertaken largely through the following ways:

(a) Efforts to conserve our national heritage of horse and donkeys.

b) Efforts at producing future equines of high potential.

(c) Efforts to protect equines from the constant threat of diseases.

Several methods are employed for realizing the above aspects, which are given below:

I. Conservation of Domesticated Equines:

(a) Improving the lot of owners.

(b) Establishment of equine industry on sound footing.

(c) Establishment of turf clubs/societies.

(d) Establishment of research/developmental institutions by Government

(e) Improving equines through import/export.

(f) Cryo-preservation of semen and embryo.

II. Conservation Of Wild Equines:

(a) Protection by law

(b) Establishment of sanctuaries/refuges.

(c) Restoration of the original habitat.

(d) Better living conditions

  (i) Provision of cover

  (ii) Provision of good quality fodder .

(e) Raising of attractive animals.

(f) Educating the common man.

Conservation of Domesticate Equines:

(a) Improving the lot of owners:- In India, it is generally the landless and marginal farmers, who own native horses or donkeys which are primarily used as pack animals and for moving around. They lack capability to look after animals due to poverty and governmental efforts along with those of equine industry and various breed societies will be required to improve these animals by providing free breeding/health cover, subsidized good quality feed and providing ideal, supportive market conditions.

(b) Establishment of equine industry on sound footing:- Equine breeding should be given the required governmental support to start breeding good quality equines. They should be guaranteed good prizes for generating competitive sense and better managemental and training conditions. A healthy equine industry will be able to support the development of native equine breeds by joining the government in sponsoring various equestrian programme and breed shows, which act as morale booster for those engaged in such works. In India, presently more than 155 stud owners are present. It is essential that those entering into equine breeding for the first time be given the required help by the governmental set up from time to time.

(c) Establishment of turf clubs/societies:- In India, there are 6 turf clubs authorities. Of these, *Royal Western Turf Club Limited* was founded in 1800 and conducts racing in Bombay, Pune and

New Delhi. The *Royal Calcutta Turf Club* started in 1803. Bombay Turf Club initially presented a prize of 100 gold mohurs with the primary idea of encouraging breeding of horses. The turf clubs play their role by encouraging breeding and by maintaining modern lab and hospital facilities.

A variety of clubs have been established in various countries as Pony Enthusiast's Club, Breed Clubs, Horse Societies, and Riding Clubs. These clubs are related with conducting pony shows, breed shows, and Native Pony Championships, which go long way in improving the various breeds.

In India, the like-minded people from various parts of the country who were interested in the preservation, promotion and International recognition of the Indigenous breed of horses founded the *Indigenous Horse Society of India* on *19th March 1999* at Jodhpur (Rajasthan) for conserving 5 Indian breeds i.e. Marwari, Kathiyawari, Manipuri, Spiti and Zanskari. Similarly, the other breeding societies are also working to conserve the indigenous equines in India.

Horse Rescue trusts involve directly with the animals and ensure that over use of animals is not related with their ill-health, ensure proper care and good food to these animals, prevent mares heavily in foal from going for meat and also prevent half starved ponies at work. The functioning of International league for protection of horses is also more or less of similar nature. Brooke Hospital for Animals, an NGO from UK is functioning at few places in India to safeguard equine interest on the same lines.

(d) Establishment of research /development institutions by Government:

Independent institutions looking into equine development with all its related problems, and suggesting measures to get over them and an independent body looking into all aspects of equine development are essential to bring in necessary improvement in future. The *Indian Council of Agricultural Research* has set up *National Research Centre on Equines* at Hisar to carry out research relating to all aspects of equines including their breeding.

ICAR established *National Bureau of Animal Genetic Resources* who will have information on equine breeding stock in the country with them.

The MacDonald Institute of Archaeological Research, Cambridge University, UK is doing the research work on the Marwari and Kathiyawari horses since January 2006.

Equine Development Board with Union Minister of Agriculture as chairman was constituted in November 1991 for proper coordination of equine breeders, users, scientists and others. The board advises government on equine development.

(e) Import of Equines and their Export: In order that Indian thoroughbreds and native breeds improve and start excelling the foreign breeds, import of quality horses are controlled by CCI&E in consultation with Department of Agriculture.

The Indian economy will gain a lot and equine industry also will gain a boost when Indian thoroughbreds start capturing foreign market. A start was made for export when in 1980-86, 22 thoroughbred horses were exported to Kuwait by M/s Usha Stud and Agricultural Farm Private Limited, Gurgaon, Haryana which earned the country a foreign exchange of Rs.6,60,000/-.The armies of neibouring countries are importing the equines from India for their use.

(f) Cryo-preservation of Semen and Embryo:- Since native Indian breeds of equines are facing threats of shrinking genetic base, their conservation involves

(I) Establishing nucleus studs in the breeding tracts and

(ii) Storing required number of embryos and doses of semen of these breeds for generating the required population as and when needed.

(iii) There should be linkages between farms of ICAR/State/Central Government and Army Stud & Depot to achieve success. International agencies like FAO and EAAP and developed nations should help developing nations in conserving their species.

II.CONSERVATION OF WILD EQUINES:

(i) **Protection by law:-** Stringent laws are required to ensure that there is no trespass into the habitats of endangered species nor anyone interfere with their habitats.

(ii) **Establishment of sanctuaries/refuges:-** After the establishment of Indian Board for wild life in 1952, there is clear-cut provision to convert the natural tracts of breeds with their original habitats to be converted into sanctuaries to permit un-interfered breeding.

(iii) **Restoration of the original habitat:-** Towards this a missing lake is recreated, reforestation can be carried out; polluted rivers are chemically cleaned; Roads and Railways deviated from the heart of tracts of breeds to permit them to live without interference of modern civilization.

(iv) **Better living conditions:-**

(a) **Provision of cover:** A habitat will be ideal only if it is accompanied by presence of
shrubs and trees that offer cover to these animals.

(b) **Provision of food:** Such plants should be abundant that can be ideal as food to animals.

In the Rann of Kutch where a wild life sanctuary for wild ass (*Khol*) exist, Babul shrubs have been provided as cover and Dhub grass as the ideal grazing for wild asses which are the native habitat of the area.

(v) **Raising of attractive animals:-** This is possible mainly in domesticated equines.where due to machinery, some equines are least in demand, by modifying the breed through selective breeding, advantages of hair quality, height, colour etc., can be taken, which will create fresh demand and usher a new life to these breeds. The Army studs and Depot could be the ideal place for such activities with financial assistance from national and international organization.

(vi) **Educating the common man:-** Illustrated books, video/ TV coverages, encouraging tourisms, use of museum, encouragement for pet keeping, are methods whereby the common man is made aware of the importance of habitat and the details of endangered species so that he willingly participates in wild life conservation. On the same lines for the promotion of the Marwari and Kathiyawari breeds, the Dancing with Horses show choreographed and created by Francesca Kelly was performed at Jaipur at the Rajasthan Polo Club Grounds Jaipur on 27th and 28th March 2007 under the aegis of IHSI (Indigenous Horse Society of India) is a good example.

State Specific Equine Development Programme

(a) **Gujarat:** Government of Gujarat is maintaining Kathiawari horse breeding farm in Junagarh. They have also initiated formation of Breeders Society for Kathi breed of horses. They have created service centres in the state for Kathi breed where pure farm-bred Kathi stallions are kept for breeding purposes. One more Kathi breeding farm is being established at Inaj.

(b) **Manipur:-** North Eastern council is making constant efforts for conservation and further development of Manipuri breed.

(c) **Himachal Pradesh :-** Government of Himachal Pradesh has initiated horse and mule breeding scheme for preserving Chamurthi breed of horses found in Spiti sub-division.

(d) **Jammu & Kashmir :-** Government of Jammu & Kashmir has taken up conservation and intensive development of Zanskari breed so as to save this breed from extinction

(e) **Uttar Pradesh:-** The government of Uttar Pradesh is maintaining two breeding farms of Kathiawari breed, one at Pashulok (Rishikesh) and another at Chak-Ganjaria (Lucknow). From these two units, stallions are made available to different locations for breeding of indigenous horses.

(f) **Rajasthan:-** In order to conserve the Marwari/Malani breed, the horse breeders of Rajasthan have established the *Marwar Horse Breeding & Research Institute in Chopasni, Jodhpur.* This institute works to save the breed from extinction and to build respect for the horse breeders of the area. It registers horses and conducts educational programmes to maintain and improve the breed. Fairs held in Rajasthan, especially the Tilwara and Pushkar Animal Fair, encourage breeders with certificates, cash prizes and trophies awarded to the best-quality animals.

MODERN APPROACH TO EQUINE CONSERVATION PROGRAMME

Principles for Preservation of Endangered Species and Breeds in the Tropics

Although, specific information is not available on decline in numbers in various tropical breed populations, indiscriminate crossing with temperate exotics is putting many of these populations in danger of extinction. The need for preservation/conservation of breeds and local populations with specific adaptations, some of which are clearly endangered for various reasons, has now been clearly established.

A number of methods for preservation have been identified and costs worked out for each. There are two main categories:

Advantages of the *in situ* method are:

- the animals are visible, and so pleasing to the eye, and have some cultural value;
- they are a gene bank for future use;
- they are a constant reminder that the needs of posterity must be considered;
- the herd may have some economic advantage (e.g. disease resistance) which can be exploited and so render the enterprise economically viable.

The costs of *in situ* preservation worked out so far in Europe are not applicable to many tropical countries; these could be much less and need to be estimated for each ecosystem.

Disadvantages of the *in situ* method are:

- small population size, leading to inbreeding and random drift. Many models are now available which reduce inbreeding to a minimum, but some scientists argue that random drift over long periods (say hundreds of years; may lead to a population very different in genetic composition from the initial one).

- gene x environment interactions.

Because of random drift and possible gene environment inter actions, *ex situ* methods are generally preferred over *in situ*.

Ex situ storage can be of semen, ova or embryos. At present, embryos are preferred for obvious reasons, as the breed can be reconstructed at any time. There is agreement, however, that it is desirable to store semen as well as embryos.

The fast growing science of biotechnology may lead to newer techniques of gene preservation. DNA recombinant techniques, embryo manipulation, cloning of desirable genes from the same or other breed populations may one day become common.

Molecular characterization:- It is an essential prerequisite to developing an effective and meaningful conservation programme. At gene level several DNA-based technologies have been developed in the last decade to type polymorphic loci, including random amplified polymorphic DNA (RAPD), restriction fragment length polymorphism (RFLP), variable number of tándem repeats (VNTRs), single-strand conformational polymorphism (SSCP), and methods that make use of polymorphisms of short tandem repeats called microsatellites. Among the array of molecular markers, microsatellites are considered especially suitable for biodiversity evaluation, owing to their codominant inheritance, high heterozygosity, ease and reliability of scoring, ubiquitous presence throughout the genome, and high degree of polymorphism. Gupta *et al.*, (2004) have assessed genetic variation in the Spiti breed of Indian horses, using 25 microsatellite markers

The FAO Panel of united Nations has recommended the following guide lines for equine conservation programme:

HORSES

i. Although, other species may be more important for the

economics of developing countries the breeding of Equidae not be neglected.

ii. A survey should be made of various breed populations in the tropics to identify rare or endangered breeds for which action programmes for preservation need to be initiated immediately.

iii. Generally speaking, indigenous horse populations that are free of English and Arabian Thoroughbred genes should be studied and where necessary, preserved. This is because all the light horse populations (even the ponies) seem to have a high level of English and Arabian Thoroughbred genes, which are not endangered.

iv. In the regions having distinct horse breeds or lines well adapted to harsh conditions (e.g. in North Africa and the Arabian Peninsula), these breeds should be maintained under their original environmental conditions, even when they are also used as improvers in developed countries.

v. The developed countries should preserve the genetic variation of light and heavy, horses and ponies. The large scale of their utilization ensures the use of some of them also in developing countries.

vi. The programme for saving the Przewalski horse in its natural habitat in Mongolia should be supported.

vii. The international and national organizations should continue to foster inter-country cooperation in the exchange of germplasm, with due regard to quarantine precautions.

DONKEYS

The Panel recommends that:

i. The maintenance and improvement of donkey populations of the world should also be surveyed, since in the tropics and for some developing countries this species is more important than the horse. The different breeds should be evaluated and preserved where necessary; the first steps have been taken in Brazil and France.

ii. In the evaluation of donkeys, not only draught power but also meat production, the extent of other uses and above all, the adaptability of the breeds should be emphasized.

The Cryogenic storage of embryos/germ plasm should be organized on a regional basis under international control. Problems of access to the gene bank, and how the access is to be arranged between donors and recipients, need to be clarified

Precautions to be taken for cryo-preservation of genetic material.

There is a substantial risk of transferring contaminating agents when cryo-preservation of genetic material is used for breeds not kept under strict hygienic control.

- semen may be contaminated;
- viruses may stick to the zona pellucida of the embryos;
- contaminating agents are effectively frozen with semen or embryos and may be preserved indefinitely;
- contaminating agents cannot be removed from semen;
- addition of antibiotics does not offer guarantee of neutralization of contaminating agents.

Therefore, it is always recommended that:

i. Only specific pathogen free animals as semen donors should be used.

ii. Embryos should be treated according to the rules of the International Embryo Transfer Society (Organisation Epizootique International).

References

1. Kundu, P.B. (1992) Equine Development in India. Proceeding of Seminar on "Latest trends in Equine Breeding" on 28-29 Nov 1992 pp 120-129.

2. Harbans Singh and Moore E. N. (1978) Livestock and Poultry Production. (Second Edition) Prentice Hall of India Private Limited, New Delhi. pp 361-373.

3. National Research Centre on Equines, Sirsa Road, Hisar, Annual Report 1991-92. pp, 70.

4. Rastogi, V.B. and Jayaraj M.S (1984-85) Animal Ecology and

Distribution of Animals. Fifth Edition, Kedarnath, Ramnath, Meerut pp, 325-336.

5. Gupta, A. K., Dhillon, S. and Mamta Chauhan (2004) Genetic characterization of Indian Spiti horses. Journal of Genetics, (Vol. 83) (No. 3). 291-295
6. Indigenous Horse Society of India, News letter 2005-2007
7. Reports of FAO/UNEP Expert panel on animal genetic resources.

Chapter 31

Equine Management in Nuclear, Biological and Chemical Disaster

The *Nuclear, Biological or Chemical munitions* are used to cause large-scale casualties, destruction and damage to animal and man during war by enemy country/ terrorist organization. The mass casualty / damage producing effects of these weapons and attacks have given a new dimension to modern warfare, and all major countries have NBC weapons development programme. There is every possibility of such weapons being employed in future wars.

After the *9/11 terrorist attack* at New York, the US Govt planned an extensive training programme to educate its public to how to survive NBC attack in case of eventuality.

It is being able to survive such a threat is not enough? We must also be prepared to operate in an NBC (Nuclear, Biological, and Chemical) environment. The animal/veterinary management professionals should have some basic understanding of various aspects of NBC Warfare/Disaster to protect precious equine population. The accidental exposure of horses by chemical contaminants and hazardous substances in cities where horses are kept in vicinity of industrial areas cannot be ruled out.

NBC Environment

Mass Casualties - The number of casualties occurring practically instantaneously will be too great. Apart from the direct effects of NBC weapons, the fallout can be transported due to wind to greater distances from the actual site. Biological and chemical agents find their way into bunkers and under thatch covers.

Delayed Causalities - Chemical and Biological agents are especially useful in this way. Casualty producing effects can be made to last from a few moments to few weeks depending upon the type of agents, the dissemination method used and the meteorological conditions.

Large Area Contamination - Creation of contaminated environment including pastures will be obstacle to animal transport. The contaminated areas would have to be marked and avoided. Alternatively working in these areas would require special equipment.

Effects Even When Not Fired – The threat NBC weapons forces the use, NBC defensive measures. Measures like dispersion, high degree of hygiene, checking of contaminated area and use of protective gear particularly respirator will reduce the working capability of both men and animals.

Nuclear Warfare

Nuclear, or **atomic warfare**, is a war in which nuclear weapons are used. This has only happened once - the atomic bombings of Hiroshima and Nagasaki by the United States of America against the Empire of Japan near the end of World War II. Today the term usually refers to confrontations in which opposing sides are both armed with nuclear weapons.

Fig. 31.1 : The Titan II ICBM carried a 12 Mt W53 warhead, making it one of the most powerful nuclear weapons fielded by the United States during the Cold War.

The accidental nuclear war, in which a nuclear war is triggered unintentionally. Possible scenarios for this have included malfunctioning early warning devices and targeting computers, deliberate malfeasance, accidental straying of planes into enemy airspace, reactions to unannounced missile tests during tense diplomatic periods, reactions to military exercises, mistranslated or miscommunicated messages, and so forth.

Rogue states may acquire or manufacture nuclear weapons and use them to attack a foe indirectly through terrorism. Nuclear terrorism by non-state organizations may be more likely, as states possessing nuclear weapons are susceptible to retaliation in kind. Geographically-dispersed and mobile terrorist organizations are not so easy to discourage by the threat of retaliation

Nuclear weapons can be fired in a variety of ways depending upon the type of target and the effect to be produced. The major type of burst are: exoatmospheric, high air, low air, surface, deep underground, air burst over water, shallow underwater and deep underwater. A high airburst is one where the weapon is detonated at such a height that the fireball does not come into contact with the ground.

The chronology of events following a 20-kilo tonne high air burst is described here in brief to understand the phenomenon of nuclear explosion. After a nuclear explosion (the spot on the ground surface vertically beneath or above which a nuclear weapon has exploded is called Ground Zero or GZ) the surrounding atmosphere is heated to extremely high temperature and forms a brilliantly hot sphere of air and gases resulting in the 'fireball'. Immediately after the fireball is formed it begins to grow rapidly and rises like a balloon.

This fireball severely compresses the surrounding atmosphere producing 'Blast Wave' along with enormous amounts of 'Radiation'. As the fireball reaches its maximum height, there is cooling, condensation and formation of the characteristic 'Mushroom Shaped Cloud '. The cloud rises and depending on wind and atmospheric condition it spreads causing fallout.

Fig. 31.2 : Characteristic Mushroom Cloud due to Thermonuclear Explosion

Biophysical and Biological Effects of Nuclear Explosion

There are four principal immediate effects around the point of detonation of a nuclear weapon. These are *flash, thermal radiation, blast and nuclear radiations.* These effects are very intense close to the point of burst, but become progressively less severe farther away.

Flash - the fireball of a nuclear explosion emits very intense light. One metric tonne bomb explosion produces flash of light 20 times brighter than the sun at noon, to an observer 60 miles from the place of explosion. The flash consists of ultra- violet and infra - red radiations which cause eye injuries producing temporary flash blindness or permanent blindness as chorio-retinal burns. Protection against eye injury is difficult especially for animals facing the burst. Blinkers may provide some degree of protection. Use of antibiotic eye drops after exposure will check secondary infection.

Electromagnetic Pulse (EMP)

Electromagnetic pulse is an intense burst of radio frequency radiation that can be picked up in power lines and through antennas. The electronic equipments will get damaged, if not ruined, by a pulse that occurs at the time of detonation and continues to be a possibility throughout an attack with multiple weapons. To keep from damaging the FM and CB radios it is advisable to use only the internal antennas that are 10 inches or less and wrap the radio in aluminium foil and store in a freezer bag.

Thermal Radiation - When a nuclear device is set off, the surrounding atmosphere is heated to extremely high temperatures and causes burns by two ways:

(a) ***Flash Burns (Primary Burns)*** – These are caused by direct absorption of the heat energy through the exposed skin.

(b) ***Flame Burns (Secondary Burns)*** – These are caused by indirect action of fire caused in the immediate vicinity. Conflagration effects such as asphyxiation may cause further casualties.

IDENTIFICATION AND TREATMENT OF BURNS.

Nuclear and Chemical Warfare has the potential for producing serious burns and secondary infection.

First Degree: Also known as "superficial" or "minor". Like "sunburn". Aloe Vera lotion will soothe. Does not require medical attention unless symptoms of infection (coloured drainage, fever, increased pain) become apparent. Generally, it heais on its own within a week.

Second Degree: Also known as "partial thickness" burns result in blistering. The Blisters should not be opened. They are the body's own best defence. Do not put ice on the burn! cold water for 15 minutes (running water is best, but immersion is OK). Do not put butter on the burn! Aloe Vera lotion will soothe without irritating. Xeroform (petroleum in gauze), zinc oxide, or Silvadene cream can be used on blisters once opened. If allergy to Sulfa, be cautious with use of Silvadene. Wrap gauze loosely around/on burn. Expect healing in 2 weeks. Watch for infection.

Third Degree: Also known as "Full Thickness" or "major" require medical attention as quickly as possible, as this type of burn affects internal organs and can result in shock quickly. The appearance of third degree burns varies from pearly white to dark leathery brown.

***Burns to mucous membranes*:** Eyes, nose, mouth, genitalia require much more attention than burns to dry skin. Flush these areas with cold water for at least 20 minutes, and seek available medical / veterinary treatment as soon as possible.

Large Areas of Burns: For multiple burn areas of more than two to three inches treat as if they were a grade up. i.e. treat a large area of second degree burns as a third degree burn, as there may be risk of compromising internal organs.

***Chemical Burns*:** Treat as above, but in addition, continue to flush with cold water for at least 20 minutes break the blisters after 20 minutes flush) for as long as moderate to severe pain persists.

Prevention: If possible consists in seeking underground shelter. Blankets and rugs (preferably light coloured and multi layered) provide some degree of protection.

Blast - Two distinct, though simultaneous, phenomena are associated with blast wave in the air: -

(a) Static Over Pressure - This sharp increase in the pressure is due to compression of atmosphere.

(b) Dynamic Pressure – This is the force exerted by strong transient blast winds associated with the movement of air following the blast wave.

The differential passages of blast wave through media of varying density causes rupture and hemorrhage in human / animal body. Indirect blast injury as a result of flying debris hitting the body or the animal being flung against an object causes contusions, lacerations and fractures. Ear drum rupture occurs at 5 psi and lungs and internal organs can be damaged at 15-20 psi.

Keeping animals in underground shelter provide considerable protection against blast effect. When caught in open, position of the animal facing the head towards or directly away from explosion significantly decreases the risk of blast.

Radiation - The release of ionizing radiation is a unique feature of nuclear explosion. It is an additional casualty producing factor and basically of two kinds - electromagnetic (gamma rays and neutrons) and particulate (alpha and beta particles). It is emitted not only at the time of detonation (initial radiation) but also for a long time afterwards (residual and induced radiation). Only the neutron and gamma radiation components are of significance. The intensity of initial nuclear radiation decreases rapidly with distance from the point of burst. Fall out is the processes in which radioactive material rises into the atmosphere with the fireball and falls back on to earth over a period of time due to effect of gravity, rain or snow.

The biological response to ionizing radiation is wide, ranging from rapid death to delayed radiation effects depending upon the dose absorbed. Veterinarians are concerned with the effects of radiation injury to animals at two levels, the somatic dose resulting from acute, direct exposure to irradiation and the cumulative dose due to accumulation of radioactivity in tissues resulting small gradual exposures to radioactive materials.

Acute Radiation Syndrome (ARS) - ARS is a combination of syndromes occurring in stages during a period of hours to weeks after exposure, varying with dose. It occurs in three successive phases.

(a) **Prodromal Stage -** Appearing within first few hours, lasting for a day or more. This stage is manifested by signs of acute irritation of the alimentary tract which include anorexia, fatigue, malaise, drowsiness and diarrhoea in severe cases. With high lethal doses the animals may die at this stage of apparent normality.

(b) **Latent Period -** Relatively symptom free period may last up to three weeks.

(c) **Main Manifest Phase -** In this recovery or death occurs within 8 weeks of exposure. There is profound depression of bone marrow activity. The clotting mechanism and antibody production are impaired and facilitate bacterial infection. Progressive necrosis of the gut-wall is characteristic. This phase can be classified into three major syndromes viz., haemopoetic, gastro-intestinal and neuro-vascular. Main symptoms are fever, knuckling, swelling of one or more legs and diarrhoea developing to melanin and dysentery sometimes with tenesmus, weakness, rapid respiration and profuse nasal discharge, which may be blood stained. Death occurs in about 20 days.

Minimum Lethal Dose (MLD) – MLD for most domestic animals is 500 rads received during a period of 24 hours.

Chronic Exposure - When fallout contaminates pasture, there may be sufficient fissionable material on the leaves of the plants to produce the same effects as those, which occur with direct irradiation except that radiation sickness does not occur.

Delayed Effects of Radiation – May appear months to years after irradiation and include life shortening, cataract formation, chronic radio dermatitis, leukemia, tumors, infertility/sterility and genetic mutation.

Combined Injuries - Following a nuclear explosion radiation injuries will be superimposed upon other injuries like burns, lacerations, fractures and other injuries. Generally, each will be treated individually. Infectious complications are the most worrying features of combined injury syndrome.

Symptoms of Radiation Sickness in Man /Animal Handlers

Radiation illness develops slowly. It is not contagious and cannot be spread to other people. Except for temporary nausea shortly after exposure, evidence of serious effects from radiation may only appear after an interval of a few days to three weeks. These effects include:

Loss of hair;

Loss of appetite;

Increasing paleness;

Weakness;

Diarrhoea;

Sore throat.

Bleeding Gums and Easy Bruising

A combination of the above symptoms indicates that the individual requires medical attention.

Nausea and vomiting may be caused by fright, worry, food poisoning, pregnancy and other common conditions and is not an indicator of radiation sickness by itself.

Treatment of ARS – Only symptomatic treatment will be given. Lot of fluid administration is indicated. Resuscitation and cardiovascular stabilization are important and so is control of hemorrhage.

Prevention of Radiation Injury

The only methods of protection available are by shielding, by removal to a distance from the source, by reduction of dose through reducing the time exposure and by decontamination. In the event of fallout shelter and simple decontamination means can afford a degree of protection. The possibility of sustaining a radiation does as a result of ingesting contaminated feed or water or grazing on contaminated pastures must be borne in mind. Discipline of feed and water is essential to minimize the risk of radiation in fallout area.

Potassium iodide if given prior to nuclear attack can protect the thyroid gland. Respirator and rugs provide protection from fall–out.

Decontamination - Presence of fallout contamination upon animals constitutes a hazard to the animals as well as to the attendants. Radio monitoring instruments are used to detect the contamination level. Decontamination procedure will vary from brushing off the dust, washing with detergent to surgical debridement of contaminated wounds or drugs to increase excretion.

Chemical Warfare

Chemical warfare is the use of chemical compounds to kill or incapacitate the personnel / animals or to deny the use of ground for military operations. They can be delivered by aircrafts, rockets, field artillery and mortars, either by airburst / spray or surface burst.

Types of Chemical Agents

The types of chemical Agents are as follows: -

(a) Nerve agents, e.g., Soman (GD), Tabun (GA), Sarin (GB) and Vx.

(b) Blister Agents, e.g., Mustards and Arsenicals.

(c) Choking agents, e.g., Phosgene gas(*COCl2*) (causes lungs to fill water),Chlorine gas (destroys the cells that line the respiratory tract)

(d) Blood Agents, e.g., HCN

An important characteristic of chemical agent is its persistency. Non- persistent agents like G agents, blood agents and choking agents are used to produce immediate effects. Persistent agents like Vx and blister agents contaminate materials/ground and pose both contact and vapour hazard for a longer duration. Lethal agents e.g., nerve agents are used with the primary object of killing maximum number of men/animals. Incapacitating agents e.g., BZ and HD, on the other hand, make men/animals temporarily unable to perform their duties.

NERVE AGENTS

Nerve agents disrupt the nervous system, thus inhibiting the signals that the body needs to perform automatic functions. Nerve agents affect the body the same way snake and insect venom does. Nerve agents are the hardest to detect. Nerve agents enter the body either by inhalation or through skin and eyes. Nerve agents act by binding acetyl cholinesterase, thereby permitting continuous cholinergic stimulation and excessive autonomic and muscular activity.

Symptoms and Signs - The manifestation of nerve agents poisoning in various species of animals may vary. In horse the early symptoms include frequent urination, increased peristalsis reflected as colic and patchy sweating. Salivation may be moderate to profuse. Para-sympathetic stimulation produces defecation, urination and uneasiness. The heart rate is slow; respiratory efforts become exaggerated and animal may develop severe abdominal pain. A stiff legged gait and muscle tremors occur as the syndrome progresses. In severe cases respiratory failure is the sign. Death is due to anoxia. Death may occur within few minutes to several hours after the initial signs develop.

First Aid and Treatment – NBC protection masks should be used to protect the horses, if available (It is in service with the erstwhile Yugoslav armed forces). If mask is not available, head of the animal should be covered with wet cloth. If drops of nerve agent get into the eye, the eye should be washed immediately with water. Any liquid nerve agent on skin should be washed with soap and water or decontaminated with Fuller's earth.

Inject Atropine and repeat every 15 minutes unto 3 injections. Oxime can be administered orally or parentally. Anti-convulsants like Diazepam can also be administered. Artificial respiration increases chances of survival. If respiratory tract is involved the animal should be kept quiet and fed from the floor. This helps the nasal discharge to come away and prevents accumulation. Pre-treatment consists of administering pyridostigmine prior to exposure to nerve agent.

Prevention - It is important to seek shelter. Collective protection shelters are best. Keep all doors and windows tightly shut. Prohibit grazing on contaminated pasture. No watering from pool/ ponds in suspected areas.

BLISTER AGENTS

Blister agents irritate and inflame the skin and mucous membranes of the respiratory system or any other parts of the body that can get wet, or are wet.

Parts of our body that readily become wet also readily absorb liquid, or vapours.

These agents act on the eyes, lungs and skin, and burn and

blister the skin or any other part of the body they touch. The horn of the hoof including the frog is, however, sufficiently resistant to protect the sensitive structures of the foot.

Most blister agents are dispersed in white or yellowish clouds, and have a pungent odor, like ammonia, chlorine, or mustard (vinegar). Blister agents, (with the exception of tear gas), however are rather obsolete and can be defended against more effectively than other agents. Though not normally fatal, blister agents can debilitate and demoralize. They are also short-lived and have a short range of effectiveness. Mother Nature neutralizes them to their basic elements relatively quickly.

Symptoms and Signs

(a) Effects on eyes – Watering, redness and swelling of eyelids are noticed when eyes get exposed to vapours. A drop falling in the eye causes serious injury and may result in blindness.

(b) Effects on skin – Liquid drops falling on the skin cause hairs in the vicinity of the drop to stand erect followed by localized swelling. The swelling subsides in 4-5 days to leave a thickened, wrinkled area of skin, which separates to leave a sore. Heavier splashing cause early sloughing and suppurating sore.

(c) Effects on Respiratory System – Inhalation of vapours cause spasms of coughing and a profuse nasal discharge.

(d) Effects on Digestive System – Eating contaminated forage causes serious injury to the mouth, stomach and intestines which may be manifested by diarrhoea and colic.

First Aid and Treatment: - Slow rate of healing is characteristic of mustard injuries. To shorten the healing time, speed is of most importance in first aid treatment. The attendants applying the treatment should put on protective clothing with gloves and respirator. First aid involves:-

(a) Removal of gear and fixing of tail.

(b) Eyes should be washed with normal saline or water. Antibiotic drops can be instilled in the eyes after washing.

(c) Decontaminate the skin with Fuller's earth.

(d) If localized, anti blister ointment should be well rubbed into the skin and wiped after 5 minutes.

(e) In case large area of skin is involved, scrub vigorously with soap and water, and then rinse with lot of water.

(f) If respiratory system is involved, feeding from the floor helps in cleaning respiratory passage. Steam inhalation if possible. Parenteral antibiotic therapy in severe cases.

(g) If digestive system is involved, a liberal diet of clean forage should be given with plenty of water at frequent intervals. Later the diet should be light and of laxative nature.

(h) Forge, contaminated with liquid mustard must be destroyed. If destruction is by burning, care should be taken to protect aerosol formation.

(i) Contaminated harness and saddlery should be subjected to decontamination before use.

Prevention - Shelters provide important protection. A good deal of protection is gained by gas-proofing the stable. Use can be made of barns, stables and other building. Blankets and rugs should be used to cover the body and removed as soon as possible. Contaminated area should be avoided and grazing on contaminated pastures should be prohibited. Contaminated water should not be allowed for drinking. Some ointments like Dimercaprol and Dimethicone cetrimide cream are available which can be smeared on the legs below knee if passing through contaminated areas that cannot be avoided. Move should avoid under splashing. Use of protective mask will prevent inhalation of vapours.

CHOKING AGENTS

They attack respiratory tract causing pulmonary oedema and are used as delayed action casualty agents.

Symptoms – No symptoms may develop until 12th to 24h hour after exposure. Slight spasms or coughing may be observed. Breathing becomes hurried and difficult, the nostrils are widely dilated. The temperature rises and a nasal discharge appears which is foamy to start with and later becomes thick and blood stained. Death may occur in 48 hours.

First Aid Treatment – Don't mask immediately. Animals should be given complete rest after being moved to protected place. Any form of exercise will aggravate the condition. Animal carrier should be used to transport the animals, if available. Harness and saddlery is removed and animals be kept in open air. Bronchodilators such as aminophyllin, deriphyllin are helpful. Beclomethasone inhalation and perineal antibiotics are advocated.

Prevention - Collective protection shelters provide real protection. Gas proofing the stable can serve the purpose. It is necessary to have the sealing material in the building so that it can be put quickly into operation. Blankets or cloth curtains will be used on the inside of windows and doorways. For metal window frames gummed paper strips should be used and drainage exits should be stopped. Horses do not suffer any ill effect from such a confinement for a time long enough to ensure the dispersal of these non-persistent gases. If in open, horse lines should be sited on high grounds or hillside. Low lying valleys should be avoided.

BLOOD AGENTS

Blood agents prevent the body's blood from carrying oxygen as needed, and attack primarily the respiratory system. Blood agents act just like carbon monoxide poisoning. Common respirators cannot protect against blood agents. They are unstable and short-lived, therefore not economical to use.

These agents enter the body through respiratory tract. They inhibit cell respiration by acting on *cytochrome oxidase* enzymes. Onset of symptoms is within few seconds and death ensues in a few minutes.

Symptoms and Signs – In sub lethal doses, the signs noticed are initial excitement, muscle tremors followed by pronounced polypnoea and dyspnoea, salivation, lacrimation and voiding of faces and urine. There is gasping for breath and clonic convulsions. Blood is bright cherry red.

First Aid Treatment - If contact with a blood agent is suspected (tightness of chest, loss of breath, redness of overall skin hue, bluish lips) get the affected individual to fresh air, or give oxygen. If it survive the first 60 to 90 seconds of blood agent inhalation, it will most likely live.

Don't mask immediately. Immediate inhalation of Amyl nitrite. Crush 4 ampoules in hollow of the palm and hold close to the nostrils of animal. Artificial respiration is of help if possible. Treatment consists of Parenteral administration of sodium nitrite plus sodium thiosulphate.

Prevention - Blood agents severely degrade the efficiency of the mask. Therefore, filter should be discarded / replaced after single exposure. Animals should be moved to collective shelters.

BIOLOGICAL WARFARE AGENTS

Biological Warfare is perhaps the terrorist's best means of delivering a heavy blow to large populations. Anthrax is probably their agent of choice. Anthrax is persistent and easily manufactured. In layman's terms, biological warfare is simply germ warfare.

Biological weapons include any organism or toxin found in nature that can be used to incapacitate, kill, or otherwise impede an adversary (it's man, animal or crop). Biological weapons are characterized by low visibility, high potency, substantial accessibility, and relatively easy delivery. Biological agents represent a whole range of weapon systems rather than a single weapon. Genetic engineering techniques have been utilized to modify the potential of BW agents to render them more virulent, resistant to drugs and easier to store.

Today's modern technology and scientific capability, however, has refined these agents to include ***Smallpox-Vee,*** which is a combination of Smallpox and Venezuelan Equine Encephalitis virus. ***Ebola pox*** is combination of the Smallpox virus and Ebola virus. Finally, but certainly not the least is the ***Mar burg Virus,*** a virulent "Variant U" that is reported to be a genetically engineered anthrax bacteria. It is 1000 times more lethal than natural anthrax. Most of these agents were products of Soviet research and manufacturing, but with the collapse of the soviet regime it is thought that other nations have acquired the research. If such weapons are deployed, those stricken by the diseases may overwhelm our medical/veterinary facilities.

The mode of delivery of biological weapons may be the same as for conventional weapons. The additional mode being spread by vectors (mosquitoes, fleas and ticks etc.). Sabotaging of feed and water supply is another method of biological warfare.

The potential spectrum of bio-terrorism ranges from hoaxes and use of non–mass casualty agents by individuals or small groups to state-sponsored terrorism that employs classic biological warfare (BW) agents and can produce mass casualties. Such scenarios would present serious challenges for patient treatment and for prophylaxis of exposed persons. Environmental contamination could pose continuing threats.

The use of biological agents is not a new concept, and history is replete with examples of biological weapon use. Before the 20th century, biological warfare took on 3 main forms: (1) deliberate poisoning of food and water with infectious material, (2) use of micro-organisms or toxins in some form of weapon system, and (3) use of biologically inoculated fabrics.

Attempts to use BW date back to antiquity. Scythian archers infected their arrows by dipping them in decomposing bodies or in blood mixed with manure as far back as 400 BC. Persian, Greek, and Roman literature from 300 BC quote examples of the use of animal cadavers to contaminate wells and other sources of water. In 190 BC, at the Battle of Eurymedon, Hannibal won a naval victory over King Eumenes II of Pergamon by firing earthen vessels full of venomous snakes into the enemy ships.

In the 12th century AD, during the battle of Tortona, Barbarossa used the bodies of dead soldiers to poison wells. In the 14th century AD during the siege of Kaffa, the attacking Tarter force hurled the corpses of those who died of plague into the city to attempt to inflict a plague epidemic upon the enemy. This was repeated in 1710 when the Russians besieging Swedish forces at Reval in Estonia catapulted plague cadavers.

In the 18th century AD during the French and Indian War, British forces in North America gave blankets from smallpox patients to the Native Americans to create a transmission of the disease to the immunologically naïve tribes. In 1863, a confederate surgeon was arrested and charged with attempting to import yellow fever-infected clothes into the northern parts of the United States during the Civil War.

Biological warfare became more sophisticated against both animals and humans during the 1900s. During world war I, the Germans developed *Anthrax, Glanders, Cholera,* and a wheat fungus for use as biological weapons. They allegedly spread plague in St Petersburg, infected mules with Glanders in Mesopotamia, and attempted to do the same with the horses of the French Calvary.

In 1925, the Geneva Protocol was signed by 108 nations, including the 5 permanent members of the UN Security Council. This was the first multilateral agreement that extended prohibition of chemical agents to biological agents. No method for verification of compliance was addressed.

During world war II, the Japanese operated a secret BW research facility in Manchuria and carried out human experiments on Chinese prisoners. They exposed more than 3000 victims to *Plague, Anthrax, Syphilis,* and other agents. Victims were observed for development of disease, and autopsies were performed.

In 1942, the United States formed the War Research Service. Anthrax and botulinum toxin initially were investigated for use as weapons, and sufficient quantities of botulinum toxin and anthrax cattle cakes were stockpiled by June 1944 to allow limited retaliation if the Germans first used biological agents. The British tested anthrax bombs on Gruinard Island off the northwest coast of Scotland in 1942 and 1943 and then prepared and stockpiled anthrax-laced cattle cakes.

In India during post world war II period, the British India started research on anthrax and developed first animal vaccine at Imperial Veterinary Research Institute at Mukteshwer to safe guard the animal health from Anthrax Bomb.

The United States continued research on various offensive biological weapons during the 1950s and 1960s. From 1951-1954, simulants (*Bacillus globigii, Serratia marcescens*) were released off both coasts of the United States to demonstrate the vulnerability of American cities to biological agent attacks. This vulnerability was tested again in 1966 when the simulant *Bacillus globigii* was released in the New York subway system.

In 1957, the British government decided to end its offensive BW capabilities and destroy its weapon stockpiles.

The United States terminated its offensive biological weapons programme in 1969 for micro-organisms and in 1970 for toxins. The United States is a signatory nation of the Biological Toxin Weapons Convention of 1972. This convention addressed the prohibition of the development, production, stockpiling, and destruction of bacteriologic and toxin weapons. Signatories to this agreement are required to submit information annually to the United Nation's concerning faculties where biological defense research is being conducted, scientific conferences that are held at specified faculties, exchanges of scientists or information, and disease outbreaks. American stockpiles of biological weapons were destroyed completely by 1973.

The Soviet Union (USSR) continued to develop biological weapons from 1950-1980. In the 1970s, the USSR and its allies were suspected of having used "yellow rain" (trichothecene mycotoxins) during campaigns in Loas, Cambodia, and Afghanistan. In 1979, an accidental release of anthrax from a weapons factory in Sverdlovsk, USSR, killed at least 66 people. The Russians denied this accident until 1992.

Since the 1980s, terrorist organizations have become users of biological agents. The most frequent bioterrorism episodes have involved contamination of food and water. In September and October of 1984, 751 persons were infected with *Salmonella typhimurium* after an intentional contamination of restaurant salad bars in Oregon by followers of the Bhagwan Shree Rajneesh.

In 1985, Iraq began an offensive biological weapons programme producing anthrax, botulinum toxin, and aflatoxin. During Operation Desert Shield, the coalition of allied forces faced the threat of chemical and biological agents. Following the Persian Gulf War, Iraq disclosed that it had bombs, Scud missiles, 122-mm rockets, and artillery shells armed with botulinum toxin, anthrax, and aflatoxin. They also had spray tanks fitted to aircraft that could distribute 2000 L over a target.

Currently, 17 countries are suspected of having an offensive BW program. In 1992, 20 people were administered chemoprophylaxis after a Virginia man sprayed his room mates with a substance that he claimed was anthrax. In 1994, a Japanese sect of the Aum Shinrikyo cult attempted an aerosolized release of anthrax from the tops of buildings in Tokyo. In 1995, 2 members of a Minnesota militia group were convicted of possession of ricin, which they had produced themselves for use in retaliation against local government officials. In 1996, an Ohio man was able to obtain bubonic plague cultures through the mail.

From September to November 2001, a total of 23 confirmed or suspected cases of bioterrorism-related anthrax (10 inhalation, 13 cutaneous) occurred in the United States. Most cases involved postal workers in New Jersey and Washington DC, and the rest occurred at media companies in New York and Florida, where letters contaminated with anthrax were handled or opened. As a result of these cases, approximately 32,000 persons with potential exposures initiated antibiotic prophylaxis to prevent anthrax infections.

The threat that biological agents will be used on military forces and civilian populations is now more likely than at any point in all of history.

Types of biological warfare agents

The various types of the BW agents could be

(i) ***Bacteria*** e.g. Anthrax, Glanders, Plague (Bubonic and Pneumonic), Cholera, Tularemia, Brucellosis, Pertussis Typhoid, Diphtheria, Pulmonary Tuberculosis

Francisella tularensis, which is causative agent for Tularemia, has been considered an important BW agent because of its high infectivity after aerosolization. However, in case of Cholera it does not spread easily from human to human; therefore, it appears that major drinking water supplies would have to be contaminated heavily for this agent to be effective as a biological weapon. The easy transmission of Brucella species by aerosol suggests that it may be useful as a BW agent. The potential of Coxiella burnetii, the causative agent of Q fever as a BW agent is related directly to its infectivity. It has been estimated that 50 kg of dried Coxiella burnetii would produce casualties at a rate equal to that of similar amounts of anthrax or tularemia organisms.

(ii) ***Virus*** e.g. Varicella, Ebola, Hantavirus (causes fatal kidney disease), SARS plague, Avian flu virus (may cause pademic flu to man and other spp) Viral Encephalitis virus, Venezuelan equine encephalitis (VEE) virus, western equine encephalitis (WEE) virus, and eastern equine encephalitis (EEE) virus.

Viral Hemorrhagic Fevers: Viral hemorrhagic fevers are caused by 4 families of viruses, which include the Arenaviridae (Lassa, Argentine, Bolivian, Brazilian, Venezuelan hemorrhagic fevers), Bunyaviridae (Rift Valley, Crimean-Congo, Hantaan), Filoviridae (Marburg, Ebola hemorrhagic fevers), and Flaviviridae (Yellow, Dengue, Kyasanur Forest, Omsk hemorrhagic fevers). The best known of the viral hemorrhagic fever agents is Ebola virus. First recognized in Zaire in 1976, the virus has been linked to 3 outbreaks in Africa and is associated with a 53-92% mortality rate. A related virus was discovered in Reston, VA, in 1989 in association with an outbreak of illness among cynomolgus monkeys imported from the Philippines. No human cases occurred with this latter outbreak.

During the year 2006 in several parts of India especially Kerala, Tamilnadu, Karnataka, Maharashatra, MP, UP outbreaks of Chickengunia (type of viral fever with severe joints and muscular pain) among human population have occurred.

These viruses each are characterized by an acute generalized illness that includes malaise, prostration, increased vascular permeability, and abnormalities of circulatory regulation. All agents are highly infectious via the aerosol route, and most are stable as respiratory aerosols. Thus, they possess ideal characteristics to be used by terrorists.

Variola virus responsible for small pox is highly infectious by aerosol, environmentally stable, and can retain infectivity for long periods and hence a potential BW as currently the majority of human population has no immunity for the disease as the same has been eradicated from the world in 1980 by WHO. SARS plague virus and Bird flu are emerging agent for biological warfare in recent years.

(iii) ***Fungus*** e.g. wheat fungus

(iv) **Rickettsia** e.g. Q Fever

(v) **Biological Toxins**: These may be of microbial or plant origin. Few important toxins are described below:

Staphylococcal Enterotoxin B (SEB) is one of the most common causes of food poisoning. Nausea, vomiting, and diarrhoea normally occur following ingestion of contaminated food stuffs. The toxin causes a markedly different clinical syndrome when exposure is through a nonenteric route. In a BW or terrorist situation, the toxin is likely to be acquired through inhalation of an SEB aerosol. SEB is stable as an aerosol, and the inhaled dose necessary to incapacitate individuals is small (0.004 mcg/kg). Within 24 hours of inhalation of SEB toxin, exposed individuals are likely to be incapacitated by systemic illness created by the toxin.

Botulinum toxin: The anaerobic, spore-forming, gram-positive bacillus *Clostridium botulinum* produces botulinum toxins. Botulinum toxins are the most lethal toxins known, with an estimated lethal dose to 50% of the exposed population (LD50) of 0.001 mcg/kg in humans. Since botulinum toxin is so lethal and easy to manufacture and weaponize, it represents a credible threat as a BW agent. When used as a BW or terrorist agent, exposure is likely to occur following inhalation of aerosolized toxin or ingestion of food contaminated with the preformed toxin or microbial spores. Recently, Iraq admitted to active research on the offensive use of botulinum toxins and to weaponizing and deploying more than 100 munitions with botulinum toxin in 1995.

Trichothecene mycotoxins are highly toxic compounds produced by certain species of filamentous fungi (*Fusarium, Myrotecium, Cephalosporium, Trichoderma, Verticimonosporium, Stachybotrys* species). These mycotoxins (eg, T-2, nivalenol) cause multiple organ effects, which include emesis, diarrhoea, weight loss, nervous disorders, cardiovascular alterations, immunosuppression, hemostatic derangements, skin toxicity, and bone marrow damage. Because of their antipersonnel properties, ease of large-scale production, and amenability to dispersal by various methods (dusts, droplets, aerosols, smoke, rockets, artillery mines, portable sprays), mycotoxins have an excellent potential for weaponization. Strong evidence suggests that trichothecenes ("yellow rain") have been used as a BW agent in Southwest Asia and Afghanistan. From 1974-1981, numerous attacks resulted in a minimum of 6310 deaths in Laos, 981 deaths in Cambodia, and 3042 deaths in Afghanistan.

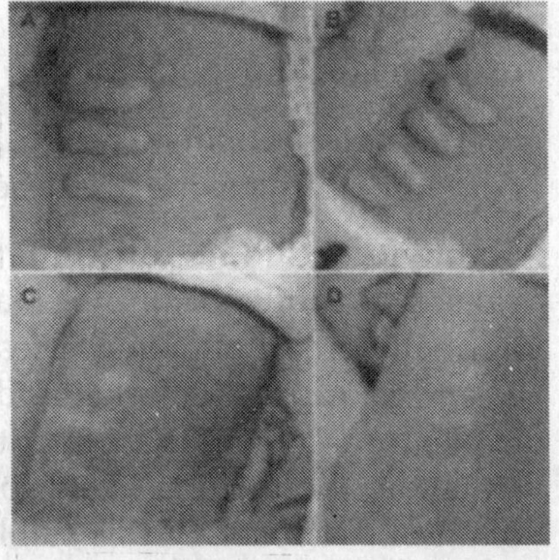

Fig 31.3 : Vesicles and erosions on the back of hairless guinea pigs at (a) 1 day, (b) 2 days, (c) 7 days, and (d) 14 days after application of (bottom to top) 25 ng, 50 ng, 100 ng, or 200 ng of T-2 mycotoxin in 2 mcL of methanol

Ricin, a plant protein toxin derived from the beans of the castor plant, is one of the most toxic and easily produced plant toxins. Although the lethal toxicity of ricin is approximately 1000-fold less than botulinum toxin, the worldwide ready availability of castor beans and the ease with which toxin can be produced, gives it the status of significant potential as a biological weapon. Since ancient times, more than 750 cases of ricin intoxication have been described. Ricin may have been used in the highly published assassination of Bulgarian exile Georgi Markov in London in 1978. He was attacked with a device that implanted a ricin-containing pellet into his thigh.

Method of Disseminating BW

Biological agents are easy to acquire, synthesize, and use. The small amount of agents necessary to kill hundreds of thousands of people in a metropolitan area make the concealment, transportation, and dissemination of biological agents relatively easy. In addition, BW agents are difficult to detect or protect against; they are invisible, odorless, and tasteless, and their dispersal can be performed silently.

Dissemination of BW agents may occur by aerosol sprays, explosives (artillery, missiles, detonated bombs), or food or water contamination. Variables that can alter the effectiveness of a delivery system include particle size of the agent, stability of the agent under desiccating conditions, UV light, wind speed, wind direction, and atmospheric stability.

The use of an explosive device to deliver and disseminate biological agents is not very effective, since such agents tend to be inactivated by the blast. Contamination of municipal water supplies requires an unrealistically large amount of agent and introduction into the water after it passes through a regional treatment facility.

To be an effective biological weapon, airborne pathogens must be dispersed as fine particles less than 5 μm in size. Infection with an aerosolized agent usually requires deep inspiration of an infectious dose. Advanced weapons systems (eg, warheads, missiles) are not required for the aerosolized delivery of biological agents. Low-technology aerosolization methods including agricultural crop-dusters; aerosol generators on small boats, trucks, or cars; backpack sprayers; and even purse-size perfume atomizers suffice. Aerosolized dispersal of biological agents is the mode most likely to be used by terrorists and military groups.

Fig. 31.4. : The Aerobiology Chamber of 1 Million Capacity Used for BW Experimentation and Development.

Detection of biological agents: It involves either finding the agent in the environment or medical diagnosis of the agent's effect on human or animal victims. Early detection of a biological agent in the environment allows for early specific treatment and time during which prophylaxis would be effective. Unfortunately, currently no reliable detection systems exist for BW agents. Methods are being developed and tested to detect a biological aerosol cloud using an airborne pulsed laser system to scan the lower altitudes upwind from a possible target area. A detection system mounted on a vehicle also is being developed in some of the advanced countries. This system will analyze air samples to provide a plot of particle sizes, detect and classify bacterial cells, and measure DNA content, ATP content, and identify agents using immunoassays.

A BW agent attack is likely to be covert. Thus, detection of such an attack requires recognition of the clinical syndromes associated with various BW agents. Veterinarians must be able to identify early victims and recognize patterns of disease. This requires integrated epidemiological surveillance systems performing real-time monitoring with information shared at many levels of the health care system (e.g., ED to ED, ED to public health officials). Preliminary criteria for suggestive outbreaks of disease that could provide indications of a possible biological weapons event include the following:

- Disease (or strain) not endemic
- Unusual antibiotic resistance patterns
- Atypical clinical presentation
- Case distribution geographically and/or temporarilly inconsistent (e.g., compressed time course)
- Other inconstant elements (e.g., number of cases, mortality and morbidity rates, deviations from disease occurrence baseline)

Indications of possible BW agent attack include the following:

- Disease entity that is unusual or that does not occur naturally in a given geographic area or combinations of unusual disease entities in the same patient population;
- Multiple disease entities in the same patients, indicating that mixed agents have been used in the attack;
- Large numbers of both military and civilian casualties when such populations inhabit the same area;
- Data suggesting a massive point-source outbreak;
- Apparent aerosol route of infection;
- High morbidity and mortality rates relative to the number of personnel at risk;
- Illness limited to fairly localized or circumscribed geographic areas;
- Low attack rates in personnel who work in areas with filtered air supplies or closed ventilation systems;
- Sentinel dead animals of multiple species;
- Absence of a competent natural vector in the area of outbreak (for a biological agent that is vector-borne in nature).

PROTECTIVE MEASURES

Protective measures can be taken against BW agents. These should be implemented early (if warning is received) or later (once suspicion of BW agent use is made). Currently, available masks such as the military gas mask or high-efficiency particulate air (HEPA) filter masks used for tuberculosis (TB) exposure filter out most BW particles delivered by aerosol. **Multi-layered HEPA masks** can filter 99.9% of 1- to 5-mm particles, but face-seal leaks may reduce the efficacy by as much as 10-20%. Individual face-fit testing is required to correct seal leak problems.

Most aerosolized biological agents do not penetrate unbroken skin, and few organisms adhere to skin or clothing. After an aerosol attack, simple removal of clothing eliminates a great majority of surface contamination. Thorough showering with soap and water removes 99.99% of the few organisms left on the victim's skin after disrobing. The use of sodium hypo chlorite is not recommended over soap and water.

The use of special suits by health care providers is not necessary. Normal clothing provides a reasonable degree of protection against dermal exposure. Latex gloves and universal precautions provide sufficient protection when treating most infected patients. Place patients in a private negative-pressure room and practice proper sanitation with universal precautions. Proper disposal of corpses is essential. In the case of anthrax spores, this should be performed by incineration.

Of the potential BW agents, only plague, smallpox, and viral hemorrhagic fevers are spread readily person to person by aerosol and require more than standard infection control precautions (gown, mask with eye shield, gloves). Regardless, place all potential victims of BW agents in isolation. Medical personnel caring for these patients should wear a HEPA mask in addition to standard precautions pending the results of a more complete evaluation.

The entry and exit points of animal shelter should be provided with Footbath.

Broad-spectrum intravenous antibiotic coverage is recommended initially for victims when a BW agent is suspected. Institute this even prior to the identification of the specific BW agent. Vaccinations currently are available for anthrax, botulinum toxin, tularemia, plague, Q fever, and smallpox. The widespread immunization of non-military personnel has not been recommended by any governmental agency. Immune protection against ricin and staphylococcal toxins may be feasible in the near future.

In short depending upon the type of biological agent the following measure are required to be implemented:-

(a) Quarantine

(b) Mass immunization

(c) Chemoprophylaxis - useful against some agents.

Medical Management - The management of affected animals will not differ significantly from that required for animals acquiring same disease through natural means. The problem will be management of mass casualties for which improvised treatment centres may have to be established.

Procedure and Essential Items Required to Protect from NBC Attack

The **essential items** such as survival kit, must be provided for man and animal to survive a serious NBC attack:

- Personal Protective Equipments.

  Mask (full face, half mask respirator type and/or the disposable cloth type).

Fig : 31.5 Biohazard suits

  Goggles (for handlers) if using half mask or disposable mask.

  Rubberized Rain Suit.

  Hood (impermeable).

  Gloves for handlers (outer and inner) butyl and surgical

Boots (rubber)

Biohazard Suits

For maximum protection against chemical and biological warfare agents, soldiers use sealed biohazard suits, which protect the entire body.

Gas Mask

A gas mask allows a person to breathe normally in an area contaminated by chemical or biological warfare agents. The mask also protects the user's face and eyes from harmful substances.

Fig-31.6 Gas Mask

- Expedient Suit;
- Ready Kit;
- Decontamination Kit;
- Sealed Room or shelter for man and animals separately;
- Air Filtration System in the accommodation including HEPA Filter;
- Water;
- Food;
- Alternative Heating;
- Alternative Lighting;
- Medical Alternatives.

The effects of biological, chemical and radioactive agents will have a greater impact on one whose health is poor. The stress of the situation complicates matters. General good health of animals is first defense. Certain medical items should be kept handy. These are

Beta 1,3/1,6 glucan

Usage: An immune system booster

Colloidal Silver

Usage: Natural antibiotic

Hobes Instant Hand Stabilizer

Usage: Antibacterial soap for personal hygiene

Penicillin-vk and Doxycycline

Usage: Antibiotics

Stabilized Oxygen

Usage: An immune system booster and additive to drinking water to kill harmful bacteria.

Terramycin Soluble Powder

Usage: Antibiotic

Thieves and Lavender Oil

Usage: Black Plague Medicine

Radblock

Usage: Thyroid protection radiation blocker

Potassium Iodide (KI) Solution

It saturates the thyroid gland. This prevents the thyroid from absorbing radioactive iodine if exposed to radiation. This will help to prevent damaging contamination and poisoning. It is best-used three days prior to exposure, but the effects of radiation are lessened if taken once receiving the announcement of radiation being detected and present in the air.

Pre-Attack Preparation

The very first step is to prepare *psychologically*. Commit to memory exactly what you intend to do the instant you see or hear of an attack in your area. The decisions you make within the first few seconds are critical ones. Rehearse over and over in your mind exactly what you must do. This same procedure is used, along with physical practice, by military personnel to create almost automatic responses for any given situation.

General Instructions for Man to Protect from Nuclear Attack

When in the Open

Drop to the ground. **Stay there for at least 2 minutes!**

Lay face down toward the detonation and keep arms tucked up under your sides. If you are some distance away from the detonation, lie in a culvert or depression in the earth. Get under a car or truck or up against the wall of a strong building.

Cover your nose and mouth with handkerchief or any filtering material you may have.

Keep down until the blast wave passes and debris stops falling.

When all clear, seek good shelter.

Get your gear on! Use your "Ready Kit". (Expedient Suit, Mask and Ready Kit.)

If Away from Home

If away from home take protective cover immediately.

If traveling, stop and take protective cover immediately, or if you are only a few minutes from a safe destination, proceed and take protective cover immediately

If at some distance away from the detonation, lie in a culvert or depression in the earth. Get against the wall of a strong building.

Listen to your radio for further instructions

When in the Home or Shelter

If there is a Public Warning before Attack

If sirens or warning systems signal impending attack, regardless of where you are or what you are doing, take the best available cover against the blast, heat, and light effects of nuclear explosions.

If you are at home and do not have a fallout shelter, go to the basement or Strongest part of your house or a building, which offers the best protection.

If material is handy, improvise blast protection.

Take your battery radio with you or turn up the house radio so that you can hear it while under cover.

Stay away from windows.

Lie down and protect yourself from flying glass and falling debris.

Shield your eyes from the flash of an explosion.

Keep down until the blast wave passes and debris stops falling.

Monitor your radio for civil defense broadcasts

If There is no Public Warning Before the Attack

Drop to the floor away from windows and close to a wall. **Stay there for at least 2 minutes!**

Cover your nose and mouth with handkerchief or any filtering material you may have available.

Keep down until the blast wave passes and debris stops falling.

Go to your shelter.

Monitor your radio for civil defense broadcasts.

After the Attack

Stay in your sealed room or shelter for at least 2-3 weeks, longer times for very high fallout areas.

Radio broadcasts will identify areas that will be affected by the fallout and give instructions and advice. These might include:

Location of nuclear explosions causing local fallout.

Information about the parts of the country to be affected by fallout.

Length of time before fallout is likely to reach specific communities or areas.

Ways to increase fallout protection.

Supplies to take to your fallout shelter.

Whether it is safer to stay in your community or area or to go to other areas.

Advice on which areas are free of danger.

Advice on when to leave shelters and for how long as danger from radioactive contamination diminishes

Requests for help in rescue operations, such as rescue, fire fighting and medical assistance.

Advice on conservation of food, water, and fuel.

How to keep warm when power is off and the weather is cold.

Get the dust and debris off yourself as soon as possible.

Use your mask during this operation, or at least some sort of covering over the mouth and nose

DON'T USE TELEPHONE

When the sirens sound don't use the telephone.

Listen to a radio or television for information. In the event of an attack, "warning" telephone lines will be required for official use.

If You are Away from your Sealed Room or Shelter, Get Out and stay out of the contaminated Area.

If you are already upwind of the area, that is good. Stay there!

If you are downwind, get upwind as soon as possible and remain upwind.

Seek shelter.

Note: Learn the prevailing winds in your area (they change with the seasons).

Learn how to determine wind direction at any given time. Hold up a piece of light material. The direction the wind is opposite to the direction the material of is trailing. Observe the direction flags are trailing from their flagstaffs.

Turn until the wind is in your face, which is the direction from which it is blowing.

Weather forecasts give wind direction as the direction the wind is coming from, not blowing to!

Evacuation

Early in the attack and during the aftermath, it may be far better to stay where you are rather than risk further contamination by evacuating with others who are contaminated.

Sit tight and listen to the radio. There may be large traffic jams and mass panic.

If you decide to evacuate, put on your gear and leave it on until you reach designated safe area.

How to Get Rid of Radioactive Dust and How to Decontaminate:

Contaminated particles can be like sand, flakes, or a powdery substance. If it is suspected that the clothes have fallout on them, remove the outer clothing before the animal and handlers come inside the accommodation and leave it outside. Don't shake these clothes inside the house or shelter. This would only scatter the fallout grit and create unnecessary danger to others. If water is available, wash thoroughly, particularly exposed skin and hair. But do not scrub the skin as this might rub in the radioactive particles.

International agreements to control/destroy biological and chemical warfare

Three international agreements deal explicitly with chemical and biological weapons. The first, the ***1925 Geneva Protocol,*** prohibits the use in war of poison gas and bacteriological weapons. The second, the ***1972 Biological Weapons Convention,*** bans not only the use, but the development, production, and stockpiling of biological and toxin weapons. The ***1993 Chemical Weapons Convention*** does the same for chemical weapons. Unlike the earlier treaties, however, the chemical pact provides for methods to verify that countries are complying with the agreement and penalties for countries that do not comply.

The Biological Weapons Convention was the first international agreement to ban an entire category of weapons. It was established three years after a unilateral decision in 1969 by the United States to eliminate its own biological arsenal. Most major powers, including the former Union of Soviet Socialist Republics (USSR) and the United States, had become parties to the biological treaty when it went into force in 1975. Later, more countries joined in the agreement and the world appeared about to be rid of germ weapons. However, illegal program came to light in 1979 when international medical experts learned of a mysterious outbreak of respiratory anthrax in the Soviet city of Sverdlovsk, the site of numerous secret military facilities. More than 60 civilians and an unknown number of military personnel died. After the breakup of the Soviet Union in 1991, the Russian government revealed that the Sverdlovsk anthrax outbreak had resulted from an accident at an illegal biological weapons facility.

In the 1991 Persian Gulf War, the United States and other coalition leaders were worried that Iraq. The experience again prompted efforts to strengthen international agreements against these weapons. One result was the 1993 Chemical Weapons Convention, which contains an intrusive inspection system. Parties to the treaty have to allow outside monitors to visit suspected sites. By June 2001, 174 nations had signed the chemical treaty. To go into effect, the national legislatures of most countries must ratify, or approve, the treaty. As of June 2001, 143 of the signing countries had ratified or acceded to the treaty and had become binding parties to the agreement. The United States signed the treaty in 1993, and the U.S. Congress ratified it in 1997. Canada signed the convention in 1993, and Parliament ratified it in 1995.

The methods of destruction of chemical weapons include chemical neutralization (adding other chemicals to form a nonlethal substance) and incineration. There is also need for safety and environmental protection during the process.

Biological agents can usually be more easily destroyed than chemical agents. Ultra-violet light or disinfectants like formaldehyde are effective against most microorganisms. But some, like anthrax bacteria, are harder to kill and can persist in an environment indefinitely.

References

Christopher, G.W., Cieslak, T.J., Pavlin, J.A., Eitzen, E.M.: Biological Warfare : A Historical Perspective. JAMA 1997 Aug 6; 278(5): 412-7.

Headquarters, Department of the Army, Washington, D.C.: Field Manual 8-284, Treatment of Biological Warfare Agent Casualties. 17 July 2000.

US Army Medical Research Institute of Infectious Disease: Medical Management of Biological Casualties Handbook, 4th ed. Fort Detrick, Frederick, Maryland: February 2001.

The ABCs of NBC Warfare Survival: A public guide to surviving Nuclear, Biological and Chemical terrorist attack. (2002). Published by NBC Warfare Survival Training Group,USA ;(www.survival- nbc.org).

Index

A

Acute Radiation Syndrome 607
Ancient Horse Types 14
Animal Protein 325
Anoestrus 176
Anovulatory-Hemorrhagic-Follicles 177
ANTHRAX 435
Antibacterial Drug 416
Antimicrobial Sensitivity Test 417
Antimicrobial Therapy 415
Arboviral Encephalitis 467
Artificial Insemination 100
Artificial Vagina 136
Ascorbic Acid 354

B

Barley 318
Bedding 265
Bhutia 25
Biological Warfare Agents 615
Biotin 353
Biting 270
blood vessels 282
BREEDING 102
Breeding Soundness 235
Breeding Stock 93, 124
Bridling 395
Brood Mares 355

C

Caecum 306
Calcium 342
Calkin Shoe 293
Carbohydrates 340
Care of Feet 279
Cartilages 281
Centrifugation 150
Cereal Grains 318
Cervicitis 181
Chemical Disaster 601
Chloride 344
Choline 353
Circulatory System 225
Clipping 257
Cloned Mule 27
Clothing 260
Cobalt 345
Coital Exanthema 191, 472, 473, 474
Cold Shoeing 296
Colostrum 121
Colostrum Feeding 362
Common Reproductive Disorders 175
Concave Shoe 293
Concentrate Feeding 311
Contagious Equine Metritis 187
Copper 345
Corpus Luteum 81
Corrective Trimming 302
Cottonseed Meal 324
Covering of the Mares 107
Creep Feed 364
Culture Media 167
Curried Leather 401
Curry Combs 249

D

Dental Problem 37
Dental Quadrants 38
Dentition 29

Dermatomycosis 479
Digestive System 225
Donkeys 7, 589
Donor Mares 164
Doping 550
Draught Horse 68
Dress Rule 524
Dressage 511, 519
Drug Abuse 549
Dystocia Management 116

E

Ectoparasites Of Horses 502
Ejaculation 76
Electromagnetic Pulse 604
Embryo Recovery 167
Embryo Recovery Rate 170
Embryo Transfer 172
Embryo Transfer Technology 163
Endometritis 182
Energy 340
Eohippus 11
Epizootic Lymphangitis 442
Equestrian Sports 511
Equine Feeding 305
Equine Herpes Virus Infection 470
Equine Infectious Anaemia 460
Equine Influenza 448
Equine Management 601
Equine Piroplasmosis 481
Equine Rabies 446
Equine Viral Arteritis 195
Equine Viral Arthritis 455
Equine Viral Rhino Pneumonitis 195
Equus 11
Equus caballus 1
Estrogens 83
Exercise 96

F

Fat Soluable Vitamins 349
Feeding Standards 329
Fertilization 88
Fish Meal 326
Fluorine 345
Foaling 90
Foaling Mares 113
Fodder 317
Folacin 353
Food and Water 569
Food Contaminants 558
Foot care 576
Forelimb Lameness 230
Forelimbs 232
Freezing extenders 151
Frozen Semen Technique 133, 148
Fungal Metritis 190

G

Genetic Disease of Horses 70
Gestation 88
Glanders 423
Grading Up 43
Gram 319
Grooming 97, 247
Grooming Equipments 248
Groundnut Meal 325

H

Hayracks 246
Helminth Parasites 488
Hind Leg Lameness 231
Hominy Feed 322
Hoof 282
Hot Shoeing 295
House Flies 504
Humane Death 579
Hybrid Vigour 45

Hyperkalemic Periodic Paralysis 70

I

Inhibin 85
Insemination 156
Iodine 345
Iron 346
Isoxsuprine 559

K

Kathiawari 4
Kicking 271

L

Lameness 226, 227
Large Intestine 306
Leptospirosis And Dermatomycosis 476
Line breeding 47
Linseed Meal 324
Lipids 341
Locomotory System 226
Lucerne Hay 326
Luteal Function 179
Luteal Insufficiency 180

M

Magnesium 344
Malani 20
Manganese 346
Manipuri 5
Marwari 4
Mating Management 98
Meat Meal 326
Melioidosis 444
Mesohippus 11
Metazoal Diseases 488
Metritis 181
Microbial Digestion 307
Minerals 342
Mixed Lameness 227
Modem Breed of Horses 16
Mollasses 321
Mule 7

N

Nail-Holes 290
Native Breeds 587
Navicular Bone 281
NBC Environment 601
Negative Genetic Association 64
Neoplasia 192
NERVE AGENTS 610
Nervous System 226
Neurological Disease 474
Niacin 352
Nuclear Warfare 602
Nutritional Requirments 329

O

Oat Hay 327
Oats 318
Oestrous Cycle Irregularities 175
Oestrous Cycles 81

P

Pantothenic Acid 352
Peat Moss 268
Periodontitis 41
Persistent Corpus Luteum 179
Phantom Mare 140
Phosphorus 342
Photostimulatory Method 86
Pinworm Infection 501
Piroplasmosis And Trypanosomiasis 481
Placenta and Placentation 89
Placental Barrier 89
Placentitis 194
Pliohippus 11
Polo 539

Polo Pony 69
Population Trend of Equines 3
Postpartum Oestrus 90
Potassium 343
Premature Luteolysis 180
Progesterone 84
Prohibited Substances 552
Prostaglandin 85
Protection from Disease 578
Protein 341
Pulps 322
Pyometra 191

R

Rapeseed Meal 325
Reproductive Cycle 73
Respiratory Disease 474
Respiratory System 225
Riboflavin 352
Rice By-products 322

S

Saddle Tree 383
Saddlery 383
Saddlery Rule 524
Saline Infusion 86
Salpingitis 182
Selenium 347
Semen Characteristics 134
Semen Collection 135
Semen Examination 103
Semen Production 74
Sexual Behaviour 73
Sexual Maturity 74
Shoeing Tools 286
Show Jumping 512
Show-Jumping 526
Silage 327, 377
Silent Oestrus 176
Singeing 258
Single Cell Protein 326
Sodium 343
Sorghum 319
Soundness 219
Soyabean Meal 323
Spiti 5, 25
Stable Routine 97
Stabling 239
Stallion variability 149
Stallion's Fertility 93
Stomach 306
Storage of Feed 375
Strangles 427
Straw Labelling 153
Straw packing 152
Straw Size 150
Strongylosis 490
Sulphur 344
Sunflower Seed Meal 324
Sweet Itch 505

T

Tanned Buff Leather 400
Tarpan 14
Teeth Labeling 38
Tent Pegging 538
TETANUS 438
Thawing of frozen semen 155
Trace Minerals 345
Transportation 409
Transportation by Air 413
Transportation by Rail 411
Transportation by Road 412
Transportation by Sea 413
Trichothecene mycotoxins 622
Trypanosomiasis 484

U

Ulcerative Lymphangitis 441

V

Vaginitis 181
Vegetable Protein Sources 323

Ventilation 244
VESICULAR STOMATITIS 475
Vitamin C 354
Vitamins 348

W

Washing 256
Water Requirements 313
Water Soluble Vitamins 351
Weanling Mares 123
Wedge Heel Shoe 293
Wheat Bran 320
Wheat Straw 266
WILD EQUINES 593
Windsucking 269
Wisping 252
Wood Shavings 267
World Anti-Doping Code 549

Y

Yeast Culture 327

Z

Zanskari 26
Zinc 347